Homes&Interiors

Seventh Edition

Ruth F. Sherwood

 **Glencoe**

New York, New York   Columbus, Ohio   Chicago, Illinois   Peoria, Illinois   Woodland Hills, California

Contributors:

Christine Venzon, Eunice, Louisiana **Linda Perrin**, Yardley, Pennsylvania

Dale Anderson, Newtown, Pennsylvania

Safety Notice

The reader is expressly advised to consider and use all safety precautions described in this textbook or that might also be indicated by undertaking the activities described herein. In addition, common sense should be exercised to help avoid all potential hazards and, in particular, to take relevant safety precautions concerning any known or likely hazards involved in using the procedures described in *Homes & Interiors*.

Publisher and Author assume no responsibility for the activities of the reader or for the subject matter experts who prepared this book. Publisher and Author make no representation or warranties of any kind, including but not limited to the warranties of fitness for particular purpose or merchantability, nor for any implied warranties related thereto, or otherwise. Publisher and Author will not be liable for damages of any type, including any consequential, special or exemplary damages resulting, in whole or in part, from reader's use or reliance upon the information, instructions, warnings or other matter contained in this textbook.

Brand Name Disclaimer

Glencoe/McGraw-Hill does not necessarily recommend or endorse any particular company or brand name product that may be discussed or pictured in this textbook. Brand name products are used because they are readily available, they are likely to be known to the reader, and their use may aid in the understanding of the text. The publisher recognizes that other brand name or generic products may be substituted and work as well as or better than those featured in the text.

The McGraw-Hill Companies

Send all inquiries to:
Glencoe/McGraw-Hill
3008 W. Willow Knolls Drive
Peoria, Illinois 61614-1083

13-digit ISBN 978-0-07-874420-4
10-digit ISBN 0-07-874420-2

Printed in the United States of America
1 2 3 4 5 6 7 8 9 10 071 09 08 07 06 05

Contents in Brief

Reviewers

Carolyn Carrier
Family & Consumer Sciences Teacher
Lockwood High School
Lockwood, Missouri

Sarinda Leverett
Family & Consumer Sciences Teacher
Americus-Sunder High School
Americus, Georgia

Melinda Blair
Family & Consumer Sciences Teacher
Hoover High School
Hoover, Alabama

Heidi Linden
Family & Consumer Sciences Teacher
Mineral Point High School
Mineral Point, Wisconsin

Gladys Insko
Family & Consumer Sciences Teacher
West Liberty High School
West Liberty, Iowa

Marcella Bentley
Family & Consumer Sciences Teacher
Jackson County High
Gainesboro, Tennessee

Elaine Snow
Family & Consumer Sciences Teacher
Pleasant Valley High School
Brodheadsville, Pennsylvania

Contents

Unit 1: Homes Are for People

Unit 2: Making Housing Decisions

Unit 3: Understanding Construction

Unit 4: Architectural Design

Unit 5: Using Design

Unit 6: Designing Interior Environments

A Visual Guide

Careers in Focus

Consumer Considerations

The Impact of Technology

Commercial Design Applications

Homes Are for People

Chapter 1

The Universal Need for Housing

Objectives

- Define housing and briefly describe how it has evolved.

- Analyze the basic physical and psychological needs that housing satisfies.

- Compare and contrast housing needs among people of different ages and life stages.

- Assess the importance of building homes that follow the concept of universal design.

Vocabulary

- housing
- archaeologist
- nomads
- physical needs
- psychological needs
- lifestyles
- universal design
- barrier-free design
- adaptable design

As the late afternoon sun dips into the treetops, Julienne and her grandmother finish weeding their garden and head toward the front porch to enjoy the sunset. On the other side of the world in Shanghai, China, Guofang steps out onto the balcony of their apartment building to join her husband and watch the city waking up. While each of these people's surroundings are quite different, they each live in a place they call home.

The Development of Housing

A home is a place of great importance in people's lives. The basic role of a home is to protect people and provide them with a safe environment in which to live. As you will learn, a home meets many other needs as well.

The need for housing is one that people share around the world. **Housing** is any structure built for people to live in. Three basic types of housing that historically have been built are natural shelters, portable shelters, and permanent shelters. Throughout the world, housing has varied greatly from place to place and from one time period to another. Regardless of time or place, people have always tried to create comfortable shelters for themselves and their families.

Natural Shelters

Before primitive people created tools, they relied on the landscape for protection and shelter. Early people often camped out in the open and sought shelter from the wind by digging pits. By about 100,000 years ago, people in cold climates were living in caves. In warm climates, trees and thickets gave shelter.

With the invention of simple tools, primitive people were able to improve their shelters. They covered openings with tree limbs. They built ladders to reach caves high on cliffs. They used levers to move rocks in front of the entrances to their caves to close out cold air.

Archaeologists (ahr-kee-AH-luh-jists) are scientists who study history through the relics and remains of old civilizations. By examining bones, charcoal, rock paintings, and pottery chips found in caves, they know that humans occupied some caves thousands of years ago. Archaeologists have also found the remains of elaborate underground dwellings. These shelters had sturdy roofs, fireplaces for cooking, and places to store food.

Portable Shelters

Primitive people survived by hunting, fishing, and gathering wild fruits and seeds. In some parts of the world, the hunters and food gatherers had to move frequently to be near new sources of food. These people learned to devise shelters that could be taken apart, moved, and reassembled at the next location. Such shelters were usually built around a collapsible framework of wood or other materials. The framework was then covered with animal skins, branches, or grasses.

Today, portable shelters are still used by **nomads**, people who wander from place to place in search of food for their grazing herds. For example, some Bedouins of the Sahara region of North Africa live in tents made from camel hides or palm branches. Nomads in Kenya, a country in East Africa, live in portable huts. The huts can be easily taken apart, put on an animal's back, and set up in a new location. In Turkey and Mongolia, shepherds often live in yurts—transportable circular dwellings made of thick wool felt covering a wooden frame. See Fig. 1-1.

Fig. 1-1 The Mongolian herders periodically move their families and animals to new grazing areas. The family's portable home is a wooden framework, or yurt, covered by felt made from the wool of their animals.

Permanent Shelters

With the development of farming and keeping herd animals, early people no longer had to move continually to find food. They could stay in one place as they planted and harvested their crops and tended their herds. They began to select locations for permanent shelters and chose areas with good soil and water supply. Two of the earliest known villages have been found in present-day Israel and Syria. These villages date back to 8000 and 7500 B.C.

The kinds of shelters that were built depended on usable materials in the area. In Southwest Asia, for instance, farmers in the region of Tigris and Euphrates rivers used giant reeds that grew along the riverbanks. The tall grasses were bound together to make a cone-shaped hut. Today, in New Guinea, an island in the Pacific Ocean, people follow a similar construction method using native bamboo.

As agriculture methods improved, farmers began producing surplus grain. They needed a place to store and preserve the grain until it was needed. A new type of shelter, called a *granary*, was devised to meet this need. The granary established the idea of building shelters for possessions.

As the centuries passed, people improved their methods of constructing housing, but using readily available materials remained a basic principle. See Fig. 1-2. For example, in areas where building materials were scarce, mud bricks were made, dried in the sun, and used to build shelters. European peasants used the stones they had dug out of their fields to construct stone cottages. Natives of the Arctic

Fig. 1-2 The Native Americans in the Southwest built pueblos from native clay. These multifamily dwellings provided permanent shelter for generations of families. Some are still in use today.

learned that ice blocks, with their insulating properties, could serve well as a building material for temporary or permanent shelters.

Distinctions Within Communities

In primitive societies, individual shelters were very much alike. As communities began to form, however, distinctions in housing developed. These differences were largely based on an individual's standing in the community. A good example of this gradual change can be found in ancient Mesopotamia.

As early as 3500 B.C., a people known as Sumerians settled between the Tigris and Euphrates rivers in an area that is now part of Iraq. Their farming flourished because they learned how to control the rivers to irrigate their fields, and food supplies increased. Fewer people were needed to produce food, so they began to do other jobs such as making pottery and cloth. In time, they became more organized and set up governments. As the population grew, they built cities.

In the center of a city were the two-story houses of the upper class—the priests and merchants. Their homes were symbols of their wealth. Behind these houses were the one-story homes of the middle class—government officials, shopkeepers, and skilled workers. On the outskirts of the city were the crude mud-brick homes of the farmers, unskilled workers, and people who made their living from fishing.

Other civilizations, including the ancient Greeks and Romans, developed in a similar way. Even in China, which was cut off from Western civilizations, archeologists have found evidence of the same type of community development. The wealthy and the powerful Chinese lived in cities in stately wooden houses. The poor people lived in the countryside in mud huts or caves scooped out of the ground.

As rich people gained more possessions, they became interested in protecting their increased wealth. They wanted housing that would protect them from robbers and enemy attacks. They chose building sites that could be protected from intruders, such as a cliff, a mountainside, or a river or lake. See Fig. 1-3. There they would build their homes of sturdy materials. For example, in medieval times in Europe, a castle was constructed of thick stone walls to withstand battering rams. A moat and high battlements were additional security features.

Fig. 1-3 The site of this castle is not only beautiful, it's also very secure. Why was a lakeside location considered a secure location?

Fig. 1-4 The large Italian villas of the 19th century were ideal for entertaining guests.

Comfortable Shelters

In earlier times, even the homes of the rich were not especially comfortable. Medieval castles, for example, appeared imposing but offered little more comfort than a primitive cave. Cold wind blew through the rooms and passageways. Stone floors were cold. Light came dimly through narrow windows fitted with small bits of thick glass.

It was not until the Renaissance that housing generally became more comfortable. The Renaissance, which began in Italy in the 1300s, was a time of increased interest in art and great advances in technology. Applied to housing, the new technology made homes brighter, better ventilated, and more sanitary.

The growth of a prosperous middle class during the Renaissance also influenced people's expectations of housing. With more leisure time, people began to use their homes for relaxation, entertainment, and privacy.

By the 19th century, many homes—particularly in industrialized nations—had become centers of social activity. See Fig. 1-4. For instance, in England, families, neighbors, and friends would frequently be entertained in the elaborate homes of the rich and the middle class. Guests would often stay for months at a time.

Housing to Fit Human Needs

People's needs throughout the centuries have determined what their housing has looked like. As their needs have changed, their housing has kept pace. Individuals may vary from place to place, but there are fundamental types of needs that are universal— the basic needs of human beings that help determine the housing they require.

Housing is designed to fulfill both physical and psychological needs. Some needs may fit into more than one category for some people. In addition, some needs are more complex than others.

Physical Needs

When you eat a hamburger or take a nap, you are helping to satisfy your physical needs. **Physical needs** include all the things the body needs to survive: air, sunlight, shelter, sleep, and food. Housing helps meet physical needs by protecting people from the weather. It also provides a place to eat, sleep, and be safe.

Shelter

Protection from nature is the most obvious physical need that housing fulfills. Throughout the world, the elements of nature—temperature, humidity, rain, snow, wind, and sunlight—have influenced how people build their housing. **See Fig. 1-5.**

In the United States, the climate varies widely, creating a need for many housing styles across the nation. For example, the North has cold, snowy winters, so homes in that region tend to have low ceilings to contain the heat. Steep roofs help shed snow. The hot, dry air of the Southwest has led to a different style. One type of southwestern house has thick clay walls and a flat roof of timber and clay tiles. This construction helps keep the interior cool.

Sometimes people can take advantage of natural features, such as a hillside or a grove of trees, to help meet the need for shelter. High in the mountains of Switzerland, villages are built on the sunniest slopes, and the main living areas of homes face southward. The sun's warmth helps heat the homes.

Sleep

Regular sleep is another need that housing helps to fulfill. Without a safe, comfortable place to sleep, people may not get the rest that they need to function or to perform well at their jobs. In North America, most people are fortunate to have their own homes in which to sleep.

In North American homes, specific rooms often are set aside for sleeping. In other countries, sleeping arrangements vary. In Japanese homes, for instance, sliding paper screens separate rooms. People sleep on the floor on padded quilts that are taken out at night and put away during the day. This practice enables rooms to be used as living rooms during the day and as sleeping areas at night. It is similar to our idea of sofabeds and futons that convert living space into sleeping areas.

Food

Most housing provides a place for food preparation and eating. In some countries, homes have a separate room—a kitchen—for cooking. In other countries this is not the case. In Indonesian homes, for instance, living rooms also serve as kitchens.

People can eat almost anywhere in a typical home, but usually a specific space is reserved for this activity. Americans usually have their main meals in a kitchen or dining area.

Fig. 1-5 The natural environment influences housing styles across the country.

Fig. 1-6 Preparing meals together is an opportunity for families with busy schedules to spend time with one another.

Safety and Security

Early homes helped keep their occupants safe from animals and people who might harm them or steal their belongings. Safety was one of the reasons people grouped homes together and formed the first towns and villages. By living together, they could help protect one another. The Pueblo people of the American Southwest built their homes in the sides of cliffs so that hostile tribes could not attack them easily. On the American frontier, early pioneers built homes in settlements, but they moved inside the nearby *stockade* for safety during attacks. The stockade had walls of logs, and inside were small sheds or cabins to house new arrivals or to shelter pioneers from danger.

Today, people still look to housing to provide a place of safety for their family and their possessions. People may increase their sense of security by building fences or installing special locks. However, communities also must take action to increase everyone's safety. When neighbors work together, they send a message that their neighborhood is organized and people look out for one another.

Psychological Needs

There is more to life than eating, sleeping, and staying safe. Human beings also have psychological needs. **Psychological** (sy-kuh-LAH-jih-kuhl) **needs** are needs related to thoughts and emotions. They include the need for love and belonging, fun and relaxation, and comfort. They also include the need to feel a sense of identity and to express oneself. Housing that provides opportunities to meet psychological needs is more than just a structure—it becomes a home. See Fig. 1-6.

Love and Belonging

The need for love and belonging to a group is satisfied by family, friends, and coworkers. In addition, this need also includes wanting to be a part of a larger community, perhaps as a volunteer. The need to feel connected is often considered a social need. Depending on its type and location, housing can play an important role in providing people with a sense of belonging.

Housing is, of course, the primary setting for the family. In most cultures, the family home is where children first learn how to interact with other people. Children learn skills and cultural behavior by observing their parents and other family members. Homes give family members space to live, work, and play together—sharing experiences that help build affection and closeness. Central areas—such as a living room, family room, or the kitchen table—are favorite places for people to be together.

Housing also provides opportunities for interaction with friends. You might invite a friend home to watch a video or work on a school project. When you do, you are using housing to meet your need to be with other people. Human interaction provides fun and relaxation, mental stimulation, and emotional security.

Many people also feel the need for some time alone in a personal space to think, daydream, or work without interruption. **See Fig. 1-7.** In some homes, bedrooms are viewed as personal space for privacy. Privacy can also be achieved through furniture arrangement. For example, tall bookcases can divide a living room into a gathering space and a more private reading area.

When choosing a place to live, people often consider their need to be a member of a group. Some may decide to live in a large city because it offers many social and cultural activities and opportunities to meet people. Others prefer to live in a small town where they can get to know everyone personally. Some want to live in a particular neighborhood because they feel welcome and comfortable there.

Not all people experience a sense of community in their daily lives. There is actually a growing trend toward isolation in North America. Studies show that people within neighborhoods don't interact as much as they did in the past.

Some housing designers are creating planned communities intended to provide a sense of neighborhood that many areas have lost. These communities often resemble older city neighborhoods because all of the homes are close to one another. Features may include attached homes, roomy front steps or stoops, and front porches designed to encourage people to get together with neighbors. You will read more about planned communities in Chapter 16.

Fig. 1-7 Many people like to have a personal space in their home.

Fig. 1-8 Even though these homes are similar, residents have personalized them with distinctive touches.

Identity

Imagine a neighborhood where all the houses are white with black roofs and each house has exactly the same kinds of trees planted in exactly the same location. Wouldn't this sameness be uninteresting? Could a person accidentally walk into the wrong house?

Most people like to personalize their homes. Even people living in rental units can add individual touches. Putting out a decorative welcome mat or hanging a door wreath personalizes the exterior. Creative arrangements of potted plants and outdoor furniture on balconies also express individuality. **See Fig. 1-8.** Inside their homes, people use many creative decorating ideas to express their personal identities.

People's tastes, values, attitudes, and personalities show others who they are and determine how they live their lives. These qualities help form the lifestyle that people choose. **Lifestyles**, or ways of living, influence people's choice of housing.

Housing meets the need to express personality in several ways. First, people choose housing styles and furnishings based on their likes and dislikes. They select housing that reflects their image of themselves. One person may choose an ultramodern style, while another wants a more traditional look. People also choose housing that reflects their values. A family that values a simple, natural lifestyle might live in a rustic cabin in the mountains—or at least decorate their city apartment to resemble one.

Housing can also be a symbol of achievement. A young adult's first apartment represents independence. As people achieve financial success, they might choose larger, more expensive housing. Some people select housing to convey a certain image. They choose a home that they feel others will recognize and admire. Most people, however, are more interested in choosing a home that suits their needs and lifestyle, rather than one that will impress others.

Early Learning Environments

With their colorful equipment and varied activity centers, preschools and child care centers may simply look like fun places to be. In reality, a lot of research and planning goes into designing early learning environments. Good design promotes learning in several important ways.

- **Active Play.** Large, open indoor areas encourage energetic toddlers to engage in physical activity without fear of injury. Sound-absorbing carpeting and walls allow children to play freely without having to be told to "keep the noise down."

- **Quiet Play.** Design features that promote quiet activities include low ceilings, soft lighting, and lofts and corners with soft, plush furnishings. Partitions can be used to enhance learning. For example, a low wall around a learning center reduces distractions and helps children focus.

- **Independence.** Bathrooms with low fixtures encourage children to learn self-care skills. Easy-to-use storage for personal items and play materials teach responsibility and organization. Meal areas with easy-to-clean surfaces allow for the fact that young children tend to make a mess as they learn to feed themselves.

- **Physical Safety.** Children need to be safe and feel safe. Varying floor or wall surfaces may identify different areas without obstructing view or traffic. If space is limited, some areas might be designed for "double duty." For instance, a reading area might also be used to store outdoor toys or other items not used on a daily basis.

- **Attitude.** Color choices can affect a child's attitude toward the learning environment. Warm and cheerful colors help to create an exciting and stimulating atmosphere that promotes positive feelings and improves a child's ability to focus and learn.

Apply It!

Imagine that your neighbors are adopting a three-year-old girl. They ask for your ideas on how to convert their screened-in porch into a playroom for the child. Identify three concerns about the space they have chosen to convert and offer a design suggestion that meets each one.

Creativity

Another psychological need is the need to be creative, which lets people use their imagination and skills to express themselves. With a little imagination, people can add a unique look to their homes. Even pioneers on the American frontier were creative when building housing. Although materials and supplies were limited, they built their own log cabins and made many of the furnishings.

You don't have to build a house to express your creativity. Deciding what color to paint the walls and how to coordinate the furnishings requires imagination. Rearranging furniture and adding accessories can be a creative outlet. Making art to hang on the walls or even the refrigerator is a good way to exercise creativity. Housing also provides space for hobbies and other creative outlets.

Housing & Individual Needs

While people may have the same basic physical and psychological needs, they also have unique needs individual to them. For example, an artist may want a home with plenty of northern light. A big family may choose a home with a large dining area so they can enjoy meals together. People's housing needs are also influenced by their stage of life, their family situation, and their personal or special needs. Some people list among their top priorities having one home they can live in through all the stages of their life. Others look forward to the mobility of moving around from place to place.

Housing Needs Through the Life Span

It is not uncommon for people to move a number of times and live in different types of housing during their lives. They may move to different cities or just change residences within an area. Changes in housing often correspond to situations that occur during a person's life span. Sometimes the life span is referred to as the life cycle—the stages of life from infancy to old age. Individuals move through their own life cycle as they grow through infancy to childhood to young adulthood to adulthood. Many adults make the choice to marry, and they then enter into a *family life cycle*. These are the stages many families go through during their lifetime together.

The early years of marriage for a couple are called the *beginning stage*. At this point, the two people are getting to know each other better and are learning to act as a team. They may be actively making career plans. One important choice they need to make together is where to live.

The next stage for many families is the *parenting stage*. During this stage, the family expands. **See Fig. 1-9.** Children are born and develop. While raising

Fig. 1-9 In the parenting stage of the family life cycle, parents are raising their children.

children, the parents' focus is on home and family life. The end of the parenting stage is marked by the grown children leaving the family home. This process is often called the *launching stage*.

With the children grown and on their own, parents become a couple again. They move into the *aging stage*, also called "middle age." During this time, many couples find new interests they enjoy together. Their careers may reach an all-time high. Sometimes grown children return home due to economic conditions or a change in the child's life, such as divorce. Often parents become grandparents during this stage. In some cases, the parents care for their grandchildren on a regular basis.

The family life cycle is completed with the *retirement stage*. Changes in income and health as well as lifestyle interests often bring about new housing needs during this stage.

Of course, every person and family does not follow this cycle exactly. For example, not everyone marries or has children. Not every family goes through the stages of the family life cycle in the same way. Remember, everyone and every family is unique.

Let's look at a few examples of how housing needs tend to change as family members age and move into new life situations.

- Michael and Rose just got married and are moving into their first apartment. They have chosen an affordable, small place close to their jobs. They are interested in saving money for a place of their own.

- Marie and Antonio have been married for five years and have a two-year-old son. They are buying a home in a neighborhood with other families with young children.

- Estella has a two-bedroom apartment next to a community park. Her two grandchildren live with her.

- Andre and Diana, whose children are grown and living in different cities, plan to sell their large two-story home and move into a one-story home with a small yard.

- Sam is retired and thinking about selling his house and moving to a retirement community.

As you can see from these examples, each family managed to select a home that fits its needs.

Special Housing Needs

Many people have special needs that affect their housing choices. For example, some older people have difficulty living alone and need help with such things as preparing meals or cleaning a home. The number of people age 65 or over in the United States continues to grow and is expected to double between the years 2000 and 2030, by which time older people will account for 20 percent of the population. The percentage of older people who live well beyond age 85 is also growing. One impact of this growth is an increased demand for housing that's suited to the health-related needs of these people. Senior housing choices used to be limited to nursing homes and care facilities. Today, a broader range of options is available. Retirement housing in which elderly people maintain an apartment, yet are assisted, is one solution. In many such arrangements, senior citizens are served meals, can socialize with others, and can enjoy transportation and shopping services. **See Fig. 1-10.**

Fig. 1-10 Many seniors opt for housing that offers opportunities to socialize.

Fig. 1-11 This bathroom is an attractive example of how universal design can be incorporated into new homes. **How many universal design features can you identify?**

People with disabilities also want comfortable, efficient housing that meets their requirements. Technological innovations have assisted them in this goal. A person with a hearing impairment can be warned of a fire by a smoke detector that lights up rather than just sounding an alarm. A visually impaired person may have a microwave with a braille control panel. A person in a wheelchair can conveniently use a kitchen sink with an open area underneath. Some people with mental disabilities reside in group living centers. This living situation provides them assistance with meals and supervision, and meets daily care needs.

Universal Design

Until recently, most homes were designed and built for "average" users—able-bodied adults of average height. People with different needs had to endure the inconvenience, make changes to their homes, or move to more accommodating quarters. Today, many home designers and builders are taking a different approach. They have adopted a philosophy called **universal design**—designing interiors and products to accommodate all people with a variety of requirements, needs, and abilities.

Universal design acknowledges that people are of different sizes, ages, and abilities. When homes are built to suit many different people, residents are less likely to require special adaptations, even if their needs change. **See Fig. 1-11.**

One aspect of universal design is **barrier-free design**. This means that living spaces are designed without structures that would prevent access by people with special needs. Some owners choose to include **adaptable design** features—design features that are temporary and can be easily changed. For example, a landlord may install a wheelchair ramp or special cabinets for a tenant with special needs. The ramp or cabinets can be removed when the tenant moves out.

Since needs are individual, how can homes be built to accommodate many different needs? Here are some common approaches.

Exterior Design

- Rather than steps, use a ground-level entrance or a ramp with nonskid surface. The ramp should be wide enough to accommodate a wheelchair easily with turn-around space.

- Provide secure handrails for both ramps and stairways.

Interior Design

- Wide doorways, hallways, and space within each room accommodate someone who uses a wheelchair, walker, or crutches. Thresholds should be flush with the floor.

- Light switches and electrical outlets should be mounted at levels easily accessible from a wheelchair. These might benefit people of different heights, too. For better visibility, outlets should contrast with the wall.

- Lever-type doorknobs are easier for children and people with arthritis to use, yet they cause no inconvenience for others.

- Built-in flexibility is another way to achieve universal design. Instead of having a fixed shelf and rod, a closet can include adjustable shelving units.

Kitchen Design

- Vary the heights of the counters. Some counters can be higher, allowing tall users to work without bending over. Other countertops can be lower, making them convenient for children, short adults, and people who are seated. **See Fig. 1-12.**

- Knee space under the kitchen sink or cook top allows wheelchair use.

- Appliance controls and water faucets should be easy to use.

- Space should be sufficient for a wheelchair to turn around.

- Cabinets with pull-out shelves are easiest to use. Cabinet knobs should contrast with the cabinet color for clear visibility.

Bathroom Design

- Enough open space should be allowed for people in wheelchairs to turn around easily and for parents to help children with baths.

- Single lever controls for sinks and tub faucets are easiest to operate.

- Grab bars in the tub or shower may be built in, or walls may be reinforced for adding grab bars later.

People have many reasons for choosing homes with universal design features. For some, it is the only housing that suits their present needs. Others may not have physical challenges themselves but want their homes to be usable for visitors who do. Many people who choose universal design want to avoid the disruption of moving or remodeling in later years. Cost is also a consideration. Although some universal design features add to the cost of building a home, savings are realized in the long run. Designing wide doorways when a home is built, for example, is less costly than replacing narrow doorways with wide ones later. By designing homes to better accommodate individual needs, universal design benefits everyone.

Fig. 1-12 A low counter makes it easier for a person in a wheelchair to prepare meals.

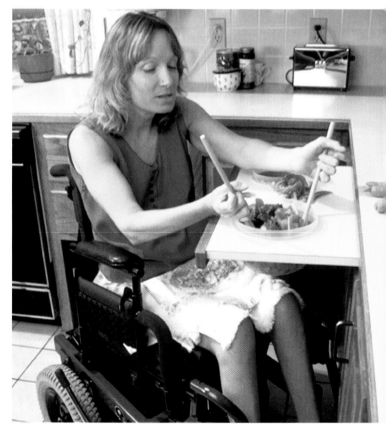

Challenges for Tomorrow

There are significant issues in housing for the future. One is to create housing that is useful to the greatest number of people. Universal design can help meet that need. Architects, planners, and builders must make sure that they meet the challenges of designing and building usable housing to meet a variety of needs. In the future, universal design features may be included in every new home.

A second challenge is to find ways to make better housing available to low- and middle-income people and to improve the social environment. For example, there is a desperate need for good housing in the older, low-income areas of many cities. Housing problems are closely related to other social problems, such as delinquency and crime. Some experts believe that providing good housing is a key to solving these problems. To foster a better social environment, homes need to be in locations where residents will be close to such conveniences as schools, parks, and shopping.

A third challenge is to conserve energy and natural resources. Builders and housing designers need to create living spaces that better relate to the natural environment. This means making careful use of land and natural resources. Every year in the United States, homes account for more than 30 percent of the total energy consumption and produce nearly 20 percent of all air pollution emissions. Designing, building, and operating homes to use materials, energy, and water efficiently is essential to ensure adequate housing in the future. See Fig. 1-13.

Fig. 1-13 Using solar energy is one way to conserve resources.

Profile of a
Healthcare Interior Designer

Some interior designers specialize in designing healthcare facilities, such as doctors' offices, clinics, and hospitals. Their goal is to create a space that healthcare professionals can use to treat patients efficiently while also providing patients and family members with a comforting atmosphere.

Education & Training

- A bachelor's or master's degree in interior design is preferred.
- Courses in interior design, healthcare design, and psychology are useful.

Skills & Aptitudes

- Solid design and presentation skills are important.
- The ability to create flexible designs is necessary because plans may have to be changed to adapt to changing medical technology.
- Healthcare designers must learn about special materials, finishes, equipment, and technology used in healthcare and must be familiar with code requirements.

Healthcare Interior Designer

José Benson

Think about the times you sat in a waiting room before seeing a doctor. How did that room make you feel? Did the colors and light make you feel comfortable or uneasy? Did the sounds soothe you or make you anxious? These are some of the issues that healthcare interior designers face. We try to create an environment that helps patients become well.

I did not start out in this specialty. I did office design at first, but then my mother became very ill. I went with her to the cancer treatment center many times, and each time the environment there impressed me. The waiting area was pleasantly lit. Soft carpets helped keep the noise level low, and paintings of people enjoying themselves offered the promise of better times to come. Patients and family members could stroll through a garden area while they were waiting for care. I could see how the space helped encourage my mother and other patients, and I decided I wanted to design environments like that one. So, I contacted the firm that had designed that treatment center to learn more about the specialty of healthcare design. It happened they were hiring, and with my background in office design, I got the job.

Healthcare designers also have to make the facility workable for the doctors, nurses, and technicians. We design intake and discharge units, examining rooms, lab spaces, offices, record storage—a whole range of spaces.

Still, my favorite part of the job is the patient areas. Now I lead design teams that can play a major role in shaping those areas. You might think that we use standard approaches for all doctors' offices or all clinics, but that is hardly the case. Each design task is unique. It depends on the ages of the patients, their conditions, the setting of the building, and even the personality of the doctors.

I take my own children to a pediatrician's office we designed. When I see how that cheerful interior brightens the faces of sick children and worried parents, I feel proud of my work.

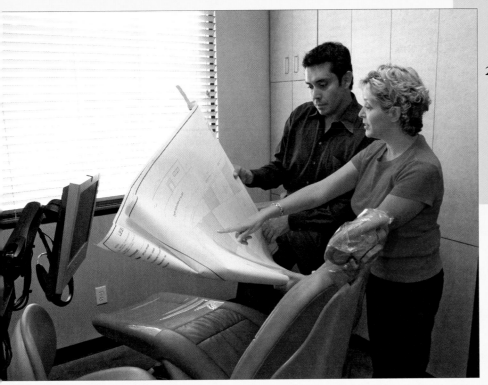

Design Portfolio

1. Visit a doctor's office or a health clinic and take notes on its color, lighting, furniture, layout, and other design features. Use a CAD program to reproduce the design. Then redesign the facility to make it more appealing to patients.

2. You have been hired by a doctor of sports medicine. Design a new reception area and waiting room for the doctor's office.

Chapter Summary

- **Housing** has evolved from natural shelters to permanent, comfortable shelters.

- Housing should satisfy people's basic **physical needs**.

- Housing that satisfies basic **psychological needs** can encourage interaction with family and friends and help people's feeling of well-being.

- As people move through the family life cycle, their housing requirements change.

- The goal of **universal design** is to make housing useful for people of all ages, sizes, and physical abilities.

- The challenge for the future is to create affordable, comfortable housing for all people and to conserve our natural resources.

Checking Your Understanding

1. How would you define **housing**?

2. What caused people in ancient times to change from portable to permanent shelters?

3. Give two examples of how housing changed during the Renaissance.

4. How does housing help meet people's **physical needs**?

5. Identify three **psychological needs** that housing can satisfy.

6. How can housing encourage interaction with others?

7. Explain how housing can reflect personal identity.

8. Why do housing needs tend to vary during the course of the family life cycle?

9. What challenges do housing designers face in making homes that meet **universal design** standards?

10. What is the goal of **barrier-free design**?

Thinking Critically

1. **Identifying Cause and Effect.** List three types of housing that you consider inadequate for your needs. For each type, identify the physical or psychological needs that this housing does not satisfy.

2. **Making Hypotheses.** What would be the advantages of having all new homes incorporate the principles and guidelines of universal design?

3. **Defending Your Position.** Do you think that the housing industry has a responsibility to build houses that conserve natural resources? Why or why not?

Applying Your Knowledge

1. **Personalizing Rooms.** Imagine you just moved into an eight-room historic home with blue interior walls and yellow ceilings. Write a report detailing how you would personalize each room and explaining how these changes reflect your personality.

2. **Housing Ages and Stages.** What kind of housing do you imagine you will live in when you are 21, 45, and 70? Find two interior and exterior pictures that show the kind of home you think you will want to live in at each age. Use magazines, real estate ads, travel brochures, and other sources. Briefly explain how these pictures reflect your goals at each of these stages of life.

3. **Universal Design.** Draw a simple sketch of a room that includes at least five universal design features. Label the features, and explain why they make the room universally usable by adults, children, the elderly, and people with disabilities.

4. **Building a Better Future.** Using Internet or print resources, find examples of innovative building techniques designed to use materials, energy, and water efficiently. Working with three or four other students, combine your findings and prepare a presentation that you can share with others.

Design Challenge

You have been hired by the assistant curator for a large museum. The museum is planning an exhibit on the evolution of housing in America. The curator has asked you to create a plan for the exhibit. Think about the materials that you will include, and answer the following questions in your written plan:

1. Should the museum display photographs, drawings, or scale models?

2. How will the exhibit be organized?

3. How much space will you need?

4. Will you include an interactive computer display?

5. Will you include a virtual tour of the exhibit on the museum's website?

Include sketches or pictures to illustrate your ideas.

Chapter 2

Housing & Society

Objectives

- Describe how housing reflects cultural views and values.

- Point out ways in which cultures influence each other.

- Identify social trends that affect housing.

- Explain the major ways in which government influences housing.

Vocabulary

- culture
- household
- nuclear family
- extended family
- single-parent family
- status
- demographics
- baby boomers
- telecommute

In your mind, take a snapshot of your home. Imagine three people on various parts of the globe doing the same thing. If the snapshots were put together in a scrapbook, your home might look quite different from the other three. What similarities might you expect to see? What would account for the differences?

How Culture Influences Housing

Traveling around the world, you would see a vast array of types of housing—from houseboats to apartment blocks to palm-covered huts. What accounts for these vast differences in housing styles? Of course, the physical environment has an important impact. As you learned in Chapter 1, geographic characteristics—such as altitude, climate, and terrain—greatly influence housing design. In addition, the building materials available play an important role.

Culture is another major influence. **Culture** is a combination of all the customs, beliefs, and ideas of a group of people. It includes people's values, traditions, and social habits, as well as their arts and religion. Culture affects every aspect of life, including housing. It affects the types of homes people build, the style of individual homes, and the arrangement of the rooms and furnishings within the home.

Cultural Views & Values

Because different parts of the world have different cultures, home design varies from place to place. In addition, cultures often change over time. As they do, people's housing needs and preferences may also change.

For thousands of years, for example, most of the people in Saudi Arabia lived as nomads in the desert, using tents for shelter. Some still live that way, but many Saudis have adopted a different lifestyle.

A typical new house owned by an upper- or middle-class Saudi Arabian family has central air conditioning and electric appliances. However, these homes, though modern, have been designed to preserve Middle Eastern cultural traditions. For instance, many Saudi homes have two living rooms. This feature makes it possible for women and children in the family to remain separate from male visitors, according to Saudi custom. A visitor to some homes would also find a dining room without furniture, and would instead find a rug on the floor on which to sit and eat a meal.

Fig. 2-1 The living arrangements in a typical household in some countries would seem crowded to most people in North America.

Different Kinds of Households

When discussing housing features, not only homes but also households must be considered. A **household** is made up of all the people who live together in one housing unit. The size and makeup of households vary from culture to culture. **See Fig. 2-1.**

One type of household is the **nuclear family**. The traditional nuclear family has a father, a mother, and one or more children. There are fewer nuclear families today than in the past.

In many cultures, households more typically consist of extended families. An **extended family** includes other relatives in addition to parents and children. For example, a mother, a father, children, perhaps an aunt or an uncle, and grandparents may all live together. On the island of Sumatra, housing is built to accommodate very large extended families. As many as 100 people, all related, share a long, rectangular house. The house is on stilts with space underneath for cattle stalls, chicken coops, and storage. In rural Nigeria, members of an extended family build their huts next to each other inside a compound or walled area. The women and children tend the gardens, and the men herd livestock.

In North America, households made up of extended families are becoming increasingly common for several reasons:

- Many people who come to North America from other countries continue the extended family tradition of their native culture. This is often true of people from countries of Southeast Asia, for example.

- Aging parents who need assistance because of poor health or physical limitations may move in with their children.

- Adult children may move into their parents' homes for financial reasons.

Situations like these affect people's housing choices. For example, the Diaz family purchased a large older home. They converted part of the space into a small apartment for Mr. Diaz's mother. This arrangement provides the elder Mrs. Diaz with privacy and independence, yet it retains the benefits of shared housing.

Still other household patterns are increasingly common in Western societies. Three-generation households, in which grandparents, parents, and children live together, are more common now than in recent decades. **See Fig. 2-2.** It is anticipated that the number of three-generation—and four-generation—households will continue to increase.

Other families, called **single-parent families**, have only one parent living with one or more children. As a result of these patterns, the demand for smaller homes, or those with fewer bedrooms and more living space, may increase.

Another change, especially in North America, is the increase in the number of people who live alone. Some are young people who have recently graduated from high school or college. Others are people of any age who have never married or are widowed or divorced. Many of these people like the independence that living alone offers. Some single people, especially in large cities, like the economy and simplicity of small apartments. Other single people choose larger living quarters that provide space for hobbies and entertaining.

Fig. 2-2 A growing number of American children live in a home where three generations are present.

Many people today share houses or apartments. By doing so, they may reduce their housing expenses or live in better housing than each person could afford individually. Other advantages include companionship and shared household responsibilities.

Whatever the makeup of the household, one of the main goals of its members is to have satisfactory housing. While individual priorities vary, satisfactory housing usually means a home that helps people meet their physical and psychological needs, is affordable, is economical to maintain, and provides the space and surroundings in which they feel safe and comfortable. Unsatisfactory housing can lead to stress, conflict, and social problems among the household members.

Attitudes Toward Privacy and Individualism

The design of housing in particular places is often determined by the attitude of the society toward privacy and individualism. Most people in North America value privacy. Walls and separate rooms provide household members with a chance to be alone when they choose. Individualism is also valued. Family members often personalize their areas of the home by decorating to suit their tastes and lifestyle.

In some Asian countries, more emphasis is placed on working together to accomplish group goals rather than on privacy. For example, at one time people living in cities in China used public bathing facilities. Cultural changes have occurred, however, and now city residents live in homes with private bathrooms.

Some people in Israel also value group goals, but in a different way. Some Israelis live in farming communities called *kibbutzim*. People in a kibbutz all work to support the group. They live in separate homes, but all the homes are owned by the group, not by the individuals.

Fig. 2-3 Some people choose large homes in prestigious neighborhoods.

Housing and Status

The way a person's importance in society is perceived by others is called **status**. A person's job, income, and social position are main factors that influence his or her status. The size of the person's home and its location, design, and furnishings can also be symbols of status. See Fig. 2-3. For example, status can be reflected in such housing characteristics as:

Building Materials. In India, for example, there are two types of houses, called *pucca* (superior) and *kacha* (inferior). Pucca homes are generally made of birch or stone held together with mortar, and they have wood, tile, or cement roofs. Kacha homes are usually made of brick or stone held together with mud, and they have straw-covered roofs.

Types and Numbers of Rooms. New houses for the middle and upper classes in India generally have a separate kitchen and a modern bathroom. In the houses of poorer people, however, cooking is usually done in the central living room, and there is rarely a bathroom with plumbing.

The Amount of Land Surrounding a House. In many cultures, people perceive the quantity of land around their house as a symbol of status. For example, in England many people live in one of a series of identical houses situated side by side and joined by common walls. These structures, called terrace houses, were originally built for factory workers. They have small rooms and usually a small garden in front. People with more money often live in two-family houses. These houses have bigger rooms, open land on one side, and a larger garden or lawn in front. Some people live in detached houses, which stand alone on a plot of land. These houses are usually much more expensive and are therefore regarded as status symbols.

Influencing Other Cultures

What people learn from other cultures influences their own homes, both in terms of building designs and methods of construction. When one group's habits and beliefs spread to another group in this way, cultural influences occur. For instance, whitewashed walls and red-tiled roofs are characteristic of Spanish architecture. Early Spanish settlers brought this style to the New World, where it became popular in the southern and southwestern areas of what is now the United States. Similarly, other European settlers brought their European styles to North America. These styles were gradually adapted all over the country.

Fig. 2-4 Cultural exchange from countries around the world has influenced housing styles in the United States. What part of the world do you think influenced this housing style?

Because of advanced communications and increased trade and travel, cultures are influencing each other far more rapidly today than at any time in the past. See Fig. 2-4. Although this process can add to the variety and richness of cultures, it doesn't always have positive results. At one time, the natives of a tropical region of Peru decided to replace the straw roofs of their huts with metal roofing. They believed that the metal roofs symbolized a more modern way of life. However, the high humidity in the region made the metal rust. Moreover, the metal roofs made the huts unbearably hot. The Peruvians realized that the environment, not status, is most important in choosing building materials.

On the other hand, there are positive influences. In this time of concern about the environment, builders in North America are studying energy conservation techniques used in countries with limited natural resources. For example, North American homes traditionally have a hot water heater that keeps hot many gallons of water. Today's energy-conscious builders are more often using on-demand water heaters that heat water at the point it is needed. This technology has been used in other parts of the world for decades.

Cultural change happens most rapidly in large cities, where many people from different parts of the world meet and share ideas. Since rural areas usually have a smaller influx of people from other cultures, the traditional local culture tends to be preserved.

Modern high-rise apartments in Dallas, Paris, and Cairo may all be built of the same materials (steel and concrete) in a similar style. On the other hand, houses in rural areas tend to be built in traditional local styles. For example, you might find a log cabin in the north woods of Minnesota, while you would see a house made of stone and cement in the countryside of Guatemala.

Societal Trends Influence Housing

Societal trends that influence housing vary from culture to culture throughout the world. The history of the kitchen in North American homes provides a good example of the influence of social change on housing.

In the homes built by English settlers during the colonial era, the kitchen was the only room in most houses that was continually heated. Consequently, it was used as the main room for many indoor activities. It was the place where family members ate meals, did their work, and socialized. The kitchen was an important gathering place for friends and neighbors, since there were few forms of entertainment outside the home. Because so many activities took place there, the kitchen was often the largest room in the house.

Compared to the colonial kitchen, a typical kitchen of the 1940s occupied a much smaller portion of the home. It also had a much more specific purpose—meal preparation—reflecting society's emphasis on efficient work methods. Other former functions of the kitchen were taken over by other rooms. Socializing took place in the living room. Families ate meals together in a separate dining room.

Today, jobs, sports, and school activities often take family members away from home. Because families eat fewer meals together, separate dining rooms have become less popular. Often the kitchen is a place where family members cross paths, preparing and eating informal meals and snacks as they follow their own schedules. Some kitchens are now designed to allow more than one person to cook, making meal preparation a family activity. The kitchen is often now the social gathering and entertainment area in the home. Interestingly, many modern kitchens are open to an adjoining family room, bringing to mind the multipurpose kitchen of colonial times.

Many families have also taken the concept of the kitchen outdoors. See Fig. 2-5. By equipping backyards with barbecues and outdoor furniture, they extend their living space and expand opportunities to socialize while cooking.

Fig. 2-5 Cooking does not have to be confined to the kitchen. Barbecues provide a great opportunity to cook and socialize at the same time.

As the history of the kitchen shows, many different societal trends can affect housing. Some of the trends affecting housing today, discussed on the next few pages, include:

- Changing family structures and roles.
- Changing fashions and personal tastes.
- Longer life spans.
- Changing economic conditions.
- Increasing environmental awareness.
- Mobility and diverse communities.
- Working at home.

Family Structures & Roles

Family structures and roles within the family continue to change. In a large percentage of nuclear families, both husband and wife have full-time jobs outside the home. Meanwhile, the number of single-parent families is increasing. Because of the time demands faced by most working parents, children often help with household duties.

Many home designers and builders are looking at these trends and planning housing to fit present and future needs. As you read in Chapter 1, the concept of meeting all family members' needs through universal design is influencing housing today. For example, kitchens in many homes are being designed with children in mind. A work area with lower cabinets and counters and a microwave oven allows children to prepare their own snacks or to help with family meals.

Fashion & Personal Taste

Fashions affect housing design, just as they influence clothing styles. Certain colors or themes are popular for a few years and then the styles change. For example, during one period, bright colors were very popular in interior design. Later, subtle tones became more common. You can usually spot these trends by observing the furnishings that are currently featured in magazines and newspaper articles.

Another current trend is that people are spending more time at home, and entertainment is an increasing function of the home. Consequently, home entertainment centers and computers are popular additions in homes.

Although styles change as fads and fashions come and go, certain elements in American design remain constant. Many Americans seem to prefer simplicity and comfort in their homes. They tend to like informal settings, light interiors, and open spaces. Others like traditional touches in their home design. Housing and design choices will always be determined by people's personal tastes.

Population Trends

Demographics—the statistical characteristics of a population—have a great impact on housing. Demographic information comes from the U.S. Census Bureau and many other public and private surveys. Such information is used both to learn about people today, and also to predict future trends. The number of people in various age groups affects the type of housing built, where it is built, and specific design features. See Fig. 2-6. In general, the average age of Americans is rising. People age 65 and older now outnumber teens. The U.S. Census Bureau estimates that older Americans will account for about 20 percent of the total population by 2030.

The fact that Americans are now living longer has created special housing needs. The majority of older adults continue to live independently, alone or with a spouse. Many retired Americans move to the warm regions of the southern United States. This has resulted in a housing boom in these regions. Even if they do not relocate to new areas, many retired people move to smaller, more manageable housing units. Older adults may require homes that accommodate physical disabilities, such as poor vision, arthritis, or hearing impairments. Some older adults move to retirement homes or other buildings that offer a higher level of assistance. Others move in with family members.

Fig. 2-6 Baby boomers' desire for new housing brought about a surge in construction. **What impact will this large segment of the population have on American housing in the future?**

People born in the 20-year period immediately following World War II, the **baby boomers**, form the largest group of Americans. As the baby boomers age, a larger number of Americans will be over age 65 than ever before. In 2003, nearly 36 million people were age 65 and older. In 2050, the number is projected to be more than 85 million. Baby boomers have also affected housing design. As they grow older and become "empty nesters" (families whose children have grown and left home), they are looking for smaller homes with fewer stairs and less maintenance. These houses are sometimes called patio homes because they feature low-maintenance patios and relatively small yards.

In contrast to the large number of baby boomers, your generation is much smaller. Although it is uncertain exactly how your generation will affect housing design, you may have an easier time buying a home than did the generation before you. As baby boomers move out of the housing market, a surplus of homes may be available. Noting that there may be fewer first-time buyers, some experts predict that the price of housing may decrease sharply in some areas of North America.

Economic Conditions

The economy affects people's choice of housing and the value they receive when they buy a home. These economic conditions include the level of interest rates for home loans, unemployment, inflation, and the cost of living. One or more of these can determine if people choose to delay home purchases and what type of home they choose to buy.

For example, the state of the economy affects interest rates for home loans. Depending on the amount of money available for home loans, interest rates vary. Interest is money paid for using borrowed money. Interest rates are usually given in percentages. Interest rates may go up when loan money is scarce or go down when loan money is plentiful.

Prices of homes also affect affordability. Housing prices have risen drastically during the last 50 years. In general, 30 to 40 percent of people's income is now spent on their monthly home payments. In some parts of the country, population increases are outpacing available housing. In those locations, people are bidding for homes and sometimes offering more than the sellers' asking price. The same holds true for renters in areas of the country where rental property is scarce.

In some cases, the cost of housing has risen faster than people's income. One result is that some people must live in substandard housing. **See Fig. 2-7.** Problems with substandard housing include overcrowding, unhealthy and unsanitary conditions, unsafe situations, and lack of contact with any natural environment such as parks. Substandard buildings and homes can have poor plumbing, dangerous electrical wiring, rats and insects, fire hazards, and deteriorating structures. Housing problems are linked to violence, vandalism and destruction of property, and theft and crime. Substandard housing has an impact on us all.

Environmental Awareness

Rising fuel costs, concern over pollution, and an interest in recycling are some of the environmental concerns that impact housing today. For example, insulation in homes was not used in the early 1900s. Today, builders wouldn't think of constructing a home without it. Proper insulation cuts down on the cost of heating and cooling a home and conserves resources. Materials that once collected in landfills are being used in a variety of home products. For example, recycled plastic is used for many home products such as porch decking and roofing.

Solar panels are no longer an oddity found on just a few homes. Future projections promise more innovative heating and cooling concepts. In Chapter 3, you'll learn about other techniques builders and homeowners use to conserve our resources.

Mobility Creates Diverse Communities

If you had a bird's eye view of the country, you would see heavily populated cities, suburban areas, small towns, and homes out in the country. Our nation offers people the opportunity to choose from a variety of lifestyles. Many people choose to live in a city to be near their work and cultural activities. They enjoy being at the center of city activity. Some people prefer small towns because of the neighborliness and feeling of safety. You'll find many families in suburban areas enjoying pleasant yards and more spacious surroundings. In rural areas, you'll find families living on farms, but also many families simply choose to live in a rural environment. Nationally, non-metropolitan areas are growing three times faster than they did 20 years ago. Many people want to live outside of congested cities and are choosing small towns and rural areas. **See Fig. 2-8.**

Fig. 2-7 When living conditions are undesirable, the result can be destruction of property and increased crime. **How can a sense of community help lessen these problems?**

Fig. 2-8 Moving to rural areas has become increasingly common. **Why would some people prefer country living?**

Working at Home

Many of today's homes do double duty as offices. Some people start their own home-based businesses, such as writing or consulting. Others **telecommute**, or work from home while keeping in touch with an employer's office. A telecommuter might attend a meeting with a conference telephone call, access the company's sales data using a home computer and a cable modem or satellite connection, and use e-mail to send a report to a colleague hundreds of miles away. Technological advances have made working from home easier and more efficient.

Some people feel that there are tradeoffs in working at home. Although people who work at home gain a quiet, independent place to work, some may feel isolated. In addition, some people find it more difficult to separate their work and personal life when living and working in the same environment.

Today, many people adapt existing spaces—such as an unused bedroom or part of a basement—to incorporate home offices. More homes being built today may be designed with space for a home office.

Each year, approximately one out of every five people in the United States moves. The average American will have 12 to 13 homes in his or her lifetime.

People in their mid-20s move more than any other group. In fact, each year one-third of all people in their 20s move. Why do you think young adults move so often? **See Fig. 2-9.**

People age 45 and older are less likely to move. In fact, fewer than one-tenth do. Therefore, as the population ages, experts predict that more people will tend to stay in their homes longer. This decrease in mobility may have an impact on new housing in the future.

The trend toward working at home is another factor that may decrease mobility. Instead of relocating to take a new job, more people may telecommute or start their own businesses.

Fig. 2-9 Some people relocate because of a new job opportunity. **What are other common reasons people move?**

The Government's Role

In the United States and Canada, as in most countries, government bodies are involved in many aspects of housing. For example, governments provide a legal system for the buying and selling of property, impose taxes on homeowners to pay for community services, and are involved in funding new housing.

State & Local Governments

In the earliest North American settlements, few regulations affected housing. Towns simply expanded as more people needed homes. Laws did not restrict where houses could be built. No one checked to see whether the homes were safe.

State and community officials now take a much more active role in controlling development by adopting comprehensive plans for future growth. Officials look at how available space can best be used for housing, business, and industry in the future. By setting aside certain areas for particular uses, the planners attempt to provide the best living and working environments possible. **See Fig. 2-10.** Space is set aside for parks. Plans are made for schools and shopping areas. Public transportation is made accessible.

Local government officials also play a role in ensuring that housing meets minimum standards for safety, sanitation, and space. Every unit, for example, must have a bathroom. Local codes require fire exits for multi-unit buildings.

Many state and city governments have enacted laws that control expansion of housing developments in certain areas. These "open space" laws, in most cases, are designed to limit development so that overbuilding does not occur. This strategy aims to prevent such problems as water shortages and traffic congestion. Other laws have been passed to revitalize inner cities. As a result, many cities, such as Chicago, Illinois and Atlanta, Georgia, have seen their inner-city neighborhoods revive.

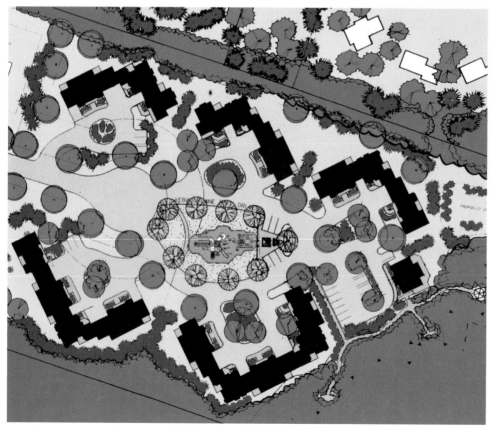

Fig. 2-10 Most new developments have plans that outline where houses can be built, along with other features such as parks. **What is the importance of green space?**

Federal Government Actions

Prior to the 1930s, the U.S. government provided little help in solving housing problems. People who could not find or afford housing turned to their families, charitable organizations, or sometimes local government. The economic hardship of the Great Depression of the 1930s, though, left millions without adequate housing. Poverty and homelessness are still intertwined today. The U.S. government has stepped in to help.

Public Housing

The U.S. government works with local housing agencies to help provide housing for those in need. The local agency identifies the need for low-income housing and determines how it can best be met.

In the past, the most common solution was to build large buildings with many apartments. The local housing agency managed the building and determined who was eligible to live there. Residents usually paid a set percentage of their income for rent, and the government paid the rest. However, that type of housing project has been criticized for isolating low-income families from the rest of the community. In many communities, the deteriorated public housing is being demolished.

In the place of those large buildings, new public housing programs are incorporating low-income housing throughout communities. Residents are encouraged to become part of their new neighborhoods. In some programs, new buildings contain no more than 20 apartments. In other programs, housing agencies work with private owners to rent to low-income families. The government guarantees the owner fair rent and may help pay part of it. In other instances, those in need are given housing vouchers that they may use to move closer to job opportunities.

In Canada, the government provides funds to build accessible housing for elderly people, low-income families, and people with special needs. In addition, the government provides funding for personal support and homemaking services for these people and for those with specific medical conditions.

Urban Renewal

Urban renewal programs attempt to redevelop run-down urban areas. The U.S. government has provided much of the money needed to make major improvements in large inner-city areas. In some cases in the past this meant clearing and rebuilding whole neighborhoods. Families and businesses had no choice but to move. Since the 1960s, more emphasis has been placed on saving and repairing existing buildings whenever possible. For example, the federal government has bought homes that were in poor condition and given them to a local housing agency for repair. The homes can then be sold to needy families at affordable prices.

Providing for the Elderly and the Disabled

Government programs provide funding to house the elderly and the disabled, and ensure that individuals with disabilities can obtain housing and participate in community life without unnecessary barriers.

The U.S. Department of Housing and Urban Development (HUD) provides funding for rent assistance, group housing, adapting an existing home for all needs, and construction of new barrier-free homes. HUD often funds programs that help aging adults and people with disabilities live on their own in independent facilities.

The Fair Housing Amendments Act protects people with disabilities from unfair and discriminatory housing practices. It also provides for architectural accessibility and adaptable design requirements in new multiple-family housing.

Fig. 2-11 The Americans with Disabilities Act has helped to ensure that public buildings, such as this library, are accessible to the disabled.

The Americans with Disabilities Act (ADA) bans discrimination against Americans with disabilities and requires that all people must be considered equally when it comes to new construction or changes to existing public structures. This means that builders must take into account the needs of all Americans when designing or adapting public or commercial buildings. See Fig. 2-11.

Emergency Shelter Grants for the Homeless

Many people, either briefly or for the long term, are without adequate housing. Estimates reveal that 3.5 million people will experience homelessness in one year. See Fig. 2-12. Families make up about half of the homeless in the United States, with children accounting for almost one-third of all homeless people. Homelessness is not directly related to not having a job. A recent study found that one out of five homeless people has a job. The number of homeless people in North America seems to be growing. Because of this, greater emphasis is being placed on developing housing for the homeless.

Poverty and the lack of decent affordable housing underlies the problem of homelessness. HUD, through Special Needs Assistance Programs, grants states and communities funds for housing the homeless. These funds can be used to renovate or convert buildings to be used as homeless shelters.

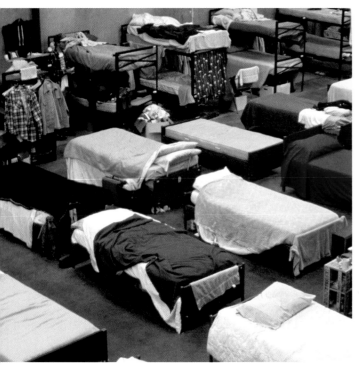

Fig. 2-12 Most American cities have implemented programs to help the homeless, but unfortunately the problem has not been erased.

Partnerships for Housing

Partnership is empowering. That is the simple philosophy behind Habitat for Humanity International. Habitat for Humanity is a nonprofit housing ministry dedicated to eliminating poverty housing and homelessness around the world. See Fig. 2-13.

Habitat houses are built through partnership. Volunteers from all walks of life contribute their time and skills to build or renovate homes. For example, former U.S. President Jimmy Carter is an active Habitat volunteer. The family that will become the homeowners are also partners in the process. They contribute hundreds of hours of "sweat equity" to help construct their own homes. By investing themselves in the building process, homeowners gain self-esteem and new skills. In addition, the new homeowners make a down payment and modest monthly payments that are used to build more housing through a revolving Fund for Humanity.

By bringing people together to work on a project, Habitat builds new relationships and a sense of community as well as new housing. Thanks to Habitat for Humanity, thousands of families in the United States and in countries around the world are able to own their own homes.

Fig. 2-13 Relying on volunteer labor and donations, Habitat for Humanity has built more than 175,000 homes around the world.

Profile of an Urban Planner

Urban planners, sometimes called community or regional planners, develop programs that help promote growth and the best use of a community's land and resources. They help a wide range of public officials and civic leaders make decisions on social, economic, or environmental problems. Planners present programs and reports to interested agencies, businesses, and citizens. They use computers to gather and analyze information, record and project costs, and forecast future trends.

Education & Training

- An advanced degree in urban or regional planning is desirable. A bachelor's degree in planning, architecture, or civil engineering and related work experience may be acceptable.
- Courses in housing, urban design, economic development, engineering, law, and finance are helpful.

Skills & Aptitudes

- Effective communication skills in both public presentations and written reports are important.
- Flexibility to effectively reconcile different viewpoints is helpful.

Urban Planner
Eduardo Martinez

As an urban planner, I help public officials and civic leaders in my city plan development projects. We want to make sure that projects will make the city a better place to live. As you might expect, everyone has different ideas and concerns. Each person's needs—and those of the community as a whole—must be evaluated.

I can't point to any one person or event that prompted me to become an urban planner. It was really a whole series of things. In high school I learned about the different ways people live in different parts of the country and in other cultures. That got me thinking about how the buildings, houses, shops, and parks in my own neighborhood influenced how neighbors felt about themselves and each other. By the time I entered college, I was beginning to realize that community planning is a two-way street. I began to be interested in how local government worked. A college internship in a nearby town opened my eyes to the responsibility elected officials and business leaders feel to provide the community with ample housing and building space, jobs, and recreational and healthcare facilities.

My first job as an urban planner was for a small city wishing to expand and yet maintain its historic neighborhoods and downtown area. Right away I had to work with people with widely varying points of view. I met with elected officials and civic leaders to discuss their concerns and hopes. I met with citizen groups, too. Many people wanted to save the abandoned downtown and see older neighborhoods rejuvenated, but I had to decide if that could be done economically and to the long-range advantage of the whole city. With the help of my staff, I gathered the data we needed and suggested projects that I thought would work for the city.

That involved designing plans and proposing budgets.

An urban planner must listen to the dreams of developers but also take into account the concerns of residents. You have to be able to work closely with other people but you also have to be able to work on your own. I spend a large amount of time reading, analyzing statistics, and writing and revising reports.

Design Portfolio

1. You are an urban planner who has recommended that your town replace two separate high schools with a single, larger school. A town council member has objected to your plan. Write a letter to the council member explaining the benefits of the plan.

2. Using CAD software, draft a design of the new high school. Be sure to address the needs of students, teachers, and the community.

Chapter Summary

- A group's **culture** affects the type, style, arrangement, and furnishings of its homes.

- Housing is influenced by different **household** patterns and by different attitudes toward privacy and status.

- Because of increased travel, trade, and communication, cultures often influence housing styles.

- Changing family structures and roles, economic conditions, and environmental awareness are some factors that affect housing choices.

- State and local governments can develop and enforce regulations that control the growth and quality of housing.

- Government programs can help people with a wide variety of housing needs to obtain safe, secure, and affordable homes.

Checking Your Understanding

1. What does the term **culture** refer to?

2. Give examples of three different types of **households**.

3. Explain how the land surrounding a house reflects **status** in England.

4. Give an example of how one culture's housing traditions have spread to another culture.

5. Identify four societal changes that have affected housing in America.

6. By the year 2050, how will the number of Americans over age 65 affect the housing market?

7. Identify the economic factors that affect people's housing choices.

8. How might the trend toward home offices and **telecommuting** affect housing needs?

9. Describe three kinds of federal housing programs.

10. If a family wants to own a Habitat for Humanity home, what must they do?

Thinking Critically

1. **Making Hypotheses.** How might the increase in the number of people who live alone affect the housing market? How might increased numbers of extended families affect it?

2. **Making Predictions.** What do you think might happen to the housing market when large numbers of baby boomers retire?

Applying Your Knowledge

1. **Analyzing Housing Needs.** In the classified section of your local newspaper, find descriptions of homes that would be suitable for each of the following households: a young single person, an extended family, a couple without children, and a single-parent family. Explain why each home might suit the needs of that household.

2. **Designing for Privacy.** Using CAD software, design a modest single family home for a family of four that includes private space for each family member. Prepare a brief description of the home that explains your decisions about allocating space.

3. **Working from Home.** Choose a home with which you are familiar—it can be your own home or that of a friend or relative. Figure how you would reorganize it for someone who wanted to work from home. Make a list of the factors you would need to consider when drawing up a new floor plan.

4. **Community Living Conditions.** During the early years of the 20th century many immigrants moved to the United States in search of better lives. Many lived in crowded apartment buildings known as tenements. Research tenement living and explain the harsh conditions under which these immigrants lived.

Design Challenge

You have decided to enter a contest. The theme of the contest is "Designing the Ideal House." Here's what you have to do to enter the contest:

1. Describe in 250 words or less a new home that would be ideally suited for the 22nd century.

2. Make sure that the home could be used by many types of families or could be changed to adapt to a family's needs.

3. Include facts about societal changes that support your design.

4. Create a drawing of the ideal house.

   Entries will be judged on practicality and originality.

Housing & Technology

Objectives

- Evaluate the benefits and drawbacks of different natural and manufactured materials used in home construction.

- Describe the three basic methods of home construction.

- Evaluate the role of high technology in homes today.

Vocabulary

- technology

- engineered wood products

- biomaterials

- green building

- site

- computer-aided design (CAD)

- conventional construction

- systems-built homes

- modular homes

- manufactured homes

- biometrics

- automated management systems

It's hard to realize all the planning, hard labor, skills, and time it took to construct a home in the 1700s. Families and friends often combined their skills and resources to make the task of building a home less difficult. Even a one-room house presented many challenges. Today's builders utilize new materials, specialized tools, and state-of-the-art construction methods to assemble homes in record time.

The Technology Revolution

Since the Stone Age and the dawn of tool making, people have worked to improve the quality of life. State-of-the-art tools advanced from axes with stone blades to hardened iron and steel machinery. The Industrial Revolution, which began about 1750 and lasted until about 1900, spurred on many techno-logical advancements that benefited the building industry. In 1885, for example, builders in Chicago completed construction of the first metal-framed skyscraper. Today major advances in technology continually change building materials, tools, and techniques of housing construction. In the past, *technology* was often described as "the study of making and doing things." It focused on tools and machines. Today, **technology** is defined as the prac-tical application of knowledge—people using what they know to change their environment. See Fig. 3-1.

Fig. 3-1 Unlike photo IDs and keycards, this biometric hand-recognition system only allows authorized people to enter the building. It automatically compares the 3-D size and shape of your hand to those stored in memory.

Materials & Construction Technology

For centuries, people were forced to build with locally available materials. Today, builders can import materials from other locations and even create new materials. Builders have access to the broadest range of both natural and manufactured materials. In addition, advances in technology have led to the development of more effective and efficient tools and building methods for use in home construction.

Natural Materials

Natural building materials are resources provided by nature that have been adapted for use in construction. The three most commonly used natural building materials in home construction are wood, stone, and brick.

Wood

Almost every home contains some wood in its construction. Lumber—boards and large pieces of wood cut from logs—is the basis for many interior house frames, floors, woodwork, doors, and other building parts. The construction industry uses approximately one-half of all the lumber produced from trees in the United States. About one-quarter of all lumber is used in the repair and remodeling of homes.

Wood is divided into two classes: *softwood* and *hardwood*. Although these terms sound as if they relate to the hardness of the lumber, they actually refer to the type of tree the lumber comes from. In fact, some softwood lumber is actually heavier and harder than hardwood.

Softwood lumber comes from trees of the conifer family. These trees, more commonly known as evergreens, include various pines, cedars, redwood, and spruce. The wood from these trees is used for flooring, walls, and roof supports as well as for door frames and window frames. See Fig. 3-2.

Hardwood lumber is the product of broadleafed trees. These trees, which generally lose their leaves in autumn, include oak, walnut, maple, and birch. Hardwoods are used mainly in furniture making, although they are also found in flooring, paneling, and trim.

Even though the United States is one of the major producers of lumber in the world, it imports more lumber and wood products than it exports. Imported wood products include teak, mahogany, bamboo, and cork.

Fig. 3-2 Wood adds to the beauty of a home's interior. Whether using wood to surround a sunroom hot tub or panel a family room wall, the choice of grain and color affect the feel of the room.

Stone

Although wood is perhaps the most commonly used natural material for building homes, it is not always available. People who live in rocky, treeless areas, such as southern Italy and western Ireland, traditionally build their homes from local stone. Homes built hundreds of years ago are still standing today, as evidence of the strength and durability of this natural building material.

Stone is taken from natural deposits in the earth. It is mined through *quarrying*, the excavation of a large stone deposit. Quarried stone used for building construction is called *dimension stone*. This stone is cut, often at the quarry site, into large blocks or slabs of different sizes and shapes. The most common types of dimension stone used for residential construction are limestone, sandstone, marble, and slate. Limestone and sandstone are used primarily in heavy construction, such as exterior walls. Marble, which is often polished to a high luster, is used to decorate stairways, fireplaces, and floors. Slate, a fine-grained rock, appears most commonly in roofing shingles and flagstone flooring.

In many countries, housing styles vary from region to region, depending on the type of stone quarried. In the Cotswold Hills of central England, for example, houses are typically made of cream-colored limestone, while in southwestern England, whitewashed stone cottages are common. In other areas of the country, houses are built of red sandstone.

Brick

Still another natural material widely used in home building today is clay. In primitive times, clay was applied wet, like plaster, and allowed to harden. Today, clay used for construction is made into bricks.

The first bricks, used more than 5,000 years ago, were made of molded clay that was permitted to bake hard in the sun. Today, bricks are baked—or "burned"—in ovens that reach temperatures of 2200°F (approximately 1200°C). The heating process gives the bricks their characteristic color.

Bricks are used in the construction of many types of homes. They can form a building's structure or be used for fireplaces, chimneys, and decorative facings for interior or exterior walls. Bricks are a strong, versatile, and durable building material. **See Fig. 3-3.**

Fig. 3-3 Bricks come in a variety of colors, shapes, and textures, and can be used indoors and outdoors in a variety of applications.

Fig. 3-4 About 30 friends and neighbors helped form the walls of this unique Illinois home. Walls were made from straw bales and held in place by bamboo. Three coats of stucco were then applied. What would be the environmental benefits of the house?

Manufactured Materials

Although wood, stone, and brick are widely used in home construction today, natural materials have their limitations. Some natural materials are not suitable for particular uses. Another limitation of natural resources is that their supply is limited. The massive cutting of trees in the 20th century has led to a scarcity of lumber. This shortage has, in turn, led to yet another problem: higher cost. When resources, such as lumber, are in short supply, the price goes up. Concerns such as these have prompted some innovative approaches to building. See Fig. 3-4. More importantly, they have led to the development of manufactured building materials.

Engineered Wood Products

In addition to dwindling resources, builders have been concerned with the low quality of lumber being produced. To conserve resources, keep prices down, and develop more reliable products, technology has provided home builders with **engineered wood products**, or manufactured materials formed from wood. One type, called composite lumber, is made by applying high pressure to paper-thin strips of wood that have been sprayed with glue. Composite lumber is made from trees such as poplar and aspen, which have trunks too slender to make good conventional lumber. Because these trees are fast growing and short-lived, their use does not interfere with conservation efforts.

In home construction, engineered wood products are used for beams, joists, studs, and window and door frames. Although they are more expensive than standard wood products, they are stronger and less likely to warp or shrink.

Concrete and Cement

Of all manufactured building materials, concrete—a mixture of gravel, cement, and water—is the oldest. It is also one of the most durable. In fact, concrete columns built by the Egyptians 3,600 years ago are still standing.

Concrete used in home construction today is often delivered in the form of blocks. These blocks have a wide range of uses. Liquid concrete is also used. It can be poured to form the foundation, or underlying support, of homes as well as exterior elements, such as porches, patios, and steps. Precast concrete is used to provide energy-efficient walls to frame homes.

Concrete provides builders with many advantages over wood and brick. It is twice as strong as brick. It is also relatively inexpensive to produce, slow to disintegrate, and fire-resistant.

A new type of aerated concrete was recently introduced in the United States. Aluminum powder added to the concrete during manufacture causes it to expand dramatically. The result is a lightweight building material with significantly higher insulation properties than regular concrete. It is also a better sound barrier, making it well suited for interior walls and partitions.

Steel

More and more homes are being built with steel. See Fig. 3-5. Steel is often used as the internal frame of a house because it can withstand severe weather, insect attacks, and fire. Steel framing is longer lasting than other materials. It won't crack, warp, twist, rot, split, or settle like wood framing might. Steel-framed houses are strong. For example, steel provides outstanding resistance against earthquakes and hurricane winds up to 110 mph. Since steel is stronger than wood, fewer building materials are required. Steel can benefit indoor air quality because it does not need to be treated with chemicals or resins.

Other Manufactured Metals

Aluminum, another manufactured metal, is commonly used in North America in the form of siding to cover frame houses. This metal provides insulation, prevents rotting, and eliminates the need for repainting. In addition, many modern homes have metal window frames, which require less maintenance than wooden frames.

Foam

Home builders only a few years ago would never have thought of using foam, but today rigid plastic foam products as well as spray foam are finding their way into many homes. One new technology features snap-together rigid foam blocks and concrete. Interlocking blocks are snapped together to form the foundation and walls of a house. Then steel rods are passed through the blocks to reinforce the walls and concrete is poured into the block cavities. The result is a very strong and energy-efficient house that uses 50 percent less energy than similar-sized houses.

Fig. 3-5 Using steel in homes has many advantages. Steel is lighter than wood, and is economical. A steel-framed home will also resist termites and withstand rugged environmental conditions.

Fig. 3-6 For the homeowner who doesn't want to repaint a deck every few years, vinyl is an option. This product maintains its color, holds up well in harsh climates, and is completely recyclable.

Some homes are being built with structural insulated panels (SIPs). Structural insulated panels consist of two exterior panels adhered to a rigid foam core. The SIPs provide excellent insulation and soundproofing.

Spray foam is another energy-efficient way to insulate a home. It's sprayed into place and expands to fill even small cavities. Spray foam is safe for the environment, too.

Plastic

Because plastic is light and flexible and can be formed into nearly any desired shape, it has been gaining acceptance in recent years as a building material. In fact, the United States building industry is now the world's second largest user of plastics. The disadvantage of using such materials as plastic and metal is that they are not *biodegradable*—they will not break down over time if they become refuse, so they are not kind to the environment.

Plastic is used in many ways and forms in home construction. For plumbing, it is lighter in weight and less expensive than copper, the metal traditionally used for pipes. Plastic is also being used in sheets for siding and roofing. It's used as insulation for cables and wires. There is even plastic "lumber" from recycled plastic. Builders find it provides a low-maintenance option for residential decking and other outdoor uses. See Fig. 3-6. Durable plastic lumber can also be used for interior framework on homes.

Recycled Materials

Today, people consider recycling such products as newspapers, plastic, and glass an essential part of their daily lives. Recycling has also found its way into the home-building industry. **Biomaterials**, organically-based building materials manufactured from recycled matter, are being used in construction in a number of ways. Construction experts have found that, like plastic, biomaterials can be molded into a variety of shapes and forms. One type of high-strength biomaterial is made from wheat straw, wood shavings, recycled newspaper, and recycled plastic. This material has been used to build interior walls and outdoor decks. Floor tile made from recycled car windshields is another example.

Biomaterials offer several advantages over wood. These new materials typically last much longer and do not warp or split. Biomaterials are also less costly than lumber yet they can be drilled, nailed, and screwed.

Yet another advantage of biomaterials over conventional building materials is that they can be customized to meet specific uses and climate conditions. For example, if a more flexible material is needed for a particular use, more fiber in the form of extra newspaper or straw can be added.

When biomaterials were first introduced, there were some disadvantages. They often didn't look like wood, and glues used in their manufacture produced dangerous fumes. Strict regulatory controls helped eliminate most problems.

The Impact of Technology

Fuel Cell Energy

Imagine a home powered by clean-burning energy that comes from the most abundant substances on earth. That vision may become reality, if fuel cell technology continues to advance.

Fuel cells convert energy produced by chemical reactions into electricity. Several different models exist, all using the same basic process. Like a battery, a cell consists of two terminals, or electrodes. Under pressure, hydrogen gas is forced to one electrode, and oxygen to the other. Reactions inside the cell split the hydrogen and oxygen molecules into their components, including atoms and electrons. The freed hydrogen electrons are channeled as an electric current outside the cell, where it can be harnessed to run machines and other devices. Actually, one cell makes just enough energy to light a bulb. For practical use, single cells are combined into fuel-cell stacks.

The only byproducts of the fuel cell process are electricity, water, and heat. It generates no pollutants. Moreover, with further refinement, it may become possible to capture the heat and use it for hot water, heating, and industrial processes.

Despite these advantages, one major limitation has kept fuel cells from common use. Pure hydrogen doesn't exist in nature, so it must be extracted from other fuels, including natural gas and methanol. This process decreases efficiency and may increase pollution. Nonetheless, many people foresee a day when cities will use fuel cells in electric power plants to provide clean, reliable electricity. Eventually, individual homes may have their own fuel cells.

Tech Trends

Learn how fuel cells are currently being used. What other future applications are most likely? What obstacles must be overcome to make them practicable for widespread use?

Green Building

Every year, housing in North America accounts for more than 20 percent of the total energy consumption and contributes to the problem of pollution. The average home produces more air pollution than the average car. Housing construction, renovation, and demolition create millions of tons of waste a year. In response to these problems, more and more builders and home buyers are looking toward green building. **Green building** is designing, building, and operating homes to use materials, energy, and water efficiently. Green building results in lower heating and cooling costs, less maintenance, and healthier indoor environments. Some green-building techniques include:

- Using alternative energy technologies such as solar energy and geo-thermal heat pumps.

- Using more insulation and insulating properly.

- Using energy-efficient heating and cooling systems as well as lighting, windows, and appliances.

- Choosing recycled and recyclable building materials. For example, steel-framed houses can be made from recycled steel. A typical 2,000 square foot wood house requires about 40 to 50 trees, while a steel-framed house can be made from 8 recycled cars. In the last decade, more than one trillion pounds of steel scrap has been recycled and kept out of landfills.

- Designing homes to use less material. Steel provides advantages in this area, too. Because steel is stronger than wood, less material is needed.

One organization leading the way in green building is the Partnership for Advancing Technology in Housing (PATH). PATH is a public/private partnership that works with industry leaders to advance the home building industry. PATH provides the latest information on innovative building materials, processes, and systems. It also publicizes innovative housing projects that might serve as models for builders, and it promotes cooperative research among industry, government, and academic partners.

Tools & Methods of Construction

As you have seen, technology has changed the types of materials used within the construction industry. There have also been changes in the tools and methods used to build homes.

Tools

For centuries, the only tools available to construction workers were simple ones, such as the hammer and the handsaw. Labor by hand was the only construction method used. Homes were built slowly and one at a time.

Today, although hand labor continues to play a vital role in construction, new tools and methods are making the process more efficient. Heavy equipment, such as cranes and bulldozers, is commonplace at construction sites. This equipment saves time and cuts down on the number of workers needed for a job. See Fig. 3-7.

Fig. 3-7 A skilled crane operator can move building materials into place with speed and ease. There are different sizes of cranes to match the weight of the material and the height of the structure.

Even hand tools have changed. For example, on a construction site you'll find that power nailers are taking over the work of hammers. The handheld tools used today for home building are more powerful and efficient than their predecessors. They are also far more specialized, with each tool designed to perform a particular task.

Many companies making new tools are designing them to be light and portable, eliminating the need for attached cords or hoses. Lighter tools also cause fewer injuries than heavy ones do. New batteries have been developed to boost power for power tools so that they can perform for longer periods of time.

Methods

Many of the labor-intensive tasks were once painstakingly done by hand at the housing **site**—the land and surrounding environment on which the home will be built. Now many tasks are accomplished by machines more quickly and less expensively at the factory. For example, kitchen cabinets and other fixtures are precut, and bathroom fixtures can be molded in one piece. Workers in factories can even produce entire homes in sections and transport them to the housing site. In some cases, robots handle much of the labor.

Imagine building your dream house or seeing remodeling plans before a worker ever picks up a saw. Computers make it possible and are becoming increasingly important in planning home building. **Computer-aided design (CAD)** programs—software that enables designers, architects, and drafters to make construction drawings, interior designs, and other drawings using a computer—are very useful. Designers can complete their plans more quickly and efficiently than ever before. These programs help builders identify design flaws and correct them before construction begins.

Regardless of technological advances, human skills will always be required in home building. Skilled workers must operate the tools and make sure that the methods and materials used are the best ones available for the jobs to be done. Skilled workers also must make sure that the finished homes meet high quality standards.

Types of Construction

As mentioned previously, some homes are made from assembled sections built in a factory. That method is just one of the options available for building homes today. In general, newly built homes fall into three categories, based on their method of construction: conventional construction, systems-built homes, and manufactured homes.

Conventional Construction

The most common way of building a house, which for centuries was the only way, is through conventional construction. **Conventional construction** is a building method in which materials are cut and assembled piece by piece at the home site. Houses constructed in this fashion are sometimes referred to as *stick built* or *site built*. See Fig. 3-8.

Fig. 3-8 In conventional construction, lumber and other materials are brought to the site where they are measured, cut, and assembled.

Disaster-Resistant Buildings

From hurricanes in Florida to wildfires in California, extreme weather conditions can cause extensive damage. No building is disaster-proof, but technology can make a structure more disaster-resistant.

- **Hurricanes and tornadoes.** How does a tall building stand up to 150-mph winds? Builders today may pour cement walls into concrete forms with foam insulation, which are left in place as reinforcement. Alternatively, they might use a newly developed concrete that is five times stronger and 75 percent lighter than conventional types. Windows that have a vinyl film bonded between layers of glass offer greater resiliency than conventional windows.

- **Fire.** Brick and stone walls offer the best resistance to fire, as do roofs made of metal or concrete. Shingles made of cement and fiberglass are also effective in protecting against fire. Metal shutters over small windows with double-glazed, tempered glass offer two layers of protection. Beams, columns, and other structural steel may be coated with cement-based fireproofing plaster.

- **Floods.** In areas that are prone to flooding, designers might recommend concrete, clay, and ceramic floors and walls, which are less penetrable than wood and less likely to warp. Supporting walls should be reinforced to withstand the pressure of water and floating debris. Watertight door closures and polyurethane sealants help to reduce seepage.

- **Earthquakes.** Many buildings, such as the TransAmerica building in San Francisco, are constructed with built-in seismic dampers to help them "ride out" earthquakes. There are two types of dampers. Passive dampers act like shock absorbers to reduce the impact. Active dampers use computerized sensors to register the amount of movement and trigger dampers to release energy to counter it. Active dampers need electricity, however, and power outages are common in earthquakes.

Apply It!

Imagine that you are part of a team responsible for designing a new home in San Francisco. What actions might you take to ensure that the building is as disaster-resistant as possible?

Systems-Built Homes

A **systems-built home** is a dwelling whose parts are manufactured in a factory, with the building completed at the site. In a systems-built home, quality is tightly controlled and waste is kept to a minimum. These homes are well built and usually cost less than conventionally built homes. They are ready to be occupied in much less time than a home built on-site. The three major types of systems-built homes are built from precut packages, series of panels, and coordinated modules. **Modular homes** are homes made up of separate boxlike sections, or modules. See Fig. 3-9. The various modules contain separate sections of the home, such as the master bedroom and bath in one module and the kitchen and dining room in another. The modules are built at a factory and then transported to the site of the home. There they are set in place on a foundation and fastened together.

Manufactured Homes

A **manufactured home** is a dwelling completely assembled at a factory and transported to the site. Another term for this type of housing is *mobile home*. The majority of these homes, however, are never moved once they have been installed at a site.

Manufactured homes are generally less expensive than conventionally built ones, but the cost varies, depending on size and features. Manufactured homes are fully equipped with major appliances, draperies, lighting fixtures, and carpeting. Homeowners may add such extras as skylights, shelving, and tile.

Although manufactured homes can, in theory, be placed almost anywhere, in certain areas they are restricted to designated parks. This situation, however, is changing. In the future, it may become common to find manufactured homes in almost any neighborhood.

The United States Department of Housing and Development (HUD) has strict requirements for manufactured homes. These standards cover all equipment and installations, including plumbing, heating, electrical systems, and fire safety.

Fig. 3-9 A modular home begins as several boxlike sections, or modules. The modules are manufactured and transported separately, and then assembled on-site.

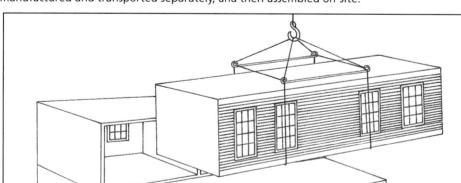

Technology in the Home

Technological advances in construction have created homes that are assembled quickly and efficiently in factories. Technology has also expanded inside the home, changing the way people live.

Advances in Home Technology

The term *high technology* or *high tech* describes advanced developments in such areas as electronics and computers. High technology has introduced the use of the integrated circuit, or computer microchip, into the home. These microchips are small enough to fit on the fingertip, yet can control many important functions in home entertainment, lighting, maintenance, communication, and security systems. Other technological advances have improved appliances and heating and cooling systems, making them more convenient and more energy efficient. **See Fig. 3-10.**

Fig. 3-10 Roomba, the robotic vacuum cleaner, represents a new phase in home technology. It is the first mass market robot designed to do its job while you are otherwise engaged.

Appliances

Today's appliances are more automated, provide more convenience, and save more energy than past models. For example, some refrigerators can alert you if a door is left ajar or if maintenance is needed. Dishwashers can sense how dirty the dishes are and provide the appropriate level of cleaning. What other types of "smart" appliances would you like to see developed?

Lighting

Home lighting has been improved in recent years. Fluorescent lighting is more energy efficient than regular incandescent lightbulbs. Solar lighting, which captures and uses the sun's energy, is often used outdoors. Now there are LED (light emitting diode) lamps that consume less than a quarter of the electricity a fluorescent lamp does. LED lamps last about 10 times as long, too.

Programmable Heating and Cooling

Guidelines for conserving energy in the home suggest turning down the heat or air conditioning at bedtime and when no one is home during the day. To handle these temperature changes, some people install a programmable thermostat. See Fig. 3-11. With this device, people can have the computer in the thermostat turn down the temperature after everyone is in bed and then turn up the heat in the morning before people wake up. The heating temperature can then drop again if everyone is out for the day and return to a more comfortable temperature as people start to arrive home. Programmable thermostats can even allow for variations between weekdays and weekends.

Another energy-saving technique divides a house or building into zones or areas in which heating and cooling are controlled independently. That means when the temperature drops in the kitchen and family room, more heat is directed there instead of the whole house. Separate thermostats monitor each zone. When this method is combined with programmable thermostats, significant reduction in energy use is possible.

Entertainment

High technology has redefined people's idea of entertainment. Home entertainment systems—including plasma, LCD, and digital TVs, DVD players, video game systems, and computer game software—change frequently in response to innovations in technology. See Fig. 3-12. Digital cameras and digital movie cameras offer many people the opportunity to create their own electronic entertainment. Satellite dishes and digital cable systems offer more channels and better reception to television viewers at increasingly lower costs.

Fig. 3-11 Heating or cooling your home while you're away wastes energy and costs money. With a programmable thermostat, you can set temperature settings to change automatically according to your schedule.

Fig. 3-12 Among the latest offerings in television technology, plasma screen TVs offer a wide screen, high quality picture, and low operating costs. Moreover, they hang on a wall and take up no more space than a picture.

Communication

Personal computers offer many ways for people to share information. See Fig. 3-13. Electronic communication has made the world accessible. E-mail is a popular means for family members and friends to stay in touch. Parents can share new photos of their children with far-away grandparents in only moments. Friends can share their latest thoughts through instant messaging, or see and talk to each other over the computer using webcam technology.

Computer users can log on to the Internet to read the latest news stories and sports scores, listen to music, or shop for everything from books to clothing to food from a local grocery store. People with common interests can "chat" online or post messages for help about hobbies, computer problems, and many other topics.

Electronic communication in the home can extend beyond the personal computer. For example, there are electronic picture frames that hook up to a phone line and family and friends can download new photos to each other. Memos and notes to other household members can be left in an electronic organizer rather than posted on the refrigerator.

Computers also offer people a wealth of information about housing. On the Internet a person can take a virtual tour of houses for sale, find a place to rent, or learn about new building techniques.

People needing information about housing programs can visit the government's various websites. People in the market to buy new furniture can visually try out different fabric coverings and make their purchase online.

Fig. 3-13 For communication and information gathering, computers are almost indispensable. They have become fixtures in many homes.

Security

Electronic door locks are a very reliable method of securing a home. They allow doors to be locked or unlocked with the push of a button or by entering a combination on a keypad. Locks can even be hooked up to a timer, or they can be activated from a remote location. If a person doesn't want to use keys to lock a door, a lock that is powered by a battery and an infrared light is available. When the user touches the doorknob, a small light appears just above it. Then, to lock the door, the person enters an access code.

One high-tech method uses **biometrics**—reading the physical characteristics of a person to allow entry. One system scans the iris of a person's eye and matches it by computer to a list of people with authorized entry. Fingerprints, palmprints, and voice can also be used. So far this technology is used primarily in business and industry.

Motion-sensitive lights can be installed outdoors and inside a home. When a sensor detects movement, the light turns on to deter intruders. Motion-sensitive lights are also an energy-efficient way to light less frequently used rooms inside the home.

Closed-circuit television (CCTV) is a system gaining popularity for use in those areas of a home that owners would like to keep secure. The system installs in a television set, and separate cameras are placed in the areas to be observed. With a remote control, a homeowner can check each site and view the home area on the television screen.

Consumer Considerations

How Much Security?

Technology has provided sophisticated options for securing our homes, ranging from video surveillance systems to intrusion detectors. It's not surprising, then, that many people wonder how much technology they really need.

Home security experts agree on certain essential steps, some of which are relatively low tech, to guard against intruders. For example, deadbolt locks on exterior doors and window bars with quick-release levers provide added security.

Preventing burglars from entering is one approach to security; another is to deter them. Burglars tend to rely on the element of surprise, so anything that takes away that advantage can be a good deterrent. For this reason, some people

believe that alarms and motion-sensitive spotlights are reasonable investments. Animal lovers might prefer a loud dog.

Whatever security technology is chosen, all family members should learn how to use it. Otherwise it may be used incorrectly or not at all. Meanwhile, joining a neighborhood watch group offers a low-cost, low-tech solution that has the added benefit of making a whole neighborhood safer.

The Automated Home

The advances described on the preceding pages are only a small part of home technology. Some homes are equipped with **automated management systems**, central control units that oversee daily functions in a home. Such automated systems are designed to maximize comfort, convenience, and safety while minimizing energy use.

Here are some examples of what an automated management system can do.

- Sensors can automatically turn lights on when someone enters a room and off when the room is unoccupied.
- The water heater can be set to turn itself off when it is not needed and to have hot water ready when it is required.
- Baths and showers can be programmed to deliver water at a preset temperature.
- A single home entertainment center can send signals to any audio or video outlet in the home.
- People can awaken each morning to find the room temperature automatically adjusted, the motorized blinds opened to let the sun in, and coffee brewing. See Fig. 3-14.
- The system can monitor the efficiency and performance of appliances and alert occupants to any problems.
- If a sensor detects smoke, the system's "brain" can sound an alarm, light a safe exit path, turn off unneeded electricity, and call for help.

Installing an automated home system adds considerably to the cost of building a home. In the long run, however, the system may reduce energy bills and insurance costs.

Fig. 3-14 Technology has made thousands of new products available. This system opens and closes drapes by remote control or at preset times.

Profile of a CAD Specialist

CAD specialists prepare technical drawings and plans on the computer for architects, interior designers, and engineers. Drawings include floor plans, elevations, sections, electrical plans, mechanical system plans, specifications, and perspectives. The drawings may be for residential or commercial buildings.

Education & Training

- Drafting training from a technical institute, community college, or four-year college or university is preferred.
- Courses in drafting, computer-aided drafting, interior design, mathematics, and engineering technology are essential.
- Keeping up to date with CAD software changes is important.

Skills & Aptitudes

- Mechanical aptitude and computer skills are required.
- Visual and spatial aptitude are important.
- Being good with details and able to work accurately is vital.

CAD Specialist
Jason Kim

I've been interested in computers as long as I can remember. About two years ago I started working for an architectural/engineering firm in Miami. The firm designs buildings and interiors for commercial buildings and residences. Our architects develop the designs of the buildings, and the engineers figure out how to meet the mechanical needs like heating, ventilating, and air conditioning.

As the architects and engineers make their designs, they give me their ideas and sketches. As a computer-aided design (CAD) specialist, I turn their sketches into detailed plans using the CAD software. The program saves the drawings, which makes it simple to revise and duplicate them. Our last project involved a new hotel in Puerto Rico. I had to draw the floor plans, elevations, sections, electrical plans, mechanical system plans, specifications, and perspectives. During the design process, I had to redo the drawings over and over as different team members reacted to the plans. If I had to do that work manually, it would have required a huge amount of time and expense. We probably never would have finished the project on time! By using the CAD software, I was able to make most of those revisions quickly and easily.

Working as a CAD specialist requires a variety of skills. Obviously you have to really enjoy working at a computer. I am in front of the monitor at least 30 hours a week. You have to be good at working with other people too. Some of my time is spent talking with the architects and engineers. We have to work as a team. That means you have to be able to compromise and build consensus.

I think our firm is able to develop better designs by using CAD software. And the software makes it easier for clients to visualize our concepts.

Since technology is always changing, I have to keep up with the changes in CAD software. I take special classes at least twice a year to learn about new software. I also use the Internet to learn about changes in the field and new products.

Design Portfolio

1. Locate a copy of a residential floor plan. Draw the floor plan using CAD software.

2. Choose a room from the floor plan and select furniture for it. Place the furniture on the plan. Show the furnished room from two different perspectives.

Review & Activities

Chapter Summary

- **Technology** will continue to play an increasing role in improving home construction.

- Both natural and manufactured materials are used to build homes.

- **Green building** techniques conserve natural resources and protect the environment.

- Technology continues to improve the tools and methods used in the construction industry.

- Three main types of construction are used by the housing industry today.

- Technology is helping to create more useful and efficient features and systems in homes, often while lowering energy use.

Checking Your Understanding

1. Define **technology** and explain the role it plays in housing construction.

2. Identify two natural building materials and describe the uses of each in home construction.

3. What is the difference between softwood and hardwood lumber?

4. Identify two advantages of using brick and stone in building.

5. What are **engineered wood products**? What advantage do they have over standard wood products?

6. What advantages does steel framing have over wood framing?

7. What are **biomaterials** made from? Give two examples of construction products made from biomaterials.

8. What makes **green building** different from conventional building?

9. What are three ways that technology has contributed to energy conservation in the home?

10. What is an **automated management system**? What are some of the advantages and disadvantages of building a house equipped with such a system?

Thinking Critically

1. **Predicting Outcomes.** Research the high-tech features of Bill Gates' home. Predict how long it will be before the technology used in that home will be available in retail stores.

2. **Defending Your Position.** Do you think that architects and builders have an obligation to use more recycled materials in building homes? Give reasons for your answer.

3. **Summarizing Information.** Describe the overall effect of high technology on the quality of life at home.

Applying Your Knowledge

1. **What's New?** Using the Internet, identify a tool, building material, construction method, or technology for the home that is not mentioned in this chapter. Share your findings in an oral report.

2. **Green Building.** Many manufacturers use recycled materials to make products such as ceiling tiles, carpeting, and paneling. Visit the Internet to learn more about green building products. Then visit a local building supply center to compare the prices of green products to other brands. Which are more costly and why?

3. **Surviving Earthquakes.** After the San Francisco earthquake of 1906, builders reevaluated the building materials that had been used. Find out about the differences between building materials and construction methods used before and after that catastrophe. Then, research the 1989 San Francisco earthquake to determine the fate of buildings that were constructed to withstand earthquakes.

4. **Perfect Material.** Imagine that you have developed the perfect building material. Based on current trends in home construction technology, write an article in which you describe this new product.

Design Challenge

Imagine that you run a home-building company that uses only recycled materials. Prepare a brochure promoting your company to potential home buyers. In your brochure, provide details about the following:

1. The various building materials your company uses and why they are the best choices.

2. The types and styles of home construction you specialize in.

3. The ways in which your company uses the latest technology to create advanced interior systems.

Design and print your brochure.

Chapter 4

Careers in Housing & Interiors

Objectives

- Explain how personal characteristics relate to career decisions.

- Identify resources for career information.

- Explain the different classifications of jobs and give examples of each.

- Develop a career plan.

- Describe the characteristics needed by entrepreneurs.

- Identify the steps in getting a job.

- Describe the skills necessary for keeping a job.

Vocabulary

- aptitude
- ability
- entrepreneurs
- career ladder
- job shadowing
- apprenticeship
- employability skills
- workplace readiness

- networking
- résumé
- portfolio
- job application
- references
- interview
- mentors

The future is now—at least when it comes to planning your career. Thinking ahead to your future work life can be both exciting and scary. Figuring out your career interests and then finding and keeping a job in a competitive market can be difficult. That's where this chapter will help you. The best way to avoid worrying about your prospects is to plan ahead and prepare for the career you want.

Career Opportunities

With hundreds of different jobs in the areas of housing and design, you have a lot to consider. Where do you start? The best place is to think about your hopes and dreams for the future. Where do you want to live? Do you want to travel or work from your home? What do you want from a career? A high salary? Personal satisfaction? Plenty of free time? Only you can answer those questions, but with a career search you don't stop with your dreams. There are other factors to consider.

Your Personality & Interests

Consider how your personal characteristics pertain to a career. Are you enthusiastic? This is a requirement for most sales positions. Are you in good physical condition? Construction workers must spend many hours doing physical labor. If you like working with people, information, or data, there are housing and interiors careers for you, too.

Now think about your interests. What are your favorite activities? Make a list of the top ten activities you enjoy. These interests might guide you to a career you'll enjoy. Many people find work much more rewarding if it's something they enjoy.

Another helpful way to identify interests is to take an interest survey. You simply choose from a long list of activities those you might most enjoy. The survey results identify types of careers that might suit you. A vocational counselor can help you find an interest survey.

Your Aptitudes & Abilities

Next consider your aptitudes and your abilities. An **aptitude** is a natural talent or your potential for learning a skill. An **ability** is a skill you already have developed. For example, you may have an aptitude for design. This is demonstrated in your ability to arrange and decorate your room attractively.

Think about the school subjects you enjoy the most and in which you do best. If you do well in graphic arts classes, you could think about a career as a drafter or architect. **See Fig. 4-1.**

To get a clear picture of your aptitudes and abilities, make a chart with the headings *Intellectual*, *Physical*, and *Social*. List your aptitudes and abilities in each category.

Your Values

Becoming aware of your values is an important way of getting to know yourself better. Your values are the principles that you want to live by and the beliefs that are important to you. For example, if you spend time mastering new computer software programs, you may value learning and challenging yourself to acquire new skills. You might be interested in a career involving technology, such as designing new building materials. You need to keep your values in mind as you think of your career options.

Many people never consider how their career and their personal and family life are related. A person who values time with her or his family but chooses a job requiring extensive overtime won't be happy. Someone who likes independence and flexible work hours won't like a highly structured nine-to-five job. Choosing a career that meshes with your values makes it more likely that you will find your career satisfying.

Fig. 4-1 Artistic ability is helpful for many careers in housing and interiors. **Can you think of some examples?**

Learning About Careers

With your personal characteristics in mind, start investigating careers. To make the best career choice, you must know the responsibilities, skills, and knowledge required for the job. You can learn more about careers in several different ways. This chapter and the *Careers in Focus* features throughout this book highlight a variety of related careers. The object is to find the careers that match your personality, interests, aptitudes, abilities, and values. See Fig. 4-2.

Researching Careers

Don't stop your investigation here. Talk with people who are working in jobs you think you might enjoy. Ask what they like and dislike about their jobs. School counselors and teachers can suggest sources of information about jobs.

The Internet is another valuable resource. You can find websites for companies in the housing and interiors industry; newsgroups; and bulletin boards created by trade organizations, companies, and individuals—all helpful for career research. You can search for everything from job descriptions to company profiles. Newspaper classified ads from other cities and online versions of trade publications are also available.

The *Dictionary of Occupational Titles, Occupational Outlook Handbook*, and *Occupational Outlook Quarterly* are good references that you can find in a library or on the Internet at the U.S. Department of Labor site. These websites provide detailed information on thousands of jobs, including descriptions of the kind of work done, wages and benefits, and the kind of education and training needed. They also discuss the prospects of these jobs in the future. One thing you need to consider is whether a career you're thinking about entering will offer plentiful job opportunities. You might wish to avoid choosing a career that does not show strong future growth.

Fig. 4-2 This remodeling specialist plans how to modernize homes. After meeting with clients to talk about their ideas, she spends time creating designs and preparing cost estimates.

Fig. 4-3 Job shadowing is a great way to find out more about a career. By spending time with a person on the job, you learn firsthand what a typical workday is like.

As you learn more about careers, you'll see that jobs are often classified into the following four categories:

- **Entry-Level.** These jobs require little training but may require a high school diploma.
- **Technical.** These jobs require special knowledge of a technical skill, which can be gained through education or on-the-job training.
- **Professional.** These jobs require a bachelor's or advanced degree.
- **Entrepreneurial.** These jobs call on the special skills of **entrepreneurs**—people who start their own business.

Some of these jobs fit together to create a **career ladder**, a group of jobs related in terms of the skills and nature of the work and that can lead to more advanced positions. In a retail store, for instance, entry-level sales clerks can, with experience, become sales associates first and sales supervisors later. With the addition of a business education and training in managing others, they can become department heads. These jobs are all connected in a career ladder. Of course, all entry-level sales clerks do not move on to more advanced jobs. The opportunity is there for them, however.

Job Shadowing

The more firsthand knowledge you have before you make a decision, the better the chance of a positive outcome. One excellent way to learn about a job firsthand is job shadowing. **Job shadowing** means spending time with a person at work and learning by watching as he or she performs the functions of the job. The person you are observing follows a regular workday while you stay quietly nearby—like a "shadow." **See Fig. 4-3.**

How do you arrange for job shadowing? Sometimes your teacher or counselor can help. You can also make your own arrangements by contacting companies and asking to job shadow a person with a specific position. You can use the experience to evaluate whether you are interested in that career. You can also ask the worker you shadowed for advice on how to prepare to enter that field.

Work Experience

On-the-job experience can be very helpful in learning more about various career areas. If you can, take advantage of a work-study program while you are in school. This may help you explore your interests and skills. There are also many part-time and summer jobs in the housing and interiors fields. You can also gain helpful general knowledge and skills from other jobs. For example, you gain experience working with people when you do volunteer work in a hospital.

Developing Your Career Plan

If you do your research well, you'll turn up several career choices that interest you. Now you can narrow the field by comparing your personal data with the career information you've gathered. For instance, if you are interested in working outdoors, you might consider such careers as construction worker and surveyor. If you also like planning and have a talent for growing plants and for design, the career of landscape architect might be a good fit. Keep in mind that your choice is flexible. As you grow and change, your choice may change, too.

Setting Goals

You have already accomplished goals in your life. You achieved them step-by-step. You reach a long-term goal by accomplishing a series of short- and medium-term goals. Use the same strategy when working toward your ultimate career goal. To get started, set some short-term goals. For example, your long-term goal might be a career as a public relations specialist who handles consumer, community, and media relations for a company. You will need excellent communication skills. A short-term goal might be to improve those skills by getting a position on the school newspaper. Another might include a summer job working with consumers. You also know from your research that you will need a college degree. You set a medium-term goal of attending a college with a good public relations or journalism program.

Education & Training

To reach your long-term career goal, you need the necessary education and training. Almost every job requires some special training. Having advanced education and training means you'll have more career opportunities to choose from. **See Fig. 4-4.**

You may get your start with an entry-level job. For entry-level jobs, many companies offer on-the-job training. This may consist of a few days of orientation or more formal long-term instruction.

At the next level are jobs that require specialized training. Workers may need vocational-technical or trade school training or a two-year college degree. Some careers require an apprenticeship.

Fig. 4-4 Learning how to use computer-aided design (CAD) software is a positive step toward developing a design career.

An **apprenticeship** program combines on-the-job training by a skilled worker and classroom instruction. See Fig. 4-5. Completion may take from several months to several years, depending on the craft. In some cases, workers must pass a state licensing exam.

Still other jobs require advanced education. A training period of several years after college may also be required. In some instances, the worker must take an examination to become licensed in his or her field. The research you have completed for your career choices will tell you how much education and training you need.

Basic Job Skills

What does every employer want in an employee, no matter what the job is? The answer is employability skills. **Employability skills** are those general skills required to acquire and retain a job. Many employers put dependability, responsibility, and a positive attitude at the top of the list. Along with those, the following skills are essential:

- The basics—reading, mathematics, writing, speaking, and listening.
- Thinking skills—problem solving, decision making, creative thinking, visualizing how to accomplish a task, and reasoning.
- Personal qualities—integrity, honesty, self-esteem, sociability, and self-management.

Strong communication skills, for example, are vital to the success of workers in any job. These skills are needed to interact successfully with supervisors, coworkers, and customers. Employees who can speak clearly are valuable to employers. Equally important, workers must be able to listen closely to a manager's instructions or a client's questions so they can respond appropriately. In addition, some jobs require the ability to make effective written or oral presentations.

Fig. 4-5 For some careers, you learn on the job and are trained by a master in the profession.

Workplace Readiness

Employers also look for behaviors that indicate a person will be able to function well in their workplace. **Workplace readiness** refers to a person's ability to do the various tasks required for a particular job. They include:

- Having a good work ethic—showing up on time each day and focusing on work during working hours.
- Working effectively as a team member.
- Having good presentation skills.
- Showing initiative, the ability to make suggestions to improve work.
- Computer literacy, or the ability to work effectively using computer software.
- Understanding the "big picture," knowing how each worker contributes to the overall mission and goals of the company.

Did you notice that many of these skills have to do with attitude? Employers want workers with a positive attitude toward their work. Such an attitude helps people do their work more smoothly—and keeps clients happy.

The Impact of Technology

Designing in Three Dimensions

Picture this scene: A designer and his clients sit before a computer screen, looking at a room in the house they are designing. The client says, "It looks a little dark. What if we change the stain on the wood from mahogany to beech? That's better. Now let's change the curtains from forest green to lime green. Perfect!"

Until lately, making such detailed revisions to a design required a lot of time and work. With computer-aided design (CAD), design professionals now do the work with just a few clicks of a mouse.

Flexibility. Unlike older methods of showing design, such as scale or miniature models, CAD software can generate numerous views of a single room. Clients can take a virtual tour, allowing them to see rooms from different points of view.

Efficiency. Using CAD is faster and easier than making drawings or models or even simple floor plans. This saves time and money for both designers and clients. It also makes it easier for people with disabilities to realize dreams of a career in home design.

Detail. CAD means that details once left to the client's imagination can be more fully realized. An image can be fine-tuned to show the play of natural lighting on different surfaces at different times of the day or year. Program features allow designers to display different textures to provide a better sense of a room's look.

These features make CAD software an important tool of designers in today's world. Developing strong CAD skills has become vital to any designer's career—and to success in that career.

Tech Trends

Visit the website of a CAD software dealer that shows examples of CAD-generated images. Identify three features of the CAD program. For each, write a scenario illustrating how a design professional could use that feature to better meet a client's needs.

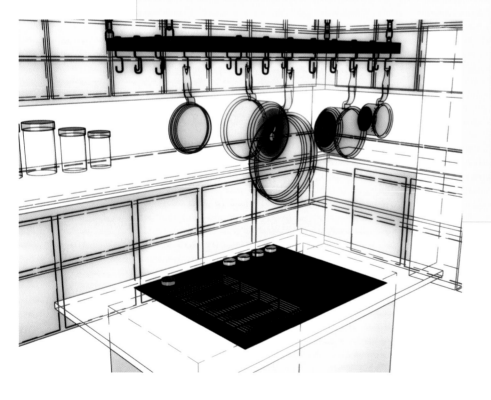

Owning Your Own Business

Do you dream of running your own business? The housing and interiors industry offers many opportunities for entrepreneurs.

Most entrepreneurs share certain traits, such as the following:

- **Motivation.** Successful entrepreneurs are self-motivated. They know how to set and achieve goals.
- **Foresight.** Entrepreneurs see problems and find ways to solve them successfully.
- **Decision Making.** Those who make sound decisions stand the chance of being more successful.
- **Relationship Skills.** Being able to get along with others and the ability to negotiate and resolve conflicts are vital skills.

Many people start their own business as a second job. When the business becomes more established, they become self-employed.

Are you cut out to be an entrepreneur? Consider the advantages and disadvantages. Some aspects of working for yourself are appealing. You make the rules, set the schedule, and make the decisions. The potential for financial gain depends on how hard and wisely you work. You receive all the profits. Entrepreneurs generally feel a lot of personal satisfaction.

On the downside, managing your own time requires that you be self-disciplined and a self-starter. See Fig. 4-6. Many entrepreneurs work alone and are on the job long hours. You'll also need to wear many hats. You'll probably be the manager, the worker, the advertiser, the accountant, and the one in charge of maintenance. You are also the one responsible for meeting all local, state, and federal workplace requirements. This involves taking responsibility for safety, security, and environmental factors. Reporting accidents, maintaining inventory, and managing cash flow are critical tasks. Most entrepreneurs have variable incomes, and without a steady income you must be an excellent money manager.

Fig. 4-6 Entrepreneurs often have to work long hours, even holidays, and not take any vacation—expecially when they are getting a business started. **Do you have the commitment to be an entrepreneur? Would the personal sacrifices be worth being your own boss?**

Finding a Job

Congratulations! You've done your personal evaluations and your research. You've gotten the education or training you need. Now you are ready to make the move into the world of work.

Finding the right job begins with a job lead. This can be a tip from a friend, an ad on an online job site, a help-wanted ad in a newspaper, information from a counselor or teacher, or the result of networking.

Networking

Networking is communicating with people you know or can get to know to share information and advice about jobs. See Fig. 4-7. Networking is not as difficult as you might think. Start by making a list of all the people you know, even casual acquaintances. Then contact those people, let them know you are looking for a job, and ask for any information that may lead to a job. Some won't be able to help you, but others will be able to direct you to another person who can help. Research shows that more than one-third of the jobs people get results from networking.

The Internet

The Internet is an excellent source for job leads. When you are online, hundreds of job-listing sites are just a few keystrokes away. Type in any of these search words to access worldwide opportunities: *employment opportunities*, *jobs*, *job listings*, or *careers* along with words describing the field or job you're interested in. You can also check to see if there are any job openings at companies where you would like to work.

Job Advertisements

Job ads are another way to find a job. Look in the classified ads in local newspapers or in magazines that cover your field of interest. Study an ad carefully to determine the necessary skills and qualifications. Do you have the skills the ad specifies? If so, follow the directions in the ad to respond.

As you think about the job, consider what you could learn from it. How could this job help you meet your long-term career goal? Some jobs will not apply directly to that goal, but you can still learn valuable skills from them.

Fig. 4-7 If the people you meet through networking don't know of any job openings themselves, they may be able to put you in touch with others who do.

Employment Agencies

Employment agencies match job seekers and companies with job openings. Job seekers fill out applications at the agency. Businesses call the agency when they have openings. The agency then matches qualified applicants to the positions available. There is normally a fee for jobs found through an employment agency. Sometimes the applicant pays the fee; other times the employer pays. Be sure to ask the agency before giving them your name.

Preparing a Job-Winning Résumé

Developing a résumé and keeping it up-to-date will make it easier for you to land the housing job of your choice. A **résumé** is a brief summary of your personal information, education, skills, work experience, activities, and interests. You will send your résumé to an employer when applying for a job, or you may post it on the Internet. Think of your résumé as an advertisement about yourself. In it you cover the facts of your experience and education in a positive way that will tell an employer at a glance how you can contribute to the workplace. A well-written résumé helps convince the employer that you are the right person for the job.

The best résumés are brief, usually only one or two pages. Carefully choose what to include and what to emphasize. If you don't have any work experience, focus instead on your skills and education. Be sure to include any volunteer work you have done. That can let an employer know you are reliable and have a good attitude toward work.

Résumés may be organized in many ways. Most common is the *chronological résumé* that lists work experience and education in a specific order. The most recent job is listed first, followed by the previous one, and so on. Educational achievements are listed in the same order. **See Fig. 4-8 on page 92.** On a *skills résumé*, you organize the information around your skills and accomplishments. After each heading, such as *Knowledge of CAD* or *Design Experience*, you provide a description of what you know.

You may need to send your résumé as an e-mail attachment. For the best results, keep it simple and avoid italics, underscores, and other type elements that might get garbled in transmission.

When you send your résumé to an employer to apply for a job, you'll also send a cover letter. This one-page letter introduces you, tells what job you are applying for, and explains why you think you are qualified for the job. If you learned about the company from someone, say so. In the body of the letter highlight why you are right for the job. Conclude by asking for an interview. Be sure to include your phone number and e-mail address.

Building Your Portfolio

You can use a design **portfolio**—a collection of examples of your best work—to show potential employers what you are capable of doing. Written work, drawings, CAD design projects, and photographs of work you have created or built all belong in your portfolio.

Start building your design portfolio now, in high school. There are many design assignments throughout this book that could contribute to your design portfolio. Review your work and choose the best examples. Having a range of work enables you to show varied skills.

You may also ask teachers or employers to write a letter of recommendation. They should explain how long they have known you and in what capacity before discussing your strong points. You can place those letters in your design portfolio too.

Fig. 4-8

Josephine Sapphire

8131 Sunshine Road
Woodruff, Illinois 80002
555-555-5555

Your **contact information** goes at the top of the page.

Career Objective states what you would like to achieve in the workplace.

Career Objective

- A creative position in the housing and interiors field that will allow opportunities for career growth and development.

Skills & Abilities list your qualifications

Skills & Abilities

- Accomplished in CAD software
- Artistic and creative
- Flexible team member
- Detail-oriented and committed

Work Experiences list your current and past employment, beginning with your most recent job.

Work Experience

- 2005-Present, Apprentice, 2Chez Designs
- 2004-2005, Receptionist Remax Realty
- 2003-2004, Part-time Clerk, Hobbit Art Supplies

Education & Training lists your education and training achievements, beginning with your most recent achievement.

Education & Training

- 2006 Certificate, Real Estate
- Apprenticeship, 2Chez Designs
- 2005 Graduate, Royal Community College
- 2003 Graduate, Woodruff High School

Activities & Honors list your extra curricular activities and achievements, beginning with your most recent achievement.

Activities & Honors

- 2005 Star Apprentice, 2Chez Designs
- Chair of the 2004 MS Smile Campaign
- President of the Woodruff Art Club, 2003
- Student Council Member, 2001-2003
- Woodruff Hospital Volunteer, 2000-2002

References are either listed at the end of the résumé, or a statement tells the reader that references are available upon request.

References

- Available upon request

Job Applications

A **job application** is a form employers use to ask questions about an applicant's skills, work experience, education, and interests. Employers do not have the right to ask about your race, religion, gender, children, or marital status. Always fill out an application completely and accurately. Follow these job application tips:

- Follow directions exactly.

- Print neatly. Answer all the questions. If you have nothing to write, draw a line or print "Not Applicable" or "NA" in the space provided.

- Make your statements positive.

- Never lie or exaggerate on a job application.

- Keep your options open. If asked to state the salary you want, write "Negotiable." If asked if you will work nights, write "Will consider."

- Prepare lists of information you will need in advance. This includes schools you have attended and jobs you have held along with addresses.

- Prepare references in advance. **References** are people, such as teachers and former employers, who will recommend you to an employer. Ask permission of the people before you use their names as references. Take along their addresses and phone numbers to complete the application.

The Interview

All your hard work has paid off! You've been asked to come in for an **interview**—a formal meeting between an employer and a job applicant. This is the employer's chance to meet you in person and learn more about your qualifications. It is your chance to show how your career research can pay off.

Before the Interview

Before you go on a job interview:

- Find out everything you can about the company. Visit the company's Internet site. Talk to anyone you know who works for the company.

Fig. 4-9 People tend to feel more confident when they look their best. It's a great way to help get an interview off to a good start.

- Practice your interviewing skills. Have a friend ask you typical questions and comment on your answers.

- Plan what you will wear. The first impression you make when you walk in the door is based on your smile and your clothes. Being well-groomed and dressing appropriately are important. Match your clothes to the job. See Fig. 4-9.

- Make sure your portfolio is in order. Take along an extra copy of your résumé, cover letter, and list of references.
- Plan to arrive a little early. You may need to make a trial run the day before so you are certain how long it will take you to get to the interview. Make sure you add extra travel time for unexpected conditions.

During the Interview

When you meet the employer for the interview, project a positive attitude. Remember the employability skills and workplace readiness behaviors employers are interested in and convey those. A firm handshake will show you have confidence. Maintaining eye contact lets the employer know that you are paying close attention. Speak clearly and avoid using slang. Give specific answers. Always be honest, but don't undersell yourself. Stress school activities and volunteer work that show you are dependable, able to work as part of a team, and responsible. Some questions may be asked to assess your problem-solving skills, or you may be asked to role-play a situation. Keep in mind that the employer is not looking for one right answer but is evaluating your thinking skills.

Be prepared to ask your own questions, too. This is one of the reasons you did research on the company. You may ask questions about the business, such as "What plans do you have for selling your new line of furniture over the Internet?" You may also ask questions about employee benefits, such as "What does the health plan cover?"

Interviews can be stressful, but don't let yourself be overwhelmed. See Fig. 4-10. Relax and be yourself. The worst thing that can happen is that you don't get the job. There are other jobs. The most important point is to be certain that you and the company will be right for each other.

At the end of the interview, you may be offered the job then and there. If not, thank the interviewer and ask when the decision will be made. Ask when would be a good time to check back.

Follow Up

The interview process doesn't end when you leave. You need to follow up. Ask yourself, What went well? How could I improve for the next time? Did I forget anything important? Is there additional information about me that might be beneficial to give to the employer? Also, send a follow-up letter to the employer. Thank the interviewer for the time, reinforce how your skills could help the company, and restate your interest in the job. Don't forget to check back.

Fig. 4-10 As you begin an interview, take a deep breath, smile, and let the interviewer take the lead.

The Offer

You've done it! You've been offered a job. Believe it or not, you don't have to rush into saying yes. If you want to think about it, ask for a day to make your decision. List the job's pros and cons and evaluate them carefully before calling back to accept. If you are offered the job but at a lower salary than you were looking for, think it over. You might change your mind or be able to negotiate the salary.

Remember, though, just because you have been offered a job, you don't have to take it. You may decide that the job isn't for you, or you may have been offered a better position in the meantime. If you decide not to take the position, let the employer know. You don't have to give reasons for turning the job down. Just say, "Thank you for considering me, but I am not interested in taking the position."

If an employer doesn't offer you the job, try to learn from the experience. Ask why you weren't hired. Do you need more training? How did you come across in the interview? Any feedback you get will help you in future interviews.

On the Job

You've got the job, and now the work starts of keeping and advancing in the job. Now is the time to demonstrate your employability skills and workplace readiness.

Always arrive at work on time. Make sure that you practice good personal hygiene. While you are on the job, produce quality work and maintain productive work habits. Manage your time wisely. Perform job tasks efficiently without wasting energy. Identify the goal of the job you are given and try to visualize the steps to reaching it. Some jobs require handling more than one task at a time. Set priorities or ask your supervisor for help in doing so. Be cooperative, no matter how unimportant a task may seem to you. Entry-level jobs often involve the worst tasks and little responsibility. If you find yourself in such a position, smile and do the job well. When you really demonstrate your skills, you will advance in the job.

Show willingness to learn and to follow directions. Listen carefully to your instructions and take notes if possible. See Fig. 4-11. Use good communication skills. Speak clearly. Before submitting written reports, always proofread your work to catch any errors. Always demonstrate pride in the work you perform.

Fig. 4-11 When you're on the job, listen carefully as your responsibilities are explained. If you don't understand the instructions, ask for more information. Most supervisors are happy to give you the help you need to do the job correctly.

Teamwork

Getting along with your coworkers as well as your manager is an important part of any job. Treat others fairly. Be courteous and kind. Remember, though, you are on the job to work, not to socialize. Do your fair share, and pitch in to help someone who is behind.

Teamwork is essential on every job. **See Fig. 4-12.** You can be a positive and productive part of any team by doing your tasks well and on time. Always pay attention to the directions of the team leader and to the comments and ideas of other members. Show respect for team members' skills and expertise. If someone is having difficulty with an assignment, help brainstorm solutions. The whole team's success depends on the work of each member.

Leadership

If you are asked to take the leadership role, you will want to foster these qualities:

• Generate a plan based on the tasks needed to be done, the resources your team has, and the alternatives. Communicate the plan clearly to the team and make sure all members understand their roles.

• Promote teamwork. Include the team in decision making. Ask for feedback and listen carefully when it is given. Understand the needs of your team, and adjust your plans to accommodate the team's goals.

• Keep the team on track. Provide guidance when team members need it, watch to make sure goals are being met, reevaluate the plan as necessary, and help everyone achieve her or his full potential.

• Set the example. If you want others to give their best, give your best. Show initiative, help others, act with maturity, keep a positive attitude, and always act ethically.

• Be a team player yourself. Respect others' ideas, and show their input is valued. Praise good work, and thoughtfully offer constructive criticism when necessary.

• Use your problem-solving and decision-making skills to develop creative solutions.

One way you can gain leadership skills is by participating in Family, Career and Community Leaders of America (FCCLA). FCCLA is a national organization of students enrolled in Family and Consumer Sciences courses. FCCLA activities and skill events provide opportunities for leadership development. Membership will also help you gain invaluable experience and help you develop teamwork, leadership, communication, and employability skills.

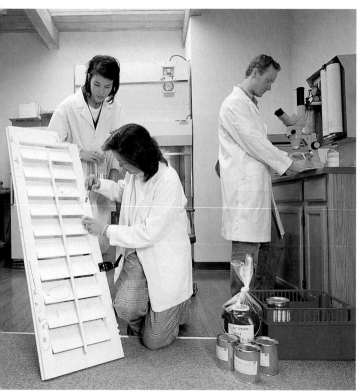

Fig. 4-12 These workers are part of a team researching new kinds of paint. **What are some problems that can prevent team members from working well together?**

Ethical Behavior

Ethical behavior is crucial to success. Two important aspects of ethical behavior are being trustworthy and honest. One of the most common ways employees demonstrate honesty concerns work hours. For example, if a worker takes an extra 15 minutes at lunch every day, the employer is being cheated. Those 15 minutes a day add up to over 5 hours in a month.

What about honesty over money? Obviously stealing money from a company is dishonest. It is also dishonest for employees to overcharge employers on expenses for which they are reimbursed.

When employees lie to their supervisors or coworkers about work they haven't done or don't admit when they have made a mistake, they are not being trustworthy. Would you want to work with someone you couldn't trust?

Remember to respect the property of others and be fair. Don't go along with the wishes of other people because they pressure you. If the company ethics don't match yours, don't hesitate to leave the job. Always treat your employer with the same respect and trust as you would like to receive.

Resolving Conflicts

There will be times on the job when conflicts will arise. You may disagree with your team on how to accomplish a task, or you may have a personality conflict. Don't assume you know the other person's point of view. Ask and give the other side time to talk. Respect the opinions of others. Try to understand their needs. Keep any discussions professional. Keep your body language, such as gestures, nonthreatening. Don't make personal remarks. Treat others fairly and ethically. Be open to creative solutions and be willing to compromise. Sometimes both sides have to give a little to reach a solution everyone can accept.

Managing Multiple Roles

Everyone has multiple roles in life, each with specific responsibilities. You may juggle work, family, community, and social obligations. Sometimes you may feel that there isn't enough time to do everything that is important to you. For example, if your job requires frequent travel or you work two jobs, family time may be limited.

Pressure from multiple roles can make a person less effective in each of them. A frustrating situation at home may cause you to have trouble concentrating at work. A problem at work can interfere with enjoyment of social activities.

What's the solution? Unfortunately, there's not one that fits every situation. Learning how to prioritize, effectively manage time and energy, and handle stress all help. However, sometimes it's necessary to cut out some activity or even find a different job. The way you balance your work with the other roles you have in life will influence your satisfaction with your career.

Mentors

Have you ever been in a position to help someone learn how to do a task? If so, you have a glimpse of what it is like to be a mentor. **Mentors** are successful workers who share their expert knowledge and demonstrate correct work behaviors. **See Fig. 4-13.**

Fig. 4-13 A mentor can both provide helpful advice and suggest ways to improve your skills.

Some companies assign mentors to new employees. Mentors introduce employees to their coworkers and help them learn the procedures for their new jobs. They may help new workers develop key skills such as conflict resolution, negotiation, teamwork, and leadership. Sometimes these programs are called corporate coaching.

If your company doesn't have a formal mentoring program, you may want to work at developing a mentor relationship. With a trusted mentor, you can show your ignorance and ask "dumb" questions without feeling judged or embarrassed. You will learn from the mentor's experience, advice, and wisdom. Your mentor's guidance can help you advance in your career. The mentor can gain from the relationship, too, by having the opportunity to strengthen his or her leadership skills. Your mentor may also get recognition from the company when you succeed.

Maintaining Your Design Portfolio

As you gain work experience, keep your portfolio up-to-date. Include your best work. Some examples of what to include in a portfolio are:

- Photographs of projects. A builder could display homes in the process of being built as well as completed houses.

- Letters of recommendation. An interior designer may include letters from satisfied clients.

- Awards and certificates. A researcher could have an industry award for outstanding work.

- Certificates of completion. Workers who attend training seminars or take continuing education classes could add certificates or diplomas to their portfolios.

Leaving a Job

At some point you may choose to explore new job opportunities. Be certain, though, to leave your present job on good terms. You never know when you may need this employer as a reference for a future job, or when you may be working with a coworker or manager again. Also, you may want the option of returning to this company if your next job doesn't work out. Follow these guidelines:

- Leave your work in order and as completed as possible. Explain to your replacement or your manager the status of any work in progress.

- Give a reasonable amount of notice. Two weeks notice is standard.

- Offer to answer questions from your replacement. This gesture is appreciated by managers.

- Be tactful about why you are choosing to leave. Even if you did not get along with your boss or disagreed with the ethics of the company, don't air that news. You can merely state that you were given an offer "too good to pass up."

- Sometimes your present employer will make a counteroffer of a bigger salary to encourage you to stay. If money was your reason for leaving, you may choose to accept the offer. If other reasons have affected your decision, know what your requirements are for staying around. If you have definitely made up your mind to leave, let your employer know up front that your decision is non-negotiable.

Novel Designs

An imaginative designer can enhance a structure's commercial and aesthetic value alike. A well thought-out concept adds appeal for workers and customers and even serves as advertising. A hotel might have a multi-story atrium that lets sunshine flood a breakfast buffet area. At a local ice cream stand, you might pick up orders at a window inside a fiberglass, double-dip cone. Think of how these businesses stand out:

- **Theme Restaurants.** Like movie sets, some eateries are built and furnished to evoke a specific time and place. At one restaurant chain, diners enter a simulated jungle, complete with waterfalls, tropical fish, and the occasional "thunderstorm." Retro diners bring back the 1950s with rotating stools set at long counters and bright neon signs. A steak house offers décor that reminds customers of ranches and cowhands.

- **The Capitol Records Tower.** This building's unique design has made it a Los Angeles landmark for over 50 years. The designer actually chose the rounded, layered look to use space efficiently. The fact that it recalls a stack of old vinyl records is a bonus.

- **Retro Ballparks.** Reacting against the trend of multi-use stadiums that were popular in the 1960s and 1970s, designers of newer baseball parks try to recapture the charm of much earlier ones. These baseball-only facilities are often located in the center of the city, not the suburbs. Fans may enter under brick archways and eat in picnic areas. Playing fields feature asymmetrical dimensions and natural grass. Existing buildings may be incorporated into the design. A renovated warehouse attached to one park includes a team merchandise store, a restaurant, luxury suites, and rooftop bleachers.

Apply It!

Imagine that you're designing a building honoring a famous person. How would you design the building's exterior and interior? What special or unusual features would you include? Sketch your ideas. Explain why the design is appropriate.

Careers in Housing & Interiors

On the following pages you will read about a few of the various job levels within several different career areas. See Figs. 4-14, 4-15, 4-16, 4-17, 4-18, and 4-19. Keep in mind that these charts represent only a sampling of careers in each area. Many more opportunities exist in the field of housing and interiors.

Fig. 4-14

Careers in Real Estate			
Job Title	Description	Skills & Aptitudes	Education & Training
Real Estate Clerk	*Entry-level:* assists in office; compiles lists of homes for sale; copies contracts; answers the phone.	Computer, time-management, and communication skills; ability to work well with others.	High school diploma.
Appraiser	*Professional:* determines and reports on the value of individual properties.	Good organizational skills; ability to pay close attention to detail; good writing and math skills.	College degree in business administration, math, or accounting; appraisal training.
Real Estate Office Manager	*Professional:* keeps office running smoothly; tracks sales; keeps records; manages sales and office staff.	Ability to work well with others; organizational, computer, and communication skills.	College degree in business administration is desirable.

Fig. 4-15

Careers in Home Furnishings & Interior Design			
Job Title	Description	Skills & Aptitudes	Education & Training
Interior Designer	*Professional:* plans and furnishes interiors; prepares and presents design ideas; develops ideas into design concepts.	Creativity; knowledge of color, design, and furnishings; good communication and presentation skills.	Interior design training at a two- or four-year school; work experience; state licensing required in some states.
Buyer	*Professional:* determines which merchandise a store will carry; chooses the suppliers; negotiates prices; awards contracts.	Creative thinking and problem solving; trend forecasting; time-management, communication, and computer skills.	College degree in business or merchandising.
Furniture Designer	*Professional:* designs functional and appealing furniture for manufacturers, design firms, and furniture shops.	Artistic ability; uses design software; ability to visualize; good problem-solving skills.	College degree in art and design.

As you read these career descriptions, think about how workers in this field promote the quality of people's lives. Consumer writers provide information that helps people save money. Designers make clients' dreams come alive. Industrial designers create new shapes for products that make them easier to use. If helping others gives you satisfaction, then a career in housing and interiors might be for you!

Fig. 4-16

Careers in Home Construction & Design			
Job Title	**Description**	**Skills & Aptitudes**	**Education & Training**
Surveyor's Assistant	*Entry-level:* helps measure distances, directions, and angles of land.	Must be in good physical condition; aptitude in math and physics helpful.	High school diploma; can advance with further training and education.
Heavy-Equipment Operator	*Technical:* drives bulldozers, cranes, and other large construction equipment.	Ability to judge spaces well and handle multiple controls at the same time; aptitude in physics helpful.	Apprenticeship or certified operator training credential required.
Construction Technologist	*Professional:* supervises construction work; performs technical work; may specialize in estimating, quality control, specifications, or purchasing.	Technical knowledge of construction; aptitude in science; communication and leadership skills.	College degree in construction technology; experience in construction is helpful.

Fig. 4-17

Careers in Home Care & Maintenance			
Job Title	**Description**	**Skills & Aptitudes**	**Education & Training**
Entry-Level Maintenance Worker	*Entry-level:* cleans homes and offices.	Good physical condition; ability to work well alone and with others.	Education and training may lead to higher wages.
Home Remodeling Specialist	*Technical:* plans and estimates the cost of remodeling projects; carries out the job.	Math, communication, and people skills; ability to visualize; problem-solving and construction skills.	College degree in construction technology. Some specialists also have experience as carpenters or construction workers.
Industrial Designer	*Professional:* develops products such as home appliances, garden tools, and office equipment.	Artistic talent; research skills; knowledge of design software; good problem-solving skills; ability to visualize; knowledge of current trends.	College degree in industrial design, engineering, or architecture.

Fig. 4-18

Careers in Retailing & Entrepreneurship

Job Title	Description	Skills & Aptitudes	Education & Training
Department Store Advertising Worker	*Entry-level:* assists photographers, designers, artists, and writers; proofreads material; gathers samples; helps plan special projects.	Good writing and communication skills; ability in the areas of art and design.	High school diploma.
Sales Associate	*Entry-level:* interacts with customers; provides information on merchandise; carries out sales.	Good interpersonal skills; accuracy with details, especially financial.	High school diploma; on-the-job training often provided.
Home Furnishings Store Owner	*Entrepreneurial:* owns and operates store; keeps the business financial records; manages staff.	Good organizational and communication skills; ability to lead and motivate others; ability to understand and respond to market needs.	College degree in business, management, marketing, or retailing.

Fig. 4-19

Careers in Communications

Job Title	Description	Skills & Aptitudes	Education & Training
Consumer Advocate	*Technical:* provides a link between consumers and companies that manufacture, sell, and repair products; writes publications and answers questions.	Good writing and speaking skills; ability to work well with others; ability to remain calm under pressure.	High school diploma; a college degree in communications, law, or community education preferred.
Public Relations Specialist	*Professional:* writes reports, news releases, booklets, and speeches for the people or organizations represented.	Good speaking and writing skills; ability to work well with others; organizational skills.	College degree in public relations, journalism, or communications.
Consumer Writer	*Professional:* covers developments in housing and interiors for magazines, newspapers, and radio and television stations. This can also be an entrepreneurial position for freelancers.	Good writing skills; organizational skills.	College degree in English, journalism, or consumer education; courses in marketing and business are useful.

Staying on the Cutting Edge

Change is a constant in our technological world. Today, it is difficult to find a job that doesn't involve computers in one form or another. Salespeople use computers to track accounts, demonstrate new products, and keep records of sales. Carpenters may use handheld computers to help them determine how much material to purchase for a particular project. Workers in many jobs use the Internet to research new advances in their industry or simply as part of routine information gathering.

Job-related technology is constantly changing. Companies develop new software and machines that can cut the time it takes employees to do their work. Workers who know how to make use of these new tools become very valuable to employers. Those workers who aren't willing to make the effort to stay up-to-date are less likely to earn raises or be promoted. They might also be the first ones a company lets go if it scales down. For these reasons, it is vital for each worker to keep up-to-date on technology and other changes in the industry.

Some employers play a major role in keeping their staffs up-to-date. They send workers to training seminars or help pay for continuing education classes. See Fig. 4-20. Other times it is up to each employee to shoulder that responsibility. Fortunately, there are plenty of opportunities for workers to find the needed training. Community colleges offer classes that benefit many workers in a wide variety of careers. Magazines devoted to particular industries have ads or articles about seminars teaching new techniques.

Open your mind and keep learning about the world around you. Not all learning has to be formal. Whenever you learn how to operate new software or read a book to develop a new skill, you are advancing your education and training. Remember that by doing so, you're building a better chance for success in your career.

Fig. 4-20 These real estate workers are taking part in a seminar paid for by the agency. **Where can workers go to gain knowledge and skills if their employers do not offer such programs?**

Profile of a Visual Merchandiser

Visual merchandisers design, construct, and install displays in store windows and showcases in order to direct customers' attention to the merchandise being sold. They construct backdrops, choose and install background settings, gather props, arrange mannequins and merchandise, and place descriptive signs. Holidays and big sales events provide the busiest times of year for a visual merchandiser.

Education & Training

- A high school diploma is required.
- College courses that would be beneficial include merchandising, business administration, marketing, art, CAD, and psychology.
- Some stores provide on-the-job training.

Skills & Aptitudes

- Good communication and teamwork skills are needed.
- Creativity with a good eye for color and detail is important.
- A strong sense of balance and proportion is essential.

Visual Merchandiser
Kyle Owen

As a child, I loved to window shop during the holiday season. All of the big stores in town were so beautifully decorated. Some had lights all around the display windows. Department stores even wrapped up the appliances with bows and ribbons. They seemed more like toys than dishwashers or washing machines. What I liked best, though, was to walk by the big toy store. The owner would place battery-operated toys together in the display case. Watching these toys run was like watching a parade.

I got started in the field with a summer job at a smaller department store. It helped that I had worked in set design for my high school's plays. In high school, I took courses in art, woodworking, and mechanical drawing. Many visual merchandisers go on to community or junior colleges. Fashion merchandising schools, fine arts institutes, and interior design schools are also good places to get valuable training.

Some visual merchandisers specialize in one area. I started out arranging furniture displays at a department store. After several years I accepted a job as a display director in a home furnishings store. I'm responsible for supervising and coordinating all activities connected with display. I consult with the store manager and decide which items should be displayed. My long-term goal is to be a sales promotion director or head of store planning for a major department store.

Today, as a visual merchandiser, I'm responsible for putting together the very scenes that I used to admire. I try to create for other people that same sense of delight and excitement. I start working on the design months before a holiday or event.

We construct backdrops, install background settings, gather props, arrange mannequins and merchandise, and place descriptive signs.

A store's success is affected by its visual merchandisers because they can often encourage people to come into the store. My goal is to get shoppers to notice products they might not have considered buying otherwise.

Design Portfolio

1. Choose a product and design a display area for it. Create a visual showing your design.

2. Choose a season of the year. Decide what decorative home accessories you would display in a shop window for that season. Create a visual of your window display. Give a rationale for your choices.

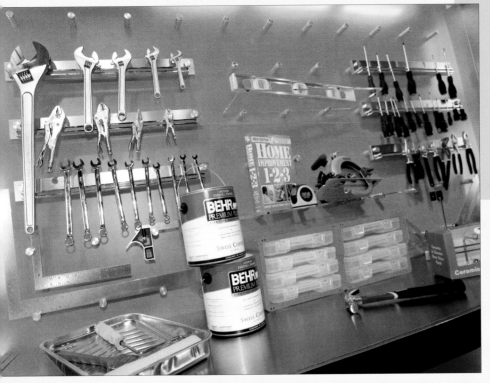

Chapter Summary

- Knowing your **aptitudes**, **abilities**, personality, interests, and values is the first step toward choosing a career.
- Many resources can provide information about careers, which you can use to find those that appeal to you.
- A career plan including short- and medium-term goals will help you accomplish your ultimate career goal.
- Developing your **employability skills** and **workplace readiness** behaviors will prepare you for getting a job.
- Many people in housing and interiors own their own business, which is challenging but can be rewarding.
- Getting a job includes making a **résumé** and a **portfolio**, having **references**, and doing well in an **interview**.
- Successful workers act responsibly and ethically, are good team members, and work to resolve conflicts.

Checking Your Understanding

1. What are **aptitudes** and **abilities**? How do they relate to career decisions?
2. What are some resources for getting career information?
3. Describe each of the four classifications for jobs.
4. What is an **entrepreneur**?
5. What are the steps in developing a career plan?
6. What are the steps in finding a job, and how can **networking** help?
7. What are examples of items that could be included in a design **portfolio**?
8. What are some skills needed to succeed in a job?
9. Give an example of a behavior that would help promote smooth teamwork.
10. How does the design industry relate to the quality of people's lives?

Thinking Critically

1. **Predicting Outcomes.** Refer to the list of workplace readiness skills on page 87. Which of those skills would an entry-level sales clerk most need? Why? What about an architect who is a partner in an architectural firm? Why?

2. **Analyzing Information.** What factors do you think contribute to the success of an entrepreneur? What responsibilities do entrepreneurs have? What managerial skills would an entrepreneur need to operate a business? What are the advantages and disadvantages of being an entrepreneur?

Applying Your Knowledge

1. **Job Shadowing.** Working within the rules of your teacher and school, design a job shadowing day for a career you're interested in. Carry out the project and report on it.

2. **Creating a Résumé.** Assemble information about jobs you have held in the past, your educational experience, and any volunteer work you have done. Use that information to create a résumé. Proofread your résumé carefully before turning it in to your teacher.

3. **Writing a Cover Letter.** Suppose you find an ad for a job that fits your career goal. Write a cover letter to the company's personnel director that explains why you believe you are qualified for the position.

4. **Analyzing Careers.** Refer to the information in the charts on pages 100-102. Try to find at least one additional entry-level, technical, professional, and entrepreneurial job among the six career areas. Create a similar chart that describes the job and lists the skills, aptitudes, education, and training required.

5. **Studying Job Trends.** Use the Internet or other sources to learn about future employment opportunities and job trends for the six jobs you researched in #4 above.

Design Challenge

You have been given the task of designing a "Career Center" about housing and interiors. It can include fact sheets, images, presentations, and other sources of information. You could even involve real people by inviting workers in the industry to answer questions from students about their jobs.

1. Develop a list of the elements that you will include in your career center.

2. Explain what kinds of information students can learn from each element you have chosen.

3. Draw a design showing how the center will look and where each element will be located.

4. Present your career center plan to the class.

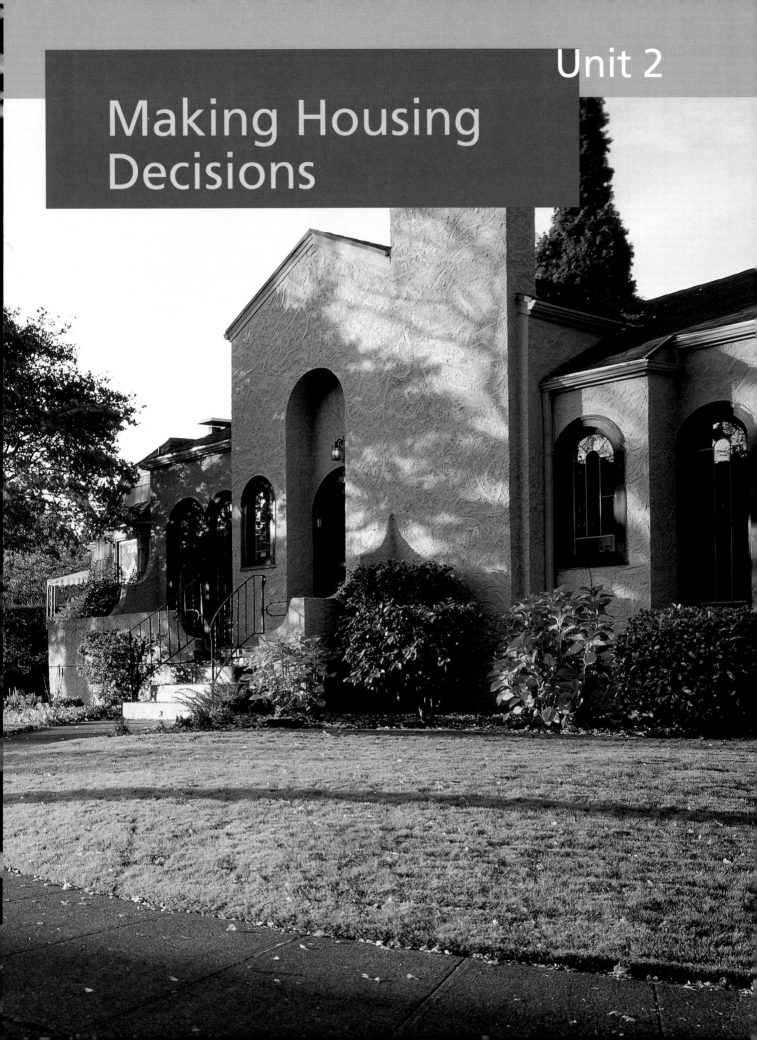

Unit 2

Making Housing Decisions

Chapter 5

Choosing a Place to Live

Objectives

- Explain the steps in the decision-making process.

- Analyze the impact of housing needs, wants, and priorities when choosing a place to live.

- Identify human and material resources that influence housing decisions.

- Contrast different types of community environments.

- Analyze the factors that should be considered when selecting a neighborhood.

- Evaluate the importance of public services in choosing a place to live.

- Compare and critique multifamily and single-family housing options.

Vocabulary

- human resources
- material resources
- utilities
- high-rise apartment
- low-rise apartment
- garden apartment
- efficiency apartment
- town house
- duplex
- triplex
- fourplex

Imagine that your family has decided to move. How would you begin to find a home? How could your family find a place that would suit every member's needs and as many of their wants as possible? This chapter will help you learn how to make the best choices regarding housing. Whether you will be moving soon or in the future, you'll learn how to prepare to handle the situation.

Making Housing Decisions

Choosing a place to live is one of the most important decisions a family or individual can make. One reason is that the costs involved in housing greatly impact people's financial picture. Beyond that, the choice of location affects the daily lives of every person living in the home, possibly for years to come. Such a decision deserves serious consideration.

The Decision-Making Process

You've made many decisions in your life. Major decisions—and even many smaller ones—are more likely to give satisfying results if you follow this process.

Step 1: State the Situation. Ask yourself: "Why do I need to make this decision? Who else needs to be involved in the decision? Who will be affected by it?"

Step 2: Identify Your Resources. Think about how resources such as time, energy, and your budget might be helpful in this situation.

Step 3: List the Options. Identify all of the alternatives you can think of. The more you can come up with, the more likely that one of them will be a satisfying solution.

Step 4: Weigh the Options. Consider how each alternative will affect the final outcome. Ask: "What might be the positive and negative results?" Think about what is most important to you, but also how each option will affect others.

Step 5: Choose the Best Option. There may not be a "perfect" solution, but look for one that meets as many of your goals as possible.

Step 6: Carry Out Your Decision. Your decision won't do any good unless you put it into action.

Step 7: Evaluate the Decision. Ask yourself: "How well did this decision turn out for me and for others? What might I do differently next time?" If you made a poor choice, accept responsibility for it and learn from your mistakes.

Influences on Housing Decisions

Many factors enter into the housing decision. The specific needs of a household or an individual may determine the location or size of housing. Wants and priorities affect housing choices as well, especially in terms of appearance and special features. Also, people take into consideration their resources when they choose a place to live.

While all people have the same basic needs for shelter, their specific needs differ. For instance, a family of seven people needs more bedrooms than a single person. What other examples of differing needs can you think of?

People choose housing that satisfies their current needs and those they expect in the near future. When people's life situations change over the years, their housing often changes too. Housing that may have suited a couple when they were first starting out may no longer be suitable when they have children.

Needs

Probably the most important factor in making a housing decision is need. As explained in Chapter 1, housing fulfills a variety of basic human needs. See Fig. 5-1.

Fig. 5-1 Evaluating your needs should be the first step in choosing a place to live.

Wants & Priorities

Whenever possible, people make choices that also fulfill their wants. Wanting something is not the same as needing it. People may *want* their shelter to provide a swimming pool or a recreation room, but they usually don't *need* either.

Since it's rare to find a home that fulfills all their wants, people must often make choices based on their priorities. To one person, a home's appearance might be more important than its comfort. Another person might make the opposite choice. Considerations such as privacy, economy, and convenience might rank differently in importance for you than for someone else.

Resources

A resource is something that can be used to accomplish a goal. People generally use resources to meet their needs and wants. Both human and material resources are used in making decisions about housing.

Human resources are personal qualities that people possess, including creativity, imagination, knowledge, skills, talent, time, energy, and experience. Knowledge and skills can be especially useful when making housing decisions. For example, a person with knowledge and skills in carpentry might use these resources in updating or remodeling a home. **See Fig. 5-2.**

Human resources are often overlooked. For example, you might think you don't have any skill or talent when it comes to gardening or decorating, when you just haven't had the opportunity to try. By trying your hand at different projects, you may discover talents and skills that you didn't know you had.

Human resources can also be increased. Many community colleges and trade schools offer noncredit classes and workshops in woodworking and in home maintenance and repair. Employees at home improvement centers, garden supply stores, and paint and wallpaper stores can offer advice about many types of projects. Some stores offer free classes, demonstrations, and project plans. You can also find expert advice and detailed instructions for projects on the Internet. A willingness to increase knowledge and skills can be a valuable resource when making decisions about housing.

Material resources are tangible assets, such as money, property, supplies, and tools. Perhaps the most essential material resource is money, which plays an important role in the choices people make about housing. Whether an individual or family decides to rent or buy, the choices will be limited by the amount of money available. The challenge comes in using money wisely to best meet housing needs.

Fig. 5-2 People who have time, energy, and "do-it-yourself" skills may choose to buy a home that needs some work and fix it up.

Material resources other than money can come from communities and other sources. For example, to help maintain an attractive environment, some communities offer free or low-cost trees and shrubs to homeowners. Some people borrow needed tools from neighbors or rent them from rental centers.

Before making a decision on where to live and what type of home to live in, individuals and families need to carefully evaluate all of their resources. Sometimes tradeoffs can be made. For example, you might use time and skills to do a project yourself in order to save money. Having a strong understanding of all available resources helps people make the best housing decisions.

Choosing a Location

One of the choices people make about housing is its location. A person may need to choose a region of the country, a particular town or city, and a neighborhood. These decisions are based on personal preferences as well as practical concerns.

The location of housing has a major impact on its cost. Generally speaking, certain trends can be seen across the United States:

- Housing tends to be more expensive on the East and West Coasts than in the interior of the country.

- Housing costs tend to be higher in areas with the most desirable climates and lower in areas with severe winters. **See Fig. 5-3.**

- Housing within and near major cities tends to be more expensive than in smaller cities and towns.

- Within major cities, housing costs are generally higher in downtown areas and sections under development.

- Single-family homes in suburbs often cost more than those in cities.

- Housing costs in rural areas tend to be the lowest of all.

While these general trends are true, variations can occur in any specific location. A city may have an older neighborhood with single-family homes that cost more than homes downtown. One suburb may have houses that cost less than those in a nearby resort area in the country.

Fig. 5-3 Climate is one factor to consider when choosing a region in which to live.

Inner City Revival

The empty factory was so neglected that fire officials said if a fire were to break out they would plow the building down rather than try to save it. Yet that run-down factory became the core of an award-winning development of apartments, businesses, and public buildings. Such is the promise of a trend called urban infill. In this movement, developers transform a blighted urban area into a thriving community asset. The result halts urban decay and renews civic pride and prosperity.

Urban infill projects range from a single building on a few acres to a cluster of structures on several city blocks. The Fan District in Richmond, Virginia, shown in the photograph on this page, is a prime example of inner city revival. Designers of these projects may face several issues:

- **Architectural Integrity.** The architectural style of the new structures should be distinctive but should still blend in with the style of those nearby. Restoring a building's original look or preserving a traditional style may be a key part of the plan.

- **Accessibility.** For the new project to succeed, it must be convenient. Existing roads may need upgrading and parking added. Areas have to be designed to accommodate people with a range of physical abilities.

- **Mixed Use.** Balancing private, commercial, and public elements encourages more people to make use of the space. That fosters a sense of community—and helps provide a strong economic base for the future. A complex may include housing, shops and restaurants, and public spaces open to all.

- **Community Character.** The businesses brought in should build on the strengths of the community to help ensure success. With an area near a university and research hospital, planners might base a project on health technology firms. In a district with a tradition of arts, they might choose galleries and independent, uniquely styled hotels.

Apply It!

Imagine you're on a design committee that will present ideas on how to renovate a stately, three-story, brick hotel that sits on two acres in the middle of a city. Generate ideas of its restoration and use, based on the factors described above.

Types of Locations

In general, the locations in which people live can be described as urban, suburban, or rural. Although there are general characteristics for each type of area, it is important to remember that there are variations within each of the three categories. Chicago, Illinois, and Fargo, North Dakota, are both urban areas, but the lifestyle in each is quite different.

The convenience of living close to work, shopping, and cultural opportunities appeals to most people who live in cities. Other people choose the slower-paced life available in rural areas. Rural, or country, living offers wide open spaces, less industry (and therefore less industrial pollution), and fewer people. For families who enjoy the outdoors and more privacy, rural living is an attractive choice.

For some people, living in a suburb—a residential area adjacent to a city—provides the best of both city and country living. Suburban living generally offers more open space than city living, while offering some of the same work, transportation, and entertainment opportunities.

How Did They Choose?

Choosing where to live is a decision based on many factors. Work situations, lifestyles, and stages in life all contribute. The following renters and homeowners describe why they chose the location for their homes.

Fig. 5-4 Gary Talbron.

Gary Talbron: See Fig. 5-4. "My daily schedule in the city is full and hectic. When I was living in the suburbs, I spent too much time traveling to and from work. I decided to move to an apartment within walking distance of my office. Although my rent is a little more, I've saved money by not having to commute. I'm enjoying the city more—the sporting events, concerts, restaurants, and the interesting people I've met."

Luis and Carmen Dominguez: See Fig. 5-5. "About five years ago, Carmen and I were feeling cramped living in the city. The houses in our neighborhood were very close together and allowed for little privacy. We chose to move to one of the suburbs. We haven't regretted the move for a minute. Although we had to pay more for our home, the real estate taxes are less. There are plenty of recreational opportunities, good schools, and life is a little more peaceful here."

Fig. 5-5 The Dominguez family.

Fig. 5-6 Carol and Bill Frakes.

Carol and Bill Frakes: See Fig. 5-6. "Once my husband and I were both retired, we decided to move to the country. We wanted a place that would allow us to pursue our hobbies. We rented a property with just enough land for my garden and a barn for Bill's pottery studio. The peace and quiet appeals to us, but life can be challenging at times—like digging out after a heavy snowfall in the winter. It was the right decision for us. We enjoy the fresh fruits and vegetables I raise, and Bill is doing what he loves best. Plus, we've made new friends."

Neighborhood

Once the general location has been selected, those who choose city, suburban, and small town living will need to choose a neighborhood. The housing units in a neighborhood are of similar design and price range. Some neighborhoods are made up only of homes, while others include housing, supermarkets, and small shops.

Knowing as much as possible about your future neighborhood is just as important as selecting the right dwelling. When choosing a neighborhood, consider its convenience and condition, the neighbors you would have, and any drawbacks.

Convenience

Most people do not want to spend a lot of time traveling to and from their daily activities. Finding a home close to their place of employment and basic services, such as food stores, is very important to them.

Parents with school-age children might want to live close to schools and recreational facilities. Some families choose a home that is convenient to child care services.

Many residents of cities don't own cars and rely heavily on public transportation. Living near bus or train stops is essential for these people. Suburban housing that is located near major highways might be significant for people who drive into a city or to another suburb to work.

Condition of the Neighborhood

The condition of a neighborhood affects the value of the housing in it. Before moving to a new neighborhood, take a walk around the area. Are the roads and sidewalks in good repair? Is there adequate street lighting and parking? These factors can tell you much about the condition of a neighborhood.

Also try to determine the pattern of improvement and growth in the area. If residents are painting, landscaping their yards, or renovating their homes, that's a good sign. Is there much new building going on? Such questions can help you determine whether the quality of the neighborhood is likely to improve, worsen, or stay the same. Many city planning offices can assist you in finding the answers to these questions.

All of these factors are of special concern to people who are buying a home. The value of a home increases or decreases with the value of other homes in the area and with the amount of community involvement shown by residents of the neighborhood.

Fig. 5-7 Friendly neighbors make the transition of moving to a new neighborhood or community much easier.

Neighbors

When neighbors share interests and can rely on each other in an emergency, the entire community benefits. It may be a good idea to learn about the people living in a neighborhood before making a final decision about moving there. Are the neighbors friendly? Do people seem to know and help each other? Families with children should find out whether there are other children in the neighborhood. The ability to form friendships helps people feel more at home in their surroundings. **See Fig. 5-7.**

Drawbacks

No location is perfect. All neighborhoods have problems, but it's best to know about them before moving in. Check the amount of noise and air pollution in the area. Is one street less noisy than another? What plans are there to deal with any vacant buildings that could lead to vandalism or other problems? You might also ask the local police about any safety concerns and whether a community watch program exists. Drive around, ask questions, and be aware of the activity in a community before making a decision.

Assessing Community Services

Imagine what you would do if the trash were not collected from your neighborhood. If your home were to catch fire, would you be able to save it yourself? Like most people, you depend on the community to provide you with certain services. Services vary from community to community. Check out the availability and quality of these services before choosing a place to live.

Utilities & Public Services

Utilities are the electric power, gas, water, and telephone services people use. Public services generally include trash collection, street repair, and sewer systems.

Prospective residents should investigate the services that are available in the neighborhood they are interested in. They should also find out which of these services are paid for by property taxes, which services residents pay for separately, and how much they cost. These items can, in some cases, add a significant amount to housing expenses.

Get Involved in Community Services

One way to make sure that your community gets the services it needs is to get involved. Here are some possible options for making a contribution in your community:

Local Government. Members of city councils, county boards, and other local government groups pass laws that affect the entire community. Individual members may head different committees, such as public safety or recreation. Citizens can call, write, or meet with these leaders to make their voices heard on current issues.

Park and Recreation Department. Park and recreation departments provide a range of services. Individuals can help out by giving nature tours, teaching sports, or demonstrating crafts, among other possibilities.

Neighborhood Association. You can help improve the quality of life on your own street and those nearby. Neighborhood associations sponsor cleanup campaigns, community gardens, holiday events, and tutoring programs. By uniting, people from the same neighborhood give a stronger voice on issues facing local government.

Citizen's Utility Board (CUB). A citizen's utility board represents consumers' concerns to the companies that provide electricity, water, gas, or telephone service. A CUB can also help people understand proposed laws on utility-related issues.

Local Cable Stations. Some cable television systems offer programming time to people in the community. Shows may highlight community groups or notable individuals.

Public Safety

A community should have well-trained and well-staffed fire and police departments. See Fig. 5-8. Rural areas often depend on a volunteer fire department and a county sheriff for protection. The number of staff and distance from your home are factors that can affect response to emergencies. Another consideration is the location of the nearest hospital and ambulance service.

Education

For families with children, the quality of the schools in a neighborhood or community holds significant weight when choosing housing. When moving to a new community, it is a good idea to visit local schools, meet the principals, and talk to people in the neighborhood about their experiences with the school system.

There are several things to look for when evaluating a particular school. Are classes overcrowded?

Fig. 5-8 Why do utilities, public services, and public safety services vary according to community or neighborhood?

What is the ratio of students to teachers? What is the graduation rate at the high school? What does the school spend per student on instruction? Is there an active parent group associated with the school? What plans for improving the school are in place? Is there a community college or university nearby for continuing education? The answers to these questions and more can indicate the quality of education in a community.

Transportation to school is also a concern. If schools are not within walking distance, find out whether adequate busing is provided.

Recreation

An ideal neighborhood includes space and facilities for recreational activities. These might include soccer and baseball playing fields, basketball courts, parks, and open areas. See Fig. 5-9. You might check to see if there is a park or playground nearby, a community swimming pool, a well-stocked public library, museums, movie theaters, or concert halls.

Some of these facilities are provided by residents' tax dollars; others will be paid for by individuals as they are used. A good neighborhood has a mix of both kinds of recreational opportunities.

Tax Policies

Tax policies indirectly influence the quality of life in a community. Some communities have much higher taxes than others. These taxes generally pay for better public services and for maintaining neighborhood schools and recreational facilities.

The tax rate, and its impact on the household budget, may directly influence the decision to buy a home in a particular community. Tax rates can also influence rental decisions by increasing the cost of rent.

Fig. 5-9 Convenient recreational facilities are an important factor as families choose a neighborhood or community.

Housing Alternatives

People can choose among a variety of housing options available, ranging from single-family homes to multifamily housing. To some people, maintaining one's privacy is the most important consideration when choosing housing. Others look for freedom from maintenance.

Multifamily Units

Multifamily dwellings are designed to be used by more than one household. Each household within the dwelling has a private living unit. The units may be attached side by side or one above the other, or both.

Multifamily units make the most economical use of land. They frequently offer lower housing costs than single-family housing and come in a variety of styles.

Apartments

The apartment building is the most common form of multifamily unit. Apartments range from a separate living unit within a house to several large rooms in a high-rise complex.

A **high-rise apartment** is one of many separate living units in a multistory building generally equipped with elevators. This form of housing is most often found in cities. High-rise apartment buildings may or may not provide extras such as off-street or covered parking, recreational facilities, resident managers, and other services.

A **low-rise apartment**, or an apartment in a building with few floors and no elevators, offers the benefits of apartment living in a more personal setting. A low-rise apartment building may or may not offer laundry facilities, covered parking, or recreational facilities.

A **garden apartment** is a unit in a low-rise building that includes landscaped grounds. **See Fig. 5-10.** These apartment buildings are often clustered around a patio with a fountain or a swimming pool, or an open lawn area sometimes called a commons.

Fig. 5-10 Apartment buildings efficiently house many people on a small amount of land.

Fig. 5-11 Town houses consist of several stories. What are the advantages and disadvantages of living in a town house?

Garden apartment buildings, more open than traditional low-rise buildings, often have balconies and outside stairs leading to individual units.

An **efficiency apartment** is a unit with one main room, a small kitchen area, and a bathroom. The main room functions as a living, dining, and sleeping area. An efficiency apartment is also known as a *studio apartment*. This is usually the least expensive apartment option in a given location.

Some apartment complexes are built especially for senior citizens or other people with special needs. These complexes may offer assisted living services, such as medical facilities, housekeeping, a central dining room, transportation, and special safety features.

While some apartments can be very costly, for many people apartments are the most affordable form of housing. Another advantage is that apartment dwellers usually don't have to take care of outdoor maintenance. On the other hand, apartments offer less privacy than other dwellings.

Town Houses

A **town house** consists of several houses attached together at the side walls. See Fig. 5-11. Town houses generally have identical floor plans and are two or more stories high. Each unit has its own separate entrance from the street, and some have a private backyard or patio. Town houses offer more privacy than most apartment units. In addition, town houses require less maintenance than single-family homes since they have only two or three exterior sides and tend to have smaller yards.

Older town houses located in cities are sometimes called *row houses*. Row houses usually have no recreational facilities of their own, and parking may be limited. In suburban areas, some town house complexes provide a swimming pool, tennis courts, or other facilities. These extras tend to increase the cost of the housing.

Duplexes

A **duplex** is one building that contains two separate living units. The units may be attached side by side, with one or two stories per unit, or there may be one unit on the first floor and one on the second floor. Each unit has its own outside entrance.

While a duplex is less private than a single-family home, it may offer some of the same advantages, such as yard space and a quiet residential location. A duplex does not offer the recreational facilities that larger multifamily complexes sometimes do, but is also less impersonal.

Other Multifamily Units

The popularity of multifamily housing has led to the availability of other forms. One option is a **triplex**—three housing units that are attached at the side walls. Another is a **fourplex**—four housing units that are attached at the side walls. These living units generally have two levels and a garage. Often these structures are designed in unique shapes. Each entrance often faces a different direction, giving the residents a measure of privacy.

Single-Family Housing

A single-family house is a detached, or separated, dwelling designed to be used by one household. Single-family homes may be large or small, new or old. For example, a manufactured, or "mobile," home (discussed in Chapter 3) is a single-family dwelling; so is a two-story Colonial-style house or a 1930s bungalow.

One of the most attractive advantages of a single-family home is privacy. The walls, ceiling, and floor are not attached to any other living unit, and a plot of land separates each home from the next. However, the land surrounding the home adds to its cost. Owners are responsible for their own outdoor maintenance. Renters may be responsible for maintenance or may have an agreement with the landlord to have maintenance provided.

In areas where many people must be housed in a limited amount of space, single-family homes are probably not the best choice. Multifamily housing uses land more efficiently. However, as explained in Chapter 16, cluster homes and zero-lot-line homes are designed to use land more efficiently than traditional single-family housing developments.

People often choose single-family housing when they have young children. They want to raise their children in a place that they find comfortable and welcoming. That need is very important to Art and Suki Tung. As Art says, "Every day that I come home from work and see the children playing in the backyard, I give thanks that we found our home. At night, we all gather in the living room and read or talk or watch movies together. On weekends, we all work together in the garden. Over time, we've repainted some of the rooms and made some other changes. That helps the place seem more like it's ours." Suki agrees. "My family moved around a lot when I was a child," she says. "I like knowing that our son and daughter have a place that they can feel they belong to."

The Choice Is Yours

Choosing a place to live is one of the most important decisions people make. People put large amounts of money into housing. It also costs money to move your belongings into a new home—and to live in and maintain the home once you are there. For these reasons, the decision of where to live should be made carefully and with as much information as is available. **See Fig. 5-12.**

Needs, wants, priorities, and personal resources should all be identified. The options, in terms of both location and type of housing, should be examined carefully. It's wise to invest some time, energy, and thought before making a decision. By thinking carefully about this important decision, you too can choose a place you're happy to call home.

Another decision that must be made by people looking for housing is whether to rent or buy. Renting lets people choose a place to live without making a long-term commitment. They also do not need to come up with as much cash as someone buying a home. Owning provides financial advantages, though, and many homeowners have a feeling of security and of putting down roots. The decision to rent or own is explored further in Chapter 6.

Fig. 5-12 The decision-making process is particularly helpful when you make an important decision like choosing a place to live.

Profile of a Real Estate Agent

Real estate agents help people go through the process of buying or selling a home. This includes locating and showing possible homes to buy, arranging inspections, helping clients price a home they are selling, marketing a home on sale, doing appraisals, and taking part in settlements.

Education & Training

- A high school diploma is required.
- Agents must pass a written exam to become licensed by the state.
- Most states require a specified amount of formal training in real estate.

Skills & Aptitudes

- Knowledge of the housing market, marketplace, and financing and mortgage options is important.
- A good understanding of people is vital.
- The ability to negotiate successfully is helpful.

Real Estate Agent
Sharon Thomas

House hunting can be one of the most exciting experiences in your life. It can also be one of the most confusing—especially the first time. I have a knack for dealing with first-time buyers. That's because I'm a good listener. I draw out buyers' needs, preferences, concerns, and finances. Knowing that one client wants a large dining room or objects to electric heating can help me make better suggestions. I try to get feedback about every house we look at. Then I keep those comments in mind when looking for other homes to show.

After all, my goal is to help my clients find the home they think is right for them. That's good business sense too. Since I work on commission—a percentage of the sale price of the home—I'm paid only if a home is sold. If I show people houses they aren't interested in, I'm just wasting time.

You have to be well informed to be a real estate agent, not just about the housing market but also about the community. Buyers ask questions about everything from the quality of the schools to the availability of recycling pickup.

Most important, though, is an understanding of people and how to deal with them. My success depends on my ability to gain buyers' confidence. This is especially true of first-time buyers, who sometimes judge me almost as much as they judge the houses they see. If they don't trust my ability or my integrity, the relationship will not work.

First-time buyers can become anxious as they consider the financial and other demands of owning a home. I always begin by helping them find a comfortable price range.

In some cases I even advise clients to wait to buy a home. It's better to lose the commission than to wind up with unhappy clients. This makes good business sense in the long run. Fewer of my sales collapse at the last minute, and my clients are more likely to recommend me to their friends. Then, when they're in the market for another house, they call me again!

Design Portfolio

1. You are a real estate agent who often works with first-time buyers. Design a questionnaire you could use to learn what features buyers are looking for in a home.

2. Suppose a family signs a contract with you to sell their home. They have a three-bedroom, two-bath house with a finished basement, a single car garage, and new kitchen appliances. The home is in good condition. Design an ad for the sale of their home.

Chapter Summary

- The decision-making process is a useful tool for making housing choices.
- Before making housing decisions, identify your needs, wants, and priorities. Then determine what **human resources** and **material resources** you can use.
- Evaluate various locations to determine whether you prefer an urban, suburban, or rural environment.
- Consider the advantages and drawbacks of a neighborhood before deciding to live in it.
- The quality of community services can vary widely and should be evaluated carefully as part of a housing decision.
- Many types of housing, both multifamily and single-family, are available.

Checking Your Understanding

1. What specific steps can you use to make major decisions?
2. Give examples showing how a need, a want, and a priority could affect housing decisions.
3. Identify two **human resources** and two **material resources** that may enter into a housing decision.
4. Rank the following locations from most expensive to least expensive: small town; downtown of a large city; rural.
5. How do urban, suburban, and rural lifestyles differ?
6. What are four factors you should consider when looking at a neighborhood?
7. Why are public services important to the choice of where to live?
8. How do **high-rise apartments**, **low-rise apartments**, and **garden apartments** differ?
9. How do **town houses** differ from **duplexes** and **triplexes**?
10. What are the advantages and disadvantages of a single-family home?

Thinking Critically

1. **Establishing Priorities.** Suppose you had two young children who were nearing the age for starting school. List five or six factors you would consider in choosing an area to settle. Rank them from most to least important.

2. **Identifying Cause and Effect.** Explain how tax rates in a community are related to public services.

3. **Defending Your Position.** Explain whether you would prefer living in a high-rise apartment, a low-rise apartment, or a garden apartment. Identify the advantages and disadvantages of each and give reasons for your preference.

Applying Your Knowledge

1. **Housing Through the Life Cycle.** Briefly describe appropriate housing options for a person at these stages of the family life cycle:

   • Starting college at a university in another state.

   • Age 30, married with two children ages 6 and 3.

   • Age 55, married, still working, but with no children at home.

   • Age 75, retired, traveling often.

2. **Using Resources.** Imagine that your family has decided to build a deck. List ways you could find out how to build the deck. Explain what human and material resources are involved.

3. **Making a Checklist.** Compile a personal checklist of features to investigate before selecting a neighborhood in which to live. Identify which features are most important to you and which you might be willing to give up.

4. **Planning an Assisted-Living Facility.** Imagine that you are working on plans for an assisted-living facility for seniors. What type of housing would you build? How many units would the facility include? What extras would you include? Give reasons for your choices.

5. **Comparing Housing Options.** Make a display that compares the different housing options described in this chapter. Use photographs, drawings, and floor plans to show the exterior and interior of each option.

Design Challenge

You are helping a husband and wife look for housing for themselves and their two children, and for the husband's parents. The parents are in their late sixties and still healthy and able to live independently. The couple and the parents want to live as near each other as possible.

1. Find floor plans for town houses, a duplex, and a single-family home with an in-law suite—a separate living area typically used by older adults.

2. Evaluate the three floor plans in light of the family's current and future needs and wants.

3. Choose the type of housing you think would be best and design a family/living room that the entire family could use.

Chapter 6

Renting versus Buying

Objectives

- Compare and contrast the advantages and disadvantages of renting or buying a home.

- Assess the advantages and disadvantages of condominium and cooperative ownership.

- Analyze costs involved in renting and buying.

- Describe how to determine a realistic housing budget.

- Analyze ways to reduce housing costs.

Vocabulary

- landlord

- tenant

- interest

- condominium ownership

- cooperative ownership

- security deposit

- renter's insurance

- earnest money

- down payment

- closing costs

- mortgage

- principal

- gross income

- fixed expenses

- flexible expenses

Some people dream of owning their own home and being able to customize it as they choose. Others prefer to rent and have the flexibility of changing residences on short notice without the concerns of selling. Renting and owning a home each have advantages and disadvantages. Understanding these will help you analyze the pros and cons of renting versus buying.

Renting: Pros & Cons

Renting means paying money to live in a dwelling that is owned by someone else. **Landlords**, or owners, offer renters—called **tenants**—many types of housing, from small efficiency apartments to single-family houses. Rental housing is available either furnished or unfurnished and in all price ranges.

Advantages of Renting

A young college graduate with a new full-time job needs a small, inexpensive place to live. A couple with two children want to live in a single-family house, but they know they will be making a job-related move within a year. A retired couple want to try living in a warmer climate for a few months before deciding whether to move there permanently. For these people, and for many others, the best choice may be to rent a home. Rental housing offers several advantages.

Predictable Housing Costs. Renters typically know what their monthly housing cost will be. They don't have to worry about unexpected repair bills. Money that otherwise might be spent for maintenance and improvements can be saved.

Limited Maintenance. For some, a major reason for renting is the limited maintenance responsibilities involved. Yard work, snow removal, painting, and household repairs are generally the responsibility of the landlord. Those who rent single-family dwellings, however, may have to provide their own lawn care and some basic home maintenance. **See Fig. 6-1.**

Mobility. Some people don't want to commit themselves to the long-term responsibilities of home ownership. They may have to move often because of their careers, or they may be unsure of the type of housing that will be most comfortable for them. Others may not be sure their income will remain steady for a long period. Renting gives them flexibility.

Fig. 6-1 Landlords provide appliances like refrigerators and ranges. Tenants have the responsibility of caring for them properly.

Disadvantages of Renting

While renting a home has many advantages, there are also some possible disadvantages. Renters have limited control and freedom. They also may feel a lack of stability or permanence. In addition, people are at a financial disadvantage when they rent.

Limited Control and Freedom. The major disadvantages of renting relate to control over living space. Renters may have little or no voice in how the building is managed or maintained. They often do not have the freedom to make changes in decor, such as painting and papering walls, without getting the landlord's permission. Some landlords prohibit pets or restrict the number and type of pets that tenants can keep.

Lack of Permanence. Tenants may move in and out so often that there's no feeling of permanence or belonging. Unlike homeowners, renters often view their neighbors as strangers and may not get to know them as well.

Financial Disadvantages. Money spent on rent is not applied toward ownership. After paying rent for years, renters have no investment in property to show for their payments and no tax savings. At the end of the rental agreement period, a landlord often raises the rent. The renter must pay the increase or face the disruption and expense of moving. In many cases, monthly rent can cost more than a monthly loan payment for a similar size home.

Building in Flexibility

The phrase "built to last" has new meaning in commercial design. A structure must not only last over time, but also through changing tenants and varying business needs. Solid construction must be balanced with flexible design to allow for a variety of uses and give the building a long and productive lifetime. Several features promote flexible design:

- **Workspace Layout.** In some businesses, employees work both alone and in teams. Temporary workers, from consultants to data entry clerks, may be brought in from time to time. To meet these needs, designers might choose moveable interior walls over stationary walls. Electronic sound-masking systems are often chosen to reduce distractions and add privacy.

- **Connectivity.** Businesses need electronic connections, from computer networks to Internet access to security cameras. Wiring must be sophisticated enough to keep up with the growth of a single company or to meet the needs of several different companies. Advances in wireless technology may eventually eliminate this challenge.

- **Lighting.** Lighting may need to change with the way a space is used. Overhead panels may work for a conference room but produce glare on computer screens when the space is converted to a data-entry room. Adjustable features like occupancy sensors are one solution. Use of natural lighting is another.

- **Temperature.** Local, rather than centralized, temperature controls allow employees to make the space that they occupy more comfortable. Occupancy sensors can be used to adjust an area's temperature. Likewise, innovative air-ventilation software senses increases in carbon dioxide and draws in more outside air when needed.

Apply It!

You've been hired by a company to design its office space. The company has a permanent staff of 12, but for three months of every year it hires 20 additional temporary workers. What would you suggest regarding surfaces, lighting, and other design features to provide the needed flexibility? Sketch your ideas. Give reasons for your choices.

Buying: Pros & Cons

Owning a home has been a traditional dream for many people because it offers a unique sense of satisfaction. The most common type of housing that is purchased is the freestanding, single-family house set on its own lot. However, units in multifamily dwellings may also be purchased. Those options are explored at the end of this section.

The purchase of a home is a major decision. Like renting, buying has advantages and disadvantages that need to be carefully weighed.

Advantages of Home Ownership

When choosing home ownership, there are several significant advantages. Some of these advantages include:

Feeling of Belonging. Home ownership provides a feeling of stability and a sense of "putting down roots." Many homeowners develop a sense of community awareness and responsibility. Homeowners often participate in local government to help protect the value of real estate in their area and help determine how tax money will be spent.

Independence. While some homeowners must comply with regulations about the exterior designs of their homes, most are free to adapt their homes to meet their needs. They can redecorate to suit their tastes. They can remodel as the household grows or as their needs change. These improvements can also add to a home's value.

Investment Value. Buying a home is an investment. The cost of the home and the money put into maintaining it are not lost, as they are with renting. Rather, the homeowner is exchanging one form of wealth (cash) for another (real estate). Over the last several decades, the value of real estate has generally risen. If a home is kept in good condition, and if the economy is sound, its value will probably rise. **See Fig. 6-2.** Chances are, the owner will be able to sell the home for more than he or she paid for it.

Some people buy a multifamily dwelling—such as a duplex or fourplex—and live in one unit, renting out the rest as a source of income. These owners become landlords.

Fig. 6-2 A well-maintained home in a desirable location has the best chance of providing a return on the owner's investment.

Good Credit Record. Making regular monthly home loan payments to a bank or other institution helps homeowners build good credit records. Prompt payments establish a reputation for reliability that can help people qualify for loans in the future.

Tax Advantages. Homeowners enjoy income tax savings. With home loans, **interest**—the money that the lending company charges the buyer for a loan—is tax-deductible. This means it can be deducted from the income amount used to figure taxes. Property tax payments are also deductible.

Disadvantages of Buying a Home

While owning a home has benefits, there are possible disadvantages to think about, too. These include:

Unexpected Expenses. With home ownership comes the responsibility for maintaining the home. Although improvements such as adding a deck or remodeling a kitchen can be planned and saved for, many maintenance expenses arise without warning and need immediate attention. For example, a water heater may need replacing, or a roof may develop a leak. These problems can be expensive. If damage is due to an accident, insurance may pay a portion of the cost of repair. Often, however, problems arise simply as a result of wear and aging of the home.

Time Spent on Maintenance. The owner of a single-family home is responsible for day-to-day and week-to-week upkeep. Such tasks as yard work, painting, and snow removal must be done periodically to protect the appearance and value of the home. These tasks take time and must be repeated often. Before investing in a house, potential homeowners should realistically assess the amount of time, energy, and money they are willing to spend on maintenance. **See Fig. 6-3.**

Limited Mobility. Buying a home should be considered a long-term investment. It can be costly to sell a home shortly after buying it, because the costs of selling and buying a home are high. A person who knows that he or she may need to move within a year should consider renting rather than buying.

Fig. 6-3 Homeowners who are not able to do some home maintenance chores often hire others to do the chores for them.

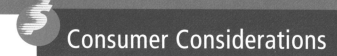

Shopping for a Home from Home

Using the Internet, you can compare any number of homes for sale or rent around the world without leaving the one you live in. On their websites, realtors and real estate companies routinely offer virtual tours and details on properties for sale or rent. You can view available homes based on location, price, and size. If you don't see anything you like, you can sign up for e-mail updates when new homes go on the market. You can often use these sites to learn about schools, crime rates, and housing values in a particular neighborhood. Some people take their research a step further using online satellite map sites. These "bird's-eye views" can reveal features that might not be mentioned elsewhere, such as a lack of trees or the presence of a nearby electric tower.

Of course, websites are just one tool for narrowing the search. Most people visit a home that they are considering before deciding whether to buy or rent. Though the Internet can provide extensive information about a home, neighborhood, and community, nothing beats walking through the space yourself.

Condominium and Cooperative Ownership

What combines the advantages of owning and of renting? For many people, buying a condominium or into a cooperative meets that description. However, these two forms of ownership also have some of the disadvantages of both buying and renting.

Condominiums. With **condominium ownership**, a person buys a unit in a multifamily dwelling, such as an apartment building, town house, or a duplex or triplex. Like any homeowner, that person is responsible for home loan payments, property taxes, and interior maintenance. The owner can sell the unit and move whenever he or she desires.

The owners of individual units also are part-owners of common areas, such as hallways, the building exterior, and the outer grounds. All owners share in the rights and responsibilities of using and keeping up these areas. All owners become part of an owners' association. That group collects fees that are used to cover the upkeep of the common areas and provide services such as trash pickup. All owners can vote on important issues concerning the property, such as whether to install additional lighting or landscaping.

Cooperatives. Instead of owning a unit directly, **cooperative ownership** allows people to buy shares of stock in a nonprofit corporation. That corporation owns the property. The price of each unit determines how many shares a person owns.

Some members of the cooperative sit on the board of directors. That group arranges for maintenance and services, which are paid for by fees collected from each owner. All the owners have the power to accept or reject any sale of shares—in other words, the sale of a unit in the building.

A Closer Look at Costs

Finances are a major factor to consider when deciding whether to rent or buy. Both buyers and renters need to consider two types of costs: the initial costs that must be paid once, and the continual costs that must be paid every month or year.

Renter's Initial Costs

When looking for a place to live, first-time renters usually pay close attention to the monthly costs that will be involved. Many, however, don't realize that they need to set aside some cash for the initial expenses of moving into rental housing. Typical initial costs include:

Application Fee. A prospective renter may have to pay a fee when filling out an application to live in a unit. The fee helps ensure that the renter is seriously interested in taking the unit.

Fig. 6-4 Planning ahead for such expenses as renting a moving truck can reduce financial stress.

Credit Check Fee. A landlord will probably obtain a credit check on a prospective renter. A credit check tells the landlord whether the renter pays bills on time and whether or not the person has large outstanding amounts charged on credit cards. This kind of confidential information is researched by a credit agency.

Security Deposit. Before moving into a rental unit, a renter is usually required to pay a **security deposit**. This fee covers the cost of any future damage the renter might cause to the unit. The deposit may be equal to one or two month's rent. Renters who own pets often must pay an additional security deposit called a *pet deposit*. When the renter moves out, the security deposit is returned if the unit is left in good condition. However, if the renter has damaged the property, the landlord keeps part or all of the deposit to pay for repairing the damage. The pet deposit may or may not be refunded depending on the landlord's policy.

Advance on Rent. Some landlords require payment in addition to a security deposit. A renter may have to pay one month's rent (or more) in advance before moving in. A landlord considers this advance as a type of "insurance" if a renter moves out unexpectedly, leaving a unit vacant.

Moving and Other Costs. Renters should not forget the costs of actually moving into their new home. Professional movers charge a fee to move furniture and other household goods. For an extra fee, they will also pack items in boxes. Renters can save money by renting or borrowing a truck and doing the packing and carrying themselves. See Fig. 6-4. In addition to actual moving expenses, there may be a one-time fee for installing or turning on any services that are the tenant's responsibility, such as telephone service, electricity, or cable television.

Renter's Continual Costs

After moving in, a renter has certain housing costs to pay each month. These include the rent payment, insurance, and perhaps utilities and parking.

Monthly Rent. Rental costs depend on many factors such as the size of the unit, the age of the building, the neighborhood, and the services that are included. Renters who do not already own furniture might consider paying slightly more to rent a furnished apartment.

Insurance. Since the landlord's insurance on the building does not cover the tenant's belongings, tenants should purchase **renter's insurance**—a policy that covers their personal property against loss by theft, fire, or other hazards.

Utilities. Sometimes the costs for services such as water, sewer, and trash collection are paid by the landlord and are included in the rent. Other times, the tenant pays for some or all of these utilities, as well as for electricity, natural gas, and telephone service.

Parking. Some rental units charge an additional fee for covered parking. This is particularly true in a city apartment building that has an underground parking garage, where space is at a premium.

Buyer's Initial Costs

The initial costs of buying a home are usually much higher than those involved in renting. As a result, most people plan for many years before buying a home.

Few people can save up enough money to pay the purchase price of a home in cash. Most people must borrow money to pay for a home. A number of costs associated with financing the purchase of a home arise at the time the purchase is made.

Earnest Money. **Earnest money** is a deposit that a potential buyer pays to show that he or she is serious about buying a home. The money is held in a trust until the deal is final. When the deal goes through, the earnest money is applied toward the payment of the total price. If buyers cannot secure a loan, the money is usually refunded. Buyers may lose the earnest money if they back out of the agreement.

Fig. 6-5 It is always an advantage to have a home inspection performed prior to buying a home.

Application and Credit Check Fees. Before loaning a substantial amount of money to buy a home, banks and other financial institutions check the buyer's credit to see whether that person has any large outstanding debts and has the income to pay the monthly bills. The buyer usually has to pay the fee that covers the cost of this credit check.

Inspection Fees. When a buyer is seriously interested in a particular home, it is wise to have it inspected. Many buyers hire a professional home inspector. A certified inspector will check the foundation, the roof, and the plumbing, electrical, and heating systems. The inspector also checks for pests, such as termites. Some firms will estimate the cost of any needed repairs. See Fig. 6-5.

Down Payment. People are rarely allowed to borrow the entire price of the home they buy. They are usually required to make a **down payment**, or a partial payment of cash, at the time of purchase. The down payment may be from 5 to 25 percent or more of the purchase price, depending on what the financial institution requires. The more money a buyer puts down, the less expensive monthly payments will be.

Closing Costs. In addition, buyers are required to pay certain **closing costs**—fees due at the time the purchase is finalized. These fees usually total several thousand dollars. You will read more about closing costs in Chapter 8.

Moving and Other Costs. Like renters, homeowners should plan for the expenses of moving and connecting utilities. In addition, they may want to, or need to, spend money on appliances, lawn and garden tools, and other useful items. If they have purchased a newly constructed home, landscaping may be a major expense. Doing landscaping work in stages over several years can reduce initial costs.

Buyer's Continual Costs

Once buyers move in, their monthly costs begin. These include a monthly mortgage payment, property taxes, insurance, utilities, and maintenance of the property. See Fig. 6-6.

Monthly Mortgage Payment. Unlike a loan to buy a car or television, a **mortgage**, or home loan, is long term. Most require making monthly payments for 15 or 30 years, although some are offered for other periods of time.

A monthly mortgage payment includes two components. Part of the payment directly repays a portion of the **principal**—the original amount of the loan. The rest is interest.

At first, most of each mortgage payment goes toward paying the interest on a loan, with a small amount going toward paying the principal. Near the end of the loan term, more money goes toward the principal. This can vary with different types of home loans. Chapter 8 gives more information about types of home loans.

Taxes. Homeowners are required to pay property, or real estate, taxes. Often this cost is added to the monthly mortgage payment. The taxes are based on the value of the home and are used to pay for such community services as schools, libraries, street repairs, and parks.

Fig. 6-6 Careful budgeting for rent, insurance, taxes, and utilities can help you meet the regular costs of owning a home.

Insurance. Homeowners should carry property and liability insurance. Property insurance covers the cost of repairing or replacing objects damaged by fire, theft, or other hazards. Liability insurance covers any claims filed against the homeowner by persons who are injured on the property. Most lenders require the buyer to protect the home by purchasing insurance. Sometimes, one-twelfth of the estimated yearly insurance premium is added to the monthly mortgage payment, and the lending company makes payments to the insurance provider.

Utilities. Homeowners pay for their own utilities, including water, sewer, telephone, electricity, natural gas or heating oil, trash collection, and cable television fees. The cost of some utilities may be included in property taxes, but most are separate expenses.

Maintenance. As mentioned earlier, homeowners are responsible, directly or indirectly, for the cost of upkeep on their property. A home inspector can point out any possible trouble spots for the buyers. This way, they will be aware of the possibility of any major repairs that may be coming up.

What Can You Afford to Spend?

Before looking for a place to rent or buy, you should decide how much you can afford to spend on housing. One rule of thumb is to spend no more than about 28 percent of gross monthly income on a mortgage payment or rent payment. **Gross income** is the full amount you earn before taxes are taken out. However, this varies according to your situation. Some people may want to stretch their budget to spend more on housing, while others prefer to spend less.

Careful planning can help you obtain affordable housing that meets your needs. Take a close look at your financial picture and determine how much you can spend. Also consider what other resources might be available to help you. **See Fig. 6-7.**

Analyzing Your Finances

As you read in Chapter 5, a careful account of material resources is a significant factor to consider when making housing decisions. Keep records of your current finances. Be sure to analyze the following:

Income. Income is the money received for work done or from investments made. For purposes of housing, it is important to determine monthly and yearly income. Is it steady, or does it vary from month to month? Remember, monthly mortgage or rent payments must be paid whether or not you received income that month.

Fig. 6-7 People thinking about buying a home can meet with loan officers at banks to learn about how much of a mortgage loan they can afford to take on.

Expenses. There are two kinds of expenses—fixed and flexible. **Fixed expenses** must be paid regularly, and the amount is fairly constant. Rent is a fixed expense. Many people look upon regular deposits to a savings account as a fixed expense. Other types of expenses are referred to as **flexible expenses**, that is, they vary in amount and do not occur regularly. Clothing is a flexible expense. Remember to include payments on existing debts, such as an installment loan for a car, as expenses.

Savings. Both homeowners and renters need to consider the significance of savings as part of their financial plans. Life is full of unexpected—and often expensive—surprises. Without savings, it can be difficult to cope with unplanned needs. To become homeowners the first time, people must save money for a down payment and closing costs. After they buy, they might need money suddenly for expensive home repairs. Both homeowners and renters should ask themselves: "How much savings do I have now?" and "What can I save each month?"

Strengthening Your Finances

After looking at your finances, you may decide to make some changes. Here are some ideas:

- Make a budget—a financial plan.
- Set aside savings first instead of saving what's leftover.
- Reduce flexible expenses.
- Reduce current debt.
- Limit impulse buying. Stick to your plan.
- Continue keeping records so you know how your money is used.

Fixed and flexible expenses change as work and lifestyles change and as households expand and contract. Good money management adjusts spending according to these changes. Knowing exactly where your money is spent can give you better control in using available financial resources to deal with expenses, including housing.

Using Other Resources

Human resources can be used to lower the costs of buying and maintaining housing. **See Fig. 6-8.** People who are willing to invest time, energy, and talent in their homes can save money and increase the livability of their homes. Some save by completing their own home repairs and maintenance. Consumer-friendly products—such as self-adhesive floor tiles, water-based paint, and precut and prefinished wall panels—have encouraged this trend.

People can also use their skills to make things for their homes that might be expensive to buy. For example, a person who sews can design and make window treatments. Someone with plumbing skills can update a bathroom. The money saved can be invested or spent for other needs and wants. Making good use of your human resources can also give a great deal of personal satisfaction and enjoyment.

Fig. 6-8 Homeowners can save quite a bit of money by doing some maintenance and decorating tasks themselves.

Deciding to Rent or Buy

Making the decision whether to rent or buy a home is a major one. It is also a personal one that will vary from individual to individual. There are many factors to evaluate, compare, and analyze when considering housing. See Fig. 6-9. Keeping careful records and learning to manage your finances will make your financial picture clearer. Recognize that the decision to rent or buy takes knowledge and planning—tools you will use to make an informed, sound housing decision.

Even if you choose to rent when you first move into a place of your own, you will not necessarily always rent. As your circumstances change, your housing needs will change. So, too, will your financial situation.

If you do buy a home, you will not necessarily stay in that home for the rest of your life. Many young people buy a smaller home, called a "starter home," when they begin life as homeowners. They often don't need a large home at first. As time goes on, you might feel the need for more space. Your income might be increasing by that time, making it possible for you to buy a larger home. Also, the money you invested in the starter home can help you. When you sell that home, you're likely to receive more than you paid for it. The additional cash can be used as the down payment on your next home.

You might also have to change housing because a new job or a job transfer sends you to another part of the country. When you make that move, think carefully through your needs, wants, and priorities by looking thoroughly at all your options.

Fig. 6-9 The decision to rent or buy is based on personal and financial considerations. Each person's situation is different.

Profile of a Relocation Specialist

Relocation specialists help people move from one part of the country to another, and sometimes to other countries. They use knowledge of housing and real estate to find suitable homes. They often use computers to explore options and ensure a cost-effective move.

Education & Training

- Classes and work experience within the real estate industry are desirable.
- In some areas, relocation specialists need to have a real estate license.

Skills & Aptitudes

- Knowledge of the housing industry, real-estate related documents, sale negotiations, the mortgage process, and relocation tax law is important.
- The ability to work carefully and to be detail oriented is useful.
- The ability to carry out real estate and service-related Internet searches is vital.
- The ability to track and analyze financial data is useful.

Relocation Specialist
Matthew Kingfisher

The corporation I work for has offices around the world. That's why it has its own relocation department. Smaller employers hire companies that specialize in relocation to help move their employees.

Before getting this job, I had moved a number of times myself, so I know firsthand how tough moving can be. Changing jobs is stressful in the first place. When someone has to find a new home, too, the stress goes up.

When I'm notified that an employee is being transferred to another city, I arrange an orientation meeting. Most of the time I meet with the employee and his or her spouse. Sometimes when several workers are moving to the same location, I schedule a group orientation.

First, I cover our employer's rules and regulations for moving. I explain how expense claims should be filled out. It's extremely important that this be done correctly. We talk about trips they will be allowed to take for house-hunting purposes. I also assign them a moving company, though they contact the movers and meet with them.

Our employees have the option of selling their home themselves or having us help. They are given a guarantee of a minimum selling price for their home. If it sells for less, we make up the difference.

Our company pays a moving bonus of an extra month's salary. Employees can use it to cover relocation expenses. If their move is to what we classify as a high-cost area, they receive more money.

Sometimes I handle international moves. They are even more complex. Those orientations last all day—and they include the children. I also help arrange for passports, tax advice, handling pets, and language tutoring. Most of our employees stay abroad for three to five years. When they're ready to move back to the United States, I'm back on the job!

Design Portfolio

1. Suppose you were a relocation specialist learning about housing costs in different parts of the country. Use the Internet to find the cost of a three-bedroom home in at least ten different states across the country. Use a graphic to present your findings.

2. Suppose you're helping a family with two teens relocate to Madison, Wisconsin. Use the Internet to learn facts about the area that would be helpful to the family. Create a brochure that presents the facts.

Chapter Summary

- **Landlords** and **tenants** are the two parties involved in renting a home.
- Renting and buying both have advantages and disadvantages. Individuals must analyze the pros and cons of each.
- **Condominium ownership** and **cooperative ownership** are two options for buying a unit in multifamily housing.
- Both renters and buyers have both initial and continual costs, which people must budget for.
- Keeping financial records can help people budget.
- Human resources can be used to lower housing costs.

Checking Your Understanding

1. What are the advantages of renting?
2. What are the disadvantages of renting?
3. What are the financial advantages of buying?
4. What are the financial disadvantages of buying?
5. Which arrangement provides more mobility—**condominium** or **cooperative ownership**? Why?
6. What initial costs might a renter face?
7. Why do renters need insurance?
8. What are **down payments**, **closing costs**, and **mortgages**?
9. What general guideline is given for how much an individual should spend on housing?
10. How do you make a budget?
11. What are three ways families can strengthen their finances?
12. What are three human resources that can be used to reduce housing costs?

Thinking Critically

1. **Comparing and Contrasting.** What do you think would be preferable, renting in a duplex, owning half of the duplex, or owning the entire duplex and renting half of it out? Why do you prefer that arrangement?

2. **Evaluating Information.** What are the biggest advantages and disadvantages of condominium and cooperative ownership? Why?

3. **Analyzing Information.** Identify the continual costs for renting and home ownership. Identify which of those costs are fixed and which are flexible.

Applying Your Knowledge

1. **Developing Case Studies.** Write a fictional case study about two different families or individuals, one that chooses to rent and one that chooses to buy a home. Include a description of the characteristics that played a role in each decision, such as family size and future plans. Explain why each person or family made the decision they did.

2. **Analyzing Housing Decisions.** Interview at least three adults about housing decisions they made in the past. Find out what housing alternatives were available to them, what circumstances they had when they made each decision, how long they lived in the housing they chose, and how they felt about the decisions. Share your findings with the class.

3. **Analyzing Local Rent Costs.** Research the costs of renting a two-bedroom apartment in your community. Prepare a chart of at least 10 apartments ranked by cost from highest to lowest. Include a column for extra features in each. Write a brief analysis that explains why—based on features, location, or other factors—the apartments vary in price.

4. **Calculating Taxes.** Property taxes are based on the tax rate and a home's assessed value, or the amount of money the tax agency says the home is worth. Suppose a house is assessed at $85,000. Calculate the tax that would be owed if the property tax rate is 86 cents on each $100 of assessed value. Explain why it is important for homeowners to know the assessed value of their homes.

Assume that you have decided to start your own housing locator service.

1. Answer the following questions: What characteristics will make your company attractive to potential clients? How will you meet the housing needs of your clients? What fees will you charge for your service?

2. As you create your plan, you may want to contact housing locator services in your area or on the Internet to find out about the services they offer.

3. Design a brochure in which you promote your company and identify the services you offer.

4. Place the finished brochure in your design portfolio.

APT
FOR
RNT
545-7007

Chapter 7

Renting a Home

Objectives

- Identify factors to consider when assessing rental housing.

- List sources of information about available rental housing.

- Compare three categories of rental housing.

- Give guidelines for evaluating rental housing.

- Analyze the features and conditions of rental agreements.

- Explain the roles and responsibilities of tenants and landlords.

- Describe how to successfully share housing with a roommate.

Vocabulary

- subsidized housing
- floor plan
- lease
- sublet
- breach of contract
- evict

When you rent a place of your own, you need to make many decisions before you move in. After that, the way you handle your responsibilities as a tenant will affect how you get along with your landlord and with others in the building. If you decide to share with a roommate, you'll need to ensure the arrangement goes smoothly. Planning and thought can help you make wise decisions about renting.

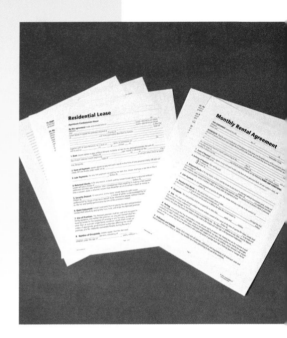

Selecting Rental Housing

Selecting rental housing is worth the time it takes to make an informed choice. Most landlords require tenants to sign a rental agreement for at least one year. Also, the cost of moving can be high. Following a plan of action will help you make the best possible selection.

The first step is to think about what your requirements in a home are. Then you need to find out what's available. After this, you will inspect and compare rental units you are interested in. Finally, when you are close to a decision, you will need to review the rental agreement carefully.

Assess Your Housing Requirements

Before beginning to search for rental housing, think about your housing requirements. As you do, remember to consider your needs, wants, and personal priorities. Here are some questions you need to think about:

- What can I afford to spend? Some financial experts say to allow about 28 percent of your monthly gross income for rent, depending on the cost of housing in your area. The information in Chapter 6 can help you analyze your finances.

- What location am I interested in? As you read in Chapter 5, location influences the cost of housing as well as its convenience.

- What type of housing unit would suit me—a house, an apartment, a town house? You may want to review the advantages and disadvantages of various types of housing in Chapter 5.

- How much space do I need? How many bedrooms do I require? What other rooms must I have?

Fig. 7-1 Rental properties have varying levels of security. **What types of security measures would be important to you if you were renting an apartment?**

You may need to think about other questions too. For example, suppose you have decided to look for an apartment. Do you prefer a low-rise or high-rise building? Would you rather live on an upper floor or at ground level? Each has advantages and drawbacks. Although you may not always have a choice, you need to think about such issues as convenience, environment, and security. **See Fig. 7-1.** Consider the following factors:

- Apartments located near stairways, elevators, or entrances may be noisy. Heavy drapes or carpets may muffle some noise.

- Apartments that face a busy street tend to be noisier than those facing quiet areas.

- Apartments in the upper portion of the building may be warmer and have poorer air circulation than those on lower floors.

- Ground-floor apartments may be more convenient than those on upper floors.

- Upper apartments may be more secure because they are harder to get to from the street.

- Apartments close to elevators and stairs may have greater risk of theft or burglary.

What Is Available?

How do you find out what rental housing is available? You can use various sources of information. Drive or walk through areas in which you would like to live and look for "For Rent" signs. A landlord might advertise vacancies on a bulletin board in a local convenience store or other gathering spot.

Friends who live in the area you're interested in may know of housing vacancies. Tell them you are looking for a place to live, and describe the kind of place you want.

Newspapers print advertisements for rental housing under the headings "Apartments for Rent" or "Houses for Rent." In some larger cities, rentals are grouped according to the area of the city where they are located. Rental ads usually use abbreviations to save the advertiser space and, therefore, money. **Figure 7-2 on page 152** shows some common abbreviations found in real estate ads.

You can also check for online listings of available rental housing. These may be posted by newspapers and real estate services. You can search for ads with certain criteria, such as location, number of bedrooms, and price range. Some online listings also have a service that will notify you via e-mail of new ads posted to the site. Because space isn't at such a premium as it is in newspaper advertisements, online ads tend to use fewer abbreviations.

Fig. 7-2

Reading Rental Advertisements

6th & Butler Incredible corner apt. with wide-open views of river and city! 2BR, 2 baths, sep DR, big kit, hrdwd flrs, gar, utils pd. 1 mo sec dep.

Riverside Rented by owner, 1 BR, 1 bath, furn, immed occ. Nr. bus. W/D in basement $500/mo + util.

Silverdale Immed occ! 2BR, 1 bath, grt vw, no lse. LR w/fpl, EIK, pvt entr. Call soon to find your great new home!

Capitol Park 3 BR ranch, xtra lg MBR, hrdwd flrs, c/a, attached gar, refs req'd Incl h/hw. Great location. Appt only.

E. 13th & Main Studio apt. Grt vw! Cpts & drps, grt clst spc, BB heat. No pets! New WWC. Avail Nov 1.

22nd & Birch Cozy efficiency w/grt vw. D/W, ldry in bldg, c/a. Conven all trans. No lse, $400/mo, utils pd.

7th & Park Spacious new 2 BR, 1 1/2 bath. This garden apt has hrdwd flrs, W/D, LR w/fpl, and cpts & drps. BB heat and c/a. Appl incl. Immed occ, call now! No lse.

Abbreviation	What It Means
appl incl	appliances included
appt only	can be seen by appointment only
apt	apartment
avail Nov 1	available November 1
BB heat	baseboard heat
bldg	building
BR	bedroom
c/a	central air conditioning
conven all trans	convenient to all transportation
cpts & drps	carpets and drapes
D/W	dishwasher
EIK	eat-in-kitchen
furn	furnished
gar	garage
grt clst spc	great closet space
grt vw	great view
hrdwd flrs	hardwood floors
immed occ	immediate occupancy
incl h/hw	includes heat and hot water
kit	kitchen
ldry	laundry
LR w/fpl	living room with fireplace
MBR	master bedroom
no lse	no lease
nr bus	near bus
pvt entr	private entry
refs req'd	references required
sep DR	separate dining room
+ util	utilities paid by tenant
utils pd	utilities paid
w/	with
W/D	washer and dryer
WWC	wall-to-wall carpeting
xtra lg	extra large
1 mo sec dep	1 month's rent as a security deposit
$400/mo	rent is $400 a month

Fig. 7-3 Public housing makes it possible for people with low incomes to live in homes that they could not otherwise afford.

Real estate agencies and apartment-finding services often have lists of apartments that are vacant or soon will be. These services provide great help in narrowing down your search in a short time. Some agencies charge renters a fee for their services; others charge the landlord. In some large cities the fee can be as high as one month's rent.

If you are moving a long distance, finding housing may require more research. Some communities have a relocation service to help newcomers find housing. You can also find out what is available by subscribing to the local newspaper, contacting the Chamber of Commerce or a real estate service, or using online resources.

Affordable Options

As you look for rental housing, keep in mind that there are three basic categories of rental units. Which ones are available to you depends on your income and the portion of it you can pay for rent.

Privately Owned Housing. Most rental property is privately owned by individuals or companies. Rental properties are generally owned as investments and are used as sources of income. Tenants pay the full amount of the rent, which is determined by whatever the market will bear.

Public Housing. Public housing complexes with low-cost units are typically found in large cities. **See Fig. 7-3.** This type of housing is designed for low-income families, senior citizens, and those with disabilities. The government builds public housing and rents it to those who cannot afford private housing. The amount of rent paid is usually set as a percentage of the renter's monthly income. To qualify for public housing, a person cannot earn more than a certain amount, which can vary with each public housing building.

Subsidized Housing. In the case of **subsidized housing**, the government helps low-income families live in private housing by paying part of the rent. Payments go directly to the owner of the housing. Government money makes up the difference between what the tenants can afford to pay and what the rent would normally be. Families who live in subsidized housing must meet certain income guidelines. In many areas, the demand for subsidized housing is greater than the supply.

Inspect and Compare Units

Once you have a list of available units that interest you, the next step is to call the landlords so you can take a look at them. Never rent an apartment or house you have not seen, and be sure you see the specific space that is available. **See Fig. 7-4.** Some landlords keep a well-maintained display unit to show prospective renters. Because it's not lived in, the display unit doesn't show signs of normal wear and tear as other units will. Discovering that your unit has cracked walls, peeling paint, or a badly stained carpet after you have rented it would be an unpleasant surprise.

You may want to talk with some of the tenants who would be your neighbors. Ask them whether they feel the building is properly maintained and if they enjoy living there.

A good way to keep track of the various units you visit is to compile an inspection checklist. Make notes on the list for every apartment you inspect. Then compare the lists to see which units best meet your needs. In addition to cost and condition of the unit, here are some features to note on your list:

Living Space. Evaluate the overall layout of each unit you look at. Will your furniture fit? Is there enough storage space? Ask whether a copy of the floor plan is available. The **floor plan** is a diagram of an apartment or home that shows the arrangement of rooms. It may also include dimensions of each room. Comparing floor plans can help you determine whether there is enough living space to meet your needs and whether that space is arranged conveniently. If a floor plan is not available, you may want to sketch your own or take pictures of each room.

Facilities. Does the complex provide facilities such as covered parking, laundry areas, a swimming pool, or storage areas? Is there an extra fee for any of these facilities?

Safety and Security. If there is a main entrance to the building, is it kept locked at all times? Is there an intercom system for admitting visitors? Are entrances well lighted? Do apartment doors have deadbolt locks, and are locks changed when tenants move out? Are there smoke detectors, a carbon monoxide detector, sprinkler systems, and clearly marked fire exits?

Fig. 7-4 Always visit a rental property in person before agreeing to rent it. **What features would you look at when inspecting an apartment?**

Fig. 7-5 Many apartment buildings are accessible to people with disabilities.

Maintenance. Whom do the tenants contact if maintenance is needed? Does the landlord or building manager live on the premises? Are there provisions in the rental agreement that state when the landlord or maintenance workers may enter the unit? Is there a policy on scheduling routine maintenance services?

Individual Needs. If you own a waterbed or have a pet, be sure to ask prospective landlords if either is permitted. You may also want to consider how accessible the building is for people with disabilities. See Fig. 7-5.

It may be difficult to find an apartment that meets all your requirements. Be realistic and reasonable when making your final decision. Prioritize your needs and wants to identify ones that are most important. Don't be afraid to ask to see a unit for a second time. You should feel satisfied that the unit you select meets as many of your requirements as possible.

Review Rental Agreements

Once you've found the place you want to rent, you and the landlord must agree about the terms of the rental. It's essential that you carefully review all the terms to be sure you understand them. Rental agreements take three basic forms: verbal agreements, written agreements, and leases.

Verbal Agreement

A verbal agreement is reached through discussion between the landlord and the prospective tenant. The discussion should cover such things as the amount of rent, the date payments should be made, and maintenance and repair service. Remember, however, that a verbal agreement will not hold up in a court of law. Verbal agreements are not common. Most people realize that it's wiser to put a rental agreement in writing.

Written Agreement

A basic written agreement outlines certain provisions, such as rental cost. It allows a tenant to rent for an indefinite period of time on a month-to-month basis. This arrangement is a good alternative for renters who move frequently. Landlords may dislike the month-to-month agreement because it does not guarantee long-term occupancy. Some written agreements state that a landlord may tell tenants to move out at any time. This could be a disadvantage for renters.

Lease

A **lease** is the legal document tenants and landlords sign when agreeing to rent housing for a specific period of time. It is the most binding type of rental agreement. **See Fig. 7-6.** A lease states the rights and duties of the landlord and the tenant. Many landlords require a one-year lease.

The lease should include the following details:

- Address and number of the unit.
- Date tenant will move in.
- List of contents if unit is furnished.
- Cost of unit per month, date monthly payment is due, and where to send the payment.
- Penalty for late payment and date on which the penalty is assessed.
- Amount of security deposit and conditions for refund.
- Amount of additional fees for such services as trash collection and indoor parking.
- Whether the landlord or the tenant pays for specific utilities, such as electricity.
- Length of time the lease is valid.
- Procedures for renewing the lease.
- Tenant's and landlord's rights to end the lease.
- Statement of responsibility for repairs and maintenance.
- Restrictions, if any. For example, some landlords do not allow pets. There may be regulations about window treatments, putting nails in walls, and painting.
- Landlord's action for tenant's failure to pay the rent.

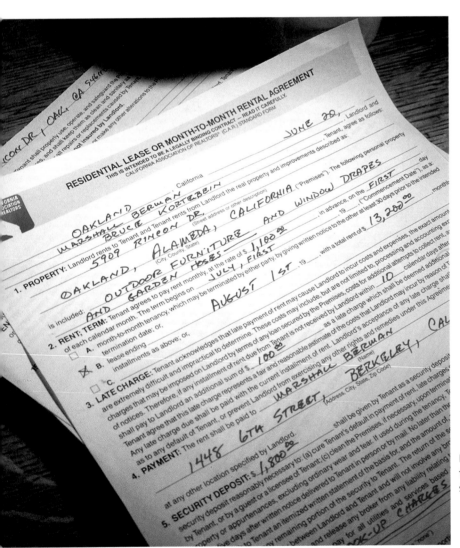

Fig. 7-6 Make sure you understand the rules, rights, and restrictions specified in a lease before you sign it.

You should read a lease carefully, even the small print, before signing it. If you don't understand its terms, ask someone who is familiar with rental agreements to explain them to you. A legal aid service or renters' association in your community or state may be able to provide assistance. You should be able to take the lease with you to check it over before you sign it. Beware of any landlord who tells you that you must sign the lease on the spot. If there are provisions in the lease you don't like, discuss them with the landlord before signing. Also, never sign a lease until all blanks have been filled in and all your concerns have been answered in writing. If you want additional guarantees, such as installation of appliances, have the landlord add them to the lease before you sign it.

Make sure that any damages you find in the apartment are recorded in the lease by the landlord before you move in. Otherwise, you may be held responsible for this damage when you move out.

The lease should state the options you have if you must move out before the lease expires. Some leases require the tenant to pay the rent for the duration of the lease, which can be expensive. A second option is the right to assign, or transfer, the lease to someone else. In this case, the original tenant is no longer responsible. A third option is for the tenant to **sublet**, or rent the unit to someone else. In this case, the original renter's name remains on the lease, and he or she is still responsible if the rent is not paid or if damage occurs.

The landlord should sign the lease at the same time you do. You should get a copy of the signed lease so that you have proof of the terms and conditions agreed to.

Consumer Considerations

Planning a Move

With moving, as with any project, planning can make the work proceed more smoothly and with less stress. These are the kinds of details people need to think about when planning to move:

What to Take. You may not want or be able to take all your possessions. Some people use moving as an opportunity to decide which things they really value and which they can give away or sell. Once you've chosen what to keep, gather needed supplies, such as boxes and tape, before you begin packing. Be sure to wrap breakables well.

Transportation. You can rent a truck to do the move yourself or with friends or you can hire professional movers. Either way, you'll need to make reservations in advance.

Services. Utilities must be canceled at one address and turned on at the new one. You may need to change banks and other services as well.

Mail. Send a "change of address" card to companies that bill you regularly. You can find this card at the post office. Most of your mail can be forwarded to the new place for up to one year.

Survival Kit. Pack separate bags of personal items, batteries, food, and small kitchen tools to help you through the first days of settling in at the new place.

Tenant Rights & Responsibilities

By signing a lease or written agreement, a tenant agrees to assume certain responsibilities. He or she also has certain rights.

Tenants have the right to a safe, habitable rental unit. The landlord is responsible for providing plumbing and heating systems that work, installing smoke detectors, and making necessary repairs. Tenants also have the right to privacy. The landlord cannot enter a unit unless proper notice is given or in an emergency. In addition, a landlord cannot discriminate against a tenant because of race or color, national origin, religion, gender, family status, or disability.

Responsibilities of a tenant include abiding by the rules and regulations set forth in the lease. He or she promises to pay the rent on time and to take proper care of the rental space.

If either party fails to fulfill his or her responsibilities, a breach of contract exists. **Breach of contract** is a legal phrase for failure to meet all terms of a contract or agreement. Tenants who find that they cannot keep promises agreed to in a lease should talk to the landlord and try to work out the situation. If tenants breach the contract, landlords can **evict** them—legally require them to move out before the lease has expired—and bring a lawsuit against them. Landlords must provide tenants with written legal notice of the eviction. The notice must include the reason for the eviction and the amount of time tenants have to remove themselves and their belongings from the property.

Relationship with the Landlord

A tenant may or may not deal directly with the landlord. A landlord may hire a housing manager to handle daily business. Landlords and housing managers are in charge of managing repairs and maintaining building safety. Tenants must know whom to call in case of a problem, as well as who will be collecting the rent.

If repairs are needed on a rental unit, one of a tenant's rights is to receive a written statement discussing the repair, what will be done, and when it will be done. See Fig. 7-7. The statement should be signed and dated by the landlord or manager. A specific date should be noted by which all repairs are to be made. If the repairs are not done, the landlord may be guilty of breach of contract.

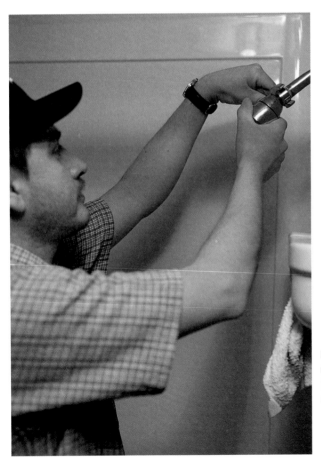

Fig. 7-7 It is the tenant's responsibility to report any repairs that need to be made to a rental unit. It is the landlord's responsibility to make sure the repairs are made in a timely manner.

Misunderstandings sometimes occur between landlords and tenants. In many cases, tenants bring these problems on themselves by not understanding the rights of landlords. For example, a lease may state that rent is due on the first of the month and that a late charge will be applied if the rent has not been paid by the tenth. Some tenants think this means they have a "grace period" and don't have to pay until the tenth. This is incorrect and can put the tenant at risk for eviction.

The security deposit is another common area of misunderstanding. Some tenants think they should automatically get the security deposit back. Actually, the landlord can pay all or part of the security deposit back within 45 days of the tenant's moving out or keep it to repair any damage. Some people think it's all right not to pay the last month's rent if they have paid a security deposit. These are two separate aspects of a lease. Withholding rent is illegal at any point in the rental period.

When tenants move out they should always return the keys directly to the landlord or housing manager. Keys should never be left in the rental unit. In return, tenants should ask for a receipt for the returned keys.

Relationships with Neighbors

Sharing a building with others requires tenants to respect everyone's rights. Tact and courtesy help create good relationships with other renters. Tenants should follow building policies about such concerns as assigned parking spaces, misplaced mail, loud music, and visitors.

Tenants often develop friendships with others in the building. In some complexes, tenants meet to discuss common concerns. They may also meet socially. Often tenants pitch in to help one another out.

When renting a single-family home, it is equally important to develop good relationships with neighbors. Even though you don't own your home, you are a part of the neighborhood. You might join the neighborhood association or community neighborhood watch.

Sharing Housing

Several factors can influence a person's decision to share housing with others. **See Fig. 7-8.** Finances are a common reason, especially for those who live in large cities in which housing tends to be more expensive. A group of people in the same situation, such as a group of students sharing housing while at school, is another reason. Some of the advantages of sharing housing include lower housing costs, the chance to rent a larger space than could be done alone, and companionship.

Fig. 7-8 Sharing rental housing means sharing the cost, which can make a unit more affordable.

Choosing a Roommate

"How do I choose a roommate?" you might ask. In some cases, roommates have known each other through school, work, or just growing up in the same neighborhood. If you don't know someone who wants to share housing, you can still find a roommate with needs similar to yours. Here are some tips you might find helpful in choosing a roommate:

- Read the newspaper classifieds section titled "Roommate Wanted." College newspapers and workplace bulletin boards often have such ads as well.

- Talk with people you know about your need to find a roommate. Others often know of someone else in the same situation.

- Select a few people who seem to be potential roommates and set up a time to meet them and talk with them.

- Discuss your living habits during the room-mate interview. Talk about your schedules. How do you each spend your leisure time? Are you neat and tidy or is clutter okay?

When you are ready to make your decision about a roommate, look over your notes. Which person or persons seem to be the most compatible? If you're thinking of choosing someone you don't know well, ask for references from previous land-lords and roommates. It's also a good idea to verify the person's place of employment.

Roommate Relationships

Roommate relationships can work out well when mutual respect is part of the relationship. Roommates need to respect each other's schedules, privacy, personal items, and other needs. As in any relationship, there will be ups and downs, but most problems can be solved with clear communication.

Dividing Expenses

Roommates should agree on how to divide their expenses. For the rent payment and monthly utility bills, the easiest method is to divide the expenses equally among the people living in the unit. One exception might be the telephone bill, with each roommate paying for his or her own calls.

Allocating Responsibilities

When establishing household responsibilities, make a list and divide the jobs fairly. Roommates might each have certain jobs they do consistently, such as one roommate shopping for food and cooking, and another cleaning and taking out the trash. Another possibility is to take turns performing tasks. Roommates should come to an agreement about household responsibilities based on what might work best for them.

Be sure that all people involved are in mutual agreement about the living situation. Establishing some "ground rules" for household routines and shared expenses is essential for successful roommate relationships. **See Fig. 7-9.**

Fig. 7-9 It is important to select roommates who are compatible. Why is it a good idea for roommates to agree in advance on household routines and responsibilities?

Feeling at Home

People need to consider a variety of factors to determine what kind of place they want to rent. Those factors include the type and size of the housing, the location, the additional services desired, and the monthly cost that their budget allows. They need to inspect each place personally before finally selecting a place to live. And tenants need to make sure they understand the lease or rental agreement before signing their name to it. These documents are enforceable in a court of law, and it is vital that tenants enter into such agreements with full knowledge of their rights and responsibilities.

Think of the research and information-gathering involved in finding and selecting rental housing as a challenge. Your final reward for meeting that challenge is to find the right place to live—a space that becomes home. See Fig. 7-10.

If you decide to share housing, clear and open communication is important to building a successful relationship with your roommate(s). Working out agreements about how to divide costs and responsibilities and how to use shared space fairly can prevent problems from arising. When difficulties do come up, all parties need to be willing to compromise.

The result of all this planning and communicating is a rewarding one. Each day when you wake up or come home from school or work, you will feel that you belong there. By taking some time to make decisions carefully and by acting responsibly, you can find the right place for you.

Fig. 7-10 This family certainly looks "at home" in their rented town house.

Profile of a Resident Manager

Resident managers collect rent payments and handle other finances of a rental property. They also purchase supplies and equipment for the property and schedule repairs either by the maintenance staff or by outside contractors. Resident managers must follow the provisions of such laws as the Americans with Disabilities Act and the Federal Fair Housing Amendment Act.

Education & Training

- A high school diploma with some experience in real estate is desirable.

- College graduates with degrees in business administration, accounting or finance, public administration, or related fields are preferred.

Skills & Aptitudes

- Good communications skills and the ability to deal tactfully with people are vital.

- Computer and financial skills are useful.

- Knowledge of a building's mechanical systems is helpful.

- Ability to do minor plumbing and carpentry repairs is desirable.

Resident Manager
James O'Neill

Home ownership is high on the list of the goals for many American families. Why pay rent, people say, and have nothing to show for it? Yet there's another side to this issue, and I prefer apartment living. I appreciate the conveniences it offers—no major repairs to make, no yard work to do.

We'd lived here for about three years when the owner asked me to become the resident manager. It was a great deal. I could live rent-free and earn a small salary. Plus I had time for a part-time job and to volunteer at my daughters' school. Having worked in customer service, I had plenty of experience in dealing with people and felt confident that I could do the job.

Rapport is the real key to managing an apartment building. I try to maintain a good relationship with the residents of each of our 18 units. It takes a lot of skill to monitor the building without disrupting people's privacy or getting too caught up in their demands. We have one chronic complainer, for instance, who even expected me to change his light bulbs! I finally had to explain to him, very tactfully, where my responsibilities began and ended.

A description of this job would be hard to write. Basically, I do whatever is needed to run the building. I make minor repairs—such as fixing a leaky faucet—but hire professionals when a job is beyond my skills, like electrical problems. I handle all the books and pay all the bills.

I also monitor safety—watching for fire hazards and taking steps to prevent burglaries. I've taken first-aid training in case of emergencies. I try to keep an eye out for our older residents. If I see that their newspaper hasn't been picked up, I knock or call and ask how they're doing. It's an extra that people really appreciate and that I feel good about.

Apparently, the residents are pleased with the way the building is operated. Our turnover rate is low, in spite of the inevitable rent increases. Now, my daughter and son-in-law rent a two-bedroom unit here. That's great for me because I can spend more time with my young grandson while doing a job that I enjoy.

Design Portfolio

1. Design a checklist of tasks that would need to be done when a tenant moves out of an apartment in order to prepare it for the next tenant.

2. Suppose you are the resident manager of a new apartment complex that will have one- and two-bedroom apartments. Design an ad to be placed in the local paper advertising the new building and its most attractive features.

Chapter Summary

- Before looking for a rental unit, determine your needs, wants, and priorities.
- Many sources provide information on available rentals.
- Three basic housing options are privately owned housing, public housing, and **subsidized housing**.
- Evaluating a rental unit involves checking its living space, services, and facilities and learning about any special restrictions that apply to it.
- **Leases** are legal documents that a prospective tenant should read and review carefully before signing.
- Both tenants and landlords have rights and responsibilities.
- Choosing a roommate carefully, setting ground rules, and communicating openly can make home sharing succeed.

Checking Your Understanding

1. What four factors should you consider before looking for rental housing?
2. What are three sources of information about available rental housing?
3. How do privately owned housing, public housing, and **subsidized housing** differ?
4. What features of rental housing should you look at when inspecting and comparing units?
5. How does a **lease** differ from a verbal or written rental agreement?
6. What does it mean to **sublet** a rental unit?
7. What is **breach of contract**, and how is it related to a landlord's right to **evict** a tenant?
8. What are the rights and responsibilities of tenants and landlords regarding repairs?
9. What are three advantages of sharing housing?
10. What actions could you take if you needed to find a roommate?

Thinking Critically

1. **Giving Examples.** What mistakes do you think people might make when looking for rental housing? What advice would you give people to avoid those mistakes?

2. **Understanding Viewpoints.** As a tenant, would you prefer to assign or sublet an apartment? Why? If you were the landlord, which arrangement would you prefer? Why?

3. **Solving Problems.** You share an apartment and your roommate is out of work and having trouble contributing money to the monthly bills. Your landlord has been calling about the late rent. What would you do? Explain your answer.

Applying Your Knowledge

1. **Finding Available Housing.** Choose a community in a state in which you would like to live. Using Internet resources, find out what type of rental housing is available there and identify at lease five potential rental units. Describe them and explain why you do or do not find each one appealing.

2. **Inspecting Rental Units.** Create a checklist showing the items that you would check when inspecting a rental unit.

3. **Understanding Leases.** Obtain a copy of a lease from a local rental office. Reword each clause of the lease in your own words. If you are unsure what any of the clauses means, find an adult who can explain it to you.

4. **Evaluating Rights.** Suppose you were a landlord drawing up a standard lease for your eight-unit apartment building. What are five rules—other than those related to rent payment—that you would put in the lease? Explain why you would choose each one.

5. **Interviewing Roommates.** Suppose you are looking for a roommate to share a two-bedroom apartment. Draw up a list of questions you would ask. Then interview a classmate, with each of you asking questions from your lists. From your classmate's responses, do you think you would be compatible roommates? Why or why not?

Design Challenge

You have been given an opportunity to design a new rental housing complex in your community. Write a proposal that includes the following information:

1. The area of the community in which you would build.

2. The type of buildings (low-rise, high-rise).

3. The number of units.

4. The sizes of the units (numbers and types of rooms).

5. The types of tenants you would wish to attract (age group, income level).

6. Special features, if any (such as pool or health club).

Draw up a plan showing the layout of a typical rental unit in your planned complex.

Chapter 8

Buying a Home

Objectives

- Explain factors people use to determine an affordable price for a home.

- Compare and contrast various ways to finance the purchase of a home.

- Evaluate the advantages and disadvantages of new and older homes.

- Identify factors that affect the resale value of a home.

- Summarize the steps in the home-buying process.

- Describe the various inspections that potential home buyers should have performed before purchasing a home.

- Identify the closing costs that home buyers may have to pay.

Vocabulary

- credit history

- amortization

- equity

- escrow

- conventional mortgage

- adjustable rate mortgage

- graduated payment mortgage

- points

- homeowner's insurance

- closing

Buying a home is a serious financial decision. For many people, a home is the most expensive item they will ever buy. As your housing needs change throughout your life, you will most likely buy and sell more than one home. Real estate agents, lenders, home inspectors, and lawyers help guide many consumers through the home-buying process and help them become proud homeowners.

Financial Planning: The First Step

Before they began shopping for a home, Seth and Mandy Walsh sat at their kitchen table one evening and discussed their finances. They asked themselves such questions as: How much have we saved for the purchase of a home? What monthly payment will fit in our budget? How much debt do we currently have? The answers to these questions helped them estimate how much they could afford to pay for a home. By determining the price range they should focus on, buyers can make their search for a home more efficient. **See Fig. 8-1.**

Fig. 8-1 Buying a home is a critical decision. Whether it's the first time you've purchased a home or the fifth time, it should involve much thought and financial planning.

Fig. 8-2

Down Payment on a Home		
Cost of Home	**Down Payment**	**Amount of Loan**
$90,000	10% = $9,000	$81,000
$90,000	20% = $18,000	$72,000

Income and Budget

A prospective buyer's income is one of the factors that lenders look at carefully to determine how much money they are willing to lend. As you learned in Chapter 6, one commonly used formula states that the monthly mortgage (home loan) payment should be no more than about 28 percent of the household's monthly *gross income* (total earnings before taxes and other deductions are taken out of paychecks). For example, if a prospective buyer makes $2,000 a month, the monthly mortgage payment should not exceed $560. Knowing this makes it possible to calculate how much money a buyer may borrow, based on the length of the loan and the current interest rates.

While the 28-percent guideline is used by many lenders, prospective buyers should also consider their own situation. How much are they willing to spend on housing compared to other items in their budget? How much do they want to set aside each month for other financial goals? Questions like these can help families and individuals decide what price range they will be comfortable with.

Savings

Another consideration is how much cash the buyer has for initial expenses. The largest of these is the *down payment*—the portion of the purchase price that must be paid in cash at the time of purchase. The down payment and the mortgage work together. As you can see from **Fig. 8-2**, a larger down payment means a smaller mortgage. A standard down payment is 20 percent.

Buyers also need enough cash on hand for the *closing costs*—fees due at the time of purchase. In addition, buyers must keep in mind the cash they may need for other expenses that arise when purchasing a home. Prospective buyers who qualify for a loan on the basis of their income but lack cash must either postpone buying a home or look for a home in a lower price range.

Debt and Credit History

Prospective buyers should also take a look at how much debt they currently have. If their credit card balances or other debts, such as car loans, are high, they might not be able to get as large a mortgage as they want. As a general guideline, lenders want to make sure that total monthly debt, including mortgage payments, is no more than about 36 percent of gross monthly income.

Lenders also look at prospective buyers' **credit history**, or their record of paying loans and bills. They want to know whether the buyer makes payments reliably and on time. This information is available to them from credit reporting agencies. Would-be buyers who have a history of skipped or late payments will find it difficult or impossible to get a mortgage loan until they improve their record.

Understanding Financing

To a first-time homebuyer, obtaining a mortgage loan is often one of the most unfamiliar and challenging aspects of the purchase. The process is easier if buyers understand how mortgages work.

Mortgage Basics

A mortgage contract outlines the terms of a loan between the lender and the borrower. The lender agrees to lend a certain amount of money at a specified interest rate. The borrower agrees to repay the loan according to the terms of the contract, usually by making monthly payments. If the borrower fails to repay, the lender can take possession of the home.

As explained in Chapter 6, only part of each mortgage payment goes toward repaying the *principal*, or the original loan amount. The rest is interest, the fee charged for borrowing the money. Early in the loan, most of each payment is interest. With each payment, a larger portion goes toward principal and a smaller amount toward interest, as shown in Fig. 8-3.

Each time a mortgage payment is made, the principal balance—the amount owed to the lender—is reduced. Finally, with the last payment, the principal of the loan has been completely repaid. This gradual elimination of the principal is called **amortization**.

As the loan principal is gradually paid off, the homeowner builds equity. **Equity** is the difference between the market value of a property—the price it might sell for—and the principal still owed on the mortgage. You might think of it as the home's "cash value" at any given point. For example, suppose a home has a market value of $150,000. If the remaining principal on the mortgage is $100,000, the owner has $50,000 of equity.

In some cases, the monthly mortgage payment includes not only principal and interest, but also a portion of the yearly cost of property taxes and insurance. These are deposited in an escrow account. **Escrow** refers to money held in trust by a third party until a specified time. When the taxes and insurance payments are due, the lender withdraws money from the escrow account and makes the payments on behalf of the homeowner.

Types of Mortgages

There are several types of mortgages that buyers can choose from:

Conventional Mortgage. This is the most common type of mortgage offered. With a **conventional mortgage**, the borrower pays a fixed interest rate for the length of the loan, usually 15 to 30 years. A conventional mortgage is a particularly good choice when interest rates are relatively low, since the rate remains the same for the length of the loan.

Fig. 8-3

Principal and Interest		
Sample mortgage: $75,900 for 30 years at 10% interest		
Payment Number	Principal	Interest
1	$33.58	$632.50
48	49.60	616.48
180	148.33	517.75
240	244.04	422.04
300	401.52	264.56
360	654.06	5.45

Special Financing Alternatives

Besides conventional financing, alternatives exist that can make home buying more manageable. Buyers need to weigh the risks and benefits of each option to decide whether one is right for them.

Government Programs. The U.S. Department of Housing and Urban Development (HUD) helps buyers get loans by insuring them against default. HUD promises to pay the lender if the buyer cannot. If that should happen, the homes are opened to bids from low- and middle-income families. Also, teachers and law enforcement officers can buy homes at reduced prices to spur development and community stability in special "revitalization areas." Current and former members of the armed forces can obtain financing with no down payment through the Veterans Administration.

Contract for Deed. Buyers and sellers can deal directly without involving a lending institution. The buyer pays the principal and interest in regular installments. The seller signs over the deed, or legal title, to the property when the full amount is paid. State laws on this arrangement vary, but include complex issues related to ownership rights and tax liabilities.

Rent with Option to Buy. The buyer starts as a renter, with part of the rent going toward the down payment. When the agreed-on amount has been paid, the buyer obtains financing for the balance of the purchase price from a lender.

Tapping Retirement Plans. People who have a retirement account through their employer can borrow against the money they have invested in it. They can also withdraw money saved in an individual retirement account (IRA).

Adjustable Rate Mortgage. A loan in which the interest rate changes after a certain length of time, usually every one to five years, is called an **adjustable rate mortgage**. Changes in the rate depend on current rates in effect at the time; rates are not determined in advance. How much the rate changes depends on the terms of the mortgage. There is usually a limit on how high the rate can go. Often there is also a limit, or cap, on how much the rate can increase in any given year. As with conventional loans, adjustable rate loans are generally paid off over 15 to 30 years.

An advantage of an adjustable rate loan is that the interest rate usually starts out lower than the conventional mortgage rate. An adjustable rate mortgage might be a sound economic choice for people who are not planning to stay in a home for a long period of time. It might also be a good choice for people who are not earning enough to afford a conventional loan at the time they take the loan. When interest rates are high, buyers might choose an adjustable rate loan with the expectation that rates will come down in the future.

The disadvantage of an adjustable rate mortgage is that the rate changes are unpredictable. Buyers do not know in advance whether their monthly payments will increase or by how much.

Graduated Payment Mortgage. An option that appeals to many first-time buyers is a **graduated payment mortgage**. With this type of loan, the payments start out low and increase in the later years of the loan, when people are likely to have more income. The advantage over adjustable rate loans is that buyers know in advance how much they will owe each month for the length of the loan.

Shopping for a Mortgage

Mortgage loans are available from many sources, including banks, savings and loans, credit unions, finance companies, and lenders that specialize in mortgages. Prospective buyers are wise to begin shopping for a loan even before they begin their home search. **See Fig. 8-4.** They can compare interest rates and other loan features by phone, on the Internet, or by visiting lenders in person.

Buyers should compare not only the interest rate of mortgage loans, but the number of points. **Points** refer to a one-time fee charged by lending companies to increase their yield on a mortgage. Each point generally equals 1 percent of the mortgage amount. For example, if a lender charges three points on a $50,000 loan, this adds $1,500 to the cost. Although points are usually paid in advance, sometimes they are added to the mortgage and paid out over the length of the loan. In some cases, no points are charged. The decision to charge points is up to the lender.

Prequalifying for a Loan

Many lenders are willing to prequalify a buyer for a loan. This means that after obtaining information from the buyer, the lender provides a written estimate of how large a mortgage is likely to be approved. The buyer is not obligated to apply for a loan from that lender, and the lender does not promise to approve one. Still, prequalifying has several advantages for buyers. It lets them know how much they can expect to borrow and a maximum price range they can afford. Once the buyer finds a home to purchase, having a letter of prequalification can make it easier to negotiate with the seller. It can also save time in the final loan application process.

Fig. 8-4 Meeting with a mortgage loan officer can be a wise first step in the home-buying process. The loan officer can determine a realistic price range for you based on an analysis of your finances.

Deciding What to Look For

After determining an affordable price range and investigating loans, interested buyers should review the kinds of housing available. There are many housing sizes, styles, floor plans, and methods of construction to choose from.

Buyers must think about what size home would best suit their needs. First-time buyers often start with a smaller home so that their mortgage payments won't be too high. Buyers can't always purchase their "dream home." They can, however, set their sights on a comfortable home in a neighborhood they like with the possibility of moving up to another home later.

Even within a limited price range, there are many types of homes to choose from. By considering their needs and wants, buyers can determine the options that best suit them. Seth and Mandy, whom you read about earlier, decided they would rather have a small home in good condition than a larger one that needed a lot of work. They did, however, want two bedrooms so they could use one as an office. They also wanted a home with more privacy than the apartment building in which they currently lived. Seth and Mandy looked at conventional single-family houses, manufactured homes, and town house condominiums. By agreeing to consider more than one type of home, Seth and Mandy increased their chances of finding an affordable home that would fulfill their needs and wants.

New Home or Old?

One of the choices home buyers face is whether they would prefer an existing home or a new one. To make this decision, it helps to understand the different ways in which new homes enter the housing market. Buyers should also be aware that both old and new homes have advantages and disadvantages.

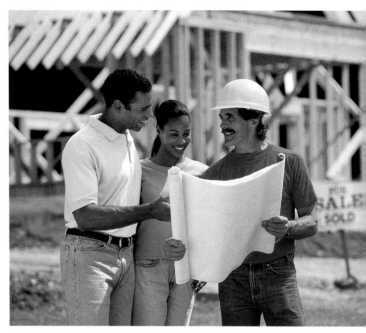

Fig. 8-5 People often have to rely on construction plans to envision what their new home will be like.

New Home Options

People who are interested in becoming owners of a new home can do so using one of four basic approaches. These options vary in cost and in the amount of design freedom they offer the buyer.

Development Homes. New homes are often part of a housing development. A housing development is created when a developer, builder, or real estate company buys a large area of land and subdivides it into individual lots on which to build homes. Typically, prospective buyers are recruited before their homes are actually built. They are offered a limited number of similar home designs to choose from, which helps keep building costs down. Buyers make their choice by viewing model homes and reading information supplied by the developer. See Fig. 8-5. Once they select a lot, choose a home design, and sign a contract, their home is constructed.

Homes Built on Spec. Some builders construct new homes on "spec," which is short for speculation. Construction begins before a specific buyer is found. The builder hopes that the finished home will appeal to buyers and be sold. An advantage for prospective buyers is that they can view the home before agreeing to purchase it. A disadvantage is that buyers have no say in the design and construction of the home.

Stock Home Plans. Many books, magazines, and websites offer stock home plans—predesigned, pre-approved plans that are ready for a builder to use. Buyers can select a design that will meet their needs and fit their budget. In most cases, they must also purchase a lot and hire a builder. Some buyers, however, choose to do some of the work themselves to save money.

Custom-Built Homes. People who desire a one-of-a-kind home may have one designed for them by an architect. This option is the costliest but offers buyers the most freedom. They can specify the number of rooms, how they should be arranged, the exterior style, the materials to be used, and hundreds of other details.

Buyers who decide to build a new home should find out how reliable the builder is. The local Better Business Bureau keeps records of complaints that have been filed against a building company. Also, the buyer can ask the builder for names and addresses of people who are living in homes built by the company. Buyers should contact these people and ask them if they are satisfied with the builder and the quality of work in their homes. While the home is under construction, buyers should visit the site often to check on construction progress.

Advantages of a New Home

The advantages of new homes are fairly obvious. They are clean and in good condition. They have modern kitchens and usually more than one bathroom. For some new homes, the purchase price may include major appliances, such as a dishwasher and built-in oven. Depending on the situation, the buyer may have freedom to choose exterior and interior materials and designs. **See Fig. 8-6.**

A new home is usually easier to finance than an older one. Sometimes buyers can arrange financing through the developer or builder. Some lenders may accept a smaller down payment for a new home than would be required for an older home.

Since the home is new and in good condition, maintenance costs should be minimal for the first several years. New homes usually cost less to heat because they have been built to follow energy-saving guidelines established by the federal government. They generally have more insulation and more efficient heating systems than older homes.

A new home may also be protected by the Homeowner's Warranty Plan established by the National Association of Builders. This plan provides 10-year protection against defects in the quality of work or major construction flaws. Should such a problem occur, the builder must make the repairs at no cost to the owner.

Fig. 8-6 Fixtures such as towel racks aren't always provided in new homes. This allows the owner to personalize the space.

Finally, a new home is often constructed in a neighborhood in which other new homes of equal quality are built. A new home's value will be similar to that of surrounding homes.

Disadvantages of a New Home

One disadvantage of buying a new home is that there are often additional costs. In many cases, the land on which the home is built is not landscaped with shrubs and trees. Fortunately, most builders seed or sod a lawn to make the home look more appealing and to prevent damage to the soil.

Advantages of an Older Home

Many people prefer preowned homes. The age of these homes ranges from several years to a century or more. Many older homes were built at a time when labor and material costs were lower than they are today. Because of this, buyers may get more space for their money. Some older homes provide up to 30 percent more living space than a new home of the same selling price.

Older homes often have more character than new ones. Today, most new homes are built in large quantities by developers. Because of this, many of these development houses look alike. Many older homes, on the other hand, vary more. They may also utilize quality construction and materials, such as plaster walls and hardwood floors, that would be costly to duplicate today. Some older homes also have special architectural touches that can appeal to buyers. **See Fig. 8-7.**

Older homes are usually in well-established neighborhoods. Streets, curbs, and sidewalks have been installed. Landscaping throughout the neighborhood is generally well developed. The buyer can enjoy the beauty of mature trees and lawns.

Fig. 8-7 Older homes often include unique features that are part of the architectural structure of the home.

Disadvantages of an Older Home

A major disadvantage of older homes is the costs of repairs. Wiring, plumbing, and interior and exterior surfaces all deteriorate with use and age. Repair or replacement can be expensive. Do-it-yourselfers who have the knowledge, interest, and time to do the necessary repairs can reduce these costs. It's a good idea to check with the seller to find out about any repairs that have recently been made. Some home sellers purchase a special kind of "home warranty" that covers the cost of major repairs on the home for the first year after its sale. This protects buyers from facing an unexpected expense.

An older home may also have structural problems. The basement or roof might leak, or the home may be infested with termites. There may be wall or foundation cracks that need extensive repair work.

Many older homes have little or no insulation and inefficient heating and cooling systems. These can result in high utility bills. Depending on when the home was built and whether it has been updated, it may not meet today's high standards for energy efficiency.

Some older homes may actually present a health hazard. For example, until the mid-1970s, lead-based paints were used in homes. Lead was used in plumbing systems until the late 1980s. Flaking or chipped lead-based paint and water from lead pipes can cause lead poisoning. Stripping walls and woodwork of lead-based paint and replacing lead water pipes is expensive. If the stripping is not done carefully, homeowners and their children will breathe in poisonous lead dust.

Lenders may require a larger down payment on an older home. However, a buyer may be able to negotiate with the seller to lower the price or change the terms of the deal. The price of a new home is often set by the builder and is usually firm.

Moving into an older home means inheriting whatever decorating features are there. These may or may not agree with the tastes of the buyer. In addition, floor coverings, paint colors, or wallpaper might be worn or faded. Buyers can change these backgrounds, but doing so adds to the cost of moving into the home. Some homeowners spread that cost out by making the changes over a period of years. Others save money by doing the work themselves.

Understanding Resale Value

A home is a large investment. Because of this, buyers will want to choose a home that will increase in value and be easy to resell. Several factors can enhance or detract from a home's *resale value*—the value of the home when resold. The condition and size of the home is one such factor, as well as any special features it may have, such as a pool, outside deck, or oversized family room. Other important factors in resale value include location, design, taxes and assessments, and improvements.

Location. Many factors determine the value of a location. These include desirability as a residential area; its closeness to public transportation and shopping; the appearance, age, and condition of homes in the area; the quality of the school system; and the distance from industrial and commercial areas. Two homes of similar age and style will be priced differently if one is in a desirable residential location and the other is in a deteriorating area.

The site and lot size can also affect the value. Attractive landscaping, a large lot with many trees, or a decorative fence will enhance a home's appearance and make it more valuable. This is part of what real estate agents call *curb appeal*, or the visual appeal of a home when viewed from the street.

Design. Generally, it takes no more material to build an attractive dwelling than a poorly designed one of the same size. However, a good design may make a home more desirable and increase its value because people are willing to pay more for an attractive home. Some styles, too, are more acceptable than others in a particular setting. For example, in a neighborhood of stately old Victorian homes, a split-level home may be more difficult to sell, which can force the price down.

Lending agencies tend to be conservative in their judgment of architectural style. Since the value of a home is determined partly by the price a buyer will pay, the lender is apt to look with greatest favor on a design that has wide appeal. **See Fig. 8-8.**

Fig. 8-8 This home has a lot of curb appeal. **What exterior features add to its curb appeal?**

Taxes and Assessments. Owners pay a yearly property tax to the city, town, or county. This tax is based on *assessed property valuation*, the value of the property as determined by the local government for tax purposes. This is not necessarily the same as market value, which is the amount the property might bring when sold. The market value can be higher or lower than the assessed value. Although the property tax does not add to the initial price of the home, it may affect the price an owner gets when the home is put up for sale. If property taxes are very high, the owner may have difficulty finding a buyer or have to accept a lower selling price.

Assessments, too, add to the cost of owning a home and may affect the price. An assessment is a charge made to the homeowner by the local government. This might pay for the owner's share of the cost of an improvement such as widening a street or installing new sewers. Such assessments are more likely in older neighborhoods. Neighborhood association fees are charged to people living in some town houses and single-family homes in particular developments.

Improvements. For many reasons, the possibility of remodeling a home may enter into the decision to purchase it. Perhaps a prospective buyer has finally found the "perfect" home—except that the kitchen hasn't been updated since the 1950s. Another buyer may choose a home that can easily be adapted to meet future needs by converting the attic to extra bedrooms. Still another buyer may be looking for a run-down home that can be fixed up and sold at a profit.

Prospective buyers should be aware that remodeling projects affect the resale value in different ways. For example, owners who put in a new kitchen will probably get back about 80 to 95 percent of its cost when they sell the home. The percentage depends on many factors: the style of the home, the cost of the home, and the location, among others. Return can be lower if unusual cabinets, colors, or layouts are used. Types of improvement projects that generally have a high rate of return are major kitchen and bathroom remodeling, a family room addition, and new vinyl or aluminum siding.

Owners should be careful to keep improvements in line with neighborhood housing values. A remodeling project that will cause the price of the home to exceed the average in the area might not be a wise investment. **See Fig. 8-9.**

Fig. 8-9 Weigh the risks and benefits before deciding to make costly improvements to a home. **What is a possible drawback to making improvements that exceed neighborhood housing values?**

The Home-Buying Process

Buying a home is a long and complicated process. If you know the basic steps, however, the procedure becomes much easier. In addition, real estate agents and lenders are ready to help home buyers.

The Role of Real Estate Agents

Some homeowners sell their homes directly to buyers. They advertise in newspapers or put up a "For Sale by Owner" sign in the front of their home. The buyer and seller negotiate the details of the purchase between themselves or with the assistance of their lawyers.

Most homeowners, however, prefer to sell their homes though a real estate agent. A good real estate agent screens prospective buyers and shows the home only to people who are truly interested in buying a home and can afford a home of that price.

When listing a home with a real estate agency, the owner agrees to pay the agent a *commission*, or fee, when the home is sold. The fee is usually from 5 to 7 percent of the selling price of the home. To cover this cost, the owner usually raises the asking price for the home. The buyer, then, actually pays the cost of the agent's fee.

Good real estate agents can also help buyers. An agent helps buyers determine which homes fit their needs and budgets. Effective real estate agents are familiar with local conditions. They can answer questions about neighborhoods, schools, churches, and shopping centers. They should also discuss the advantages and drawbacks of various areas.

An agent can also help negotiate the price with the seller or the seller's agent. However, prospective buyers are often surprised to learn that the real estate agent they are working with may be obligated to protect the seller's interests. This is usually the case unless there is a written agreement that the agent will represent the buyer as a *buyer's agent*. If you're not sure who the agent represents, ask. In either case, the real estate agent who helps a buyer find a home usually shares the commission for selling the home with the seller's agent.

Finding Homes for Sale

Prospective buyers can learn about homes for sale in several ways. They can drive through neighborhoods they like and look for "For Sale" signs on front lawns. They can scan real estate websites, read newspaper ads, and go to open houses to walk through homes that are for sale. However, the most efficient way to locate suitable homes for sale is usually to work with a real estate agent.

Real estate agents keep files with photographs and descriptions of the homes that are listed with them. By looking at these listings, buyers can see what homes are available. At many real estate offices today, buyers can view videotapes of homes or scan computer files that include many photos. Most communities also have *multiple listing services*, an all-inclusive list of homes for sale in the area. This allows buyers to see homes listed by all real estate agencies that are part of the multiple listing pool.

Many real estate services are available on the Internet. Online listings of properties for sale may include photos, descriptions, lists of amenities, maps, and agent contact information. Some services also offer "virtual tours" of homes for sale. These allow prospective buyers to see many different views of the home, almost as if they were walking through it. Using these types of services from the agent's office or their own homes can help buyers quickly narrow their search. **See Fig. 8-10.**

Affordable Alternatives

In addition to traditional ways of finding a home to purchase, other options are available to prospective buyers. These include auctions and urban homesteading.

Auctions. When a homeowner cannot pay the mortgage on a home because of financial difficulties, the lender and the owner may put the home up for auction. In another typical situation, an elderly person who is moving to a retirement home may decide to auction off the home along with many home furnishings. In either case, the home then becomes the property of the highest bidder. Buyers can often acquire homes through auctions at relatively low prices.

Fig. 8-10 An online service can help prospective buyers narrow their search for a home.

Urban homesteading. Urban homesteading is one solution to urban decay. In this program, people buy old or abandoned homes at very low prices. They agree to make repairs and live in the home for a specified period of time. The new owners often save money by doing their own carpentry, plumbing, and painting.

These homes can be a good investment. The owners can usually sell the homes for more than the sum of the original buying price and repair costs.

Evaluating Homes

Buyers should look at as many homes as possible to get a good sense of the options available within their price range. There will be many that don't measure up to their hopes. It takes time to fit people with the homes that are best suited to them.

When looking at homes, buyers should pay attention to the layout and the number and types of rooms. These factors greatly affect a home's livability. Buyers should also be alert to possible trouble spots.

Making an Offer

When a buyer finds the right home, he or she can have a lawyer or the real estate agent draw up an *offer-to-purchase contract*. In this contract, the buyer bids for the home by offering a price to the seller. The offer-to-purchase contract includes a legal description of the property to be purchased. It also states the date on which the buyer proposes to assume ownership of the home and other details of the sale. See Fig. 8-11.

Along with the offer-to-purchase contract, the buyer submits a check for the *earnest money*. This is the deposit the buyer makes to show he or she is serious about buying the home.

The buyer may ask that the offer-to-purchase contract be worded with certain *contingencies*, or conditions that must be met in order for the sale to become final. For example, most contracts state that the offer is *contingent upon financing*. This means that the buyer agrees to buy the home only if he

or she can qualify for an appropriate loan. Another common contingency is a satisfactory report from a certified home inspector. If the specified conditions are not met, the contract between buyer and seller is declared void. The earnest money is returned, and the seller puts the home on the market once again.

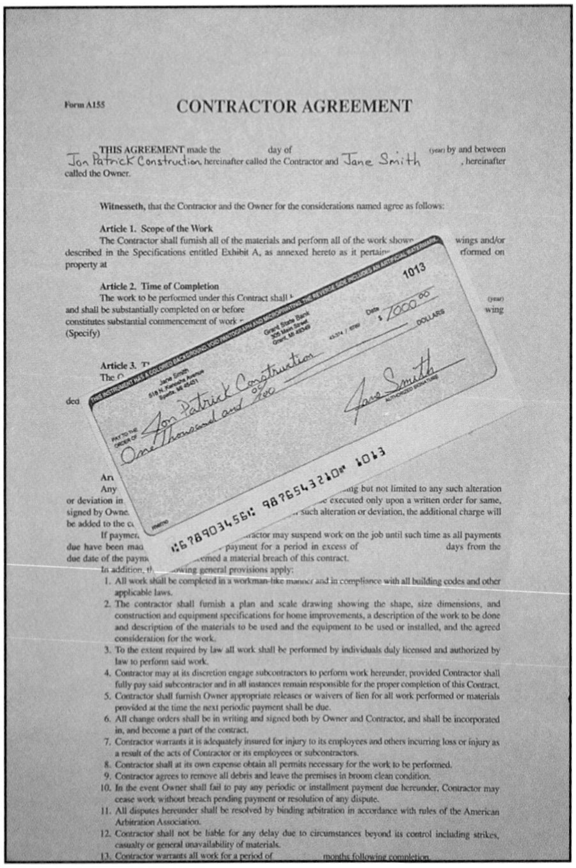

Keep in mind that the advertised price of the home is an asking price. Owners usually set an *asking price* that is somewhat higher than the price they actually expect to receive from the sale. Asking prices allow for bargaining.

The amount of bargaining and the final price depend on local economic conditions. In a *buyer's market*, there are more homes for sale than there are buyers. This condition favors the buyer and pushes prices lower. The buyer can usually purchase the home for below the asking price. In a *seller's market*, there are more people who want to buy homes than there are homes for sale. This condition favors the seller. The buyer may have to meet or exceed the seller's asking price.

Current mortgage interest rates are also a factor in a buyer's or seller's market. If rates are high, people are not as likely to buy homes as when rates are low.

Agreeing to Purchase

If the buyer and seller agree on a price, the offer is accepted. The seller signs the offer, which becomes a binding sales contract. The earnest money is deposited in an escrow account until all the conditions of the sale are finalized.

Once the seller has accepted the earnest money, he or she may not sell the home to someone else even if that person offers more money. If the buyer decides not to buy the home, the seller is allowed to keep the earnest money but is not required to. When the purchase is finalized, the earnest money becomes part of the down payment.

Fig. 8-11 The deposit that a potential home buyer puts down on a home is called "earnest money."

Obtaining Financing

Now that there is a sales contract, the buyer is ready to apply for a mortgage loan. The buyer fills out an application form and provides the lender with information from the sales contract. The buyer must also make a final decision on the type of loan and the amount, depending on the size of the down payment. The lender provides the buyer with information about the loan terms and begins the process of finalizing the loan.

The lender may give the buyer a choice of when to "lock in" an interest rate. A buyer who thinks interest rates may go up in the near future would probably accept the rate that is offered on the day of application. If the buyer thinks interest rates are on their way down, he or she may wait a few days or weeks before locking in an interest rate.

Obtaining Homeowner's Insurance

One of the last steps in the home-buying process is obtaining insurance coverage for the home. **Homeowner's insurance** is a package of insurance protection for the home and its contents. A basic homeowner's insurance policy combines two types of insurance coverage: property insurance and liability insurance.

Property Insurance. This coverage protects the structure and its contents from damage or loss caused by a variety of hazards. These usually include fire, lightning, smoke, windstorms, hail, vandalism, and theft, among others. Depending on where you live, supplemental insurance against floods, earthquakes, and certain other hazards may be purchased in addition to the basic policy.

How much property insurance is needed? The lender will require an amount of coverage at least equal to the mortgage principal. Many experts recommend purchasing an amount between 80 and 100 percent of what it would cost to replace the structure if it were destroyed.

Besides insuring the structure itself, it's important to insure the personal property that it contains—furniture, electronic gear, clothing, and so on. An insurance agent can help the homeowner obtain an appropriate amount of personal property coverage. In addition, to help ensure that personal belongings will be replaced in the event of a disaster, it's a good idea to make a household inventory. The inventory should include a record of items owned, when they were purchased, and what they cost. Pictures or videotape of possessions are good proof of ownership, as well as cancelled checks and credit card receipts. The inventory should be stored in a safe place away from the home, such as in a safe deposit box.

Personal Liability Coverage. This type of coverage protects the homeowner in case of an accident. For example, if someone slips and falls on the property, homeowner's insurance would cover any medical expenses. If a tree on the property falls and causes damage to a neighbor's property, the insurance company will likely pay for the damages.

Having the Home Inspected

Although buyers should examine a home carefully before making an offer to purchase it, professional inspections are also part of the home-buying process. **See Fig. 8-12 on pages 182-183.** Several types of inspections and tests can be involved. Some of them may be required by the lender or by state law; others are optional.

Fig. 8-12

Home Inspection

A Visual Guide

When buying a home, there are a number of trouble spots that a home inspector should check. Many problems can be taken care of with little work or expense; other problems can be costly. If you are seriously considering a home that shows signs of trouble, consult an expert to determine the extent of the problem, possible remedies, and the estimated cost of repair.

Roof. Ask the age of the roof. Signs of age and possible leaking include curling asphalt shingles, dry and deteriorating wood shakes, and cracked and broken tiles. Water spots on interior ceilings may be a sign of roof problems. Roof replacement can be expensive. Check with a roofing company about the life expectancy of a roof.

Exterior Walls. Look for blistered or peeling paint, which indicates that paint may have to be removed and new paint applied. On exterior brick walls, look for signs of mineral deposits and cracked or disintegrating mortar joints. These signs may indicate that the mortar needs to be replaced. Repairs can be expensive.

Foundation and Grade Level. Look for standing water or ground that slopes toward the foundation. These indicate improper drainage that can lead to uneven settling, foundation cracks, and basement leaks. Check the vertical distance between the ground and wood framing or siding. If there is little or no foundation showing, the wood is susceptible to damage from rot or insects.

Interior Walls. Stains on walls and ceilings may result from plumbing leaks, condensation, or missing gutters and flashing. Cracks in walls or ceilings may indicate structural defects or settling of the structure. Both conditions may be minor or serious. Some repairs can be expensive.

Floors. Check for spots that squeak or bounce when you walk on them, or places in the floor that dip or sag. These factors may, but do not always, indicate defects such as sagging floor joists, insect damage, inadequate framing, or concealed fire damage. Repairs for this type of damage can be expensive.

Insulation. Check under the attic floor and between rafters for insulation; try to learn its R-value. Remove a switch plate cover to check for insulation in exterior walls. Inadequate insulation means higher heating and cooling costs.

Home Inspection (continued)

A Visual Guide

Wiring. Identify the age of the wiring. Adequate service includes a 3-wire, 220-volt, 100-ampere capacity. Signs of inadequate wiring include double or triple plugs in a receptacle; old knob-and-tube wiring visible in the attic or basement; use of extension cords; the need to disconnect one appliance in order to use another; the dimming of lights when a major appliance starts up.

Water Heater. Check the capacity on the label to be sure the size is adequate for your family. Look for leaks and water on the floor around the unit. Most leaks are not repairable, requiring replacement of the water heater.

Plumbing. Determine the material used for water supply pipes and their approximate age. Lead pipes are found in some older homes and may cause serious health hazards. Galvanized iron or steel pipes can eventually rust from inside, causing clogs and leaks. Flush each toilet to be sure the tank and bowl fill properly. Turn on the faucets to be sure the water pressure is adequate. Low pressure may indicate corroded pipes or problems with the water pump.

Sewage Disposal. Ask whether there is a municipal sewage system or an underground septic system. If there is a septic system, ask where the underground tank and drain field are located and the last time it was cleaned out.

Basement. Look for signs of moisture (such as mineral deposits) on columns, walls, or floors; cracks in walls or floor; signs of insect infestation, such as cockroaches; and poor drainage around floor drains. These repairs can be expensive.

Furnace. Ask about the age of the furnace. Check for rust and cracks. An older furnace may not produce enough heat or may quit working during a period of intense cold. If you have doubts about the furnace, request a thorough inspection from a reputable service.

Termite Inspection. This is the most commonly required inspection. Most purchase contracts state that the seller pays for this inspection and for repairing any termite damage that is found.

Radon Testing. Radon is a naturally occurring gas that can pose a health hazard. If present in soil, it can seep into buildings through cracks in slabs or basement floors and walls. Tests can determine whether radon is collecting in the home at dangerous levels. **See Fig. 8-13.** If so, steps should be taken to reduce the levels. Usually this involves sealing cracks and installing a system of vent pipes and fans.

Asbestos Inspection. Asbestos was formerly used as a building material, most commonly for insulation, but is now known to be hazardous. An inspector should look for the presence of any asbestos—particularly damaged asbestos. If it's found, the seller must decide whether to hire an expert to repair the asbestos or to perform the costly process of removing it. You will learn more about radon and asbestos in Chapter 28.

Lead Testing. In older homes, the inspector should check for lead water pipes and lead-based paint.

General Home Inspection. A certified inspector can check the home for structural soundness and ensure that plumbing, electrical, and heating systems are in good working order.

Inspections are well worth their cost to the buyer. It's far better to learn of any problems before the purchase than after. If problems are found, what happens next depends on how the sales contract is worded and the seriousness of the problems. The seller may agree to take care of needed repairs, the buyer and seller may agree on a lower price, or the buyer may be able to legally back out of the purchase.

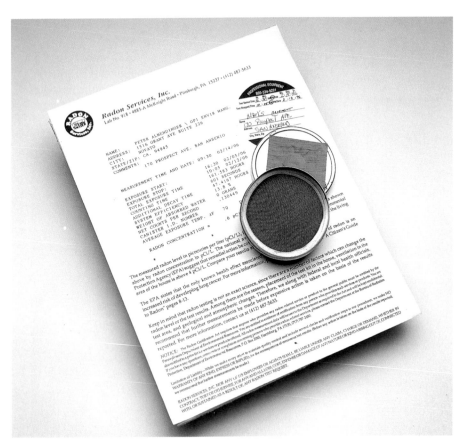

Fig. 8-13 One way to test for radon is by using a canister. It is opened in the house and left undisturbed for a specific period of time. The canister is then mailed to a testing lab.

Closing the Deal

The last step in the home-buying process is the **closing**. This is a meeting at which legal papers are signed and money changes hands, finalizing the deal. The closing is typically attended by the seller, buyer, lender, and any real estate agents involved in the purchase. Sometimes buyers and sellers choose to have their lawyers attend as well.

The buyer must bring funds to pay the down payment and closing costs in the form of a cashier's check. For this reason, the buyer is given a written list of the closing costs ahead of time. Closing costs that must be paid by the seller are also noted and are deducted from the amount the buyer must pay. Here are the typical costs a home buyer can expect to pay at the closing:

- Origination fee—a fee paid to the lender to process the mortgage application. Sometimes this fee includes the survey, appraisal, and title search.
- Survey fee—for a check to determine the exact boundaries of the property.
- Appraisal fee—for an estimate of the value of the property. This can determine the amount of the loan a lender will agree to.
- Title search fee—for an investigation to make sure that the seller actually holds the title to the property and that no one else has any claims against the property.
- Fee for the credit report that details the buyer's credit history.
- Points—the one-time fee sometimes charged by lending companies.
- Home inspection fee(s) (unless paid by the seller).
- Attorney's fee—money paid to a lawyer to represent the buyer during the home-buying process.

Once the buyer has signed the mortgage contract, the loan officer issues a check for the purchase price of the home and gives it to the seller. The seller signs the deed to the home, which transfers the title to the buyer. See Fig. 8-14. The lending institution generally holds the title to the home until the buyer pays off the mortgage in full.

Fig. 8-14 Once they have taken possession of their new property, most home buyers experience a feeling of pride.

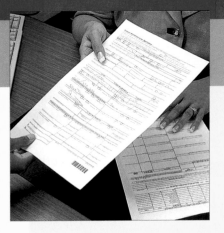

Profile of a
Mortgage Loan Officer

Mortgage loan officers help people apply for loans to purchase real estate or refinance an existing mortgage. Mortgage loan officers seek to develop good working relationships with real estate agencies in the hope that agents will refer people buying properties to them.

Education & Training

- A bachelor's degree in finance, economics, or a related field is required.
- Training or experience in banking, lending, or sales is advantageous.

Skills & Aptitudes

- Ability to develop effective working relationships with others is useful.
- Knowledge of spreadsheet programs, bank applications, and loan terms is important.
- Sales experience can be very helpful.

Mortgage Loan Officer
Judy Flores

The greatest single investment that most people ever make is the purchase of a home. Most buyers need a mortgage loan to make that purchase. My job is to determine whether my bank should make that loan.

Part of my decision concerns the prospective buyers—whether they are financially able to meet the expenses of the home they want to buy and are good financial risks. My ability to make sound judgments is crucial.

I start by gathering information on the person's financial status, such as annual income and other assets like savings or stock holdings. I run a credit check and contact the person's employer to verify income.

Next, I find the projected monthly mortgage payments, real estate taxes, and homeowner's insurance. I put this information into standard formulas to determine whether the amount the applicant wants to borrow is realistic.

We also thoroughly investigate the property. Part of my job is making sure the home is worth the asking price and that the seller has clear title. I make sure that the applicant hires experts to inspect the home to confirm that it is structurally sound and free of insect infestation. Copies of all these reports are then submitted for my review. Each application involves a lot of phone calls, paperwork, and attention to detail. Since I handle many applications at one time, I have to be well organized.

If the facts and figures produce a borderline result—showing that the applicant may have trouble paying off the mortgage—I have to make a judgment call. My interviewing skill helps me to put the person enough at ease to gain some insights about character, values, and other issues that may become significant.

If paying the mortgage will present a real difficulty, I have to reject the application. Approving it would be a disservice to the lender and probably to the applicant. I have to go with the facts and figures, not emotions. Luckily, I get to say "yes" pretty often. Working with the first-time buyers is especially gratifying. I feel good helping them realize their dreams.

Design Portfolio

1. Obtain a copy of a mortgage application form. Analyze it to determine what kinds of information lenders look for. Create a chart that groups the information under different headings. Make notes about each heading to help homeowners gather this information easily.

2. Write and design a brochure about mortgages and the mortgage application process that is aimed at helping first-time home buyers understand the process.

Chapter Summary

- Looking at income, savings, and credit situation helps people see how much they can afford to pay for a home.
- Home buyers can choose from several different types of mortgages.
- Buyers decide what size, type, and age of home they want.
- Buyers need to look at the advantages and disadvantages of new and older homes.
- Several factors affect the resale value of a home.
- Real estate agents, lenders, home inspectors, and lawyers all help people through the several steps of buying a home.
- **Homeowner's insurance** protects owners from financial loss.

Checking Your Understanding

1. How do income and savings affect the price range that potential buyers can afford?
2. How do **conventional mortgages**, **adjustable rate mortgages**, and **graduated payment mortgages** differ?
3. What are **points**? How much would 2-1/2 points add to the cost of a $50,000 home?
4. What are the benefits of being prequalified for a loan?
5. What are two advantages and two disadvantages of buying a new home?
6. What are two advantages and two disadvantages of buying an older home?
7. What six factors affect the resale value of a home?
8. What are the steps in the home-buying process?
9. Why might a buyer's market produce a lower cost for a home?
10. What do the two parts of **homeowner's insurance** cover?
11. What are four types of problems that a home should be inspected for?
12. What are three examples of **closing costs**?

Thinking Critically

1. **Evaluating Information.** A friend who's shopping for a home says, "I don't see any difference in having a 15 percent or a 20 percent down payment. The home is going to cost the same regardless." How would you explain this important difference to your friend?

2. **Comparing and Contrasting.** Compare the four different options for new homes in terms of cost, freedom of choice for the buyer, and other factors.

3. **Making Decisions.** Suppose you were selling a home. Would you sell it yourself, or list your home with a real estate agent? Explain the reasons for your choice.

Applying Your Knowledge

1. **Comparing Mortgage Rates.** Research current interest rates. Make a chart showing the following comparisons: 15-year conventional versus 30-year conventional; conventional versus adjustable rate; adjustable versus graduated. Explain how you would use this information if you were buying a home.

2. **Studying Development Housing.** Visit the website of a developer building homes in your area. Gather information on one development the builder is constructing. Include price information, copies of the different floor plans available, data on the features of the homes, images of the different exteriors, and facts about the choices that buyers can make to customize their homes. Explain why you think this development would or would not appeal to home buyers.

3. **Comparing Newer and Older Homes.** Use real estate listings to find six homes for sale in the same community—three that are less than 5 years old and three that are 30 or more years old. Based on the asking price and the stated size, calculate the cost per square foot of the six homes. Are the results what you expected? Why or why not?

4. **Analyzing Resale Value.** Find three homes for sale that are comparable in size and in the same county. Analyze why the prices of the three homes vary. Write a paragraph explaining your conclusions.

You have been hired by a local real estate agency to create a pamphlet called *A Beginner's Guide to Home Buying*. The agency plans to give copies of the pamphlet to first-time buyers. Its goals are to inform them about the home-buying process and to promote its services.

1. Outline and briefly describe each step in the home-buying process.

2. Explain how the real estate agency is equipped to help new buyers.

3. Design a cover and include illustrations that will help get the information across.

4. Place the finished pamphlet in your design portfolio.

Home Maintenance

Objectives

- Identify four cleanliness standards that should not be compromised.

- Develop a cleaning schedule.

- Identify actions that will trim time spent on cleaning chores.

- Identify routine outdoor maintenance tasks.

- Explain the importance of preventive maintenance.

- Describe some emergency home repairs.

- Identify issues involved in caring for and repairing appliances.

- Describe ways of making cleaning and maintenance tasks enjoyable.

Vocabulary

- caulking
- warranty
- defect
- damage
- service contract

A home cannot maintain itself. When you keep your home clean and in good repair, living there is more pleasant and healthful. Learning how to do minor home repairs yourself can save you money and give you a feeling of accomplishment. Regular cleaning and maintenance schedules can help keep your home clean and attractive, both inside and out.

Home Cleaning

People have different standards of neatness and cleanliness. Some like to have everything in its place, while others have a much more casual attitude. People who share a house need to agree on standards of cleanliness. If views of what is and isn't acceptable vary greatly, compromise will be necessary. Although there's room for give-and-take in how much clutter is tolerable, the following cleanliness standards should never be compromised. They protect both health and safety.

- To avoid attracting insects and rodents, food wastes should be kept in closed containers and removed daily or at least every other day.

- To prevent the growth of bacteria, dishes should be rinsed after use, and all dirty dishes should be washed in hot soapy water at least once a day. Cutting boards should be washed with hot water and soap after every use.

- To prevent falls, spills should be wiped up immediately.

- To prevent falls and to ensure quick exit during emergencies, nothing should be stored, even temporarily, on stairs or in front of doors.

Cleaning Schedules

Maintaining the standard of cleanliness you decide on will be much easier if you set up a cleaning schedule. **See Fig. 9-1.** How frequently a cleaning task needs to be done depends on the task, on circumstances, and on personal preferences. For example, dishes should be done more frequently than laundry. A person with few clothes and towels will need to do laundry more often than someone who has more.

The suggested cleaning schedule on the facing page offers recommendations for organizing a cleaning schedule. Once you have decided on your schedule, getting the correct tools and supplies and working out efficient cleaning routines for each area will help you stick to the schedule.

Fig. 9-1

Suggested Cleaning Schedule	
Time Frame	**Tasks**
Daily	• Wash dishes • Clean kitchen sink • Sweep or vacuum kitchen floor • Make beds • Straighten all rooms • Take out garbage
At Least Weekly	• Vacuum carpeting • Shake out small rugs • Dustmop, sweep, or vacuum noncarpeted floors • Clean bathroom fixtures • Wash kitchen and bath floors • Clean inside of microwave • Dust furniture; polish if needed • Dust accessories • Change bedsheets • Do laundry • Clean washer and dryer lint filters
Monthly or Bi-Monthly	• Wash mattress pads and turn mattresses • Wash windows and mirrors • Clean refrigerator (defrost if needed) • Clean oven • Vacuum drapes, upholstered furniture, and lampshades • Clean dust buildup from ceiling fans • Wipe blinds • Straighten and clean kitchen shelves and drawers • Straighten closets
Every Four To Eight Months	• Clean closets • Wash blankets, bedspreads, bedskirts • Clean drapes and curtains • Clean woodwork, walls, and ceilings • Vacuum refrigerator coils

Tools & Supplies

The right cleaning tools can make a job go faster and often give more satisfactory results. See Fig. 9-2. The following list includes some basic cleaning tools and products as well as a few items you may not have thought of using for cleaning. Which items on the list do you use?

- Vacuum cleaner for vacuuming rugs and carpeted floors.
- Hand-held vacuum for vacuuming furniture and stairs.
- Soft paintbrushes for dusting hard-to-reach places such as pleated lampshades.
- Disposable foam paint applicators for dusting blinds and between slats on louvered doors.
- Putty knife for scraping hardened splashes and drips on kitchen counters.
- Dust mop for noncarpeted floors.
- Stiff bristled brush for scrubbing floors and tile; an old toothbrush for getting to corners.
- Mop for cleaning floors.

Fig. 9-2 Having the right tool for the job is essential to getting the job done efficiently.

- Brush for cleaning toilet.
- Sponges and dust cloths.
- Cleaning solutions and polishes. Read labels when selecting products to be sure they're appropriate for the material to be cleaned. Ammonia, for example, may remove the finish from no-wax floors.
- Step stool or stepladder for reaching high places.

Storing cleaning supplies in a convenient place for use makes cleaning more efficient. If you have two or more bathrooms, you may find it practical to buy a toilet bowl brush and a set of cleaning products for each bathroom and store them there.

Another solution is to store cleaning supplies and products in a basket that can be easily moved from room to room as you clean.

Many cleaning products are poisonous if taken internally; some can cause serious damage to the skin and eyes on contact. To prevent accidents, follow these rules:

- Always read and follow label directions when using cleaning products.
- Never mix cleaners together.
- Wear rubber or plastic gloves when cleaning.
- Store all cleaning products out of the reach of children.

The Impact of Technology

Cleaning with Microfibers

Even floor cleaning has gone high-tech! Cleaning cloths and pads are made with special *microfibers*—polyester fibers that are about one-sixteenth the thickness of a human hair. Microfibers are split in wedge shapes, so a cross-section resembles a pie cut into pieces. This creates a rough surface area that snags even tiny particles of dust, dirt, and grime. What's more, the fibers produce a positive electrical charge, which attracts the negatively charged dirt particles. They are literally dirt magnets, needing no chemical cleaners or sprays.

To use a microfiber mop pad, for instance, you wring it out once in water and then mop the floor. It absorbs water better than cotton mops due to the fibers' dense composition. When the pad is dirty, you just replace it with a clean one. Dirt particles, and the germs they harbor, remain trapped in the fibers until they're washed away when the pad is laundered.

Microfiber cloths and pads are safe for almost all surfaces found in a home and can be used on most types of soil. They are washed with warm water and mild detergent.

Cotton Fiber **Microfiber**

Dirt, Dust, Grime, Liquids

Residue   No residue

Tech Trends

Investigate the history and technology of microfibers. What are some early examples of their use? What fibers and processes are involved? For what other purposes are microfibers used? What applications might they have in the future?

Fig. 9-3 Donate all the useful belongings you never use. You'll appreciate being free of clutter and other people will be able to make good use of the items.

Reducing Cleaning Time

How much time are you willing to devote to cleaning your home every week? Think about this question before you go furniture shopping. Select furnishings with maintenance requirements that match the time you have to maintain them. You can also reduce cleaning time in other ways.

Choose Easy-to-Maintain Furnishings. Although all furnishings need some care, many products are now designed to be kept clean with a minimum of time and effort. For minimum-care kitchen flooring, choose a color that doesn't show dirt readily. For furniture, carpeting, and window treatments, look for stain-resistant fabrics and fibers.

Stop Dirt at the Door. Keep dirt from ever entering the home. Place doormats outside and inside every entrance. Choose sturdy, rough-textured mats that will remove dirt from shoes and boots and hold up in all kinds of weather.

Reduce Clutter. The fewer items you have, the less there is to clean. First, get rid of things you don't need or really want. One way to weed out clutter is to get three medium-sized cartons. Label them "Keep," "Toss," and "Can't Decide Today." Go through an area and sort items into the appropriate box.

Once the area has been cleaned, decide on the best place to store or display the things in the "Keep" box and put them there. Take another look at the items in the "Can't Decide Today" box; if you still aren't sure, date the box and store it out of sight. In a few months, check these items again. Sell or give away all usable items in the "Toss" box. **See Fig. 9-3.**

Once your home is de-cluttered, keep it that way. These rules will help:

- Put things away. Don't leave something where it doesn't belong, even temporarily.

- Don't keep a broken object that you might fix someday. Fix it now, or give it to someone who will.

- Before buying anything, decide where it will be stored or displayed. If you can't think of a place, don't buy the item.

- Keep only what you need. If you want a magazine article, for instance, clip it and recycle the rest of the magazine.

Clean as You Go. Keep cleaning jobs from building up by taking time to clean as you go through the day. Straighten rooms before you leave them—stack magazines, fluff cushions, and remove items that don't belong there. Store dirty dishes in the dishwasher, if you have one. Rinse and stack them by the sink, if you don't. To prevent soap scum buildup after a bath or shower, quickly wipe off the shower door or curtain and rinse out the bathtub.

Outdoor Maintenance

It is just as important to keep the outside of your home well maintained. Making outdoor tasks part of your regular maintenance schedule will keep the outdoor spaces attractive and comfortable.

Special tools are needed to perform some outdoor maintenance tasks. These include lawn mowers, trimmers, weed cutters, pruning shears, rakes, and shovels.

Depending on where you live, outdoor maintenance tasks will vary. For example, a person who lives in a warm climate may have to mow the lawn for a longer season than someone who lives in a climate where it snows in the winter. However, a person who lives in a cooler climate may have to shovel snow in the winter. See Fig. 9-4.

Other factors that affect the amount of outdoor maintenance tasks are the size of the lawn and the amount of landscaping. Generally, the more landscaping materials and plants there are, the more maintenance is required.

Some outdoor maintenance tasks are only done at certain times of the year. In the spring, for example, summer-blooming flowers are planted. Raking fallen leaves and removing dead foliage after a frost are done in the fall.

Fig. 9-4 Some outdoor maintenance tasks can be very time consuming. What outdoor maintenance tasks would homeowners have to perform in your region during different seasons of the year?

Preventive Maintenance

"A stitch in time saves nine" is an old proverb that certainly holds true in the case of home maintenance. Fixing something at the first sign of trouble is a lot easier than fixing it after the damage has gotten worse. The primary purpose of preventive maintenance is to deal with home repair problems as soon as you're aware of them. That way you will prevent minor problems from becoming major ones. A secondary purpose is to keep up the appearance of the home. Several areas of the home benefit from regular preventive maintenance. Some special tools are needed to carry out some of these maintenance tasks. See Fig. 9-5.

Fig. 9-5

Basic Maintenance Tools

A Visual Guide

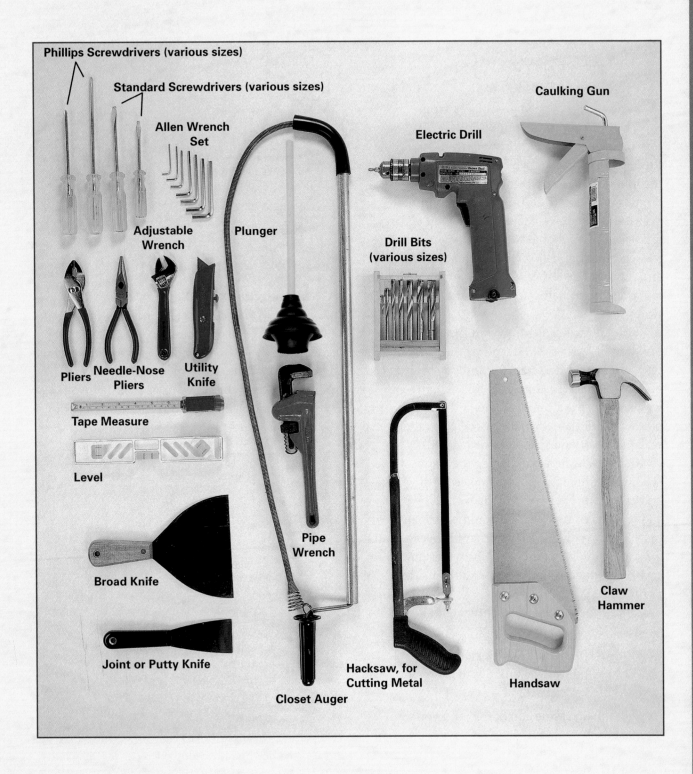

Phillips Screwdrivers (various sizes)

Standard Screwdrivers (various sizes)

Allen Wrench Set

Adjustable Wrench

Plunger

Pliers

Needle-Nose Pliers

Utility Knife

Tape Measure

Level

Broad Knife

Joint or Putty Knife

Pipe Wrench

Closet Auger

Hacksaw, for Cutting Metal

Caulking Gun

Electric Drill

Drill Bits (various sizes)

Handsaw

Claw Hammer

Fig. 9-6 One easy home maintenance task is applying caulk around windows. **How does caulk help cut down on energy consumption?**

Joints

Where two housing surfaces come together at a joint, an opportunity exists for moisture, air, and insects to enter. Problems may occur where siding meets the foundation or roof, where plumbing or electric lines enter the home, and around doors and windows. Many of these joints are sealed by caulking. **Caulking** means applying a sealing compound to make a joint watertight and airtight. See Fig. 9-6. A variety of caulking compounds are available in hardware and home improvement stores.

Over time, as caulk dries with age and the joined building materials swell and shrink at different rates, the caulk often cracks or pulls away from one or more surfaces. Damaged caulk is fairly easy to repair. You need a caulking gun and caulking compound. Acrylic latex caulk is a good general-purpose sealant that dries fast and can be painted.

Caulking is necessary inside the home, as well. Seal joints where interior walls meet with windows and exterior doors, along the edges of resilient floors, and to fill gaps between walls and baseboards. You can buy heavy-duty, water-resistant caulk in a tube for sealing the joints around tubs, sinks, and showers. Check interior and exterior caulk at least once a year.

Follow these steps when applying caulk:

• Remove old caulk with a paint scraper, putty knife, or screwdriver. Load a caulking gun with the appropriate kind of caulk. Cut the tip to the size needed.

• Place the tip at one end of the joint you want to caulk.

• Hold the gun at a 45-degree angle. Squeeze the trigger lever as you pull the gun toward you or downward in a smooth motion.

Gutters & Downspouts

Uncontrolled water from rain and melting snow can ruin roofs and siding, seep into windows and do interior damage, and erode lawns. To control drainage, gutters should be installed at the bottom of all sloped roofs. Connected to the gutters are downspouts that carry the water to ground level. See Fig. 9-7. Downspouts may lead directly to underground

Fig. 9-7 This downspout needs to be repaired. The splash guard needs to be reconnected or replaced. Splash guards prevent erosion by directing water away from the foundation.

drainage systems or simply release the water onto the ground some distance from the house. Concrete or heavy plastic slabs, called "splash guards," are often placed at the outlet of a downspout to direct the water flow away from the foundation. If the gutters or downspouts are broken or clogged, or if splash guards are broken or missing, water may collect in an area where it can seep into the foundation or basement.

Roofs and roof drainage systems should be checked at least twice a year. After autumn leaves have fallen and before spring rains start are the best times. Check for missing shingles, loose sections, and leaking joints.

Roof drainage systems can become clogged, especially if leaves fall nearby. Using a sturdy ladder, inspect and clean out gutters. To prevent further accumulation, you can install mesh guards or wire cages. **See Fig. 9-8.**

Fig. 9-8 Homeowners can avoid clogged gutters by covering them with mesh guards.

Water Heaters

Drain water heaters once a year to allow sediment that collects in the bottom of the tank to drain out. **See Fig. 9-9.** Also check the thermostat on the water heater. If your hot water must always be cooled with large amounts of cold water before it can be used, you're wasting energy and money. Turn the thermostat down.

The water in the water heater is under pressure. As a safeguard, most water heaters have a pressure relief valve located at the top. The valve is designed to leak water if the pressure inside builds up beyond a predetermined level of safety. Excess pressure could result in a dangerous explosion. Every six months, test the pressure relief valve by lifting the test lever. When you lift the lever, it should release hot water through the overflow. When doing any maintenance on a water heater, remember that the water is very hot—usually between 120° and 150°F (49° and 66°C). These temperatures can cause serious burns and scalds.

Fig. 9-9 Draining the water heater on a regular basis can help prolong its life.

Furnaces

More than half the heating systems in the United States are forced-air systems. These systems warm air with a burner and circulate it through a network of ducts with a fan or blower. Cool air returns to the furnace through a return duct. Forced-air heating stirs up dust and dirt. A filter in the return duct catches these particles and sends clean air through to the furnace. If the filter becomes clogged, it blocks the flow of air. This makes the furnace work harder. It also wastes energy and may lead to insufficient warming.

If your home uses forced-air heating, check the furnace filter every month. Open the filter compartment door, slide the filter out, and hold it up to the light. If you can see through the filter, it's good for another month. If not, replace it.

Air Conditioners

Routine maintenance of air conditioning systems is important to help keep them operating efficiently. Air conditioning units should be cleaned and checked at the beginning and the end of each season. **See Fig. 9-10.**

A room (window) air conditioner, like a furnace, contains a filter that traps pollen, dust, and dirt. If the filter becomes dirty or clogged, cooling performance is affected. A dirty filter can be washed with warm soapy water. If the filter has deteriorated, replace it.

A central air conditioning system is a split system, with some of the components installed outdoors and some indoors. Because it sits outdoors, dirt, leaves, grass, and other debris can easily get into the condenser unit and reduce the unit's efficiency.

Clean both room and central air conditioning units to remove leaves, dirt, and other debris. Always follow the manufacturer's instructions when cleaning a room air conditioning unit. Also check the manufacturer's instructions about any other maintenance tasks that are necessary.

Fig. 9-10 Air conditioners run more efficiently when they are clean. At the beginning of the season, remove leaves and dirt from the condenser unit.

Living in a Historic Home

Like many antiques, historic homes need extra attention. Original materials like brick and brass were chosen for durability, but the years take their toll. Yet, owners may not be able to replace the original materials with modern options. If the home is located in a historic district, owners may be limited in the changes they can make, especially to exteriors.

Weather. Vulnerability to water and dampness is one major challenge to maintaining these homes. Regular gutter cleaning and roof repair prevent water from pooling and seeping into attic timbers, where it can start a cycle of decay. Efficient heating and ventilation systems reduce humidity that can also damage the home.

Wear. Water, wind, creeping ivy, and air pollutants can wear away the softer lime mortar used in exterior brick walls and chimneys. However, cracks and gaps must be repaired with more lime mortar. Cement would seal in moisture and salts, causing greater damage.

Insulation. Inadequate insulation in some historic homes can add to maintenance concerns. In cold weather, water can freeze and burst pipes, especially in unheated areas like crawlspaces and exterior walls. Some homeowners cover the pipes with fiberglass insulation or foam rubber sleeves to prevent this problem.

Home Repairs

Normal wear and tear, pests, and natural decay occasionally result in a need for home repair. There are numerous home repairs that you may be able to handle yourself. You might tighten hinges to fix a sagging door or install a new lock. Books, magazines, newspaper articles, and Internet sites give step-by-step directions for doing some home repairs. Home improvement centers, as well as some hardware and lumber stores, have experts who will give you advice on specific problems.

As you do more repairs yourself, your skill and confidence in handling repairs will increase. There are some repairs, however, that should always be left to professionals. Leave such work as rewiring a home or replacing water supply pipes to qualified electricians or plumbers. Gas-leak problems should be handled immediately by your gas supplier. Air conditioner and furnace repair should be done by a qualified technician. Major structural repairs—replacing a roof, for example—are also probably best left to professionals.

Emergency home repairs, such as an overflowing toilet, need immediate attention. When the toilet overflows, for example, it must be attended to immediately. Everyone should learn to handle home repair emergencies. **Figure 9-11 on pages 202-203** shows what to do if a pipe bursts, the lights go out, there's no hot water, a sink stops up, or a toilet overflows. Before an emergency strikes, locate and label the main shutoff valves for water, natural or propane gas, and electricity in your home.

Fig. 9-11

Emergency Repairs

A Visual Guide

Water Pipe Bursts

1. Place bucket under pipe to catch water. If water is shooting up, place a large towel over the top to direct water down.

2. Turn off water at main shutoff valve. (Located near the point where the main water supply pipe enters house. Could be outdoors or in basement.)

3. Turn on all faucets in the home to drain pipes.

4. Call a plumber to replace damaged pipe.

Lights Go Out

1. If you were using a small appliance, unplug it.

2. Determine how widespread the problem is. If it's the entire neighborhood, call your electric company to report the power failure. If it's your home, go to Step 3.

3. If you have a breaker box, check to see whether any breakers have been tripped (usually has a red marker showing). Flip it to "off," then back to "on."

4. If you have a fuse box, check for blown fuses by looking at the thin metal filament inside the glass. If it's blackened or broken, unscrew the fuse and replace it with a new one.

No Hot Water

1. If there is water on the floor around the water heater, shut off the water inlet valve and close the gas shutoff valve or cut off electricity to heater. Call a plumber.

2. If there is no water on the floor, and the heater is gas, check to see if the pilot light is lit. If it's electric, check the fuse box or circuit breaker box to make sure it's getting power. (See "Lights Go Out.") Follow the manufacturer's directions to restart the heater. If it doesn't work, wait 15 minutes, then try again.

Fig. 9-11

Emergency Repairs (continued)

A Visual Guide

Sink Stops Up

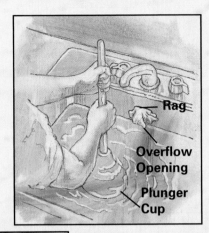

1. Bail out the sink until it's about half full of water.

2. Reach in and remove the pop-up plug (bath sinks) or the strainer (kitchen sinks). For a bathroom sink, stuff a rag tightly into the overflow opening.

3. Place the cup of a plunger over the drain and pump it at least 12 times to force the clog down or up.

4. If the clog doesn't budge, remove the trap, insert a trap-and-drain auger into the drainpipe, and crank the handle. Clean the trap and fasten it securely in its original position.

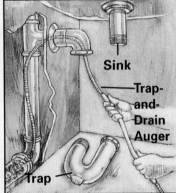

Toilet Overflows

1. Turn off the water supply to the toilet. Remove the lid from the tank behind the toilet bowl. Reach inside and push the stopper closed at the bottom of the tank.

2. Put on rubber gloves. Use a small container to scoop water out of the toilet bowl and into a bucket until the toilet is half full.

3. Place the cup of the plunger over the drain trap. Pump the plunger rapidly at least 10 times and then abruptly pull it out of the bowl to release the clog.

4. If the toilet remains clogged, place the end of a closet auger, or snake, into the drain trap. Very slowly turn the handle of the snake clockwise as you push it toward the clog. As the head of the snake works into the clog, move it in a back-and-forth motion until the clog breaks up.

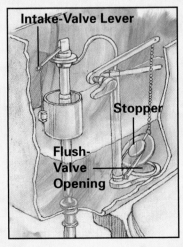
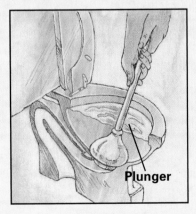

Home Repair Safety

When making home repairs yourself, remember that safety is crucial. **See Fig. 9-12.** Any time you are working with tools, substances, and electricity there are potential hazards. To make sure that you make home repairs safely, follow these safety tips:

- Read and follow the directions that come with power tools and other equipment.
- Unplug power tools before making any adjustments.
- Never touch electrical tools, appliances, or outlets with wet hands or when standing on a wet surface.

- Wear safety goggles when working with power tools, even for a short job.
- Wear a breathing mask when working with materials or tools that give off toxic fumes, such as paint remover, or particles, such as sawdust.
- Use only a sturdy step stool or stepladder to reach high places. Never place the ladder or stool on an unstable surface or in front of a door that might open.
- Keep small children away from the work area.
- Don't attempt electrical repairs unless you are absolutely sure that you can do them correctly. Before working on power switches, outlets, or light fixtures, turn off the power supply to that area by switching off the circuit breaker or pulling the fuse. Post a sign on the fuse box or circuit breaker panel so no one will restore power. Use a voltage tester to make absolutely certain the power is off.
- Before attempting to repair an appliance or fixture, read and follow the manufacturer's instructions.
- Unplug electrical appliances before you work on them.

Fig. 9-12 When making home repairs, you need to know the safe way to do each task and have the right equipment for the job.

Professional Servicing of Appliances

Large appliances are another area of home repair that should generally be left to professionals. Unfortunately, service calls for appliances are always expensive even if minimum service is given. You can cut down on service calls by giving your appliances proper maintenance. Clean the appliance according to the manufacturer's recommendations. For example, vacuum refrigerator coils every few months and empty the lint screens on the dryer after every load. Check electrical appliances for worn plugs and frayed cords, and replace them immediately.

Many appliances are sold with a warranty. A **warranty** is a written statement of the manufacturer's promise to replace defective parts at no charge for a certain time. Most warranties distinguish between "defect" and "damage." A **defect** is any flaw that exists in the product when it is sold, or that develops within a certain period of time. **Damage** is a problem that is the result of improper treatment by the buyer or the result of natural disasters. Defects are the manufacturer's responsibility; damage is the homeowner's.

Remember—a warranty is a promise included in the purchase price of an appliance. Read warranties carefully, and keep them in a safe place. Then, if the need arises, take advantage of them.

Many manufacturers and stores offer an extended warranty, usually at an extra charge, when you purchase an appliance. These warranties extend the time limit on a warranty. Most financial advisors recommend that you not pay for an extended warranty. Statistics show that only 12 to 20 percent of the people who buy extended warranties ever need to use them.

Heating and cooling systems should be inspected periodically by technicians. You may want to purchase a **service contract**, which is an agreement purchased from a dealer or manufacturer under which regular inspections and repairs are made at no extra charge or for a small fee. Before buying a service contract, carefully evaluate whether it is a wise investment for you. One thing to consider is the age of your system and its history of problems. Older appliances are more likely to need repair than new ones. You should also weigh the cost of the contract against estimated yearly costs for individual service and repair. See Fig. 9-13.

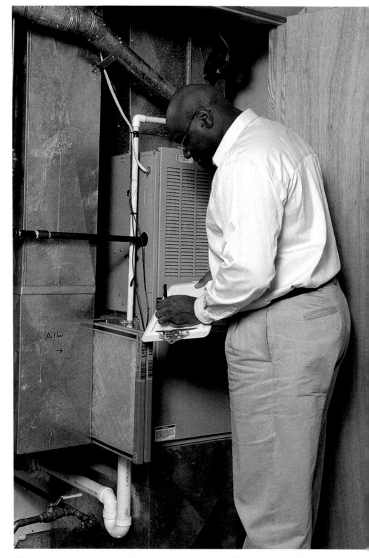

Fig. 9-13 Furnaces need to be inspected and maintained on a regular basis.

Be a savvy consumer. Although most professional service companies are honest and efficient, many are not. Millions of dollars are wasted each year on needless home repair work. Never agree to expensive repair or replacement until you have checked with two other companies or independent contractors.

Cleaning & Maintenance Routines

Cleaning and doing home maintenance may not be your favorite activity, but there are ways to make time spent on these activities seem shorter and less of a task. First, enlist help. Everyone should help keep the home clean. Even children can be assigned cleaning jobs such as dusting, emptying wastebaskets, and straightening.

When dividing up cleaning chores, consider work or school schedules, abilities, and preferences. One method that works for many people is to have everyone choose items from the cleaning schedule that he or she will be responsible for. The items that no one chooses can be written on slips of paper and drawn from a hat. To keep everyone happy, renegotiate the list of cleaning responsibilities every four to six months. That way, no one will feel stuck forever with a job they particularly dislike.

The cleaning process can be less like work if you approach it with a positive attitude. Set a timer and see how fast you can finish a room. Make the atmosphere cheerful. Play music and work to the rhythm. Think of cleaning as an opportunity to improve your health. Use cleaning sessions as part of your exercise program. Pay attention to your body movements and work on your posture. Finally, remember that cleaning, like most vigorous activities, is an excellent way to reduce stress.

A positive attitude toward cleaning can help lighten your cleaning chores. However, the best attitude in the world will not hold up long with an inefficient cleaning routine. Although periodically you'll want to take a little more time to do a more thorough job, you can clean major areas of your home in minutes if you have an efficient routine. See Fig. 9-14.

Routines are important for maintenance tasks as well. Some jobs are clearly seasonal. Many homeowners simply set aside a day each fall to clean their gutters. Checking the heater and air conditioner before the heating and cooling season starts can become a regular chore. Doing this can help prevent the possibility of the system breaking down when you need it most.

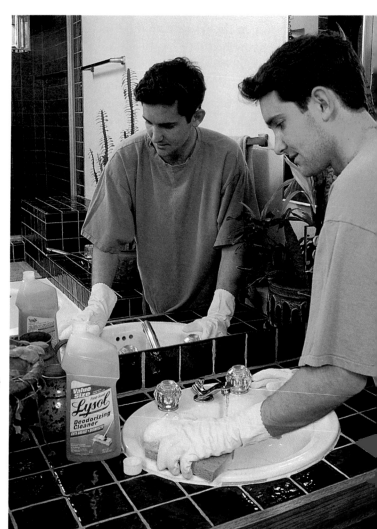

Fig. 9-14 Bathroom fixtures should be cleaned at least once a week.

Home Maintenance Checklist

A home cannot take care of itself. Whether you live in a small apartment, a town house, or a single family home, you will have to take care of certain maintenance tasks on a regular basis.

The best way to make sure that the necessary tasks get done is to create a home maintenance checklist. See Fig. 9-15. The tasks on your checklist and the way they are organized will depend on the type of home you have and on where you live. Many people find that the most efficient way to organize a maintenance checklist is by season. The climate often determines when certain tasks need to be performed. In fact, for most people, spring and fall are the busiest maintenance seasons.

Everyone's home maintenance checklist will be different. The important thing is to create a list that takes into account the maintenance needs of your home, and to make sure you follow it.

Fig. 9-15

Maintenance Checklist	
Spring	**Fall**
Clean siding	Clean gutters and check downspouts
Check roof and gutters	Clean and store yard tools and equipment
Plant summer flowers	Turn off water to outside faucets
Trim shrubs and bushes	Have heating system checked
Check batteries in smoke detectors	Check batteries in smoke detectors
Remove storm windows and install screens	Trim shrubs and bushes
Caulk windows	Rake fallen leaves
	Have chimney cleaned
	Remove screens and install storm windows
Summer	**Winter**
Paint outside surfaces	Check furnace filter monthly
Repair cracks in drive	
Clean air conditioner	
Drain water heater	
Mulch, mow, weed	

Careers in Focus

Profile of a Usability Engineer

Usability engineers, sometimes called accessibility designers, make sure that a home or building is fully accessible to the occupants. These professionals may work on an existing building to make it more accessible by adding wheelchair ramps or lowering cabinets. They may also work with construction companies to make sure new buildings will be accessible.

Education & Training

- A bachelor's degree is required. A master's degree is needed to work in special needs design.
- A background in design and architecture is necessary.
- One to three years of on-the-job training is generally needed for advancement.

Skills & Aptitudes

- Good problem-solving skills are vital.
- Ability to read blueprints and technical drawings is important.

Usability Engineer
Pearl Biden

While I was in high school, my brother was severely injured in a car accident. He needed a wheelchair to get around. Unfortunately, our home had narrow doorways and two stories with all the bedrooms and bathroom upstairs. That's when I learned the meaning of the terms *barrier-free* and *accessible*.

Today, as a usability engineer, I make homes truly accessible for those living in them. It's a job that gives me much satisfaction.

When I'm hired to modify a home, I start by meeting with the family members. I listen to their needs and concerns, discuss possible options, and help them plan their choices. I also meet with the people who will do the work to make sure they understand the family's desires and needs.

Sometimes a usability engineer is hired by the owner of rental housing.

The owner may want to make a unit temporarily accessible to a tenant who requires a wheelchair ramp. Other owners convert their rental units to be fully accessible at all times.

While the unique needs of an individual determine some design features, some elements are common to all accessible homes. They include wide doorways; smooth, hard flooring; maneuvering space in bathrooms; and kitchens with an open central floor area and pullout storage shelves. Other universal features include remote control units at the bedside and light switches, thermostats, and appliance controls that are accessible to all.

The courses in architecture that I took in college help me understand what accessible features are suited to particular kinds of home construction. I have also learned about the characteristics and needs associated with various disabilities. My design training and creative skills help me visualize and plan a home to meet the needs of individuals. I have to stay current with the latest advances in accessible home design; ongoing research shows usability engineers how to do their job better.

Design Portfolio

1. Identify design ideas that could be incorporated into the dining area of a retirement home to make it fully accessible to all residents. Create a drawing that shows your ideas.

2. Create a bedroom and kitchen design for a resident's personal living space in the same retirement home. Make sure a wheelchair could be accommodated in both rooms.

Review & Activities

Chapter Summary

- Although standards of neatness and cleanliness vary from person to person, some minimum guidelines must be met for health and safety.
- Following a schedule for cleaning and maintenance makes the work easier.
- Efficient routines can cut the time spent on cleaning.
- Outdoor maintenance should be done regularly to make the outside of the home attractive and comfortable.
- Doing regular preventive maintenance is less expensive and time-consuming than facing major repairs.
- Homeowners should be able to do some emergency repairs.
- Major appliances should be serviced by professionals.

Checking Your Understanding

1. What four rules of cleanliness should never be compromised for reasons of health and safety?
2. What are three examples of household cleaning chores that should be done daily?
3. What are three examples of household cleaning chores that should be done every four to eight months?
4. What techniques can you use to reduce cleaning time?
5. What are three routine outside maintenance chores?
6. Give one example of preventive maintenance that can be used in each of the following areas: joints, gutters and downspouts, water heater, furnace, and air conditioner.
7. What are two examples of repairs that should be done by professionals?
8. What should you do if the lights go out?
9. What steps should you follow to fix a clogged kitchen sink?
10. What is the difference between a **defect** and **damage** in terms of a **warranty?**

Thinking Critically

1. **Identifying Cause and Effect.** What are the benefits of preventive maintenance? What are the drawbacks of not taking these steps?

2. **Distinguishing Fact from Opinion.** An appliance salesperson tells a customer the following: "Our extended warranty protection plan costs only $159. The plan covers your new range for three years. It's a great idea because you won't have to worry about costly repairs." What statements are fact and which are opinion?

Applying Your Knowledge

1. **Developing a Cleaning Schedule.** Make a list of all the cleaning and maintenance chores that two friends would have to do to care for a two-bedroom apartment they share. Consider only those tasks that have to be done daily, weekly, or monthly. Develop a cleaning schedule that gets all needed tasks done and distributes the work equally.

2. **Identifying Unneeded Goods.** Make a chart with two headings—Need and Don't Need. List each item in your room under the appropriate heading. Review your list to determine which things you can get rid of. Give them away or throw them out to reduce clutter.

3. **Finding Alternative Cleaning Supplies.** Some common substances, such as vinegar and baking soda, can be used as cleaning products. Identify at least five other cleaning alternatives. Explain how they can be used and why they are better for the environment than typical cleaning products.

4. **Designing a Maintenance Calendar.** Create a seasonal calendar that homeowners can use to remind themselves of regular indoor and outdoor maintenance tasks they need to perform. Share your calendar with family members.

5. **Reading a Warranty.** Obtain a copy of a warranty for a major appliance. Read the warranty to determine what problems are covered, how long the warranty lasts, and what procedure must be followed to make use of the warranty. Summarize your findings.

Design Challenge

You have been asked to design a bedroom for a young child that's easy to maintain. Think about the kinds of furnishings and other objects that children 6 to 8 years old may have in their rooms.

1. Research materials for wallcoverings, floorcoverings, and furnishings that are easy to clean.

2. Develop a system that the child can use to store possessions. Choose something that would be easy for the child to use and that promotes cleanliness.

3. Use CAD software to draw a floor plan of the bedroom.

4. Write an explanation of the room's easy-to-maintain features.

5. Place a copy of the report and the floor plan in your design portfolio.

Understanding Construction

Chapter 10

Construction Basics

Objectives

- Analyze how a site influences the dwelling that sits on it.

- Describe and interpret the information shown on a building plan or blueprint.

- Analyze construction materials, methods, and workmanship in basic construction.

- Describe major components of a home's basic structure.

- Evaluate materials used to finish the exterior of a home.

- Analyze factors to consider when selecting insulation, windows, and other components.

Vocabulary

- topography
- orientation
- cross-ventilation
- windbreak
- floor plan
- elevation
- footing
- clapboard
- stucco
- veneer
- shingles
- flashing
- R value
- vapor barrier

*I*magine that you are preparing to build your dream home. How do you prevent that dream home from turning into a nightmare? Careful planning and learning as much as possible about home construction are the keys to avoiding costly mistakes. You can play an active part in building your dream house by starting with a basic understanding of construction.

Understanding Construction

A basic understanding of construction principles is useful even if you will never build a home. Knowing the basics of how homes are constructed can help you evaluate existing housing or tackle home maintenance tasks.

As you explore this chapter, you will discover the way a home is built, from planning the site and structure to laying the foundation, building the frame, and installing the insulation, roof, windows, and doors. You will see that many different materials, people, and technologies work together to build a home that will last a long time. See Fig. 10-1.

Fig. 10-1 A home that ideally suits its owners requires selecting the best place to build, carefully choosing a design, and using quality construction materials and methods.

Planning the Housing Site

In building a new home, one of the first points to be considered is the housing site—the specific parcel of land on which the home will sit. Every housing site, or lot, has certain characteristics, such as size, shape, contour, and soil type. The natural conditions of the site can influence how the home is situated on the lot, as well as the style of architecture used. For example, a small lot won't have space for a large one-story home, but a two-story house would work well.

Local zoning laws also affect how the site is used. For example, they may specify the setback distances (how far the building must be from the property lines). Chapter 16 explains zoning laws in more detail.

Analyzing Characteristics of the Site

The topography of the land is one aspect of the site. **Topography** refers to the contour, or slope, of the land and its other physical features. A site might be flat and low-lying, or it might be sloped. Topography influences the housing style a person can choose when building a home. Sloping land might lend itself to a multilevel home, whereas such land might not be suitable for a long, rambling ranch style. See Fig. 10-2.

The characteristics of the ground on which the housing will rest affect planning, construction, and maintenance. Land that is flat, well drained, and free of rocks is generally the easiest and least expensive to build on. Not all sites are like that, however. Poorly drained soils may cause swampy yards, wet basements, sewage problems, and poor plant growth. In a cold climate, water trapped in poorly drained soils will freeze and expand, sometimes causing sidewalks, driveways, and foundations to crack and bulge. People shopping for land should visit the site while it is raining to check for drainage problems. Any special design or construction modifications required to counteract poor drainage will increase building costs.

Fig. 10-2 Building a house on a hillside requires special plans to protect the land from erosion and keep the house on solid footing for years.

Sick Building Syndrome

A commercial designer may be hired to address sick building syndrome (SBS). SBS is a condition caused by contaminants in a building's environment. Depending on the source, SBS may affect an entire structure or just one area. SBS can cause a host of flu- and allergy-like symptoms. People may feel dizzy, tired, or nauseous. They may have chills, headaches, and muscle aches. SBS may be suspected if all those who suffer symptoms work in the same area and if the symptoms disappear when they leave the building. It can be verified by indoor air quality specialists, using visual inspection and sensitive testing equipment.

In order to offer design solutions, the designer must address the causes of SBS.

- **Causes.** Ironically, technology meant to increase comfort can produce SBS. Central heating and air conditioning provide a sealed environment. As a result, chemicals common to workplaces build up. These include obvious hazards like cleaning agents and insecticides and even unexpected sources, such as fumes from carpet fibers, copier ink, and other items. Mold, mildew, and dust mites are biological culprits.

- **Solutions.** Eliminating the sources of SBS solves the problem. For example, installing finer air filters removes more contaminants. More intensive measures include replacing carpets or water-damaged ceiling tiles. Designing new buildings to combat SBS includes commonsense measures like locating air-intake vents away from heavily traveled roads. Planning natural cross-ventilation can keep mold-prone areas dry and allow other contaminants to dissipate. Trees planted near a building can serve as natural air purifiers by exchanging oxygen for carbon dioxide.

Apply It!

Suppose a grade school wants to convert its basement, now used for storage, into an after-care center for students. What potential triggers for SBS do you see in this arrangement? What would you suggest to design a healthy space?

Planning the Orientation

The **orientation** of a home is its position on the lot and the direction the home faces. Ideally, a home should be oriented so that residents can enjoy sunshine, gentle breezes, and the natural beauty of the housing site. The principles of good orientation apply to all types of housing. For instance, awareness of orientation can help a person choose one apartment unit over another.

Using Sunlight Effectively

For natural warmth and light, homes need exposure to sunlight. Sunlight and fresh air help prevent dampness, mildew, and rot. A home oriented to receive maximum sunlight will need less artificial lighting. Also, the general placement and angle of a home can make a great difference in home energy use and conservation. **See Fig. 10-3.**

In regions with cold winters, exposure to the sun is especially important. The south and west sides of a dwelling receive the most sunlight. For this reason, rooms that are the center of family activity—usually the kitchen and the family room, living room, or great room—are best located on the south or west side. Such design features as large windows can combine with the orientation to make the interiors of these rooms bright and sunny.

Homes also need some protection from the hot summer sun. An overhanging roof or the use of awnings to provide shade, may help screen the direct rays of the sun. The roof overhang should project far enough to shield windows from the summer sun, yet allow the rays to penetrate windows in the winter, when the sun is low in the sky. Limiting sun exposure is especially important in hot climates.

Planning Effective Air Flow

As climates vary, so do the methods used to create air flow in housing. In warm climates, a dwelling should be oriented so that it takes advantage of pleasant breezes. Ideally, natural cross-ventilation, or the air flow created when air travels in one side of the home and out another, should be a significant factor when building any home. Windows are the major means for providing **cross-ventilation**. Cross-ventilation is a natural way to keep a home cool during warm weather.

Fig. 10-3 Properly situating a house on the building site allows natural heating and cooling from shade, sunlight, and gentle breezes. **How could the porch protect the interior of this house in the summer?**

In areas with cold winters, the home should be protected from strong, cold winds. As few windows as possible should face north. A garage could be placed on the north side of the home to shelter the home from winds.

In both hot and cold climates, the natural elevation of the housing site may influence the effect of winds. A home on a hilltop is more likely to be exposed to strong winds than one nestled in a valley. This can be an advantage in a warm climate and a disadvantage during winter months in a cold climate.

Something that protects a housing site from strong winds is called a windbreak. Rows of trees and shrubs are often planted around isolated homes to act as **windbreaks**. See Fig. 10-4. Walls and fences may also be used for this purpose. In cold climates, some people even build a home in the side of a hill to shield it from the winter wind.

Fig. 10-4 A line of trees or shrubs is an excellent way to shelter a house from cold winds. If planting trees or shrubs along the north side of a home is not possible, what other feature could provide protection?

Choosing the Best View

Whenever possible, homes should be oriented to take advantage of desirable views. Large windows can help. A porch or patio will also add to the residents' enjoyment of attractive surroundings.

Sites with an unattractive view may be creatively changed to hide the undesirable features. For example, if a home is next to a commercial parking lot, building a fence or planting trees can camouflage an unattractive view.

Architectural Drawings

Once the building site is chosen, the owners select a floor plan that best suits their needs and the site's topography. (Guidelines for evaluating a floor plan are discussed in Chapter 16.) Architectural and construction drawings—sometimes referred to as *prints*—are drawn up or selected. They are thoroughly checked to be sure they meet all building codes and regulations. Building codes specify construction techniques and materials to ensure that the home is safe and well built.

Architectural drawings are technical drawings that provide information about the appearance and construction of a building. There are several kinds of architectural drawings. The most common are floor plans and elevations. Other drawings give information about the foundation, framing, and other aspects of construction.

Floor Plans. A **floor plan** is a scale diagram of one or more rooms as if seen from above. A basic floor plan includes information about the size and location of walls, doors, windows, stairs, closets, fireplaces, cabinets, and major appliances. From the basic floor plan, specialized floor plans are developed. For example, there may be separate floor plans for the electrical, plumbing, and heating and air conditioning systems. If all of the information were placed on one floor plan, the drawing would be too hard to read.

Consumer Considerations

Do-It-Yourself Homes

Having a house built is a big job. However, people who like to get involved in the building process can call on a variety of resources for help.

Design Software. To better communicate ideas to an architect, home buyers can use software to create floor plans and elevations. These programs let you specify everything from the plumbing to exterior trim. After scanning or downloading a photo of an existing home into the computer, you can experiment with different colors as well as wall and floor coverings. You can even "plant" a tree to see how it might look in 10 years.

Home Kits. Some companies sell packaged kits of prefabricated components. Customers choose from the plans offered or design their own home from a choice of features. All needed materials—from roof trusses to insulation—are transported to the site for assembly. Many people hire professionals to do the actual construction. However, a construction guide is included for those who want to do part of the work themselves.

Consultants. Home buyers may hire consulting firms to guide them through the process of choosing a site, comparing floor plans, and buying materials. They may help with finding financing and hiring plumbers, electricians, and other professionals. The clients make the final decisions, of course, ensuring that they get the home they want.

Elevations. An **elevation** shows vertical surfaces as if viewed by someone standing on the ground or on the floor. See Fig. 10-5. Exterior elevations show the front, back, or sides of the structure. Interior elevations show interior walls.

Many architects use computer-aided design (CAD) programs to generate drawings. With a CAD program, architects can make drawings on a computer, change the plans as needed, and print multiple sets of the finished plans in a fraction of the time it would take to draw them by hand. Several sets of prints are usually required for the construction of a home. One set of prints is filed with the local government. The builder also needs prints at the job site.

Since there's only a limited amount of space on a print, it's impossible to show all the information needed. Symbols are used as a type of building shorthand. Common architectural symbols are shown in Fig. 10-6 on page 222.

Fig. 10-5 This is a front elevation of a two-story home with two attached garages.

Fig. 10-6

Common Architectural Symbols

A Visual Guide

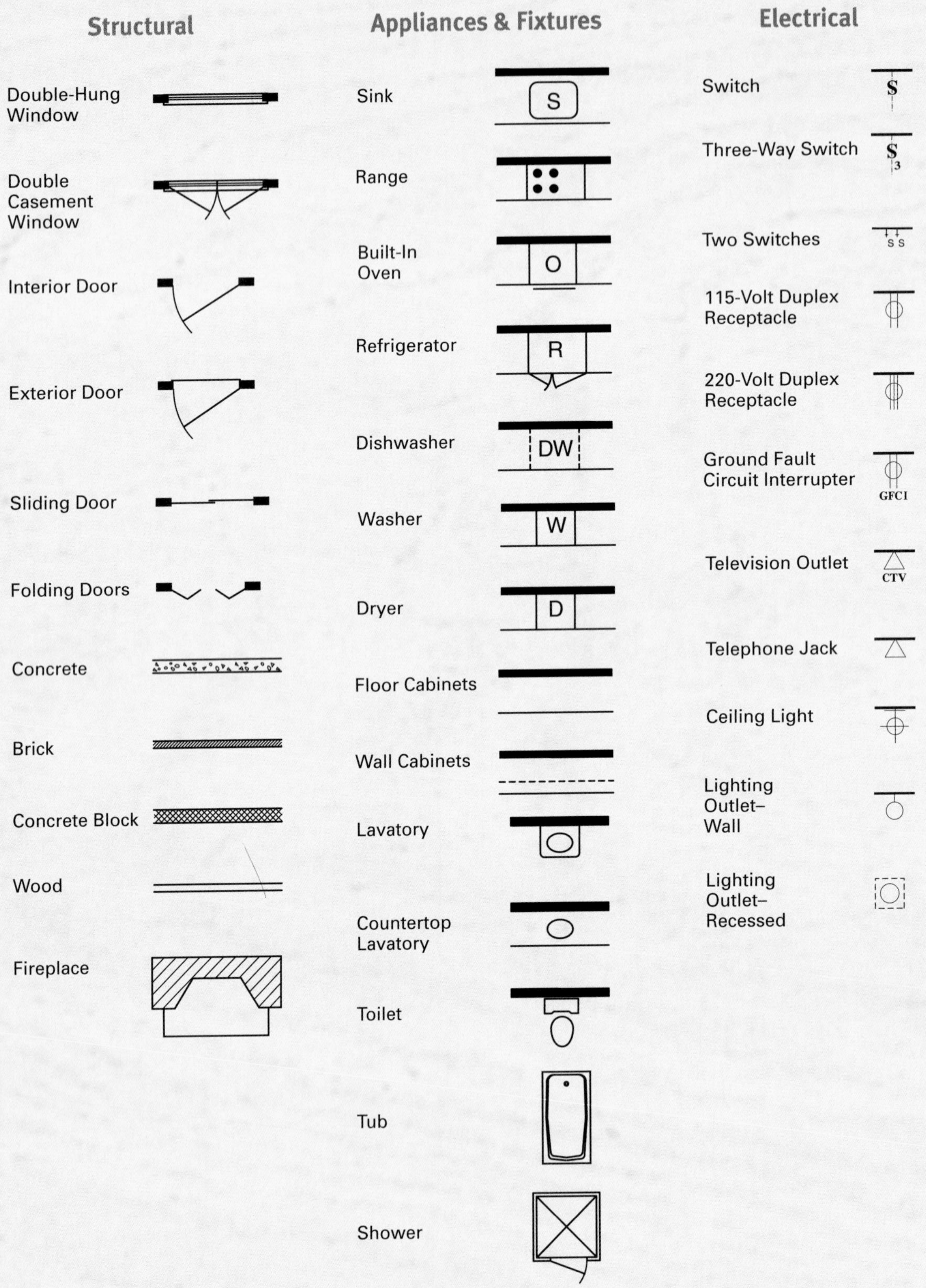

Structural

Double-Hung Window

Double Casement Window

Interior Door

Exterior Door

Sliding Door

Folding Doors

Concrete

Brick

Concrete Block

Wood

Fireplace

Appliances & Fixtures

Sink — S

Range

Built-In Oven — O

Refrigerator — R

Dishwasher — DW

Washer — W

Dryer — D

Floor Cabinets

Wall Cabinets

Lavatory

Countertop Lavatory

Toilet

Tub

Shower

Electrical

Switch — S

Three-Way Switch — S₃

Two Switches — S S

115-Volt Duplex Receptacle

220-Volt Duplex Receptacle

Ground Fault Circuit Interrupter — GFCI

Television Outlet — CTV

Telephone Jack

Ceiling Light

Lighting Outlet–Wall

Lighting Outlet–Recessed

The Basic Structure

Once plans are drawn up or selected, the builder transforms that set of plans into a solid structure that will provide shelter, and more, for years to come. The process begins with the home's underlying structure: the foundation and frame.

The Foundation

The foundation is the underlying base and support of a home. It consists of the footing and the foundation walls. The **footing** is a continuous concrete base that supports the foundation walls below ground level. Foundation walls extend from the footing to the floor and support the load of the structure above.

The type and size of footings should be suitable for the climate and be located from 1 to 6 feet (0.3 to 1.8 m) beneath ground level. They should be placed on solid, undisturbed soil below the *frost line*—the depth to which frost penetrates soil in that climate. If footings are placed above the frost line, the soil under them could freeze and expand, possibly causing the foundation to crack. Homes built in areas prone to natural disasters, such as earthquakes, must follow stricter building codes. This may include placing foundations on flexible and reinforced moorings that absorb the wave of the earthquake.

There are three types of foundation construction. Homes may be built with a basement, a crawl space, or a slab foundation. The type of foundation for a home may be a matter of choice, but location might limit these options. Basements are rare, for instance, in areas with low terrain, frequent rain, and high humidity. To prevent moisture from entering the home, houses in these areas are often built off the ground.

Basements

After the exterior dimensions of a home with a basement have been staked out, the earth is excavated down to the proper level, often about 7 feet (2.1 m). Once the excavation is dug, the footing is poured for the perimeter of the building. The footing is generally 12 inches (30 cm) thick and 24 inches (60 cm) wide. Other footings are also poured to serve as a base for interior columns that help support the floors. When the basement wall will be concrete, the footings are made with a groove called a *keyway*. This helps form a solid connection between foundation and wall and prevents moisture from entering the basement from the outside. See Fig. 10-7.

Fig. 10-7

Basement Wall Construction

A Visual Guide

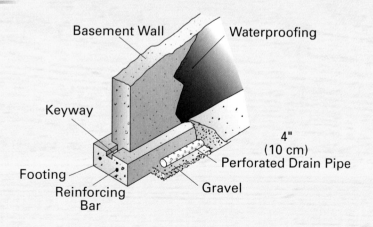

Basement Wall
Waterproofing
Keyway
4" (10 cm) Perforated Drain Pipe
Footing
Gravel
Reinforcing Bar

Most foundation walls are made from poured concrete or concrete block. They are built upon the footings and form the walls of the basement. The foundation walls are generally 10 to 12 inches (25 to 30 cm) thick and about 8 feet (2.4 m) in height. They extend above the ground level 4 to 12 inches (10 to 30 cm) to protect the frame structure of the home from soil moisture and insects. The concrete floor of the basement is poured at a later time after parts of the plumbing and possibly heating systems are installed.

Foam plastic inserts can be placed inside the concrete blocks as the basement walls are being constructed. The inserts provide additional insulation to improve the energy efficiency of the home. Pre-insulated concrete blocks are also available. Builders can also use *insulating concrete forms* (ICFs) to improve insulation of poured concrete walls. Forms are temporary walls put up on each face of the wall. When the concrete is poured, the forms keep it in place until it dries. Usually forms are then removed, but ICFs are left in place to give the wall better insulation.

Waterproofing the foundation is the next step to seal it against damage by moisture. Waterproofing material is applied on the outer face of the foundation wall starting just below the final ground level down to, as well as on top of, the footing. In addition, to reduce the danger of water damage, many builders customarily place drain pipes around the footings and, in some areas, under the concrete floor. The pipe collects any water and directs it to nearby drains.

Crawl Spaces

A home with a *crawl space* has about 18 to 24 inches (45 to 60 cm) of space between the ground and the bottom floor of the home. That means the foundation walls are much shorter for a home with a crawl space than for one with a basement. The crawl space leaves just enough room to crawl under the structure to reach electrical wiring and parts of the plumbing and heating systems.

The floor of a crawl space may be soil or gravel. It is covered with a plastic material that runs up onto the foundation walls to prevent moisture from rotting the wood floor above it.

Slabs

A home with a slab foundation has no basement or crawl space. The concrete footing and short foundation walls under the home hold up a slab—a poured layer of concrete about 4 inches (10 cm) thick. In warm climates where frost is not a problem, a thickened edge slab—which combines the footing and concrete slab into one unit—may be used. Figure 10-8 shows a slab foundation.

Parts of the plumbing and heating systems are often put in place before the slab is poured. A system of welded wire rods—called *rebarring*—is also put in place before the concrete slab is poured. These rods reinforce the concrete and prevent cracking.

Fig. 10-8

Slab Foundations

A Visual Guide

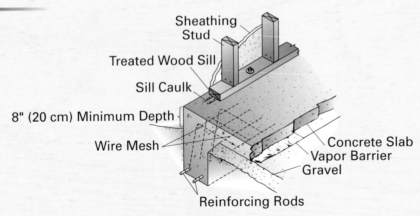

Sheathing
Stud
Treated Wood Sill
Sill Caulk
8" (20 cm) Minimum Depth
Wire Mesh
Concrete Slab
Vapor Barrier
Gravel
Reinforcing Rods

Fig. 10-9

Floor Framing

A Visual Guide

Sill Plate The first piece of lumber, called a *sill plate*, is bolted to the foundation wall with galvanized steel *anchor bolts*. (Anchor bolts are set about 6 ft. (1.8 m) apart into the concrete of the foundation walls before the concrete hardens.)

Band Joists The ends of the floor joists are nailed to the *band joists* (also called *rim joists*).

Bridging *Bridging* consists of wood or metal braces, either horizontal or crisscrossed, nailed tightly to the joists. Bridging distributes the load from one point over several joists, making them all work together. (If floors squeak, it often means that bridging is not nailed tightly or is missing entirely.)

Subfloor The floor frame is covered by the *subfloor*—rough flooring made of plywood sheets or other panel stock or tongue-and-groove boards. Subflooring is nailed directly to the floor joists to hold them in line.

Girders *Girders*—major support beams—help support the floor joists. A girder is made of wood or steel and placed at right angles to the floor joists about halfway between the foundation walls.

Floor Joists *Floor joists* are attached to the sill plate and support the flooring.

Termite Guard A sill sealer (strip of insulation) and sometimes a *termite guard* are placed on top of the foundation wall.

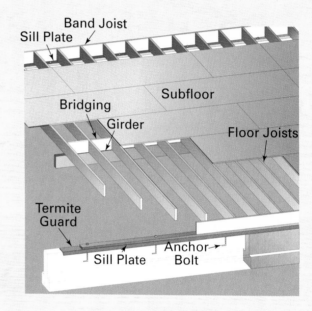

The Frame

The frame is the skeleton of the housing structure. It supports the wall and roof materials and distributes their weight to the foundation. If the frame is not constructed properly, the structure may sag or even collapse.

Most home framing is done with wood or engineered wood products. However, builders are increasingly using alternative building materials, such as steel. Nearly every wood-framing component has its steel counterpart. Steel framing is more expensive than wood but the quality control is much tighter. Steel can withstand termites, fire, and severe weather and will not shrink or settle over time. Steel framing also can be designed to withstand earthquakes and hurricanes. Chapter 3 describes other materials that are used for framing homes, such as engineered wood products and plastic.

The Floor Frame. The first piece of the floor frame attached to the foundation wall is the sill plate. The floor frame is built on top of the sill plate. When a second or third floor is added, those floors are built on top of wall frames. The floor frame consists of girders, joists, bridging, and subflooring. Standard floors are built to hold a uniform load of 100 pounds per square foot. In areas where homes may need to withstand natural disaster, floors are designed to hold 185 pounds per square foot to help minimize damage. See Fig. 10-9 for more information on floor frames.

In parts of the country where termites are common, a termite guard should also be installed. A *termite guard* is a metal shield fastened on the top of the foundation walls under the sill. This shield prevents termites from getting into the wood structure of a building.

Fig. 10-10

Wall Framing

A Visual Guide

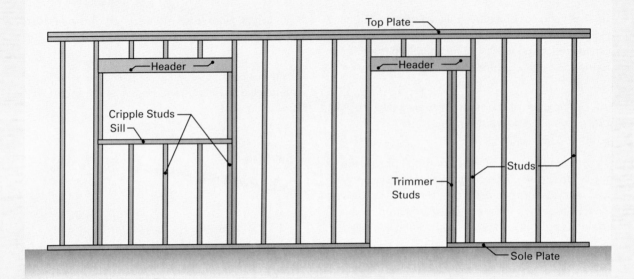

Header The *header*, or lintel, supports the load above a door or window opening. The header is supported by a *trimmer stud*.

Plates Studs are attached at the top and bottom to horizontal members called *plates*. A double *top plate* consists of two lapped pieces of lumber spiked together. The bottom plate is also called the *sole plate*.

Stud A *stud* is a vertical wall framing member. Wood studs are generally spaced every 16 inches (40 cm). If larger wood members or steel framing is used, walls may be framed at 16 or 24 inches (40 or 60 cm). A cripple stud does not extend all the way from the bottom plate to the top one. *Cripple studs* are used above window and door openings and below window openings.

Sill The *sill* provides the support below a window; the cripple studs below the window are attached to it. Since the sill supports only the window and not structural loads, it does not need to be as strong as the header.

The Wall Frame. The wall frame is built on top of the floor frame. The wall frame supports the ceiling, upper floors, and roof and serves as a nailing base for wall finishes. It includes the vertical studs and horizontal plates, as well as headers above doors and windows. **Figure 10-10** shows and explains these components of the wall frame.

Standard construction practices use 2 x 4 wood studs placed every 16 inches (40 cm). If steel framing members or the deeper 2 x 6 wood studs are used, the spacing can be increased to 24 inches (60 cm).

Some interior walls support the floors and roof above, in addition to separating rooms. These interior walls are known as *load-bearing walls*. A load-bearing interior wall should never be removed unless a beam is put up to take its place. Otherwise the upper floor or roof will lack sufficient support. On the other hand, a *nonbearing wall* does not support any weight from the structure and it may be removed. Homeowners will want to keep this in mind if they are planning to remodel, especially when changing the size or shape of a room.

Fig. 10-11

Ceiling and Roof Framing

A Visual Guide

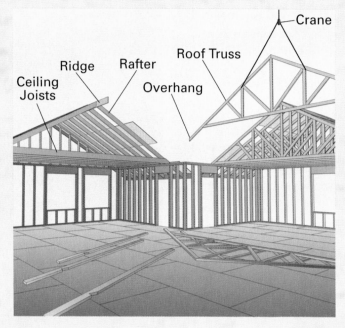

Crane
Roof Truss
Ridge   Rafter
Ceiling   Overhang
Joists

Ceiling Joists *Ceiling joists* support the ceiling and often act as floor joists for second floors and attic floors. They also support the bottom ends of the rafters.

Rafters *Rafters* support the roof. They extend from the exterior walls to the ridge.

Ridge The *ridge* is the horizontal beam at which the two slopes of the roof meet. It is the highest point of the roof frame.

Roof Truss A *roof truss* combines a joist, rafters, and supports in one preassembled unit. Trusses are assembled at a factory and delivered to the job site, where they are attached directly to the top plate.

Overhang Rafters or roof trusses often extend past the edge of the exterior wall to provide an *overhang*.

The Ceiling and Roof Frames. The roof frame consists of a series of rafters that support the weight of the roof. Carpenters nail the bottom outer end of the rafters to the top of the outside walls. If steel framing is used, joints are fastened with screws rather than nails.

The slope of the rafters establishes the roof pitch, the angle of the roof. In general, the steeper the slope of a roof, the less likely it is to leak. On most roofs the rafters extend past the edge of the exterior wall to provide an overhang, which prevents water from running down the walls and also shades the home. **See Fig. 10-11** for more information on ceiling and roof framing.

Finishing the Exterior

Once the basic structure and frame have been built, work on the exterior of the home begins. The care that is taken in finishing the exterior, and the materials that are used, will greatly affect the home's appearance and the safety and comfort of the occupants.

The Walls

The rough finish and final finish of exterior walls are important for the home to be fire-resistant, waterproof, and energy-efficient. Various materials are used.

The Rough Finish

Rough boarding, also called *sheathing*, is applied to the outside of the roof and wall framing. It usually is in the form of 4 ft. x 8 ft. (1.2 m x 2.4 m) panels. Sheathing is generally moisture-resistant and helps brace the frame against the wind by joining the floor framing and studs. Sheathing can consist of plywood, foam, or *oriented strand board* (OSB). OSB is a product made from strands of wood fibers that are bonded together with water-resistant or waterproof adhesives.

Fig. 10-12 Once a house is framed, the sheathing is applied to the outside face of the walls and roof. A waterproof barrier provides further protection. **How does the waterproof barrier also reduce heat loss from the home?**

After the sheathing is up, builders usually wrap the home with a heavy waterproof material. See Fig. 10-12. This creates a protective envelope that keeps out water and moisture. Wrapping the home also helps reduce heat loss by keeping insulation dry and closing the small cracks and holes in the rough boarding to keep out wind.

The Final Finish

Since exterior wall coverings have a tremendous impact on the appearance and overall maintenance of a home, homeowners should select them with care. See Fig. 10-13. The most common materials are wood, aluminum, and vinyl. Masonry siding materials are also used. The choice depends on the area's climate and the preference and budget of the homeowners.

Fig. 10-13 Cedar siding can be used to give a home an attractive exterior appearance. **What other products could a homeowner choose for siding a house?**

Wood and OSB Siding. Wood is a commonly used siding material. It's strong, a good insulator, easy to assemble, and suitable for a wide variety of exterior styles. Wood siding is milled from cedar, redwood, pine, or cypress. One side is smooth and the other rough. Wood siding may be made into clapboards, vertical boarding, or horizontal boarding. **Clapboards** (KLA-buhrds) are narrow overlapping boards that are thicker on one edge than the other. They are more weatherproof than vertical and horizontal boarding, which are applied without overlapping.

OSB siding is a popular alternative to the high cost of wood. It is available in a variety of styles. Plywood siding is another economical type of wood siding that comes in a variety of textures.

Manufactured Siding. Siding is also made from materials other than wood. See Fig. 10-14.

- Siding made of aluminum or steel is durable and resists weather and corrosion. Because of metal's reflective qualities, this type of siding helps lower heating and cooling costs. Aluminum does dent, however, and it may conduct electricity. Steel, on the other hand, is dent-resistant. It is one of the most durable of all prefinished siding materials.

- Vinyl siding is also fairly durable and requires no maintenance. It is less likely to dent and doesn't conduct electricity. However, it is brittle and more likely to crack or break under extreme weather conditions. Although vinyl and aluminum can suit many geographic locations, you may not want to use them if you live in areas where hailstorms are common.

- Fiberglass siding looks like wood shingles and comes in a variety of natural wood colors. It does not need to be finished or painted.

Masonry Siding. Masonry products include brick, clay, tile, stone, concrete block, and stucco. **Stucco** is a plaster material made with cement, sand, and lime. In some situations, masonry products are used to construct the entire exterior wall. In other situations, a **veneer**—an overlay material that provides an ornamental finish—is used to create the look of a masonry wall. Masonry veneer walls are used in many areas of the country. Masonry construction is often more expensive than wood construction. However, it is usually less expensive to maintain and lasts longer.

Fig. 10-14 Manufactured siding is available in several materials and many colors. From a distance, it is difficult to identify what type of siding has been used.

Paints and Finishes

Siding made of wood products must be protected against the elements. Wood and plywood siding can be either painted or stained and sealed, while OSB siding must be painted.

Primer should be applied to exterior wood before painting. A coat of primer serves as a sealer and prevents paint waste that occurs from untreated wood absorbing the paint.

For paint, the choice is between water-based and oil-based. Good water-based paints expand with changing temperatures without cracking the paint film. They are easy to spread, dry quickly, and have good color retention.

Oil-based paints are harder to spread and take longer than water-based paints to dry. They can, however, hide imperfections better than many water-based paints and offer good stain resistance. Many oil-based paints are harmful to the environment because they are a major source of *volatile organic compounds* (VOCs). VOCs combine with sunlight to form ground-level ozone, an ingredient in smog. Paint manufacturers are developing hypoallergenic paints, sealers, and finishes that are durable, much safer, and VOC-free.

The Roof

Since the roof protects the home's interior from the weather, roofing materials must be strong and weatherproof. Light-colored roofs are popular in hot climates because they help keep the home cool. By reflecting sunlight, lighter roof colors can reduce cooling loads 20 to 50 percent. Common roofing materials include asphalt, fiberglass, wood, clay tile, slate, concrete tile, and metal. See Fig. 10-15.

Shingles. Shingles are thin pieces of material laid in overlapping rows that cover roofs. Asphalt shingles are the most widely used roofing material because of their fire-resistant qualities, attractive appearance, and low cost. In general, the heavier the shingle, the longer its life will be. Asphalt is also the easiest type of shingle to install and the most economical to repair. Fiberglass shingles are similar to asphalt shingles and come in a variety of textures and colors.

Wood shingles and *shakes*, a thicker shingle, are attractive but may cost from 50 to 100 percent more than asphalt. They are treated with fire-retardant and decay-resistant chemicals. Wood shingles and shakes are most often used in parts of the country where cedar, redwood, and cypress trees grow.

Fig. 10-15 Roofing materials vary, depending on the climate. For example, a steel roof is very durable and weather resistant. **What types of roofing materials are on the homes in your neighborhood?**

Slate and Tile. In places with hot sun and little snowfall, roofs are often covered with clay tile, slate, or concrete tile. Slate and tile are usually chosen for their design qualities. If properly installed, they are fireproof and make the strongest roofing materials. However, they tend to crack in a cold climate. An alternative to slate is cement fiber, which costs less and is not as heavy.

Steel. Steel roofs are very durable and provide excellent protection against severe weather, even hailstorms. A steel roof can last longer than 50 years, and the metal can be recycled. Steel roofing materials can be made to look like traditional materials and come in a variety of colors. The initial cost of a steel roof is higher than shingles, but considering that the steel roof lasts over twice as long, the long-term cost is less.

Other Metals. Metal roofing made of lead, zinc, copper, or aluminum tends to be popular in warm, dry climates. Metal roofing is fireproof, but can be noisy in heavy rain, hail, or sleet.

Installing the Roof

Most roofing materials are applied in a standard way. First the roof frame is covered with sheathing, then with roofing felt. This process keeps out moisture. Then, starting at the outer edge of the roof, a starter strip of shingles (or other roofing material) is applied. The roof should be shingled in straight lines, and the distance between the shingles should always be equal. Wind-resistant roofing materials and methods are often used on homes in areas prone to hurricanes or tornadoes.

Flat roofs are not shingled. Instead, several layers of building paper may be applied with a special compound and then covered with gravel or marble chips. Flat roofs are economical to build. They are most practical in areas where there's little or no snowfall. The weight of snow can damage a flat roof.

Fig. 10-16 Metal flashing, such as that used around chimneys, protects the home from water seepage.

As a construction crew finishes applying the roofing materials, flashing is installed around some areas. **Flashing** consists of strips of sheet metal. It is placed where the roof meets a vertical surface, such as a chimney or a second story wall; around openings in the roof, such as for skylights or vent pipes; and in roof valleys. Flashing prevents moisture from leaking through roof openings. Flashing around chimneys also insulates the roof from the heat of the chimney when in use. See Fig. 10-16.

Insulation

Proper insulation is one of the keys to a comfortable, energy-efficient home. The purpose of insulation is to reduce the passage of heat through the walls and roof. If the insulation is installed properly, the home will feel warmer in winter and cooler in summer.

The effectiveness of insulation depends on its **R value**. The R value of insulation is a measure of its capacity to resist winter heat loss and summer heat gain. The higher the R value, the better the insulation. **See Fig. 10-17.**

The R value of an insulation product is generally given per inch. To determine the total R value a product will provide, multiply the thickness of the insulation by its R value per inch. For example, if an insulation product has an R value of 5, you can use 2 inches (5 cm) of it to get an insulation value of R-10.

Builders and home buyers have learned that it is easy and cost effective to increase insulation beyond the minimum levels required by building codes. The R value of exterior walls can vary from R-9 to R-24 depending not only on climate but also on the wall material used. Depending on the climate, other desirable R-value ratings range from R-30 to R-49 for attics and ceilings, R-13 to R-25 for floors, and R-11 to R-19 for basements and crawl spaces.

Vapor Barriers

Vapor barriers are materials that help reduce drafts and prevent moisture from getting into a home. Barrier materials include asphalt-laminated paper, aluminum foil, and foil-backed gypsum board. Rolls of plastic film are also used as vapor barriers to envelop entire walls and attic areas. The vapor barrier can be part of the insulation.

Vapor barriers should be properly installed to prevent moisture damage in walls and ceilings. A vapor barrier should face the warm side of the wall. This means placing the barrier toward the *inside* of the wall in cold climates and toward the *outside* of the wall in warm climates (assuming the home is air conditioned).

Fig. 10-17 Properly installed insulation at the recommended R value will provide years of comfort in this new home. It will also help hold down heating and cooling bills.

Insulative Siding Systems

Two new siding systems are improving the look and performance of vinyl siding. In one system, conventional vinyl siding is installed over a layer of rigid foam insulation. This layer is preshaped exactly to the contours of the siding. In the other system, the siding and insulation are bonded into one piece.

These new products use *polystyrene*, better known by its trade name, Styrofoam®. Polystyrene starts as an oil-based liquid called styrene. It is chemically changed into tiny beads, which are steam-heated to expand like popcorn. This airy, light texture makes polystyrene an excellent insulator.

Tech Trends

Interview a local home construction professional about the use of insulative siding systems in your area. Research what, if any, changes or improvements in this technology are likely in the future.

Both siding systems are considerably more costly than conventional siding because of higher production and shipping costs. However, both promise lower maintenance and utility costs. The snug fit with the insulation helps the siding resist sagging, waving, and dents. It can boost the R value of the siding and make a home more soundproof. The insulation is "breathable," allowing moisture to escape. This reduces the chances of mold growth and deterioration. Like other plastics, polystyrene resists insect attacks.

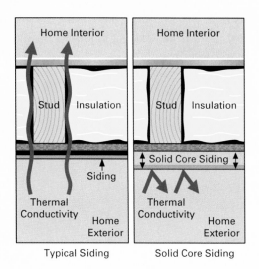

Typical Siding   Solid Core Siding

Forms of Insulation

There are several common kinds of insulation. The basic types include flexible, loose-fill, foam, rigid, and reflective.

Flexible Insulation. This type of insulation comes in two forms: blanket and batt. Both types consist of a fibrous, porous material that is usually made of fiberglass. *Blanket insulation* is covered with paper on one side and a vapor barrier material on the other side. Blanket insulation comes on a long roll. Tabs on the sides of blanket insulation allow it to be fastened easily to the studs.

Batt insulation (blanket insulation cut into shorter lengths) is often uncovered and is also made of a fibrous material, such as fiberglass. It may or may not have a vapor barrier on one side. Some forms of batt insulation are made to stay in place without the usual fastening method.

Loose-Fill Insulation. Loose-fill insulation can be poured, blown in, or packed by hand. The most effective use is in floors. Materials used are fiberglass, vermiculite, perlite, and cellulose. Because loose fill is made up of short fibers, it tends to settle. This can cause cold spots to occur. When part of a wall is warm and part is cold, condensation may cause paint to blister and wood to rot. Care must be taken to distribute loose-fill insulation evenly and to replace the insulation when it begins to break down with age.

Foam Insulation. Foam insulation is pumped through a tube to the location where it is to be applied. Foams generally expand after application to fill all cracks and crevices. A newer type of foam insulation is *CFC-free foam*. It has no *chlorofluorocarbons* (CFCs), which deplete the earth's ozone layer. One advantage of foam is that it always fits perfectly, conforming to the shape of the space. Spray foam insulation is typically easier to install, safer for the environment, and more energy efficient than traditional batt insulation. Foam works particularly well in steel-framed buildings. Care must be taken when using foam in existing structures since the foam can crack existing walls as it expands.

Rigid Insulation. These rigid foam panels can serve as rough wall boarding as well as insulation. An aluminum foil facing is sometimes attached to the panels as a vapor barrier.

Reflective Insulation. Reflective materials include aluminum foil, tin-coated sheet metal, and coated paper. Because these thin materials are very effective in keeping heat from entering a home, they are more likely to be used in warmer climates. These materials may be used between studs and in attics. The reflective surface should face an air space at least ¾ inch (2 cm) deep to maintain reflective and insulating properties.

Windows

There are many types of windows from which to choose. Since they are both functional and decorative, windows should be chosen with care. Windows come in many different styles. See Fig. 10-18 on page 235 to learn more about window parts and styles.

Frame Materials

Over the years, wood has been commonly used for window frames and sashes. Both the inside and outside of plain wood frames must be painted or stained every few years. All-wood frames are generally more expensive than other types of frames.

Aluminum and vinyl window frames are lightweight and come in a variety of factory finishes and designs. Their light weight makes them easy to install and remove. However, metal frames conduct heat and cold. Wood frames are better insulators than metal frames.

Many people prefer window frames that are a combination of wood and another material. Aluminum-clad and vinyl-clad wood frames don't need to be painted and are good insulators. Whatever type of frame material is chosen, the windows need to be installed correctly so there is no air leakage that causes drafts.

Fig. 10-18

Window Parts and Styles

A Visual Guide

Sash The *sash* is the framework that surrounds the window glass. If the window can be opened and closed, the sash is the part that slides or swings open.

Lights The *lights* are the areas of glass. If each sash has one continuous glass area, it is described as *single light*. A *divided light* window has several smaller areas of glass within each sash. In a true divided light window, *muntins* are the strips that hold individual small pieces of glass within the sash. In modern windows, muntins are more likely to consist of a decorative grid that fits over a single light. The grid gives the look of divided lights but may be removable for easy window cleaning.

Frame The frame surrounds and holds the sashes. The *head jamb* is the top of the frame. The sides are called *side jambs*. The bottom is called the *sill*.

Trim Decorative trim can be added around the window after installation. The trim around the top and sides of the window is called *casing*. Some windows have casing along the bottom as well. Others have a ledge at the bottom, called a *stool*, with an *apron* below the stool.

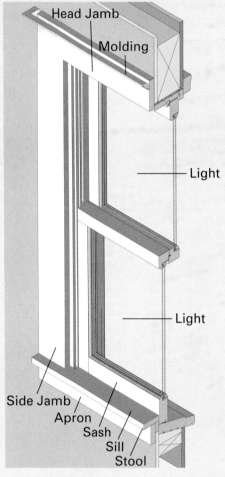

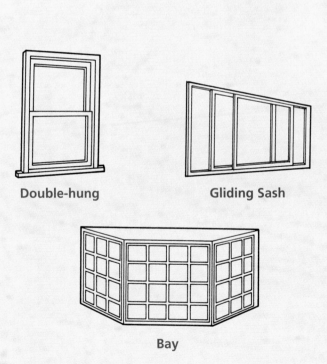

Double-hung   Gliding Sash   Hinged (Casement)   Jalousie

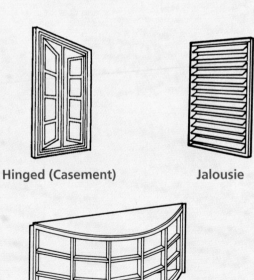

Bay   Bow

Types of Glass

A single thickness of glass is a poor insulator. By sealing two or three panes together as a unit, much better insulation is provided. The sealed air space between panes provides the insulation and reduces heat loss. This space can be filled with argon gas to further improve the insulating qualities of the window. With double- or triple-pane windows, moisture is less likely to condense on the side of the window that is indoors, as often happens with single-pane glass.

Low-emissivity (or low-e) glass is often featured in newer thermal windows. It has a clear coating that helps keep heat inside in winter and outside in summer. Low-e glass blocks out ultraviolet rays and helps reduce fading of upholstery fabrics and drapes. However, because it keeps out the sun's warmth, low-e glass may not be desirable in the south windows of homes designed for passive solar heating.

On older windows, insulation can be improved with storm windows. These are second windows installed outside the regular window. The air space created between the two windows provides insulation.

Certain other kinds of glass are used for special purposes. Tempered plate glass is made to be extra strong. Because of its strength, it is used for sliding glass doors. Patterned glass, sometimes called obscure glass, has a textured surface. It allows light to pass through, but no one can see through it. It may be used for privacy purposes in bathroom windows or for windows in exterior doors. Laminated, shatter-proof glass is recommended for homes in hurricane and tornado areas.

Doors

Many styles of doors are available. They may be made of wood, metal, fiberglass, or some combination of these materials. Flush doors have a smooth surface. Panel doors have sunken or raised sections. Molding may be added to a flush door to give the appearance of panels. Some styles include windows. See Fig. 10-19.

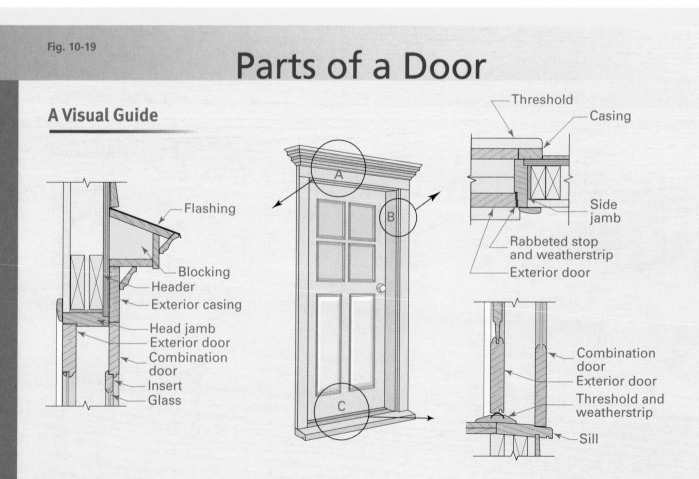

Fig. 10-19

Parts of a Door

A Visual Guide

Threshold

Casing

Flashing

Blocking
Header
Exterior casing
Head jamb
Exterior door
Combination door
Insert
Glass

A

B

C

Side jamb

Rabbeted stop and weatherstrip
Exterior door

Combination door
Exterior door
Threshold and weatherstrip
Sill

Most doors come prehung in a wood or metal frame that consists of a head jamb and side jambs. Exterior entrances also have a threshold at the bottom.

Doors are either solid or hollow. Hollow doors are lighter in weight than solid doors and are generally used only for interiors. They are less expensive, but they are also less sound-resistant.

For exterior use, a solid door is recommended. It provides greater security and is more weather-resistant. **See Fig. 10-20.** An insulated door, such as one with a steel outer "skin" and a polyurethane foam core, conserves energy better than a wood door.

For extra protection from the weather, a storm door may be installed in front of an exterior door. Storm doors include glass for protection from cold weather and a screen for ventilation during warm weather. The frames are made of metal, fiberglass, or wood. Storm doors are not recommended for areas of the home that are exposed to more than a few hours of direct sunlight each day. Heat trapped in the space between the storm door and the exterior door can damage the exterior door.

Building codes require some areas to have fire-rated doors. For example, the door between the living space and an attached garage should be fire-rated. The fire rating indicates how long it would take the door to burn. Common ratings are 20, 60, and 90 minutes.

Exterior doors are hinged so that they swing inward. Whenever possible, they should swing against a blank wall. The same is true for interior doors. For safety, interior doors should never be hinged to swing into a hallway.

Water Protection

Additional details for the exterior of a home are important in keeping rainwater or melting snow from damaging the structure. These include the finish grade, gutters, and downspouts.

Fig. 10-20 The design of the main entrance to a home affects both its appeal and level of weather protection.

Finish grade. To raise the level of the ground around the home or to eliminate holes that often result from excavation, sand and gravel are usually used as fill. The *finish grade*, or finish level of earth next to the foundation, should be contoured to slope away from the home to prevent rainwater from seeping into the basement or crawl space. The finish grade should also be kept below the top of the foundation. This will keep ground moisture from coming into contact with any of the wood construction, which could eventually cause the wood to rot.

Gutters and downspouts. Rain-water falling from a sloping roof will erode the soil and damage plants and shrubs close to a home. A *gutter*—a horizontal open trough, generally at the eaves or edges of the roof—catches rainwater that drains off the roof.

The gutter is attached to a vertical pipe called a *downspout*, or a *rain leader*. It carries the water down to the ground. At the bottom, the downspout is connected to a ground drain or to a downspout extension to carry rainwater away from the foundation of the home. Gutters need to be kept clean and clear of leaves, sticks, and other materials that can block the water from draining off. See Fig. 10-21.

Fig. 10-21

Gutters and Downspouts

A Visual Guide

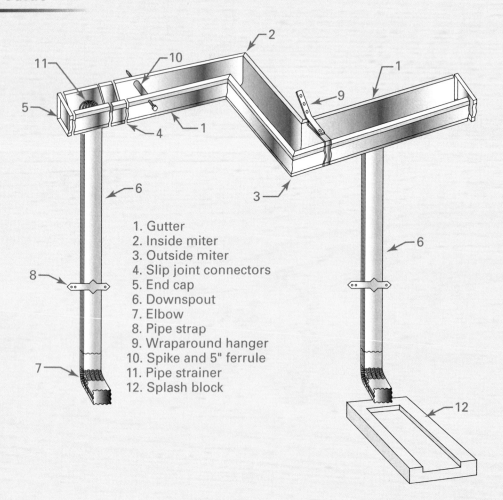

1. Gutter
2. Inside miter
3. Outside miter
4. Slip joint connectors
5. End cap
6. Downspout
7. Elbow
8. Pipe strap
9. Wraparound hanger
10. Spike and 5" ferrule
11. Pipe strainer
12. Splash block

Understanding Construction Basics

Countless decisions go into building a home, from those about major issues such as where to locate the structure to those about details such as what kind of windows to install. All these decisions affect the look of the home, the comfort of the people living in it, and the ease or expense of maintaining it.

For many decisions, builders and home owners can choose among a great variety of materials. These choices involve trade-offs. That is, one choice offers certain advantages, such as durability and energy efficiency, but also has disadvantages, such as higher initial cost. Thinking about these issues can help you avoid making costly decisions.

Now that you understand basic construction decisions, you can use this information to evaluate housing options in the future. See Fig. 10-22.

Fig. 10-22

Construction Basics		
Feature	**Types/Materials**	**Key Issues**
Site	Not applicable	• Topography • Orientation to sun and wind • View
Foundation	Basement; crawl space; slab	• Make footing suitable to climate • Provide sufficient support for home • Basement may need to withstand natural disaster
Frame	Floor frame; wall frame; ceiling and roof frame	• Floor should hold 100 pounds per sq. ft. (185 per sq. ft. in areas prone to natural disaster) • Wall frame: support needed for load-bearing walls • Rafters support weight of roof; include overhang
Walls: rough finish	Sheathing; waterproof covering	• Sheathing material should be moisture-resistant • Waterproof covering keeps out moisture
Walls: final finish	Wood, manufactured, or masonry	• Wood: needs finishing or painting; clapboards give more weatherproofing; OSB, plywood less expensive • Manufactured: aluminum can dent; vinyl can break; fiberglass doesn't need finishing • Masonry: more durable, expensive than wood
Roof	Asphalt, fiberglass, wood, clay tile, slate, concrete tile, or metal	• Asphalt: easiest to install, most economical to repair • Wood: 50 to 100 percent more costly than asphalt • Slate, tile: unsuitable for cold climate • Steel: costly but very durable
Insulation	Flexible, loose-fill, foam, rigid, reflective	• Vapor barriers improve waterproofing • Use R value to evaluate • Loose-fill can settle over time, producing cold spots • Foam tricky to use in existing structures • Reflective useful in warm climates
Window	Frames (wood, all metal, aluminum or vinyl over wood); glass	• Frame: wood better insulator; metal lighter; aluminum or vinyl-clad wood easier to maintain • Installation: ensure no air leakage • Glass: double- or triple-pane for insulation; tempered for extra strength; patterned for more privacy
Doors	Wood, metal, fiberglass, or combination	• Solid doors for exterior; hollow for interior • Storm doors provide weather protection • Fire-rated doors for some areas

Profile of an Ergonomic Designer

Ergonomic designers create products that are shaped to the people who use them every day. They link technology and design with how people function at work and at home. These specialized designers can work in such fields as furniture and environmental design, computer animation and special effects, medical products, consumer electronics, and building and transportation design.

Education & Training

- At least a bachelor's degree is required. Advanced degrees are becoming more necessary as employment opportunities increase.
- Courses in ergonomics, biomechanics, engineering principles, physical science, and interior design are helpful.

Skills & Aptitudes

- Creative problem-solving and excellent communication and presentation skills are required.
- Mechanical aptitude and the ability to convey concepts with quick sketches is essential.
- Proficiency with CAD is also necessary.

Ergonomic Designer
Shane Dillard

The day you realize that one size does not fit all is the day you start to appreciate ergonomics. Ergonomics is the study of designing space and products to meet people's needs. Ergonomic designers adapt tools, appliances, and furniture to accommodate differences in people's size and shape and in their physical and mental strengths and limitations.

I'd always been interested in engineering and design. I was working for a manufacturer as an industrial designer, adapting offices and assembly lines to help workers be more productive and happier. This work gave me the chance to be both analytical and creative and to work with both technology and people.

My focus changed because of my grandfather. He was having trouble doing everyday tasks but was determined to live independently. I began to see that many of his problems could be solved by ergonomics. For instance, he had trouble turning the round, knob-like faucets in the bathroom. We put in new faucets with handles he could grasp more easily.

That led me to find work with a firm that designs consumer products using universal design. Our goal is to make products accessible to as many people as possible. We've designed a convection oven with legroom so people in wheelchairs can do their own cooking. We've developed visual cues to tell people with hearing impairments when someone is at the door.

People without disabilities also hire us. We plan how to arrange a space, like a kitchen, bathroom, or home office, more efficiently and comfortably.

I start a project by talking with the clients: what isn't working in the environment? What improvements do they envision?

I like to see the product or space myself for a hands-on assessment. Sometimes the solution is new technology I can use, but I prefer simple, standard modifications whenever possible. A refrigerator door that's difficult to open might need only a slightly less powerful vacuum seal. As I see it, ergonomics is a continuation of our attempts to conform the environment to our needs.

Design Portfolio

1. Think of an elderly person who has little strength or flexibility. Make a list of the everyday tasks that would be difficult for that person to perform. Design ergonomic solutions for three of the tasks.

2. Study how students at your school use their backpacks. Draw a sketch or create a prototype of a new backpack and explain why you think it would be an improvement.

Chapter Summary

- The characteristics of the site and the home's **orientation** affect a home's comfort and appeal.
- Architectural drawings provide information about the appearance and construction of a building.
- The foundation forms the base and support of a home.
- The frame is the skeleton of the housing structure.
- Exterior construction includes covering the frame and applying a final finish to the walls and roof.
- There are many types of insulation, windows, and doors to choose from, each with its own characteristics.
- You can use knowledge of basic construction to evaluate homes when making renting or buying decisions.

Checking Your Understanding

1. Give an example of how a building site affects a home.
2. What do a **floor plan** and an **elevation** show?
3. What are three kinds of information shown on an architectural drawing?
4. What is the function of a **footing**?
5. How is floor framing constructed?
6. How are load-bearing and nonbearing walls similar and different?
7. How do OSB and plywood siding compare to wood siding?
8. What are advantages and disadvantages of manufactured and masonry siding compared to wood?
9. Why are slate and tile used as roofing finishes in warm climates and not cold ones?
10. Where is **flashing** needed? Why?
11. What does the **R value** of insulation mean?
12. What are the advantages of using low-emissivity glass?

Thinking Critically

1. **Evaluating Alternatives.** What are the advantages and disadvantages of having a home built with a basement, a crawl space, or a slab?

2. **Analyzing Information.** Imagine you are building a home in a southern coastal area. What climate-related conditions would you need to consider in choosing siding, roofing, and windows?

3. **Defending Your Position.** Write a brief report defending the need for more people to use energy-efficient construction materials when building residential or commercial buildings.

Applying Your Knowledge

1. **Architectural Symbols.** Draw 10 architectural symbols on a piece of paper. Exchange papers with a partner, and identify the 10 symbols your partner drew. When both of you have finished, check each other's work and identify any corrections needed.

2. **Construction Checklist.** Imagine that you are having a new home built. Develop a checklist you could use to keep track of the progress the builder is making on the home and to ensure that the builder is using good workmanship in the construction.

3. **Construction Decisions.** Make a chart with the following column headings: *Climate, Foundation, Roofing, Siding,* and *Windows*. Choose three different climates and write them in the first column. Fill in the other columns with options suitable for each climate.

4. **Using R Values.** For each of the following thicknesses and R values of insulation, find the total R value that the product will provide. Then determine where in the home that amount of insulation is most suitable.

   a. $1^1/_2$ inch (3.8 cm) thick with R-7 per inch.

   b. $1^1/_2$ inch (3.8 cm) thick with R-11 per inch.

   c. $2^1/_2$ inch (5.7 cm) thick with R-16 per inch.

Design Challenge

You are about to design your dream home. Find a photograph or make a drawing showing the topography of the site where your home will be located and indicate the direction of the sun's rays as well as the climate of the area.

1. Sketch the general size and layout of the home, indicating where it will sit on the home site.

2. Draw a floor plan for the home.

3. Draw an elevation showing the front of the home.

4. Create a chart that shows what materials you would use to construct the walls and the roof; what kind of insulation you would use; and what features the doors and windows would have. Explain why you would make each choice.

Chapter 11

Interior Construction

Objectives

- Explain the roles of contractors and subcontractors.

- Analyze construction materials, methods, and workmanship in interior construction.

- Describe safety features of electrical systems.

- Summarize characteristics of the plumbing, heating, cooling, and ventilation systems.

- Evaluate options for interior features such as stairways, walls, ceilings, and floors.

Vocabulary

- contractor
- subcontractor
- panel box
- fuse
- circuit breaker
- ground wire
- ground fault circuit interrupter (GFCI)

- recovery rate
- septic tank
- cesspool
- conduction
- convection
- radiation
- thermostat
- flue

The construction of your new house is going great. The contractor says that the builders are ready to start work on the inside. This is your chance to find out all about the inner workings of a home. Even if you are not going to be the owner of a newly constructed house, you'll benefit from knowing what goes on behind the walls and under the floor of a home.

The Inner Workings

In Chapter 10, you learned about the framing of a home; the finishing of the exterior; and the installation of insulation, windows, and doors. Now you will learn about the hidden inner systems: electrical, plumbing, heating, cooling, and ventilation. You'll also find out about finishing the interior of a home.

Contractors and Subcontractors

Many people work together to construct a home. A **contractor** oversees a construction project. This person may own the construction company or may be an employee hired by an owner, developer, or management firm. Contractors are also called general contractors or construction managers. Contractors oversee construction supervisors and workers, coordinate building schedules, and supervise all design and construction processes for the duration of the project. See Fig. 11-1.

Fig. 11-1 The contractor ensures the success of a construction project by coordinating the work of subcontractors and workers.

Tsunami-Resistant Homes

In December 2004, a devastating *tsunami*—a giant wall of water produced by an earthquake—swept over Indonesia and other areas on the shores of the Indian Ocean. Hundreds of thousands of people were killed. Survivors found their homes and businesses utterly wiped out.

Viewing the destruction, a team of structural engineers was inspired to identify simple, sustainable technology that could be used to build tsunami-resistant housing and lessen such tragedy in the future.

Construction began by placing the wood or concrete foundation several feet off the ground to allow for rising floodwaters. Steel-reinforced concrete columns, about $3^1/_2$ feet (1.1 m) wide, support the house at each corner. Engineers recommend using bamboo for walls, instead of cement blocks. Bamboo allows water to wash through, decreasing the likelihood of collapse.

Computer models indicate that the new design is five times more resistant to tsunamis than the older one. As a bonus, the homes are also more comfortable. The porous walls let in breezes and let out heat.

Tech Trends

Research another example of disaster-resistant housing design that is used today. What are the feature's advantages? Has it been improved by modern technology? In what ways?

One of the contractor's main jobs is to supervise subcontractors. **Subcontractors** are workers hired by contractors or homeowners to perform a specific function in the construction of a home. Bricklayers, electricians, drywall installers, carpenters, heating and cooling specialists, plumbers, painters, floor-covering installers, and other subcontractors work together to complete a home. Before choosing subcontractors, owners or contractors need to check on reliability and past performance on other jobs.

The contractor must be very careful in scheduling subcontractors so that all the work can be completed according to plan and on time. Unfortunately, some problems can't be anticipated, such as delays in deliveries of materials. These problems can sometimes cause building projects to fall behind schedule. It's the job of the contractor to see if time can be made up on some other part of the project.

By planning carefully, the contractor is able to coordinate the installation of the internal systems that make up a home. These systems include electric wiring, plumbing, heating, cooling, and ventilation.

Electric Wiring

One of the first systems to be installed is the electrical system. Codes set by state and local governments generally require that home wiring installations meet high safety standards because electricity is potentially dangerous. **See Fig. 11-2.**

Electric power is sent to communities through a network of overhead wires or underground cables. Underground service is considered more desirable since there is less chance of storm damage that may interrupt power.

The main electrical supply line runs from the public lines to each home, entering through an electric meter that measures the amount of current used. A power company worker reads the meter to determine the amount of electricity used during a certain period. This is typically done once a month. The power company then bills the resident according to usage.

Circuits

A **panel box**, also called a service entrance or fuse box, is a device that controls the distribution of the electricity to the home wiring system. This system is made up of circuits. Each circuit carries electricity to a specific area of the home. Heavy-duty appliances, such as refrigerators, ranges, and clothes dryers, usually require separate circuits. Lights and small appliances within the same area may share one circuit.

The number of circuits depends on the lighting system, the number of electric *receptacles*—or outlets—needed, and the number and types of appliances to be used. The popularity of home computers and entertainment centers has resulted in an increased need for circuits and receptacles in homes. A good electrical plan provides an ample number of circuits so the owner can add new electrical devices and appliances in the future without costly rewiring.

For safety, a main switch at the panel box can be used to disconnect all the home's power from the main supply line. Fuses or circuit breakers in the panel box control power to each circuit in the home. **Fuses** and **circuit breakers** are safety devices that stop the flow of electric current in an overloaded circuit. Newer homes have circuit breakers, but older homes may still have fuses. Circuit breakers are preferred because fuses can be used only once. If a fuse blows, it must be replaced. A circuit breaker, on the other hand, can be reset and used many times.

Fig. 11-2 Electricians wire a house in accordance with strict codes that ensure a safe supply of the necessary power to handle the variety of electrical appliances inside.

Here's how fuses and circuit breakers work. Each circuit is designed to carry a specific amount of electricity. If too many appliances are used on one circuit, the demand for electricity is too great and the circuit becomes overloaded. This could cause the wires to overheat and start a fire. Fuses and circuit breakers prevent that from happening. When a circuit is overloaded, the fuse melts or the circuit breaker switches off, cutting off the power. The homeowner can then reset the circuit breaker or replace the fuse. See Figs. 11-3 and 11-4. If overloads occur often on the same circuit, steps need to be taken to have fewer devices drawing power from that circuit.

A *surge protection device* (SPD) can be used to protect equipment, such as computers, from damage due to power surges. It filters out sudden increases in power created by a local power company or a storm. Several types are available. For best protection, use a central unit that protects the whole home at once. It is installed with its own circuit breaker as close as possible to the panel box. SPDs can be installed in new or older homes.

Receptacles

Current building codes require that wall receptacles, or outlets, include a ground wire connection. A **ground wire** is an electrical conductor that is connected to the earth. The ground wire provides protection in case there is an abnormal flow of electric current. Electricity naturally seeks the ground, so a grounding system provides a safe path for the electricity. If this safe path were not provided, any problems in the circuit could produce a shock that could seriously injure or kill a person. An electrician can tell you whether the receptacles in your home are grounded.

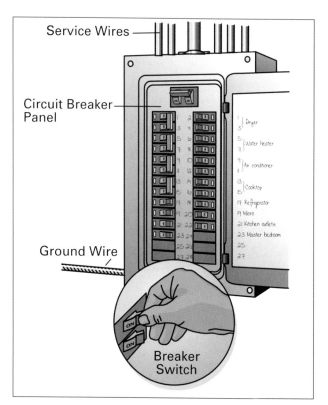

Fig. 11-3 To reset a circuit breaker that has tripped, move the switch to the ON position. With some models, you may need to move the switch all the way to the OFF position first, and then to the ON position.

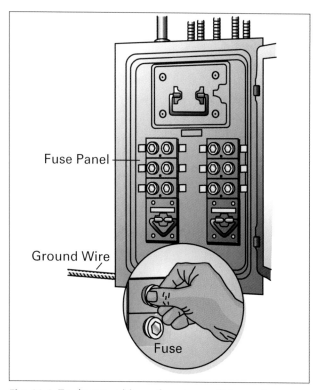

Fig. 11-4 To change a blown fuse, turn off the main power supply. Grasp the blown fuse and turn it counterclockwise until it is free of the panel box. Replace it with a new fuse that has the same capacity, measured in amps.

Some appliances have plugs with two flat prongs and one round one. The round one serves as a ground connection. These plugs are designed to be used in modern receptacles that have three slots. People who live in older homes that do not have three-slot receptacles can use a grounding adapter plug to convert a two-slot receptacle for three-prong use. A grounding adapter plug should be used only if the electrical service is grounded. To ground the adapter plug, loosen the screw on the receptacle's cover plate. Slip the adapter's grounding wire under the screw, then tighten the screw again.

Present building codes require that all electrical receptacles near plumbing or water have **ground fault circuit interrupters** (GFCIs). See Fig. 11-5. GFCIs are receptacles that guard people against electrical shock. For example, if a current makes contact with water and a person comes into contact with the current, normally the result would be a serious shock to the person. However, a GFCI senses the drop in current through the receptacle, and the circuit interrupter stops the current flow before injury can occur. People who live in older homes without GFCI receptacles can have them installed.

Some homes need additional safety devices. Families with small children should place safety covers over the receptacles. These prevent a child from putting a metal object into an outlet and receiving a shock. For outdoor use near a yard or patio, weatherproof receptacles help keep out moisture.

Fig. 11-5 Building codes require that all electrical outlets in bathrooms have a ground fault circuit interrupter. **How does a ground fault circuit interrupter work?**

Office Design Trends

Offices of the future will likely look quite different from offices today. Business trends are changing the way many offices operate—and designers are responding.

- **Mobility.** More and more office work is being performed by telecommuters. Telecommuters can work anywhere they can plug in a laptop computer; they need office space only to meet with clients. One trend is to build a space that several telecommuters can share, an arrangement often called *hoteling*. Thus a cost-effective design may use more versatile, open spaces that can be easily and temporarily divided. Companies may also rent workstations off-site in telework centers. These areas come fully equipped with communication and information technology. They are located in the suburbs, near where many workers live. Workers appreciate going to a work center that reduces the time they spend in traffic.

- **Globalization.** Designers may also get ideas for using space efficiently from counterparts in Asia and Europe, where companies often have much less land available for building. International agreements on environmental protection may require greater use of sustainable practices.

- **Productivity.** Designers and employers now better understand how acoustics, lighting, air quality, and spatial design affect productivity. They're finding ways to use these elements to promote worker performance, health, and satisfaction. For instance, wiring individual workspaces for desktop video-conferencing adds convenience and fosters a sense of connectedness. Advances in ergonomics may result in new furnishings and arrangements that reduce physical and emotional stress.

- **Integration.** Designers are integrating office spaces with the production floor of many industrial facilities. This connects "behind the scenes" office workers with the product being created at that facility. This new design trend tends to have a motivating effect on the workforce as they view the impact of their contributions to the product being developed.

Apply It!

Imagine that a small book distributor currently has a floor of offices over its warehouse. What design changes can be made to the offices to improve productivity and integration? Present your ideas to the class.

Plumbing

The term *plumbing* refers to the system of pipes used to carry water into the home and water and waste materials out of the home. The plumbing system must be built according to regulations established by state and local boards of health. This set of rules, called the *plumbing code*, is designed to ensure that the community has pure drinking water and adequate sanitary waste disposal.

In most cities, water is supplied by a publicly maintained system with water from wells, lakes, or rivers. The water goes through a purification process that destroys disease-producing microorganisms and makes it safe to drink. Generally stored in a reservoir, the water either flows to consumers by gravity or is pumped through service pipes.

Pipes

Plumbers install pipes that supply water to a home (*supply pipes*) and carry off wastes and odors (*waste and vent pipes*). Supply pipes have shutoff valves that make it possible to turn off water in part of the system when repairs are needed. Pipes may be made of copper, brass, iron, steel, or plastic. **See Fig. 11-6.**

Plastic has become very common for plumbing pipes. It resists rust and corrosion and is economical to install. Plumbers can bend plastic pipes between wall studs, floor joists, and other obstructions for faster, easier installation than is required for metal piping. However, these benefits should be weighed against possible drawbacks. In the event of a fire, plastic pipe can release toxic chemicals. In addition, plastic waste pipes tend to be noisier in use than metal ones.

Fig. 11-6 Water supply pipes carry hot and cold water to fixtures in bathrooms, kitchens, and utility rooms.

Fixtures

Various plumbing fixtures are available for use in bathrooms, kitchens, and utility rooms. Popular materials for fixtures include cast iron or steel with a porcelain coating, china, stainless steel, prefabricated plastic, acrylic, and fiberglass. **See Fig. 11-7.** Each type has its advantages and disadvantages.

Porcelain Enamel. Porcelain enamel on cast iron or steel is often used for bathtubs, toilets, and sinks. These fixtures come in colors to fit any decorating scheme. Porcelain-coated sinks are easy to clean, but they can chip and may become permanently stained by some substances. Scouring powder and drainpipe cleaner shouldn't be used on porcelain.

China. China fixtures are made of clay fired at a high temperature. They are resistant to ordinary acids and cleansers and are used for toilet bowls, toilet tanks, and sinks. China fixtures are available in many colors and styles. They are heavy and durable but can crack or break.

Stainless Steel. Stainless steel is commonly used for sinks. It is durable and rust resistant. A satin finish is usually used to hide water spots. Compared to other types, stainless steel sinks are easier to install because they are lighter in weight.

Prefabricated Plastic. Bathtub and shower units made of prefabricated plastic are popular in new home construction and home improvements. The entire unit is molded in one piece. These units install easily and don't require costly on-the-job trim and finishing. Countertops with molded sinks are good choices for bathrooms and kitchens. They offer easy care and come in many patterns and colors. Chapter 22 has more information on other types of materials used for countertops in kitchens.

Fig. 11-7 Kitchen and bathroom fixtures come in a variety of styles and materials. **What materials can you identify in these fixtures?**

Acrylic. Acrylic is colored and then molded into the desired shape. This material is often used for bathtubs. The tubs have a good finish that is easy to clean, though it can scratch and color can fade. Acrylic is light, so the material is good for large fixtures like tubs. Adding fiberglass makes the surface less likely to chip or crack.

Fiberglass. Some fixtures are made entirely of fiberglass. This lightweight material is the least expensive of all options, but the fixtures are not as durable or long-lasting as those made of acrylic. Because it is so light, this material is often used for units that work as both bathtubs and showers.

Water Heaters

Homes need a reliable supply of hot water for bathing, washing dishes and clothes, and other uses. There are two basic types of water heaters: storage and on-demand.

A *storage water heater* is the most common type. It consists of a tank to hold the water and a burner or unit underneath the tank to provide heat. Water can be heated by electricity or gas. The size of the water heater needed depends on the appliances and the number of people in a household. Generally, a 50-gallon (190-L) water heater is recommended for most households.

In addition to a storage water heater's capacity, it's important to consider the recovery rate. The **recovery rate** indicates the average amount of water that will be heated in the tank in one hour. The higher the recovery rate, the more hot water will be available during peak demand periods. Since a water heater is a long-term investment, homeowners should try to anticipate future needs before buying a unit.

New storage water heaters come with an energy-efficiency rating on the outside. High-efficiency water heaters can use 10 to 50 percent less energy than conventional models. Some models have insulation built into the shell. Insulation is important because storage water heaters keep water constantly heated even when no one is using water. The efficiency of older models of water heaters can be improved by wrapping a layer of insulation around the unit.

If there is consistently not enough hot water in the home when it's needed, the storage water heater may be too small or its recovery rate may be too low. Perhaps sediment has formed on the inside, decreasing the storage tank's capacity. The tank should be drained periodically to remove sediment.

On-demand, or tankless, water heaters are another option. These units hook up directly to a supply line and heat water only when needed. This can result in great energy savings. The drawback is that on-demand heaters have a lower flow rate.

Other energy-efficient models include:

- A heat pump water heater moves heat from the surrounding air into the water, cooling and dehumidifying the air surrounding the unit. This produces the equivalent of about $1/2$ ton of air conditioning. See Fig. 11-8.

- Models that capture "waste" heat from air conditioners and deliver it to hot water storage units.

- Solar water heaters, which often can provide nearly half of a household's hot water demands.

Fig. 11-8 Heat pumps can cut the amount of electricity needed to heat water by 50 percent, but these units cost more than traditional water heaters. They also put more demand on your heating system. **Explain why heat pump water heaters are a more popular choice in warm climates.**

Sewage Disposal

Wastewater and sewage flow from fixtures to a system of underground piping. This piping is connected to a public sanitary sewer, a septic tank and disposal field, or a cesspool.

In many public sewer systems, sewage is carried through cast-iron piping for a distance of at least 5 feet (1.5 m) from the building. Then it may be carried through another type of piping. Sewer pipes and water supply pipes should be kept as far apart as possible in order to prevent any leaks in the sewers from contaminating the water supply.

For buildings not connected to a public sewer system, the sewage may be disposed of through a **septic tank**. This tank is a large concrete box, generally buried underground. See Fig. 11-9. In it, solids settle and eventually decompose due to bacterial action. The liquids overflow into a system of pipes or drain tiles laid underground in an area called the *disposal field* or *drain field*. The liquids gradually seep out of the pipes or tiles and into the soil. After several years of use, the septic tank must be cleaned and the residue removed.

A cesspool is another way to dispose of sewage. A **cesspool** is a system that collects sewage and lets it gradually seep into the surrounding earth. In many urban areas, local health regulations don't allow cesspool use because of the dangers of contaminating nearby soil and water.

Septic tanks and cesspools may develop problems. Overloading can occur if gutters and swimming pools are connected to the system. High-foaming detergents and other cleaning products may interfere with the necessary bacterial action in septic tanks and cesspools. Mechanical waste disposers fill cesspools very quickly, resulting in the need for more frequent cleaning.

Fig. 11-9 Houses not on a public sewer have a septic system. Strict standards must be met for homes using this system in order to avoid polluting nearby groundwater, rivers, and lakes.

Heating the Home

People living in cold-weather climates require efficient heating systems designed to keep them comfortable. Most people feel most comfortable at temperatures of 70-75°F (21-24°C). However, *humidity*—the amount of moisture in the air—affects the temperature at which people feel comfortable. When the right amount of humidity is in the air, people may feel just as comfortable at 65-70°F (18-21°C).

To see how home heating systems work, it helps to understand the three types of heat movement: conduction, convection, and radiation. Some heating systems use more than one type of heat movement. **See Fig. 11-10.**

Conduction is the transfer of heat from a body of higher temperature to one of lower temperature by direct contact. When you step on a cold floor with your bare feet, the heat leaves your feet through conduction.

Convection is the transfer of heat by means of air flow. For example, warm air naturally rises to the highest point in a room or home. The most common way to provide heat in a home is through convection. Air that has been warmed by a furnace is circulated through each room.

Radiation is the transmission of heat by means of rays traveling in straight lines from a source. The classic example of radiation is the sun. Its heat does not come through physical contact, nor is it blown. People receive warmth directly from the sun's rays.

Types of Heating Systems

Do you know what type of heating system is used in your home? Common systems include warm air, steam, hot water, and radiant heat. **Figure 11-11** on page 257 and 258 explains how each type of system works.

Heating systems may be fueled by gas, oil, or electricity. Gas and oil are usually used with furnaces and boilers. Furnaces and boilers are rated for energy efficiency. The rating is the ratio of heat produced to the energy consumed on an annual basis. Electric heat is usually the most expensive and inefficient way of heating a home. In Chapter 12, you'll learn about alternative heating methods that are energy efficient.

Most heating systems are controlled by a thermostat. A **thermostat** is a temperature-activated switch that turns the heating system on and off to keep the temperature of a home at a set level. Programmable thermostats can save energy and money by reducing the amount of time a heating system operates. When a home is not occupied, or when everyone is asleep, less heat is needed. A programmable thermostat can be set to raise and lower the temperature at certain times each day. Some programmable thermostats allow different times and temperatures to be set for each day of the week.

Fig. 11-10 Radiators for a steam heat system heat the room through a combination of radiation and natural convection.

Fig. 11-11

Heating Systems

A Visual Guide

Forced Warm Air System

Air is warmed by a furnace, then propelled by a blower through ducts to registers in each room. The air circulates, heating the room by convection. Cooler air returns through another system of ducts. For best efficiency, the hot-air ducts need to run through the center of the building and be insulated. A filter usually cleans the air before it is reheated and recirculated.

- Provides the fastest method of raising room temperature.
- The same ducts can be used for a central air-conditioning system.
- Leaky, uninsulated ducts allow heated or cooled air to be lost in attics, crawl spaces, and unfinished basements.
- Heated air may dry out skin and furnishings unless a humidifier is added.
- Circulating air tends to stir up dust, which can aggravate allergies.
- Ducts take up valuable space.

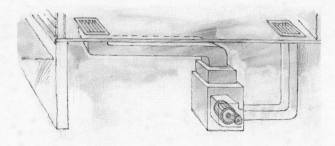

Warm Air Gravity System

Similar to a forced warm air system except that there is no blower. Warm air from the furnace rises upward through the ducts and into the rooms by natural convection. When the air cools, it becomes heavier and drops to the floor of the room, then into return ducts by gravity.

- Quieter than a forced warm air system.
- Can't be installed in a home that does not have a basement.
- Ducts take up valuable space. Leaky ducts cause loss of heat in unused spaces.
- Air cannot be filtered or humidified by the furnace.

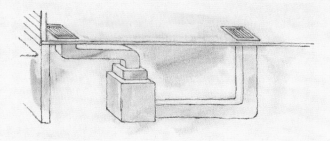

Fig. 11-11

Heating Systems (continued)

A Visual Guide

Steam System

Water is heated in a boiler, which generates steam. The steam is forced by its own pressure through pipes to heating fixtures—either radiators or convectors. *Radiators* (shown here) heat the room by a combination of radiation and natural convection. *Convectors* are upright or baseboard fixtures that heat the room by convection.

- Raises room temperature quickly.
- Clean—doesn't stir up dust.
- Difficult to maintain an even temperature in the home.
- Heating pipes may freeze during severe weather.
- Doesn't provide for cooling and ventilation.
- May be noisy.

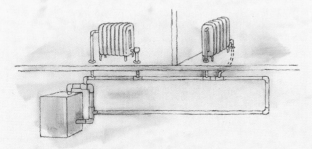

Hot Water System

Water is heated in a boiler, then circulates through pipes to radiators or convectors. In a forced hot water system, the water is circulated by a pump. In a hot water gravity system, the boiler must be located in the basement; warm water rises by natural convection, and cool water drops by gravity.

- Quiet and clean. Efficient and economical.
- May take longer for rooms to reach the desired temperature.
- Heating pipes may freeze during severe weather.
- Doesn't provide for cooling and ventilation.

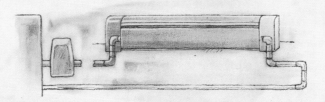

Radiant Heat System

Heating elements—either hot-water piping or electric wiring—are hidden in the floor, ceiling, or baseboards. Heat radiates from the elements.

- No registers, radiators, or convectors to affect furniture placement.
- Quiet and clean.
- Hidden heating elements can be difficult and expensive to repair.
- Electric radiant systems lose efficiency over time.

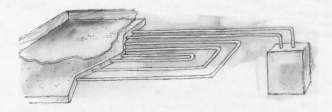

Choosing A Heating System

Based on its location, building materials, and method of construction, each home has specific heating needs. Designers of quality systems can help in the selection of a system.

For most people, choosing a heating system is a financial consideration. However, the purchase price is really less important than the operating costs. Those costs are determined by the level of heat required, the climate, the type and cost of the fuel used, the home's insulation, and the efficiency of the system.

Another important consideration is indoor pollution. To reduce the buildup of harmful fumes within a home, homeowners need to select heating equipment that uses sealed combustion technology, which means an air supply directly vented into and out of the appliance. Many people are also concerned about the heating system's impact on world pollution and conservation. Expert advice is crucial to the selection and installation of a heating system.

Fireplaces and Stoves

Would you want to have a fireplace or a wood- or coal-burning stove in your home? Fireplaces and stoves have many advantages. Some homes use these as a supplemental—or even main—source of heat.

Heating a home with wood requires work. Wood must be cut or purchased and stacked. The fire must be fed continually to maintain heat. Wood prices are generally lower than gas and oil or electricity, but burning wood does contribute to air pollution. Environmental regulations in some areas control the use of wood furnaces and stoves.

Traditional built-in fireplaces are made of masonry. Many modern fireplaces are made of metal or metal encased in stone to give a more traditional appearance. These fireplaces are often less costly to install, and the metal case provides a safer, more durable unit. **See Fig. 11-12.**

Fig. 11-12 Some fireplaces burn gas rather than wood. Can you tell which type of fireplace this is?

Fireplaces contain a *firebox*, the recessed area in which the fire is built. The floor, or *hearth*, extends out in front as a precaution against flying sparks. The *mantel* is the facing around the fireplace, including any shelf above it.

When the fire is burning, smoke goes up into the smoke chamber to the chimney flue. The **flue** is a vertical shaft through which smoke and hot gases rise from the fireplace to the open air. Every fireplace must have its own flue. Otherwise, smoke from one fireplace may be carried to another by drafts. At the top of a fireplace, as it meets the chimney, there should be an adjustable damper. When the fireplace is not in use, close the damper to prevent heated or cooled air from escaping up the chimney.

Although popular, fireplaces have disadvantages. They are expensive to build, can cause drafts, and require attention and maintenance. In addition, they waste heat (up to 90 percent) and create a potential fire hazard. To help prevent heat loss, glass doors are available to cover the fireplace opening when not in use. Glass doors with vents along the top can be kept closed while a fire is burning; the vents allow heat to enter the room.

Fig. 11-13 Wood-burning stoves require less attention than fireplaces and hold their heat longer.

Gas-fired and electric fireplaces don't use wood, yet produce fires that look like wood-burning ones. Gas fireplaces are increasing in popularity for several reasons. They are cost-effective and provide continuous high heat. Gas fireplaces can be vented directly outside; they require no chimney or indoor air.

Wood- or coal-burning stoves are also popular. These may be made of steel, cast iron, or soapstone. See Fig. 11-13. In many cases, stoves are used as supplements to a home's central heating system.

A stove may be placed inside an existing fireplace, using the fireplace flue for venting. Freestanding stoves can be placed within a room to radiate heat in all directions. There must be adequate clearance between a freestanding stove and the floors, walls, and ceiling. The stove also must be placed on a fireproof base, such as metal, brick, or concrete.

Stoves have the advantages of fireplaces without some of their disadvantages. They don't cause drafts, require less attention, and hold heat for several hours. They also use less fuel.

Cooling & Ventilation

Cooling systems are important to people who live in areas with warm seasons or year-round warm temperatures. Equally important is ventilation in the home.

Cooling

Air conditioners remove excess moisture while they cool and circulate air. There are two main types of air conditioners: room air conditioners and central air-conditioning systems.

A room air conditioner is enclosed in a cabinet that fits into a window or wall. These units cool the air and blow it into a room. Room air conditioners come with different cooling capacities, measured in Btus (British thermal units). Choose a unit with the right capacity for the room. A general rule is that 12,000 Btus are needed for every 500 square feet (46 square meters) of floor space.

A central air-conditioning system has a large unit located outside the home that, with the help of the furnace blower and ducts, supplies cool air to each room. See Fig. 11-14. Central air conditioning can be built into a new home or installed in some older homes by adding it to a compatible heating system. The home may need additional insulation to help the air-conditioning system operate efficiently and economically. Central air conditioning is controlled by a thermostat, just as heating systems are. For the best energy efficiency, the size of the air conditioner needs to be matched carefully to the size and cooling needs of the home.

Newer air conditioners use a refrigerant that does not deplete the ozone. Federal appliance standards require that all new air conditioners be rated for energy efficiency. The Seasonal Energy Efficiency Ratio (SEER) helps consumers choose air conditioners with less energy consumption.

Fig. 11-14 Efficient air conditioners have SEER ratings in the range of 10 to 17.

Ventilation

Ventilation refers to supplying a home with fresh air and keeping air circulating throughout a home. This can help to reduce odors, stale air, and indoor pollution levels. A whole-house ventilation system consists of a fresh air inlet to bring in outside air, ducts to distribute the air, exhaust fans to remove the stale air, and a timer to control the system cycle. See Fig. 11-15. The benefits include improved indoor air quality, fewer drafts, improved health, and lower utility bills. In some areas, active ventilation systems are required by the building code.

Ventilation can also help cool a home. Many homes have a *whole-house fan* installed in the ceiling to pull air from the living space into the attic. A switch is used to turn on the fan when the outdoor temperature is lower than the indoor temperature. The fan pulls hot indoor air up into the attic, allowing cooler outdoor air to enter through open windows. Whole-house fans are most effective in climates with warm days, cool nights, and low humidity.

Fig. 11-15

Active Ventilation Systems

A Visual Guide

This active ventilation system brings fresh air into the home and distributes it. Stale air is exhausted to the outside.

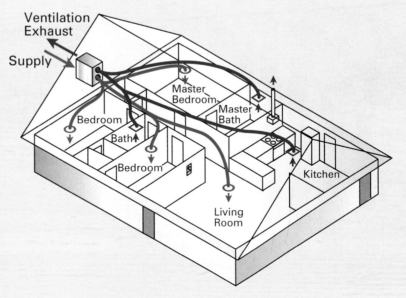

- Balanced Heat-Recovery Ventilation (HRV) Unit
- Ventilation Control
- Direction of Air Flow
- Intermittent Range-Hood Exhaust Fan
- Ceiling Exhaust Grill
- Ceiling Supply Grill
- Ventilation Exhaust Duct
- Ventilation Supply Duct

Roof vents are another important component of ventilation. Attics must have roof vents so that warm, moist air can escape. Roof vents may be installed in the soffit area, along the roof ridge, or in gable ends. Crawl spaces, too, must have vents to provide air flow.

Some rooms in a home require special ventilation for health, as well as for comfort. These rooms include the kitchen and bathrooms. In kitchens, indoor pollution and humidity levels can be high. Cooking smoke can leave walls and cabinets hard to clean. It can irritate your eyes, nose, throat, and lungs. Gas appliances can produce toxic fumes as well. Exhaust ventilation solutions include range hoods and ceiling or wall fans that vent heat, smoke, moisture, and odors outside.

The big problem in bathrooms is water condensation, which can allow mold and mildew to grow. It can also rot drywall, moldings, and window frames, as well as rust fixtures and damage insulation. When an exhaust fan ducted to the outdoors is used, moisture is removed ten times faster than without such a system.

For safety, the room in which the furnace and the water heater are kept must be well ventilated. If necessary, this can be accomplished through ducts and fans that bring fresh air in or draw room air out.

Finishing the Interior

Fig. 11-16 Stairs need to be easy to walk up or down for people of all ages.

After all the mechanical systems are in place, work can begin on more visible interior components: the finish construction. This includes the addition of stairways and finished walls, ceilings, and floors and then the more decorative elements, such as floor coverings.

Stairways

A home may have one or more main stairways connecting different levels of living space. See Fig. 11-16. It may also have a service stairway leading to the basement. Most main stairways are assembled with premade parts constructed of hardwoods, stone, metal, or tile. Service stairways are usually constructed on site from softwoods.

Each step consists of both a *riser*, the vertical part, and a *tread*, the horizontal part you walk on. Three features are needed for stairway safety. The size of risers and treads should be uniform on a stairway so people won't stumble. Generally, risers are $7^{1}/_{2}$ inches (19 cm) high and treads are 10-11 inches (25-28 cm) deep. Short stairways should have one or three steps. Research shows that people fall more frequently if there are only two steps. Handrails should always be installed and securely fastened.

Fig. 11-17

Interior Wall Finishes		
Material	**Characteristics**	**Advantages and Disadvantages**
Brick	Warm, earth look; forms interesting patterns.	Resists fire; durable; low upkeep; poor insulator for its thickness.
Concrete	Massive appearance; may look institutional; can be colored and textured.	Durable; low upkeep; fireproof; can be painted; poor insulator unless separate insulation added.
Plaster	Smooth; no joints; can be given texture.	Durable; can be finished in many ways; may crack.
Plastic (Panels, Tile, Sheets)	A variety of textures and colors.	Durable; easy to clean; easy to install; moisture-resistant.
Tile (Glazed, Clay)	A variety of sizes, shapes, and colors.	Easy to clean; durable; reflects noise; resists water and stains; requires strong base such as cement or plaster.
Drywall (Wallboard)	Smooth finish; joints must be taped.	Durable; can be finished many ways; fire-resistant.

Walls

Figure 11-17 summarizes the characteristics, advantages, and disadvantages of common wall finish materials. One of the best materials for interior wall and ceiling finishes is plaster on lath. *Plaster* is a hard, white finish made of lime or gypsum, sand, and water. *Lath* is the base to which the plaster adheres.

Today, lath is made of metal mesh or sheets of drywall that are nailed to the studs. The joints between the sheets of drywall are concealed with tape and a thin coat of plaster, then the surface is painted, wallpapered, or covered with tile. Special tools make it possible to texture plaster walls.

Decorative wall coverings are discussed in Chapter 24.

Consumer Considerations

Salvaged Interiors

A used countertop, floorboards, or stained glass window are just a few items that can be successfully salvaged and incorporated into a new home design. Using salvaged materials has the same benefits as other types of recycling—less waste and lower costs. It can also add character to a room and may even inspire the rest of a design. Think of planning a dining room around a built-in mahogany wall cabinet or an entranceway around an octagonal stained-glass window.

Finding attractive items in good condition can take some detective work. You might try classified ads, online exchanges, and even demolition sales. There may be a reuse retailer in your area, like the ReStores run by some chapters of Habitat for Humanity. The group sells quality donated items at low cost to help fund its homebuilding projects.

Not every item is a good candidate for a second life. Inefficient pieces like single-pane windows and older appliances cost more money in the long run by wasting energy. Potential hazards, such as plumbing fixtures with leaded brass, have no place in any home, no matter how appealing.

Ceilings

Most ceilings are flat and set at right angles to walls, but innovative designs are sometimes used instead.

- *Shed ceilings* expand vertical space. They ascend diagonally from one side in a single slope.

- *Gabled ceilings* expand space in the center of the ceiling and have two sloping sides. Both shed and gabled ceilings are sometimes referred to as *vaulted ceilings*.

- *Coved ceilings* have walls and a ceiling that flow into each other by means of a curved surface.

- *Dropped ceilings* are lower than the rest of the ceiling area. This type of ceiling accents or defines an area of a room, such as a dining area.

- *Tray ceilings* feature edges that angle out and down to walls. See Fig. 11-18.

Ceilings may be constructed from materials such as plaster or drywall. The following are some other options:

- *Acoustical tile ceilings* are ceilings with a porous material that can absorb sound. They are useful in high-noise areas, such as recreation rooms.

- *Stamped metal ceilings*, which were popular in the 19th century, are being manufactured again. They are durable and offer a high-tech look. They can be perforated and backed with a fabric liner that absorbs sound to provide soundproofing.

- *Wood ceilings* are also becoming popular. They provide a rich, warm look. Like metal ceilings, they can be cut into unusual shapes to bring drama to a room.

- *Beamed ceilings* feature decorative wood beams over a plaster ceiling. Lightweight materials finished to look like wood are also used.

- *Ceramic tile ceilings* are popular in bathrooms, especially above showers.

Fig. 11-18 The crown molding used in this room draws attention to the ceiling and adds to the overall visual appeal.

Floors

When it comes to flooring, people are concerned with comfort, convenience, durability, and appearance. They have many styles and materials to choose from, each with its own characteristics. Materials for floors can be divided into two types: finish flooring and floor coverings.

Finish Flooring

Finish floor materials are considered a permanent part of the floor. These materials include wood, engineered wood, ceramic tile, concrete, slate, stone, and brick.

Wood. Wood is the most popular finish flooring. It is attractive and comfortable to walk on. Oak is the most commonly used hardwood.

Wood flooring is usually made in strips that fit together with *tongue-and-groove joints*. The tongue-edge projection of one board fits into a groove cut along the edge of another board. Strip flooring is fastened to the subflooring with nails. It comes in prefinished (factory-stained and sealed) and unfinished styles.

Hardwood planks, which are wider than strips, are also used. They are usually attached to the subfloor with screws. The screws are covered with wood plugs, giving the floor an Early American look.

Wood floors may also be laid with small pieces of wood arranged in different designs, such as herringbone and checkerboard. This type is called *parquet* (par-KAY). **See Fig. 11-19.** Parquet is available in prefinished squares that can be easily installed.

Whatever type of wood floor is chosen, the finish is also important. A low-gloss finish hides scratches better than a glossy finish. Polyurethane finishes provide excellent protection for wood.

Fig. 11-19 Parquet wood floors can be arranged in different geometric patterns. **Why is this style of flooring often used in a small area such as an entryway?**

Engineered wood floors consist of several layers of wood glued at right angles to each other (similar to plywood). The top layer is a hardwood veneer. Unlike solid wood, engineered wood floors can be used in areas that may be damp. They are stapled to subflooring or glued directly to a concrete floor slab. Some tongue-and-groove boards can also be glued to each other and then installed over a foam pad. This type of installation is called a floating floor because it is not nailed or glued to a subfloor or concrete slab.

Ceramic Tile. Ceramic tile is often used in bathrooms, kitchens, and entryways because it is durable, moisture-resistant, and easy to clean. It can also be used in other rooms, such as dining areas and sunrooms. Tiles come in many sizes and shapes. The spaces between the tiles are filled with a cementlike substance called *grout*. Tiles should be installed on a solid, even surface in order to prevent cracking.

Concrete. Flooring made of concrete is easy to clean and extremely durable. However, the hardness of concrete can make it hard to stand or walk on for long periods of time. Previously, concrete was used only in garages and utility areas. New technologies for coloring concrete and creating textures have made concrete an attractive finish floor option for other rooms as well. **See Fig. 11-20.**

Slate, Stone, and Brick. Slate, stone, and brick may be used on both indoor and outdoor floors. These materials are often used for patios, porches, and entrance halls. Like concrete, they are not comfortable to stand on for lengthy periods.

When choosing a floor material, consider how a room will be used and how much traffic there might be. For instance, brick wouldn't be the best choice for a bedroom because it is cold and hard. There may be architectural limitations as well. For instance, a stone or brick floor is very heavy. A room where these are used requires special framing to carry the additional weight.

Floor Coverings

Unlike finish flooring, floor coverings are not considered permanent. When a floor covering becomes worn, it is removed and replaced. Floor coverings may be installed directly over the subfloor or over a finish flooring material, such as a hardwood floor.

Carpeting is a popular floor covering. It creates a warm feeling in a room, absorbs sound, and is comfortable to walk on. For areas that require a nonabsorbent floor surface, such as kitchens and bathrooms, vinyl or laminate floor covering is often used. These are durable, are easy to clean, and come in a wide range of colors, patterns, and textures. Floor coverings are discussed in greater detail in Chapter 24.

Finish Trim

Toward the end of the home construction process, carpenters generally install the finish trim. They put up *moldings*—the decorative strips of wood around a room. For example, crown molding might be installed around the top edges of walls along ceilings, baseboards along floors, and trim around windows and doors.

Fig. 11-20 Concrete flooring isn't just for garages anymore, as you can see from this attractive great room flooring. **What are some advantages of concrete flooring?**

From the Inside Out

Understanding the interior construction of your home and its systems can make living there easier and more enjoyable. Many repair problems can seem overwhelming unless you know something about a home's hidden mechanical systems. This knowledge can help you understand what is involved in maintaining, repairing, or replacing home systems. See Fig. 11-21. In addition, understanding a home's systems and construction enables renters or potential buyers to recognize possible trouble spots and to deal with them—whether that means patching a crack in a plaster wall or calling an expert to repair a heating system. It all adds up to being informed and knowing that you can deal with any home maintenance or repair situation that arises.

Fig. 11-21 Knowing what goes into building a home can help you decide what actions you need to take to maintain one.

Profile of a Model Home Designer

A model home designer plans the space and selects the furniture, wall coverings, floor coverings, lighting, and accessories for model homes. They order these furnishings and coordinate the installation. These workers also coordinate the materials chosen for the home's exterior.

Education & Training

- A bachelor's degree and interior design certificate are preferred.
- Courses in interior design, art, drawing, ergonomics, architectural drawing, CAD, and business practices are helpful.

Skills & Aptitudes

- Creativity, a sense of design, and an eye for color are required.
- Ability to sketch and use CAD software is necessary.
- Visual and spatial aptitude and a working knowledge of the principles and practices of interior design are very important.
- Good interpersonal skills are valuable for working with other professionals.

Model Home Designer
Shawna Holt

For me, completing the interior design work on model homes is a dream job. In college, I liked learning about architectural styles from the past, but modern interiors are my favorite.

For each construction project I'm involved with, I might design the interiors for five or six different model homes. I also help select colors for brick, siding, shutters, doors, and even the roof. It's vital that these homes have excellent curb appeal. Coordinating the colors is one important key to that success.

Inside the homes, my work usually involves developing the furniture plan and selecting wall coverings, window treatments, floor coverings, lighting, and accessories. I order these items and coordinate the installations. Generally, I have very little time to do all of this work and must complete the project within a reasonable budget.

The work is challenging, but it's exciting. Over time, I have learned which suppliers I can count on. I know which companies will deliver items, such as furniture, in a timely manner and at a reasonable cost. My schedules mean that I can't wait to have walls painted or window treatments installed. My painters and installers are reliable and able to complete a job with little notice.

I have to be very sensitive to trends and to which designs appeal to a broad audience. The designs I select must use colors, fabrics, patterns, and styles that are current and popular. I can't overdo it though! The designs I select have to appeal to a variety of people with diverse tastes. The developer I work for builds model homes in different states. That means I have to select designs that appeal to people in a specific region. For example, styles in Arizona are quite different from styles in Oregon. I have to know those style differences and adapt to them.

To keep up to date I attend national conferences and workshops. I also read several trade publications and monitor new building trends and technologies. Our computer system has been very important in managing our business transactions, records, and maintaining a product resource database.

Design Portfolio

1. Obtain the floor plan for a home in your area. Use CAD software to execute a model home design for the master bedroom and the living room.

2. Design the same rooms for a model home in a different region of the country. Explain why you think the different design selections are appropriate.

Chapter Summary

- **Contractors** schedule and supervise the work done by **subcontractors** in a construction project.
- Safe, efficient home electrical systems are regulated by state and local codes. New systems should be adequate for the needs of the home's occupants.
- Plumbing systems, which bring water into the home and wastes out of it, also need to meet building codes.
- Energy efficiency and the cost of operation are important in choosing heating, cooling, and ventilation systems.
- Finishing the interior involves installing stairways, walls, ceiling, floor finishes, floor coverings, and trim.

Checking Your Understanding

1. Give two examples of tasks **contractors** and subcontractors perform.
2. How does a **panel box** work? What safety devices does it have?
3. How does a **ground fault circuit interrupter** work?
4. How do plastic and metal compare for plumbing pipes?
5. What materials are used for plumbing fixtures?
6. What is the **recovery rate** and what does it tell you?
7. Give an example of a heating system that uses **convection** and one that uses **radiation**.
8. What factors affect the operating cost of a heating system?
9. With what type of heating system would a central air conditioning system work well? Why?
10. What are the benefits of a ventilation system?
11. What three safety features are important in stairways?
12. What materials are used for interior wall finishing?
13. Why is ceramic tile better than wood for bathroom floors?

Thinking Critically

1. **Sequencing Construction.** Suppose you are a contractor building a new home who had scheduled a trusted electrician to install the electrical system. You learn that the electrician is ill and cannot work for two weeks. How would you resequence the construction work flow to allow for this setback?

2. **Evaluating Alternatives.** What heating system would you recommend for a new home being built in Florida? What about in Maine? Explain the reasons for your choices.

Applying Your Knowledge

1. **Sewage Alternatives.** Find out what the rules are regarding public sewage systems, septic tanks, and cesspools in your community. Write a summary of your findings.

2. **Water Heaters.** Use print or Internet resources or visit a store that sells water heaters. Find three models—a standard storage water heater, an energy-efficient storage water heater, and an on-demand water heater. Determine the price of the unit, including installation, and the annual operating cost based on the Energy Guide label. Create a chart that compares your findings. Which unit is most economical? Why?

3. **Fireplaces and Stoves.** A homeowner wants to include a fireplace or stove in the new home he is having built. Research the advantages and disadvantages of the alternatives. Recommend a particular option to the homeowner, explaining your reasons.

4. **Background Materials.** Find photos of different interior wall and floor finishes. Use them to create a design brochure that new homeowners could use to choose among their options. Include information on the advantages, disadvantages, and best uses of each material you include.

Design Challenge

You have been hired to design an office lobby. The telecommunications company hiring you wants to present a high-tech, but friendly image when customers and business clients enter the lobby. The lobby must include a reception desk.

1. Think about what other features the lobby should have and make a list.

2. Research alternatives for ceiling, wall, and floor finishes as well as lobby furnishings.

3. Create a chart showing the materials you choose for each area and why.

4. Prepare a design showing your recommendations.

Chapter 12

Landscaping & the Environment

Objectives

- Define resource management.

- Identify and evaluate traditional and alternative energy sources.

- Explain the features of energy-efficient heating and cooling systems.

- Describe ways home designers, builders, and consumers can conserve resources.

- Give examples of ways outdoor living areas can expand living space.

- Explain how landscaping can enhance a home.

- Incorporate natural and manufactured elements in a landscape design.

- Explain the relationship between conservation and comfort.

Vocabulary

- resource management
- fossil fuels
- geothermal energy
- active solar heating systems
- passive solar heating systems
- U value
- retrofitting
- energy audit
- landscaping
- xeriscaping

Do you turn off the lights when you leave a room? Do you turn down the heat at night in the winter? If so, you are already helping protect our natural environment. The environment provides people with just about everything they need to live, including food, water, fuel, and building materials. As you'll see in this chapter, there are many steps in building and maintaining a home that can be taken to preserve these resources.

Housing & Resources Management

For years, people assumed that sources of food, heat, and housing materials would always be there when needed. As supplies decreased and prices rose, however, people became more conscious of conserving resources—that is, using them wisely.

Throughout the country, scientists, engineers, and architects have created model homes designed to make the best use of the environment. **See Fig. 12-1.** These homes are virtually self-sufficient, using very little energy from outside sources. Almost everything, including waste products, is recycled. Solar water heaters, solar ovens, devices that convert sewage to fertilizer, greenhouses, and gardens all help provide food and fuel with a minimum of pollution.

Fig. 12-1 This earth-sheltered home in Marquette, Michigan is very energy efficient and has bright airy rooms.

Even though not all people can work this closely with nature, they can still use natural resources wisely. Whether people build their own homes, buy them, or rent them, they are making decisions that affect the environment.

Preserving the natural environment is essential for our future well-being. It's a matter of resource management. **Resource management** is the wise use of natural resources—that is, the building materials, energy sources, and everything else that nature supplies. When it comes to your home, resource management covers a wide range of issues: everything from insulation to energy-efficient argon-filled windows to energy-saving appliances to less-polluting paint. As you learned in Chapter 3, green building is a way to design, build, and operate homes to use our resources efficiently. Conserving land, water, and energy and managing consumption extend beyond building a home. In our daily lives, we need to strive for sustainability. *Sustainability* means meeting the needs of people today without forfeiting the well-being of future generations.

Managing resources means making tough decisions. Is it worth spending more on extra insulation and a heat pump to reduce your heating bills? Do you spend the time and effort sealing the home against cold drafts each winter, or do you just turn up the heat? This chapter discusses environmental issues and describes solutions for sustainable living. It's up to you to make choices that are right for you.

Using Energy Efficiently

People use huge amounts of energy to heat, cool, and light their homes and to operate appliances. Every time you turn on the television, blow-dry your hair, or run the dishwasher, you are using energy. Two steps you can take immediately to reduce your household's energy needs are to lower the thermostat in cold weather to 68°F (20°C) or below and raise it to 78°F (26°C) or above when using central air conditioning.

Some homes, buildings, and products are designed to be more energy efficient. Those with outstanding energy efficiency earn the honor of being labeled Energy Star. The rating was created by the Environmental Protection Agency (EPA) and the Department of Energy to identify energy-efficient products and homes. Energy Star labeled homes are inspected and tested by an independent third party. These are some of the features that contribute to this status:

- Improved insulation and windows that help maintain a constant temperature in the home.

- Heating and cooling systems designed to work with minimum waste. Some builders guarantee that, with this equipment, utility costs will not exceed a certain amount.

Energy efficiency may increase the purchase price of a home, but lower maintenance and energy costs will create savings over time. These homes can use up to 30 percent less energy than other homes. The investment may also pay off with a higher resale value.

The Energy Star label is also given to various appliances, televisions, computers, and even light bulbs. Along with reduced energy use, these products provide another benefit—they tend to last longer and need fewer repairs. Chapter 22 includes more information about energy-efficient kitchen and laundry appliances.

Fig. 12-2

Sources of Energy

Fuel	Type	Uses in Home
Natural gas	Nonrenewable	Heating homes, water; in ranges, clothes dryers
Butane and propane	Nonrenewable	Heating homes; cooking
Fuel oil	Nonrenewable	Heating homes, water
Coal	Nonrenewable	Heating homes, water; generating electricity in power plants
Wood	Renewable	Heating homes
Hydroelectric	Renewable	Generating electricity in power plants
Nuclear	Nonrenewable	Generating electricity in power plants
Solar	Renewable	Heating or generating electricity in homes; generating electricity in power plants
Geothermal	Renewable	Heating; generating electricity in power plants
Wind	Renewable	Generating electricity in homes or power plants

Energy Sources

Many different sources of energy are used in the home. Some are used directly. Others fuel power plants that generate the electricity that runs many systems and devices within the home. See Fig.12-2.

Traditional sources of energy have been oil, coal, and natural gas. They are called **fossil fuels** because they were formed in the earth from the remains of prehistoric animals or plants. These fuels are nonrenewable, which means they can be used up. As the supply diminishes and demand continues, fuels become more expensive. Burning fossil fuels also adds pollution to the environment, increasing health hazards and contributing to climate change.

Hydroelectric and nuclear power plants do not depend on fossil fuels, but they do have other limitations. To help meet future energy needs, researchers are developing alternate sources of energy, such as solar, geothermal, and wind power.

Traditional Fuels

Natural gas, a clean-burning fuel, is the fuel used by most households in the United States. Natural gas does not require storage space in the home because it is brought in through underground pipelines. Therefore, natural gas can be used only in areas that have gas pipelines.

Two other types of gas—butane and propane—are forms of liquid petroleum (LP gas). They are sold in pressurized tanks. The gas is liquid in the tank but burns as a vapor.

Fuel oil is also used by millions of people. Fuel oil is stored in tanks, either in the home or in the yard, often underground. Oil does not burn as cleanly as natural gas, which adds to air pollution. Because of this factor, some people do not want to use it.

Although the United States has large coal reserves, only a very small percentage of households use coal directly. However, large utility companies burn coal to generate electricity, which reaches homes to power lighting and appliances and for heating and cooling. Burning coal pollutes the air. These pollutants can contribute to health problems such as asthma and lung disease. They are also a major cause of urban smog and acid rain, which harms trees and pollutes lakes hundreds of miles from the place where the coal is burned. Burning coal also releases carbon dioxide into the atmosphere, contributing to global climate change. Coal can be treated to make it burn more cleanly, but the process is expensive.

Fig. 12-3 Hydroelectric plants can produce huge amounts of energy.

Until about 1850, wood was the major source of fuel. Although wood alone could not supply enough fuel to serve modern needs, it can be a second source of home heating. Wood is a renewable resource; users can plant new trees. Unfortunately, heat from wood fires escapes up the chimney along with the smoke.

Alternative Energy Sources

Other sources are being used to supply energy as well. Forms of energy that are renewable and do not pollute are often referred to as *green energy*.

Hydroelectric Power. Hydroelectric plants use the moving water of rivers to drive electrical generators. Hydroelectric plants supply 9 percent of the power generated in the United States and account for about half of all renewable energy used. **See Fig. 12-3.** Hydroelectric power is clean and renewable. Water is not destroyed in the production of electricity. Building dams and reservoirs, however, can significantly impact surrounding areas and affect wildlife. The amount of hydroelectric power is not likely to increase significantly because there are few remaining sites in the United States that are appropriate for new hydroelectric plants.

Nuclear Power. In a nuclear power plant, reactors fueled by uranium produce heat. The heat is used to make steam, which drives turbines. The turbines in turn power the generators that produce electricity. There are many difficulties and dangers in operating nuclear plants. Radiation leaks have occurred in nuclear plants in several countries. Such accidents can pollute the local land with radioactive material. Because the contaminated material is also vented into the atmosphere, the pollution can spread farther. Nuclear waste is hard to dispose of because it remains hazardous for centuries. Finally, nuclear plants are very expensive to build.

Solar Power. The sun is the most powerful energy source available to us. The energy the sun delivers in only 40 minutes could operate all the factories, machines, and vehicles and heat all the buildings on the earth for an entire year.

Because it is clean and plentiful, solar power is an appealing alternative energy source. With advances in technology, ways to use solar energy will increase.

Geothermal Energy. Heat from the earth's interior is **geothermal energy**. Beneath the surface of the earth, the ground remains at a relatively constant temperature throughout the year. Home systems that use geothermal energy take advantage of this by transferring heat stored in the earth or in ground water into a building during the winter, and transferring heat from the building into the ground during the summer. The ground, in other words, acts as a heat source in winter and as a natural air conditioner in the summer.

Wind Power. More and more utility companies are building "wind farms" to supply clean, renewable energy. See Fig. 12-4. Colorado now offers most residents the option of using wind power. Parts of California are well known for the windmills that line the highways. More than 1.2 million homes in the United States use power generated by wind turbines, and that number is expected to continue to increase.

Fig. 12-4 These wind turbines are reliable sources of energy. Are there wind turbines in your region of the country?

Energy-Efficient Heating & Cooling Systems

Although alternative energy sources are becoming more widely used, Americans still rely primarily on traditional fuels. As a result, we all need to use these fuels wisely. On the average, heating accounts for about one-third of home energy use—twice that in colder areas. Choosing wisely in the areas of home heating and cooling is very important. Heating and cooling systems are broadly referred to as *HVAC* (heating, ventilating, and air conditioning). Each of the heating systems you learned about in Chapter 11 is available in energy-efficient models. Remember to look for the ENERGY STAR label on furnaces, boilers, air conditioners, and other HVAC systems. ENERGY STAR-labeled equipment uses 10 to 20 percent less energy than standard-efficiency models.

In addition to the traditional heating systems, engineers have developed more advanced heating and cooling systems to conserve fossil fuels and reduce pollution.

Geothermal Heat Pumps

A study by the United States Environmental Protection Agency (EPA) named geothermal heat pumps (GHPs) as more efficient heating and cooling systems than other types of equipment, including high-efficiency gas furnaces and air conditioners. While geothermal heat pumps initially cost more than a gas furnace, money is saved in operating and maintenance costs. These heat pumps can reduce energy consumption 25 to 75 percent compared to older or conventional replacement systems. For further savings, GHPs can be equipped with a "desuperheater" that provides hot water. Geothermal heat pumps are environmentally clean, too. All heat pumps require electricity to run the compressor. However, GHPs use less electricity than conventional systems.

Fig. 12-5 Solar energy is an environmentally friendly way to provide energy for a home.

A geothermal system consists of a series of pipes buried in the ground. Liquid circulates through the pipes and absorbs the heat from the ground. A geothermal heat pump removes the heat from the fluid in the pipes and transfers it to the house. In the summer, excess heat is sent into the ground. Conventional ductwork is generally used to distribute heated or cooled air from the geothermal heat pump throughout the building. About half a million geothermal heat pumps are now being used throughout the United States in residential, commercial, and government buildings.

Solar Heating

Another option is to use solar energy to heat homes. This process can be either active or passive. **Active solar heating systems** require mechanical devices that collect and store the sun's heat and then distribute it throughout the house when it is needed. **See Fig. 12-5.** Active solar heating systems are usually designed to provide 40 to 80 percent of the home's heating needs. This type of heating system is expensive, for two reasons. First, the components are often costly and must be custom fitted to the house, so installation costs are high. Second, the house needs a backup heating system for periods of cloudy weather and severe cold. Small systems, such as wall air panels and window box collectors, are a simpler and less expensive option for those who want to heat only one or two rooms.

Passive solar heating systems make direct use of the sun's heat without mechanical systems. They use features such as windows and masonry walls to collect and store heat. **Figure 12-6** on page 280 further explains solar heating systems.

Heat Recovery Ventilators

A *heat recovery ventilator* is an energy-efficient device that uses heat energy that would otherwise be wasted. Heat recovery ventilators remove stale air from the house in winter, but first they extract the heat from the air and keep it indoors. Similar technology transfers heat outside to cool a home. Heat recovery ventilators are popular in Canada and are gaining popularity in the United States.

Fig. 12-6

Solar Heating Systems

A Visual Guide

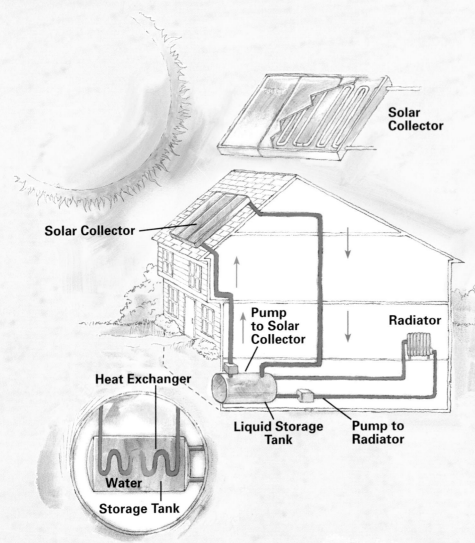

Solar Collector

Solar Collector

Pump to Solar Collector

Radiator

Heat Exchanger

Water

Storage Tank

Liquid Storage Tank

Pump to Radiator

Active Solar Heating System. Large solar collectors are located on the roof. The solar collectors contain absorber panels, usually copper with a black coating that absorbs the sun's heat. If a liquid system is used, liquid passes through pipes coiled behind the panels and transfers the heat to a storage tank of water. The storage tank is heavily insulated to reduce heat loss. When the room temperature in the home drops, the thermostat activates a pump that brings the heated water from the storage tank to radiators. Some systems use air rather than liquid for heat transfer. In an air system, the sun's heat is moved via fans to a storage bin filled with rocks. The rocks absorb the heat. When the room temperature drops, fans distribute the heat from the rock bin through ductwork in the house. Another type of system uses roofing materials with built-in photovoltaic cells that turn sunlight into electricity.

Passive Solar Heating System. Large south-facing windows allow sunlight to enter the home and heat masonry walls and floors. These materials collect and store warmth for times when the sun is not shining. An overhang above the windows shades them from too much heat in the summer. However, in winter the sun is lower in the sky, so its heat penetrates the windows when it's needed most.

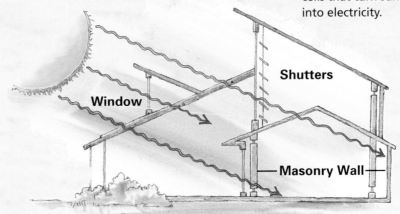

Window

Shutters

Masonry Wall

Fig. 12-7 These solar panels convert sunlight into electricity. Research the economic and environmental benefits of solar panels.

Conserving Energy Through Design & Construction

The ongoing energy use of a building is probably its greatest environmental impact, so designing buildings for low energy use is a priority. While it costs money to make a home energy-efficient, those who live in it will save on energy costs for years to come. In addition, these homeowners will enjoy greater comfort, better indoor air quality, and lower maintenance costs.

As you've learned, improved insulation, advanced windows, tightly sealed and insulated ducts, high-efficiency heating and cooling, and reduced air infiltration from drafts are important ways to conserve energy. There are also basic design features that can contribute to energy conservation.

The need to design for energy conservation is likely to grow in the future. As the population grows, demand for resources will grow also. Yet resources such as fossil fuels are available in limited supplies. Minimizing the resources used in building and operating homes will help make supplies last longer.

Energy Efficient Design

Architects and builders know that, by following certain principles, they can reduce a home's heating and cooling costs. **See Fig. 12-7.** Consider these factors when choosing a new or existing home:

- The smaller the roof, the less the heat loss. Compact, two-story houses are best in cold climates because there's less roof in proportion to the total floor area.

- The color of the roof also affects the amount of heat a home loses or retains. Light colors reflect heat and dark colors absorb it. Therefore, light-colored roofs are better in warmer climates because they lower air-conditioning needs. Dark roofs are better in colder climates because they reduce heating needs.

- Sunrooms, skylights, and large windows provide passive solar energy if they face south. Dark walls absorb light and store heat. In regions with cold weather, family rooms and living rooms should be placed where they get afternoon sun.

- Storm windows or insulated glass block hot or cold outside air from entering the house.

- Window shades and awnings can help keep out sun and heat. Overhangs and porches can keep out sunlight during summer months. Light-colored walls also reflect heat.

- The smaller the wall area, the more easily a structure can be heated or cooled. Square buildings are energy efficient. Rambling L-shaped and T-shaped homes are the most difficult to heat or cool efficiently.

- Rooms such as the kitchen, family room, and living room, where most activities take place, should be in the same part of the home. That way, other areas of the home can be closed off to conserve on heating and cooling.

- Ceiling height can influence room temperature because warm air rises. In warm weather, high ceilings collect rising room heat that can be pulled outside by exhaust fans. In cold weather, however, high ceilings make a room more expensive to heat. Ceiling fans can be used to move heat back down into the living space.

- A *vestibule*, or entryway with an outer and inner door, reduces heating and cooling costs. When people enter through the outer door, they close it behind them *before* opening the inner door. This helps prevent outside air from entering the home.

- Closets and storage areas placed on the coldest side of the house (the north side) act as insulation for the living areas. This can save on heating costs.

- An attic fan or whole-house fan will help cool the house.

Earth-Sheltered Homes

The earth-sheltered home features an energy-efficient design. It is usually built into the side of a hill so that only the south wall is exposed. **See Fig. 12-8.** The south wall has large windows to let sunlight in, allowing passive solar heating. The tops of the other walls may be exposed enough to let light in through smaller windows. The roof area of the home is covered with a layer of earth to insulate it. Since the ground temperature stays around 50-55°F (10-15°C) all year, this natural insulation greatly reduces heating and cooling costs.

Construction of an earth-sheltered home may cost more, since it must withstand great earth pressures and moisture. However, in the long run, the energy savings may make up for the initial costs.

Despite its energy efficiency, the earth-sheltered home does not yet enjoy widespread acceptance. One reason is that it doesn't fit into traditional residential neighborhoods.

Fig. 12-8 Earth-sheltered homes are designed to be energy efficient. What design features make this earth-sheltered home energy efficient?

Fig. 12-9 Getting a home ready for the winter takes time but the effort shows up in lower utility bills.

Insulation and Blocking Air Leaks

High-quality insulation, caulking, and weatherstripping can save energy. By reducing heat loss, they decrease fuel consumption and lower heating and cooling bills.

Insulation, discussed in Chapter 10, is laid, sprayed, or blown into areas in walls and ceilings, wrapped around pipes, or otherwise used to keep a home warmer in cold weather and cooler in warm weather. One area that is often overlooked when insulating is the ductwork that distributes heated and cooled air through the home. The ductwork is usually located in attics, basements, and other spaces not heated or cooled. Leaky, uninsulated ducts waste energy. Foil tape, fiberglass tape, or advanced duct tape need to be applied to seal the joints, and ducts need to be insulated.

Weatherstripping is a strip of material installed around the edges of windows and doors to exclude outside moisture and air. Some types of weatherstripping for windows are adhesive-backed foam rubber or vinyl. Interlocking metal sections of weatherstripping are often nailed around doors. *Caulking* is a pastelike substance, often made of silicone, that can be applied inside or outside a home wherever air or moisture can enter. On the outside of a home, this might be around windowsills or any location where the siding meets window or door frames. See Fig. 12-9.

Another approach to improving a home's energy efficiency is called *weather blocking*, or reducing energy waste. Here are several ways to do so:

- **Insulating electrical outlets.** You can place foam rubber pads and gaskets beneath cover plates and around electrical outlets to prevent air from seeping from these boxes. Some utility companies give these materials away to customers who request them.

- **Sealing windows.** Placing plastic film over windows helps form an airtight seal. Inexpensive indoor and outdoor kits are available.

- **Installing door sweeps.** These hinged devices attach to a door jamb to draw the door across the frame for a tighter fit. They can be cut to fit different sized doors and can close gaps of up to $1/2$ inch (1.25 cm).

Energy-Efficient Windows

Research shows that windows account for about one-quarter of a house's heating load and half of the cooling load. Energy efficiency needs to be one of the main concerns when selecting windows. One way to tell a window's energy performance is the U value. The **U value** is the measure of a window's capacity to resist winter heat loss. The lower the U value, the better the window. For example, a window with a U value of 0.15 means high thermal performance. In warm climates, windows need to prevent heat gain. This measurement is called solar heat gain coefficient, SHGC. Lower SHGC numbers mean better performance. Here are several ways windows can be made energy efficient.

- Windows with a layer of air between the panes of glass help prevent heat or cooling loss.
- Double- or triple-paned windows that have argon gas sandwiched between the panes can cut down substantially on heat loss in cold weather or heat gain in warm weather.
- "Cool windows" save on air-conditioning costs. They use a tinted, coated glass (such as low-e glass) to let light in but filter out the heat.
- Windows with another type of coating on the glass absorb solar heat in cold weather and reflect it in warm weather.
- Tubular skylights through the roof use the sun for lighting interiors but avoid the drawbacks of leaks and energy loss that can be associated with regular skylights.

Experts predict that windows will soon be as well insulated as walls. Consumers should choose the types that best fit their climates.

Retrofitting Homes

The process of making a home that is already built more energy efficient is called **retrofitting**. Many steps can be taken to conserve energy, from using weatherstripping on windows and exterior doors, to sealing leaky ducts, to building a solar room to collect heat. Insulation can be added to attics, outer walls, and heating ducts. See Fig. 12-10. Windows can be replaced with new energy-efficient designs, or storm windows may be added.

For a small fee, most utility companies will evaluate the energy efficiency of a home. This **energy audit** is an inspection of the home to determine where heat loss may be occurring. The energy advisor will suggest ways to seal leaks and reduce energy use.

Fig. 12-10 While new homes are usually well insulated, many older homes lack adequate insulation. They can be retrofitted by adding insulation to exterior walls and attics.

Energy Conservation in Commercial Buildings

If the average homeowner appreciates the money saved by conserving energy, imagine how important it is to business owners. Money spent on utilities directly affects their ability to stay in business. Besides their own wise practices, they rely on energy-saving design in these areas:

- **Location.** Locating a site near existing parking, public transportation, or bike paths saves energy needed in parking areas for lighting and security cameras. Taking advantage of prevailing winds along lakefronts and in other areas adds natural ventilation.

- **Heating and Cooling.** Commercial heating and cooling systems grow ever more efficient. Zonal controls, which can be adjusted to the temperature needs of different areas, are common features. Economizer cycles increase or decrease outside air intake to warm or cool the inside environment. Underfloor systems may offer greater savings and comfort than those installed in a ceiling. Radiant heat may be chosen over forced warm air for factories and other large, hard-to-heat spaces. Structural elements such as reflective roofing can be used to cut the demand for heating and cooling as well.

- **Lighting.** Efficient design often requires a blend of different types of lighting. Long-lasting compact fluorescent bulbs come in a variety of shapes to fit numerous applications. Red-glowing light-emitting diode lights are a logical choice for exit signs. Natural lighting, where available, is enhanced by lowering or eliminating walls and by using ceiling tiles with high light reflectance. Designers consider a building's outdoor lighting needs in the same way. For instance, putting motion sensors or timers on security lighting saves energy while still providing protection.

Apply It!

A drapery maker wants to open her own business in the vacant second floor of a warehouse. Given the location and type of business, what special heating, cooling, and lighting needs should she consider? What design strategies might be most efficient?

Using Water Wisely

Water is essential to daily life. People use it for drinking, cooking, bathing, washing clothes, scrubbing floors and windows, and flushing the toilet. In fact, households in the United States use 40 billion gallons (151.4 billion L) of water every day. Considering that two-thirds of the earth is covered by water, you might think that conserving water is not necessary. Think again. Less than 1 percent of the world's water is suitable for people to drink. About 97 percent is in the oceans and therefore has a high salt content. Another 2 percent is in the form of glaciers and polar ice. With the growth of world population, it is important to conserve water. In many areas, periodic droughts result in water shortages. Pollution is another threat to the water supply. To conserve and protect water, governments, businesses, and individuals must work together.

Government agencies manage and protect the water supply. They regularly test all major sources of water. They also monitor potential sources of contamination, such as housing developments with septic systems or industries with chemical storage tanks.

Through zoning and building codes, septic system permits, and other measures, local governments can control the amount of water used. One county in California prohibits lawns from taking up more than 20 percent of the landscaped area in some housing developments. This helps cut down on the amount of water used for lawns. See Fig. 12-11. Many other communities have issued watering schedules, such as permitting residents to use water for lawns only on odd or even days, according to their street addresses.

Many cities and towns have water-treatment plants that help recycle water. In some plants, wastewater is treated and purified, then discharged into the ground where it seeps back into natural places. In this way, water is sent back to its original sources and later converted again into drinking water.

Fig. 12-11 One way to conserve water is through water-wise landscaping.

Fig. 12-12 Remember to do the laundry only when you have a full load. **How else can you conserve energy when doing the laundry?**

Water-Saving Fixtures & Appliances

Many manufacturers are redesigning fixtures and appliances with water conservation in mind. For example, a new "smart" dishwasher constantly monitors wash load conditions. Grinding mechanisms remove food particles; so there's no need for prerinsing, which saves both water and time. The dishwasher runs just long enough to get the dishes clean, then shuts off automatically. This saves both water and energy.

A front-loading washing machine uses the same tumbling action as a dryer and uses over 40 percent less water than a standard washer. Its electronic controls monitor tumbling and spin speeds and keep clothes from balling up. These machines have an added convenience: because there's no agitator in the way, it's easy to wash bulky items like bedspreads and parkas. One model saves 19 gallons (72 L) of water per load, or about 8,000 gallons (30,283 L) a year.

Water-saving fixtures for the bathroom and kitchen are available. Modern toilets are designed to use only 1.6 gallons (6 L) of water per flush. An electronic faucet that reduces water usage by 85 percent runs only while hands or objects are beneath it.

Water-efficient showerheads use less than 2.5 gallons (9.5 L) of water per minute. That saves the typical household 12,000 gallons (45,425 L) of water a year. It also means that less energy is needed to heat water and clean and process wastewater, reducing the carbon dioxide emitted into the atmosphere by water treatment plants.

Conserving Water Daily

You and the members of your household can take measures to conserve water in your home. You can also encourage government action. Here are just a few things you can do to help preserve water supplies.

- Run washing machines only with full loads. Use the water-saving feature if your machine has one. **See Fig. 12-12.**

- Wash dishes by hand with minimal water use or use the energy-saver cycle on a dishwasher.

- Take shorter showers. If taking a bath, fill the tub with only a few inches of water.

- Contact a pollution-control agency or county extension agent for advice on how to dispose of hazardous household waste. Don't dump toxic substances, such as oil-based paints, paint thinners or solvents, cleaning fluids, or motor oil, on the ground or into storm sewers.

- Fix leaky faucets and toilets that run continuously. Even a small leak can waste gallons of water.

Using Building Materials Wisely

People have always used materials from the environment to construct their homes. Many of these materials, such as stone and metals, are nonrenewable. With the construction of 1 to 2 million new homes in the United States each year, some supplies of natural building materials are running out.

As discussed in Chapter 3, much can be done to conserve building material. When natural resources are processed into building material, by-products such as wood chips and sawdust can be used to make particleboard for flooring, shelves, and ready-to-assemble furniture.

For more efficient use of materials, builders can use plentiful materials in place of those that are scarce. Materials that are easier to process can be substituted for those more difficult to manufacture.

Recycled Building Materials

Recycling helps the environment. Many communities collect materials such as paper, aluminum, and glass or plastic containers, which can then be processed to make new products. Many building materials make use of recycled goods. See Fig. 12-13.

Fig. 12-13 Materials that are recycled don't add to the problem of overflowing landfill.

- Old newspapers can be made into material for subflooring, wall paneling, and insulation.
- Steel from old automobiles can be used for framing and roofs.
- Aluminum beverage cans can be processed into material for house frames.
- Glass bottles can be crushed and used to make brick, driveway pavement, and floor tile.
- Plastic soft-drink bottles can be made into polyester carpeting.
- Discarded car tires can be melted and mixed with crushed glass for driveway surfaces.
- Ashes can be used in making concrete.

- Clay soil contaminated with petroleum products (possibly from the ground around a gas station) can be used to make paving bricks.
- Old wooden doors can be remilled to make stair rails and hardwood floors.
- Door and window moldings can be constructed of recycled materials. One such material is made from wheat straw, newspaper, wood, and plastic. It is stronger and less expensive than wood, and it doesn't warp, split, or need painting.
- A lumberlike material for outdoor decks is made from plastic bags, industrial sawdust, and other wood waste. It needs no preservatives and won't crack, splinter, or rot.

Permeable Pavement

Green space around your home is not only attractive, but also helps the environment—especially when it rains. Seeping through soil rids rainwater of some impurities and slows its return to lakes and streams. However, water runs off pavement into a series of gutters and pipes. It arrives at waterways still carrying any pesticides, bacteria, and other contaminants it picked up along the way. The rush of water can cause erosion and flooding along banks and shores. These problems are apt to worsen as cities expand and more land is paved.

A partial solution may lie in permeable, or porous, pavement. *Permeable pavement* mimics soil in allowing water to trickle through.

For roads and driveways, the effect may be achieved by changing the paving material used. Porous concrete uses larger gravel and less water than conventional concrete. Porous asphalt contains less tar. For landscaping, decorative paving stones allow water to escape into the spaces between them.

Layering materials also improves drainage. The surface material may be laid over another porous substance, such as sand, gravel, or crushed limestone. A heavy-duty plastic lattice also gives support under gravel or clay that gets regular foot traffic and occasional wheeled traffic, such as fairgrounds.

Permeable pavement does have drawbacks. Porous concrete and asphalt are more expensive and require special maintenance. The pores must be kept clean, so permeable pavements are less useful in regions where wind or runoff from fields frequently deposits soil or dirt on the roads.

Tech Trends

Explore the future use of permeable pavements and other solutions to erosion. What are some design advantages and disadvantages of each solution?

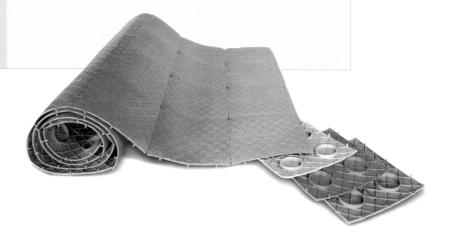

Outdoor Living

As people have developed more awareness of protecting the environment, they have also developed a greater appreciation of enjoying the environment. More and more people are finding that when good weather arrives they want to spend time outdoors. Outdoor living spaces have become extensions of a home's interior. By making good use of outdoor living spaces, people can even cut down on how much space they need inside their house.

Designing Outdoor Living Space

The first step is to consider the best place for an outdoor living space. Most people prefer outdoor living areas to be accessible easily from the home. Does the house design facilitate adding a large front porch or a porch that wraps around the side? What about a multilevel deck on a sloping building site? Some homes are ideal for a patio that extends off the main living area. Screened porches are popular in some areas of the country, and interior courtyards are found in many Southern and Southwestern homes.

Fig. 12-14 Adding a three-season porch can bring the outdoors in.

Just as when originally planning the house, designers create their plans for outdoor living areas based on the terrain of the site and how much space is available. They must consider where the house is on the lot, what people will see from the street, what household members will see from inside the house, where the active-use areas are, and the location of existing trees and shrubs. They spend time studying the sun and shade, wind and breeze, and sights and sounds.

Three- or four-season rooms are increasingly popular. See Fig. 12-14. These rooms are meant to be permanent. The walls feature lots of energy-efficient windows that can be opened for fresh air or closed to shut out the weather. Such rooms have doors leading to the main part of the home that can be left open or closed off.

Homeowners need to think about how the outdoor space will be used. In some cases, the homeowners want an area for casual entertaining. A brick fireplace or barbecue grill may be the main feature of the area. See Fig. 12-15. Some homeowners even go to the extent of adding an outdoor kitchen, which makes the most sense in parts of the country that remain warm most of the year. A family with small children might set aside an area for a swing set, sandbox, or playhouse. Sometimes people just desire a place to sit back and enjoy the fresh air.

Imagine the pleasure of sleeping outdoors on a breezy summer night. A screened-in porch can be an ideal fair weather bedroom. A couch or futon that easily turns into a bed provides comfortable seating during the day and a cozy bed at night.

Remember energy conservation for outdoor areas, too. Trees provide needed shade in the summer and good windbreaks in the winter. Shading the area also can be done by extending the roofline on the house or with awnings and umbrellas.

Fig. 12-15 More and more people are adding outdoor living areas to their homes and using them for casual entertainment.

Walls with screens may be added to define the space, or a fence may edge the space. For safety reasons, raised areas need railings. Wood or plastic lumber can be used here as well. Plantings and rocks can also be used to frame a space naturally.

Of course, seating will need to be provided. In some instances, seating is built into the deck design. Freestanding outdoor furniture is available in a wide variety of styles and price ranges. Look for materials that can withstand the use they will be given. For example, furniture that will be outdoors on an open patio needs to be more durable than pieces inside a covered porch.

When nighttime use of outdoor living spaces is desired, lighting can be added. Solar-powered lights work well in many cases. Electricity can be added to some spaces easily, or lights from the house may be directed to the outdoor living area. One final important aesthetic consideration for outdoor living areas, as well as the house, is the landscaping.

Constructing Outdoor Living Space

Once the outdoor living space is thoroughly planned, construction can begin. This can range from a simple concrete pad for a patio to an elaborate structure that would follow the same construction process as a house. See Fig. 12-16.

Flooring for a patio or interior courtyard could be concrete, brick, tile, or paving stones. Wood decks offer the homeowner a readily available and relatively simple way to create functional, pleasing outdoor features. Wood for outdoor space must withstand all kinds of weather as well as insect attacks. It must be strong and resist wear, splintering, and warping. Naturally decay-resistant woods are redwood, cypress, and western red cedar, but they are expensive. Treated lumber is more economical and is satisfactory for most projects. Pressure-treated wood is the best choice. Recycled plastic is an environmentally wise and economical choice as well. It is made to resemble wood and does not warp or rot.

Fig. 12-16 More homes are being designed with porches, decks, and patios to allow people to enjoy the outdoors.

Landscaping—The Finishing Touch

Landscaping refers to the ways people use plants and objects to enhance or change the natural environment around the exterior of their homes. Landscaping should be planned carefully. It needs to take into account the basic characteristics of the housing site.

The Purpose of Landscaping

Well-planned landscaping enhances the exterior appearance of the home and the outdoor living spaces. Landscaping can serve a variety of purposes. For example, it can enhance the privacy, safety, and beauty of a property. It can provide shade, block unpleasant sights and sounds, affect wind patterns, reduce maintenance, and provide areas for specific uses. **Figure 12-17** illustrates some landscaping ideas.

Landscaping plans are usually determined by the amount of space available and the needs and wants of members of the household. Most houses have plantings close to the building, which can make the house look more appealing. Landscaping around an outdoor living area increases its appeal. People who enjoy gardening might clear a sunny area with good soil for growing flowers and vegetables.

Designing the Landscape

Whether a landscape is designed by a professional or by homeowners, good planning is the key to a successful outcome. Here are some of the steps involved in planning a landscape design.

- Determine how much time will be spent taking care of landscaping. Areas that are orderly and elaborate require more time to keep looking attractive. Natural plantings require less time.
- Assess the site over a period of time. Observe and keep track of details, such as which areas get sun and shade at different times of year.
- Consider the needs, wants, and lifestyle of the residents.
- Sketch a plan that shows the general location of landscape features, such as existing and planned trees, hedges, patios, flower beds, and play areas.
- Choose specific varieties of plants. To do so, first identify the characteristics desired (for example, a low-growing, red flowering annual). Check gardening books and catalogs to find plants that match those characteristics and are suitable for the climate. Local plant nurseries and county extension offices can also help you learn which types will grow best in your area.

Fig. 12-18 Attractive landscaping can add a lot of visual appeal to a property, as well as extend the living space. **What natural elements are used in this landscape design?**

Using Natural Elements

Natural elements—whether found on the site or added—are a major part of most landscaping plans. They include materials such as soil and rock as well as various types of plants. **See Fig. 12-18.**

Soil and type of terrain are basic features a landscaper must begin with. Landscapers can either work with the existing terrain, or they can alter the terrain to make it more attractive. Soil containing the right nutrients and the correct balance of sand, silt, and clay encourages plant growth. Landscapers who work with soil that lacks these qualities must fertilize the ground or look for other ways to enhance the land.

Fig. 12-17

Landscape Planning

A Visual Guide

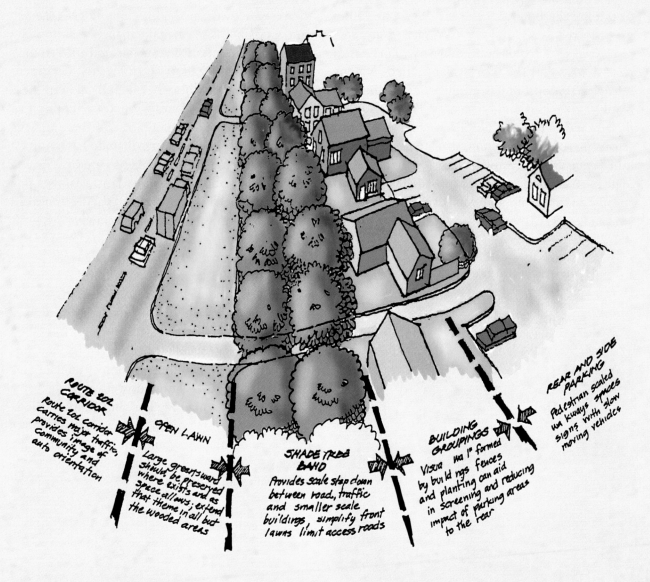

Route 202 Corridor. Route 202 corridor carries major traffic, provides image of community and auto orientation.

Open Lawn. Large greensward should be preserved where exists and as space allows; extend that theme in all but the wooded areas.

Shade Tree Band. Provides scale step down between road, traffic and smaller scale buildings; simplify front lawns; limit access roads.

Building Groupings. Visual "wall" formed by buildings; fences and planting can aid in screening and reducing impact of parking areas to the rear.

Rear and Side Parking. Pedestrian scaled walkways, spaces, signs with slow moving vehicles.

Trees and shrubs can serve to accent the landscape design and provide natural shade. Depending on the type, trees may also provide flowers, fruit, fall color, or winter greenery. When planted in rows, trees and shrubs can serve as a natural privacy fence or outline the boundaries of specific areas within the property.

Flowers add color and beauty to a landscaped area. **See Fig. 12-19.** They can be planted in beds along hillsides, around borders of lawns, or in pots and planters on patios and courtyards. Flowers vary in the amount of care they need. Some flowers, called *perennials*, continue to bloom year after year. Others, called *annuals*, must be planted each season. The climate of an environment affects whether you should add flowers to a site and your decision about the kind of flowers to plant.

Groundcovers include grasses and various types of low-growing plants. Grass is the most common groundcover. Some grasses are suited to particular climates. In dry areas, having grass lawns is not ecologically sound since watering is required. Certain grasses grow well in shade, while others need full sun. Grass needs more maintenance than do other groundcovers. Vines, woody plants, and other groundcovers are perennials. Depending on the variety, groundcovers may bloom with tiny flowers, lose their leaves, or sprout cones. Groundcovers other than grass are often used in shady areas or where mowing is difficult. Choose plantings that are natural to an area because they will require less watering.

You might not think of rock as a landscaping element, but it has many uses. Flat paving stones can be used to form walkways or a decorative driveway. Small colorful rocks can keep weeds out of planting beds. Large rocks can serve as accents in a landscape design. Rock gardens are attractive and easy to maintain. In dry climates, combinations of rock and native plants are a popular—and often necessary—alternative to grassy lawns.

Don't overlook the possibilities of edible landscaping. Popular plantings include fruit and nut trees, strawberries as groundcover, and blueberry bushes. Consider planting for wildlife, too, such as birds, squirrels, and other small animals. Contact the extension office in your county or a local plant nursery for tips on which edible landscaping varieties grow best in your area.

Fig. 12-19 Many homeowners enjoy planting flowers and tending to their yards.

Fig. 12-20 Lighting can make a house look more attractive by illuminating landscaping and structural features.

Using Manufactured Elements

Few landscape designs rely exclusively on natural elements. Manufactured elements such as fences and walkways often play a role in design.

Fences are used for decoration as well as privacy. Several types of fences are available, but two of the most popular are the *picket fence* and the *rail fence*. A picket fence is made of small vertical stakes held together by horizontal bars at the bottom and near the top. A rail fence is made of horizontal boards or bars supported by vertical posts.

Walkways and footpaths help define the space by adding a framework, and they make moving around a landscaped yard easy. Railroad ties, paving stones, and bricks are popular choices.

Outdoor lighting can have two purposes. It's a practical way to add beauty to a yard or common area. Certain types of lights can also provide safety and security at night. Low-voltage, solar, or spotlights can illuminate flowers and plants. Lights on stairs and along walkways help prevent falls. Spotlights— some motion-activated—can add to the security of entrances, garages, and outdoor areas. **See Fig. 12-20.**

Hiring a Landscaper

Hiring a landscaper is like finding a dentist. You can read ads in the phone book or newspaper, but they can't tell you how comfortable or confident you will feel with that person. You need to do some detective work. What facts do you need? Whom do you ask? The process starts at home.

Identify Your Goals. You may not know exactly what is doable given your budget, but define your ideas as specifically as possible. If you want a stone patio, choose a color and an approximate size. That will help the landscaper suggest certain types of paver stones and estimate the job.

Prepare Yourself. Learn what to expect from people who have professional contact with landscapers. Workers at nurseries and home improvement stores can suggest standard questions to ask a landscaper— whether the landscaper replaces plants that die, for instance.They often know which individuals and companies have a good reputation. Neighbors who have used landscapers can describe their satisfaction with the work and overall impression of the service.

Narrow the Field. To identify the most promising candidates, ask relevant questions, such as how committed are they to sustainable design. Also be sure the landscaper is qualified for the job. Adding an in-ground sprinkler system, for example, takes an irrigation specialist.

Landscaping to Save Water

Landscaping to conserve water is called **xeriscaping** (ZIHR-uh-skay-ping). The key is choosing plants that are native to a geographic area or to another region with a similar climate. These plants need extra watering the first year, but once established, they thrive on nothing more than natural rainfall. Here are some other water conservation tips.

- **Water early or late.** If you must water lawn and garden, do so in the early morning or in the evening to reduce evaporation.

- **Choose locations of plants carefully.** Plants that are sheltered from strong winds and glaring sun need less water.

- **Keep only a small lawn area.** Lawn grass soaks up water like a sponge. It needs more water and more pesticides than most other plants,

and it requires more maintenance. For an open look, try wildflowers or prairie grasses instead. Groundcovers, such as vinca and pachysandra, look invitingly green and are easy to care for. Include decks and patios as part of the landscaping to reduce mowing and watering.

- **Keep grass long.** If you do have a patch of lawn, don't mow it too short. Taller (3-inch [7.6-cm]) grass blades shade the ground and reduce evaporation of soil moisture. They also develop deeper root systems that use water more efficiently.

- **Don't overfertilize.** Too much fertilizer makes plants need watering more often.

- **Avoid using sprinklers.** About half the water from a sprinkler evaporates before it ever touches the ground. A soaker hose or drip irrigation system works more effectively.

You & the Environment

Housing and the environment can work together. Architects and builders can create successful, energy-efficient housing with methods and materials that do not harm the earth. People can make their homes energy efficient by using alternative energy sources, installing better insulation, sealing ducts, and purchasing equipment that works more efficiently. They can also conserve energy and water in many ways in their daily lives. Thought, planning, and access to environmentally friendly materials and methods can enable people to respect the environment while retaining the quality of life they want. See Fig. 12-21.

These steps can also increase the comfort of the people living in the home. Energy-efficient appliances that run more quietly cut down on unpleasant noise. Lower fuel costs increase the share of a family's income available for other uses. Longer-lasting ENERGY STAR appliances that require fewer repairs mean people can enjoy an uninterrupted use of the equipment. Creating outdoor living areas and landscaping increase comfort too. These spaces encourage people to enjoy the fresh air, and gardening can be good exercise that helps people stay fit.

Fig. 12-21 Solar systems are one example of environmentally friendly materials and methods that enable us to live in harmony with the Earth. **What landscaping practices could be used to add to this home's appeal while maintaining the environment?**

Profile of a Landscape Architect

Landscape architects design projects and conduct impact studies to ensure building and recreational space is used safely and well. Projects can be as basic as creating "green space" within an industrial complex or as exotic as designing the landscaping for a resort or wildlife refuge.

Education & Training

- A bachelor's degree, including an internship, is required. Master's degrees are desirable for areas of specialization.
- Licensing is required in most states. Contact the Council of Landscape Architectural Registration Board for more information.
- Courses include surveying, CAD, site design and construction, and ecology and environmental science.

Skills & Aptitudes

- Communication and presentation skills are essential.
- The ability to draft and design using CAD software is essential.
- Strong analytical skills, along with artistic talent, help landscape architects look for the right plantings for a site.

Landscape Architect
Grant Shepherd

Landscape architects help others enjoy life. That's how I see my job. We use our hands and our heads to analyze an outdoor space, and then we create and present a design project for approval and implement the final plan. The goal is to give our clients a usable outdoor space that they will want to be in.

My interest in landscaping started in high school when I took part in a volunteer project to improve the grounds of a nursing home. We removed litter and planted trees, shrubs, and flowers. We put in safe walkways so the residents could enjoy time outdoors. It was great to see people take a renewed interest in their surroundings.

That experience—along with the yard work I did to earn money for college—helped me realize that what's outside the home matters too. I chose a university with a strong landscape architecture program that included lots of emphasis on CAD design.

My internship with a state agency gave me experience with the whole range of work that landscape architects do, and I decided that this was the career for me. We had to redesign a park campground. We visited the site time and again to analyze the land. We took soil and plant samples and met with contractors. CAD drawings helped us visualize and convey plans for new roadways, camping areas, hiking trails, and scenic views.

Many landscape architects are self-employed, but I work for an engineering firm that offers landscape services. The projects people hire us for are many and varied. Some of my colleagues are busy creating the landscaping for a proposed shopping center. Others are designing a golf course. I've worked on single-family homes in a new subdivision and indoor gardens in a downtown high-rise.

As I've worked in the field, I've realized just how important "people skills" are in my work. One thing we have to do is to help clients figure out what they want. We also have to work closely and smoothly with other professionals including architects, engineers, contractors, urban planners, and environmental scientists.

Design Portfolio

1. Take a walking tour of a local business or retail district to study landscape design. Sketch out the design. Then create a second version of your drawing showing what you would change. Explain why you would make those changes.

2. Design the backyard garden of a single-family home in your climate zone.

Chapter Summary

- **Resource management** is important in home design and daily life.
- ENERGY STAR homes and equipment conserve energy.
- Each energy source has advantages and disadvantages.
- A home can gain energy efficiency through choices made in design and construction.
- **Retrofitting** can cut energy needs of an existing home.
- Water, a vital resource, needs to be conserved as well.
- Recycled materials reduce waste and save resources.
- Outdoor living areas can extend a home's interior.
- **Landscaping** can improve a home's outside environment.

Checking Your Understanding

1. Why is **resource management** important?
2. What are two simple steps people can take to reduce energy use in the home?
3. What are two features of ENERGY STAR rated homes?
4. What are three traditional energy sources, and what is a disadvantage of each?
5. Why is the use of hydroelectric and nuclear power unlikely to grow in the future?
6. Why is a geothermal heat pump an energy-efficient device?
7. Why will resource management be even more important in designing the future?
8. Give two examples of energy-conserving design choices appropriate for a new home in a warm climate.
9. What are two steps that can be taken to use less water?
10. What are two examples of recycled building materials?
11. Identify three purposes that **landscaping** can serve.
12. What is **xeriscaping**? In what parts of the country might it be especially important?

Thinking Critically

1. **Analyzing Information.** Identify three criteria you think are important in evaluating energy sources. Analyze these sources—natural gas, coal, hydroelectric power, nuclear power, geothermal power, solar power, wind power—and determine which you think is superior. Explain why.

2. **Suggesting Solutions.** The owner of a 40-year-old home complains about rising energy bills. What steps would you recommend for cutting those costs?

3. **Synthesizing Information.** How is conservation related to comfort? Explain this in a brief essay.

Applying Your Knowledge

1. **Analyzing Materials.** Look around your classroom at the walls, ceiling, floor, windows, and door(s). Identify what material you think is used in each. Then suggest what type of recycled material or energy-efficient product could be used to replace it.

2. **Energy-Efficient Homes and Products.** Choose an energy-efficient product that has been used in, or would be suitable for, housing in your area. Identify the advantages and disadvantages of the product.

3. **Planning a Family Room.** Plan a family room for a home in a cold climate. Identify the exterior and interior features you would include to make the room energy efficient. Explain why each feature would help achieve that goal.

4. **Thinking about the Future.** Use print or Internet sources to research an energy conservation issue likely to arise in the future concerning home design. Report your findings.

5. **Outdoor Living Spaces.** Assume you work for a design firm specializing in outdoor designs. Use print or Internet sources to find images showing different outdoor living spaces. Create a brochure aimed at potential clients that includes the images plus descriptive text.

Design Challenge

A client of your landscaping firm wants to include a deck or patio plus a mix of trees, bushes, and flowers to her backyard. She wants to incorporate a variety of colors and textures. Her home is in central North Carolina, so the plants chosen should be suitable to that climate.

1. Write down what additional questions you would need to have answered before designing the plan. Then, take the role of the client and answer those questions.

2. Research plant materials that fit the client's criteria.

3. Draw a landscape design that includes an overhead view and at least two ground-level elevations.

4. List the materials you chose to include and explain why each is appropriate.

5. Include the finished design in your design portfolio.

Chapter 13

Remodeling & Renovating

Objectives

- Identify possible reasons for remodeling a home.

- Identify points to consider when deciding whether to remodel.

- Give examples of various types of remodeling projects.

- Summarize the components of a remodeling project.

- Describe how to select a contractor.

- Compare professional remodeling with do-it-yourself remodeling.

Vocabulary

- remodeling
- renovation
- restoration
- conversion
- setback
- variance
- home equity loan
- performance bond
- bid
- contract

Deciding to remodel a home is a much bigger decision than deciding to redecorate. Redecorating—painting rooms a different color, replacing drapes with blinds, or rearranging the furniture—will give the home a new look. Such changes don't, however, affect the structure of the home. Remodeling is much more time-consuming and costly. A successful remodeling project requires careful planning.

Reasons for Remodeling

Any project that involves changes to a home's structure or systems can be considered **remodeling**. This can include knocking down walls to make two small bedrooms into one larger room or building a breakfast nook off the kitchen. It includes changing basic systems to make them more energy efficient and finishing a basement.

Change is often both the cause of remodeling and its result. As people's lifestyles and levels of physical ability change, their housing needs also change. Families become larger or smaller, requiring adaptations in the home. Some homeowners want more storage space; others need more bedrooms or an updated kitchen. **See Fig. 13-1.**

Fig. 13-1 This kitchen remodeling project shows how a new design can update and transform a room.

Fig. 13-2 Sometimes a home is sold as a "fixer-upper," and the new owners are people who enjoy tackling a variety of jobs from a fresh coat of paint to major renovation.

Some homeowners remodel just before putting their home on the market, hoping to increase the home's value. Because certain features such as an updated bath or kitchen can increase the sale price, these rooms are popular choices for this type of remodeling. Keep in mind that the costs of other remodeling projects, such as adding a sunroom, may not be completely recouped by a higher selling price.

Remodeling Versus Buying

Remodeling is one option when an existing house no longer meets its owners' needs and wants. Buying or building a new home is another possibility. There are several factors to consider when deciding whether to move or to remodel.

Costs. The expense of remodeling should be weighed against the cost of moving. Moving costs are estimated to be at least 8 to 10 percent of a home's value. If owners can make the changes they want for around this amount, they will save money by not moving.

The length of time you plan to stay in the home should be considered. Many housing experts suggest that many remodeling projects are not a worthwhile financial investment if the owners plan to move within two years. Remodeling kitchens and baths are usually an exception to this rule. They are likely to immediately add enough to the home's resale value to equal the costs involved. On the other hand, finishing a basement may have only a 15 percent payback over time.

Still another consideration is taxes. Property taxes are based on a home's value, which generally increases with remodeling. Therefore, the homeowner who remodels will probably face a higher yearly property tax bill. On the other hand, buying or building may also result in increased taxes. If budget is to be the deciding factor, it's important to get accurate tax estimates for all options.

Convenience. Many homeowners choose to remodel because they are pleased with the home except for its few flaws. The home may be convenient to a school or job or be in a desirable neighborhood. It may be simpler to remodel than to go through the inconvenience of moving. With careful planning, homeowners can remodel their homes to get the new features they want without losing the features they already have.

Commitment. Finally, homeowners must decide whether they are willing to put in the time and energy needed to complete a project. Thinking about commitment is even more important if the homeowners will do the work themselves. Then they must be prepared for weeks or months of work as well as for major disruption. **See Fig. 13-2.** Remodeling can be messy and disorderly while the work is being done. It's important to anticipate the stress caused by changes in daily routines. Add in hours of research and planning, attention to such matters, and concerns about liability for injury to workers.

Types of Remodeling Projects

Remodeling projects can be categorized as one of four types: changing a lived-in area, making unused space livable, adding on, and buying to remodel. Each type of project has a different cost, amount of time required for completion, and complexity of work required.

Changing a Lived-in Area

Changing a lived-in area involves altering space that is already occupied. Most projects of this type involve kitchens and bathrooms. In a kitchen, new cabinets might be installed, appliances moved, or a door closed off to provide more wall space. In a bathroom, a skylight could be cut in the ceiling or new fixtures installed. Other lived-in areas can also be remodeled. For example, a wall might be removed between the living room and dining room to make a large open area.

Remodeling a lived-in area usually involves less complex changes than the other types of remodeling, but inconvenience is greater. Often rooms being worked on are unusable at least part of the time.

Making Unused Space Livable

Unfinished areas of a home—such as an attic, basement, porch, or attached garage—may be remodeled. See Fig. 13-3. These spaces have a roof, walls, and floor but may need further structural work to make them livable. For example, the foundation under a garage or porch may not meet the requirements of the local building code.

Insulation, heating, wiring, plumbing, and lighting may also be required. Basements can be gloomy if there's no access to natural light. Even with extensive changes such as these, it is usually less expensive to remodel the spaces than to add rooms to a house.

Fig. 13-3 Finishing a basement to create work space or a recreational area is a popular remodeling project.

Fig. 13-4 Extra space on a lot may be used to add a room onto a home.

Adding On

Another type of remodeling consists of adding one or more rooms to an existing home. **See Fig. 13-4.** Adding on includes enlarging a room. Early in the planning stage, the homeowner should check local zoning laws. Many contain restrictions on the size and placement of home additions. When there's not enough space on the property for a ground-level addition, a second-story addition may be the answer.

Adding on is more complex than altering space already built. To add on to a home, a foundation must usually be dug or a slab laid and exterior walls removed. Sometimes walls that are removed contain plumbing or electrical wiring that must be relocated. For a second-story addition, the roof must be removed and replaced. A stairway may also need to be constructed.

The addition must be carefully planned to blend architecturally with the existing house. If additional doors and windows are added, they should match the style of the rest of the home, to keep the exterior consistent. How the addition connects to the existing rooms should also be given some thought. Placing a bedroom adjoining a noisy family room, for instance, may not be a good choice.

Buying to Remodel

Some people buy an older home in need of repair because they plan to repair and modernize it. The process of extensively repairing and modernizing a home is called **renovation**. When searching for a home to renovate, look for one that has a sound basic structure. A home with a sound structure, though in need of repair, can gain value that will exceed the cost of the renovation. **Restoration** is a type of renovation in which an older home is returned to its original state.

Another type of major remodeling is **conversion** —buying a building for the purpose of converting it or changing its use. An example is a large single-family house converted to a duplex; another is a warehouse converted to loft apartments.

In some urban areas, old, run-down houses are sold at low cost by the government. The owners agree to make repairs within a certain period of time. In many cases, low-interest loans are made available to finance the cost of these repairs. With such programs, old neighborhoods are rehabilitated and preserved. These programs also make it possible for people with a small or modest housing budget to afford a comfortable home.

Adaptive Reuse

In commercial design, *adaptive reuse* means converting older buildings for a new use while retaining their historical features. Two main factors help convince preservationists, community officials, and financial investors to undertake adaptive reuse.

First, the building must be structurally sound, although renovation to meet modern standards may be needed. Second, the intended use must fit the neighborhood and be welcomed by the neighbors. For example, when the Allentown Public Library in Allentown, Pa. wanted to move into a 19th-century church building on the same street, the idea had wide community support. The adaptation included replacing basement timbers with concrete columns.

The United States Department of the Interior standards regarding adaptive reuse projects include:

- **A building can be used for its original purpose, or a new purpose that requires little or no change to its historical features.** For example, the Los Angeles Union Station, once a train station, has been preserved as an Art-Deco, Spanish-style hub for bus, trolley, and commuter rail lines.

- **Changes in the property that have become part of its history must remain.** Suppose a Civil War-era home was partly rebuilt in the Queen Anne style after a fire in the 1900s. Any reuse would have to respect both architectural styles.

- **Distinctive construction and design features must be preserved.** The new Allentown Library kept the old church balcony. The light fixtures, paint colors, and furniture all reflect the structure's 19th-century roots.

- **Only the gentlest cleaning methods may be used on the building.** Sandblasting, chemical treatments, and other destructive procedures are forbidden.

- **New construction is permitted only if it can be added and removed without damaging the original property.**

Apply It!

Imagine that residents of a rural community wanted to save a 1920s era hotel on the town square. What uses might be successful options? What concerns should be addressed before tackling adaptive reuse?

Planning a Project

A home remodeling or renovation project is a major undertaking that can bring great satisfaction. See Fig. 13-5. However, it also has the potential for equally large problems. The project may be delayed when materials or workers do not arrive on time. Unexpected work may need to be done, adding to the cost of the project. Bad weather may cause delays. Even worse, the homeowner may be dissatisfied with the finished work. Problems will be greatly reduced if the remodeling project is well planned and carefully organized ahead of time.

Fig. 13-5 The kitchen in the upper photo was remodeled. The lower photo shows the result. **What updates give this kitchen a more spacious appearance?**

Evaluating the Area

Before beginning a complex remodeling job, homeowners should evaluate the area to be remodeled. If a new foundation is to be dug for an addition, the utility companies should mark the location of existing underground wires and pipes. If an existing area is being converted, it needs to be examined to make sure it is suitable for the desired changes. A contractor, structural engineer, or architect should check it to make sure it can support the new addition or equipment.

Plumbing, heating, and wiring should also be checked. If these systems will need updating soon, it may be more convenient and less costly to do the upgrade during the remodeling process. When adding rooms to the home, homeowners need to know whether the existing plumbing, heating, and electrical systems will be adequate after the job is done.

Awareness of structural and systems problems is particularly important for older homes. People who are planning to purchase an older home to remodel or renovate should make sure the foundation and structure are sound. Many prospective homeowners hire engineering inspection firms to check a home for structural problems. A professional can also advise a buyer about the age and efficiency of the home's plumbing, heating, and electrical systems. If the home isn't sound to begin with, remodeling might cost too much to make it a worthwhile investment.

Deciding on Design Goals

Homeowners often begin a remodeling project without a clear idea of what they want done. As a result, they're easily swayed by the preferences of designers and contractors. These homeowners may end up with a living space that doesn't suit them. Doing some advance research can help homeowners identify their preferences.

Some good sources of ideas are home decorating and remodeling magazines. People considering remodeling should clip pictures of materials, styles, equipment, and arrangements they like. It's also a good idea to clip things that are *not* acceptable. Put both types of information in a resource file.

Such files help people communicate their ideas to a designer or a contractor. In addition, a resource file allows members of the household to show each other how they envision the remodeled space. See Fig. 13-6.

Using the four-step process that follows will help further define goals for the project.

1. Examine the present home layout and identify any problems.

2. Analyze the family's habits in using the home as well as their design preferences.

3. Use the information gathered in Steps 1 and 2 to draw up a list of remodeling goals.

4. Consider all possible options for meeting the goals. Think through each potential decision before finalizing the choice of design.

These points must be established before moving forward into the next areas of project planning. Figure 13-7 on page 311 shows how one family worked through this process to establish kitchen remodeling goals.

Fig. 13-6 A remodeling project has a higher satisfaction rate when the whole family participates in major decisions.

Fig. 13-7

Kitchen Remodeling Goals

A Visual Guide

Julia and Michael Parker liked everything about their house except the kitchen. Last year they decided to remodel. To help organize their goals for the remodeling project, they worked their way through the following steps:

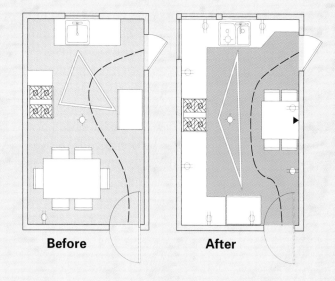

Before   **After**

Step 1—**Examine the Present Layout and Identify Problems** The Parkers measured the kitchen and drew a floor plan to scale on a piece of graph paper. The floor plan included the dimensions of the kitchen and the location of all receptacles, switches, furniture, and appliances. Studying the floor plan helped the Parkers identify the following problems:

- Work triangle—refrigerator to sink to range—is interrupted by the traffic between the two doors.
- Not enough electrical receptacles.
- Kitchen table is the only available work space for preparing food.
- Not enough storage space for kitchen items.
- Sink is too small.

Step 2—**Analyze Habits and Preferences** By thinking about how they wanted to use the kitchen, the Parkers made the following list:

- Want to eat most meals in the kitchen.
- Want to be able to look out the window while working at the sink.
- Want to use back door to enter and exit home.

Step 3—**List Remodeling Goals** The Parkers used their list of problems and preferences to draw up a list of remodeling goals.

Step 4—**Consider Possible Options and Make Decisions** The Parkers made another floor plan of just the room area. They made templates to help them try out ideas. For each remodeling goal, they tried out possible options before making a final decision. The result was a well-defined plan they could take to a building contractor.

Remodeling Goals	Considerations	Decisions
Eat-in kitchen	Space taken up by table and chairs needed for work triangle.	Build a low eating counter with four stools between the two doors.
Larger sink, under a window	Relocating water pipes would be costly.	Install new double sink in place of current sink.
Eliminate traffic from work triangle	Avoid placing appliances between the doors; three walls remain.	Change basic design of kitchen to U-shaped.
Add cabinet and counter space	Putting standard-size cabinets on the wall next to the outside door would block the entryway.	Install cabinets under the new countertops to maximize storage.
Add electrical receptacles	Need for major appliances as well as small ones.	Add receptacles for appliances and at regular intervals.

Checking Local Regulations

Homeowners should know about any zoning regulations or aesthetic codes that will affect the planned remodeling job. If they proceed without proper approvals from the local government, they may have to pay a fine or even tear down an addition or make other exterior changes. **See Fig. 13-8.**

As you will learn in Chapter 16, zoning laws and aesthetic codes in a community regulate the types of structures that may be built and the appearance of their exteriors. In some cases, zoning laws limit how much of a building lot may be occupied by a structure. They also define **setback**, or the distance any part of a building must be from the property line. If remodeling plans do not meet zoning requirements, the homeowner may have to apply for a variance. A **variance** is a license to waive the zoning law. It is a time-consuming process, so many people prefer to change their plans.

Homeowners should find out whether they need a building permit for their proposed job. **See Fig. 13-9.** A building permit is required for any alterations that affect the framework, size, or safety of the building. Inspections may also be necessary to ensure that the remodeling meets the building codes. As you will read in Chapter 16, building codes establish minimum standards for construction in an area. Most often, national codes—such as the Uniform Building Code, National Electrical Code, and Uniform Plumbing Code—are followed.

Fig. 13-8 A good contractor makes sure that a project meets all national and local regulations, thereby saving the homeowner time, money, and potential headaches.

Deciding About Financing

Some remodeling jobs are costly. A home improvement loan may be needed to meet expenses. Many people finance their remodeling projects by taking out a home equity loan. A **home equity loan** is money borrowed from a lending institution based on the current market value of a property, minus the amount owed on the mortgage. A competitive interest rate can often be obtained with these loans. A drawback of this type of loan is that if the homeowners cannot repay the loan, the home may be taken by the bank and sold for payment of the loan.

When obtaining a loan, homeowners should shop around to find the best rate of interest. They also need to know the length of the waiting period before approval of a loan. Waiting for money can affect the building schedule. When homeowners are calculating the costs of their projects, it is often recommended that they include an additional 20 percent in the budget to cover unforeseen costs.

Fig. 13-9 Local building codes may require a building permit before construction begins. The permit must be displayed during the project and inspections may also be necessary. **How do building codes affect the quality of homes in an area?**

Hiring Professionals

Professional designers, architects, general contractors, and subcontractors can help with a remodeling project. Homeowners should choose these professionals carefully.

Designers

Interior designers, kitchen planners, and other design professionals translate people's ideas into concrete plans. They draw up floor plans done to scale. Designers may also suggest ways to improve a plan submitted by the homeowner. In addition to planning projects, some designers and architects supervise the entire construction process.

A good way to find a designer is to ask for referrals from friends and relatives who have had remodeling done. Listings of local designers are available from professional associations such as the American Society of Interior Designers.

Homeowners should check the designer's portfolio, which contains photographs and descriptions of completed projects. If possible, it is often informative to visit the homes of clients for whom the designer has completed projects. See Fig. 13-10.

Fig. 13-10 Check the references of the professionals you are considering hiring for a project.

Contractors

Finding an experienced, reputable contractor is crucial to the success of a remodeling project. The National Association of the Remodeling Industry offers information on selecting a professional remodeling contractor. Other sources of referrals are friends and relatives, lumberyard managers, plumbing dealers, and other suppliers. The state licensing board and Better Business Bureau are other sources of information.

Questions to Ask. There's important legal information you should find out before hiring a specific contractor for the job. Ask such questions as:

- Does the contractor carry liability insurance? If not, and an accident takes place on your property, you are liable.

- Does the contractor carry the appropriate workers' compensation? *Workers' compensation* is a payment into an insurance fund which compensates, or pays, employees for injuries they suffer on the job.

- Does the contractor have the proper credentials to work in your state? Some states require a license.

- Is a permit needed for the job? If a permit is needed, who will obtain it?

It's wise to find out whether performance bonds are required in your area. A **performance bond** is a sum of money a contractor puts up to provide insurance that a job will be completed. For example, a community might require that a contractor working on a large job post a bond; then, if that contractor fails to finish the job, the performance bond covers the cost of completion.

Checking References. Asking questions of the contractor is a good start, but the contractor's references should be checked with others. Ask the contractor for business and bank references. Determine how long the contractor has been in business. In addition, it's important to visit homes at which the contractor has done work.

Request a list of previous clients for reference. Visit some of the homes your contractor has worked on. You'll probably want to ask the clients such questions as:

- Was the contractor easy to work with?
- Was concern shown for the client and property?
- Was the job completed on time?
- Were the workers easy to deal with?
- Did they do a good job?
- Were there any safety problems on the site? (OSHA regulations are meant to protect workers.)

During your visit, ask the client to point out examples of the contractor's work. Examine the quality of the work. Look at architectural elements. Is the placement of the doors and windows good? Are elements such as cabinets square and level? Look at construction details. Does the drywall or plaster have a finished look? Is the wood grain smooth? Look at the joints. Are they tightly mitered? Are the materials quality ones? Does the overall space give you a sense of a good design and workmanship?

Bids and Contracts. Contractors submit bids for projects. A **bid** is an offer from a contractor to complete a project for a certain price. The bid states the work to be done and estimates the cost of labor and materials. To make the bid, the contractor uses the homeowner's plans and any specifications from the designer or architect.

A homeowner should get bids from three separate contractors for a remodeling project. The lowest bid is not always the best choice. The bids must be compared carefully to be sure nothing was omitted from any bid that would affect cost. Experienced contractors will be able to estimate the total cost of a project quite closely.

After choosing the contractor, the homeowner and the contractor should sign a contract before any work begins. The **contract** is *a legally binding agreement* that states what work the contractor will do and the amount the homeowner will pay. The contract also lists the date work is to begin and when it is expected to end. It may also include details on the materials that will be used, including the brand and model number for appliances and fixtures. If subcontractors are to be used, their responsibilities should be clearly spelled out. The homeowner's obligation to them, should the contractor fail to pay, should also be detailed.

Once a contract has been signed, the contractor must complete the work for the specified amount, even though the finished project may actually cost more or less than this amount. If either party breaks the agreement, legal action may be taken.

Acrymax Roof Coatings

A valuable antique that needs extra protection might be put under glass. That's not an option for the roof of an older home—or is it? A line of coating products, sold under the trade name Acrymax®, offers a chemical version of a glass case for metal roofs. As the name suggests, Acrymax liquid coatings are based on acrylic, an oil-derived product known for standing up against harsh weather. Even steel, aluminum, tin, and other types of metal are prone to damage from intense heat, severe cold, sea salt, and acid rain. For roofs in good repair, two or three applications of Acrymax provide weatherproofing.

Badly aged roofs get a sandwich of protection—a layer of high-strength fabric added between the acrylic layers. The fabric fibers consist of a polyester core wrapped in nylon, lending elasticity and durability. The fabric expands and contracts with heat and cold. In fact, depending on the products used and the outdoor temperature, the Acrymax system can stretch from 50 to 150 percent of its original dimensions.

Looking at a roof preserved or restored with Acrymax products, you probably wouldn't know you weren't seeing the original construction. The entire process adds no more than about 1 mm (0.045 inches) in thickness. The coatings come in a variety of colors, which can be blended to create an authentic appearance.

Tech Trends

Research another type of engineered, or synthetic, roofing material that imitates traditional roofs. How is the product made? How is it used to reinforce or cover the original roof material?

Some contractors prefer to work on a time and materials basis, which means they get an hourly rate. Homeowners are at a disadvantage with this system because they're not sure at the outset what the total cost of the project will be. A better arrangement is a contract that divides the project into stages and pays the contractor a percentage of the total cost at completion of each stage. Be wary of contractors who demand large amounts of money before they begin work.

When the job begins, it's to the homeowner's advantage to establish a good working relationship with the contractor. Keeping the channels of communication open is essential. The homeowner should oversee the various steps of the project, especially when building inspections are being made. That way, there is less chance that the homeowner will be surprised or disappointed.

Planning the Schedule

Deciding when to do a remodeling project can have a great impact on its outcome. Avoid starting a large-scale remodeling job near a major holiday season or after a significant change in your life. The season of the year may be a factor as well. In a northern climate, late fall or winter is not a good time to start an addition to a house. An exposed exterior wall or roof could greatly increase heating costs. On the other hand, winter is a slow time for construction. Some contractors are willing to do jobs for less money just to keep busy.

It's also very important that you order all materials well in advance of the starting date. Delivery of custom-made kitchen cabinets, for example, can take four to six months. If materials aren't on hand when needed, costly delays may result.

 Consumer Considerations

Living Through Remodeling

Anyone who has remodeled can admit to experiencing some stress. Things do go wrong. Since most people are living in the home during remodeling, the place that is normally a haven may become a noisy, chaotic mess. Developing a good working relationship with the professionals to whom you have entrusted the job can make it less trying and more enjoyable—for you and for them.

Prepare for the Work. You can do a few things to help the project start off smoothly. Have duplicate keys made for the contractor. Clear out space for the supplies. Make sure the materials that arrive are the ones you ordered. If not, notify the contractor so they can be replaced as soon as possible.

Respect Safety Rules. A remodeling project is a construction zone. It may be filled with hazards both recognizable and hidden —from exposed wires to wet paint. Respect the workers' instructions and requests about your safety and theirs.

Take an Interest. Skilled tradespeople are expert in their field. If approached at the right time, they may be happy to share useful, interesting information about your home's inner workings. They can answer questions that might otherwise cause concern—for example, how long you'll be without water while they install a new bathtub. Understanding their work also helps you appreciate their talents.

Keep Things in Perspective. If the job seems to drag on and you're growing impatient, remember that you're getting a new and improved home. That's a goal worth waiting for!

Doing the Work Yourself

People who do their own remodeling or renovating can save about half of what the project would cost if it were done by professionals. Also, many people take pride in being able to do the work themselves. See Fig. 13-11.

A disadvantage of doing the work yourself is that the project will probably take longer to finish. This means that your home and family life will be disrupted for a longer period of time. Also, taking care of all aspects of the project may be more complicated than expected. You must obtain permits and schedule inspections, jobs normally done by the contractor. You'll also have to buy materials and fixtures, and you won't get the professional discount that contractors often receive. Some homeowners choose to hire professionals to do the complex work and then do the finishing work themselves.

Whether they hire a contractor or do it themselves, homeowners who plan well in advance, stay within budget, and stay involved are usually well satisfied with their new living space. The benefits—more room, updated or personalized fixtures, and increased housing value—outweigh the disadvantages.

Fig. 13-11 For homeowners with the time and the skills, doing remodeling and renovating projects themselves is a great way to save money and get the results they want.

Profile of a
Home Remodeling Specialist

A home remodeling specialist oversees home improvement projects. The planning is often done in collaboration with construction trade and design professionals. The specialist has to estimate costs, gather the appropriate materials, and work with the client and workers to see that the remodeling project is done on time and on budget.

Education & Training

- Experience as a construction worker or completion of an apprenticeship program is required.
- An advanced degree in construction is desirable since some projects call for specialized knowledge.

Skills & Aptitudes

- Knowing how to read blueprints, organize construction tasks into logical steps, follow building codes, and work with different materials is essential.
- Supervisory skills are important since the specialist must direct the work of contractors and make sure that work meets standards for quality.
- Good communication skills help the specialist work smoothly with homeowners and professionals.

Home Remodeling Specialist
Hector Emeralde

Who would have thought that I'd ever be running a business of my own? But that's exactly what I'm doing. As home remodeling specialists, my partner and I help people make their dreams come true.

It all started back in high school when I helped my family remodel our basement. We wanted to divide the unfinished area into a family room and a laundry/utility room. We drew up plans and hired people to check the foundation, seal the walls and floors, do the wiring, and put up the drywall. Then the whole family painted, hung wallpaper, and laid flooring. When we were done, we all felt a lot of pride.

After graduating from high school, I started working in a paint store. A contractor who often bought paint there told me about an apprenticeship program, so I signed up for it. After three years of paid work-study, I became a journey-level painter, wallpaper hanger, and drywall taper. But I began to think I'd like to be in business for myself.

A few years later, I was ready to do it. I joined forces and finances with a friend with eight years' experience in remodeling. With a bank loan, we found a modest location and opened our own business.

At first, we took on smaller projects. Then one day a client asked us to attach rooms to an existing home. We jumped at the chance. We presented a cost-effective plan for the new structure, inside and out. When our bid was accepted, we organized the work of specialists in foundation, framing, plumbing, electricity, architecture, and interior design. We finished the addition under budget and on time. That led to referrals, and soon our business was growing!

We've been able to team up with a developer who wants to turn an old, abandoned building into several independent units. We're figuring out how to bring the structure up to code while also creating ideas for ways to combine work and living space. This is the kind of project that makes our work so interesting.

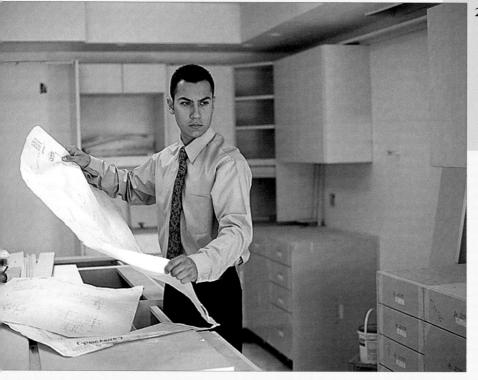

Design Portfolio

1. Choose a room in your home and create a presentation showing how you would remodel it.

2. Develop a work plan to carry out the remodeling task you designed in the first project.

Chapter Summary

- **Remodeling** involves structural changes to a home; redecorating simply gives an area a new look.

- Homeowners should compare remodeling and moving to a new home in terms of cost, convenience, and commitment.

- Four typical remodeling projects are changing a lived-in area, making unused space livable, adding space, and buying a home in order to remodel it.

- Several steps are needed to plan remodeling projects.

- Homeowners should consider carefully whether to hire professionals or do the remodeling themselves.

- Doing a remodeling job yourself saves money but gives the homeowner added responsibilities.

Checking Your Understanding

1. What are typical reasons that people want to remodel?

2. What are three cost factors that should be considered before undertaking a remodeling project?

3. Why is commitment an important issue to consider regarding remodeling projects?

4. Give one example of each type of remodeling project.

5. What is the difference between **renovation** and **restoration**?

6. What are the components of a remodeling project?

7. What is a **home equity loan**?

8. Describe a process for selecting a remodeling contractor.

9. What items should a remodeling **contract** between a homeowner and a contractor include?

10. What are the advantages and disadvantages of doing a remodeling job yourself, instead of hiring a professional?

Thinking Critically

1. **Comparing and Contrasting.** How does remodeling differ from redecorating? Explain the difference in a written paragraph.

2. **Making Decisions.** Under what circumstances would you use a home equity loan to finance a remodeling project?

3. **Giving Examples.** Write a description of a remodeling project you think homeowners should let professionals do. Write a second example of a project you think homeowners could do themselves. Write a summary explaining why the two remodeling projects should be handled differently.

Applying Your Knowledge

1. **Researching Renovation.** The first step in a renovation project is learning the past history of the building. Suppose you were going to renovate a home from the 1800s. Identify a location and housing style for that home. Use print resources or the Internet to develop a list of characteristics of that style home and place. Present your report to the class.

2. **Making a Checklist.** Make a checklist showing the steps you would take to ensure the quality of work done by a contractor hired to remodel a bathroom.

3. **Remodeling Advice.** Suppose you're a contractor who has a website that provides information and advice on remodeling. A visitor to the site has a problem with a contractor who is putting an addition on the home. The project is dragging due to late delivery of materials and worker absence. The visitor is pleased with the quality of the contractor's work, but is worried that the project will not be completed in time for his elderly parents to move into the room. Write a response to your website visitor.

4. **Doing-It-Yourself.** Interview someone who has done a remodeling project rather than hiring a professional. Find out what kind of project it was, what work the person did, whether he or she had any experience with this work before, whether there was any involvement from a professional, and how the person felt during the project and after it was completed. Report your findings.

A family comes to you with a remodeling project. They want to add a family room to their one-story, three-bedroom home. Two possible existing spaces are an unfinished basement and an attic. Both areas have two small windows. The family could also add the room off the living room at the back of the house.

1. Think about the three options, taking into account such factors as cost, lighting, insulation, and convenience.

2. Choose one of the options based on what you think would work best for the family.

3. Make a list of the steps needed to create that remodeled room.

4. Use CAD software to draw a design of the room you would plan for them.

5. Place your completed design in your portfolio.

Architectural Design

Early Home Styles

Objectives

- Describe how Native American housing was influenced by culture and environment.

- Explain how the early colonists created dwellings when they first came to America.

- Identify the materials used to build early American homes.

- Describe the structural features derived from early English, German and Dutch, Spanish, Swedish, and French homes.

Vocabulary

- pueblo
- adobe
- half-timbered house
- thatch
- Cape Cod house
- pitched roof
- gable roof
- gables
- ell
- gambrel roof
- saltbox house
- garrison house
- dormer
- coquina

When you look at pictures of early homes, you may find it difficult to realize that they were "home" to real families. Our country began in Native American lodges, log cabins, and quaint New England farmhouses. These homes also form the roots of today's architectural styles.

Links from the Past

Stroll down a street in an older part of town and you likely will see a wide variety of housing styles. You might see many of the same designs in a number of cities. If you were to examine these styles closely, you might find traces of homes designed hundreds of years ago.

Although some homes are truly modern creations, many are modifications of early American styles. As the country grew, regional styles spread across the continent. These styles were modified to suit the weather conditions and terrain of the colonists' new land.

The modifications made today are different from those made by the colonists. Technological advances have made it possible to adapt many designs. In the past, some designs would have been restricted by climate, terrain, and the building materials available. Most climate conditions can now be offset by central heating and cooling systems and by insulation. Building materials can be transported to almost any location. However, some regional differences in housing still exist. Homes in New England, for example, often show links to that area's Cape Cod, Georgian, and Federal styles of the past. Features such as pitched roofs fit well with the climate.

To examine the influence of Early American housing on the styles of today, this chapter describes the housing of Native Americans and of settlers from the major countries that established colonies in North America. Knowledge of the characteristics of each style will help you understand the origins of today's homes and furnishings.

The Growth of Traditional Styles

American architecture traditionally dates from colonial times. The actual history of housing in North America, however, starts much earlier. Before colonists arrived from Europe, Native Americans lived on the continent in a variety of types of dwellings, each suited to their particular tribe's needs. Eventually the colonists began to build their own structures.

Fig. 14-1 The tepee is one of the most familiar styles of early Native American homes. **What were some reasons for building this type of shelter?**

Native American Homes

Native Americans lived throughout the North American continent, from the forests of the eastern shore to the deserts of the Southwest. Each group or tribe developed a distinct way of life. Many depended on hunting or fishing for their survival. Some raised crops and domestic animals.

Environment and culture were the two main influences on the type of housing developed by each tribe. Environment determined which building materials were available and the type of protection from the elements that was needed. Some of the cultural considerations were social organization; religious beliefs; methods of obtaining food; and size of the group, family, or organization. Hunters of the Great Plains developed dwellings different from those of the farming tribes of the Northeast and the Inuit people of the Arctic.

Native American homes did, however, have some common characteristics. They were simple structures with dirt floors and no windows or chimneys. They tended to be dark and crowded. Cooking was done over an open fire. There was little furniture. Weapons, tools, and other possessions were stored on shelves or hung from walls.

Tribes that depended on hunting or on gathering food had to move from place to place. Therefore, they developed dwellings that could be easily constructed at the new site or carried from place to place. See Fig. 14-1. The tribes of the eastern woodlands carried reed mats which were wrapped around rounded wood frames to create a domelike structure called a "wigwam." A wigwam could house one or two families. The tepee was the invention of the tribes of the central and western plains who roamed in search of game. It was a cone-shaped tent covered with buffalo hides. This tent could be put up and taken down rapidly. It was perfectly suited to the nomadic life of the people who developed it.

Farming tribes established more permanent villages. They constructed homes intended to last for many seasons. The Iroquois tribes of the Northeast, for example, developed the *longhouse*, built from young trees that were bent to form a long, rectangular frame with a barrel-shaped roof. The frame was covered by overlapping strips of bark. The longhouse was designed to house several families. The public buildings of the Iroquois were also built this way. Some reached lengths of 100 feet (30 m).

The tribes of the Southwest also built more permanent structures. The Spanish people called these structures pueblos (PWAY-blohz), meaning "villages." See Fig. 14-2. **Pueblos** were houses built on top of each other into cliffs and caves and on the level ground. Pueblos were built of the only material available to these tribes, clay. The clay was formed into sun-dried bricks called **adobe** (uh-DOH-bee).

Fig. 14-2 The pueblos of the Southwest took advantage of the local geography.

Climate was a major consideration for the Inuit people of the cold North. They lived in houses built partially underground and covered with sod. These homes had long, downward-sloping entrances. This construction kept the Inuit people well insulated from freezing temperatures and served as protection against the wind. In the snowiest regions, Inuit tribes built their dwellings from blocks of ice, lightly covered with snow.

The First Colonists

The colonists who came to the New World represented many groups. Some came seeking religious freedom; others were adventurers determined to find wealth. A few were powerful aristocrats with vast land holdings. There were also individuals who had been exiled as punishment for a crime.

Upon landing in the New World, the first settlers were faced with the immediate problem of finding sources of food and building shelters. They had few tools and materials with which to accomplish these tasks. Some of them weren't able to make a home in the wilderness. In 1585, for instance, the first English settlement in North America was established on the island of Roanoke, North Carolina. This first group of settlers soon gave up and returned to England; a second group disappeared without a trace.

Those who did survive followed the example of the Native Americans. They saw how the native people adapted their dwellings to the surrounding environment and tried to do the same. Little is known of the earliest temporary shelters. Their owners usually destroyed them as soon as permanent dwellings were built. It is known, however, that huts of bark and branches, held together with clay, were used as crude shelters. Other types of early dwellings included a triangular, tentlike structure made up of logs propped up against each other, as well as a shedlike roofed house built into the side of a hill.

The Early American Period, 1640-1720

To feel more at home in a strange land, the colonists wanted to create an environment that was familiar to them. When they built their permanent houses, they patterned them as much as possible after the ones they had left behind. Modifications were made to suit the weather conditions and terrain.

As more people emigrated to North America, the workforce become more specialized. Records show that numerous experienced stonemasons and carpenters were among the first arrivals. They came with their *apprentices*—individuals who had entered into a legal agreement to work, usually for seven years, with a skilled master to learn a trade. Construction techniques began to be refined. See Fig. 14-3.

Local materials were used as a basis for construction in the New World. Wood from New England forests was made into lumber. Local stone was quarried. Settlers in Virginia, southern New Jersey, and Philadelphia found a good supply of brickmaking clay there. Handmade brick quickly became a popular building material in those areas. Lime for mortar between the bricks came from seashells.

Fig. 14-3 Early colonists learned to survive in the New World through perseverance and by adapting building methods from their homelands.

English Settlements

The first two successful English colonies were started at Jamestown, Virginia, in 1607, and in Plymouth, Massachusetts, in 1620. By 1640, a sprinkling of tiny English settlements dotted the eastern edge of North America. Between 1640 and 1720, small, isolated settlements grew into bustling towns with larger and more comfortable houses. Some roads were constructed. Trade by land and sea grew.

Many of the first permanent dwellings constructed by the English colonists were patterned closely on **half-timbered houses** found in England. In the half-timbered house, the wood frame of the house formed part of the outside wall. The spaces between beams were filled in with brick or plaster. The roof was constructed of **thatch**—bundles of reeds or straw. **See Fig. 14-4.**

Some of these early houses were covered with shingles or clapboards. Shingles are thin, oblong pieces of material, usually wood, that are laid in overlapping rows to cover the roof and sides of a structure. Clapboards are boards with one edge thicker than the other laid in overlapping rows to protect the walls from the elements. A huge chimney served one or several fireplaces, which were used for cooking and for heat in the cold winters. Windows were generally small in order to reduce heat loss and minimize the use of expensive glass.

Many English settlers in the northeastern colonies built a style of home called a **Cape Cod house**—a house with a simple rectangular design, a central chimney, and a **pitched roof**. **See Fig. 14-5.** This is a two-sided roof with a steep angle. A pitched roof is often called a **gable roof** because it forms triangular end walls, known as **gables**, on the house. The Cape Cod remains a model for many American homes.

The interior of the Cape Cod was divided into one large room, called the "great room," and one or two small rooms. The great room functioned as the center of family life. The large fireplace, used for cooking, usually furnished the only light in the dwelling. Almost all indoor tasks were performed at or near the fireplace—weaving, sewing, and furniture making. Some family members even slept there.

Although small, the Cape Cod house was built for expansion. As families grew, an **ell**, or extension built at right angles to the length of the structure, was sometimes added. The original house was frequently built with a chimney at the end of the structure. These were called "half-houses" because when an addition to the house was made, it was placed so the fireplace and chimney would be in the center and could heat every room.

One drawback of the Cape Cod style was that the simple pitched room left little usable space on the second floor. The slope of the roof restricted the size of the rooms, door locations, and furniture placement. To overcome these problems, a new type of roof was developed. The **gambrel roof** has two slopes on each side, the upper slope being flatter than the lower slope. This allowed interior space for full-sized upstairs rooms.

Fig. 14-4 This re-creation of an early English colonial home in Jamestown shows half-timbered construction and a thatched roof. This home gave much more protection from the weather than earlier colonial homes.

Fig. 14-5 This two-story, Cape-Cod house includes the traditional rectangular form, central chimney, and pitched or gable roof. Note the wood shingled exterior.

When time and material permitted, some colonists built houses that had two full stories. The **saltbox house** began as a two-story, pitched-roof house. The need for extra space prompted some owners to build an additional set of rooms along the back of the house on the first floor. They brought the roof line down to cover the addition. The long slope of the roof is similar to the sloping cover on the wooden saltboxes common in colonial kitchens. See Fig. 14-6.

The **garrison house** can be recognized by a second story that overhangs or projects from the first story. This style was copied from the Elizabethan houses (houses built during the reign of Queen Elizabeth I, 1558-1603). Such an overhang was first used on forts, or garrisons, to prevent attackers from scaling the walls.

Today, if you visit the restored town of Williamsburg, Virginia, you will see many of the English dwellings just discussed. Since Williamsburg was the colonial capital, however, the homes there are more stylish and sophisticated than the average colonial home of this period.

Fig. 14-6 The saltbox house characteristically has a long, sloping back roof and a central chimney.

Fig. 14-7 This German home has an abbreviated roof between the first and second stories.

German & Dutch Settlements

The majority of German settlers who came to North America in the late 17th century settled in southeastern Pennsylvania. The Germans built large, durable houses of wood and quarry stone. The typical German house provided entry into a first-floor kitchen. The fireplace was located in the center of the first floor. On the opposite side of the fireplace was a large family room for entertaining. Some of the larger houses had small bedrooms behind the family room. In some German houses, an abbreviated roof, or "hood," was built between the first and second stories. See Fig. 14-7.

The Dutch came to the New World more than a century earlier than the Germans. Their first settlements were in New Amsterdam (now New York City) and in the Hudson Valley to the north. The Dutch used stone and brick to build houses considered large by colonial standards. Some houses were four or five stories high. The Dutch homes were noted for their decorative brickwork and intricate stepped gables. The gambrel roof design in Dutch Colonial homes gave more usable space beneath the roof. To add light, these roofs often contained **dormers**—structures projecting through a steeply sloping roof. The window set in this structure is called a "dormer window." This feature shows up in later architectural styles. See Fig. 14-8. Also characteristic of Dutch styles were metal gutters, small windows with sliding shutters, and the "Dutch door"—a door divided in half horizontally. This design allowed the top half to stand open like a window while the bottom half remained closed.

Fig. 14-8 This modern home shows the influences of Dutch architecture. The gambrel roof and dormers give the second floor more usable living space.

Fig. 14-9 This home is modeled after early Spanish architecture in the Southwest. How does it compare with the pueblos built by Native Americans in the region?

Spanish Settlements

The Spaniards were the first Europeans to establish colonies in the New World, mostly in Florida and the Southwest, in the early 1500s. The oldest Spanish house still existing in the United States is located in St. Augustine, Florida. Built about 1565, it is made of **coquina** (co-KEE-nuh), a soft porous limestone composed of shell and coral. Many of the Spanish houses in the South were rectangular, with balconies that faced the street. Kitchens were often separate so that the heat from cooking fires would not affect the rest of the house. The interior was usually simple, with whitewashed plaster walls, beamed ceilings, and earthen floors. The more elaborate houses used tile on the floor or roof.

In the Southwest, the Spanish settlers at first adopted some of the features of the natives' housing. These early Spanish houses had thick adobe walls, flat roofs, rough-hewn beams projecting through the outside walls, and deep-set windows. **See Fig. 14-9.**

In the 17th century, a more elaborate style was created by Spanish settlers in California and other parts of the Southwest. These houses were covered with adobe, brick, or stucco. Stucco is a plaster material made with cement, sand, and lime. These homes featured rounded archways and windows and red tile roofs. Porches and balconies often went around the outside of the dwelling. Some homes of this type had inner courtyards.

Swedish Settlements

As settlers moved westward into dense, unexplored forest, the log cabin was their most common and practical shelter. These early settlers had to clear the land for farming, so they used the trees they felled to build their dwellings. This system was used by pioneers for many years as they pushed their way across the continent. The log cabin was so common that it has become a part of American folklore and is looked upon as a truly American building style. The fact that its origins were Swedish has almost been forgotten.

In Sweden, houses were traditionally made of wood. Swedes who came to the New World called on their knowledge of log construction. They felled the trees, cut them into logs, and laid them on one another horizontally. The logs were joined with notched corners and the joints were filled with clay, bark, or moss.

The log cabin was a primitive, small building. Its length rarely exceeded that of a single log. Sometimes a cabin was divided into two rooms with an attic above, but more often there was only one room. Originally, the roof was of bark or thatch. Later, wood shingles were used.

French Settlements

The early French colonists who settled along the St. Lawrence River built houses of stone or wood, with the high, steep roofs common in French country cottages, particularly in Normandy, France. The typical home had small windows and heavy wooden shutters that could be closed to protect the occupants from cold weather. Original buildings in this style are found today in New York State and Canada.

The French cottage style had to be adapted when built by settlers in the hot and humid southern Mississippi Valley. A porch was added that was covered by a broad roof extending around the house. It helped keep the house cool and protected it from the rain. Often the houses were raised on posts a full story above the ground. This was done to improve air circulation and protect the house from floods. The houses were usually painted white. The rooms had many doors and windows, which allowed for the flow of air. See Fig. 14-10.

In later versions of this style, galleries, or roofed balconies, were added, which provided shade and outdoor living space. The galleries could be reached from inside the house as well as by outside stairs. Posts supporting the balconies were made of wood or ornamental iron. Many such houses can still be seen in the French Quarter of New Orleans.

Fig. 14-10 Pierre Menard built this French colonial home in 1803 along the Mississippi River in what is now Illinois. How was the French style adapted for its location?

Roots of Today's Styles

The earliest homes were simple and practical, providing little more than shelter from the weather and a place to sleep. Their inhabitants would have been astonished at the extravagant homes of today.

Early settlers followed the lead of Native Americans, building temporary shelters and using locally available materials. Gradually, though, they built permanent structures. The early home styles of North America were as different and varied as the people who built them. By attempting to recreate the homes they had left behind, each culture made its contribution to the Early American period. At the same time, the early settlers had to adapt their building practices to their new lifestyles and environments. These adaptations made the homes distinctly American, and established the roots of the styles that were to follow. See Fig. 14-11.

Housing continued to evolve as new waves of immigrants came to America. As the population grew and spread, patterns of housing changed to meet the needs of a changing society. As you will learn in the next chapter, housing styles were influenced by a variety of factors, including political, economic, and social events.

Fig. 14-11 American housing styles reflect the roots of the early settlers and the adaptations they made to their new land.

Profile of a Home Stager

Home stagers help home sellers get the best price for their homes by recommending steps the sellers can take to make their homes more appealing. They change furniture, accessories, colors, fabrics, and landscaping to make a home look more attractive to potential buyers.

Education & Training

- A high school diploma is required.
- A college degree in interior design is very helpful.
- Experience as a real estate agent or an interior designer is also useful.

Skills & Aptitudes

- Good people skills are needed to convince the seller to accept home staging recommendations.
- Good design sense is essential.
- Knowledge of the real estate market is vital.

Home Stager
Ron Worthington

When people put their home on the market, they often want to show a place full of memories and good feelings. But when potential buyers view the home, they see other things. They may get distracted by family photos, or piles of magazines, or filled curio cabinets. Those sights make the home less appealing to a buyer who is trying to visualize their belongings in the space.

It's my job as a home stager to figure out what needs to be done to make the home appeal to potential buyers. I start by doing a thorough inspection of the home. That means going through every room and looking in every closet and cabinet. Then I develop a list of steps the sellers should take to improve the home's look. One step is to get rid of clutter. People often hang too many pictures and put too many objects on shelves. Families with children often have toys scattered around the house.

I also look closely at the furniture. Having too many big pieces in a room makes the room look smaller. I might suggest that they move furniture from one room to another, or even put some pieces in storage. If they have a special collection, like baseballs or teacups, I often advise they be put in storage too. It's better to make the house look less unique. Prospective buyers can't imagine their own things in the house if the look is too personal. This advice can be hard for a family to hear. I remind them that we're working toward the same goal—selling their home as soon as possible for the best possible price.

We also look at wall colors. A fresh coat of paint can brighten a room and help a house show better. We encourage people to paint in neutral tones—colors that are too dark or dramatic can turn people away. My clients are often shocked to see what a difference these changes make. It's almost like they're living in a different home. But home staging definitely works. I've seen houses that were on the market for months sell very quickly once I've staged them. And sellers like those results!

Design Portfolio

1. Take the role of a home stager. Create a checklist of 10 general tips you would give to all sellers about how to best present their homes.

2. Visit a real estate agency's website to find pictures of a home for sale. Print out pictures of two of the rooms and one exterior view. Prepare a presentation showing what changes you would make to the two rooms and the outside to make the home more appealing to prospective buyers.

Review & Activities

Chapter Summary

- Native American tribes' culture and environment determined the type of housing they developed.
- The earliest colonists built simple, primitive homes often based on Native American homes. Later they built sturdier one-room dwellings and larger permanent homes.
- European colonists often built their American homes in the style of housing from their country of origin.
- European styles were adapted to the climate of the New World, creating a wide range of American housing styles.

Checking Your Understanding

1. How did the shelters of Native American hunters and food gatherers differ from the shelters of Native American farmers?
2. How did climate influence the design of Inuit homes?
3. Identify three types of materials used by the first colonists to build permanent shelters.
4. Describe the construction of a **half-timbered house**.
5. What simple, early English style is still a popular model for American homes? Briefly describe this style house.
6. What advantages does a **gambrel roof** have over a **gable roof**?
7. Explain how the **saltbox house** evolved from a house with a normal pitched roof.
8. Describe three characteristics of the Dutch homes in New York State.
9. How did Spanish settlers in the Southwest adapt native building styles?
10. Describe a typical French-style house in New Orleans.

Thinking Critically

1. **Making Hypotheses.** Consider the early settlers in Jamestown who came to a strange land not knowing what awaited them. What does this say about the settlers' character and the kind of people they were? How might these qualities have influenced their housing decisions? Share your thoughts in an essay.

2. **Drawing Conclusions.** What room in a modern home would you consider most similar to the great room of an original Cape Cod house? Why? How might the needs of people today and those of the past be similar? Explain your conclusions.

Applying Your Knowledge

1. **Native American Homes.** Research one variety of Native American housing. Write a report explaining how these homes were made, what materials were used, and how the homes met cultural needs.

2. **Environmental Influences.** Briefly describe the climate and environmental conditions in your area. Then think about how these conditions have influenced construction materials, style, and location of housing. Is this influence greater on older or new homes? Summarize your thoughts for the class, using specific examples of homes in your town.

3. **Home Advertisement.** Choose an early home style discussed in the chapter. Then write an advertisement for the *Colonial Times Gazette* to offer the house for sale. Write the advertisement so that it reflects the historical period and addresses the people who would be living at that time.

4. **Housing Styles.** Take a walk down a street in your town or city. Take notes on and keep track of the number of different housing types you see in a one-block area. Note whether they are mostly multifamily dwellings or single-family. How are they similar or different to the designs of early settlers? Sharing your findings with the class.

5. **Modern Versions.** Using illustrated ads for houses for sale or a real estate company's website, find a modern version of the early home styles found in this chapter. Mount or print out at least three of these ads. Identify features that are similar to the original styles.

Design Challenge

Imagine that you are an early settler in the region where you now live. You have to design and build a home, taking into account locally available materials, environmental conditions, climate, and so on. Assume that you have a few basic tools to work with.

1. Research what construction materials were available in the early 1700s.

2. Design a home that could have been built at that time, and that meets your basic requirements.

3. Create sketches of your home, showing the exterior and interior.

4. Write a brief essay describing your home and explaining the decisions you made regarding its design and construction.

Home Styles Since 1700

Objectives

- Evaluate how events in America's history have affected housing design.

- Compare and contrast housing styles in the 18th century.

- Compare and contrast housing styles in the 19th century.

- Evaluate historical housing elements that influenced 20th century designs.

- Analyze the unique housing designs of the late 20th and early 21st centuries.

Vocabulary

- hip roof
- pilasters
- pediment
- cornice
- fanlight
- portico
- tenements
- gingerbread
- mansard roof
- bungalow

America in the 18th century was still undergoing enormous change. Waves of new immigrants continued to arrive, bringing with them rich heritages and traditions, including native home-building styles. At the same time, architects were emerging as the creators of a new discipline that would keep American housing changing and evolving. That evolution continued through the 19th and 20th centuries and into the 21st.

Understanding Period Housing Styles

Architectural history traditionally is divided into various periods. Each period is influenced by the historical events of its time and is characterized by distinctive housing styles. However, it's important to understand that one period flows into another, often overlapping; so dates are approximate. Several design movements can exist at the same time in different areas of the country. In addition, all houses of a certain style do not look identical. Architects and builders often add their personal stamp to each house they create. Variations can be seen from town to town and region to region. **See Fig. 15-1.**

The design characteristics discussed in this chapter are the most common ones for each style or period. In identifying the style of a specific house, look for the overall "feeling" of a style, as well as for particular design details. However, keep in mind that many homes—especially more recent styles—break the traditional rules, creating new, individual designs.

The historical homes you see today don't represent all the housing of a particular period. The homes that remain as examples of early architectural styles tend to be those of the middle or upper classes. Built of more durable materials, they often stayed in one family for many generations. A large number of people lived in very simple homes. Most of these homes did not last, since they typically were not built as solidly or expensively as middle- and upper-class homes.

Fig. 15-1 Compare this old stone home to the highly decorative one above. **Identify the period and style of each home.**

The 18ᵗʰ Century

Eighteenth-century life in America was filled with contrast. On the frontier, people lived in the roughest shelters. Along the East Coast, businesses and plantations grew steadily; elegant houses and furniture were in demand. Modest homes continued to be built by new arrivals to America. The three main architectural styles associated with this century are the immigrant, Georgian, and Federal styles. See Fig. 15-2.

Immigrant Styles

The new immigrants, like earlier ones, brought their styles of homes to the colonies or they created new styles adapted to the new land. They built homes in sturdy, distinctive styles that added to the variety and richness of America's housing. Materials and styles of building were then passed on to other immigrant groups, who, in turn, took them to other areas.

Fig. 15-2

18ᵗʰ Century Architecture	
Periods and Styles	**Approximate Dates**
Immigrant Styles	continuous
Georgian Period	1700–1780
Georgian Style	1700–1780
Federal Period	1770–1830
Adam Style	1780–1820
Early Classical Revival	1770–1830

The English used timber sawed into boards to build their homes. The Dutch used stone and brick, Germans used wood and quarry stone, while Swedes used squared logs. Log cabins were erected from the Carolinas westward to Texas. See Fig. 15-3. This type of cabin was modified from the original one-room style to a larger version with two rooms side-by-side, often with a breezeway between them.

Spanish immigrants, who began to settle in the southwestern United States, brought the Spanish influence of cut stone and adobe brick for home building. In addition, a new American technique was born—building homes with sun-baked adobe clay.

Fig. 15-3 This log cabin was typical housing in the 1700s. **Give some reasons why an early settler in the wilderness might have chosen to construct a log cabin.**

The Georgian Period

For many, life in colonial America was comfortable. Americans, like Europeans, were becoming more prosperous, better educated, scientifically curious, and interested in history and the arts. The link to England was still there. This factor, combined with the new prosperity, turned people to the formal Georgian style of home that was then fashionable in England. This style was very popular in America throughout most of the century. See Fig. 15-4.

Georgian Style

The Georgian style was named for the kings of England who ruled during that time: George I, George II, and George III. The colonists copied design details that had long been popular in England.

In England, Georgian-style buildings were constructed of brick and stone. American builders used these materials when available but had to adapt the style when they weren't. The walls of George Washington's Mount Vernon home in Virginia, for example, are actually made of wood. They were carved and painted to look like stone.

Fig. 15-4 This is a formal Georgian style home. How many characteristics of the style can you identify?

The main characteristics of typical Georgian houses in America include:

- A formal, balanced design. Houses are often two or three stories high.
- A gable roof, which is a pitched roof with two sloped sides, or a **hip roof**, a roof with four sloped sides.
- Large windows symmetrically placed. The windows consist of many small panes.
- Doorway details. The front door is the focal point of the house. Typically, the door is framed by **pilasters**, which are decorative flattened columns. The doorway is often topped by a **pediment** (PED-uh-munt)—a triangular or arched decoration. See Fig. 15-5.
- A distinctive cornice. A **cornice** (KOR-nuhs) is a decorative strip at the area where the roof and the walls meet. Georgian houses often have a cornice of toothlike molding.
- A central chimney or a chimney at each end of the house.
- Contrasting materials. Red brick is often used with white wood trim, but other materials are also common.

Inside the typical Georgian house, molded plaster ceilings conceal the beams of the second floor. Wood paneling or wallpaper covers the walls. An ornate rectangular fireplace, topped by a mantel, is often the center of interest.

Many Georgian houses are square or rectangular. Larger Georgian-style houses often have a central section with a wing on each side to accommodate the kitchen and offices or guest rooms. Georgian homes are generally built around a central hall with a wide staircase. These homes reflect the gracious, somewhat formal style of living that had become popular among upper-middle-class and wealthy colonists.

Pediment

Pilasters

Paneled Door

Fig. 15-5 The Georgian style was the first in this country to place major emphasis on decorative elements. **What do you think brought about this change?**

The upper classes, with much leisure time to enjoy, turned their attention to the arts. Men and women had their portraits painted. In the evenings, they entertained family and friends by playing the harpsichord or the newly invented "pianoforte" (today's piano). The formal Georgian home provided the perfect backdrop to display portraits, as well as affording ample space for entertaining.

Decorative characteristics of the Georgian style were applied to "row houses," sometimes called "townhouses." *Row houses* are a continuous line of two- or three-story houses that share a common wall with houses on either side. This kind of housing first appeared in such American cities as Boston and Philadelphia during the 18th century.

Achieving the decorative look of the Georgian style required the work of craftsmen and artisans. Many European immigrants supplied the labor to build these houses. Their skills as woodworkers, brickmakers, glassmakers, and plasterers can still be seen today.

The Federal Period

In the 1770s, American attitudes toward England changed. From 1775 to 1783, the colonists fought and won the American Revolution. This war brought to an end many of the old political and social patterns. People who had been leaders because of their ties with England died in the fighting or had been forced to emigrate. New trend-setting leaders emerged, many of them traders and merchants. Cities with busy ports grew in importance; the expanding frontier opened up new possibilities in the west; and the tide of immigration from Europe continued.

With a sense of renewed patriotism after winning the American Revolution, Americans turned away from the English Georgian style. They sought architectural styles that expressed America's newly won freedom and independence. These styles make up what is known as the "Federal period," named in honor of the new federal government of the United States. They were popular at the end of the century as the young country looked for ways to express its new identity.

During the Federal period, two distinct architectural styles developed. The more popular, often called the "Adam style," borrowed from English architects but was "Americanized" to be different from European architecture. Early Classical Revival style is a thoroughly American innovation, although it shares many characteristics with the Adam style.

Adam Style

The Adam style was named in honor of the English architects Robert and James Adam. These two brothers took the Georgian features and combined them with elements from classical Greece and Rome. They paid particular attention to decorative interior details. The style made its mark in America from about 1780 to 1820. **See Fig. 15-6.**

Some of the features of the Adam style are:

- A rectangular design with one or more stories. Some homes have a center section with a wing on each side.

- Gable roofs. The slopes of the roof generally face the front and back of the house. A decorative cornice often extends across the front and back of the house at the roofline.

- Symmetrically placed windows. As in the Georgian period, the windows have many panes. A **fanlight**—a semicircular, round, or oval window with fan-shaped panes of glass—is often above the door or in the pediment.

- Decorative interiors. Plaster and wood carvings in classical design are used on walls and ceilings. The mantels around fireplaces are especially decorative.

Fig. 15-6 These Adam-style row houses show how a new style evolved from the Georgian. The fanlight above the doorway replaces the triangular pediment. Decorative glass sidelights replace the pilasters beside the doors.

Fig. 15-7 This Early Classical Revival home has timeless appeal. The style can be adapted to small, as well as large, buildings.

Early Classical Revival Style

Between 1770 and 1830, many architects turned to ancient Rome to find new ways of expressing American independence. They were led by Thomas Jefferson, who was an architect as well as President, statesman, and inventor. Jefferson's home, Monticello, and the buildings he designed for the University of Virginia include features from the buildings of antiquity.

The style Jefferson helped develop became known as "Early Classical Revival." It was used for many government buildings, as well as row houses and other residences. These included many of the buildings in the new federal capital of Washington, D.C. The Early Classical Revival style also extended beyond the eastern United States to new states being settled, such as Texas, Iowa, Kansas, and Minnesota.

The Early Classical Revival style is similar to the Adam style in several ways. The rectangular shape of the buildings, with windows symmetrically placed, is common in both types. See Fig. 15-7. The fanlight window is another feature found in both styles. The feature that distinguishes Early Classical Revival style structures, however, is the **portico** (POR-tih-koh). This is a tall, open porch, supported by columns, over the front entrance. The portico is topped by a triangular pediment. Sometimes the porch is built up on a foundation and extends to the roof of the house or building. This revival of the classic design of the past paved the way for greater interest in classic styles as America moved from the 18th into the 19th century.

The 19ᵗʰ Century

In the early 1800s, the Industrial Revolution was sweeping America. Throughout the 19ᵗʰ century, manufacturing grew steadily. The results of industrialization changed America forever.

Along with the growth of factories came new demands. Because more workers were needed, immigrants began pouring into the country in greater numbers to provide cheap labor. Railroads were built to ship the new products to the expanding population. What effect did all this have on housing in America?

First of all, the construction industry was one of many developing at a rapid pace. With mass production, factories could make in quantity the products needed to build and furnish homes and businesses. As prices for homes dropped, more people could afford to buy them. This raised the standard of living for many people.

Not everyone was so fortunate, though. Because of low wages, many factory workers could not afford decent housing. Factory owners built row houses, which they rented to their employees. However, many more poor quality houses were built near the factories. Apartments and other multiunit dwellings also became common in cities. **Tenements**—apartment complexes with minimum standards of sanitation, safety, and comfort—were built. Workers and their families crowded into them. **See Fig. 15-8.**

At the same time, a considerable number of Americans became wealthy from the profits of industrialization. They spent their money on travel and newer and larger homes. From their travels to Europe, they returned with ideas that they incorporated in their own homes.

Fig. 15-8 Multifamily homes in the late 1800s were often crowded. To save money, several families, or a large extended family, would live together in a small apartment.

While all of this was going on, housing styles in America were also changing. During the 18ᵗʰ century, one style had dominated—the Georgian. During the 19ᵗʰ century, there were many styles, from those that imitated the classic styles of the past to the fancy designs of Victorian homes. **See Fig. 15-9.** Housing during this century reflected a mixture of ideas and a spirit of fantasy and excitement. The American housing scene was as varied as the people who came together to create it. It mirrored the many changes in the economy and in society.

Fig. 15-9

19ᵗʰ Century Architecture	
Periods and Styles	**Approximate Dates**
The Romantic Revival Period	1820–1880
Greek Revival Style	1825–1860
Revival Style	1840–1880
Italianate Style	1840–1885
Victorian Period	1860–1900
Mansard Style	1860–1880
Queen Anne Style	1870–1890

Fig. 15-10 Many mansions in the South were built in the Greek Revival style.

The Romantic Revival Period

During the first half of the 19th century, many writers and artists found inspiration in the European past. They were especially drawn to ancient Greece, medieval Europe, and Renaissance Italy as sources of inspiration. Nineteenth-century architects expressed these patterns of the past in the Greek Revival, Gothic Revival, and Italianate styles.

Greek Revival Style

The Greek Revival style flourished from about 1825 to 1860, ending around the time of the Civil War. Its features were linked to the temples of ancient Greece. One of the most famous variations of Greek Revival architecture is the Southern plantation style. See Fig. 15-10. Such homes have a two-story porch supported by columns across the entire front of the house.

Typical characteristics of the Greek Revival style include:

- A two-story rectangular house with symmetrically placed windows.
- A gable roof emphasized by wide trim at the cornice.
- Pilasters on the corners of frame houses or across the whole front.
- An elaborate entrance. The door is usually surrounded by small windows and may also have additional wood or masonry (stone or brick) framework.
- Columns supporting a small or large porch. Sometimes the columns are simply set into the entrance. Greek columns are most common.

Gothic Revival Style

One of the styles that became popular all over America during the 19th century was the Gothic Revival style (1840-1880). Designers used such European features as pointed arches and circular windows with ornamental carved stone. Many Gothic Revival homes were built of wood because stone was very expensive in many parts of America and because there was a shortage of stonemasons. Countless houses were built with high-peaked Gothic gables decorated with **gingerbread**, lacy-looking, cut-out wood trim. See Fig. 15-11.

Fig. 15-11 The pointed arches and gingerbread trim of this house are characteristic of the Gothic Revival style.

Italianate Style

Architectural features of Italian villas, or estates, were also reproduced in houses in America during the 19th century. Homes built in the Italianate style (about 1840-1885) were often square and two stories high. They featured wide, overhanging hip roofs with decorative brackets, or supports, at the cornices. Their long, narrow windows were commonly arched and crowned with an inverted, U-shaped structure. See Fig. 15-12.

The Victorian Period

The Victorian period takes its name from Queen Victoria, who reigned in England from 1837 to 1901. The entire time of her reign is often described as the Victorian period. In America, however, Victorian housing styles were most popular from about 1860 until the end of the century.

Victorian styles are often very elaborate. Their detail was largely, and loosely, taken from medieval and Renaissance European styles. Because of the new technology in America at the time, the use of complicated details and shapes in housing design was possible. The Mansard and Queen Anne are two of several styles that were popular during the Victorian period.

Fig. 15-12 This is an example of Italianate style. In what ways is the Italianate style different from the Gothic Revival style which preceded it? Are there any similarities?

Mansard Style

The Mansard style (sometimes called the *Second Empire style*) showed the French influence during the Victorian period. It was most popular between 1860 and 1880. The most notable feature of this style is the boxlike mansard roof. See Fig. 15-13. A **mansard roof** is a roof that has two slopes on all sides, with the lower slope being steep and the upper slope almost flat. Other features of the Mansard style are decorated cornices and French windows, which are long windows that open lengthwise at the middle. Dormer windows for the top story project from the lower slope of the roof. The mansard roof and other popular roof designs are shown in Fig. 15-14.

Fig. 15-13 This home has a Mansard roof. What would be the main advantage of the mansard roof? How would the dormers add to that advantage?

Fig. 15-14

Roof Styles	Gable	Hip	Gambrel	Mansard	Flat
Century	**Gable**	**Hip**	**Gambrel**	**Mansard**	**Flat**
18th	Immigrant Georgian Adam	Georgian Early Classical Revival	Immigrant Adam (rare)		Immigrant
19th	Greek Revival Gothic Revival Queen Anne	Italianate	Dutch Colonial	Mansard (Second Empire)	Italian Renaissance
20th–21st	Tudor Chateauesque Craftsman Ranch Contemporary	Colonial Revival Mission Prairie Craftsman Ranch	Colonial Revival		International Contemporary

Queen Anne Style

In the 1870s and 1880s, the most fanciful of the Victorian styles, the Queen Anne style, became popular. Some typical details of this style are an irregular steep roof with ornamental gables, overlapping decorative wood shingles for siding, and wraparound porches with railings and columns. Many Queen Anne houses have a circular tower that extends the entire height of the building. A variety of decorative woodwork was used on Queen Anne homes, from spindlework to brackets and half-timbering. See Fig. 15-15.

The End of the Victorian Period

In general, houses built at the end of the Victorian era were less elaborate than those built earlier in the period. Their architectural lines were cleaner and simpler. Homes for the wealthy, however, were built on an even larger scale. Some common Victorian features—such as irregular gables and windows, wooden wraparound porches, and patterned wood shingles—were easily adapted to the smaller middle-class homes being built at the end of the century.

Fig. 15-15 The ornamentation of the Queen Anne style showed off the greater wealth of the industrial age. Decorative details were highlighted by different colors of paint.

In addition, by the late 1800s, multifamily housing was changing. In this type of housing, many families lived in individual units within a larger structure such as an apartment building. The invention of the elevator in the 1850s and the use of steel-frame construction meant that apartment buildings could safely house several individual homes on each floor.

As was true of single-family homes at the end of the Victorian period, architects and designers of multifamily housing also started to build as simply as possible. Their designs stripped away the overwhelming amount of ornamentation and details found in the earlier Victorian period.

The Impact of Technology

Interior Storm Windows

Owners of historic homes face a dilemma. Like other homeowners, they want to control what they spend on heating and cooling. Yet they also want to maintain the home's authentic architecture, down to the last detail.

Installing interior storm windows is one way to meet both demands. Because these storm windows are mounted inside existing windows, they go unnoticed from outside. Yet their technology makes a decided difference in conserving energy.

Insulation. Made of either acrylic or glass, interior storm windows add a layer of air between the inner and outer environment. Magnetic bars hold them in place and ensure a tight fit. Acrylic windows are significantly more efficient than glass in keeping heat and cold out. Glass windows have a special glaze that filters out heat and ultraviolet rays while admitting light.

Safety. Acrylic and coated glass are more resilient than plain glass. When they do shatter, they tend to break in larger pieces that are safer to handle and easier to clean up.

Maintenance. Interior-mounted windows reduce condensation in colder months by limiting contact between warm inside air and the cold outer window. This helps prevent rotting wood, peeling paint, and mold growth. Moreover, because they are placed inside existing windows, they are less prone to damage from the elements and are therefore more durable than exterior storm windows.

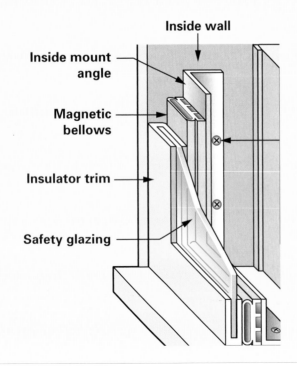

Inside wall

Inside mount angle

Magnetic bellows

Insulator trim

Safety glazing

Tech Trends

Using Internet and other resources, compare prices and insulative values of conventional and interior storm windows. Create a chart showing the advantages and disadvantages of each type.

The Early 20th Century

Early in the 20th century, America experienced one of the most creative and productive times in the history of home design. Traditional styles from various cultures and countries were being adapted to new ways of living. Architects also took bold steps in new directions. In general, two architectural movements took hold in the 20th century. One was based on traditional styles. The other, based on new ideas, was called *modern*. See Fig. 15-16.

Fig. 15-16

Early 20th Century Architecture

Styles	Approximate Dates
Period Revival Styles	
Colonial Revival Style	1880–1955
Tudor Style	1890–1940
Chateauesque Style	1880–1910
Mission Style	1890–1920
Modern Styles	
Prairie Style	1900–1920
Craftsman Style	1905–1930
International Style	1925–present

Period Revival Styles

Included in 20th-century housing designs are those that copy past styles. When Victorian architects copied the past, they mixed styles freely. Twentieth-century architects, however, wanted to copy styles in more pure form. The resulting styles came from European and American history.

Colonial Revival Style

From 1880 to approximately 1955, many middle-class Americans duplicated house styles from their own country's past. The Colonial Revival brought back such styles as the Georgian, saltbox, and Cape Cod.

The door and windows of a Colonial Revival home have distinctive features. The door is prominent, usually with a decorative pediment supported by pilasters. In some homes, the pediment extends forward, supported by slender columns, to form an entry porch. Windows appear in symmetrically balanced pairs, with double-hung sashes. See Fig. 15-17.

Fig. 15-17 With its symmetrical façade, prominent entrance, and simple classical detailing, the Colonial Revival style was popular for many years.

Tudor Style

During the period 1890-1940, the Tudor-style home was also popular. Its half-timbered look (resembling homes from very early England) is probably its most dominant characteristic. **See Fig. 15-18.**

Many Tudor-style homes feature steeply pitched gables at the front and sides; tall, narrow windows, usually placed in groups, with many small panes; and massive chimneys with decorative *chimney pots* (earthenware pipes placed at the tops of chimneys). Stucco, brick, and stone are among the most commonly used exterior wall surfaces.

Chateauesque Style

French palaces provided the model for another housing style. Chateauesque homes often featured towers, turrets, ornamental metal cresting, elaborate moldings, relief carvings, and arched windows and doorways. These castlelike details give Chateauesque homes a grand look.

Wealthy Americans hired European-trained architects to build these large, impressive homes. Many descendants of the original owners, however, could not afford to keep up the grandest of these ornate buildings. Some are used today as schools or museums.

Fig. 15-18 This Tudor house is recognized by its half-timbered exterior and distinctive chimney pot.

Mission Style

The Mission style was born in California and spread eastward from 1890 to 1920. Although the Mission style is most commonly found in the southwestern United States, examples can be found throughout the country.

Inspired by California's Hispanic heritage, its unique characteristics were fashioned after the old mission churches and houses in southern California. **See Fig. 15-19.** The Mission style includes such design details as arched doorways and windows; tile roofs often hidden by *parapets* (low walls or railings along balconies); and exterior walls made of stucco. In addition, bell towers and turrets with pyramid-shaped roofs often added charm to the Mission style's traditional shapes.

Fig. 15-19 The Mission style gained popularity after the Panama-California exposition in 1915.

Modern Styles

While some architects were looking to the past, others wanted to create something different. Modern styles developed throughout the 20th century. They began with the Prairie and Craftsman styles early in the century and picked up again later with other designs such as the International style.

Fig. 15-20 This Craftsman bungalow has very distinctive features. English architects built their bungalows with hand tools.

Prairie Style

At the beginning of the 20th century an American architect named Frank Lloyd Wright began designing homes in the Prairie style. These were very different from the homes of the Victorian era. Most Prairie-style homes were built until about 1920.

Wright's homes are characterized by their emphasis on horizontal lines, low-pitched roofs with overhanging eaves, wide porches, and such details as rows of leaded-glass windows. In the interior of these homes, rooms flow into one another, giving a feeling of spaciousness. The rooms are open and designed to connect with the outdoors. Porches, terraces, and rows of windows help draw the outside environment in. Wright custom-designed furniture and carpets to fit each home that he designed.

The Prairie style is not limited to the homes designed by Wright or the young architects he trained. Its influence can be seen in homes built throughout the United States in the first quarter of this century. One of the most common forms is the square, two-story house with a hip roof and wide front porch. This form is sometimes called "American Foursquare."

Craftsman Style

The Craftsman style originated in southern California, developing at the same time as the Prairie style and sharing many of its characteristics. The Craftsman style, however, is distinguished by the development of the **bungalow**. This is a small, one-story house with an overhanging roof and a covered porch. A variation of this style is the one-and-a-half-story type. See Fig. 15-20. The bungalow met the need for smaller, less expensive homes. The Craftsman style was adapted across the United States until the early 1930s.

The Craftsman style has the following distinctive features:

- A low-pitched gable roof (although some have hip roofs).
- Decorative beams or braces under the eaves.
- Full- or partial-width porches with the roof supported by columns or pedestals extending to the ground.

International Style

After the end of World War I, European architects began to experiment with new materials and new building methods. The result was the International style, also called Modernism or Functionalism. The International style used design elements in ways that departed drastically from tradition. Among its best-known originators were the architects Le Corbusier (luh kawr-byooz-YAY) of Switzerland, and Walter Gropius (GROH-pee-uhs) and Ludwig Mies van der Rohe (meez VAN-duh-ROW) of Germany. In the late 1930s, the immigration of Gropius and Mies van der Rohe to the United States helped introduce the style here.

Houses built in the International style emphasize function, or usefulness. Thus, elements that are purely decorative or ornamental are avoided. A typical International-style house combines simple geometric shapes to create an asymmetrical design that resembles a piece of sculpture. See Fig. 15-21. The innovative design was made possible by the use of a steel skeleton, which gave architects more freedom than traditional methods of building. The roof is usually flat. The exterior walls feature smooth, blank surfaces and large expanses of windows.

Fig. 15-21 While the Prairie style was a distinct departure from previous architectural forms, the International style, shown here, was even more radical. Frank Lloyd Wright designed this house, named *Fallingwater*, in 1935.

The Mid 20th Century to Today

The United States was involved in World War II from 1941 to 1945, so home building came to a temporary standstill. When it started up again, people wanted *modern* styles. During this time, several new styles emerged that changed the face of home building. See Fig. 15-22.

Fig. 15-22

Architecture from the Mid 20th Century to Today	
Styles	**Approximate Dates**
Postwar Modern Styles	
Ranch Style	1935–present
Contemporary Style	1950s–early 1970s
Split-Level Style	1950s–present
Shed Style	1960s–1970s
Traditional Styles	1900–present
Innovative Designs	
A-Frame	1940–present
Geodesic Dome	1940–present

Fig. 15-23 Ranch homes appeal to many people because they provide easy access to all rooms on the ground level.

Postwar Modern Styles

The styles after World War II ignored historical styles in favor of new, innovative ones. These styles include ranch, contemporary, split-level, and shed.

Ranch Style

A ranch house is a long, low, one-story house. It resembles the rambling one-story houses built by the early settlers of the West. The ranch-style home features a low-pitched gable or hip roof. Most have decorative shutters and picture windows. **See Fig. 15-23.** Some have partially enclosed patios or courtyards based on the Spanish influence. Private outdoor living areas are generally in the rear.

Although ranch-style homes appeared as early as the mid-1930s, this style dominated American home building from the early 1950s through the 1960s. It became popular as people moved to the suburbs because lots were larger. In many parts of North America, ranch homes are still popular. The one-story ranch is often preferred by people who want to make their homes accessible to all.

Contemporary Style

The contemporary style was popular among architects in the 1950s, 1960s, and early 1970s. It features wide eave overhangs, flat or low-pitched roofs with low gables, exposed supporting beams, contrasting wall materials and textures, and unusual placement and shapes of windows. This style is designed to integrate into the landscape around it. (This style is very different from the International style, which is meant to stand out from its surroundings like a piece of sculpture.) Some contemporary homes appear to be strongly influenced by the Craftsman and Prairie styles. The contemporary style is sometimes called American International.

Split-Level Style

The split-level home became popular during the 1950s as a modification of the ranch-style home. The split-level has the horizontal lines, low-pitched roof, and overhanging eaves of the ranch style—but the similarity stops there. A split-level house has at least two levels of living space, connected by short flights of stairs. Some split-levels have a basement, which adds another level.

The split-level house was originally designed to take advantage of a sloping lot. **See Fig. 15-24.** Because of the interior advantages of this house, however, it is also built on level lots. It provides the space of a ranch home without requiring as large a lot.

Shed Style

The shed style appeared during the 1960s. It grew out of the teachings of several famous architects, including Charles Moore and Robert Venturi. The roofline of a shed-style home is made up of a combination of steeply pitched *shed roofs*, each of which may slope at a different angle and face in a different direction. There is little or no traditional ornamentation. The exterior is usually wood shingle; but many of these homes feature board siding applied horizontally, vertically, or diagonally. The entrance is not obvious, and is usually set back. The windows are usually small and placed asymmetrically.

Fig. 15-24 The split-level style offers three levels of living space and needs less land than a comparably-sized ranch.

Fig. 15-25 This modern home has many traditional elements. **Identify as many traditional elements as possible in this modern house. Would you prefer a home with some traditional features or an International-style home?**

Traditional Influences

Many people are drawn to homes that reflect the traditions of the past. Traditional elements of style are often used for the exterior design on both single-family and multifamily housing. For example, an apartment building with an entrance featuring elaborate masonry framework might hint at the Greek Revival style. Row houses with pediments over each entrance may remind you of the Georgian style. A red tile roof can give a group of townhouses a Spanish flavor, while gingerbread trim brings to mind Victorian farmhouses.

Most designers and builders today are not as concerned with constructing replicas of historical styles. They do, however, borrow some elements of one or more styles to create homes with traditional appeal. Yet, traditional styles are adapted to suit today's more casual tastes and lifestyles. **See Fig. 15-25.**

Unique Designs

New designs often break all the existing rules of accepted housing designs that came before them. Two unique designs that redefined housing are the A-frame and the geodesic dome.

A-Frame

The A-frame is a design in which the gabled roof continues to ground level on two sides. This eliminates the need for separate side walls. **See Fig. 15-26.** The A-frame usually is used for vacation homes. Ease in building and the broad range of building materials that can be used during construction are the main advantages of the A-frame. The biggest disadvantage of the A-frame style is the odd interior space created by its design.

Geodesic Dome

In 1947 the American architect R. Buckminster Fuller invented the geodesic dome, an efficient home built of triangular frames that are joined to form a self-supporting roof and walls. **See Fig. 15-27.** The frame is metal or plastic covered by either a flexible skin or rigid panels. Because the dome is structurally self-supporting, interior walls are not needed. As a result, great flexibility is possible for interior floor plans.

Fig. 15-26 This A-frame home has three floors. **What rooms might be located on each?**

The geodesic dome also provides low-cost, energy-saving housing. Less building material is needed than in traditional housing. Heat loss is minimized by the decrease in exposed surface area. However, many people do not consider this style attractive.

Fig. 15-27 The geodesic dome is inexpensive to build, energy-efficient, and durable. **Explain if you would like to live in a geodesic dome.**

Influences on Housing

Many factors have influenced home design in North America. Not only the environment but also the history and the political, economic, and social conditions of the country have played a role.

Architects and builders have often looked to the past for inspiration. They combined the graceful elements of classical Greek and Roman architecture with styles from other times and regions to develop new styles found only in America. Today, cities and communities across the nation offer a variety of housing styles that illustrate and celebrate diversity.

Housing styles continue to evolve. Seeking to meet ever-changing needs and to take advantage of modern technology and materials, architects have designed new forms and shapes of housing. **See Fig. 15-28.** In the coming years, they must address the needs of a nation with an aging population and a greater concern for resource conservation. In the next chapter you will read about different ways designers are addressing social trends and lifestyle changes.

Fig. 15-28 The Sheats Goldstein house in Beverly Hills, California, is a concrete art form made up of cornerless walls and amazing arrays of light. The house was designed by modernist architect John Lautner. **Research the history of this famous home.**

Profile of a Preservationist

Preservationists restore buildings to the way they looked when they were first built. They spend a lot of time researching what the structure originally looked like, looking for historic pictures or records. They try to learn everything from what color of paint was used to what wallpaper was installed. Once the research is complete, the preservationist makes sure the restoration work is completed correctly.

Education & Training

- A bachelor's degree in historic preservation, architecture, history, or related fields is required.
- A master's degree in history, museum studies, or interior design with a concentration in preservation is helpful.

Skills & Aptitudes

- Must be able to carefully and patiently sift through historical records for information on a structure's history.
- Good communication skills are essential.

Preservationist
Tom Chaney

Sometimes, a person who buys an old house decides to restore it to the way it looked when it was first built. That's when I'm called in. As a preservationist, I find out how the house once looked and then organize and carry out the restoration work.

I start by doing research in the local community. Municipal records state the year the house was built and give details about any additions made over the years. A local historical society may have photographs showing how the house looked during different periods. Even a black-and-white picture gives an idea of color values by showing which areas were dark, medium, or light.

I also look in books about old homes and architecture. And I use my knowledge of the color schemes that were popular in various eras. Like clothing fashions, there are trends in house painting.

Next I determine the house's original paint color. On the outside of the house, I choose areas least affected by the weather—behind shutters, for example. With a small knife I carve a circle in the layers of paint. The result should look like the annual rings of a tree, with each ring indicating a new paint job. A similar technique is used inside. I check paint layers inside the closets, under moldings, and behind doorbell chimes.

Reproducing the original colors comes next. Most paint stores can custom mix thousands of different colors, and sometimes they can supply the exact shades I need. Many use a computer to analyze a scrap of the original paint color and determine its pigment formula in modern paint.

Once the colors are supplied, I can move on to wallpaper patterns, flooring, woodwork, and accent pieces. I keep a list of manufacturers, architectural dealers, and craftspeople who can furnish the items I need. The ability to establish and maintain these contacts is invaluable. Finally, I organize and oversee the work.

Of all the parts of my job as a preservationist, it's the research I like the most. I do take pride in seeing the final product emerge. But it's that initial detective work I find exciting.

Design Portfolio

1. Choose an older building in your community to research. Find out as much as you can about the design of the building when it was first built.

2. Prepare a proposal that lists the recommendations you would make if you were hired to restore the building that you researched. Include sketches, paint chips, and other visual elements in your proposal.

Review & Activities

Chapter Summary

- Historical events, such as immigration and wars, affected housing in the 18th, 19th, and 20th centuries, and still do today.

- In the 18th century, immigrant groups adapted their native styles to America.

- During the 19th century, architects copied styles from Europe's past. The Victorian period combined features from those styles.

- During the first half of the 20th century, some American architects copied traditional styles from England, France, and colonial America, while others developed Modern styles with simple, clean lines.

- During recent years, architects have adapted traditional housing styles and developed new housing forms.

Checking Your Understanding

1. What are three distinct features of the Georgian style?

2. What style is characteristic of early government buildings in Washington, D.C.?

3. How is the Early Classical Revival style similar to the Adam style? How is it different?

4. What is the main feature of a Greek Revival house? A Gothic Revival House? An Italianate house?

5. What are the main features of the Mansard and Queen Anne styles?

6. How did some buildings from the end of the Victorian period form a link to the Modern style?

7. Discuss some characteristics of Frank Lloyd Wright's Prairie-style homes.

8. How was the International style introduced to the United States?

9. Describe three advantages of a ranch home.

10. How do unique designs break architectural rules?

Thinking Critically

1. **Making Hypotheses.** Why do you think George Washington and Thomas Jefferson wanted the newly established United States to adopt Greek and Roman architectural styles for its public buildings? Defend your hypothesis.

2. **Identifying Cause and Effect.** Why do you think many Americans wanted to abandon the past and look for fresh new housing designs after World War II? Explain your answer

3. **Summarizing Information.** What values of society are emphasized by the following styles: Georgian, Early Classical Revival, Prairie, and geodesic dome?

Applying Your Knowledge

1. **Making Connections.** Make a horizontal time line for the years 1720 to the present. Above the time line, indicate major events in American history. Below the time line, indicate the periods and characteristics of American architecture.

2. **Improving on Design.** Select a housing style from this chapter. Then create a chart with the following headings:

   - Characteristics
   - Advantages
   - Disadvantages
   - How It Can Be Improved

   Fill in the chart by evaluating the housing style you chose.

3. **Persuading Others.** The year is 1950. You are an architect who advocates a new era of housing design. You want to persuade prospective homeowners to let you and your partners design modern housing for them. Write a persuasive speech about the new world of modern house design and why homeowners will love it.

4. **Creating New Designs.** Imagine that you have the opportunity to create an original housing design. Name your style and draw a sketch of it. Explain why your new housing style makes good design sense.

You have been hired to create a brochure to be given to visitors of a historic home. The brochure will help visitors visualize the home and its neighborhood when the home was originally built.

1. Choose a historic home in your area or one that you have visited, or work from an Internet site.

2. Gather information on what life was like when the home was built, its architectural details, and any modifications that were made to the building. Locate and print photos or drawings to support your research.

3. Design your historical brochure, making it as informative and attractive as possible.

4. Add the finished brochure to your design portfolio.

Designing Homes for Today's Needs

Objectives

- Explain how planning and regulation are used to assure quality of life in new housing developments.

- Describe how lifestyle changes are reflected in housing.

- Describe the various activity zones in a home and evaluate their importance.

- Distinguish between open and closed floor plans.

- Identify factors to consider when evaluating a floor plan.

- Analyze the advantages and drawbacks of various floor plan options.

- Summarize current trends in housing design.

Vocabulary

- zoning laws
- building codes
- aesthetic codes
- private zone
- service zone
- social zone
- open plan
- closed plan
- traffic pattern

T ry to imagine what homes of the future might look like. It's hard to predict the future, but housing designers and developers must try to do just that! When considering futuristic housing designs, what aspects of today's home would you like to keep? What would you like to change? This chapter explores the factors considered in designing homes and communities.

Developing Communities

People have been planning communities for hundreds of years. During colonial times, villages often grew up around a *village green*, an open grassy area that became a common gathering place. Government buildings, churches, and shops were centrally located around the green. Houses were constructed near the public buildings, with farmland developed just beyond.

Some community plans were devised by the immigrant groups that settled areas. For example, the Dutch built a wall on Manhattan Island to protect them from invasion. The large estates and plantations of the South, reflecting the French influence, were located far apart.

Another type of community plan was devised for the city of Philadelphia by William Penn, an Englishman who founded the colony of Pennsylvania in 1681. Penn brought to the colonies a *gridiron* design —straight streets crossing one another at right angles. Many communities later adopted Penn's plan.

As society became less agricultural and more industrial after 1900, cities grew as people sought jobs there. As an alternative to living in the crowded tenements that sprang up in the cities, people wanted homes of their own. Because city lots were expensive, developers began building small houses on the outskirts where land cost less. Gradually, residential districts, called "suburbs," surrounded most cities. Suburban residents who worked in the city, commuted to their jobs by car or public transportation.

Today, development continues at a fast pace. Entire neighborhoods can spring up within a year or two, complete with shopping malls. However, lessons have been learned from unregulated growth in the past. Haphazard building results in traffic congestion, pollution, loss of natural habitat, and an unending sprawl of homes, businesses, and industry. Managing rapid growth without these drawbacks is a goal of deliberate planning, often referred to as *smart growth*. **See Fig. 16-1.**

Fig. 16-1 Smart growth policies focus on creating communities that offer a wide range of housing and facilities.

Building Laws & Regulations

To make sure that growth is orderly and neighborhoods are attractive, most towns and cities have passed laws and regulations governing the use of land. Usually, these laws and regulations are created and enforced by a city council or another local government body. Most regulations include zoning laws, building codes, and aesthetic codes.

Zoning Laws

In many communities today, factories and businesses tend to be located in one area, while houses and small apartment buildings are in another. This is the result of zoning. **Zoning laws** are laws that determine the type of building that may be constructed in a particular zone, or section, of a community.

For example, some areas are set aside as residential zones. *Restricted residential zoning* means that only single-family homes may be built in the area. *General residential zoning* typically allows apartment houses, town houses, two-family dwellings, and some businesses or stores.

Commercial zoning is another type of regulation. Stores and office buildings may be located in commercial zones. Few homes are built in a zone set aside for businesses. Districts zoned as *industrial* consist of factories and warehouses. Some zoning laws set aside other areas as *greenbelts*—parklands and farmlands where no building is permitted. Many states are making efforts to preserve open space.

In addition to land use, zoning regulations may specify:

- Minimum lot size.
- The distance a building may be from property lines and other buildings.
- Maximum heights of buildings.

Zoning laws are important because they can prevent a company from tearing down houses in a neighborhood and constructing a factory next door to other homes. Zoning must make sense for the community's needs. Also, in order to be effective, it must be enforced. Most communities have maps indicating zoning. These maps are usually on display in the city hall. Real estate agents and salespeople often provide copies to home buyers.

Building Codes & Commercial Design

Commercial designers must do more than satisfy the client who pays them. Their work affects the life of the community at large, so they must also meet the requirements of commercial zoning laws and building codes. Codes vary with different types of structures, but in general they require designers to consider these factors when planning a project:

- **Safety.** The design must anticipate the safety needs of both motorists and pedestrians. Will the building block a driver's view at an intersection? Will a sidewalk café force pedestrians into the street? Should a skywalk be added for safe passage over a busy roadway?

- **Conserving Resources.** Some building codes set basic standards for energy efficiency. For instance, a lighting code might mandate the maximum wattage per square foot of space. Other rules may state that landscaping must be designed for minimum water usage.

- **Community Plans.** Commercial codes may be written to advance a community's goals. Limits on building sizes in certain areas, for example, may be used to promote small, neighborhood shops. Requiring the use of certain colors can help preserve cultural heritage.

- **Aesthetics.** Certain codes are designed to ensure that a project's design adds to the area's appearance, or at least does not detract from it. Zoning laws commonly require that commercial signs and lighting fixtures meet certain standards, for example.

- **Quality of Life.** Some statutes affect a development's overall impact on the community. When considering a location, for example, designers may be required to determine whether a new business will increase the amount of traffic in residential areas.

Apply It!

Imagine you've been hired to help design a small shopping center. The stores will face a main road. The rear will be visible to residents on the street behind it. Generate a list of concerns that you think are most important in this project. Then suggest solutions for addressing them.

Fig. 16-2 Building inspectors are responsible for making sure buildings meet building codes.

Building Codes

Usually, before construction can start, the builder must apply for a building permit. During and after construction, building inspectors visit the site to ensure that all building codes have been met. **See Fig. 16-2.** **Building codes** are rules that regulate the quality of building materials and set standards of quality and safety for construction.

Building codes can vary from area to area, since they are developed by each community to match local soil, weather, and other conditions. However, most areas have adopted some standard codes, such as the Uniform Building Code (UBC) in the United States. Other regulations include federal standards for public buildings to accommodate people with disabilities, such as the Americans with Disabilities Act.

Building codes regulate several areas of construction, including:

- Type and quality of building materials.
- Form of construction.
- Provisions for health, safety, and sanitation.
- Use of flammable materials.
- Installation of fire exits, where necessary.
- Electrical work.
- Type and installation of plumbing, heating, and ventilating systems.

Aesthetic Codes

In addition to zoning laws and building codes, some communities have **aesthetic** (es-THE-tik) **codes**, codes that regulate the appearance of buildings in order to maintain the beauty and the desired look of an area. In some condominium developments, for instance, the homeowners' association strictly controls the exterior appearance of individual units. For example, perhaps all doors must be of the same design, and they may be painted only in certain colors.

In designated historic areas, homes often must conform to standards set according to the time period in which the homes were constructed. For example, in a historic area featuring ornate Victorian homes, owners may be required to paint homes only in colors that were commonly used in the Victorian period. Owners often must have remodeling or home improvement plans approved by a neighborhood association to be sure that the proper "period look" of the home is preserved.

Many resort communities, whether near the ocean or in the mountains, have codes to protect the natural beauty of the area. One community might, for example, prohibit storing garbage containers in the open; another might restrict the use of certain materials and colors on building exteriors. Many communities have citizens participation in review boards that approve plans before a building can be constructed or the exterior remodeled.

Neighborhood Associations

In many communities, you'll see signs welcoming you to the neighborhood. The signs are evidence of a neighborhood association at work.

Technically, neighborhood associations are legally incorporated nonprofit organizations made up of residents of a defined area. Their goal is to improve the quality of life in the community in a variety of ways.

Communication. Most groups hold regular meetings to discuss issues of common interest. Members may also keep up with neighborhood concerns through print or online newsletters.

Special Events. An association may sponsor block parties, tours of homes, or talks on safety.

Care of the Environment. An association helps the neighborhood put on its best face by organizing seasonal yard clean-ups and encouraging residents to maintain their property.

Community Involvement. Associations help members stay informed about community affairs, such as proposed changes to zoning laws or new traffic patterns.

Planning New Communities

In order to manage growth and development within their communities, most towns and cities agree on a plan. Local city councils usually appoint a group, such as a *planning commission*, to make sure that land is developed appropriately. These commissions consist of local residents who may then hire a professional planner or other experts to make recommendations about present and future changes.

Rather than develop farmland or open space, many city planning commissions are now promoting infilling. *Infilling* is the redevelopment of run-down homes and construction on vacant lots within cities and mature neighborhoods. For example, in Mountain View, California, an unused shopping mall was replaced with a neighborhood that features a mix of shops, offices, and homes.

Planning commissions usually offer general recommendations about land development within a community. In contrast, some neighborhoods and communities are planned in detail from the outset. Such planned housing developments include planned neighborhoods, master planned communities, and cooperative housing communities.

Fig. 16-3 This is a planned neighborhood. From looking at this planned neighborhood, what do you think the goals of the developers were?

Planned Neighborhoods. Many housing developments can be referred to as "planned neighborhoods." The layout of the development, the type and appearance of housing units, and the use of surrounding land are all carefully planned before construction begins. See Fig. 16-3. Roads are designed to cut down on traffic. Grassy open areas, resembling private parks, may be set aside. The locations of neighborhood schools, recreation, and shopping are also determined in advance.

Some planned neighborhoods use innovative layouts to make the most of available land. *Cluster homes*, for example, are groups of homes clustered together on a development site, and surrounded by open spaces or forested land. All residents of the area can enjoy the beauty of natural surroundings. *Zero-lot-line homes* are placed on the lot line rather than in the center of the lot. This arrangement gives each home more usable yard space. See Fig. 16-4.

Some planned neighborhoods are designed for specific groups of people of similar ages or interests. Retirement housing developments are an example. They frequently offer planned recreational activities for older residents.

Planned neighborhoods are popular in North America today. The idea of smart land use and a ready-made neighborhood appeals to many people.

Fig 16-4 Zero-lot-line homes, which adjoin on the property line, offer more yard space while still protecting the privacy of residents.

Master Planned Communities. *Master planned communities* take the planned neighborhood concept one step further, creating developments that are virtually self-contained towns. The earliest and most successful experiment in a master planned community began in New York in 1946. William Levitt built "Levittown," a community of 17,450 identical houses plus community swimming pools, recreation centers, and schools. Built on the site of former potato fields on Long Island, the small, one-story, single-family homes represented affordable housing for young families at the end of World War II. This community still exists, but most of the homes now have second stories or other additions.

New master planned communities, sometimes referred to as *new urbanism*, follow the same concept. These communities feature housing, shops, public spaces such as parks, and public buildings such as a library and community center. The emphasis is on community. Rather than the suburbs of the past that were built for the automobile, new master planned communities are "walkable" neighborhoods where residents can walk down the street to mail a letter, buy groceries, or go to a movie. **See Fig. 16-5.** Both multifamily and single-family housing are included in master planned communities. The homes are designed to meet a variety of needs.

One such community is Owings Mills New Town in Baltimore. Here, the community has home dwellers with different housing needs and who are at different stages of life. The housing options include single-family homes, town houses, and apartment units. Some housing is designed especially for senior citizens. Residents have the option of either renting or buying a home.

In Owings Mills New Town, housing is organized into neighborhoods that are linked to one another by landscaped walking and jogging paths. Sports facilities—such as tennis courts and swimming pools—a day-care center, shopping, and a bordering forest preserve are within easy access.

Cooperative Housing Communities. Another form of planned communities—cooperative housing—is on the rise. These communities balance the traditional advantages of home ownership with the benefits of shared common facilities such as a large dining room, meeting rooms, recreational areas, workshops, and child care. The people in cooperative housing are committed to living as a community where people build friendships and trust among neighbors. Cooperative housing has its roots in Europe.

Fig. 16-5 Bicycle paths are a feature of many planned communities.

Housing Reflects Changing Needs

Just as our communities have changed over the years, housing styles have changed, too. Social trends help shape people's housing needs. Economic conditions, lifestyle changes, physical needs, and advances in technology are just some of the factors that influence housing design. Changes in housing and home design take place more gradually than do some other changes, such as clothing styles. A look at homes through the last century, however, shows that just as the outward appearance of a home often reflects its era, so does the way in which space within a home is designed and used. For example, some of the rooms featured in yesterday's homes are no longer used for the same purposes. Years ago, many people used cellars to store food; now they use refrigerators and freezers. Few homes today have a formal parlor for people to gather in, but many have a casual family room. **See Fig. 16-6.**

Large Victorian homes were divided into such specialized rooms as a dining room, kitchen, parlor, library, and music room. Today's houses are more likely to have open space and multipurpose rooms. The dining area, living area, and kitchen, for example, may be included in one large open area, often called a "great room."

Many homes in the 18th and 19th centuries were two or more stories high, which kept family activities separated. The bedrooms were all upstairs. Many of today's homes are on one level or have split levels. If two-storied, the home may have some sleeping space and a bathroom on the first floor, as well as on the second.

Fig. 16-6 In the Victorian era, the parlor was set aside for entertaining guests and was not used by the family on a regular basis.

A room you would not have found in most homes just 20 years ago is a home office. Today, with over half a billion people working from their homes, there is an increased need for home office space. In some homes, an extra bedroom or finished area in the basement serves as an office. Many new homes are being designed with a room specially designated as a home office.

Solar Electric Systems

In 1994, a researcher for a solar technology company showed slides of his firm's roof-mounted solar panels. An architect in the audience called them "ugly." The researcher took the remark to heart. Three years later, the first solar shingles were offered for sale, an aesthetically pleasing combination of energy collection and home protection.

Solar shingles and tiles are technically called building-integrated photovoltaics (foe-toe vawl-TAY-iks). The term *photovoltaic* refers to the conversion of light into electricity. Each shingle is a sheet of flexible stainless steel, about seven feet long, coated with silicon. Silicon is a moderately efficient conductor of electricity. It's applied to the shingle in three layers of film, each one blended with a different metal to absorb a different wavelength of light. Light particles "excite" the electrons in the silicon, generating the energy flow. Wires drop through holes drilled in the roof to carry the flow to the home's electricity system.

Like other photovoltaic systems, those using integrated shingles are still far from economical. Depending on how extensive the system is and the household's electricity uses, a system could take 10 to 30 years to pay for itself in savings from electric bills. An exception would be homes in isolated areas, where utility providers charge extra for extending power lines or cables. Some people argue the savings to the environment are worth the added expense.

Tech Trends

Explore other uses of photo-voltaics to conserve energy. What is the current state of the technology? How does it compare to other forms of home energy?

Designing Functional Interiors

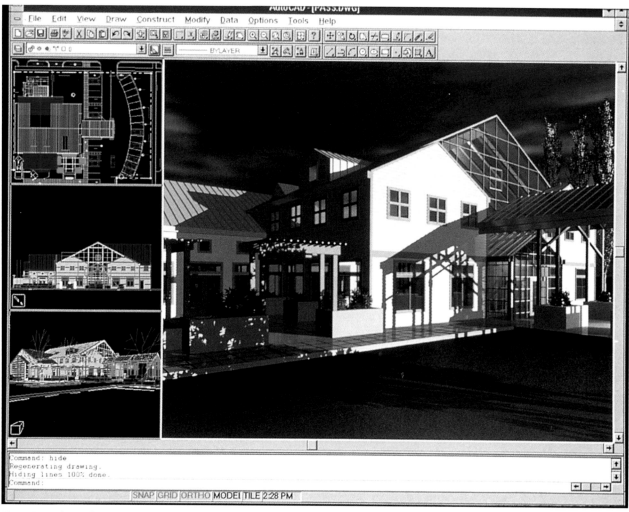

Fig. 16-7 When planning this home, the architect took into account the owner's lifestyle and interests as well as his current and future needs.

Designing and building functional homes to meet the needs of all people—regardless of age, type of family, or physical need—has become more of a challenge than ever. Home designers and builders must think through numerous situations that could have an impact on universal design. For example, how might a home with an open kitchen and family room design benefit a single-parent family or a household in which older people live independently? The single parent might want to be near the children while preparing meals. The older person would find it easier to move around in a home with a more open design. In addition to such factors as these, designers and builders must consider cost and environmental concerns in order to develop affordable, functional housing.

Most of the changes discussed in the first part of this chapter have to do with the way space within the home is organized. Well-designed homes are planned from the inside out. That is, successful architects begin by thinking about how a home will be used. They carefully consider the needs and lifestyle of the home's potential occupants in order to decide on the number and types of rooms, their size and shape, and how they should be arranged. See Fig. 16-7.

As you read through the following pages, you will discover a number of elements essential to making homes functional, livable, and comfortable for those who inhabit them.

Zones for Different Activities

Today's homes must fulfill numerous functions in a limited space. When several activities are going on at the same time, as often happens, there may be a conflict. For example, some activities are noisy, while others require quiet and privacy. The need to take different activities into account adds to the challenge of designing a home.

Well-designed homes divide the space into zones. The three most common zones are private, service, and social. Each zone contains rooms or areas with similar functions. By keeping the three zones distinct, as shown in Fig. 16-8, activities are less likely to cause conflict.

The **private zone** provides quiet, comfortable areas for sleeping and relaxing, as well as privacy for bathing and dressing. In most homes, the bedrooms and bathrooms are the core of the private zone.

The **service zone** is where household work is done. It includes the kitchen, one of the busiest and sometimes noisiest areas of the home. A laundry room, workshop, or garage may also be part of the service zone.

The **social zone** is the part of the home used for activities and entertainment. A living room, for example, would be considered part of the social zone, as would a dining room, family room, recreation room, or entrance hall. Patios, decks, and other outdoor living spaces can also be considered social areas.

Fig. 16-8

Activity Zones

A Visual Guide

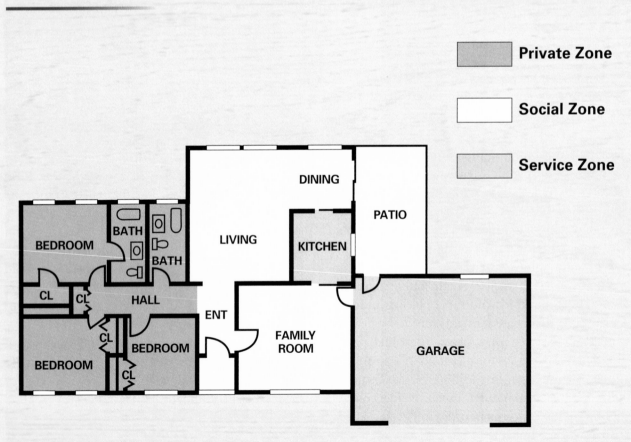

Private Zone

Social Zone

Service Zone

Fig. 16-9 In this open-plan home, the living room, dining room, and kitchen all flow together.

Setting aside separate zones for privacy, service, and socialization has advantages for daily living. For example, in the later evening, television noise or kitchen clatter is less likely to disturb a young child sleeping in a bedroom. Furthermore, zones enhance the convenience of the home because they allow similar activities to take place near one another.

There are many variations on the zone concept. In a home with two or more levels, some zones may be repeated. For example, there may be one private zone on the main floor, where the master bedroom is located, and another for the second-floor bedrooms.

In small homes, there may be little physical separation between zones. Still, a thoughtful design can establish clearly defined spaces for specific purposes. Even in a one-room apartment, a folding screen or bookcase can divide the space into private and social areas.

Open & Closed Floor Plans

As you read earlier, today's homes often include a multipurpose area. The living room and dining room may be combined into one L-shaped room. The kitchen and family room may be separated by a low divider instead of a full wall, or they may be completely open. In a **closed plan**, rooms are separated and self-contained. When few dividing walls separate rooms, that part of the home is said to have an **open plan**.

Each type of plan has advantages and drawbacks. Open plans seem more spacious. Lifestyles today tend to be more informal and many homeowners favor an open plan that offers flexibility for entertaining. See Fig. 16-9. Closed plans allow for greater privacy and better separation between zones. Many homes combine the two, with an open plan in the social zone and a closed plan in the private zone.

Evaluating a Floor Plan

Because the space in any home is limited, it's important that it be used wisely. The easiest way to evaluate how space is used in a home is to look at the floor plan. A floor plan is drawn as if the roof has been taken off, providing a downward view into the house. One-level floor plans show a single view. For a two-level home, there are two views of the floor plan, one of the lower level and a second of the upper level. Studying the floor plan enables you to evaluate the layout of a home and determine if it is suited to the needs of those who will live there.

One of the most important considerations when evaluating a floor plan is the **traffic pattern**, the paths people take as they walk from room to room during everyday activities. A well-designed floor plan provides convenient pathways to all areas of the home. At the same time, hallways should be as short as possible to avoid wasted space. Easy access should be provided between closely related areas. It should be easy to get from the kitchen to the dining area, for instance, and from each bedroom to a bathroom.

Economy of construction is another consideration. For example, having to install long runs of plumbing pipe adds to the expense of building a house. Costs can be reduced if two areas that require plumbing, such as kitchen and laundry areas, are placed back-to-back or, in a two-story home, if one bathroom is above the other. That way, the plumbing pipes for both rooms can be located in the same wall.

Floor Plan Options

Another consideration when designing or choosing housing is the number of levels in the home. Each option has its advantages and disadvantages. The choice depends on who will live in the home and their needs and preferences. **See Fig. 16-10.**

One-Level Homes

Many people prefer a home that is all on one level. Some apartments fit in this category, as do manufactured and ranch-style homes. All parts of the living area are easily accessible without going up or down stairs. Eliminating stairways also increases the usable space in the home. In a ranch home or ground-floor apartment, the architect can plan for any number of rooms to have direct access to outdoor patios. Exterior maintenance of a one-story house, such as painting, cleaning gutters, and changing window screens, is simpler than with a two-story house. A one-level home generally has more universal design appeal. Older people who do not want to contend with stairs or middle-aged people who want a home that can be adapted to their needs as they age often choose one-level homes.

On the negative side, the sprawling design of one-level homes can be a problem in areas where land is scarce. It also increases the cost of the lot, foundation, and roof construction.

Fig. 16-10

Comparing Efficiency

A Visual Guide

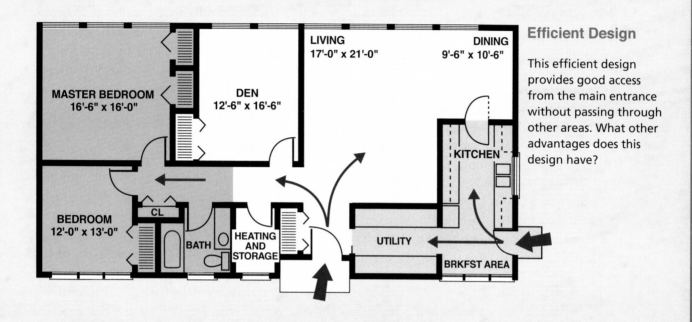

LIVING
17'-0" x 21'-0"

DINING
9'-6" x 10'-6"

MASTER BEDROOM
16'-6" x 16'-0"

DEN
12'-6" x 16'-6"

KITCHEN

BEDROOM
12'-0" x 13'-0"

CL

BATH

HEATING AND STORAGE

UTILITY

BRKFST AREA

Efficient Design

This efficient design provides good access from the main entrance without passing through other areas. What other advantages does this design have?

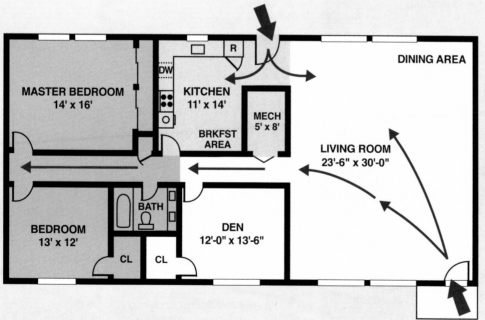

MASTER BEDROOM
14' x 16'

DW

R

KITCHEN
11' x 14'

DINING AREA

MECH
5' x 8'

BRKFST AREA

LIVING ROOM
23'-6" x 30'-0"

BATH

BEDROOM
13' x 12'

CL

CL

DEN
12'-0" x 13'-6"

Inefficient Design

This floor plan is inefficient. People entering the house from the front must always pass through the living room. The long hallway wastes space. How could you improve this design?

Two-Level Homes

Many single-family homes and multifamily units have two levels of living space. The traditional approach has been to place the social and service zones on the first floor and the bedrooms on the second floor. This floor plan option is a popular one because it maintains privacy. However, stairs must be climbed to reach any of the bedrooms. A universal design approach includes at least one bedroom on the first floor.

A different kind of design that is a variation of a two-story home is a home with a "loft." A loft is the space just below the roof of a house that can be made into an open living area. **See Fig. 16-11.** A builder can create a bedroom or another type of room and enclose it with a railing. The appearance from the lower level is similar to that of a balcony. Instead of simply a hallway, however, there is a room extending back from the railing. This plan can open up a small room, creating a feeling of space. A drawback is that, without a fourth wall, the open area lacks privacy.

Split-Level Homes

As you read in Chapter 15, a split-level home has two or more levels of living space, each separated by a short flight of stairs. The split-level design uses space very efficiently. In a typical split-level home, the entrance, living room, dining area, kitchen, and one or more bedrooms and a bath are at ground level. The garage, laundry room, utility area, family room, and perhaps a bedroom and bath, are a short flight below. Multiple levels allow for good separation between zones, yet only a few steps are required to go from one level to another.

Split-Entry Homes

A split-entry home has two levels of living space, with the lower level partially below the ground. The design is so named because the main entrance to the home is located midway between the two main levels.

Persons entering a foyer area must go either up or down a short flight of stairs to reach one of the main levels. This arrangement has the advantage of keeping the entry separate from the living room. The upper level usually contains the living room, kitchen, dining area, and bedrooms, while the lower level contains the laundry and utility area, family room, and perhaps a bathroom and bedroom. However, no part of the home is accessible to someone who cannot climb stairs.

Fig. 16-11 The family that bought this home decided to convert the loft area into a home office.

Trends in Housing Design

Housing design continues to evolve as people's priorities and lifestyles change. See Fig. 16-12. In Chapter 3 you read how new building materials have been developed because of concern about protecting the environment. More energy-efficient and environmentally friendly homes are part of the future of housing.

Other innovations in housing design are sparked by the interests of home buyers. Front porches, for example, are becoming popular again as people look for ways to make their home more inviting and their neighborhood friendlier. Homeowners now use outdoor areas as extensions of their living space. Designers have responded by creating attractive outdoor patios and decks. Some even include kitchens, with grills and sinks, in their plans. In some parts of the country, homes are being built around an interior courtyard.

An increasingly popular feature in two-level homes is a laundry area on the second floor. This is a sensible option since much of the household's laundry originates in or near the bedrooms and baths. Another growing feature is the creation of a media room that includes a home entertainment center, HDTV, surround sound, and more.

Flexibility is a prominent feature in modern housing. Homes are being designed so that spaces can be rearranged to meet changing needs. Some homes include a "bonus" room, that has no designated function, but that can be used as an office, guest room, play room, or whatever else the owner needs.

Fig. 16-12 Kitchens today have an open, efficient appearance.
What do you think kitchens will look like in 10 years?

Profile of an Architect

Architects design buildings and other structures and oversee their construction. Most architects use CAD programs to develop building plans instead of drawing them by hand. An architect's job is not finished until construction is complete and the building passes all inspections.

Education & Training

- A bachelor's or master's degree is needed from a school accredited by the National Architectural Accrediting Boards (NAAB).
- Architects must pass all sections of the Architect Registration Exam (ARE) before gaining a license.
- Most states require a 3-year apprenticeship program before becoming eligible for accreditation to practice.

Skills & Aptitudes

- Computer skills, especially with CAD software, are vital.
- Design and engineering knowledge is essential.
- The ability to focus on both small details and the big picture is necessary.

Architect
Chris Harrison

There are two things that every successful architect has to have—artistic sensitivity and engineering knowledge. Any building that I design has to be structurally sound and able to support the ways it will be used—that's the engineering side. It must also be pleasing to the eye so that the people who live or work there will feel comfortable—that's the artistic side.

When I'm designing a home, I first sit down with the clients to listen to what they want. Sometimes they come with photos of homes they like or lists of features they want included. I explain what is structurally possible and the probable costs involved. This is an important part of my work. Gaining client satisfaction at this early stage is essential if they're going to be pleased with the final product.

Making the sketches and final drawings has been greatly simplified by CAD. With a few keystrokes I can turn the design for one townhouse into a design for a 12-unit development. In seconds I can relocate the garage of a ranch home from the right side to the left. Besides speeding up my work, the CAD system has a number of special features that are great for architects. For instance, we have to create many separate drawings of the same structure. The CAD system links the information in various drawings. When I make changes to the two-dimensional floor plans, the program updates the three-dimensional view as well. I can also use the software to rotate the drawings on the computer screen. This really helps my clients see

what their new home will look like from all angles. I can even take them on a virtual "walk-through" of the house.

Once the design of the structure is complete and approved, I turn to supervising its construction. I make sure that the proper materials are ordered and used and that costs are kept within the approved budget. I have to ensure that all national and local zoning laws and building codes are followed. It's always very satisfying when the job is done and the family moves in.

Design Portfolio

1. In teams, conduct a study of your classroom. Determine how effectively the space is being used and what changes could be made to improve the area.

2. Based on your findings, develop a floor plan of your classroom, showing how you would reorganize it for greater efficiency.

Review & Activities

Chapter Summary

- **Zoning laws** and regulations that govern land use and the building quality, safety, and appearance.

- Master planned communities are similar to self-contained towns, providing nearby amenities to residents.

- Three principal zones within a home are the **private zone**, **service zone**, and the **social zone**.

- A home may have a **closed plan**, an **open plan**, or a combination of the two.

- Four primary floor plan options are the one-level, two-level, split-level, and split-entry.

- Housing design continues to evolve as people's priorities and lifestyles change.

Checking Your Understanding

1. What are **zoning laws**? Give an example of what zoning laws may specify.

2. What is the difference between **building codes** and **aesthetic codes**?

3. How do planned neighborhoods differ from master planned communities?

4. Give an example of a lifestyle-related change in housing over the last century.

5. Describe characteristics of private, service, and social zones in a home.

6. What is the difference between a **closed plan** and an **open plan**?

7. Name two basic characteristics to look for when evaluating a floor plan.

8. Compare the advantages of a one-level home and a two-level home.

9. What advantages make the split-level home popular?

10. Give two examples of recent trends in housing design.

Thinking Critically

1. **Making Hypotheses.** What are some consequences of zoning laws that allow commercial buildings in the same neighborhood as residential buildings?

2. **Identifying Cause and Effect.** What effect would an open-plan design have on the traffic pattern of a home? What is the effect of a closed-plan design?

3. **Making Predictions.** Identify as many factors as possible that will affect the way homes are planned and built in the future. Explain your reasons for ranking three of those factors as the most influential.

Applying Your Knowledge

1. **Aesthetic Codes.** Gather information and prepare arguments on whether or not aesthetic codes have a positive effect on communities.

2. **Planned Communities.** Research a preplanned community. Identify the developer's main goal, how businesses and industry were included, and the types of housing included. Share your report with the class.

3. **Floor Plan Evaluation.** Select a floor plan from a magazine, newspaper, or website. Study the floor plan and make a list of its positive design features. Write an advertisement for a home with the floor plan that you chose. Be specific about why the home is a good design choice.

4. **Plan for the Future.** Imagine that it is 10 years in the future. Design an innovative home that incorporates popular technologies. Sketch the interior layout and a view of the exterior. Write a description of the home's features and the community in which it will be built.

Design Challenge

Imagine that you work for a large relocation company. A corporate employee is being relocated due to a job transfer and you are handling the account. The client and her husband have two teenage children and an aging parent who lives with them. They want a home with an interior design that will be both comfortable and accessible for all family members.

1. Evaluate one-level, two-level, and split-level designs, keeping in mind the needs of all members of the family.

2. In your written report, indicate the advantages and disadvantages of each design option.

3. Include the floor plan of your recommended design.

4. Present your recommended design to the class and ask for feedback.

5. Make any needed revisions and place the final report in your design portfolio.

Unit 5

Using Design

The Elements of Design

Objectives

- Summarize the elements of good design and explain why they are useful.

- Suggest strategies for changing the apparent size of a space.

- Demonstrate ways to use line to create specific effects.

- Analyze the effects created by forms and shapes in particular designs.

- Explain how texture can be used to create desired effects.

- Explain why color is the most significant element of design.

Vocabulary

- space
- line
- form
- texture
- color

Have you ever walked into a room for the first time and been struck by how pleasing it looks or how welcoming it feels? Chances are the look and feel of this room—the design—didn't just "happen." The person who designed the room used the elements and principles of design to create the desired effect. In this chapter you will learn how to use the elements of design to create various effects.

Elements for Success

The guidelines used by artists, designers, and architects to create pleasing, orderly designs are called the elements and principles of design. Rather than restrict the designer, the design elements and principles provide a general roadmap to follow that helps ensure success. The elements of design include:

- Space
- Line
- Form
- Texture
- Color

As you learn to recognize these elements, you will increase your design sensitivity. You'll see how the components of a piece of furniture, a room, or an entire home combine to give an overall design impression.

With greater awareness of design elements, you can begin to look for and plan design in little things as well as large: from the arrangement of objects on a dresser to the placement of furniture in a room. When paired with the principles of design—which you'll read about in Chapter 19—an understanding of design elements can help you create pleasing, comfortable environments.

Space

Dictionaries list nearly a dozen meanings for the term *space*. As an element of design, **space** is the three-dimensional expanse that a designer is working with, as well as the area around or between objects within that expanse. The two parts of this definition state the two aspects of space that a designer must consider—the size of the overall design space and the arrangement of objects within that space. See Fig. 17-1.

Different-sized spaces convey a range of feelings. Large, open spaces give many people a feeling of freedom and sometimes of luxury. Too much empty space, on the other hand, can make people feel lonely and uncomfortable. If you've ever been alone in a room meant to hold hundreds of people, you may have felt that way. A room with a high ceiling or too few furnishings sometimes has the same effect.

The empty parts of the room look much larger than the smaller areas containing furniture. The emptiness of those areas appears exaggerated.

Have you ever felt confined in a room with too much furniture? That feeling isn't unusual. On the other hand, well-designed small spaces can make people feel snug and secure. People often seek this kind of space when they want to talk with a close friend or relax alone.

Fig. 17-1 The space was well planned in this functional room—a favorite spot for family and friends to gather.

Fig. 17-2 Even in a large loft, furniture can be arranged to make a conversation area inviting.

Arranging Space

Whatever the size of the space, people have two general design choices—fill the space or leave much of it empty. How much space is filled and how the furnishings are arranged should be determined by the effect you want to achieve. It's possible to arrange small spaces to make them appear larger, and arrange large spaces to make them appear smaller. See Fig. 17-2.

To make a smaller space appear larger, keep as much space open as possible by limiting the number of furnishings. In contrast, you might install mirrors to visually enlarge a room. Another strategy is to choose furniture that has a dual purpose. A shelf unit with cabinets, for example, might hold books, computer equipment, a television, and a DVD player.

When a space is too large for its purpose, it can be divided with permanent or temporary room dividers or screens. You can also divide space by arranging furniture in small clusters, almost as if each group were within walls. Another design trick to make the space appear smaller is to use area rugs to visually divide a large room.

As you arrange space, consider the feelings that the space conveys. Keep in mind that the effect space has on people also depends on how the other design elements are used within that space.

Line

Line is often called the most basic design element. **Line** delineates space, outlines form, and conveys a sense of movement or direction. When lines intersect they create two-dimensional planes. Examples of this are the lines that mark the edges of a wall, floor, or ceiling.

Lines can be used to convey a sense of strength, serenity, gracefulness, or action. One place to see how line conveys a sense of movement is in the distinct lines that make up some fabric and wallpaper patterns. Stripes are an obvious example. The outlines of objects and the lines formed by groups of objects also convey movement and direction. An example is a row of windows.

All lines are either straight or curved, and are placed in a direction—vertical, horizontal, or diagonal. Lines can be combined to make zigzags or other variations. Combining lines can create specific effects and feelings. Vertical lines can convey strength and stability. A horizontal line may suggest rest. Diagonal or zigzag lines evoke excitement and movement.

Creating Effects with Line

A variety of lines is desirable in a room design. For example, lines can be used either to separate or unify space. **See Fig. 17-3.** When people see a line, their eyes tend to follow along the line from one end to the other.

Another effect that line can create is increased height. If you've been inside a home with tall windows, you may have noticed they seem to add height and strength to the room. As you look at a tall window or long draperies, your eye is drawn in a vertical direction—up and down—emphasizing the vertical space.

Width can be emphasized too. Low sofas can draw your gaze around the room and create the illusion of greater width. The same effect can also be achieved with smaller objects. By aligning the tops of picture frames in a wall grouping, you can create the effect of a continuous line.

Fig. 17-3 This Mission-style bedroom furniture contains a lot of vertical lines. **What effect and feeling do these lines convey?**

Fig. 17-4 This great room combines a variety of vertical, horizontal, and curved lines. **Identify the effects of each type of line in this room.**

The characteristics of line in fabric and wall coverings are easy to identify. Not so obvious are the lines indicated by entire objects. For example, a tall bookcase, as a whole, creates a vertical line against the wall.

By placing lines in certain combinations and directions, you can create restful feelings or exciting ones. **See Fig. 17-4.** A bedroom with mainly horizontal lines and a few decorative patterns would seem relaxing. In a game room, crisscrossing lines contribute to an exciting decor. The graceful curve of an archway or a stairway will catch the eye and create a pleasing effect.

Form

Another design element that can easily be seen is form. **Form** describes the shape and structure of solid objects. Form may be two-dimensional or three-dimensional. Walls and rugs are examples of two-dimensional forms. They have length and width but little or no depth. Three-dimensional forms, such as chairs and other furniture, have depth in addition to length and width. **See Fig. 17-5.**

Creating Effects with Form

Form, like line, can be used to achieve certain effects. Large, heavy objects, such as a piano or sofa, give a feeling of stability. Their massive appearance adds a solid feeling to a room. Another way to create stability in design is to place several small objects together. Two chairs and a table placed close together, for example, have a visual effect similar to a large sofa. Long, low tables achieve the same effect because of their shape.

Fig. 17-5 The forms of this furniture give the living room a solid feeling. **What would be the effect if delicate furniture were used in this room?**

Weight is an interesting factor in considering form. A designer is more concerned with an object's *apparent weight* than its actual weight. Sometimes the same form can appear lighter or heavier based on its color or texture. For instance, the form of a beige sofa against a beige wall may not appear especially heavy. The same sofa with a denim slip-cover against that light-colored wall would have more apparent weight.

Fig. 17-6 San Francisco row houses are a classic example of harmonious design in architecture. This concept is also important in interior design.

Harmonious Design

A designer strives to combine forms in a way that creates a *harmonious design*—a design in which every item fits well with the others. Homes in some new developments or older city neighborhoods often have similar designs with only minor variations. They may be related in form, size, and color. The similarities are often the result of the homes having been built around the same time, perhaps by one builder. See Fig. 17-6.

In interior design, it's important that forms harmonize with one another. Suppose that you have a long sofa with a simple curving line and are looking for a table to go with it. Which would create a harmonious arrangement—a large table that echoes the curve of the sofa or a small telephone stand?

The telephone stand is quite different in form from the sofa. Often when forms that are very different from one another are placed together, the effect isn't satisfying. As you work with the design elements, ask yourself the following questions: Is this form right for its intended function? Does it blend well with other forms in the room? As you learn to answer these questions with ease, you'll develop an eye for good design form.

Designing with a Purpose

The elements of design in commercial buildings do more than create a pleasant setting. Here are some examples of how skillful use of design helps businesses achieve their purpose:

- **Hospitals.** For patients and their families, hospitals often arouse feelings of anxiety, uncertainty, and helplessness. Using glass opens up space. Tall windows instead of solid walls can make a long corridor feel less threatening, for example. Rounded canopies over entrances and oval mirrors in exam rooms are softer than right angles. Skillful use of colors and textures can create a more comforting setting. Design elements can also provide spatial orientation—that is, they help people know where they are. An open staircase, for example, gives a better sense of location than an elevator.

- **Restaurants.** Compare the design in a fast-food place with that of a formal restaurant. The fast-food design uses open, sunlit spaces, bright colors, and shiny surfaces to communicate cheerful efficiency. In the formal restaurant, darker colors, closer spaces, and plush textures evoke relaxation and comfortable surroundings.

- **Community Planning.** Community planners use the elements of design to direct the growth of commercial areas. Repetition or continuity of elements balance the diversity of businesses with a sense of unity. For instance, a red brick walkway visually connects buildings on a street through color, texture, and form. Selected use of contrast, such as different colored awnings on shops, adds interest.

Apply It!

Imagine that you're asked to design a new lobby for an upscale hotel. The hotel is used primarily by business people. What kind of atmosphere would you want to achieve? How would you use the elements of design to achieve this? Sketch your ideas and share them with the class.

Texture

An object's **texture** is the appearance or feel of its surface. When you run your fingers over the surface of something, your sense of touch reveals the *tactile texture*—the feeling of roughness or smoothness—of that surface. You can often predict what a surface will feel like from its appearance. Some printing techniques, however, can fool the eye. What appears to be a rough-textured wall covering may be smooth paper printed to make it look rough. These surfaces have a smooth tactile texture, but a rough *visual texture*. **See Fig. 17-7.**

Special Effects with Texture

Texture can influence the way people feel in a room. Plush carpet and furniture covered with soft fabric provide a sense of comfort. Nubby, rough materials convey a feeling of ruggedness and stability. Smooth velvets and heavy brocades suggest luxury. Glass, metal, and stone give a feeling of coolness.

Texture can also affect the apparent size of an object. For instance, a chair covered in a rough, loosely woven fabric may seem larger than the same piece covered in a smooth, satin-like fabric.

Another interesting aspect of texture is the way it affects color. In general, smooth textures appear lighter in color than rough textures. That's because smooth textures reflect light whereas rough textures absorb light. Thus, a metal chair painted green would appear lighter in color than a wicker chair painted the same green color.

Texture is useful for adding variety and interest to a room. Careful planning is important, however. Through experience, you will develop confidence in using this element of design.

Fig. 17-7

Faux Finishes

A Visual Guide

With a little imagination, you can transform walls, floors, furniture, or accessories into eye-catching *faux finishes*. Faux (foe) is the French word for "false." First, a base coat of water-based latex paint is applied to the surface. Then additional colors of paint are applied using household items such as sponges, rags, and plastic bags to create false textures. Using sea sponges will create a soft, blended texture. A rag brush, or a wad of rags, can give the appearance of lace. Plastic bags can be used to create rough textures. Dragging a dry brush over wet glazes will give the look of textured fabric. For your first project, choose a small item. After you get the knack of faux finishes, you could even create a floor as beautiful as the one shown here.

Marbling. Creating the look of marble requires careful application of a second color using a sponge. Then, a very thin artist's brush or a feather is used to create the veining. After the veins are drawn, a brush is used to soften the lines.

Antiquing. Applying stone- and sand-textured paints will create an old world look. Some antique finishes involve the use of five or more colors of paint. Certain color combinations can even create the antiqued surface known as Venetian Plaster.

Color

All elements of design are important, but most designers agree that **color** is the most significant. People are able to express their individuality with color. It's possible to set a mood or create an illusion with color. See Fig. 17-8. You can even make a warm room seem several degrees cooler—and a cool room can actually feel warmer.

The design elements you have read about so far can be used to create certain effects. When you combine them with color, however, the possibilities become much more exciting. You will see why when you read more about this important design element in Chapter 18.

Fig. 17-8 Color is a design element that most people enjoy working with. Can you pick out other elements of design in this cheerful room?

Using Design Elements

Paying attention to all the elements of design really makes a difference in design. See Fig. 17-9. Ashley was inspired to redecorate when she came home from a weekend visit at her friends' new condominium. She spent the next Saturday afternoon at the mall and came home to duplicate some of her friends' ideas. Her purchases included an ornate mirror and some paint for an old rocking chair.

After painting the large rocker and hanging the mirror, Ashley surveyed the results. She had to admit that the change wasn't what she'd anticipated. The rocking chair made the room seem crowded. The mirror took up too much space on the narrow wall.

Now that you have learned about the elements of design, you can figure out what Ashley did wrong. If Ashley had spent more time examining the space in her apartment, and had paid more attention to line, form, texture, and color before going to the mall, she would probably have achieved a more harmonious effect. Considering the elements of design is important, whether you're designing a room from top to bottom, or just adding some special touches.

Fig. 17-9 This cozy room reflects careful attention to the elements of design. **Which elements are particularly striking?**

Profile of a
Residential Interior Designer

Residential interior designers create designs that are efficient and meet homeowners' needs. Residential interior designers consider the size and shape of rooms before suggesting colors and materials to suit their clients' budget and taste. Their designs must also follow all residential building codes and regulations. Designers often use CAD software to allow the client to visualize what the final design will look like.

Education & Training

- A bachelor's degree and two years of experience are required for licensing. A license is required in many states.
- Passing a qualification exam is also required for licensing.
- Certification by the American Society of Interior Designers (ASID) is preferred.

Skills & Aptitudes

- Creativity and imagination are essential to creating a variety of designs.
- Visualizing spatial relationships is a must.
- Being adaptable to changing trends is important.
- Excellent communication skills are necessary.
- The ability to meet deadlines is vital.

Residential Interior Designer
Elizabeth Jackson

In many large cities, rents are skyrocketing. People find that the housing they can afford is much more compact than they expected. To make the most of their limited space, many of them turn to an interior designer. This is the type of challenge I enjoy.

I begin by analyzing the rooms to identify any design problems. Then, I consider the clients' needs, wants, and budget. Using my knowledge of space, color, proportion, and other elements and principles of design, I devise a plan that makes the space work for the client. Doing so requires artistic talent, imagination, good business judgment, and the ability to manage many details simultaneously.

The basic goal of interior design for a smaller room is to lighten it up—literally and figuratively. I show people how to trick the eye into believing the room is larger.

For example, smaller pieces of furniture take up less space and make a room seem less cramped. Pale shades are best for walls and ceilings because they reflect light and seem to enlarge the room.

Anything that calls attention to the spaciousness overhead also helps an area look larger. Ceiling moldings can be painted to define the upper half of the room. A patterned border, vertically striped wallpaper, and tall pieces of furniture such as bookcases all direct the eye upward.

Ample lighting makes every inch of a small room more noticeable. I usually avoid heavy draperies on windows, using sheer curtains or shades instead. Mirrors can also fool the eye into seeing more space than is actually there.

Eliminating clutter is the best—and least expensive—way to "free up" a room. I encourage clients to display large collectibles in higher locations. To avoid countertop clutter in the kitchen, I suggest storing small appliances under the counter.

I believe that attractiveness and usefulness go hand in hand. If the space is well designed, even the smallest home can feel comfortable and welcoming.

Design Portfolio

1. Choose a room in your own home that is small and cramped. Redesign the room so that it appears to be larger. List the actions you would take to achieve your goal.

2. Create before and after sketches of the room to show the problems you faced and the design solutions you came up with.

Review & Activities

Chapter Summary

- **Space** is the three-dimensional expanse that a designer is working with, as well as the area around or between objects within that expanse.

- **Line** delineates **space**, outlines **form**, and conveys a sense of direction.

- **Form** can be used to achieve stability.

- **Texture** influences how surfaces look and how people feel in a room.

- **Color** allows individuality to be expressed.

Checking Your Understanding

1. Identify the elements of design.

2. Describe one way to make a large **space** appear smaller.

3. What feelings do these **lines** suggest: horizontal, vertical, zigzag?

4. Explain one way to create the appearance of extra height in a room.

5. Give an example of a way to use **line** to emphasize the width of a room.

6. Define **form** as a design element.

7. Explain the difference between actual weight and apparent weight.

8. What term describes a design in which every item fits well with the others?

9. Describe **textures** used in formal and in informal design.

10. How can the **texture** of an object affect the appearance of its **color**?

Thinking Critically

1. **Making Analyses.** Give examples of a room that you felt was too large, and a room that seemed too small. Analyze the reasons why each space created that impression. What design changes might make the two rooms seem more comfortable?

2. **Drawing Conclusions.** What types of lines dominate your school building? Which are used most in your classroom? What design effects are created by these lines?

Applying Your Knowledge

1. **Elements Assessment.** Critique photographs of several interior room designs. Explain how the designers used each of the design elements.

2. **Space and Mood.** Find photos that illustrate the following: a large space that is mainly empty; a large space that has been divided; a large space that's filled; a small space that is rather empty; a small space that has been divided; and a small space that has been filled. Mount the photos on a poster board. Label each, indicating what you perceive the mood, or feeling, of each room to be.

3. **Harmonious Housing.** Select a street or neighborhood in your community that is an example of homes with harmonious design. Sketch or photograph the scene showing several of the homes together. Write a paragraph explaining the features that make the structures harmonious.

4. **Texture Board.** Collect fabric and carpet samples that represent different textures. Cut them so they are all the same size. Classify the samples as either formal or informal. Mount them on a sheet of poster board and label the types of fabric and carpet.

5. **Elements of an Era.** Locate photos of two living rooms, dining rooms, bedrooms, or kitchens that depict styles from two different eras—for instance, Colonial America and the Renaissance. Write a brief essay explaining how the elements of design were used differently in the two eras.

Design Challenge

Your client is an insurance agent who is leasing space in a new office building. She has hired you to design her office. While the space needs to be comfortable, the client also wants to make sure that her clients feel they can trust her with their business. The office is 10 ft. x 12 ft.

1. Draw a floor plan of her office.

2. Clearly illustrate how you plan to use each element of design in the room.

3. Present your design to the class and ask if they think it conveys a feeling of trust.

4. Make any needed revisions.

5. Place your completed work in your design portfolio.

The Role of Color in Design

Objectives

- Analyze how color can be used to create moods and illusions.

- Explain how primary colors are used to produce other colors on the color wheel.

- Describe the effects of intensity and value on various hues.

- Identify the characteristics of different types of color schemes.

- Describe factors to consider when planning a color scheme.

- Explain how to create a color sample board.

Vocabulary

- pigments
- hue
- intensity
- complement
- primary colors
- secondary colors
- tertiary colors
- value
- tint
- shade
- tone
- color scheme
- monochromatic
- triadic
- analogous
- complementary
- double-complementary
- split-complementary
- accented neutral

The duplex your cousin just rented needs to be repainted. The walls are dirty and the low ceilings give the rooms a closed-in feeling. Your cousin finds a note from the landlord offering to buy the necessary paint. "No wild colors" is the postscript at the bottom. Your cousin turns to you and asks, "Do you want to help me choose a color scheme?"

The Magic of Color

The words *color* and *magic* seem to go hand in hand. Perhaps this is because color affects how people feel. It can even play tricks on your eyes. Some psychologists study people's perceptions, attitudes, feelings, and responses to colors.

Red, for example, can make people feel bold, excited, or even nervous. Yellow can make people feel cheerful and hopeful. Blue is generally subdued and is often used to create a calm feeling. Many greens also have a calming influence.

Neutral colors such as whites and grays evoke certain feelings as well. An all-white room has a simple, clean look, but can lead to feelings of isolation. For some people, too much gray can result in feelings of fatigue. You would likely want to create different moods in different rooms. Most people enjoy living with a variety of colors in their homes.

Warm & Cool Colors

It's possible to feel warmer or cooler because of a color. In general, colors associated with the sun—red, orange, and yellow—are considered warm colors. Blues and greens—colors that capture the essence of the ocean—are considered cool colors.

Red-orange conveys the most warmth of any color. However, depending on the base, or undertones, of the color, it's quite possible to have a relatively warm green or cool yellow. Blues appear warmer when red is added to them; the opposite is true when green is added. Making a wise color selection in a design scheme can change the feeling of warmth or coolness in a room even if the temperature stays the same. **See Fig. 18-1.**

The colors you choose will depend partly on the purpose of the rooms. Cool colors are popular in bedrooms, bathrooms, and home offices because of their relaxing effect. Warm colors are especially suitable in areas of high activity, such as the kitchen and family room.

Fig. 18-1 Compare the subdued earth tones of the room above with the bright, warm colors in the room on the left. Which room reflects your personality?

Illusions with Color

Color can fool the eye. At the same distance, warm-colored objects appear closer than cool-colored ones. You can visually enlarge a small room, for example, by painting the walls a cool color.

Dark and light colors also create illusions. A high ceiling that is painted a dark color will seem lower, and a light color will cause a low ceiling to appear higher. Bold, bright colors make objects stand out. On a tan sofa, your eye would be drawn to turquoise pillows; white pillows would be less likely to be noticed. A dark walnut bookcase against an ivory wall seems to fill more wall space than a bleached oak bookcase against a deep blue wall.

Designers often rely on the psychological effects of color to help them achieve their design goals. Figure 18-2, a visual guide to color on pages 406-407, provides an overview of the effect color can have on the design of interiors.

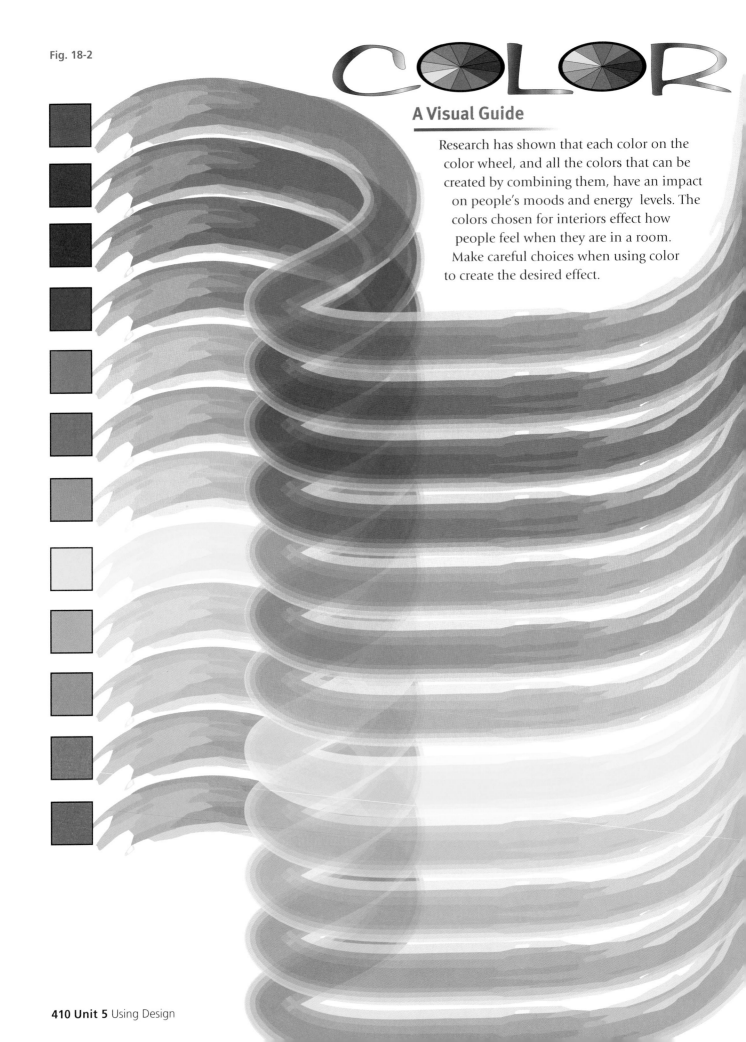

COLOR

A Visual Guide

Research has shown that each color on the color wheel, and all the colors that can be created by combining them, have an impact on people's moods and energy levels. The colors chosen for interiors effect how people feel when they are in a room. Make careful choices when using color to create the desired effect.

Fig. 18-2

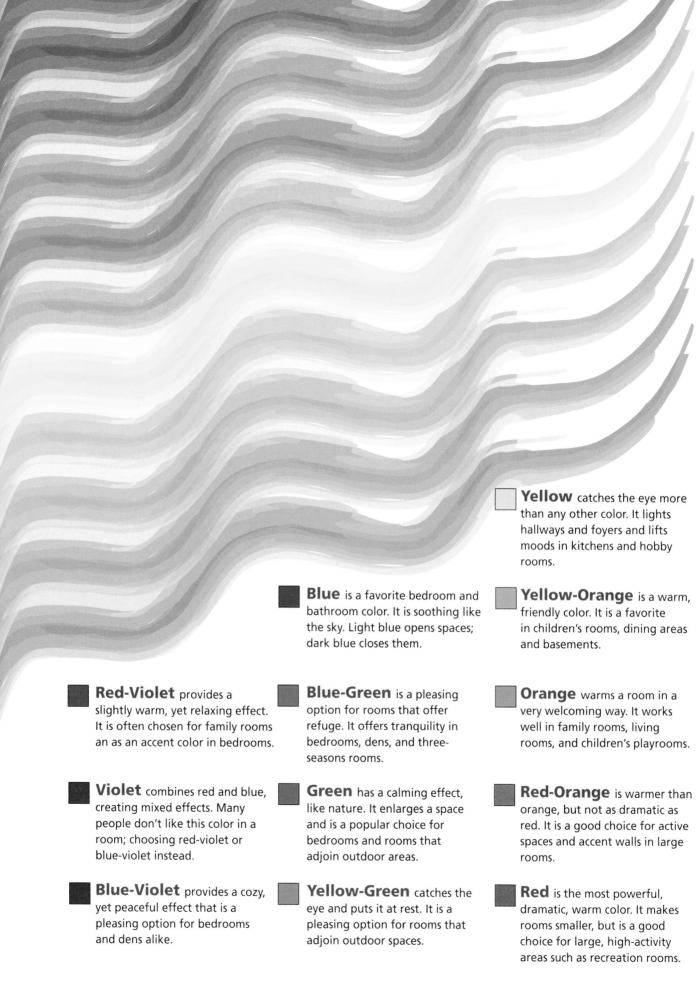

Yellow catches the eye more than any other color. It lights hallways and foyers and lifts moods in kitchens and hobby rooms.

Blue is a favorite bedroom and bathroom color. It is soothing like the sky. Light blue opens spaces; dark blue closes them.

Yellow-Orange is a warm, friendly color. It is a favorite in children's rooms, dining areas and basements.

Red-Violet provides a slightly warm, yet relaxing effect. It is often chosen for family rooms an as an accent color in bedrooms.

Blue-Green is a pleasing option for rooms that offer refuge. It offers tranquility in bedrooms, dens, and three-seasons rooms.

Orange warms a room in a very welcoming way. It works well in family rooms, living rooms, and children's playrooms.

Violet combines red and blue, creating mixed effects. Many people don't like this color in a room; choosing red-violet or blue-violet instead.

Green has a calming effect, like nature. It enlarges a space and is a popular choice for bedrooms and rooms that adjoin outdoor areas.

Red-Orange is warmer than orange, but not as dramatic as red. It is a good choice for active spaces and accent walls in large rooms.

Blue-Violet provides a cozy, yet peaceful effect that is a pleasing option for bedrooms and dens alike.

Yellow-Green catches the eye and puts it at rest. It is a pleasing option for rooms that adjoin outdoor spaces.

Red is the most powerful, dramatic, warm color. It makes rooms smaller, but is a good choice for large, high-activity areas such as recreation rooms.

Components of Color

The endless array of colors makes the process of choosing colors for a design quite challenging. Learning about colors and how they combine with one another will give you greater confidence in color selection.

Color is a property of light. Light is made up of energy rays of different wavelengths. Each wavelength is a separate color. When sunlight passes through a prism, the rays are bent. Because each wavelength bends a different amount, the light is separated into its component colors: red, orange, yellow, green, blue, indigo (a deep blue), and violet. The display is called the *visible spectrum*. The red rays, which are the longest, bend the least. They appear on one side of the spectrum. The shortest rays are violet. They are on the opposite side of the spectrum because they bend the most. A spectrum appears when the sun's rays pass through water vapor to form a rainbow.

All objects contain **pigments**, substances that absorb some light rays and reflect others. The colors that you see are the reflected light rays. For instance, when light strikes a red chair, all the rays in the light are absorbed except the red rays. The red rays bounce off the surface and we see the chair as red. Most objects reflect some of the rays in the light that hits them. If no light is reflected, the object is black. If all light is reflected, it is white.

The Language of Color

Several special terms refer to the different qualities of color. Learning these terms will help you better understand color. By using the language of color, you can better communicate your color ideas.

You have probably seen the color wheel before. It's a helpful tool for visualizing how different colors are related to one another. The placement of each color on the wheel is significant. Use Fig. 18-3 to analyze the relationship of the colors on the color wheel. Notice which colors are located next to each other on the color wheel, and which colors are opposite one another.

The specific name of a color is its hue. **Hue** is the feature of color that makes one color different from others. Each color on the color wheel is a hue.

Black, white, and gray don't appear on the color wheel because they have no hue. Technically, they are not colors at all, but often they're called *neutral colors*. Because they're neutral, they tend to blend well with other colors.

Intensity

The brightness or dullness of a color is called its **intensity**. Objects with high color intensity seem larger and closer than objects with low intensity. You can lessen a color's intensity by mixing it with its **complement**, the color that is opposite it on the color wheel. Colors of low intensity are muted and generally create a calmer effect than intense or pure colors.

Fig. 18-3

The Color Wheel

A Visual Guide

The color wheel is a circular arrangement of primary, secondary, and tertiary colors. The sequence of colors on the wheel is fixed.

Primary Colors: yellow, red, and blue. These colors are basic—they cannot be created by mixing other colors.

Secondary Colors: orange, violet, and green. These colors are made by mixing equal parts of two primary colors. Secondary colors appear on the color wheel halfway between the primary colors that make them.

Tertiary Colors: yellow-orange, red-orange, red-violet, blue-violet, blue-green, and yellow-green. Tertiary (TUR-shee-air-ee) colors are also known as "intermediate" colors. They are created by combining a primary color with a neighboring secondary color.

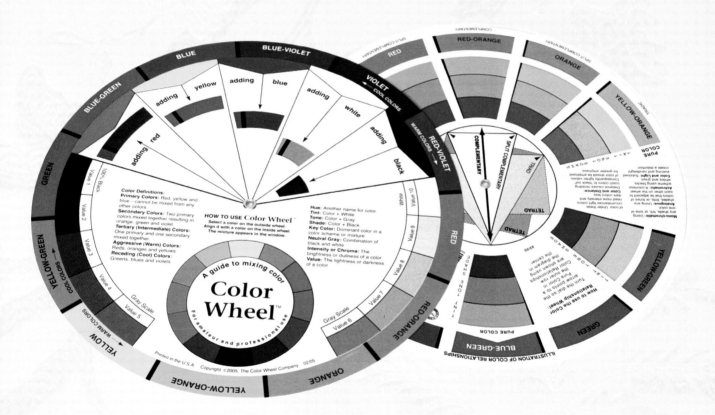

Fig. 18-4 Color chips from paint manufacturers are typically arranged by value—from tints to shades.

Value

The lightness or darkness of a color is its **value**. See Fig. 18-4. The basic hues in the color wheel are considered middle or normal values.

Adding white to a hue raises its value, or lightens it. The result is a **tint**, a hue that is lighter than its normal value. For example, pink is a tint of red. Peach is a tint of orange. Lavender is a tint of violet.

Adding black to a hue lowers its value, or darkens it. The result is a **shade**, a color that is darker than its normal value. For example, navy is a popular shade of blue. Rust is a shade of orange. Maroon is a shade of red.

Gray is created by combining black and white. Adding gray to a hue creates a **tone**, a color that is duller than its normal value, but not as dark as a shade.

Color Schemes

With so many individual colors to choose from, how can you be sure the combination you have chosen will be pleasing? Although color preferences are personal, designers have established certain tried and true ways of developing color schemes. A **color scheme** is a combination of colors selected for a room design in order to create a mood or set a tone.

You can create pleasing color schemes based on the color wheel, as described in Fig. 18-5. If you want to create a clean look, you might choose a monochromatic scheme that uses tints and shades of the same color. For a richer effect, you might choose an analogous scheme, using colors that are next to each other on the color wheel. High-contrast color schemes, such as complementary, split-complementary, and triadic schemes, can produce exciting results.

Fig. 18-5

Color Schemes

A Visual Guide

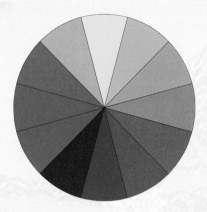

Widely used color schemes are based on ordered relationships of the color wheel.

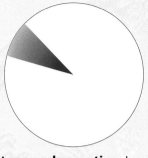

A **monochromatic** color scheme uses tints and shades of one color on the color wheel.

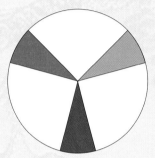

A **triadic** color scheme uses any three hues that are an equal distance apart on the color wheel.

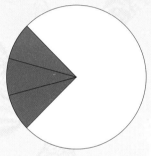

An **analogous** color scheme uses colors that are next to each other on the color wheel.

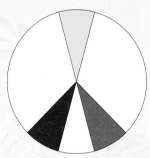

A **split-complementary** color scheme uses three colors. It combines one color with the two colors on each side of its complement.

A **complementary** color scheme uses two colors that are directly opposite each other on the color wheel.

A **double-complementary** color scheme uses four colors that are an equal distance apart from each other on the color wheel.

Fig. 18-6 Bright hues, such as red, yellow, and blue, are often seen in children's rooms. This softer look was achieved by using less intense hues. **What is this color scheme called?**

White, black, and gray can be used to create a *neutral color scheme*. Color schemes based on beige and brown are also typically regarded as neutral. It's common for people to fear making mistakes with color and feel "safer" working with neutral color schemes. Professional designers often encourage clients to use more color. **See Fig. 18-6.**

To provide contrast, a small amount of bright color is sometimes used in a neutral color scheme. **See Fig. 18-7.** The result is called an **accented neutral**, or "neutral-plus," color scheme. In a beige family room, for instance, red lamps, pillows, and picture frames might be added for contrast.

Fig. 18-7 Neutral colors dominate this room's color scheme. **What is the name of this color scheme?**

Psychological Effects of Color

How and why color affects people is not entirely understood. What is known is that certain colors do elicit noticeable responses. Warm colors, for example, increase the heartbeat and breathing rate. This may be one reason that they excite the emotions as well. It is not surprising, therefore, that designers suggest color schemes aimed at achieving an intended physical and emotional response. Their choices can make quite an impact in commercial spaces as well as residential spaces.

- **Body Temperature.** Colors can be literally warming and cooling to the human body. Yellow walls can warm up a cold warehouse. Blue walls can make a bakery feel cooler.

- **Health and Safety.** Because bright, warm colors stimulate the nervous system, they are used to warn or alert. Yet this same quality can also make them a distraction, and thus a possible safety hazard.

- **Food Appeal.** You may know that blue promotes calmness. Did you know that it also tends to dull the appetite? Scientists suggest this is related to the scarcity of naturally blue foods in the human diet. Restaurant designers often recommend full-spectrum lights and white dishes to avoid bringing out "the blues" in menu items. Fast-food restaurants often use red and orange to add excitement and stimulate the appetite.

Apply It!

Analyze the color scheme used in this auditorium. What effect will the color scheme have on students who visit the auditorium several days per week? What effect will the color scheme have on people who use this room once per year? Would you recommend any changes to the color scheme? Why or why not?

Planning Color Schemes

In many instances, a color scheme that is satisfying in one setting may be disappointing in another. One individual or family may like a color scheme that another would not. To be successful, a color scheme should suit the place, the people, and purpose for which it's intended.

Consider the following factors before choosing colors for a color scheme.

Mood. Decide on the mood you hope to create. Do you want the effect to be active or restful? Formal or casual? Sophisticated or relaxed? **See Fig. 18-8.**

People. Ask clients for their input about colors. You may not be able to please everybody, but avoid using a color in a common area if someone really doesn't like it.

Style. The style of the room and furniture may influence your choice of color. For example, a room with Spanish-style features and stucco walls is often painted a shade of white. You might choose muted tints, such as a dusty green, in a colonial-style home.

Time. The amount of time you'll spend in a room is also a consideration. Many people reserve dramatic color schemes for areas where they spend little time, such as an entryway or stairway. Another option is to use the intense color on one wall only. Such an accent wall is relatively simple to change.

Fig. 18-8 This room has a complementary color scheme. What mood do you think the designers of this room wanted to create when they chose this color scheme?

Fig. 18-9 Tints and shades of the same color have a soothing effect with a look that is elegant and easy on the eyes.

Existing Colors. Most people have to accept some room components they can't change without substantial expense: ceramic tile, countertops, draperies, and furniture. If so, plan a color scheme that incorporates the colors of those elements.

Adjacent Rooms. When there's an open passage between two rooms, you can see parts of both rooms at the same time. That doesn't mean colors have to be the same, yet you'll want to consider how they harmonize. To create a unified look, many designers believe that one color, called a signature color, should run throughout a home, even if only in small amounts.

Lighting. Lighting, both natural and artificial, has a significant effect on color. When a room has a great deal of bright natural light, for example, white walls may seem too stark and glaring. Muted or cool colors might be a better choice. On the other hand, a room without much natural light will seem brighter if a warm color is used.

Different kinds of light change the way colors appear. Natural light shows objects in their true colors. Different kinds of artificial light, on the other hand, can make colors appear more blue or yellow than they really are.

For all of these reasons, it's important to choose colors under lighting conditions similar to those in the room you are designing. Bring paint, wallpaper, flooring, and fabric samples to the room before making a purchase. Look at them at various times of the day and evening. They can look different, depending on the light.

Selecting Colors

After considering the factors that affect your color choices, you can begin to finalize a color scheme. It may begin with a color concept, such as a dominant color. This may be a favorite color, the color of a rug or a piece of furniture, or a color that sets the mood you hope to create. It should be a color the client will enjoy and can live with. Remember, a general rule of thumb is to avoid too much or too little color. Consider that large quantities of intense colors can overpower a room. Limiting their use or substituting a tint or shade of the color are alternatives. See Fig. 18-9.

To select additional colors, you can use the color wheel. For example, suppose you decide to use various shades of blue and blue-green in an analogous color scheme. A light tint of blue for the walls might be combined with brighter blue-green accents. You may also find a color scheme in a painting, some fabric, or wallpaper.

As you make choices, ask yourself if the colors you're considering have *color harmony*. The colors should relate in a way that is pleasing and satisfying when you look at them together. If you don't like the color scheme or you're indifferent toward it, keep looking for other options.

Creating a Color Sample Board

When planning a color scheme, it's helpful to make a preliminary sample board of the colors and materials that may be used. The sample board provides an idea of how the different colors, patterns, and textures will look together. To make a sample board:

- Use pins or thumb tacks to mount samples on a foam-core board so you're able to move swatches around as the color scheme evolves.

- Gather as many actual samples as you can of the materials you plan to use: paint, wallpaper, fabrics, flooring, even wood finishes. **See Fig. 18-10.**

- Vary the size of the samples so that they are in the same proportion to one another as the real objects. For instance, the carpet sample might be three times the size of the fabric swatch you're considering for a window treatment.

- Arrange the samples to reflect the relationship of objects in the room. Place the swatch of the sofa fabric next to the paint sample for the adjacent wall, for example.

- Evaluate the color scheme. Look at the sample board at various times of the day and evening. If you're dissatisfied, make changes until you find a pleasing combination.

If you're using paint, you should realize that paint samples may not accurately represent how the paint will look on the walls. Before you make a final decision, paint a large section of a wall and allow it to dry. Make sure the color meets your expectations before painting the entire room. Also keep in mind that the larger an area you cover with a color, the darker it will appear.

Fig. 18-10 Include paint chips on your sample board, but remember that the color on the chip may look different when it is on the walls.

Success with Color

Imagine that you're back at your cousin's new home, where the chapter began. During the past three weeks, you helped your cousin choose a new color scheme. Now you're here to see the results. The place has been transformed. The dark ceilings have been painted an off-white, so the closed-in feeling is gone.

The bedroom faces the sunny side of the house and is filled with light most of the day. For the walls, your cousin selected a soft, cool green that harmonizes with the room's pale blue carpeting. With her favorite shade of blue as an accent color, and the addition of some plants, the room has an airy feeling of coolness and serenity. Your cousin used the same shade of blue for the chairs and accessories in the kitchen. **See Fig. 18-11.**

When you know how to work with colors, creating pleasing effects can be fun. If you take the time to learn the characteristics of individual colors and how to work with them effectively, you can combine this knowledge with that of the other design elements to create interesting interiors that will be a pleasure to live in.

Fig. 18-11 By learning how to work with color, you can achieve the effects you desire.

Profile of a Color Specialist

A color specialist works with designers and manufacturers to select colors for fabrics, wall coverings, floor coverings, accessories, lighting, and furniture. This specialized individual can work for companies in a variety of industries.

Education & Training

- A bachelor's degree or higher is preferred.
- College courses in art, art history, color theory, interior design, and physics are helpful.
- Work experience with an interior designer is beneficial.

Skills & Aptitudes

- Creativity and an eye for design are required.
- An affinity for the subtle distinctions among colors is needed.
- Ability to keep abreast of trends in the field of interior design is essential.
- Good interpersonal skills for working with other professionals is valuable.

Color Specialist
Julia Sanchez

My interest in color started when I was taking art classes in high school. I loved mixing colors together to create new ones. I was also fascinated by how people reacted differently to colors. Some people didn't like orange, but most people seemed to like blue.

Today, I'm a trained color specialist. I work for a company that designs home and office products, including fabrics, wall coverings, paint, and floor coverings. My job is to select colors for the products the company makes.

To start, I research the theme the designer has identified for the new product. For example, if the theme is related to ancient Egypt, I research the colors associated with that culture. It's very important to be historically accurate.

Communicating a specific color can be complicated because everyone has a different impression of a color name. If I just said that a fabric should be sky blue, the manufacturer might select a different shade of blue from the one that I had in mind. So we all use the Munsell color chart. The chart includes samples of each color with a specific number assigned to each. I find the color I want on the Munsell chart and provide its number to the manufacturer. That takes away all the guesswork.

Besides communicating about color, I need to be very aware of color trends. I am a member of the Color Marketing Group and the Color Association of the United States. These groups forecast which colors will be popular in the coming seasons. Identifying future trends is important to companies in the interiors industry. Products are expensive to make. The companies want to make sure their products are manufactured in the "popular" colors so that the pieces will sell. A few years ago, black and white were popular kitchen colors. Today, earth tones are in high demand, but that will change too. I anticipate a great deal of international influence on color trends in the future.

Design Portfolio

1. Obtain photographs of at least five interiors. Identify the color schemes used in the various rooms and write an explanation of how the different colors work effectively together.

2. Using CAD software, design a master bedroom using two different color schemes. Describe the effects that each color scheme achieves.

Review & Activities

Chapter Summary

- Colors can influence your mood and create illusions.
- Color is a property of light. An object's color results from the way **pigments** reflect light that strikes an object.
- The color wheel identifies relationships between colors.
- A color can be described in terms of its **hue**, **intensity**, and **value**.
- Various types of color schemes can be created by using the color wheel.
- To design an effective **color scheme**, first consider the uses and characteristics of the room.
- Creating a color sample board can help you coordinate colors in a room.

Checking Your Understanding

1. Identify the moods that each of the following colors can create: red, orange, yellow, blue, green.

2. How can warm and cool colors be used to create illusions?

3. What happens to sunlight when it passes through a prism?

4. Explain how the **primary colors** are used to create **secondary colors** and **tertiary colors**.

5. What is **intensity**?

6. What is the difference between a **tint** and a **shade**?

7. Compare a **monochromatic** color scheme to an **analogous** color scheme.

8. Give an example of a **split-complementary** color scheme.

9. What is a signature color and why is it used?

10. Describe the factors that should be considered when choosing a **color scheme**.

Thinking Critically

1. **Suggesting Solutions.** Assume you are working with clients who want an intense red used as the dominant color for one room in their new home. Where would you suggest the intense red be used? Explain why.

2. **Identifying Alternatives.** Imagine that you are designing a color scheme for a couple's retirement home. The wife loves most shades of blue, but her husband doesn't care for blue. He prefers greens. What color scheme would you suggest? Why?

Applying Your Knowledge

1. **Expressing Personality.** Imagine that you are about to visit the home of a family you have never met. You have been told that your hosts are cheerful, friendly people. Write a descriptive paragraph to convey how you would expect their home to look and why, focusing your comments on how color would be used in their home.

2. **Effective Color Schemes.** Look through magazines or newspapers to find pictures of three rooms that use color effectively. Analyze and describe the type of color scheme in each room. Why do you think each was chosen for that particular room? What makes each color scheme effective and appealing?

3. **Light Effects.** Observe three different colored objects under natural light and artificial light. Note the changes in color under each type of light. How do these differences in color impact purchases people make when designing a room?

4. **Color Inspiration.** Choose a picture from a calendar or a piece of artwork that you really like. Plan a color scheme for a family room around your inspirational image. Create a sample board of your color scheme, placing the inspirational image at the center. Explain the color scheme you created for a family room and how you arrived at your choices.

Design Challenge

You've been hired to redesign the color scheme for a sunny kitchen. This room is the central activity zone for your clients and their six-year-old son. They want new floor coverings and are willing to have the walls and kitchen cabinets painted. Existing colors include gray cabinets, cream countertops, and stainless steel appliances.

1. Create a sample board that shows your proposed color scheme for their redesigned kitchen.

2. Explain why you selected these colors. Ask the class if they like the proposed color scheme and why.

3. Place your completed sample board and written explanation in your design portfolio.

Chapter 19

The Principles of Design

Objectives

- Identify the principles of design.

- Analyze ways that proportion is used in effective design.

- Analyze scale and the ways it is used in design.

- Explain ways to achieve balance.

- Explain ways to achieve various types of rhythm.

- Identify features that could be used for emphasis.

- Assess the importance of balancing unity with variety.

Vocabulary

- proportion
- golden section
- golden rectangle
- scale
- symmetrical balance
- asymmetrical balance
- rhythm
- repetition
- radiation
- gradation
- opposition
- transition
- emphasis
- unity
- variety
- eclectic

Learning about the various elements of design is only part of a designer's education. Knowing how to work with the design elements involves recognizing the principles of design—proportion, scale, balance, rhythm, emphasis, unity, and variety. With a little practice, you'll be able to assess how these design principles are used.

Proportion

In math class you've learned that proportions are often expressed as ratios. If a table is twice as long as it is wide, the proportion of length to width may be expressed by the ratio 2 to 1.

Ignoring proportion may be the most common reason that a room setting just doesn't look right. **Proportion** refers to the size relationships that can be found within an object or design.

It can take practice to learn to "see" proportion. Consider the example of a rectangular area rug with an intricate pattern. What proportions can you identify? You might think of these:

- The length compared to the width.
- The size of the border area compared to the middle of the design.
- The size of the middle of the design compared to the rug as a whole.
- The rug's area compared to the entire floor area.
- The amount of each different color in the design.

Each of these size relationships can be expressed as a ratio, and each is an aspect of the rug's proportions. Whether or not the rug appeals to you depends in part on the proportions that were chosen by its designer.

From experience, designers know that certain proportions create a more pleasing effect than others. For example, most people generally prefer rectangles to squares. Think about how often you see rectangular rugs, windows, picture frames, and chests of drawers compared to square ones. On the other hand, a rectangle that is too long and narrow can create a sense of discomfort—it may not "look right." In that case, its proportions are not pleasing.

Another general rule is that unequal divisions of space are often more appealing to the eye than equal divisions. For instance, suppose you decide to enhance a room design by draping a patterned throw over the back of a large upholstered chair. You could fold and place the throw so that it covers the top half of the chair's back. However, it might be more visually interesting to drape it so that unequal areas of throw and chair fabric are showing.

The Golden Section

Thousands of years ago, some of the ancient Greeks studied proportion in art and mathematics. One idea that fascinated them was a certain way of dividing a line into two segments. If you divide the line at just the right point—somewhere between one-third and one-half the distance from one end—something unique happens. The ratio of the larger segment to the smaller segment will equal the ratio of the whole line to the larger segment. This special way of dividing a line has come to be called the **golden section**.

Many designers feel that dividing a line or form according to the golden section is more visually pleasing than dividing it exactly in half or in any other way. For example, you might use this principle when deciding where to place tiebacks on a drapery—not halfway between the top and bottom of the window, but approximately at the point of the golden section. **See Fig. 19-1.**

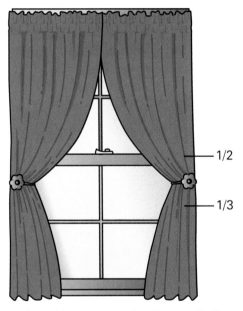

Fig. 19-1 The golden section is the division of a line between one-half and one-third of its total length. These curtains are tied back at the golden section for this window.

The Golden Rectangle

Imagine dividing two identical lines according to the golden section, then using the four resulting segments to create a rectangle. The ratio of the long side to the short side will reflect the golden section. This special rectangle is called the **golden rectangle**. It is thought by many to be the most visually satisfying rectangle—not too skinny, not too square. **See Fig. 19-2.**

1

1.618

Fig. 19-2 The sides of this golden rectangle represent a ratio of 1 to 1.618. Due to careful study of the ratio by Greek sculptor Phidias, the ratio was named "phi."

An easy way to approximate a golden rectangle is by using this pattern of numbers: 2, 3, 5, 8, 13, and so on. (To remember the sequence, notice that each number is the sum of the two preceding numbers.) A rectangle with dimensions based on two consecutive numbers in this sequence—such as 3 : 5 or 8 : 13—will be close to the shape of a golden rectangle.

The golden section and the golden rectangle have influenced design for centuries. Here are some examples:

- **Music.** Certain compositions by Mozart and Beethoven appear to be divided into parts according to the golden section. Whether this was done purposely is unknown. Another composer, Bartok, deliberately used the golden section to structure some of his pieces. The golden section even figures in the design and construction of violins.

- **Visual Arts.** The proportions of Greek sculptures often seem to be based on the golden section. In some of his drawings, Leonardo da Vinci sketched in golden rectangles to guide the proportions of human faces and figures. People have found golden rectangles in analyzing many other works of art.

- **Architecture.** The Parthenon in Athens, Greece, is the most commonly cited example of the golden rectangle in architecture. Some experts maintain that the Great Pyramids in Egypt are based on the golden section. In the 20th century, architect Le Corbusier used golden rectangles in some of his structures in various ways, such as for the shape of windows.

Look around for examples of rectangular shapes, such as desktops, windows, or picture frames. Measure each rectangle, then divide the length by the width. What items come close to being a golden rectangle?

Recognizing Good Proportion

Visually pleasing proportion is usually referred to as "good" proportion. The best way to learn how to recognize good proportion is to study the shapes and sizes of actual objects, rooms, and homes. Proportion is vital in architectural design. Well-proportioned structures are pleasing to the eye. Try to identify exteriors in which the walls, windows, and roof create a visually appealing whole. **See Fig. 19-3.**

Some proportional relationships are easier to pick out than others. The relationship between wall areas and windows is fairly obvious. Ideally, when several windows are the same size, the space between them should not be the same width as the windows. For instance, an architect would be unlikely to space three 30-inch-wide windows 30 inches (76 cm) apart from each other. Making the space between the windows narrower or wider than the actual width of the windows would appear more interesting.

Considering proportion is also important when you buy furniture and accessories. Take notice of whether the base of a lamp is in pleasing proportion to the shade, for example, or how the thickness of a table's legs relates to their length.

When you see proportions that seem pleasing to you, try to figure out why they're appealing. With practice, you'll be able to recognize good proportion.

Fig. 19-3 The architecture of this home shows good proportion. Notice the size relationships between the upper and lower windows. **What other proportions do you see?**

Scale

Fig. 19-4 The design of this child's playroom demonstrates appropriate scale for the individuals who use it.

Imagine that you're sitting at a writing desk in a swivel desk chair. The chair is so large that your feet dangle, your knees bump the edge of the desk, and you have to hunch forward to write. When you get up to leave, you try to push the chair into the knee space of the desk, but it won't fit. What's wrong? Obviously, the chair is too large for the desk—and for you. You could also say that the chair is out of scale. **Scale** refers to how the size of an object or a space relates to human beings and to other objects or spaces in a design.

Scale is not the same as proportion. A particular lamp may be well proportioned in itself, with a pleasing ratio of shade to base. However, to be in scale with a room design, it must also be the proper size in relation to the other furnishings. A large lamp might be the right scale for a heavy-looking library table, but out of scale if placed on a compact nightstand. Similarly, a miniature accent lamp on a triple dresser would also be the wrong scale.

In a small den, an oversized coffee table in front of a loveseat would be out of scale. The table would overwhelm the room and make it seem crowded.

There might be too little space for other furnishings. In contrast, a spacious room sparsely furnished with small furniture would be equally out of scale.

The Human Scale

Because homes and furniture are built for humans, it is important to use the human figure in evaluating their scale. Rooms and furnishings should be designed for the individuals who will use them. Lack of appropriate scale can cause both physical and visual discomfort. For example, pictures and mirrors should be at eye level. If they are hung too high on the walls they will not only detract from the design, but be difficult for people to see and enjoy.

Sometimes special scale is necessary, as in a child's bedroom or playroom. Here, adult furniture would be out of scale. Chairs and a table designed on a child's scale would be more appropriate. Low chests and shelves are suitable to store belongings within a child's reach. See Fig. 19-4.

Scale in Commercial Settings

Designers know that scale can have a profound effect on people. Large-scale structures can inspire or even intimidate; small-scale structures can be intriguing. Here are some examples of effective use of scale in commercial settings:

- **Schools.** Scale is downsized in grade schools. Smaller desks and chairs and lower hooks for coats create a setting that children feel is made for them. Compare these fixtures with the full-sized furnishings meant for adults in office buildings. Besides their practicality, they also use proportion to subtly communicate authority.

- **Hotels.** Some hotels use scale to impress and impart a sense of opulence. Large lobbies with central atriums several stories high may have tall trees, exposed elevators, and surrounding balconies. Plants, pictures, and wall hangings are similarly large. The scale of furnishings within these large spaces remains normal, often arranged in small groups so that the human scale is maintained at ground level.

- **Places of Worship.** Few structures use scale as dramatically as traditional cathedrals and mosques. Outside, towering steeples and minarets dwarf most surrounding structures. Inside, soaring vaulted arches and domed ceilings humble the human and glorify the divine.

- **Convention Centers.** These structures use scale to promote themselves. Huge posters promote upcoming exhibits or conferences and large entrance halls promote a sense of awe and expectation.

- **Government Buildings.** The U.S. Capitol Building in Washington, DC, has come to symbolize the American government. The Rotunda—the vast interior hall beneath the dome—gives visitors a lasting impression of the power of democracy.

Apply It!

Think of some ways the principle of scale can be used to improve the learning environment of a museum. Present your ideas in writing. Explain how scale makes the museum more useful or pleasing as a visitor walks through the exhibits, lobby area, and gift shop.

Balance

Fig. 19-5 Because symmetrical balance suggests rest and calm, it is particularly appropriate for a bedroom. **Which elements in this room contribute to its symmetry?**

Balance is the design principle that provides a feeling of equality. Balance in design occurs when the amount, size, or weight of objects on both sides of a center point is equal, or when unequal objects or groups of objects appear to be equal. The two main techniques for achieving balance are symmetrical balance and asymmetrical balance.

Symmetrical Balance

Symmetrical balance, also known as formal balance, is the most obvious balanced relationship. In **symmetrical balance**, the arrangement of forms on one side of an imaginary central line is the mirror image of the forms on the opposite side. See Fig. 19-5. Symmetrical arrangements seem to convey dignity and quiet. They suggest a feeling of rest and calm because both sides of the arrangement are of equal interest. Many impressive buildings throughout history have been designed with symmetrical balance.

Inside a home, consider a furniture arrangement in front of a fireplace. To create symmetrical balance, you might arrange two upholstered chairs facing each other in front of the fireplace, which would act as the center point. Suppose that you also placed a rug between the chairs and hung a painting above the mantel. If you drew an imaginary line through the center of the painting, fireplace, and rug, both halves would appear the same. This mirror image of one side looking just like the other illustrates symmetrical or formal balance.

Applying the basics of symmetrical design is a good place to start when trying to achieve balance. If this type of balance is overused, however, a monotonous appearance can result.

Asymmetrical Balance

A design with **asymmetrical balance** is one in which elements on either side of an imaginary central line are unmatched, but appear to be in balance. Different sizes, forms, textures, and colors can be combined to achieve asymmetrical balance. For example, a round object can balance a square object of similar size. Two or more smaller objects can balance one large one. See Fig. 19-6.

To use the fireplace example again, the two upholstered chairs could be placed on one side of the fireplace, balanced with a loveseat on the other side. Another name for asymmetrical balance is *informal balance*. East Asian design often makes use of asymmetrical balance.

When using asymmetrical balance, be sure to consider objects' apparent weight rather than their actual weight. For instance, a small, dark object could balance a larger, light-colored item, in spite of their size difference. That's because the dark object has more apparent weight.

Fig. 19-6 The objects on either side of the lamp balance the top of this small chest.

Rhythm

You can find rhythm in the back of a chair, in the pattern of a quilt, or in the folds of draperies. **Rhythm** is the principle that suggests connected movement between different parts of a design. It might be created with colors, lines, forms, or textures. Sometimes rhythm is referred to as *continuity*. It can add interest to an area, but to avoid monotony, it should not be overused. Rhythm can be achieved in various ways, including repetition, radiation, gradation, opposition, and transition.

Repetition. Rhythm is most often achieved by **repetition**, which is the act of repeating. The repeating pattern might be as simple as *A A A A*, in which the letter A might represent a spindle in a stairway railing or a pattern in a wallpaper border. The repetition might be an *alternating* pattern, such as *A B A B A B* (think of a checkerboard); or *A B C A B C*, with three different elements repeating.

Repeating rhythm helps to lead the eye from one point to another. A specific color repeated at various points in a room setting creates a sense of rhythm, as does a repeated design in flooring. Woodwork that runs around the top or base of a wall also introduces a rhythm that leads the eye around the room. See Fig. 19-7.

Fig. 19-7 The repeating window panes, the lines in the wallboard, and even the starfish develop a sense of repetition in this colorful studio.

Radiation. Rhythm in design can also be achieved by radiation. **Radiation** occurs when lines radiate, or move outward, from a central point. Chairs arranged around a round table are an example of radiation. To achieve rhythm through radiation in design, you might group small pictures around a large one. Tieback curtains, which lead the eye to the top and center of the window, are also an example of radiation. See Fig. 19-8.

Fig. 19-8 Radiation is apparent in this tile design.

Gradation. When objects increase or decrease in size, the eye tends to follow the line created. **Gradation** is a gradual increasing or decreasing of color, size, or pattern. See Fig. 19-9. For example, different sizes of candles, arranged from tall to short, lead the eye from one candle to the next.

A gradual change of form is usually more pleasing than an abrupt one. When forms gradually change from low to high, as in a pyramid arrangement, your gaze glides up the slope. On the other hand, if you see one small form perched on top of a much larger one, your gaze will dart back and forth.

Opposition. When lines come together to form right angles, the result is termed **opposition**. Examples of opposition include the square corners of a doorway and a sofa with arms at right angles to the back.

Transition. When lines change direction by flowing in a curve, or when curved lines lead the eye from one object to another, the result is called **transition**. Arched doorways, draperies with swags, and a sofa with a back that curves into the arms are examples of transition.

Fig. 19-9 Nesting tables are a classic example of gradation. Can you think of another example?

Emphasis

Fig.19-10 The purple walls serve as emphasis for this foyer. The walls provide a nice contrast with the wood flooring.

The terms *center of interest* and *focal point* can be used to describe the principle of design called **emphasis**. Dramatic structural features—such as a colorful stained glass window or a stone fireplace—are likely to be focal points because they draw attention. However, the rooms in your home don't need such features to have a center of interest. You might create emphasis with a large cabinet or an eye-catching framed poster. The focal point doesn't have to be valuable or expensive. It might be a brightly painted headboard or a large ceramic pitcher filled with tulips.

Instead of one large object, a center of interest can also be created with a collection of smaller ones. For a grandparent, it could be a framed collection of his or her grandchildren's drawings. Collections don't have to be large to be emphasized. For instance, Michelle has dozens of teapots in her collection. By displaying only five or six at a time, her teapots have more of an impact than a large, cluttered display.

The decision to emphasize a particular area or feature is a personal one. When choosing an item or feature to emphasize, keep in mind that it should be dominant, but not overpower the rest of the room. See Fig. 19-10.

Unity & Variety

Unity occurs when all the parts of a design are related by one idea. When there is unity among design elements, the result is a harmonious design.

You can create unity by choosing items with similar characteristics. For example, you might select furniture and accessories that all have curved lines. The similarity of line will help the room look "tied together." Don't confuse unity with sameness, however. It's not necessary, or even desirable, for all the furnishings in a room to match. **See Fig. 19-11.** Without some variety, rooms can be predictable and monotonous.

Variety occurs when different styles and materials are combined. Variety adds interest to a design, but confusion can result if variety is carried too far. One common mistake is to use a different decorating style in each room of a small home. Having Victorian decor in the living room, for example, and a chrome and glass table in the adjacent dining area creates a feeling of conflict. This lack of unity may make compact living quarters seem even smaller.

The **eclectic** style of decorating involves mixing furnishings of different styles and possibly from different periods. This works as long as the styles and materials are compatible. For instance, modern furniture might be mixed with more classic styles as long as all the pieces have similar proportions and a similar finish. Familiarity with the elements and principles of design helps ensure success when creating an eclectic decor.

To be effective, unity and variety must be combined to create an overall harmonious effect. For example, most homes can be unified by carrying the exterior design features inside. Traditional furnishings might be used in a Cape Cod house. The furniture in a modern home could have the same clean, simple lines and shapes as the exterior architecture.

Fig. 19-11 A quart of paint transformed these four mismatched chairs into a harmonious grouping that creates both unity and variety.

Applying Design Principles

The principles of good design apply in any setting. When David and his brother, Marco, decided to share a house, they each already had a variety of furnishings. There was a comfortable sofa that had belonged to their parents, plus several chairs and end tables they brought from their respective apartments.

They chose which pieces to place in the living room and which to move to the bedrooms. They used David's dining table and Marco's framed prints to create rhythm and balance. For emphasis in the living room, they used the collection of seven wall clocks that they had inherited from their parents. Grouping the clocks on the wall above a low bookshelf made an interesting focal point.

With some imagination, along with knowledge of the principles of design, David and Marco created a stylish, eclectic design. By paying attention to proportion, balance, rhythm, emphasis, unity, and variety, you can experience similar design success. See Fig. 19-12.

Fig. 19-12 Design principles can be combined to create a striking, yet very livable space. **What design principles are evident in this room?**

Profile of a Contract Interior Designer

Contract interior designers take part in design projects in commercial settings, including offices and stores. They are responsible for determining the client's needs and resources; developing a design concept; making adjustments based on client feedback; choosing colors, materials, and finishes that carry out the design concept; creating construction plans to implement the concept; and reviewing the installation to make sure workers follow the plan.

Education & Training

- A bachelor's degree, two years experience, and passing a qualifying exam are required for licensing.
- Certification by the American Society of Interior Designers (ASID) is preferred.
- Advanced certification can be obtained with six years of experience and passing another exam.

Skills & Aptitudes

- Creativity and analytical skills are essential.
- Ability to prepare and follow budgets and schedules is vital.
- Research and communication skills are very important.

Contract Interior Designer
Andrea Schrader

What I find most enjoyable about my work as a contract interior designer is the variety of sites I work on. One project can be an office, but the next may be a new store or a restaurant or a phone center or a warehouse fulfillment center. Each setting has a unique set of design challenges. The size, shape, and location of the space are all important factors. So are the size of the company and its future plans. Of course, the kind of work the company does also influences design decisions.

We have to ask a lot of basic questions. Do workers interact only with each other, or do they see the public? What is the nature of the work, and what special facilities do people need to get that work done? Do employees work largely alone or do they work together in teams? All these factors can affect the way we design the space.

I designed a sales office recently. That project highlights the issues we have to think about. The company's salespeople spent most of their time on the road. Still, they needed to be in the office at least once a week to meet with other staff members. The company wanted to stagger these visits to avoid ballooning space needs. So we created offices that could be shared plus meeting spaces that allowed people to interact.

The first thing we do when taking on a new project is assess the space as it exists. We spend several hours there, walking around. We make notes on what seems to work and what doesn't. We look at traffic patterns, how people work, and how they interact.

I always make a point to talk to several workers at the client company, not just the managers or top executives. People who do the work have the best idea of

what problems they face. By getting that information, you can better design a space in which they can work comfortably and smoothly.

One thing I've learned in this job is you have to listen. If you need to work too hard to sell an idea to a client, it's because the idea isn't really what the client wants. That's because you weren't paying enough attention when researching the project. There's no point in ignoring the client's needs. That just means wasted time and effort. And *that's* bad business!

Design Portfolio

1. Visit a store or an office that customers come to. Observe how workers and customers interact. Redesign the space to improve it in terms of these interactions.

2. You are a contract designer hired to design a new software support call-in center. The office needs 20 shared work stations plus space for a supervisor. Use CAD software to design the space. Explain why you chose the materials you selected.

Chapter Summary

- Combining the principles of design with the elements of design helps achieve satisfying results.

- The terms proportion and scale both refer to size relationships. **Proportion** refers mainly to relationships within an object. **Scale** refers mainly to relationships of one object to another.

- A design can use **symmetrical balance** or **asymmetrical balance** to create a sense of equality.

- Various types of **rhythm** suggest connected movement in a design.

- An item that draws attention provides a point of **emphasis**.

- Successful design utilizes both **unity** and **variety**.

Checking Your Understanding

1. Identify the principles of design.

2. What is meant by the **golden section**? Why is it significant?

3. Why might a small, antique chair not look "right" with an oversized desk?

4. What is the human **scale**?

5. What challenge does a child's room present when applying the principles of design?

6. Explain the difference between **symmetrical balance** and **asymmetrical balance**. Which is considered more formal?

7. How might you achieve **rhythm** through **repetition**?

8. How is **radiation** different from **gradation**?

9. How is **opposition** different from **transition**?

10. What is the purpose of **emphasis**?

11. Why is **unity** alone not enough to create a good design?

12. Give an example of how interior and exterior designs can be unified.

Thinking Critically

1. **Analyzing Design.** Suppose a room contained two red leather sofas, a round coffee table, one floor lamp, three large plants, and an entertainment center. The wood floors are accented with a large area rug under the seating area. The walls are dark blue and the ceiling is high. How would you use the principles of design to analyze this design? Give reasons for your approach.

2. **Establishing Priorities.** You have been asked to design the interior of an empty one-bedroom apartment. The client has given you $10,000 and the power to make all the decisions without her approval. How would you decide what to do first and why?

Applying Your Knowledge

1. **Proportion.** Choose a basic piece of furniture or an accessory such as a lamp, an end table, or a chair to illustrate proportion. Draw various examples of the item to illustrate both good and poor proportion. Ask your classmates to identify which of the objects are not in good proportion and explain why.

2. **Scale.** Design a 12 ft. x 16 ft. playroom for children ages 3-6. Describe the scale of the furnishings and explain why each item was chosen.

3. **Balance.** Think of at least three items you might display on a fireplace mantel. Sketch at least two possible arrangements using different types of balance. Explain how each of your arrangements achieve balance.

4. **Rhythm.** Find pictures of rooms that show various types of patterns. Label at least one picture that displays each type of rhythm: repetition, radiation, gradation, transition, and opposition.

5. **Emphasis.** Design a 5 ft. x 10 ft. bathroom. Describe the point of emphasis and explain why you chose it for this room.

6. **Unity and Variety.** Cut out pictures from housing magazines that demonstrate both design unity and variety. Make a poster from your clippings, labeling the items that bring unity and variety to each room.

Design Challenge

You are helping a couple whose eight-year-old grandson is coming to live with them. Their guest bedroom currently has a neutral color scheme. They want it redesigned as a bedroom for their grandson.

1. Prepare a list of questions you might ask the clients. What questions might you ask the grandson?

2. In teams of four, rotate the roles of the two clients, the grandson and the designer. Write down the responses to your list of questions.

3. From your mock interviews, create a design for the grandson's bedroom.

4. Present your design to your teammates and ask for their approval.

5. Place the completed design and the client responses in your design portfolio.

Chapter 20

Developing a Design Plan

Objectives

- Identify the steps in developing a design plan.

- Explain how to assess client characteristics.

- Describe factors to examine when taking an environment inventory.

- Complete a scale drawing of a room and its furnishings.

- Develop a preliminary design budget.

- Identify the components of a design resource file.

Vocabulary

- inventories
- multipurpose rooms
- clearance space
- prioritize
- scale drawing
- templates
- contingency fee

*I*magine a dream come true. Your family has won the grand prize in a contest—a brand new house. The builder will finish it to your specifications, within a certain budget, of course. How would you go about making this unfinished house into a home, personalized just for your family? Would you know where to start?

Good Design Requires Planning

Designing the interior of a new house is like starting with a blank canvas. You could fill your canvas by shopping at a variety of stores for materials and furnishings and then putting all the pieces together. A shopping spree like this might be fun, but without careful planning you could run into problems. Since there is a certain amount of money to spend, you must budget to make sure you can purchase all the things you need. The furnishings, window treatments, and floor and wall coverings chosen must be attractive, meet your family's needs, and be able to withstand the wear and tear that's ahead.

Everyone is more likely to be pleased with the end result if a design plan is followed. A good design plan is the starting point of designing the interior of a home. See Fig. 20-1.

Fig. 20-1 Some interior designers recommend removing everything from a room to get a fresh perspective of the room's potential.

Steps in a Design Plan

The knowledge you've gained about using the design elements and principles will be indispensable tools in creating an effective design plan. Now it's a matter of figuring out how to approach a project.

Starting a design project is exciting. You may be tempted to jump right in and choose colors and furnishings without taking time to plan your purchases. Your design will be more successful, however, if you lay a solid foundation for the project.

Fortunately, there is a process that can be used for almost any design project—an efficiency apartment, a recreation room, or an entire house. Following the process helps designers develop pleasing rooms that meet their clients' needs. This chapter introduces the ten steps of the design process. **See Fig. 20-2.** The first five steps are explained in detail in this chapter; the remaining five steps are covered in Chapter 21.

The first five steps draw on a variety of skills. You need good communication skills to gain the information you need to begin a project. Then you will use your analytical skills to evaluate the area to be designed. Have your calculator ready to estimate costs. Then use your creativity to find ideas that might work. **See Fig. 20-3.**

Fig. 20-2

	Steps in the Design Process
Step 1.	Identify the project.
Step 2.	Assess client characteristics.
Step 3.	Analyze the environment.
Step 4.	Develop a preliminary budget.
Step 5.	Compile a design resource file.
Step 6.	Plan use of space.
Step 7.	Choose a style and color scheme.
Step 8.	Select backgrounds, furniture, lighting, and accessories.
Step 9.	Present the design.
Step 10.	Implement the design.

Fig. 20-3 Working through the design process involves creativity, along with concrete activities such as measuring, calculating, and budgeting.

Step 1: Identify the Project

A designer's initial task is to help clients clearly identify the design goal. Just what is it that they hope to achieve? Perhaps they are trying to simplify their lives and want an uncluttered living area, or maybe they want to change a bedroom into a home office. **See Fig. 20-4.**

Imagine that you are a residential interior designer. Today you are meeting with a new client, Mrs. Woo, a second-grade teacher and mother of two teens. The family lives in an older home with an L-shaped formal living and dining room. Mrs. Woo wants to convert the space into a more casual space the family can enjoy and where her children can spend time with their friends.

To develop a realistic plan, you'll need to determine the approximate amount that Mrs. Woo is considering spending. Is it $1,000, or $5,000, or more? Obviously, the scope of projects can vary greatly. One may involve redesigning an entire house, including structural changes. Another might be updating a color scheme and finding new accessories to give a fresh look to a single room. How long the client plans to live in the home may also affect the scope of the project.

The desired time frame should also be assessed. Unless changes are minimal, implementing a design plan will take some time. Often people have an event driving a design project—having a kitchen completed by Thanksgiving or redecorating because of an upcoming wedding. In the Woo household, the teens would like the changes made as soon as possible, but Mrs. Woo's realistic goal is three months.

Even if you are decorating for yourself or your family, it's important to define the goal. For example, if your younger sister has asked you to help make her bedroom look more grownup, you will still need to evaluate the project and its proposed budget and time frame. What changes would she like to see? Are your parents willing to pay for new curtains and a comforter or is the plan to do more to the room? Does your sister want the room ready for her slumber party next weekend or is she willing to wait longer to achieve the new look? The timeline needs to be realistic for the amount of work to be done.

Fig. 20-4 In order to develop ideas and assemble samples, a designer needs a clear idea of the client's design goals. A notepad and a sketchbook are handy items for recording the client's needs and wants.

Working with an Interior Designer

Hiring an interior designer may sound expensive or even extravagant, but it's a move that can pay for itself. A good designer can keep you from making costly mistakes. As a client, you can help make the relationship a successful one.

Plan and Prepare. While you probably won't know all of the possibilities, jot down or sketch your ideas. Have a clear idea of what you can afford to spend. Know when the work can start and when you would like to have it finished.

Compare Portfolios. Meeting with designers and looking at photos of past projects can help you decide which designer will best carry out your plans. Notice the types of environments they have worked on. Compare their ideas on the use of color and lighting. Which designer seems to listen well and communicate clearly? Ask if you can speak to previous clients about their experience with the designer.

Ask about Expenses. Many designers charge an hourly rate, which can range widely. Others charge a flat fee. Some require a retainer, a down payment made before the project starts that is applied to the final charge. Some designers vary the payment method to suit the client's situation.

Step 2: Assess Client Characteristics

Success in a design project begins with matching possibilities for the room design with the habits, likes, needs, and wants of the people who will use it. Designers usually use one or more **inventories**— surveys that identify characteristics that will affect the design plan. You could provide a written questionnaire for clients to complete, but it's often better to interview them in person. For many projects, you will need to consider both the family's ideas and those of the individual person or persons who will use the room most. Take careful notes for future reference.

A Family Inventory

In a family home, it's important to create a design plan that pleases everyone. Sometimes, of course, compromises will need to be made. However, it's usually possible to develop a design that the family will find both attractive and functional. You will need to learn about their lifestyle and their expectations for the room or area.

Lifestyle

Lifestyle and interior design are related in several ways. Begin by discussing the family's lifestyle. Tailor your questions according to the area to be designed. For a kitchen, you might ask what their morning and evening routines are like. Where are various meals usually eaten? How is the kitchen involved in a typical weekend? Do they entertain frequently? Your clients' answers to your questions will help to formulate your design plan.

Activities. Some rooms are used for one main purpose. Others are **multipurpose rooms**, or used for many things. As the designer, your role is to identify and accommodate the main functions that take place there. One room might serve as a guest bedroom/sewing room/home office all in one! Start by asking the family members how the room will be used. See Fig. 20-5.

Entertaining Preferences. Will the room be used for entertaining? If so, are the occasions usually formal or informal? What would be the usual number of guests? The maximum number? Is there entertainment-related equipment that should be in the room—a television, DVD player, sound system, piano, game table, microwave oven, or storage for games and music? How would food be served? Knowing where food and beverages will be consumed affects choices for floor coverings and upholstery fabrics.

Hobbies. Do family members have hobbies? Do those require any special storage needs? Is there a collection that might be displayed as part of the design?

Fig. 20-5 Multipurpose rooms can help expand the available space in a home.

Fig. 20-6 Many families include a home office or study area in their design plans.

Study and Work. Where do family members prefer to read? Study? Pay bills and do household paperwork? How many computers do they have? Where are they located? Mrs. Woo needs space to grade papers and work on lesson plans. Her children have desks and computers in their bedrooms where they do their homework. See Fig. 20-6.

Preferred Atmosphere

What are the family's overall style preferences? Formal or informal? Rustic or traditional? Sleek and stylish or soft and cozy? Do they like antiques or prefer a modern look? Keep in mind that each room is part of the home as a whole. Although every room may have a look of its own, the home should have a cohesive feeling.

Ask family members about their color preferences as well. It's unlikely that all will share the same favorite color, but you can bypass any color that someone truly dislikes.

Future Considerations

Once a room is completed, it's apt to stay that way for some time. That's why the family should consider changes that might occur in the future. Is it possible that they'll be getting a pet or adding to the family? For instance, Mrs. Woo anticipates that her father will spend winters with them after he retires. Her daughter will leave for college in two years.

Nonresidential Inventories

What if your design project is not in a home? Interior designers often plan other types of interior environments as well. These may range from a corporate meeting room to a restaurant interior. It's important to query the client about the purpose of the room, the characteristics of the people who will use it, and their needs. For example, how might the decor you plan for an orthodontist's office be different from what would be suitable for a heart specialist's waiting area?

Universal design should always be considered. For instance, the payment counter should accommodate a person in a wheelchair as well as people who can stand up.

Why Businesses Remodel

A homeowner might remodel so that guests can get to a bathroom without crossing the kitchen. A business might remodel so that delivery people can get to the warehouse without crossing the showroom. As this example illustrates, commercial and residential remodeling often meet the same general needs but with distinctly different considerations. Here are some reasons that businesses remodel:

- **Expanding Facilities.** To increase production, a business might need more space for equipment or staff. If space is added, new work areas must be designed to integrate with older ones. Getting more use from the existing space might take creative reconfiguration. To enlarge a restaurant's dining room, for example, a designer might streamline the kitchen.

- **Updating Technology.** Businesses often have to install new technology to stay competitive. Changing one part of a system can affect other parts. A hospital that wants to install new medical imaging equipment may need to redesign an entire department.

- **Meeting Regulations.** Changes in zoning codes or insurance policies may call for replacing pipes or adding a newer sprinkler system. When the Americans with Disabilities Act required that public spaces be more accessible, business owners needed to install ramps and automatic doors.

- **Changing Image.** Changes in design can be part of a business's efforts to convince customers that it is still in step with their needs. A clothing store might choose trendy colors and new lighting to display items intended for younger buyers.

Apply It!

Imagine that the owner of a small hotel catering to families wants to redesign it to appeal to business customers. What challenges would this present to a designer? What kinds of changes might need to be made?

Step 3: Analyze the Environment

Perhaps you're redesigning just one or two rooms in a home. Why might it be important to walk through and assess the rest of the house? The reason is that some features in other parts of the home may very well influence your design plan.

The Environment Inventory

Start your inventory by jotting down the exterior style of the house or building. Certain styles of homes and buildings lend themselves to specific decorating styles. You shouldn't feel limited to that one style, however. Continue with the inventory by assessing these existing factors:

Number and Placement of Rooms. Note the number and type of rooms in the home. If additional space is needed, could part of an attic or basement be converted?

Activity Zones. You learned about three types of zones in Chapter 16. Identify the current private, social, and service zones of the home. Do they need to be improved? Can this be achieved within the scope of the current project?

Storage Areas. Ask whether there is adequate storage. Are there belongings, such as books or sporting goods, that need more space? Count the closets, paying attention to their size and what they're currently used for. Look at other built-in cabinets, as well.

Furniture and Accessories. Assess the current furnishings. Are there pieces in good condition that the client wishes to use in the redesign? Would they work in a new design? Would refinishing or recovering the furniture make it more desirable? What current accessories does the client want to keep in the room? Which could be moved to a different location?

Condition of Backgrounds. Try to gauge not only the condition, but also the appeal, of the current flooring, walls, and window treatments. See Fig. 20-7. What looks worn or dated? Would it be useable if it were cleaned or refinished? Are there features that the client particularly likes or does not want changed?

Fig. 20-7 A designer must determine if backgrounds such as floor coverings and window treatments can be incorporated into a new design or need to be added or replaced.

Energy Considerations. Keep energy efficiency in mind when assessing an environment. Are existing windows and doors tight? Is additional insulation needed on exterior walls? Is better air circulation needed?

Electrical and Lighting. Is the home's electrical service adequate for existing lighting and equipment and for any that might be added? If in doubt, consult an electrician. Often electrical service must be upgraded to accommodate new kitchen appliances, lighting, and entertainment equipment. Pay attention to the lighting in the various rooms. Will it be sufficient for the new design? Would it be worthwhile to increase natural light by adding or enlarging a window? You will learn about various types of lighting in Chapter 27.

Safety. Every home must meet basic safety requirements, but sometimes more specific needs must be addressed. Will young children live in the home or visit frequently? How about an older adult or someone with a disability? If so, think about features such as childproofing, grab bars, and door handles. Look for things that could be a danger to anyone—a stairway without a railing, spindles placed too far apart on a deck railing, slippery floors, and glass doors without special safety glass.

Traffic Flow. You'll recall learning about traffic patterns in Chapter 16. Does furniture placement make the current traffic pattern awkward? Perhaps furniture is too large for the space and there's inadequate **clearance space**, the additional space furniture takes up when it's in use. Figure 20-8 lists some standard clearance spaces.

Fig. 20-8

Standard Clearance Spaces	
Living Rooms/Family Rooms/Dining Rooms	
Minor traffic pathway	1.5 to 4 ft. (0.46 m–1.2 m)
Major traffic pathway	4 to 6 ft. (1.2 m–1.8 m)
Space between coffee table and chair or sofa	1 to 1.5 ft. (0.3 m–0.46 m)
Leg room in front of chair	1.5 to 2.5 ft. (0.46 m–0.76 m)
Space around table and occupied chairs for serving	2 ft. (0.6 m)
Conversational Groupings	
Sofa, two end tables, two chairs, and coffee table	6.5 ft. x 14 ft. (2 m x 4.3 m)
Kitchens	
Space in front of cabinets	2 to 6 ft. (0.6 m–1.8 m)
Space between appliances	4 to 7 ft. (1.2 m–2.1 m)
Bedrooms	
Space around bed (any size) or between twin beds	1.5 to 3 ft. (0.46 m–0.9 m)
Space between dresser and bed; space to pull out dresser drawers	3 ft. (0.9 m)
Bathrooms	
Space in front of toilet	1.5 to 2 ft. (0.46 m–0.6 m)
Space between bathtub and opposite wall	2.5 ft. (0.76 m)

Fig. 20-9 The windows in this room are large and break up the wall space. What other items do you see in this room that might restrict a redesign?

Consider Furniture Needs

For many people, arranging the furnishings in a room is a favorite aspect of the design process. At this stage of the process, your plan for furniture placement doesn't have to be definite. Before moving on to the next step, however, it's helpful to know the number and types of pieces you want to incorporate in the floor plan.

Establish Priorities

Few people are able to change everything when they redesign a room. Budget restrictions usually limit what can be done. Also, elements such as room size and location of windows and doors, which are hard to change, may limit what can be done. See Fig. 20-9.

A designer can help clients **prioritize**, or rate their wants and needs in order of preference. Prioritizing helps clients communicate what they really hope to achieve. This, in turn, helps designers develop a plan that meets a client's budgetary and design requirements.

Measure Space & Furniture

Prepare to try out furniture arrangements by measuring the room. Use a metal measuring tape. First draw a rough sketch, then transfer measurements to graph paper. Use a pencil to make a **scale drawing** with each square representing a given number of inches or centimeters. (A common scale is ¼ inch = 1 foot.) Then measure permanent features, such as doorways, windows, built-in cabinets, and fireplaces. Transfer them to the drawing, accurately portraying their locations.

Using the chart of architectural symbols on page 222, indicate any other special features. Also mark the location of heating and cooling registers.

Then measure furniture that will be kept in the new design plan. Record the length and depth of each piece at its longest and deepest point. See Fig. 20-10. Draw the pieces on graph paper using the same scale as the drawing of the room. Cut out and label each silhouette. Another option is to use ready-made **templates** of furniture and appliances.

Some designers transfer the room and furniture measurements directly to a computer software program. They complete much of the design plan on the computer. Chapter 21 discusses this option in more detail.

Make sure you have a copy of the scale drawing and a tape measure with you when you shop. This will eliminate guesswork about whether a piece will fit.

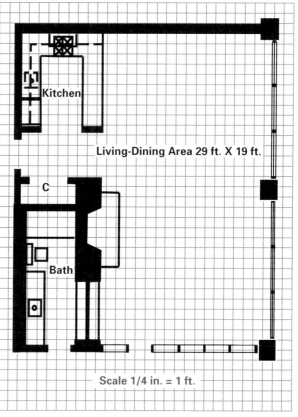

Kitchen

Living-Dining Area 29 ft. X 19 ft.

C

Bath

Scale 1/4 in. = 1 ft.

Fig. 20-10 To create a scale drawing, you will first need to measure the room and the furnishings. **Measure your bedroom and its furnishings. Then create a scale drawing to use for a sample design project.**

Fig. 20-11

Preliminary Budget for an Interior Design Project					
Item	Color/Style	Quantity	Estimated Cost	Amount Budgeted	Remarks
Sofa	Leather	1	$1,500	$ 1,500	Allow 12 weeks
Chairs	Wing	2	$800 each	$ 1,600	
Paint	Satin finish	3 gal.	$25 each	$ 75	Paint sale in June
Carpet	Berber	40 sq. yds.	$33 per sq. yd.	$ 1,320	Includes padding and installation
Window treatment	Sheers	25 yds.	$20 per yd.	$ 500	Client will sew
Lamps	Brushed steel	2	$200 each	$ 400	
Vases	Modern	3	$100 each	$ 300	
Subtotal				$ 5,695	
Contingency Fee			20% of total	$ 1,139	
Design Services			$90 per hour	$ 3,600	
Total				$10,434	

Step 4: Develop a Preliminary Budget

The budget for an interior design project may include wall coverings, floor coverings, window treatments, fabric, furniture, lighting, and accessories. The cost may also include labor for installing wall coverings, floor coverings, and window treatments. If you plan to do some work yourself, remember to factor in the cost of buying tools or renting equipment.

Architectural and interior design fees might also be included in the budget. Additional money might be needed to pay electricians, plumbers, and carpenters. To plan for unexpected expenses, it's a good idea to add a **contingency fee**, which is an additional percentage of the total cost of the project. A 20 percent contingency fee is often used.

Once you have developed a preliminary list of the items that will be changed, you can begin to estimate the cost of the project. To determine realistic costs you may visit local retail stores, review catalogs, or conduct searches on the Internet. Estimates for fabrics and for wall, floor, and window coverings will require you to perform calculations. **Figure 20-11** shows a sample preliminary budget for an interior design project.

Calculate Materials

As part of the budget process, you will need to determine how much or how many you need of particular items. If you need four dining room chairs, figuring the total cost is easy. For wall, floor, and window coverings, however, careful measuring and calculation are required. The following page explains the process for calculating various background materials.

Paint

Determine the amount of paint required for a room by measuring the room and calculating the square footage that will be painted. For example, in estimating the paint needed for a room 12 ft. x 30 ft., follow these steps:

1. Measure the length of each wall, add the lengths together, and total.

   12 ft. + 12 ft. + 30 ft. + 30 ft. = 84 linear ft.

2. Multiply the length of feet around the room (your answer in #1) by the height of the ceiling to determine the total number of square feet.

   84 ft. × 8 ft. (ceiling) = 672 total sq. ft.

3. A gallon of paint will cover approximately 350 to 400 sq. ft. To allow ample paint, divide the total number of square feet (your answer in #2) by 350 to find the number of gallons of paint.

   672 ÷ 350 = 2 gal. of paint

Wallpaper

To determine how much wall covering to order, follow Steps 1 and 2 as explained for paint. Then to figure the required number of rolls:

1. Divide the total number of sq. ft. by 36. (A single roll of wallpaper covers approximately 36 sq. ft.)

   672 ÷ 36 = 18.67 or 19 single rolls

2. For every two openings (doors and windows), subtract one roll of wallpaper. If the paper has a repeating pattern do not deduct for the openings. Example:

   19 − 2 (2 doors and 2 windows) = 17 single rolls of wallpaper

Most wallpaper is actually sold in double rolls. You would need nine rolls.

Rugs

Area rugs are priced according to size and quality. To estimate the price of an area rug, consult a catalog or check at a store. Standard sizes in feet include: 2 x 4, 2 x 8, 4 x 6, 6 x 9, and 9 x 12.

Resilient Flooring or Carpeting

To determine the amount of vinyl, plastic laminate, tile, or carpet required, measure the size of the room. For example, in estimating the amount of floor covering for a room 12 ft. x 30 ft. you would:

1. Measure the length of each wall and multiply the length by the width.

   12 ft. × 30 ft. = 360 total sq. ft.

2. Most carpet is sold by the square yard. To calculate that number, divide the total square feet by 9.

   360 ÷ 9 = 40 sq. yd.

Window Treatments

To determine fabric yardage required for a window treatment, measure the area to be covered by the window treatment.

1. Measure the width and length of the area to be covered by the window treatment.

   45 in. (width) × 84 in. (length)

2. To give fullness to the window treatment, multiply the width by 2. If you are using a sheer fabric, multiply by or 3.

   45 in. × 2 = 90 in.

3. Determine the number of widths of fabric required by dividing the width including fullness (your answer in #2) by the width of the fabric. (Home decorating fabrics are often 54 in. wide.)

   90 in. ÷ 54 in. = 1.67 or 2 widths of fabric

4. To determine the length of each width of fabric you must add 12 in. to the length of the window treatment. This extra foot is needed for the hem and heading on the window treatment.

   84 in. + 12 in. = 96 in. fabric required for each width

5. Determine the total length of fabric required for the window treatment by multiplying the number of widths (your answer in #3) by the length of fabric required for each width (your answer in #4).

   2 × 96 in. = 192 in. of fabric required

6. Fabric is sold in yards. Thus you must convert the number of inches required into yards. Divide the length of fabric required for the window treatment (your answer in #5) by 36 in.

> **192 in. ÷ 36 in. = 5 1/3 yds. of fabric required**

Upholstery Fabric

To determine the amount of fabric required for upholstery, refer to **Fig. 20-12**. It gives the sizes of common upholstered furniture and the approximate yardages. For sofas with button tufting, add two yards of fabric. More specific charts are available for special upholstery treatments.

Fig. 20-12

Approximate Yardages for Upholstery	
Furniture Piece	**Number of Yards**
Sofa, 6 ft. (1.8 m)	12 yd. (11 m)
Sofa, 7 ft. (2.1 m)	14 yd. (13 m)
Sofa, 9 ft. (2.7 m)	18 yd. (16.5 m)
Wing chair	7 yd. (6.4 m)
Club chair	8 yd. (7.3 m)
Dining chair with upholstered seat	2 yd. (1.8 m)
Square ottoman	3 yd. (2.7 m)

The Impact of Technology

Glulam: Quality + Strength

Glulam is a glued laminated timber that is used for framing that can also be used to create dramatic exposed ceilings because it can create curved archways. Glulam is as strong as steel but weighs less, so it can span greater lengths without needing support, giving architects and designers more design options. Its lighter weight also gives it a lower

Tech Trends

Learn about other engineered wood products that are becoming tools for designers to use inside the home. What are some advantages and disadvantages of using them compared to using natural wood?

thermal mass, meaning that it absorbs less heat, making it more energy efficient. Glulam also takes less energy than steel to make, and is made from a renewable resource.

While the qualities of natural wood can vary, glulam offers consistency. Individual layers are tested and graded, and each piece is designed to exact specifications. Manufacturers combine different types of wood to attain different degrees of strength and resiliency, depending on how and where the finished piece will be used. Four or more layers are glued and clamped together. The piece can be bent as the glue dries. Separate pieces can be bonded together into any length or width. Like other construction timbers, they are stained and treated to resist insects, mold, and fire.

Step 5: Compile a Design Resource File

To convey their likes and design ideas, clients often have photos and articles they have saved. Designers also maintain a design resource file for each project that they work on. **See Fig. 20-13.**

As part of the file, it's helpful to take "before" photos of the area to be designed. You'll enjoy comparing them to the finished project and they'll be useful for completing the next steps of the design process.

Find Sources of Ideas

Finding outstanding designs to include in a resource file of designs isn't difficult. There are a number of sources.

- Decorating magazines show photos of well designed rooms.

- Furniture and accessory catalogs are an excellent source of ideas.

- A growing number of informative websites are devoted to interior design.

- Sunday newspapers frequently run features on home design.

- How-to books and interior design reference books are available at bookstores and the library.

Organize your file by separating the clippings and photos into categories. You might organize it into furnishings, window treatments, floor coverings, and so on. You might also have a "general" category that includes pictures of rooms decorated in various styles. You may also include product brochures and samples of wallpaper, paint, and fabric in the resource file.

Fig. 20-13 A design resource file can provide inspiration when you're designing interiors.

The Next Steps in the Process

Following the first five steps in the design process provides you with a solid foundation for your design project. You have identified the design goal, determined the amount the client wants to spend, and established the desired time frame. By conducting a family inventory, you have learned about the lifestyle, preferences, needs, and wants of the people who will use your design. You've analyzed the space, taken all the necessary measurements, and created some drawings. These first steps enabled you to identify the items you would need to buy and calculate the materials needed, and then draw up a preliminary budget. Then, you took "before" photos of the area you'll be designing, and started to gather ideas and materials in your design resource file. See Fig. 20-14.

In Chapter 21 you'll complete the design process by following Steps 6 through 10. You'll learn how to plan use of space and select a style, color scheme, and other design components. Then you'll explore various methods of presenting your design, modifying it, and, finally, implementing your plan.

Fig. 20-14 Following the first five steps of the design process gives you the knowledge and materials to begin the more creative part of the process.

Profile of a
Hospitality Interior Designer

Hospitality interior designers create designs for businesses such as hotels, restaurants, country clubs, amusement parks, and convention centers. They aim to make a space both appealing to customers and functional for the business's staff. They often use design tools and furnishings to create a unique identity for the company.

Education & Training

- A bachelor's degree and two years of experience are required for licensing. A license is required for practice in some states.
- Passing a qualification exam is also required for licensing.
- Certification by the American Society of Interior Designers (ASID) is preferred.

Skills & Aptitudes

- Excellent communication and presentation skills are essential.
- A strong sense of the demands posed by customer service is very useful.
- Knowledge of the latest trends in technology helps in designing for the hospitality industry.

Hospitality Interior Designer
Aditya Patel

When I first started working, I joined a firm that designed a range of commercial spaces. However, I really wanted to focus on the hospitality industry because I enjoy the challenge of balancing customer needs with functionality. Also, I like to cook in my spare time, so I wanted to have an opportunity to design restaurants.

My goal is to create a design that will make customers feel welcome and special. Whether the overall goal is to help them relax, or get up and dance, or simply enjoy themselves while they dine and talk, I want them to feel that they're enjoying a special time. After all, my clients want to be sure that their customers will come back.

The key to designing for the hospitality industry is to create an environment that is attractive to the customers but also efficient for the staff. If you're designing a restaurant, you want to make sure there's enough space between tables for the serving people to pass. If it's a restaurant that families come to, you want floor coverings and furnishings that are easy to clean—because the staff will have to clean up spills frequently.

Of course, a designer must be guided by what the client wants. That's especially important with restaurant design. When chefs open a new restaurant they invest a huge amount of money, time, and creativity in the venture. They often have firm ideas about the kind of look they want. I often ask to see their menus and any décor they have already selected. I want to make sure I give them something they'll be proud to put their names on.

One thing I've learned is to make my presentations sparkle. A client once said that my firm got a project we really wanted because our presentation was the most exciting idea. You need to show enthusiasm for the design in order to convince clients that their customers will find it exciting too!

Design Portfolio

1. Design the lobby of a family-oriented resort hotel. Think about what services should be available to guests and what look would be suitable for family customers. Sketch your design and explain your decisions.

2. Design a conference center that caters to traveling business people. Explain why the materials used in this design are different from those you chose for the project above.

Chapter Summary

- There are ten recommended steps to follow in developing a design plan.
- The design process involves taking a family **inventory** to assess lifestyle needs.
- An environment **inventory** is used to assess existing factors that will affect design decisions.
- Measuring space and furniture and making a **scale drawing** enables you to try out different room arrangements.
- You need to calculate the required amount of design materials in order to prepare a preliminary budget.
- A design resource file is a helpful source of ideas and inspiration.

Checking Your Understanding

1. What are the first five steps in developing a design plan?
2. Why does a designer need to know a client's budget and time frame?
3. What topics are covered in a family **inventory**?
4. Identify five factors that should be analyzed when taking an environment inventory.
5. Why do you need to allow for **clearance space** when arranging furniture?
6. What features should you include in a **scale drawing**?
7. Why do people need to **prioritize** their design needs?
8. Explain how to measure for carpeting or vinyl floor covering.
9. What is a **contingency fee**? What is the average amount recommended?
10. What are three types of items that might be included in a design resource file?

Thinking Critically

1. **Making Hypotheses.** Some designers recommend that clients live in a new home for a while before redesigning it. Why might they make that suggestion?

2. **Drawing Conclusions.** What advantage might an interior designer have over a homeowner when trying to organize a time frame for working with painters, carpenters, plumbers, and so on?

Applying Your Knowledge

1. **Developing an Inventory.** Prepare a list of questions to pose to clients who are planning to update their kitchen. Keep in mind that your goal is to uncover their needs and wants.

2. **Drawing to Scale.** Measure a room in your home and each piece of furniture in the room. Draw the room and furnishings to scale on graph paper. Use architectural symbols to indicate doors and windows.

3. **Calculating Coverings.** You would like to give a new look to a dining room that measures 14 ft. x 16 ft. The ceiling is 8 ft. high. The room has one window and two doorways. How many gallons of paint would be needed for the room? How many rolls of wallpaper?

4. **Comparing Costs.** The paint you want to buy for the dining room cited above costs $22 per gallon. Quarts of the same type of paint are $10.99. The pre-pasted wallpaper you're considering costs $13 per single roll. How much would you spend on paint for the room? How much would the wallpaper cost?

5. **Reality Pricing.** List on a sheet of paper: leather sofa, brass table lamp, coffee table, ceiling fan, 8 ft. x 10 ft. rug, computer desk, and dining table with six chairs. Next to each item, write an estimate of how much you think it might cost. Using catalogs, the Internet, or newspaper ads, determine an actual average cost of each item. Were your estimates high or low?

Design Challenge

You are redesigning the living room of a townhouse. The client would like new floor coverings, wall coverings, window treatments, and a new sofa. However, he expects to be transferred to another city within two years.

1. What additional information would you need in order to come up with design suggestions?

2. Make at least one suggestion for each component the client wants to change. Explain the rationale for each of your ideas.

3. What would be the most expensive item in the budget? What items would you try to find at a flea market or discount store?

4. Create a preliminary budget and place it in your design portfolio.

Completing & Presenting a Design

Objectives

- Describe the final five steps in the design process.

- Identify factors to consider when arranging space.

- Evaluate different ways of drawing design plans.

- Summarize factors to consider when choosing a style and color scheme.

- Summarize factors to consider when selecting backgrounds, furniture, lighting, and accessories.

- Compare various types of drawings and visual representations used by interior designers.

- Explain how to implement a design plan.

Vocabulary

- pictorial drawing
- rendering
- overlay
- sample board

In Chapter 20 you studied the first five steps of the design process. This chapter will help you complete the process by following Steps 6 through 10. You will plan how to use the available space, and select a style and color scheme. Then you'll be ready to choose backgrounds and fill the space with furnishings. Finally, you will present and implement your design.

Step 6: Plan Use of Space

Think about your favorite room. How would it look without any furnishings? Quite different! Every room starts out as a blank box waiting to be designed. Satisfaction with the finished room depends largely on how well you use that space in your design.

A functional room arrangement is one in which the space meets the needs of its occupants. No matter how attractive a room is, if it is difficult to use or move around in, those who use it will be uncomfortable. **See Fig. 21-1.**

Fig. 21-1 Whether the space you're planning is spacious and elegant or casual and cozy, it should be designed to meet the needs of the people who will use it.

Fig. 21-2 When arranging any room you need to recognize traffic patterns and avoid placing obstacles in those paths. **Identify the traffic patterns in this kitchen and dining area.**

Arranging Space

When beginning the design of a room, review the purposes the room serves. What items of furniture go together? If you want a comfortable spot for reading, for example, you'll probably want a lamp and small table within easy reach of a comfortable chair. This could be described as a *functional grouping* because the pieces work together to meet one purpose or activity.

Next, consider the features of the room itself as shown on the scale drawing of the floor plan. Furniture needs to be arranged in a way that doesn't block doors, windows, heating and cooling vents, or electrical outlets.

On your floor plan, outline the path people would use to walk through the room. People should be able to walk easily from place to place without disrupting others. As you try out various furniture arrangements, consider their impact on the room's traffic patterns. **See Fig. 21-2.**

Remember to allow for clearance space, the space left around furniture so that it can be used. The height of furniture should also be considered.

When furniture is drawn to scale on a floor plan it may appear that you have a great deal of clearance space. However, a floor plan represents only two dimensions of an object—length and width. The third dimension—height—can reduce the apparent openness of a space. Try to visualize the bulk and height of the furnishings as they will look in the finished room.

A thoughtfully arranged room is functional and pleasing to look at. This is the time to incorporate your knowledge of design elements and principles. As you plan your furniture arrangement, keep these factors in mind:

- Don't overcrowd a room. Leave some open space for a feeling of airiness.

- Attempt to balance the room. For example, using the same size and quantity of furnishings on opposite walls can help create a feeling of balance.

- Create a focal point by highlighting an interesting feature. For instance, grouping chairs around a fireplace draws attention to that part of the room.

- Consider the views from one part of the home to another, as well as to the outdoors. You can use furniture groupings to direct attention away from unwanted views or toward pleasant ones.

- Use your imagination. Sometimes an unusual arrangement—placing a piece of furniture at an angle, for instance—will solve a problem or create an interesting effect.

Room by Room

In planning any room, always consider first how it will be used. Following are some basic guidelines.

Living Rooms and Family Rooms. In many homes, the family room serves the same function as a living room. Either room can be a place to relax and entertain. However, in a home that has both, a living room is often more formal and a family room is designed primarily for comfort.

- Sofas, chairs, and loveseats are possible seating options. Sectional sofas offer flexibility because the sections can be grouped in different ways. Arrange the seating so that people can converse without having to raise their voices.

- Provide a convenient surface for reading materials or refreshments near the seating.

You might use an end table, a coffee table, or a sofa table—even a chest, teacart, or bench. Choose pieces that are in proportion to the sofas and chairs nearby.

- The living or family room might include electronic entertainment equipment. Although these items need not be the focal point of the room, they should be placed for easy access. See Fig. 21-3.

Dining Areas. The dining table usually takes up so much space that you may be limited in the ways you can arrange other furniture, such as a china cabinet. In a small dining room, consider using a drop leaf or gateleg table, which can be collapsed to a smaller size when not in use.

Be sure to allow space for chairs and movement around the table. Provide a clear pathway between the dining table and the kitchen.

Fig. 21-3 This living room illustrates how seating can be arranged for conversation, easy access to entertainment equipment, and a great view.

Fig. 21-4 The structure of this room dictated where the bed should be placed. Notice that there is plenty of space to move around the bed.

Bedrooms. Because of its size, the bed is usually the focal point of a bedroom. Bed placement usually depends on the other furnishings that must fit in the room. The size and shape of the room, as well as the location of the doorway, windows, and closets also play a role. See Fig. 21-4. Try to leave space on both sides of the bed. If that's not possible, use casters so the bed may be easily rolled away from the wall.

- Most people want a nightstand next to their bed. If possible, place chests and dressers near the closet, leaving space to open doors and drawers. Also leave some open floor space for dressing.

- Perhaps you'd like to incorporate a sitting area or work area in a spacious bedroom. A movable screen can be a practical way to separate areas.

- A child's bedroom is often a multipurpose room. Children read, play, study, pursue hobbies, and store toys in their rooms. Modular storage units and multipurpose furniture are ideal. Consider flexibility and choose furnishings that will adapt to a growing child's needs.

Hobby Areas. A guest bedroom may double as a den, a sewing room, computer room, exercise room, or workshop for crafts and hobbies. Analyze the activities planned for the room and the needs of those who will use it. Careful choice and arrangement of furniture can make the room serve multiple functions.

Drawing Plans

In years past, design work always involved drawing by hand. To make neat, accurate drawings, designers used drawing pencils, T-squares, triangles, and compasses. They added labels and dimensions using precise hand-lettering techniques.

Planning on graph paper is still an option, particularly for fairly limited projects. However, today designers typically use CAD software to create design plans. Even amateur designers can produce plans using design software on their personal computers.

While a floor plan gives you the view from above, an elevation provides a side view. Interior elevations show one wall as seen from the center of the room. With an elevation, you can see the relative heights of furniture, walls, windows, doorways, and other architectural features.

One common use for interior elevations is to show the arrangement of cabinets on a kitchen or bathroom wall. **Figure 21-5** shows a kitchen floor plan and all four wall elevations.

Consumer Considerations

Choosing a Design Plan

Suppose you're shown several different design plans for final approval. You have considered the usual factors, such as budget and usefulness, and still feel unsure. In such cases, it could be the less obvious qualities that help you decide whether to give the go-ahead or ask for fine-tuning. Consider the following points:

Is the plan versatile? Does it lend itself to personal touches, like hanging a different piece of artwork, or rearranging furniture? If one piece or element is changed, will the design still hold together?

Does it fit your personal tastes? A design can be technically "correct" yet not feel "right" because it doesn't match your personality. Maybe you want a look that stretches the rules or conventional use of design elements. If you have a dramatic flair, for example, you might like a more striking variety of furnishings or colors.

Does it match your values and priorities? Beliefs about what is important affect more decisions than people may realize. Pay attention to yours. A design that does not conserve energy, no matter how attractive, won't sit well with someone who values environmental preservation.

Fig. 21-5

Elevations

A Visual Guide

Compare the floor plan of the kitchen in the center of this page with the four elevations placed clockwise around it. Each elevation shows how that wall will look when it is completed. The elevations include the position of the major appliances, cabinets, windows, and doorways.

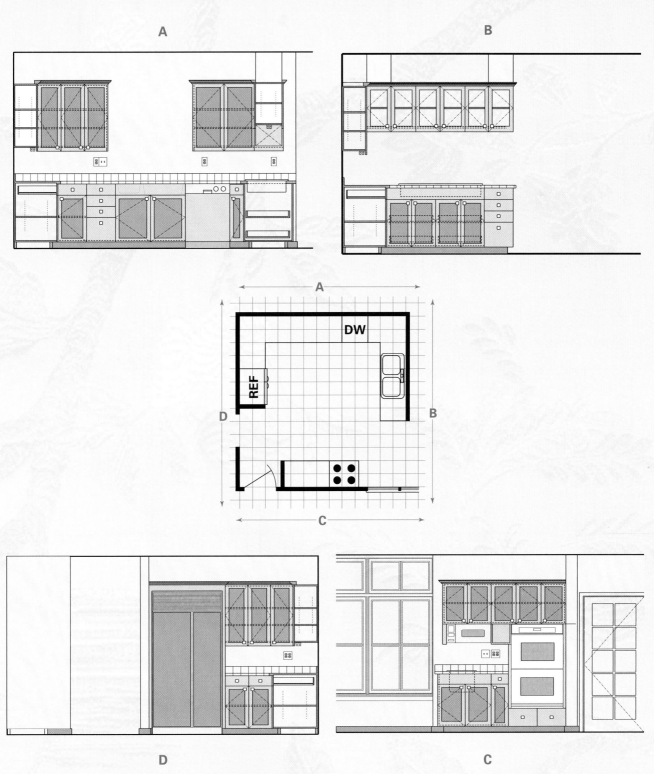

Outdoor Mall Navigation

Designers of outdoor shopping malls face special challenges when planning the use of space. The open-air design, fittingly the town-center style, needs careful attention to features that are not as significant in indoor malls.

- **Aesthetics.** Outdoors, the storefront design can be very distinctive and expressive. It helps set the tone of the shopping center as a whole, as well as individual merchants. Unifying elements must be balanced with the image that each store wants to present. After all, the overall design may need to encompass a bridal shop, an electronics store, and a family restaurant.

- **Protection from the Elements.** For shoppers' comfort, designers need to consider the area's physical environment and climate. Ideally, shops are situated at an angle to avoid strong, direct winds. Awnings and canopies may be used to offer shade from the sun and shelter from rain.

- **Orientation.** It's easier to lose your way in an outdoor shopping center than in an indoor mall, so designers must include systems to guide shoppers. Simulated "streetscapes" help orient shoppers with landmarks such as a fountain, statuary, or flowerbeds. In some outdoor malls, each street has a particular theme—based on the region's history or natural setting, for example—that is reflected in storefront colors and the architectural style. To help organize pedestrian flow, "streets" run from parking areas to a central location, such as an anchor store, food court, or green space.

Apply It!

Working in a small group, choose six types of stores where you enjoy shopping. Design storefronts that might be suitable for an outdoor mall in your area containing these six types of stores. Remember to somehow reflect a common theme, while offering convenience for shoppers. Post your completed storefront designs.

Fig. 21-6 Using CAD software, interior designers can show clients how a room will look long before a design is implemented.

Computer-Aided Design (CAD)

Designers commonly make construction drawings, interior designs, and other drawings using a computer. With CAD programs, designers can prepare drawings and make changes to them faster than can be done by hand. As a result, designers have more time to spend developing creative designs. They can also accept larger and more complex design projects. See Fig. 21-6.

Once a designer enters basic information about a room, CAD programs can produce accurate floor plans that can be changed in a keystroke. Designers can duplicate standard appliances and pieces of furniture, conventional plumbing and electrical fixtures, and identical windows, doors, and closets with ease.

CAD programs create views that seem as realistic as a photograph. This can help the designer and clients judge how pieces will actually look in a room. Color schemes can also be changed with the click of the mouse button.

Step 7: Choose a Style & Color Scheme

After completing your floor plan, the next step is to make final decisions about style and color scheme. These two aspects will dramatically impact the appearance of the space.

Style

Of all the interlocking pieces in the design puzzle that must fit together, the style probably has the greatest impact on the room's overall effect. Style refers to the overall characteristics of a design. It might reflect a specific period of time, a region, or a designer. It might also evoke a feeling, such as formal, informal, stark, or cozy. **See Fig. 21-7.**

The home itself might already have a distinctive style. Generally, architectural details help influence the style for an interior. You should not feel limited to that one style, but don't stray too far from the look, either. Here are some typical home styles that designers work with.

Colonial. This style from America's early days is very simplistic. Generally rooms are small, have low ceilings and a large fireplace as the focal point. Walls are often painted white and the ceilings have exposed beams. Floors of wide wooden planks are covered with braided rugs. Quilts are often used as accessories.

Queen Anne. This style is relatively formal. Often the rooms are large with high ceilings and classical architectural details. Walls are covered with wood paneling or wallpaper. Simple window treatments use luxurious fabrics. Known for elegance, the Queen Anne style incorporates mahogany and walnut woods, along with silk fabrics and silver accessories.

Fig. 21-7 This design evokes a cozy feeling that is very inviting.

Fig. 21-8 This large room was designed as a modern interior. What features tell you that it is designed in the modern style?

Victorian. A flamboyant and elaborate style, Victorian interiors generally have carved wooden panels. Stenciled architectural designs often form a border near the ceiling. Elaborate side and top window treatments accompany lace curtains next to the windows. Fringes, tassels, and dark, rich colors are used on furniture and accessories.

Modern. Modern interiors are simple and unify technology with art. The focus is on the horizontal line and monochromatic color schemes. Black, cream, and white are frequently used on walls and fabrics. Wood floors are often bleached. Window treatments are minimal—many windows have no covering at all. Steel, black leather, and stone are popular materials for furniture and accessories. See Fig. 21-8.

It's best to choose a style early and keep it in mind as you work through the entire design process.

In selecting a style, you'll be aided by the clippings in the design resource file that you developed in Chapter 20. Once you select a style that pleases your client, strive to make all the elements and principles of design support that selection. The colors, patterns, textures, furniture, and accessories you choose will be linked by one common denominator—style.

Color Schemes

In Chapter 18 you learned about factors to consider in choosing color schemes. At this point, you now have more to think about than which colors go well together. You must decide what colors support the style you chose and how to distribute them throughout each room.

Do you want the room to feel warm or cool, calm or vibrant, spacious or cozy? Use the color wheel as a guide in selecting a color palette for the design.

Consider the color of wood tones of furniture, floors, and woodwork and how it relates to other choices. Guard against choosing a shade or hue just because of its current popularity. You might end up with the latest fashion trend, but be unhappy if it's not the right color for your design.

Remember to consider a compatible color scheme for the entire home. Each room should have a color scheme that complements colors used in the other rooms. This is especially important for areas next to each other.

Step 8: Select Backgrounds, Furniture, Lighting & Accessories

Now you are ready to select the elements that comprise the interior. Once your choices have been made, you will be ready to revise the preliminary budget you prepared earlier in Step 4 of Chapter 20.

Backgrounds

Floors, walls, ceilings, and windows make up the background of a room. Deciding which materials, colors, patterns, and textures to use is the part of the design process that many people enjoy most. **See Fig. 21-9.**

The goal when choosing backgrounds is to make sure the choices harmonize with the overall style of the room. If you were designing a bedroom with a Victorian theme, you might choose plush carpeting, floral patterned wallpaper, and velvet draperies with swags and tassels. Different choices would be made, of course, if you were designing a country-style bedroom. You will find detailed information on choosing backgrounds in Chapter 24.

Budget is usually a guiding factor in making final choices for backgrounds. Try to focus on the changes that will have the greatest impact. For instance, you might postpone plans to add a crown molding to allow for the installation of durable laminate flooring that would visually enlarge the room.

Fig. 21-9 The warmth and softness that carpeting lends to a room setting is one reason for its ongoing popularity.

Furniture, Lighting & Accessories

Once you've chosen the backgrounds, you are ready to select the furniture, lighting, and accessories and arrange them to the best advantage. This is one of the most challenging parts of the design process, but it can also be very rewarding as the design truly takes shape.

Whether you're evaluating a room's existing furniture or shopping for new pieces, think about what styles might best contribute to the design theme. Guidelines for choosing furniture are given in Chapter 26. Focus on how the furniture will fit into the space available. Use design software to try out various room arrangements.

Finally, think about lighting and accessories. You'll find guidelines for choosing these important items in Chapter 27. If you have made good use of the elements and principles of design, the result should be a design plan you can be proud to present to a client or implement yourself.

Completing the Budget

Now that you have selected your backgrounds, furniture, lighting, and accessories, you may replace estimated costs with the actual prices of items you have selected. Figure 21-10 shows a completed budget for a sample interior design project. Note that specific information about model or style numbers is included in the budget.

Fig. 21-10

Item	Number	Color	Quantity	Estimated Cost	Actual Cost	Remarks
A Completed Budget for an Interior Design Project						
Sofa	23452	Blue	1	$1,500	$ 1,600	12 weeks to manufacture
Chairs	14530	Floral	2	$800 each	$ 1,700	
Paint	345	Blue Mist	3 gal.	$25 per gal.	$ 99	Client will paint
Carpet	47878584	Oatmeal	40 sq. yds.	$33 per sq. yd.	$ 1,550	Call installers
Sheers	34767	Ivory	25 yds.	$15 per yd.	$ 375	Paul will sew
Lighting	46763767	Brass	2	$200 each	$ 360	
Vases	3565	Red	3	$100 each	$ 260	
Rug	81	Red	9 ft. x 12 ft.	$350	$ 375	
Drapes	567243	Ginger	10 yds.	$28 per yd.	$ 280	Paul will sew
Subtotal				$5,850	$ 6,599	
Contingency Fee—20%				$1,170		
Design Services @ $90 per hr.				$3,600	$ 3,600	Actual hrs. to be charged
Total				$10,620	$10,199	

Step 9: Present the Design

Design is a visual process. Can you imagine trying to present a design using only words? Fortunately, designers can use more than words to express their ideas. Whether they are created with a computer or with more traditional tools, visual aids are useful in the design process. You're already familiar with floor plans and elevations. Pictorial drawings, renderings, samples, computer presentations, and models are other visual aids. A designer uses some or all of these when presenting a design to a client.

Types Of Drawings

Various drawings are used to help clients visualize a design concept. They include perspectives and renderings—fairly complex drawings that demand a great deal of skill and practice.

Designers use colored pens, markers, or watercolors to add texture and color to their drawings. See Fig. 21-11. Drawings can be prepared by hand or on a computer.

Perspectives

When you look at floor plans and elevations, you see only one surface at a time—either a top or a side view. These types of drawings do a good job of conveying information about the exact size and shape of objects, but they don't show how objects look in real life.

To provide a realistic view of how a finished room will look, designers may use pictorial drawings. A **pictorial drawing** shows the viewer several surfaces in the room simultaneously. This is more like a picture than a diagram. See Fig. 21-12.

Pictorial drawings typically use a one-point perspective or two-point perspective. A *one-point perspective* drawing shows what is seen when the viewer looks directly at the opposite wall. A *two-point perspective* drawing illustrates what you see when looking at the corner where the two walls meet.

Fig. 21-11 Most designers use both traditional tools and CAD software to prepare drawings.

Fig. 21-12

Perspectives

A Visual Guide

The pictorial drawing of this kitchen is shown from a two-point perspective. The photograph at the bottom of this page shows the finished design, including accessories.

Renderings

As part of the presentation, interior designers may include a floor plan, wall elevations, and pictorial drawings of the room, as well as sketches of other details. Presentation drawings are similar to the drawings used during the design process. However, they are often more detailed or have special enhancements added.

A designer's preliminary drawings may simply be rough pencil sketches that preserve ideas for later reference. To prepare drawings for the final presentation, the designer may make a rendering. A **rendering** is a drawing in which the designer adds realistic details, such as textures, shadows, shadings, and color. The designer may use pen and ink, watercolor, or CAD software to make the rendering. See Fig. 21-13.

Fig. 21-13

Renderings

A Visual Guide

A basic floor plan (top) can be made into a rendering (below) to help the client visualize the finished room.

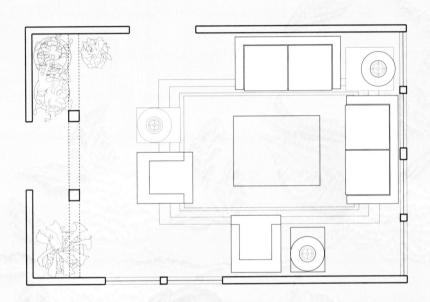

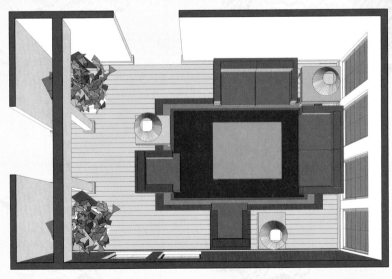

Fig. 21-14 A sample board enables clients to see and feel actual samples of carpeting, upholstery fabrics, and other design elements.

Similar techniques may be used to enhance floor plans and elevations, giving them greater depth and realism. Some presentation floor plans include not only furniture, but also figures or arrows showing the traffic flow through the room(s). Presentation elevations are useful for showing design details and the finish of materials for cabinets.

Sometimes, to avoid making changes on the basic drawing, enhancements and special details are added with an overlay. An **overlay** is a sheet of transparent material that is placed over a basic drawing. The overlay can be raised and lowered to show the drawing with and without extras. Overlays can be used to show alternative color schemes, furniture arrangements, and other design ideas.

Types Of Visual Representations

Besides drawings, designers use a variety of visual representations to help a client visualize the design concept. Designers will prepare presentation boards, samples, CAD illustrations, and models. These representations help illustrate the style, color scheme, space plan, backgrounds, furniture, lighting, and accessories. Visual representations help ensure that clients are fully aware of what the interior will look like and what they will be purchasing. It is important to make any needed adjustments at this step because it can be very costly to change purchases once items have been ordered.

Sample Boards

Most clients want to see and feel actual samples of fabrics and other materials before making decisions. For this reason, designers may prepare a **sample board**—a piece of illustration board with mounted samples of proposed wall coverings, floor coverings, fabrics, and window treatments. A separate sample board is prepared for each room being designed. See Fig. 21-14.

The layout of the sample board should reflect the elements and principles used in designing the room. The size of the samples is usually in proportion to the size of the real objects they represent. For example, the fabric swatch for a sofa should be larger than the sample for a pillow. In addition to the samples, a floor plan and pictures of furniture and accessories may be glued to the board. Information about furniture manufacturers, dimensions, fiber content, and other details may accompany the sample board.

In Chapter 18, you read about making a color sample board from samples of fabrics, floor coverings, paint, wallpaper, and wood grains. Samples allow you to see the exact colors and patterns of materials. You can also feel their textures and observe the effects of shiny or dull finishes. Even the most sophisticated CAD programs have not yet eliminated the need for actual samples.

Computer Presentations

Drawings created with CAD software can be printed out on paper for a traditional presentation. However, many designers prefer to present their designs right on the computer screen.

Some interior design software packages on the Internet allow clients to choose from furnishings and fabric samples shown in realistic detail on the computer screen. After the clients make their selections, they can view an entire room on the screen as if they were looking at a photo of the finished project. **See Fig. 21-15.**

For even greater realism, a series of images can be prepared, each showing the design from a slightly different angle. The images are stored by the computer and "played back" in sequences, like frames in a movie. This technique creates the illusion of walking through a room.

Models

A pictorial drawing provides only one view of a room. Sometimes what is needed is a three-dimensional model. A model is the best way to get an overall sense of a design because it lets you observe all the elements in the room from any angle.

In the past, the only way to create a model was to physically build one. A simple model of a room or a house can be made by gluing photocopies of the floor plan and the wall elevations to a stiff backing, then cutting them out and fastening them together.

Instead of constructing physical models, many designers now use computer models. A computer model is not really three-dimensional, since it exists on a flat computer screen. It does, however, give the illusion of three dimensions. The image can be rotated and viewed from a variety of angles. Unlike physical models, computer models can easily be changed so the designer can experiment with design alternatives. Different versions of the model can be stored in computer memory for later comparison. Computer models have become the tool of choice for evaluating how a design will look and function in real life.

Fig. 21-15 CAD software makes it possible to view different backgrounds, furniture arrangements, and other features with just a few keystrokes.

Virtual Reality Techniques

Even as computerized design presentations become more common, new developments are on the horizon. Now you can not only "walk" through a room portrayed on a computer screen, you can surround yourself in it.

Creating Virtual Environments.

Despite its futuristic name, virtual reality (VR) relies on established tools, including the animation software found in computer games and the digital imaging technology used in high-definition television. These technologies record and render visual information in minute detail. Scenes are composed from points of color called *pixels*. Each pixel can be adjusted and readjusted to contain the right proportions of color to achieve the desired result. One result is that objects seem to change position and shape, giving the illusion of movement, an occurrence called the *parallax effect*.

Tech Trends

Investigate other uses for VR technology, including ergonomics and assistive living for people with disabilities.

VisionDome®. Like an actor who goes from television shows to a movie career, VR technology has jumped from the computer screen to the big screen—literally. You've experienced it if you've watched a film in a domed theater at a planetarium or theme park. A more recent innovation is the VisionDome.

VisionDomes are portable, rounded chambers that hold from one person up to several dozen. Images are cast by a high-resolution projector. Special software and a uniquely designed lens "pre-warp" the image, so it appears realistically three-dimensional on the VisionDome's arced inner surface. Compared to the virtual home tour generated by CAD software, this experience truly places you in the artificial setting.

Unlike older immersive techniques, the VisionDome requires no headgear or viewers. In the VisionDome, the projector does the work. The scene is so real, you might be tempted to sit on an imaginary sofa.

A Professional Presentation

Once professional designers complete a design plan, they are ready to present the proposal to the client. This demonstration, or presentation, of the plan is the way interior designers communicate their ideas. Only then can the client visualize how the room or home will look when the design plan has been implemented. If the client wants to change the plan, it can be revised before actual work begins. The presentation can save time and money and help ensure the client's satisfaction. **See Fig. 21-16.**

An oral presentation of a design generally has three parts: introduction, discussion of the design, and summary. The introduction identifies the main features of the design and emphasizes how the design satisfies the client's motives and needs. The discussion section presents the designer's detailed analysis of the design solutions. A designer will generally focus on the current problems associated with the space and identify how the proposal will help solve the issues. The summary section reviews the key features of the proposed design.

After presenting the design itself, the designer will present the budget and outline a rough schedule for completing the work. A discussion will follow, in which the client may ask questions about the design or request certain modifications. The designer will then make any agreed upon changes and adjust the budget and schedule as needed.

Before beginning to implement the design, the designer will draw up a written contract that outlines costs, the items to be purchased, fees, and the responsibilities of the designer and the client.

Fig. 21-16 Good communication skills, in addition to well-organized presentation materials, are key to a successful design presentation.

Step 10: Implement the Design

The final step in the design process is implementation. This step involves developing a projected timeline, ordering purchases, and scheduling installations. The timeline for each project is tied to a budget. For example, if you are renovating an entire home you will probably have to do so in phases. If you are designing one room you might be able to complete the project in one phase.

Placing the orders for your purchases should be included in your timeline. There are many factors that can determine how long it might take to receive an item for your project. For example, if you find lamps at a local store, you can purchase them immediately. In contrast, a custom sofa could take twelve weeks to arrive from the manufacturer. As you develop your timeline, contact suppliers for estimated delivery dates.

To coordinate your project you will also want to consider when installations should occur. Generally, the first workers on the job are electricians, plumbers, and carpenters. Painters and wall covering installers do their work next. Flooring is then installed, followed by window treatments. See Fig. 21-17. The room is then filled with furniture, lighting, and accessories.

As the project proceeds, the designer should maintain frequent communication with clients to let them know when items have arrived, if there are any delays, and the actual installation dates. Communicating throughout all ten steps of the design process will help to ensure the clients' satisfaction with the finished design.

Fig. 21-17 This installer is hanging the window treatments while accessories and final touches are made to the finished room design.

Profile of a
Government Interior Designer

Government interior designers work for agencies in local, state, or national governments. They design courtrooms, meeting rooms, museums, service centers, dining halls, government offices, and many other kinds of facilities.

Education & Training

- A bachelor's degree and two years of experience are required for licensing. A license is required for practice in some states.
- Passing a qualification exam is also required for licensing.
- Certification by the American Society of Interior Designers (ASID) is preferred.

Skills & Aptitudes

- Ability to pay attention to details and work within complex regulations is important.
- Excellent skills in writing, speaking, and nonverbal communication are necessary.
- Ethical behavior in evaluating and awarding contracts is essential.

Government Interior Designer
José Guzmán

I work for the state as a government interior designer. My office is in the capitol building, but I work on projects all over the state. I like the fact that I get to travel. It gives me a chance to see different parts of the state and to meet new people.

Another thing I like about this work is the feeling that I'm serving the people of my state. Some of our projects are facilities that people never see, like data processing centers or storage areas, but even with those I see my job as creating a useful facility that is built economically and will last.

I feel very strongly about being careful with money. We must spend tax dollars wisely. The designs we choose must last. The materials have to be functional and attractive without being too expensive. Suppliers and contractors have to be reliable. Of course, when we look at bids, we have to review each one thoroughly and be completely impartial when we award contracts. We can't play favorites.

Sometimes we take on the design work for a new project. We contract other projects out to private firms. In those cases, however, we still play a role in the design of the outside projects. We take part in the needs assessment meetings and review presentations by the different design teams. We might also meet with the officials making the selection to give technical input on the designs. We have to carefully examine the designs to make sure the materials, schedule, and procedures all meet state standards. We give input on the designs and review final submissions too. We also periodically inspect the work when it's in progress.

Another area I'm involved in is refurbishing. Our state regularly reviews facilities to see if new furnishings or technology is needed to better serve the people of our state. We only update a facility if it's cost effective. Again, taking care of the taxpayers' money is our top priority.

Design Portfolio

1. A local government needs to provide a new meeting room where the town council will meet. The room must have space for seven council members to convene a meeting, space for local community members to sit, and space for guest speakers. List the questions you would need answered before you could design the room.

2. Choose a partner and answer each other's questions. Then, use CAD software to design the council room.

Review & Activities

Chapter Summary

- A good furniture arrangement is comfortable, functional, and attractive.
- Many designers use computer-aided design programs rather than hand drawings.
- The elements and principles of design are used to create a style. The color scheme, backgrounds, furnishings, lighting, and accessories in the design plan all contribute to the style.
- Designers use a variety of drawings and other visual aids to visualize and present a design plan.
- When giving a presentation, a designer can show the client enhanced drawings and **sample boards**, or present the entire design plan on a computer screen.
- Implementing a design plan includes preparing a projected timeline, ordering purchases, and scheduling installations.

Checking Your Understanding

1. What are the final five steps in the design process? List them in the order they should be done.
2. Identify four factors to consider when designing an efficient, functional furniture arrangement.
3. How does an elevation differ from a floor plan? When would a designer use an elevation?
4. What advantages does computer-aided design have over drawings done by hand?
5. Name three types of visual aids a designer might use to create a design.
6. Explain the difference between the two kinds of **pictorial drawings**.
7. Explain the purpose of **renderings** and **overlays**.
8. List three elements that could be included when constructing a **sample board**.
9. Describe the process of presenting a design proposal.
10. What are the designer's main responsibilities during the implementation phase?

Thinking Critically

1. **Making Comparisons.** Which type of room do you think would be most difficult to design—kitchen, bathroom, living room, dining area, or bedroom? Give reasons for your answer.

2. **Making Predictions.** Do you think traditional drawing methods will continue to be used in the future? Why or why not?

3. **Analyzing Information.** Why do designers need to present their designs to clients? Why can't they simply send their drawings to the client?

Applying Your Knowledge

1. **Budget Basics.** Imagine that you're working with a family who wants to convert a spare room into a home office. They would like a hardwood floor, wood paneling, new lighting, custom shades, and an oak computer desk. Their budget won't accommodate so many improvements. How would you help them settle on a design plan? What options might you suggest?

2. **Style Practice.** Identify a style for the lobby of a law firm. Based upon this style select the color scheme, backgrounds, furniture, lighting, and accessories that could be used in the lobby. Prepare drawings and a sample board for your design.

3. **Presentation Practice.** Using the design that you developed in the preceding activity, present your work to your classmates. Describe the style you wanted to achieve and explain the choices you made to achieve that style.

4. **Drawing Practice.** Make a simple pictorial drawing of one room in your home or school. You may prepare your drawings by hand or use computer software. Display your work in the classroom.

Design Challenge

The owners of a large Victorian home have hired you to redesign an area adjacent to the kitchen. Currently the space is used for storage, but the couple wants it converted into a private bedroom and bathroom for their nephew who will be attending college in their city.

1. Begin the project by making a list of questions you would ask the clients.

2. Exchange lists with a partner and answer your partner's questions while he or she answers your questions.

3. Use your partner's answers to redesign the space into a bedroom and bathroom for the client's nephew.

4. Present your completed design to your partner for evaluation.

5. Place the design and a written evaluation of it in your design portfolio.

Designing Interior Environments

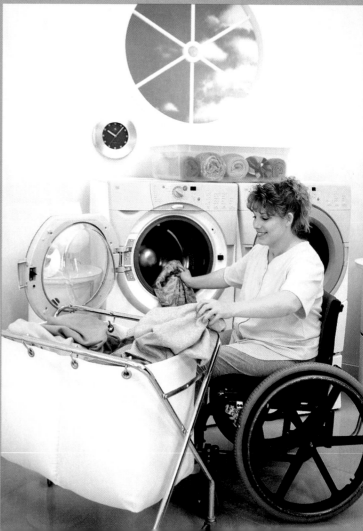

Kitchens, Laundry Areas & Baths

Objectives

- Explain basic principles for designing efficient kitchens, laundry areas, and bathrooms.

- Compare options for cabinets, countertops, and fixtures.

- Describe considerations in planning electrical, lighting, and ventilation systems for these areas.

- Identify ways to incorporate universal design features in kitchens, laundry areas, and bathrooms.

- Describe guidelines for shopping for appliances.

Vocabulary

- work center
- work triangle
- island
- peninsula
- master bath
- vanity

Of all the rooms in a home, the kitchen, laundry area, and bathroom are often the most interesting and challenging to design. Increasingly, they are called upon to be both high-tech and high-comfort, to serve multiple purposes, and to express individuality. This chapter will help you design kitchens, laundry areas, and baths that are efficient, safe, comfortable, and appealing.

Planning Kitchens

Kitchen designs should reflect the needs, wants, and lifestyle of the household they serve. Before planning a kitchen, consider the following questions.

- Which meals will usually be prepared in the kitchen? Will they be elaborate or simple meals?
- For how many people will food usually be prepared?
- Will there be more than one cook at a time?
- Should the kitchen accommodate people with physical limitations, such as vision impairments or mobility problems?
- How many appliances are to be stored in the kitchen?
- Will the kitchen be used for eating as well as food preparation?
- What other activities will be carried out in this space—such as doing laundry, accessing the Internet, or doing homework?
- How much food-centered entertaining does the household do?

Analyzing the answers to these questions can help you discover features the kitchen should have. For example, if two or more people participate in meal preparation, the kitchen must be arranged so that the cooks don't get in one another's way.

Designing an Efficient Layout

What makes one kitchen easier to work in than another? The answer is not size, but efficiency. An efficient arrangement allows meal preparation and cleanup to be completed using less time and energy. No matter how small or large a kitchen, an efficient layout will make it more convenient and pleasant to use. The first step is to plan the work centers.

Fig. 22-1 The island in this kitchen serves as a work center for cooking. How many other work centers can you identify in this kitchen?

Fig. 22-1 The island in this kitchen serves as a work center for cooking. How many other work centers can you identify in this kitchen?

Work Centers

Preparing a meal usually involves several different tasks, such as getting food from the storage area, measuring and mixing, cooking, and cleaning up. For the most efficient meal preparation, each task should be performed in a **work center**, an area of a kitchen especially equipped for a particular chore.

Most work centers are built around a major appliance or fixture and include both counter and storage space. **See Fig. 22-1.** A well-planned kitchen includes three basic work centers: food storage, cooking, and cleanup. Some kitchens also have mixing and planning centers, as well as other specialty centers.

Food Storage Center. The refrigerator is the focus of fresh food storage. Food that doesn't require refrigeration can be stored elsewhere. Some people find it convenient to store spices, sauces, mixes, and such staples as rice near the range. Canned food can be stored in cabinets or a pantry.

Cooking Center. The focus of the cooking center is the range or, in some kitchens, a separate cooktop and oven. If a microwave oven is used for meal preparation, it should also be located in this area. Other items that belong in the cooking center are small cooking appliances, such as a toaster or electric skillet; pots, pans, and utensils used for cooking; pot holders and hot pads; and serving bowls.

Cleanup Center. The cleanup center includes the sink and the dishwasher, if there is one. A garbage disposal, recycling bins, and perhaps a trash compactor might also be part of the cleanup center.

Many people prefer to store dishes, glassware, and silverware near the cleanup center so that these items can be put away easily after washing. The cleanup center also needs storage space for dishwashing detergents, scouring powder, dishcloths, and towels.

Some kitchens are designed with dual cleanup centers. One may be designed for washing dishes, while a secondary sink in another part of the kitchen handles tasks such as washing vegetables. **See Fig. 22-2.** This arrangement is especially convenient when more than one person works in the kitchen at a time.

Mixing Center. The mixing center is where much food preparation takes place. For convenience, it is best located between the refrigerator and the sink or between the sink and the range. Mixing bowls, knives, cutting boards, and utensils used for stirring and measuring should be within easy reach. Small appliances, such as an electric mixer and a blender, might be located on the countertop or in a nearby cabinet. Foods used most often in cooking and baking—such as flour, sugar, and spices—should also be within easy reach.

Planning Center. Planning centers are a convenient place to plan meals and store cookbooks. Many people also use a planning center for coordinating family messages and schedules, and paying bills. Planning centers range from a small table and chair to an office area that includes a computer.

Other Centers. Some kitchens may have additional work centers. For example, many kitchens have a serving and eating center. People who bake frequently may add a baking center with a marble surface for kneading dough and making pastry, and extra-wide storage spaces for appliances and bakeware.

A socializing center, or casual seating area, is very popular in today's kitchens. Such an area allows family members and friends to visit with the cook while he or she prepares the meal. Other specialized work centers incorporate areas for laundry, sewing, and maintaining indoor plants.

The Work Triangle

One clue to a kitchen's efficiency is its **work triangle**—the triangle formed by drawing imaginary lines to connect the sink, range or cooktop, and refrigerator. Because most kitchen work occurs in this area, it should be the basis for kitchen design. The triangle should not be so small that the kitchen is cramped or so large that the work centers are inconveniently far apart. Ideally, the total length of the sides of the triangle should be between 12 ft. and 22 ft. (3.7 m and 6.7 m). To accommodate a wheelchair, a work triangle should be 14 ft. to 24 ft. (4.3 m to 7.3 m).

A work triangle functions best when the three sides are nearly equal, with the sink located between the refrigerator and the range. If possible, traffic passing through the kitchen should not cross the work triangle.

Fig. 22-2 Some kitchens have an additional sink that allows a second cook to wash vegetables and fruits and prepare salads. The lower counter height makes it convenient for a seated user.

Fig. 22-3 An island can make a work triangle more functional in a large kitchen. **Would an island be a good idea in a small kitchen?**

Today's lifestyles may require adaptations to the work triangle. For example, more space than the recommended minimum may be needed when more than one person will be cooking at a time. The addition of extra work centers, such as a food prep sink, may affect how the basic work centers are arranged. Even with new ideas emerging, the work triangle concept remains a useful way to evaluate kitchen efficiency.

Common Kitchen Layouts

Kitchen cabinets and appliances usually are arranged in one of four basic shapes: one-wall, corridor, L-shaped, and U-shaped. In addition, any of these basic layouts can be varied by adding an island or a peninsula. An **island** is a freestanding storage and countertop unit. See Fig. 22-3. A **peninsula** is a countertop that extends out into the room, with one end attached to a wall or a cabinet. Figure 22-4 on pages 494–495 illustrates six kitchen layouts.

Fig. 22-4

Kitchen Layouts

A Visual Guide

Kitchen layouts are influenced by several factors, including available space and budget. Ideally, the layout is based on a work triangle, which is formed by drawing imaginary lines to connect the sink, range, and refrigerator.

One-Wall Kitchen

The range, sink, refrigerator, and cabinets are arranged along the wall. The one-wall kitchen is sometimes at the end of a living room and may be concealed by a set of folding doors or a screen.

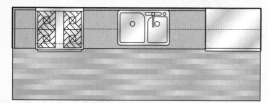

Advantage:

- Saves space. A practical choice in apartments or other small homes.

Disadvantages:

- Very limited storage and counter space.
- If stretched out to allow more storage and counter space, work centers may be too far apart.

Corridor Kitchen

Appliances and cabinets are arranged along two walls, with an aisle between them. Both ends of the kitchen may be open, or one end may be a wall.

Advantage:

- Usually has a compact, efficient work triangle.

Disadvantages:

- The work triangle may be too cramped to allow more than one person to work in the kitchen at a time.
- If both ends are open, people walking through the kitchen can interrupt meal preparation.

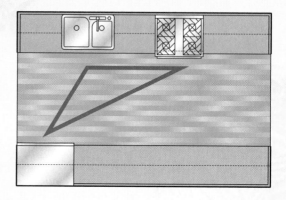

L-Shaped Kitchen

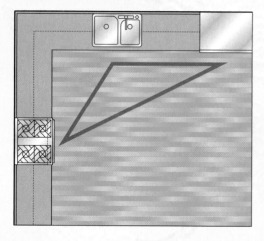

Appliances and cabinets are arranged along two adjoining walls. This arrangement permits an open area that may be used for dining.

Advantages:

- The work triangle is not interrupted by traffic.
- More than one person can work conveniently in the kitchen.
- More continuous counter and cabinet space is possible than with one-wall and corridor layouts.

Disadvantage:

- Corner storage might not be fully accessible.

Kitchen Layouts (continued)

A Visual Guide

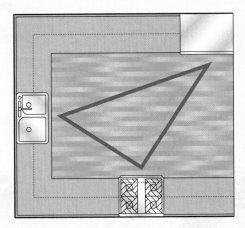

U-Shaped Kitchen

Appliances and cabinets are arranged along three adjoining walls. Some U-shaped kitchens also have an island in the middle of the U.

Advantages:

- Usually has more continuous counter and cabinet space than any of the other layouts.
- A major appliance may be placed along each wall so that the sides of the work triangle are equal.

Disadvantage:

- Corner storage may not be fully accessible.

Adding an Island

Any of the basic kitchen designs can be altered by adding an island—a freestanding base cabinet. The island may contain a second sink, a cooktop, or a chopping block. It may simply provide extra counter and storage space. It may also be used as an eating area, with stools for seating.

Advantage:

- Offers many options for making a kitchen more functional.

Disadvantage:

- Can be a traffic obstacle if not well planned.

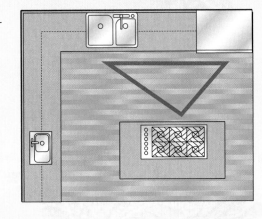

Using a Peninsula

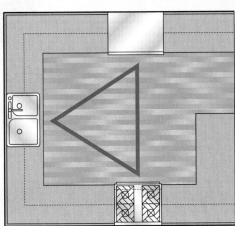

A peninsula countertop extends out into the room. Usually there's a cabinet below the peninsula countertop. There may also be cabinets suspended from the ceiling directly overhead. Like an island, a peninsula can be used for many purposes.

Advantages:

- Can serve as an open divider between the kitchen and a dining area or family room.
- Can be used to add a fourth countertop to a U-shaped kitchen, as shown here.

Disadvantage:

- Some people may not like the openness of a peninsula.

Making a Floor Plan

To plan the layout of kitchen cabinets and appliances, draw a floor plan to scale. (See Chapter 20 for directions on making a floor plan.) Use templates to determine the best locations for cabinets and appliances. Be sure to double-check the floor plan before work begins and appliances are ordered. Once the plumbing, equipment, and cabinets have been installed in a kitchen, moving them is usually complicated and expensive. Before you implement your plan, check it against the guidelines listed in **Fig. 22-5** below.

Choosing Cabinets & Fixtures

When planning the layout of a kitchen, you're working mainly with ideas, measurements, and drawings. When you begin shopping for components such as cabinets, countertops, and fixtures, the kitchen in your imagination takes its first steps toward becoming real. Looking over the available choices can be an exciting experience. For lasting satisfaction with kitchen components, be sure to consider their practical aspects as well as their appearance.

Fig. 22-5

Planning Kitchen Layouts	
Do	**Don't**
☑ Provide adequate working space for more than one person, if possible.	☒ Don't place a range under a window. Window curtains could catch fire, drafts might extinguish a pilot light or a flame, and the window would be difficult to clean.
☑ Allow enough clearance for stooping and for opening appliance and cabinet doors and drawers.	☒ Don't install cooktop burners and a built-in oven next to each other. This creates a fire hazard.
☑ Allow at least 5 ft. (1.5 m) of space between opposing counters in a corridor or U-shaped kitchen, or one with an island.	☒ Don't install a built-in oven above convenient reach. The oven will be difficult to load and unload, which could result in burns.
☑ Allow space for a chair or a stool so that a person can sit down to perform tasks.	☒ Don't place the refrigerator next to the range or built-in oven unless they are separated by insulating material. Heat from the range or the oven will cause the refrigerator to overwork.
☑ Arrange the sink, refrigerator, and range in an efficient work triangle.	☒ Don't locate a dishwasher where a person could easily fall over the dishwasher door when it's open.
☑ Allow at least 18 in. (46 cm) of counter space next to the door of the refrigerator for loading and unloading food.	☒ Don't crowd appliances into corners with little or no work space around them.
☑ Allow at least 21 in. (53 cm) of counter space on either side of the cooktop.	☒ Don't put appliances near doorways where they could be damaged by opening and closing doors.
☑ Allow 18 in. to 24 in. (46 cm to 61 cm) of counter space on both sides of the sink.	☒ Don't place a side-by-side refrigerator next to a wall. The wall will make it difficult to open the doors wide and remove the trays.
☑ Allow at least 36 in. (91 cm) of counter space in the mixing center.	

Cabinets

Most kitchens include base cabinets and wall cabinets. Base cabinets, which rest on the floor, are usually 24 in. (61 cm) deep. Wall cabinets, placed on the wall above the countertop, are usually 12 in. (30 cm) deep. Standard widths range from 9 in. to 48 in. (23 cm to 122 cm). Cabinets can also be custom made to any size.

When a kitchen is being designed, the color or finish of the cabinets is usually chosen first. This provides a starting place for selecting countertops, floor and wall coverings, and window treatments. Light-toned cabinets give a feeling of spaciousness, whereas dark-toned cabinets create a feeling of warmth and coziness.

Kitchen cabinets can be constructed of hardwood, softwood, plastic laminate, or metal. The most durable cabinets have solid hardwood doors, drawer fronts, and frames. The interiors of all cabinets and drawers should have a laminated or lacquered surface for easy cleaning with a damp cloth.

Cabinets are available with many special storage features. **See Fig. 22-6.** Kitchen designers can choose from many options.

- Cutlery drawers store knives safely.
- Deep drawers with upright dividers keep baking pans in order.
- Roll-down doors attached to the upper cabinets store small appliances.
- Turntables or hinged pullout racks improve access to corner cabinets.

Fig. 22-6 Special storage features in cabinets, such as pullout shelves (left) and a dropdown drawer (right), allow kitchen planners to make excellent use of compact spaces.

Countertops

Countertops should be attractive and durable. The ideal countertop material would withstand chopping, grinding, cutting, hot dishes, and stains. Unfortunately, there's no one material with all these features. Figure 22-7 compares several popular countertop materials.

Fig. 22-7

Countertop Materials

MATERIAL	Advantages	Disadvantages
Plastic Laminate	Economical Easy to maintain	Scratches easily Scorches easily Difficult to repair
Solid Surface (Acrylic or Polyester Compound)	Can be worked into different shapes and integrate sinks Easy to clean Range of colors and stone-like finishes Durable Resists germs and mildew	Can scorch Expensive
Wood, Butcher Block	Good for chopping and slicing	Spots easily Scorches Germs can breed
Ceramic Tile	Durable Easy to maintain Resists scratching Resists scorching	Surface can be uneven Objects dropped on it often shatter Grout must be sealed
Natural Stone (such as Granite)	Durable Resists stains	Expensive
Marble	Good for making pastry or candy	Stains easily Expensive
Concrete	Can be worked into different shapes and integrate sinks Resists scratching Resists scorching	Stains easily Prone to crumbling and cracking
Stainless Steel	Resists stains Resists scorching Easy to clean Can include an integrated sink	Shows scratches Shows fingerprints Can dent Expensive

Kitchen Sinks

Sinks and faucets are available in styles, materials, and colors to suit every kitchen design and need. Sinks may be round, square, or oval; be deep or shallow; and have single, double, or triple bowls. Some sinks are designed for special-purpose use, such as cleaning and draining vegetables. Some have a specially fitted cutting board and strainer. Materials used for sinks include stainless steel, porcelain, and acrylic.

Other Kitchen Design Considerations

For health and safety, a kitchen needs sufficient electrical circuits and outlets, proper lighting, and good ventilation. Choosing background materials for walls, floors, and window treatments is another aspect of kitchen design.

Electrical Circuits and Outlets. Electric ranges, cooktops, ovens, and other heavy-duty appliances each require a separate 240-volt circuit. If extra circuits are included in the circuit panel during installation, additional appliances can be added in the future.

Many small appliances are used in today's kitchens. Ample outlets (receptacles) make using these appliances easier. Spacing between outlets should be approximately 5 ft. to 6 ft. (1.5 m to 1.8 m) and never more than 10 ft. (3 m). Local building codes may specify the placement of outlets. To reduce the risk of electrical shock, any outlet near a water source should be equipped with a ground-fault circuit interrupter (GFCI).

Lighting. Within a kitchen, various areas have different lighting needs. For example, work centers require bright lights, but an eating area can have softer lighting. Plan the lighting as you draw the floor plan so that the necessary electrical wiring can be installed. You will probably want an overhead light for general lighting, as well as task lighting for the sink, cooktop, and countertop work areas. Refer to Chapter 27 for more information on lighting in the kitchen.

Fig. 22-8 A canopy hood over the cooktop removes steam and heat. Why is it a good idea to choose a hood that also includes a light?

Ventilation. Steam, odors, and condensation are often a problem in a kitchen. Adequate ventilation can help. Local building codes may establish the type and amount of ventilation required for kitchen equipment.

Ventilation systems are often part of the range. Whenever possible, the range ventilation system should exhaust air to the outdoors through a duct. The most common choice is a *range hood* or *canopy hood* located above the cooktop. See Fig. 22-8. Some kitchen designers save space by placing a *microwave range hood* over the range. This provides an additional cooking appliance and the needed ventilation for the range. Another option, called a *downdraft system*, uses a vent in or near the cooktop itself.

A *recirculating range hood* does not exhaust air to the outdoors, but merely filters it and returns it to the room. This type of range hood is able to remove some smoke, grease, and odors, but has no effect on steam or heat. A recirculating range hood should not be used with a gas cooktop because it doesn't remove combustion gases from the air.

Background Materials. The kitchen floor should be easy to maintain, withstand heavy traffic, and complement the rest of the kitchen decor. Options include vinyl, tile, laminate, wood, ceramic tile, and carpet. Select a wall covering that is water- and mildew-resistant, as well as easy to clean. Paint, vinyl-faced wallpaper, plastic laminate sheeting, and ceramic tile are good choices. Also be sure window treatments are easy to clean and, if used near a heat source, nonflammable. See Chapter 24 for more information on floor coverings, wall coverings, and window treatments.

Universal Design & Kitchens

There are numerous ways to include universal design features in a kitchen so that it's easy for everyone in the family to use, regardless of age or physical ability.

When designing a kitchen, remember the varying abilities of people who may use it now or in the future. **See Fig. 22-9.** To make a kitchen accessible to everyone, consider these universal design features:

Floor Plan

- Extra-wide doorways and traffic areas.
- Room for a wheelchair user to turn around 180 degrees.
- Enough clear floor space at cabinets, appliances, and work centers for wheelchair users to maneuver.

Countertops and Cabinets

- Counters with rounded edges.
- Color-contrasting borders at the edges of counters.
- Lower and higher counters for people of varying heights.
- A counter on a crank-operated unit that can be raised or lowered to a convenient work height.
- Counter areas without base cabinets, allowing wheelchair accessibility.
- Extra toe space under cabinets for wheelchairs.
- Large, easy-to-grip, D-shaped cabinet pulls.
- Lighting to illuminate cabinet interiors.
- Turntable storage aids.
- Pull-out shelves in base cabinets.
- Pull-down shelves in wall cabinets.
- Safe storage for household chemicals and sharp objects, out of children's reach.

Fixtures

- Sink in a motorized unit that can be raised or lowered at the touch of a button.
- Single-lever faucets with scald protection.
- Pull-out step under the sink for children to use.

Fig. 22-9 This kitchen has a universal design, allowing a wheelchair to fit under the sink area.

Appliances

- Side-by-side refrigerator/freezer.
- Cooktop, wall oven, and microwave oven lowered to a height convenient for all users.
- Range or cooktop with controls positioned on the side or front.
- Dishwasher installed next to a chair-accessible space.
- Dishwasher raised 9 to 12 inches (23 to 30 cm), or dishwasher drawer substituted, for easy loading and unloading without bending.
- Large, easy-to-read touch-pad control panels.

Flooring

- Nonslip, nonglare flooring.
- Color-contrasting borders on floors near solid obstacles.

Choosing Major Appliances

The cost of appliances often makes the kitchen the most expensive room in the home. When selecting any major appliance, it's important to shop carefully.

Appliance Shopping Tips

The first step when shopping for an appliance is research. Consumer information is available in print or online from many sources, including consumer magazines and product manufacturers. By studying this information, you can find out about available models and their features.

As you do your research, give careful thought to your needs and wants. Which features are most important to you? What is your price range? Keep the following considerations in mind when buying appliances.

Performance. Consumer magazines test products and publish performance ratings. You may decide to pay extra for a model that performs better—for instance, a dishwasher that gets dishes cleaner or tends to need fewer repairs. On the other hand, you may discover a bargain model that performs almost as well as more expensive ones.

Energy Use. The more energy an appliance uses, the more it will cost to run. The difference on your monthly utility bill can be significant, especially over the 10- to 20-year life of an appliance. The EnergyGuide label that appears on many appliances will help you estimate a machine's energy usage. **See Fig. 22-10.**

Fig. 22-10 The EnergyGuide is clearly posted on appliances. Why is it important to consider the energy-efficiency rating of a water heater?

Designing Commercial Kitchens

Designers who plan commercial kitchens share some of the concerns of residential kitchen designers, but they must also consider different criteria that are particular to the needs of professional cooks.

- **Appliances.** Commercial kitchen appliances are bigger, more complex, and more numerous than those in a family home. Designers may need to include space and electric wiring for everything from an espresso machine to an eight-burner oven.

- **Storage.** The food service kitchen may need room for specialty items such as 60-quart stockpots and 20-gallon ingredient bins. Open shelving and pullout drawers make utensils easy to find, while eliminating the hazard of swinging cabinet doors.

- **Work and Traffic Patterns.** Designers identify the different work areas and create a floor plan that allows for busy traffic flow. Combination work centers reduce traffic by allowing workers to do different tasks at the same place. A salad maker might chop vegetables at an island and store them in a built-in refrigerator drawer beneath the work surface. A full-service restaurant also needs space for wait staff to pick up orders.

- **Sanitation.** State and local law sets high standards of sanitation for professional food preparers. Design can help meet these needs. For example, with faucets operated by foot pedals, workers touch fewer surfaces, reducing the spread of bacteria.

Apply It!

Visit your school's cafeteria kitchen and study it. List the design features that you think make it suited to the number of people who work there and their tasks. If possible, watch the cafeteria staff prepare a meal. Were your observations correct? Why or why not?

Fig. 22-11

Money Isn't All You're Saving

Fig. 22-12

Appliances that significantly exceed DOE standards earn ENERGY STAR status. **See Fig. 22-11.** The ENERGY STAR logo may appear on the appliance, its packaging, or the EnergyGuide label. Dishwashers bearing this seal use at least 25 percent less energy than mandated by law. Refrigerator-freezers that carry the ENERGY STAR logo beat the standard by 15 percent or more.

Safety. Research the safety features of various models. On gas appliances, look for the seals of the Association of Home Appliance Manufacturers and the American Gas Association. Look for the Underwriters Laboratories (UL) certification seal on electrical appliances. **See Fig. 22-12.** This seal means that the product has been tested and meets established safety standards.

Consumer Considerations

Choosing Energy-Efficient Appliances

The U.S. Department of Energy (DOE) sets minimum standards for energy efficiency for all major appliances, but some models are more efficient than others. The technology may increase the purchase price. However, that initial expense is offset by other savings. Some states offer rebates on energy-efficient appliances; others waive the sales tax on these machines. Of course, more efficient energy use means lower utility bills as the appliance is used. How do you find these energy misers?

Size Up Your Needs.
Match the appliance size to your needs. As a rule, the larger the appliance, the more energy it uses. However, one large appliance uses less energy than two smaller ones.

If you decide you need more freezer space, for example, replacing your refrigerator-freezer with a larger one may be wiser than buying an additional freezer.

Let Labels Be Your Guide. Federal law requires that an EnergyGuide label be placed on refrigerators, dishwashers, and washing machines. The label states the appliance's estimated energy usage, given as kilowatts per hour; the range of energy used by similar models; and that model's average annual operating cost, using the national average price of energy. When you look at appliances of similar size and features, simply pick the one with the lowest energy usage. An Energy Star logo means a machine is especially efficient.

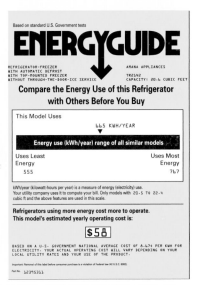

Special Features. Generally, models with more and better features cost more. If no appliance has all the features you want at a price you can afford, you'll need to set priorities.

Size. Capacity—how much it can hold—is important for some appliances, such as refrigerators and washing machines. Measure to see whether the appliance will fit through doorways and into the space you plan to put it. Allow clearance for opening the appliance door and for ventilation, if needed.

Style. Freestanding and small portable appliances are better choices for a person who moves frequently. Built-in appliances can be expensive to install.

Appearance. Choose appliance colors that will blend well with the walls and cabinets. Neutral colors work well in most color schemes and will allow you to remodel in the future without having to replace the appliances.

Purchase Price. Compare prices at several retailers to find the best buy. Ask about charges for delivery and installation of the appliance. Check to see if any stores or manufacturers are offering rebates. Some stores offer financing arrangements or special financing rates.

Warranties and Repairs. Most appliances come with a warranty, which protects you in case the product is defective. Investigate the length and type of warranty offered by the manufacturer or the retailer. What type of service does the store offer? What is the cost of a service call?

Refrigerators & Freezers

For keeping foods cold, the most common choice is the two-door combination refrigerator-freezer. The freezer compartment may be above, below, or beside the refrigerator compartment.

The recommended size of the refrigerator compartment depends on the number of people in the household. For two people, 16 cu. ft. (0.4 m^3) is recommended. Add 1.5 cu. ft. (0.04 m^3) for each additional person. Some families may want or need a roomier refrigerator than these guidelines suggest. Generally, the larger the refrigerator, the more energy it uses. The most energy-efficient size is 16 cu. ft. to 20 cu. ft. (0.5 m^3 to 0.6 m^3).

Modular refrigerators are an alternative to the traditional refrigerator-freezer. Separate drawer-type modules can be placed in convenient locations around the kitchen. **See Fig. 22-13.** The temperature and humidity in each can be adjusted to suit a particular type of food—one module for fresh fruits and vegetables, for example, and another for dairy products and meats.

Fig. 22-13 Some refrigerators include separate compartments for fruits and vegetables that allow the user to set those temperatures separately.

Fig. 22-14 Look for adjustable shelves that allow you to arrange the height according to the items.

Separate freezers enable consumers to keep large quantities of frozen foods on hand. These range from large upright or chest-style freezers to smaller models that can be installed under a kitchen counter.

Refrigerators and freezers can be purchased with a variety of special features. Here are some examples:

- An automatic ice maker.

- Ice cube and cold water dispensers on exterior doors.

- A self-defrosting freezer. This eliminates the need to remove manually frost that would otherwise build up on the freezer walls and reduce energy efficiency.

- A power-saver switch that can save energy during periods of low humidity.

- Separate compartments with individual temperature controls for fruits and vegetables, cheese, and meats.

- Movable shelves that crank up or down easily to fit in tall items. See Fig. 22-14.

- Glass shelves, a feature that prevents dripping to shelves below.

- Deep door compartments that can hold large items such as gallon beverage containers.

- Electronic controls that sound an alert when the door is left open or the unit needs repair.

- Slide-in, microwave-safe containers for storing leftovers.

- A pull-down opening on exterior doors that allows quick access to snacks and beverages. This saves energy by reducing the number of times the main door is opened.

- A built-in touch screen and bar code scanner that keeps track of the household's food inventory and can go online to order items from a local store.

Ranges, Cooktops & Ovens

Ranges combine surface cooking units and one or more ovens in one appliance. For many years a freestanding range was considered standard equipment, and it's still the most popular choice. Consumers can also choose a drop-in or slide-in range. Both are designed to give a "built-in" look when installed between cabinets.

An alternative to the range is to use two separate, built-in components. A built-in cooktop is installed in a countertop. The area beneath it can be used for storage or left open to accommodate a seated user. A built-in oven is typically installed in a wall, though it may also be installed in a cabinet or island. It may be a single or a double unit. One advantage of separate units is that both the cooktop and the oven can be installed at any convenient height.

Gas or Electric?

Debate continues as to whether gas or electricity is better for cooking. For surface cooking, many people prefer gas burners because the temperature can be adjusted instantly and precisely. However, electricity is often preferred for oven cooking because it keeps the temperature more even and is a safer heat source for children and older adults. To get the best of both options, you might choose a gas cooktop and an electric wall oven. Energy cost is another consideration. On the average, a gas appliance costs less than half as much to operate as an electric one, provided the gas appliance has electronic ignition instead of a pilot light. Check with a local utility company for a comparison of gas and electric costs in your area.

Types of Surface Cooking Units

The different types of surface cooking units vary in cost, heating characteristics, and type of cookware that can be used. **See Fig. 22-15.** Before making a selection, find out as much as you can about the options currently available. Here are some points to consider.

- Gas burners or electric coils are standard on many cooking units.
- Sealed gas burners are easier to clean than standard burners but are less energy efficient.

- Smooth cooktops are made of glass-ceramic. When not in use, they provide extra work space. The heating elements, which are below the surface, may be gas burners, electric coils, induction coils, or halogen lamps.
- Halogen and induction elements are more energy efficient than conventional electric coils. Solid disk elements and smooth cooktops using electric coils are less efficient.
- Modular cooktops can be customized with interchangeable units, such as grills, griddles, rotisseries, steamers, and woks.

Types of Ovens

Several types of ovens are available, each with its own cooking characteristics. **See Fig. 22-16.** Many kitchens have more than one oven. If a range or wall oven has two separate oven compartments, they may be of different types.

Conventional. A conventional oven uses gas or electricity to heat the air in the oven compartment. Some gas ranges also have a separate broiler compartment. With electric ovens and most self-cleaning gas ovens, broiling is done in the oven compartment.

Convection. A convection oven is similar to a conventional electric oven but uses fans to circulate heated air over the food. As a result, heat is more evenly distributed and food cooks more quickly.

Fig. 22-15 Cooktops come in many configurations to suit a cook's preference. One cook might choose fewer burners combined with a built-in grill while another may like the option of easy-to-clean burners.

Microwave. In a microwave oven, tiny waves of energy cause food molecules to vibrate against each other. The resulting friction creates heat within the food. The cooking power of a microwave oven is measured in watts. The higher the wattage, the faster the food will cook. Microwave ovens cook much faster than conventional ones, but they are not as effective at browning foods.

Halogen. In this type of oven, powerful halogen lights cook in about one-fourth the time of a conventional oven. Halogen ovens are generally higher priced than conventional ovens.

Rapid Cook. A rapid-cook oven uses a combination of convection or conventional heat and microwave energy to cook food much faster than a conventional oven. Rapid-cook ovens can bake, broil, roast, and toast foods. These ovens are more expensive than conventional or convection ovens.

Combination. Ovens are available that can be used for more than one type of cooking, such as conventional/convection or halogen/microwave.

Other Features

Special features are available on many ranges, cooktops, and ovens. Consumers must weigh the added convenience or energy savings against the extra cost of appliances with these features. Here are some examples:

• Self-cleaning or continuous-cleaning ovens. Because it has better insulation, a self-cleaning oven uses less energy for cooking than one without a cleaning feature. If you use the self-cleaning feature more than once a month, though, you'll end up using more energy than you save.

• Other features for easy cleanup, such as a lift-up cooktop, removable knobs, and a removable oven door.

• Electronic ignition on gas ranges and cooktops. This feature eliminates the need for a continuously burning pilot light, saving energy.

• Electronic touch controls.

• A warming drawer to keep foods warm until served.

• Programmable ovens that can start cooking at a preset time and shut off automatically. Some let you store frequently used settings in memory and activate them at the touch of a button.

Dishwashers

Dishwashers are available in both built-in and portable models, with a variety of wash and temperature cycles. Portable dishwashers are ideal for renters and people who move frequently. However, they must be wheeled to the sink and connected to the faucet before each use. Built-in dishwashers free the sink for other activities while the dishwasher is in operation. They make less noise than portable models because the surrounding cabinets act as sound barriers.

Some dishwashers sanitize the dishes, eliminating household bacteria. Look for certification by the National Sanitation Foundation to select a sanitizing dishwasher.

Many people believe that dishwashers waste heat and water. Actually, they conserve energy. They use less hot water than washing dishes by hand. Newer model dishwashers use as little as 4 gal. (15 L) of water and have a water preheater that adds further to the energy savings. You can store a day's worth of dishes in a dishwasher and wash them at night, when energy rates are often lower. Many models have an energy-saving switch that permits dishes to be dried by air rather than heat.

Drawer-type dishwashers are installed like drawers in a cabinet. **See Fig. 22-17.** These units use energy and water efficiently. A pair of dishwasher drawers can be run independently for small loads or together for large loads.

Disposal Units

Disposal units provide a quick and convenient way to eliminate waste. They are installed beneath the sink, where they are connected to the drain. They grind up food scraps so the particles can be flushed down the drain.

A continuous-feed disposal is turned on and off by a switch mounted on the wall. Scraps are added as the disposal is operated. Batch-feed disposals grind scraps a batch at a time. They are operated by turning or pushing a drain stopper. This type may cost less to install and is safer to use.

Washing Machines

Washing machines wash, rinse, and spin-dry clothes automatically. Most have controls that adjust the speed of agitation from delicate to heavy-duty, the temperature of the water from hot to cold, and the water level from very low to full. Some washers feature extra-large-capacity tubs. Machines are also available with automatic dispensers that add soap, bleach, and fabric softener.

Fig. 22-17 Dishwasher drawers offer space-saving features and allow users to wash just a few dishes without wasting energy and water. **Why does this type of dishwasher work well in a universal design kitchen?**

Fig. 22-18 Many front-loading washers and dryers have a larger capacity and push-button controls. They also come in several colors.

Many washers have energy-saving features. One example is separate controls for wash and rinse temperatures. Another is a suds-saver feature, which saves the wash water from lightly soiled loads for reuse.

Computer technology enables the most sophisticated and expensive machines to be programmed in advance for different types of loads. To carry out the cycle, the user merely has to press one button. **See Fig. 22-18.**

Clothes Dryers

Gas dryers are less expensive to operate than electric dryers. All dryers have time and temperature controls. Some have an energy-saving feature called "electronic sensor drying." This feature enables the machine to measure, or "feel," the degree of moistness in the clothes and shut itself off when clothes are dry. An electronic ignition on gas dryers eliminates the need for a continuous pilot light.

Most dryers feature an automatic cool-down period. This feature is especially useful for permanent-press clothes. At the end of the cycle, the clothes continue to tumble for a timed interval with the heat off. This makes them more comfortable to handle and reduces wrinkles. Some dryers feature a removable rack that permits tennis shoes, stuffed toys, and wet mittens to be dried without tumbling.

Space-Saving Laundry Appliances

Several options make it possible to fit a laundry center in a small space. For instance, a stacked washer and dryer can be used. This unit has a full-sized, top-loading washer on the bottom with a dryer stacked on top.

Washer-dryer combinations are also available. The user puts in clothes, chooses the settings, and comes back to clean, dry clothes. Small combination units can fit under a counter or in a closet.

Another solution is a portable washer and dryer. Portable washers are filled and drained at the sink. Small, portable dryers plug into any standard electric outlet and require no special wiring or venting.

The Impact of Technology

Washing Machine Innovations

Cleaner clothes and energy efficiency are twin goals driving the technology behind washing machines. The results thus far are impressive.

Water Saving. Front-loading machines, use up to 40 percent less water than top-loading models. Less water, in turn, means less energy used to heat it.

Silver Nanotechnology. This newest technology involves the electrolysis of silver solids into silver ions. These ions fill the wash and rinse water, penetrating fibers at the molecular level. Silver ions remove dirt and kill bacteria using cold water. As a result, only a small amount of electrical energy is needed.

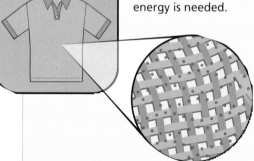

Tech Trends

Learn more about microsensors, the devices that make most washing machine functions possible. What are other possible applications? What factors may influence further growth and research in this field?

Agitator-Free Design. Machines without agitators cause less stress to clothing, while handling bigger loads. This feature has always been a selling point of front-loading machines. It's now found in some top-loading models as well. The cleaning action sometimes comes from the rapid rotation, in alternating directions, of the inner tub. Some models have plates or armlike tumblers that toss clothes, rather like a salad.

"Smart" Machines. Sensors monitor the machine's energy use throughout the washing process. They have the ability to automatically adjust the water level to the size of the load. They can detect the dominant type of fabric and choose the most efficient cleaning action and water temperature.

Customized Cleaning. Some washing machines let you save your own settings, based on personal needs. People with allergies can choose a cycle featuring a concentrated detergent solution and a longer rinse to eliminate bacteria and dust mite waste. Other settings are designed for muddy or sandy clothes. Some models offer a pretreatment option, which dissolves detergent in water and injects the mixture into clothes before washing.

Ultrasonic Cleaning. This technology cleans without water. Ultrasonic cleaning, or cleaning with high-frequency sound waves, is already used to sterilize equipment in medical and research labs. Engineers are now exploring how to use it for cleaning clothes as well.

Planning Laundry Areas

Many homes have laundry areas. They range from a closet just big enough to hold a washer and dryer to a separate room large enough to also be used for sewing and crafts.

Choosing a Location

A laundry center can be located in almost any part of the home that provides these basic requirements:

- Hot and cold water supply lines and drains. To reduce the cost of construction or remodeling, choose an area near existing plumbing lines. If possible, provide a floor drain beneath the washer in case it overflows or the hoses leak.

- A 240-volt electrical outlet for an electric dryer, or a gas line for a gas dryer.

- Proper ventilation for the dryer's exhaust system. This can be achieved by locating the laundry area near an outside wall.

A laundry area is often located on the main floor near a side, back, or garage entrance. **See Fig. 22-19.** The kitchen also can be a convenient location for a laundry center. The person washing clothes can do other household tasks at the same time. However, soiled clothes shouldn't be handled in the same area where food is prepared. Folding doors can hide the laundry equipment when it is not in use.

Another possible laundry location is in or near a bathroom or sleeping area. This might be a step saver, since these are areas where most soiled clothes and linens are collected. One drawback to a sleeping area location is that laundry equipment is noisy. Doing laundry will need to be limited to times when people are not sleeping. Insulation in interior walls can help mask the noise of laundry equipment.

A basement laundry room keeps soiled clothing and linen, as well as the noise of the washer and dryer, away from living areas. However, a basement location is less convenient. In addition, basements are sometimes damp, which promotes the growth of mold and mildew.

Fig. 22-19 Many of today's homes include laundry rooms on the main floor. **Why is this an advantage?**

Planning for Efficiency

Activities associated with laundering include storing soiled clothes and linens, sorting, washing, drying, folding, and ironing. All of these tasks can be easier when you have the right equipment and the space is arranged in an orderly manner. When planning a new or redesigned laundry area, include as many of the following features as possible:

- A washable floor covering.
- Proper lighting that does not create shadows.
- Storage space for detergent and other laundry supplies.
- Baskets, bins, or carts for sorting and carrying laundry.
- A sink near the washing machine for hand laundering or presoaking stains.
- A clothesline or rod for line drying.

Fig. 22-20 This is a drying center. It makes drying items such as hats, sweaters, and special fabrics easy.

- Horizontal racks for drying items flat. Some homes have a drying center—a traditional dryer plus a cabinet above it for drying flat items such as sweaters. **See Fig. 22-20.**

- A rod or hooks for hanging items as they are removed from the dryer.

- A countertop or other flat surface for folding laundry.

- Space to set up an ironing board near an electrical outlet. When not in use, the board can be hung on the wall or on the back of a door. Options include ironing boards that fold into their own cabinets in the wall.

Universal Design & Laundry Areas

In keeping with the philosophy of universal design, laundry areas can be planned to accommodate a variety of individual needs.

- Some compact washers are only 32 in. (81 cm) high, with the controls mounted on the front. They are easy to use from a seated position.

- A dryer door that swings to the side, rather than down, provides easier access for wheelchair users.

- Placing the dryer on a platform reduces the need to bend or stoop while loading and unloading.

- People with limited vision appreciate easy-to-read controls with an audible tone that signals when clothes are dry or when the dryer's lint screen needs cleaning.

- Braille control panel overlays and instruction books are available for some models of washers and dryers.

- Lowering the work table or counter and leaving open space underneath will accommodate seated users.

- Provide single-lever controls for faucets and D-shaped handles on storage cabinet doors.

Planning Bathrooms

Bathrooms may range from small and basic to large, multipurpose spaces. Adding or remodeling a bath is a common home improvement project. Whether you're planning a remodeling project or a new home, give careful consideration to bathroom design.

Planning the Size & Location

Bathrooms are identified as full, three-quarter, or half-baths, depending on the number of basic fixtures included. A *full bath* has a minimum of a sink, a toilet, and a bathtub. The term *three-quarter bath* often refers to a bathroom with a sink, a toilet, and a shower, but no tub. A *half-bath*, or powder room, contains only a sink and a toilet.

If a home has only one bathroom, it should be a full or three-quarter bath located off a main hallway. If there is more than one bathroom, the most common arrangement is to locate at least one full bath in or near the sleeping area and a half-bath near the living area.

Many newer or remodeled homes include a **master bath**, a full bath that is part of the master bedroom area. **See Fig. 22-21.** It often borrows design elements from the adjoining master bedroom. A large master bath can serve as a relaxing retreat or an exercise studio.

Locating a bathroom close to existing drainage pipes reduces construction costs. If that location is unsatisfactory, however, the best long-term solution may be to spend the money for pipe work and locate the bathroom where it will be most convenient.

The bathroom might also be positioned to provide a sound barrier between quieter and noisier parts of the home. For example, when placed between a family room and a bedroom, it can help prevent noisy activities in the family room from disturbing sleep.

When making a bathroom floor plan, design and measure the layout carefully. Once fixtures have been installed, they're expensive and difficult to move. Allow enough space in the bathroom for safety and comfort. Check local building codes for minimum dimensions and other requirements. Consider whether more than one person might need to use the bathroom at the same time. If so, you may want to include two sinks and perhaps partitions to separate different areas.

Fig. 22-21 Many homes have a master bath that is an extension of the master bedroom.

Selecting Fixtures & Cabinets

Much of a bathroom's decor is determined by the fixtures and cabinets chosen. Fixtures come in many colors and may be made of porcelain enamel, china, stainless steel, or prefabricated plastic.

Fig. 22-22 This bathtub is surrounded by tiled walls. Notice the creative design.

Bathtubs

Bathtubs may be rectangular, square, round, or oval. They are usually enclosed by walls on three sides. **See Fig. 22-22.** However, there are exceptions. Freestanding tubs with ball-and-claw feet are sometimes chosen for a Victorian look. Tubs may also be sunken into the floor or built into a platform anywhere in the room. Whirlpool bathtubs include water jets for massaging muscles.

For safety, some bathtubs are equipped with nonskid bottoms and grab bars. Both safety and comfort can be enhanced with a soft bathtub. This type of tub, made from the same tough plastic as automobile bumpers, becomes more cushioned when hot water is added. It has a high-density foam core that helps insulate the heat, improving energy efficiency.

Showers

Installing a shower head above the bathtub creates a *tub shower*. A walk-in *stall shower* is another alternative. A compact stall shower is a good solution for a small bathroom.

One-piece shower units made of molded plastic are an easy way to add a new shower to a bathroom. Another option for shower walls is tile. The disadvantage of tile is that the grout must be kept in good condition or the walls will leak.

The shower head may be fixed in position on the wall, adjustable, or handheld. Some shower units have multiple spray heads.

Instead of a shower curtain, sliding panels or a swinging door may be used to keep water inside the shower area. Shower doors are usually made of safety glass or plastic and may be patterned to provide greater privacy.

Toilets

Toilets can be mounted on the wall or on the floor. The water tank may be above the bowl (high-line) or at the same level (low-line). In some models, the tank and bowl form a single unit.

Building codes in some states require new or replacement toilets to be *ultra low flush* (ULF) models. These use no more than 1.6 gal. (6.1 L) per flush, as compared to older toilets that used as much as 5 gal. (19 L) per flush.

Bathroom Sinks

Bathroom sinks—also called washbasins—come in several different styles.

- A *wall-hung* sink has open space beneath, which helps make a small bathroom seem roomier.
- A *pedestal sink* is supported by a freestanding base. Many pedestal sinks are artfully shaped, giving them a look of sculpture.
- An *inset sink* is set into a countertop. The cabinet beneath provides storage.
- An *above-counter basin* looks like a decorative wash bowl set on the counter. The plumbing extends down through the counter. **See Fig. 22-23.**

Fig. 22-23 This appears to be a decorative wash bowl, but it is actually an above-counter basin with the plumbing hidden in the decorative cabinet.

The standard height for bathroom sinks is approximately 32 in. (81 cm) from floor to rim. Placing the sink at this height makes it especially convenient for children and people who use a wheelchair.

Cabinets and Countertops

Like kitchens, bathrooms may include wall and base cabinets. A base cabinet in a bathroom is called a **vanity**. It conceals sink pipes and provides counter space and storage. **See Fig. 22-24.** Materials used for vanity tops include marble, plastic laminate, solid surface, enameled cast iron, and fiberglass.

Fig. 22-24 This master bathroom has a vanity with two sinks and a walk-in shower. The vanity provides counter space and storage for two.

Other Considerations

To be safe and efficient, bathrooms, like kitchens, require a certain degree of technical planning. When designing a new bathroom or remodeling an old one, think about the following considerations.

Electrical Outlets. Bathrooms may require several electrical outlets to accommodate personal appliances, such as hair dryers, curling irons, electric shavers, radios, and clocks. Any outlet near a water source should be equipped with a ground-fault circuit interrupter (GFCI).

Lighting. For safety, bathroom lights should be wall or ceiling mounted and operated with wall switches. A lamp knocked into the bathtub or sink could cause a fatal shock..

Ventilation. Steam from a hot bath or shower causes condensation to form on mirrors and walls. Without proper ventilation, wallpaper will start to peel and mildew will grow. The best solution is an exhaust fan that vents to the outside.

Floor and Wall Coverings. Choose a floor covering that will not be slippery when wet and that can be cleaned easily. Avoid flooring that is damaged by water or shows water spots. Vinyl and tile are popular choices. As in the kitchen, select a mildew-resistant, easy-to-clean wall covering.

Universal Design & Bathrooms

When designing a bathroom, remember the varying abilities of people who may use it now or in the future. **See Fig. 22-25.** To make a bathroom accessible to everyone, consider these universal design features:

- Wide doorway and extra floor space.
- Grab bars placed near toilets and tubs.
- Elevated toilet seat added to a standard toilet.
- Shower with a seat.

- Shower doors that retract and pivot for easy access.
- No-sill, doorless shower stall and rolling shower chair.
- Hand-held shower head.
- Single-lever shower controls.
- Barrier-free sink with the faucet toward the front and a side drain that places the pipes away from the user's knees.
- Tiltable mirror at the sink.
- Faucet with a retractable spray handle to allow shampooing from a chair.
- Low counter for access by seated users or young children.

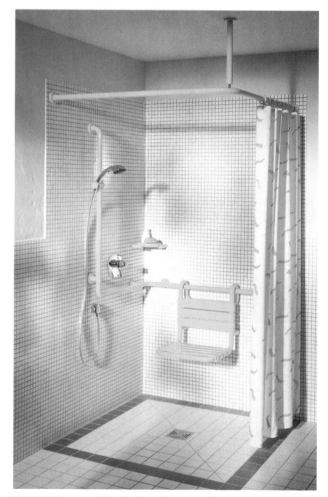

Fig. 22-25 A no-sill, doorless shower allows access to people with impaired mobility. Notice how the yellow elements highlight safety while making the shower more inviting.

Easy Updates

Making changes to kitchens, laundry areas, and bathrooms can be very expensive. Appliances are costly, and plumbing and electrical work add to the expense of remodeling. So what can people do if they want to achieve a new look but don't want to go to the expense of remodeling a room and replacing appliances? They can improve the appearance of a kitchen, laundry area, or bathroom at far less expense by using one or more of these approaches:

- Hire a professional to repaint appliances or put a new porcelain coating on fixtures. Both are much less expensive than replacement.

- Paint the walls or put up new wallpaper to give the room a new look.

- Instead of installing new cabinets, paint or refinish the existing ones, or replace just the cabinet doors and fronts.

- Brighten up the room by replacing hardware such as cabinet knobs and handles, towel bars, and faucets. See Fig. 22-26.

- To change the color scheme or add an accent color, use towels, throw rugs, a shower curtain, and window treatments.

- Choose a coordinated set of accessories that harmonizes with the room's style. Add interesting accents such as baskets or candles.

Fig. 22-26 This homeowner is replacing the faucet on her bathroom sink. Would you attempt this task yourself? Why or why not?

Profile of a Kitchen Planner

A kitchen planner works with clients to develop an attractive, practical, and efficient kitchen that fits their tastes, needs, and budgets. Kitchen planners help clients determine the most useful fixtures and appliances and the most useful and cost-effective way of organizing them.

Education & Training

- A minimum of an associate's degree is required.
- Some employers require a bachelor's degree in interior design.
- After seven years of training, a person can become a certified kitchen designer (CKD).

Skills & Aptitudes

- Knowledge of current appliance designs and cooking techniques is required.
- Knowledge of construction, electrical and ventilation systems, and building codes is essential.
- Creativity and a good eye for color and balance are essential.

Kitchen Planner
Yvette Allen

I often hear people complain that their kitchen is not "right." It's too small to move about when cooking, or the appliances or cabinets are in the wrong places, or there's no place to gather for coffee and conversation. If a kitchen doesn't meet the tastes and needs of the household, the home scores low on the livability scale.

As a kitchen planner, I design kitchens that are attractive and practical for the people who use them—including people with special needs. Whenever possible, I follow the principles of universal design: plan a kitchen for people of all physical abilities and ages. For a person with a disability, a usable kitchen can open up a world of independence.

A thorough knowledge of kitchen design principles is a basic requirement for my job. In addition, I need to keep up with the latest trends in home appliances and fixtures, ergonomics, and cooking methods. It helps to have an artistic eye, and I can't imagine succeeding as a kitchen designer without knowing how to use CAD programs for planning!

Each job begins with a meeting with the family to find out their schedules, habits, and preferences. This helps me determine the kitchen's traffic patterns and work area requirements. Together we come up with a plan to fit their lifestyle. Last year I designed a professional baking center for a woman who wanted to run a business from her kitchen.

I apply the same principles and give my best effort to all clients, regardless of how much money they want to spend. Budget, nevertheless, is a determining factor. Modest budgets require a special kind of creativity. I concentrate on useful, good quality appliances and fixtures, and a few well-chosen decorative elements, using designer tricks like revolving shelving devices for storage. In one small home I was able to convert a closet into a pantry area to store food and extend the kitchen.

Preparing and sharing meals with family and friends is a wonderful part of life; people should enjoy that to the fullest. I'm proud that my work helps people reach that goal.

Design Portfolio

1. Interview a family member or neighbor about what he or she would like to keep and to change in an existing kitchen. Create a new kitchen design that meets your "client's" desires.

2. Design a kitchen that includes areas where children 8 to 12 years old can help their parents prepare meals.

Review & Activities

Chapter Summary

- A well-designed kitchen is based on the needs of the home's occupants, has **work centers** for various tasks, and is arranged efficiently.

- Both practical factors and appearance should be considered when choosing cabinets, countertops, and fixtures.

- Universal design features can make kitchens, laundry areas, and bathrooms suitable for people of all ages and abilities.

- Research the options before choosing major appliances.

- Laundry rooms should be conveniently located.

- A home should have at least one full or three-quarter bath.

Checking Your Understanding

1. Identify three standard and three optional **work centers**.

2. What is the **work triangle**, and what principles should be followed in designing one?

3. What is the difference between an **island** and a **peninsula**?

4. How does a corridor kitchen compare to a U-shaped kitchen in terms of work space?

5. What kitchen design element is typically chosen before others? What other decisions are related to this one?

6. Why do kitchens need ventilation systems?

7. What factors are important when buying major appliances?

8. Name two advantages of gas cooktops and electric ovens.

9. What appliances are useful for people who move often?

10. What three requirements must be met by a laundry area?

11. What are two features of universal design that can be used in both kitchens and laundry areas?

12. What is the difference between a full bath, a three-quarter bath, and a half bath?

Thinking Critically

1. **Evaluating Information.** Which kitchen layout would you prefer for a family of five with two food preparers? Why?

2. **Comparing and Contrasting.** Identify the materials you think are preferable for kitchen cabinets, countertops, and fixtures and explain why you prefer each.

3. **Inferring.** How might the idea of kitchen work centers apply to a laundry room?

Applying Your Knowledge

1. **Kitchen Planning Checklist.** Make a list of questions a kitchen planner could use to evaluate a family's needs in a kitchen.

2. **Analyzing Work Triangles.** Take the measurements of an existing kitchen. Draw the layout to scale, and find the distances between the three points of the work triangle. Think about the arrangement of these three points and those distances. Write an analysis indicating whether you think the kitchen is efficiently arranged or not, explaining why. If not, describe any suggested improvements.

3. **Comparing Costs.** Compare the prices of three ranges or refrigerators of similar size and features. Compare not only the purchase price but also—using the EnergyGuide label—the operating costs for 15 years. Which appliance is the better buy based on initial price? Which is the better buy based on total cost? Compile your findings into a written report.

4. **Laundry Technology.** Choose a laundry appliance and research the technology behind it. Find information about how it works, the advantages and disadvantages, and how it is rated in *Consumer Reports* magazine. Prepare a sales presentation about your laundry appliance and present it to the class.

5. **Designing Bathrooms.** Design a stylish and efficient bathroom that includes at least five universal design features. Sketch the floor plan and create a sample board showing the materials you would use.

Design Challenge

You have been asked to design a large but efficient 14 ft. x 12 ft. kitchen for a family of six. The family eats meals in the kitchen. It is also their laundry center and where the children do their homework.

1. Develop a list of features and appliances that this family would need in their kitchen, including work centers.

2. Design a floor plan of the kitchen, showing the location of each work center and all major appliances.

3. Highlight the universal design features in your design.

4. Identify the eating and study areas, as well as the laundry appliances.

5. Present your finished plan to the class for feedback.

6. Place the finished plan in your design portfolio.

Home Offices & Storage Spaces

Objectives

- Identify reasons people set up a home office.

- Describe considerations for choosing a location for a home office.

- Explain how to arrange work zones in a home office.

- Identify and describe useful accessories in a home office.

- Identify ergonomic features of office furniture.

- Demonstrate ways to maximize efficient storage.

Vocabulary

- telecommuters
- ergonomics
- open storage
- closed storage

Imagine that you have the opportunity to work from your home. How will you create a comfortable and productive work environment? You have also been wanting to make better use of storage space to help reduce clutter in your home. This chapter will help you make efficient use of the space, fit in your new home office, and make your home more livable.

Home Offices

The dream of working at home has turned into reality for many people. There are millions of home office workers, and the numbers continue to grow. Many home workers are telecommuters, also called teleworkers. **Telecommuters** are people authorized by their employers to work from home using computers, modems, fax machines, and teleconferencing equipment to handle their work responsibilities. Telecommuters are accustomed to accessing all the information they need from their company via computer connections. Other home office workers are entrepreneurs who run their own businesses from their homes.

There are many advantages to working at home. Eliminating the need for long commutes saves hours every day. At-home workers often manage their own schedules, and many get to spend more time with their families. A home office can be a more comfortable place to work. Some people who work at home find it difficult to get away from work, however. Others must focus to avoid distractions that take them away from work.

Home office workers are in charge of creating their own work environment. They need to make careful plans to ensure they create the best surroundings for their work.

Uses for a Home Office

How do you get started creating a home office? First, consider all its uses. Not every home office is used by an entrepreneur or telecommuter. Millions of workers have created a space that serves as an after-hours extension of their business office. Some families use the home office as the place to store family records and manage finances and bills. Many people use a work station to access the Internet and e-mail family and friends around the world. Take the time to consider all the potential uses for the space to prepare the best plan.

Fig. 23-1. For families who need a home office in order to manage finances or do homework, an efficiently organized space in a corner of a room will be adequate. How has the use of laptop computers changed the look of home offices?

Location

Where should a home office be located? That depends on the type of work to be done there and the available space. Home offices range from a corner of the family room to an entire room. **See Fig. 23-1.** If the space is to be used only occasionally, a 2-ft. x 5-ft. (0.6-m x 1.5-m) space provides enough room for a work area and filing space. For example, a section of a bedroom could be used with freestanding panels to separate the work area from the rest of the room. Sometimes an extra wide hallway, storage space under a stairwell, or a closet can be converted to a functional, small office space.

For someone who works full-time at home, though, a larger, professional work space is needed. The perfect space is a separate room that encourages creativity and productivity. With a separate space, the home worker can keep business materials and equipment all in one place to promote maximum efficiency. Setting aside a room strictly for business also helps separate home activities from work activities.

One essential first step for someone planning to work full-time at home is to check the zoning laws that affect the location. Zoning laws may restrict the types of businesses that can be run from a home, particularly if clients will be visiting the home.

Today, more new homes are being designed to include space for a home office. Often, the office space has a separate outdoor entrance.

When an existing home is used, adding a separate office usually means using existing space for a new purpose. If a quiet area is needed, choose a room with a door that's away from the main activity of the home. An extra bedroom is often the first choice. A bedroom usually has closet space for storage and windows to let in natural light. Other options include converting a seldom-used dining room, finished basement, loft, attic, or part of a garage.

Perks at Work

People who must go to work don't necessarily have to miss out on some of the comforts of working from home. Some employers provide employees access to wellness, family care, and personal services within their place of business. These "perks" make most employees feel valued, increase their productivity, and reduce absenteeism.

- **Personal Services.** Some workers can accomplish everything on their "do-to" list without leaving the workplace. They can have their dry cleaning collected and delivered, their hair cut, and access to an ATM station inside the office building. The cafeteria kitchen may even provide the option of take-home meals for the family dinner.

- **Health Facilities.** Exercise rooms are becoming standard in many office buildings. Access to walking and bike paths, fitness centers, basketball courts, and swimming pools are sometimes available. Some offices provide access to massage services.

- **Family Care.** Many employers provide on-site child care facilities, where workers could drop off their children in the morning, visit them at lunch, and pick them up at the end of the day. Some companies offer elder care services as well. A few facilities have desktop video monitors so workers can literally look in on loved ones during the day. Some even provide kennels to relieve the worries of pet-owning employees.

Apply It!

Suppose a business wanted to offer employees one of the "perks" described above. What would be the most cost-effective way to add the needed facilities? How could they be incorporated into the existing design? Make a list of questions about the business facility that would help you design the added perks.

Designing a Home Office

Once the space for the home office is chosen, the next step is developing a design plan. The daily activities required to do the work, as well as the worker's habits, needs, and personality, need to be considered. Some workers like to keep things out of sight and have a clean workspace. Others prefer to have items displayed and spread out. **See Fig. 23-2.**

Jamar Adkins, an interior designer, is starting his own company and will work out of his home. He begins the design process, as he would with a client, by listing all the activities he does in an average day. He uses his computer for developing design plans and doing paperwork. While designing, he spreads out brochures and samples of items he wants to incorporate in his design. In addition, Jamar has a library of reference books and files of samples and product brochures plus business records. He also keeps backup computer disks of all of his work. Jamar meets with clients in their homes and businesses, so he doesn't need a conference table in his office.

As Jamar analyzes his list, he divides it into zones of activity, much like a kitchen is divided into work centers. Activities that are done most often will be assigned the primary work space. In Jamar's office, this includes the computer zone and the work station zone where he spreads out samples and designs. The library zone consists of the brochures, samples, and photos that Jamar uses frequently. These need to be placed in an active storage area that is easily accessible. His reference books are used less often, so they are placed in a bookcase just outside the primary work area. A file cabinet holds business-related papers. Materials that he uses less often and his backup computer disks are placed on shelves in the closet.

Fig. 23-2. When developing a design plan for a home office, consider the individual's personality as well as work habits.

Plan the Space

One benefit of a home office is the opportunity to create a space that both feels comfortable and works well for the person using it. Most people want their office to be both efficient and have a personal touch.

Before filling the room with furniture and accessories, you need to decide how to arrange the space. Measure the area carefully and make a graph paper or computer floor plan. Think about the furniture and accessories you will need to carry out your tasks. If you will work on a computer, you'll need a workstation and a chair. You'll also need space for storing software and disks. You'll probably want a file cabinet for business papers, though some workstations come with drawers that hold hanging file folders.

You'll already have some of the furniture and accessories that you need. Measure these pieces to see how much space they'll take up. You can research additional pieces by visiting an office store or looking online or in an office furniture catalog. Check out the sizes and prices of different pieces. Then try out different arrangements on your floor plan before making any final decisions or purchases.

Here are some guidelines for designing home offices:

- Keep the activity zones in mind and plan how to arrange furniture and equipment into different centers of operation.

- Arrange the main work area in an L-shape or U-shape. Start with the desk or work surface and determine placement of the computer work station, shelving, and file storage. A compact L-shape work zone takes about 5 ft. (1.5 m) on one wall and 6 ft. (1.8 m) along another. Place a swivel chair in the middle so that by turning or rolling slightly, everything is within reach. If the room is carpeted, put a plastic pad under the chair.

- When seated, the computer, telephone, and file storage should be within easy reach.

- Plan for plenty of work surface. A desk should be at least 24 in. (61 cm) deep and 36 in. (91 cm) wide.

- Strive to create an ergonomic work space. **Ergonomics** is an applied science concerned with designing and arranging things so that they are safe, comfortable, and efficient for people to use. An ergonomic work environment is an adjustable one that facilitates frequent changes of body position and avoids eye-straining glare from light sources. **See Fig. 23-3.**

- Use vertical space. For example, tall, narrow bookcases can hold many things without taking up much floor space. Consider a rolling filing cabinet that can be stored under the desk. A corner bookcase can optimize wasted space.

- Be sure to plan for enough storage space. Figure out how to put in as many cabinets, cubbyholes, and storage units as possible without overcrowding the space. No matter how organized workers are, they always need more storage space than they think. Don't forget about storage space for paper, pens, office supplies, research materials, and other work tools.

- Use storage wisely. Store similar items together. Put most frequently used items in a handy place, such as on the middle bookshelves. Put less frequently used items in less convenient places or in another room.

Fig. 23-3 This home office has an ergonomic design. Work surfaces are at the appropriate height.

Fig. 23-4 For people who plan on moving or adding to their home office, modular furniture is the answer. They can easily add on as their needs grow, or reconfigure the pieces to better fit the space.

Select Office Furniture

Few people have an unlimited budget for a new home office. As with other rooms, it's helpful to make a master plan, then decide what basics are needed now and which items can be added later. A basic office setup usually includes a desk or writing surface, a computer area, a chair, a filing cabinet, and shelving for books and references.

There are choices for every budget and for every type of space. An unused table might function as a work surface. A desk can be made by placing a flat door on top of two filing cabinets. Many companies lease furniture, as well as computer equipment. Leasing can be a viable solution for outfitting a business without putting out a lot of money all at once.

Office furniture comes in a variety of styles from ultramodern steel to classic oak. No matter what style is preferred, there are a few points to keep in mind. A computer station needs to be ergonomically designed with adjustable sections for a keyboard, mouse, and monitor. Correct placement of the components helps prevent fatigue and other problems. Adjust the top of the monitor so it is slightly lower than eye level. Place the keyboard directly in front of the user and at a height that keeps the wrists relaxed but not bent. Some desks feature legs that allow the user to adjust the height. Choose a desk with enough space to work effectively. Some come with built-in drawers; others are open. Keep overall storage needs in mind when deciding which option is best.

Modular furniture makes it easy to rearrange the office. See Fig. 23-4. Many furniture manufacturers offer office systems that create a "mix and match" plan. A person starts out with the basic plan and adds new pieces as the budget allows. Modular furniture is available in both modern and traditional styles.

Another space-saving technique is to select pieces that serve more than one function. For example, a low filing cabinet could also serve as a computer printer stand. Some desks come with an optional shelving unit at the back. What other multiuse options can you think of?

The most important part of a home office is a good chair. It is worth paying a little more to get an ergonomic design. An ergonomically designed chair has a contoured backrest, adjustable arms, and adjustable chair height and seat height. An office chair needs wheels for ease of movement.

Choose Office Technology

One reason there is such growth in home offices today is the widespread use of computers. See Fig. 23-5. The type of computer needed, and the amount of additional equipment, depends on the reason for and use of the office. One business owner might need a computer, a printer, a telephone with an answering machine, and a fax machine. Another might need more extensive equipment to compete with larger companies. For example, freelance designers use the same illustration and CAD software as a large firm. Telecommuters might need a web-cam so they can take part in conferences or meetings at other sites.

One option to save space and money is to choose one multitask machine instead of several separate ones. For example, there are printers that also serve as a fax machine, a scanner, and a photocopier.

One very important aspect of a home business is safety and security of data. Surge protectors will protect electronic equipment against loss from electric current fluctuations. Home workers need to back up all their computer data on a regular basis. A fireproof box can be used to protect electronic files, important paperwork, and legal documents.

The Power Supply

For computers and other electronic equipment, home offices often need a lot of electrical power. Additional outlets may be needed in the office space, or electrical service into the house may have to be increased. Have an electrician check out the space before moving in all the equipment. The worst time to add outlets is after the room is filled with furniture and equipment.

The office of a full-time at-home worker needs a dedicated business telephone line. Many offices also have another line used by a fax and a computer modem. Some people prefer using a cable modem for their computer, which eliminates the need for a phone line for a modem and provides faster Internet access.

Fig. 23-5 Technology enables workers to compete in a global marketplace without leaving home.

Going Wireless

Someday soon the wired home may become the unwired home. Wireless technology—a method of sending signals over the airwaves rather than through wires or cables—is nothing new. The remote control devices used with TVs and DVD players use infrared light rays. For these devices to work, the control must be in line of sight of the machine.

Wi-Fi. Wireless technology is rapidly improving. Newer technology, called Wi-Fi, uses a narrow range of low-energy, low-frequency radio waves. Like radio stations, devices on a wireless network transmit information to each other using one particular frequency. Wired devices can connect to wireless machines through an adapter. With Wi-Fi systems, a line of sight is not needed. This means you can control any "wireless-enabled" appliance or system from inside or outside the home. Through a laptop computer, for example, you could turn down the stereo and turn on the air conditioning while visiting at a friend's home. The principle is similar to that used in cell phones, which do not have to be in sight of the transmitter tower to function.

Cell Phones. Cells phones also illustrate some of the problems with Wi-Fi. Signals can be disrupted by humidity, by the presence of metal and other materials commonly found in homes, or by stronger signals. Also, radio waves are easily intercepted, putting personal information at risk. Engineers are continually refining the technology to overcome these drawbacks, however Wi-Fi promises to be a wave of the future.

Tech Trends

Research and give a short description of one of the following topics in wireless systems, explaining the technology involved: hotspots, encryption, or Bluetooth®.

Select Lighting

One important final consideration for a home office is lighting. Both glare and low light levels lead to eyestrain. A well-planned home office has indirect lighting and task lighting. **See Fig. 23-6.** Overhead lights to illuminate the entire room can provide indirect lighting. Task lighting on desks and work areas can be adjusted in angle and level of intensity to light up the papers and other materials on the desk. Natural lighting from windows can make a home office cheery and comfortable, but care needs to be taken to be certain it doesn't produce glare. Positioning the computer monitor away from the window or the screen at a 90-degree angle to the window can solve this problem. Window coverings such as blinds can further reduce unwanted light.

Fig. 23-6 The recessed downlighting in the soffit provides general lighting for this office area. **What function does the desk lamp perform?**

The Storage Challenge

Many people find they need to increase the amount of space they have to store things. There are several reasons for the growing need for storage:

- Some modern homes have less storage space than homes built in earlier times.

- Decades of strong economic growth has provided people with more money, and many have used that money to buy new things.

- Advertising, changes in technology, and fashion trends encourage people to buy new goods.

- Longer lifespans give many people more time to accumulate possessions.

Whatever the cause, people are looking for ways to tuck away things that create clutter. By devising and using a convenient system to store your belongings, you will be able to find what you need easily and it will stay in good condition.

The challenge is somewhat different in every situation. The number and type of items to be stored varies. The amount of available space and each person's natural "neatness quotient" does, too. However, it's possible for everyone to develop a workable system. It just takes time and effort to plan and maintain a good storage system.

Planning Storage

Fig. 23-7 Finding storage "opportunities" means using your creativity as well as analytical skills. **What creative storage ideas do you see in this space?**

Simply having a place to put things isn't enough. An effective storage plan draws on your analytical and decision-making skills plus your creativity. You need to identify what needs to be stored (and what doesn't). Often you must find solutions to the need for additional storage space. Then, you need to choose the best equipment and methods to make the plan work. **See Fig. 23-7.**

Assess Storage Needs

Whether you are reorganizing storage for one room or a whole house, the first step is to identify what needs to be stored. Go through the area and simply make a list of all the items.

As you make your list, identify things you no longer use. Having less to store immediately frees up space. If you find yourself saying, "This might come in handy someday," you probably don't need it. Unless something has special meaning for you, if you haven't used it in two years, you can probably give it away or sell it and not miss it.

Next look at your list of remaining items and group those that are similar. As a general rule, similar things should be stored together. Is there a specific area or room in which it would be best to store certain groups of items?

If what you have to store will fit conveniently in the storage space you have available, you can skip the next step. However, most people find they need additional storage space to organize their possessions effectively.

Find Additional Storage Options

Suppose every drawer and cabinet is already full or overflowing. Where will you find more space?

First, realize that storage can be open or closed. In **open storage**, stored items are visible. In **closed storage**, doors or drawers conceal items. Both types are important.

Next, look both for unused space that might be used for storage and for ways to maximize the space you already have. Each room's unique features need to be considered.

Possibilities in a bathroom might range from adding a shelf around the entire room to fitting in a small chest or vertical shelving over the toilet. Colorful baskets could hold often-used toiletries.

In the kitchen, you can attach a small shelf or bin to the underside of an upper cabinet. This can be used to store spices, cookbooks, or other small items. Look for small appliances that can be mounted under cabinets as well. Benches with under-seat storage might replace chairs at the table.

What about extra storage space in the family room, living room, and bedrooms? Cabinets, chests, and desks are designed specifically for storage. Look, too, for pieces that do double duty. A large stool might open to reveal storage space. An old trunk could serve as a coffee table and store games, pillows, or rarely used items. Bear in mind that it makes sense to put items that are used together in the same place. See Fig. 23-8.

In the bedroom, you might substitute a small chest of drawers for a bedside table. Some beds have drawers built into the base, but you can devise your own. Purchase storage boxes designed to fit under the bed or put wheels on old dresser drawers and roll them underneath.

Be creative! Virtually every nook and cranny can be cleverly used. Empty suitcases can store out-of-season clothes. High shelves can be added to closets for more space.

Fig. 23-8 Group similar items together and then devise a way to store them. With a convenient place for keeping items, they are more likely to be kept neatly than just piled up in the back of a closet.

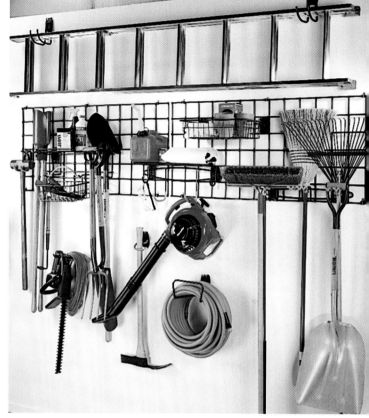

Fig. 23-9 Organized storage puts everything within reach and allows the users to get to the task at hand.

Choose Storage Organizers

Although storage may seem tight, the options for storing and organizing have never been so plentiful. Whole stores are dedicated to storage equipment. You can spend thousands of dollars on custom storage for a home or do wonders with a very limited budget.

Go back to your list of items to be stored. First, identify those that are used most often. Then identify the type of storage preferable or possible for each item. Shelves can easily hold everything from towels to canned goods. Drawers are ideal for folded clothing, kitchen utensils, and other small items. A few hooks can hold a bathrobe, belts, or coffee mugs.

Next analyze your existing storage spaces. Are there ways they can be used more efficiently? Can the items in them be stored more conveniently?

You don't have to buy an expensive, sophisticated storage system. For example, roll-out shelves might be most convenient. You could, instead, use inexpensive plastic containers for various items and pull them out to access what's in them. Maybe you don't have space for small cubbyholes, but you can add a long shoe bag to the inside of a door to hold small items.

Choose what you do buy with an eye to flexibility. For instance, adjustable shelves allow you to adapt space to the height of the objects being stored. Modular storage pieces can be assembled in different configurations as needs change. With basic carpentry skills, you can also make your own storage pieces.

Arrange Items

When your storage systems have been selected and installed, you can begin to implement your plan. The final step in organizing storage is to arrange stored items in a systematic way. See Fig. 23-9. When doing this, keep these principles in mind.

- Arrange items according to frequency of use. Items used every day or quite often should be stored within easy reach—on low shelves, near the front of shelves, in top drawers, at the front of the closet. Items used less frequently can be kept on top shelves, in bottom drawers, or at the back of a closet. Rarely used or seasonal items can be stored on high shelves or in an attic, basement, or garage.

- Arrange commonly used items in places and at levels that are accessible to everyone. For instance, in the kitchen, put the plates and bowls on cabinet shelves that are within the reach of the shortest person. Put toys and children's movies where children can reach them.

- Remember safety issues. Store medications, cleaning products, or other dangerous substances in locked cabinets.

- Devise ways to remember where things are. Items that are visible are easiest to find. Labels are a great help. When storing things in out-of-the-way places, mark the containers and keep a list of what's where.

- Arrange items for safe storage and easy access. Heavy objects are best stored at waist height because they are difficult to move. Avoid stacking items of different shapes and sizes; they could easily topple.

Consumer Considerations

Mobile Storage Solutions

If you're not ready to invest in permanent storage options, you might want to consider mobile storage. The advantage of mobile storage is, obviously, that it's mobile. Shoe racks can fit in any closet. A rolling utility cart offers great flexibility as a baking center, with supplies and cookware that slide under the work surface until needed.

Versatility. Tiered hanging baskets can hold fresh produce in the kitchen or soaps and shampoos in the bathroom. A tabletop caddy with drawers, shelves, slots, and wells might be used in the home office or the sewing room. Add-on drawers can be attached in open spaces under counters and inside cabinets.

Flexibility. You can change a design or floor plan without investing in large pieces of furniture. Storage boxes cost less than a chest of drawers with the same capacity. A rollaway computer desk with folding shelves is just as useful as a more expensive wood desk. A rolling corner floor cabinet can look as attractive in a kitchen as a built-in.

Organizing Closets

Whether you're storing clothing or hobby supplies, closets are excellent storage spaces. Some techniques can help you take advantage of this space.

Divide Space. Adapt the space to the items being stored by using rods, shelves, drawers, hooks, containers, and racks. See Fig. 23-10. You can purchase ready-made components or kits, or build your own. In a clothes closet, hanging space can be doubled by adding a second, lower rod partway across a clothes closet. Place the upper rod about 80 in. (203 cm) above the floor and the lower rod about 40 in. (102 cm) above the floor.

Use Shelves and Drawers. Use overhead shelves to store items needed less frequently. Place a small chest of drawers in a large closet to hold small items, or create your own drawer unit with stackable containers.

Use Doors and Walls. Use closet hooks and racks to make use of these vertical storage areas. A shoe rack keeps shoes in order. Hooks on the inside of a door or on a closet wall can be used for hanging brooms and mops in a cleaning closet.

Fig. 23-10 This closet divides the space vertically and horizontally, maximizing the storage area.

Profile of a Professional Organizer

Professional organizers assist people in many different areas, such as space planning, time management, business organizing, financial record keeping, or room organizing. They often specialize in one or two of these areas. These workers also train people so they can stay organized.

Education & Training

- A high school diploma is recommended.
- Noncredit courses are available over the Internet.
- Work experience is invaluable.

Skills & Aptitudes

- Strong organizational skills are essential.
- Math skills are necessary, and computer skills are helpful.
- Good communication skills are important.

Professional Organizer
Lisa Harmoning

I make my living from the clutter that other people collect in their homes and offices—and not by selling it at garage sales! I'm a professional organizer. My job is to help people sort, organize, and store their belongings to make their lives easier and their surroundings neat and attractive.

I started my business by accident. When I was home with my newborn son, I forced myself to work on my overstuffed bedroom closet. I was so happy with the results that I decided to overhaul the other six closets we had. When the results caught a friend's eye, she offered to pay me to do two of hers. That job led to two more, and word of mouth took over from there.

I have a knack for creating an environment that makes it much easier to keep things in order. While I've taken on all kinds of organization jobs, my specialty is closets. To reorganize a clothes closet, I start by removing all the contents and asking the owner to set aside all items that are used regularly—at least once every two weeks. Then I ask people to identify items they no longer need. This pile is never as big as it could be. I have to use tact and persuasion to help clients pare down their belongings.

Then I discuss possible ways of organizing and renovating the closet. Many people store things besides clothes in their closets. I always see if some can go elsewhere to make space.

The next step in the process is to decide how to organize the items to be kept. That requires analyzing the types of items and determining the best use of the space. I often make a rough sketch of the reorganized closet, using shelves, hooks, bins, and rods. For more complex jobs, I use a CAD design program to show what the finished project will look like and to determine materials and costs.

Once the client approves the design, I get the materials I need and begin installing the equipment and putting everything back in the closet. People are delighted with the results. Not only is the space more efficiently arranged with everything easy to find, but there is often room to spare to make room for new items.

Design Portfolio

1. Make a drawing of your own closet or the closet of someone you know. Then make a drawing of how you could reorganize the closet to use space more efficiently and to make regularly used items more accessible.

2. Imagine that you have been hired to design storage for a home office. Draw a design for the storage of file folders, office supplies, and reference books.

Review & Activities

Chapter Summary

- Home offices are used by entrepreneurs, **telecommuters**, and family members for many different uses.
- Home offices can be tucked in small spaces or occupy an entire room, depending on the worker's need for space.
- Daily work activities can be used to create work zones to plan a home office space.
- Office furniture and accessories should be chosen with needs, functions, and **ergonomics** in mind.
- Planning storage begins with assessing storage needs and determining storage options.
- You can maximize storage space in many ways.

Checking Your Understanding

1. What are three reasons people set up a home office?
2. What are two advantages to a full-time at-home worker of having a separate room as an office?
3. What are two examples of work zones in a home office?
4. Write two guidelines for arranging work zones in a home office.
5. What are three useful home-office electronic accessories?
6. What is **ergonomics**?
7. What are some features of an ergonomic chair?
8. How do indirect lighting and task lighting differ?
9. When planning storage, why begin by identifying items you no longer use? What should you do with those things?
10. Give an example of **open storage** and of **closed storage**.
11. What are four guidelines for arranging things in storage?
12. What are two ways to maximize the use of closets?

Thinking Critically

1. **Analyzing Information.** A parent with two young children works at home. What would be the advantages of using part of the family room as a home office? What would be the disadvantages?

2. **Suggesting a Solution.** Suppose someone has the option of setting up a home office in a rarely used dining room, an extra bedroom, or a portion of the living room. Which space would you recommend? Why?

3. **Making Inferences.** Which family is likely to have a greater need to maximize efficiency in storage, one living in a two-bedroom apartment or one living in a two-bedroom house? Explain your answer.

Applying Your Knowledge

1. **Researching Working at Home.** Use print resources or the Internet to learn more about working at home. Find out what kinds of issues home workers often confront. Develop a list of frequently cited problems with working at home. Try to identify design solutions that could be used to prevent or minimize each problem. Compile your findings into a report.

2. **Making a Presentation.** Take the role of a salesperson in an office store. Suppose a customer comes to you asking for advice on what accessories and furniture to buy to equip a home office. Write and deliver an oral presentation outlining the issues the customer should consider.

3. **Planning Home Offices.** Find the floor plan for a two- or three-bedroom home. Identify at least two different areas that could be used for a home office. Prepare rough plans for organizing the spaces you chose. What are the advantages and disadvantages of each space? Present your recommendations.

4. **Analyzing Storage Options.** Using the same floor plans as for the previous activity, take a marker and highlight all the closets and other storage areas. Then identify other areas that could be used for storage. Indicate what kind of objects could be stored in each area and what kind of storage systems would be best for those objects.

Design Challenge

A client who works at home has asked you to design her home office. As a commercial photographer, her studio space is 18 ft. x 24 ft. and houses her equipment against one wall. Props are stored in moveable bins. She has several pieces of computer equipment that are used to process and store images.

1. Research commercial photography to determine the kinds of furniture the photographer needs.

2. Draw a floor plan of the studio space that shows placement of equipment, storage, and furniture.

3. Create an elevation of the floor plan to show how the space will be used.

4. Present your plans and explain why you designed it as shown.

5. Place the completed plan in your design portfolio.

Chapter 24

Choosing Backgrounds

Objectives

- Explain what backgrounds are and why they are important.

- Assess the characteristics of various home textiles.

- Evaluate the characteristics and uses of various floor coverings.

- Compare the characteristics and uses of various wall coverings.

- Describe the characteristics and uses of various window treatments.

- Select floor coverings, wall coverings, and window treatments.

Vocabulary

- backgrounds
- natural fibers
- synthetic fibers
- plain weave
- satin weave
- twill weave
- resilient flooring
- pile
- primers
- alkyd
- latex
- stenciling
- moldings
- chair rail
- valance
- swag
- blinds

Why do many people consult interior designers? Often, they need help choosing coverings for their floors, walls, and windows. Along with the ceiling, these are the backgrounds of a room. Together, these surfaces affect more than the room's appearance. They also contribute to the feel, sound, and energy efficiency of the room.

The Role Backgrounds Play

Backgrounds—floors, walls, ceilings, and windows—fill several roles. For this reason, it is best to make some decisions about backgrounds before thinking about other parts of your design.

Backgrounds help set the mood of a room. The materials, patterns, colors, and textures you choose for the background elements make the room formal or informal, calm or exciting.

Sound is also affected by backgrounds. Soft, textured materials tend to absorb sound, while smooth, hard surfaces don't. What would the noise levels be like in a room with thick carpeting, compared to one with a wood floor?

In some rooms the background may actually be the focal point of the room. This is true when there is some special quality, such as a dramatic beamed ceiling or a floor-to-ceiling window. In other rooms the background goes almost unnoticed, serving only to provide a setting for the furnishings. **See Fig. 24-1.**

Fig. 24-1 Architectural features may be an asset or they may present special challenges when designing the background of a room.

Consumer Considerations

Choosing the Right Paint Color

Choosing paint colors can be difficult. Paint chips may offer dozens of variations of one hue. Two different shades may look identical—until you put one on your walls and realize it isn't what you wanted. How can you avoid such frustration?

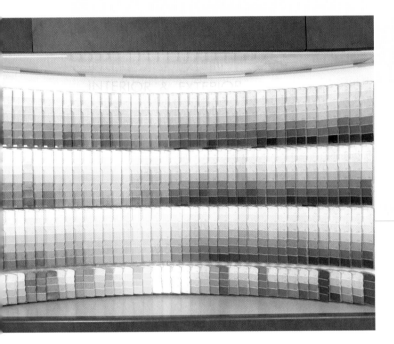

Check Websites. Paint manufacturers' websites are very helpful. Some have interactive, step-by-step instructions for finding or matching specific colors. You can also view a room in different color schemes.

Compare Colors. Comparing colors that are similar can put them all in perspective. By holding a red next to a rosy peach, you'll see if that second color is closer to rose than to peach.

Try it Out. When you find a promising color, buy the smallest container available and paint a small area where it will be used. How does the color appear at different times of the day under different lighting? How does it react with parts of the design that you don't plan to change, like wallpaper or lighting in an adjacent hallway? How do you feel about the color after a few days? Only when you're sure that the color works should you buy enough paint for the whole room.

Color Considerations

You have already studied characteristics of particular colors in Chapter 18, but there are some special factors relating to background color.

- Because the light in a room is uneven, color seldom looks the same in every spot.

- The way light strikes the wall can affect how dark or light a color appears. Colors may even appear different from one season to the next.

- Doorways, windows, and fireplaces all affect the color in a room. How does color change when it reflects through a doorway? Won't an uncovered window be black at night?

- Furniture reduces the amount of background color that can be seen. An entertainment center, for instance, covers much of a wall. A sofa obscures part of the floor.

- Remember that reds, oranges, and yellows make a room seem warmer. Greens, blues, and violets generally create a cooler feeling.

- For passive solar heat, the color of the mass that stores the heat (tile, brick, or concrete) should be dark. The surfaces that reflect the heat (walls, ceilings, and furnishings) onto the thermal mass should be light.

Textiles in the Home

Fig. 24-2 A variety of textiles are used in this room. How do they contribute to the overall design?

Imagine a home with smooth ceramic tile floors, polished wood chairs, gleaming glass tables, and shutters at every window. It sounds interesting, but isn't something missing? Without textiles most people wouldn't consider a house a home. To select backgrounds and home furnishings effectively, it's important to understand textiles and the fibers that are used to make them. See Fig. 24-2.

Types of Textiles

Consider the abundance of textiles in your home. You probably have carpeting or a rug, upholstered furniture, pillows, and curtains—and that may be just in the living room. There are many more items, of course, in the kitchen, bathroom, and bedroom. Chair cushions, placemats, towels, linens, and bedspreads are all home textiles.

Fibers

Fabrics start out as tiny fibers. The fibers are twisted together into yarns, then the yarns are woven into fabric. Fibers are classified as either natural or synthetic. **Natural fibers**, such as cotton, wool, linen, and silk, come from plants or animals. **Synthetic fibers** are made with chemicals and other materials. Examples are nylon, polyester, and rayon. Natural and synthetic fibers are often combined to blend the best qualities of both. See Fig. 24-3.

Fig. 24-3

Natural Fibers		
Material and Common Uses	**Advantages**	**Disadvantages**
Cotton Chintz and other upholstery fabric; curtains and draperies; throw rugs; towels; bedding	Strong and durable; absorbent; washable; easily dyed	Wrinkles; shrinks unless treated; soils easily; very flammable if untreated; not mildew-resistant
Linen Draperies; upholstery; tablecloths; kitchen towels	Strongest natural fiber; withstands frequent laundering; lint-free and absorbent; ages well	Wrinkles easily; highly flammable; relatively expensive; not mildew-resistant
Silk Draperies; upholstery; lampshades; wall coverings	Strong and smooth; very absorbent; dyes well; drapes and retains shape well; stain- and wrinkle-resistant; washable or dry cleanable	Weakened by bleach and light; spotted by water unless treated; not insect-resistant; yellows
Wool Plush and Berber carpeting; fine rugs; blankets; upholstery; draperies	Soft and durable; resilient; long lasting; soil- and fire-resistant; easily dyed; resists fading and abrasion	Not resistant to moths; can shrink; may cause an allergic reaction; hard to clean once deeply soiled
Synthetic Fibers		
Material and Common Uses	**Advantages**	**Disadvantages**
Acrylic Blankets; rugs; some carpets	Appearance and feel of wool; low static level; resists mildew and moisture	Subject to pilling
Nylon Very popular for carpeting; rugs	Very durable; easily maintained; resists matting; mold-, mildew-, and moth-proof	Generates static unless treated; subject to pilling and fading; attracts dirt
Olefin, Polypropylene Carpeting; decorative rugs; may be combined with acrylic or nylon	Strong, easily maintained; nonabsorbent; resists stains and static; extremely colorfast; inexpensive	Crushes easily; limited colors and designs unless combined with other fibers; sensitive to heat
Polyester Curtains; window scarves; pleated shades; draperies; fiberfill; bedding; upholstery; carpeting	Soft, durable; resists soil; resists stains; easily dyed; often blended	Generates static electricity; subject to stains and pilling; not absorbent
Rayon Draperies; bedding; slipcovers; upholstery; tablecloths	Absorbent; easily dyed; drapes well; resists insects; sometimes combined with acetate	Wrinkles easily if untreated; shrinks in hot water; highly flammable; susceptible to fading
Nylon/Polyester Blend Carpeting	Durable; easy to maintain; combines advantages of both fibers	Limited colors

Weaves and Finishes

Most home decorating fabrics are woven, although leather is an example of a nonwoven material. In weaving, two or more sets of threads are interlaced at right angles. The *warp* is the set of threads that run lengthwise. The *weft* is the set of threads that runs crosswise.

Figure 24-4 illustrates three basic weaves: plain, satin, and twill. The *Jacquard weave* is used to produce brocades and damasks, rich-looking fabrics used for draperies and upholstery. These fabrics are woven on special looms and usually feature large, elaborate designs.

Carpeting, upholstery fabrics, and table linens are treated to resist stains. Some fabrics have had a finish applied to make them flame resistant. Other fabric treatments help reduce wrinkling, shrinkage, and fading.

Textile Laws

The federal government protects consumers with regulations for textiles. The Flammable Fabrics Act established standards for home items such as rugs, carpeting, and mattresses. The act blocks manufacturers from making these products out of material that is so flammable that it is dangerous. The Textile Fiber Products Identification Act specifies what must appear on labels: fiber content and percentage, the product's manufacturer, country of origin, and care information.

Fig. 24-4

Basic Fabric Weaves

A Visual Guide

If you examine a piece of fabric under a magnifying glass you will likely discover one of these basic weaves:

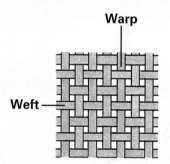

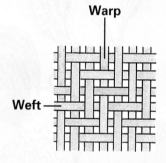

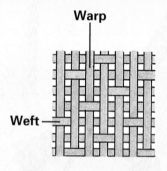

Plain Weave is a simple pattern that is as strong in one direction as it is in the other. This pattern should wear evenly. The plain weave is used for percale and muslin sheets and pillow cases. Many curtains also have a plain weave. How would you describe the way the warp interacts with the weft to create a plain weave?

Satin Weave is a pattern distinguished by long "floats," which are formed when each warp thread passes over a certain number of weft threads before passing under one. The floats give satin fabric its characteristic sheen. Satin fabric, silk, and rayon are woven in a satin weave.

Twill Weave is a pattern with diagonal lines or wales. A wale is formed when a weft thread passes over two or more warp threads before passing under a warp thread again. The twill weave produces a firm, strong fabric. Denim and gabardine are fabrics that use this weave.

Floor Coverings

Floor coverings are usually one of the most expensive components of a design project. One way to justify the cost is to regard them as the foundation of the room. Another is to realize that quality floor coverings pay off in years of good service. Durability is important because most floors are subjected to dirt and spills, the weight of furniture, and heavy traffic.

As you read in Chapter 11, finish floor materials, such as wood, brick, and ceramic tile, are laid over the structural flooring. They are often installed when the home is built and provide a durable, long-lasting surface. Finish floorings are not always desired, however. Floor coverings are popular choices.

The type of floor covering chosen depends largely on the purpose of the room, the amount of traffic flowing through it, how much maintenance the floor covering requires, and whether it coordinates with the decorating scheme of the room. See Fig. 24-5. The lifestyles of the occupants must also be taken into account. Resilient flooring, carpeting, and rugs are all possible choices.

Fig. 24-5 Wood floors require different cleaning procedures than carpeting. **Does this wood flooring seem appropriate for a child's room? Why or why not?**

Resilient Floor Coverings

Resilient flooring is flooring with a semi-hard surface that returns to its original shape after stress. For instance, if a frying pan were dropped on a resilient floor, the floor would resist denting. Resilient floor coverings are warmer and quieter to walk on than hard floor materials such as wood and ceramic tile, but they aren't quite as durable. The resilient floor coverings that are used most often are vinyl and plastic laminate flooring.

- Vinyl resists many stains, including grease and bleach. It is durable and easy to clean and comes in a vast assortment of patterns and colors. Most varieties have a no-wax finish with built-in luster. Vinyl flooring is sold in tile and sheet form. The tiles are 12 in. x 12 in. (30 cm x 30 cm). The sheets, or rolls, are sold in 6-ft. and 12-ft. widths (1.8-m and 3.7-m).

- Plastic laminate flooring is made of fiberboard that is covered with a photo reproduction of wood grain or other material. A top layer of plastic provides protection. Laminate floors are installed as floating floors over a foam pad. They are durable and comfortable to stand on. They also resist dents and scratches.

Carpeting

Carpeting is a preference of many people, in at least part of their home. Besides insulating the floor, carpeting cuts down on noise and provides a feeling of comfort. Slips and falls are less likely to occur on well-anchored carpeting than on bare floors.

New manufacturing techniques and advancements in fiber chemistry have resulted in carpeting that is more durable, attractive, and easier to maintain than ever before. People no longer have to avoid light-colored carpeting for fear of soiling. Some carpet fibers feature permanent protection against tough stains.

Carpet selection involves much more than choosing a color. You also have options in pattern, texture, and durability. There's striped carpeting, floral prints, plaids, and even some that glow in the dark! With the wide array of carpeting on the market, choosing a knowledgeable carpet dealer is essential. He or she can help you examine performance ratings of various carpets, provided by many manufacturers.

Size and Installation

Wall-to-wall carpeting provides an unbroken area of color and texture and can make an area seem spacious. The same color is often used in several rooms to help unify the design. Broadloom carpet is carpeting manufactured in rolls up to 15-ft. (4.6-m) wide, but 12-ft. (3.7-m) rolls are standard. Seams are taped or sewed together, and the entire carpet is fastened to the floor with tackless strips or by gluing.

Carpet tiles come in various sizes. They are easy to install and are convenient because an individual piece of soiled or worn tile can be replaced.

Quality

The density of a carpet's **pile**, or nap, helps determine its quality. The pile is the visible surface of the carpeting. The amount of pile in carpeting is called the average pile yarn weight. It should be sufficient to prevent crushing. Contrary to popular belief, the depth of the pile doesn't necessarily make a carpet more durable, although it might make it feel more luxurious. Carpet density can be checked by bending back a piece of carpet and noticing the amount of space between the yarns and how the yarns are attached. This is called the *grin* test.

Fiber content and construction also help determine carpet quality. While some high-quality carpeting is made of wool, more than 95 percent of carpeting today is created with manufactured fibers. Nylon is by far the most popular, followed by polypropylene or olefin.

A relatively new type of polyester called PET is being used more often because of its resistance to stains and fading. Recycled plastic containers are used in the production of PET.

Texture and Construction

In years past, almost all carpeting was woven on looms. Today, about 90 percent is constructed by *tufting*. **See Fig. 24-6.** With this method, the yarn is inserted with threaded needles into a backing material. The tufts are then glued to the backing. Carpets can also be knitted into an uncut loop pile. Another construction process, needlepunch, is used to produce a lower-cost product often used as indoor-outdoor carpeting. It has a flat surface rather than a pile.

Fig. 24-6 To make tufted carpet, yarn is threaded into a backing, secured with adhesive, and then cut or left looped.

Fig. 24-7

Carpeting Textures

A Visual Guide

Cut Pile

Cut Pile. Formal looking plush, sometimes called velvet, has a smooth surface. May flatten.

Saxony

Saxony. Similar to cut pile, except yarns have been twisted more, giving a less formal appearance.

Friezé

Friezé (FREE-zay). This informal cut pile has a "curly" texture because fibers are highly twisted. Shows minimal foot and vacuum marks.

Level Loop

Level Loop. Loops are all the same height. Sometimes has flecks of a darker color. Very durable.

Multi-Level Loop

Multi-Level Loop. Has two or three loop heights. Can have a sculptured or embossed effect. Good in high-traffic areas.

Cut and Loop Pile

Cut and Loop Pile. A sculptured effect results from some loops being cut and some appearing braided. May have various surface textures. Very durable.

Carpet yarns made of a variety of fibers can be looped, twisted, or cut to create many different textures and to influence the quality of the carpet. For example, plush carpeting has upright loops cut to form an even surface, providing a luxurious effect. **Figure 24-7** shows how other carpet textures are created.

Color and Pattern

The decorating scheme of a room is often determined by the carpet color, so it is important to choose it carefully. Examine a carpet sample at various times of the day and evening in the room where it will be used. That way you can tell what it will look like in different types and levels of light.

Chapter 18 discussed how color may be used to create different effects and feelings. You can use these principles when choosing a carpet color. Remember that light colors make areas seem larger.

It's possible to choose a neutral color and still achieve great visual interest with carpeting. New machines produce textures ranging from squares to diamond shapes. Geometric or floral designs can suggest design elements to be repeated in the wall and window treatments. A rule of thumb is to use a small pattern in a small room and reserve large patterns for larger rooms. Patterned carpets are practical, since they don't show dirt easily. Tweed can also be used to disguise footprints and dirt. Practical in high-traffic areas, tweed carpets consist of multicolored yarns looped together.

Carpet Cushion

A quality under padding, or *carpet cushion*, can extend the life of a carpet dramatically. It acts as a shock absorber and adds to the comfort, quiet, and insulating qualities of carpeting. It also prevents the carpet or rug from sliding.

Carpet cushion is typically made of polyurethane foam, fiber, or rubber. A thick cushion feels luxurious, but it should always be less than ½ in. (1.3 cm) thick. For high traffic areas, a cushion that is thinner and firmer is recommended. Berber carpet requires a thin, dense cushion. Some relatively inexpensive carpeting comes with the cushion attached to its backing.

Rugs

Most rugs are a type of carpeting. The difference is that they aren't fastened to the floor. Rugs are made in one piece and have finished edges. They are usually rectangular or oval and come in many sizes. Unlike wall-to-wall carpeting, rugs can be moved from room to room or from one home to another. They can be turned to distribute wear more evenly.

Many large rugs are made of wool and have colorful designs that can be incorporated into the style of a room. Smaller accent rugs, often made of polypropylene, add personality to a room setting. Motifs range from animals and sports to seasons and natural scenes. Carpets, rugs, and mats constructed of plant fibers, such as sisal, coir, rush, and jute, have become favorites of many designers. Softer, synthetic versions of some of these fibers are an alternate way to capture the same look.

Wall Coverings

Walls are the largest background space in a room. There are a variety of factors to consider when choosing wall coverings. These include the condition of the walls, the cost involved, the function of the room, the look desired, and lifestyle. The most common wall coverings are paint, wallpaper, and paneling. **See Fig. 24-8.**

Paint is generally the least expensive wall covering. When walls have a lot of cracks, however, it can be less time-consuming to wallpaper or panel. Fabric, mirrors, cork, and even carpeting are sometimes used as wall coverings. These wall coverings bring additional textures and patterns into a room.

Neutral colors are often used on walls, regardless of the type of wall covering chosen, because they are less overpowering than more vivid colors. However, tints, shades, and intense colors can also fit in a carefully planned design.

Washable surfaces are recommended for bathrooms, kitchens, children's rooms, and hallways, because walls in those areas tend to become soiled sooner than bedrooms or living rooms.

Fig. 24-8 Wall coverings can provide a warm, light, or dramatic background to a room. **How does the texture and color of this wall covering work?**

Backgrounds That Mean Business

Wise choices in backgrounds let commercial designers convert rooms to suit any number of functions. Compare how they are used in each of these settings:

- **Museums.** The challenge in museum design is to draw attention to a display without overwhelming it. For a collection of vintage appliances, one designer replaced "busy" wallpaper with melamine, a plastic laminate often used for kitchen countertops. The setting was still appropriate and eye-catching, but not distracting. On the other hand, an exhibit honoring a well-known painter featured a dramatically paint-splashed floor and walls with chipped plaster, recreating the look and feel of his studio.

- **Hotel Guest Rooms.** After a day of travel, work, or play, hotel guests want comfort and privacy. The hotel housekeeping staff appreciate easy care. A wool, cut and loop carpet fills both needs: it feels plush, increases soundproofing, and resists soil. It can also be sculpted to hide less noticeable stains. Drawn draperies add to both the décor and privacy.

- **Hospital Patient Rooms.** Combining a homelike feel with patient health and worker efficiency is the aim of hospital room design. Textured walls seem less sterile than plain ones, for instance, but are easy to clean. In one children's hospital, the ceiling is painted sky blue with fluffy white clouds. One novel feature is a stretched fabric ceiling cover. It creates a softer, arced effect, yet can be pulled down and laundered for sanitation.

Apply It!

Analyze the backgrounds used in a local museum, hotel, or hospital. Using the factors described on this page, explain why each material or treatment was used. Would you suggest any changes? Why or why not? Present your report to the class.

Paint

Properly preparing walls to paint often takes more time than actually applying the paint. Walls should first be washed. Then tiny cracks and nail holes should be filled with spackling compound and a putty knife. Sometimes a special primer needs to be applied before repainting. Usually white in color, **primers** are sealants that make surfaces nonporous and keep out humidity. Some are formulated to cover stains.

A gallon of paint covers 350 to 400 sq. ft. (28 to 37 sq. m). Many premixed colors of paint are available. However, paint can be specially mixed to match almost any color. Consumers can buy paint that dries in 30 minutes, doesn't drip, has little or no odor, and resists rust and mildew. There are two main types of paint.

- **Solvent-based paint.** This type of paint may be oil or a synthetic resin called **alkyd** (AL-ked). Alkyd dries more quickly than pure oil paint and doesn't contain lead. It produces a durable and washable surface and is often chosen for walls and ceilings in bathrooms and kitchens, where splatters and grease are likely to build up. A solvent, such as mineral spirits, is used to clean paintbrushes.

- **Latex paint. Latex** is a water-based, quick-drying paint. It is easy to apply. However, latex does not adhere well to some surfaces, such as bare wood and surfaces previously painted with alkyd paint. In such cases, the surface should be sanded and/or a primer should be applied first. Cleanup with warm water is fairly simple. Latex paint is considered more environmentally safe than solvent-based paint.

Paints are available in various finishes: gloss, semi-gloss, satin or eggshell, flat (dull), and textured. Glossy paints are easiest to clean, but flat paints typically look more formal. Textured paint adds interest, but may be difficult to clean and to remove.

Decorative Painting

An array of special effects can be created by using a sponge or fabric to apply color over a contrasting base coat. Usually more affordable than wallpapering, the techniques can add a richness and transform a plain background. See Fig. 24-9. One technique involves spattering paint; others involve removing wet glaze from a surface by dragging or combing with a tool.

In **stenciling**, patterns are created by using a special brush to apply paint through cutout areas in a template. An up-and-down motion of the brush is used with very little paint to create shading and to prevent the paint from seeping under the stencil. Stenciled designs are often applied along the top border of a wall or around windows and doors.

Fig. 24-9 Several painting techniques and wall coverings were used in this kitchen and eating area. **How many can you find?**

Molding

Moldings are strips of shaped wood used for trim or ornamentation in a room. Their main purpose is to finish off a window, door, or wall. Providing an elegant finished look, *crown molding* is a wide trim used on walls next to the ceiling. Some moldings are more functional than decorative. For example, baseboard moldings hide the break between the wall and the floor, keep dirt from accumulating in the crack, and prevent damage to the wall at floor level.

A **chair rail** is molding that runs horizontally across the wall about 3 ft. (0.9 m) from the floor. See **Fig. 24-10**. Chair rails prevent the backs of chairs from damaging walls, but are installed mainly for their decorative appeal. Paint might be applied below the chair rail.

Wallpaper

Decorative paper has been used to cover walls since the 16th century in Europe—and since colonial times in America. Today's wallpaper is available in an almost limitless assortment of patterns and colors. Wallpaper can change the apparent dimensions of a room, making it seem smaller or larger. Wallpaper and paint can also be combined in the same room—and even on the same wall.

Types of Wallpaper

Vinyl and vinyl-coated papers are the best-selling wallpapers today. They are especially suitable for kitchens, bathrooms, and children's rooms. Most are water- and stain-resistant, making them easier to clean.

Specialty papers are also available. Foil paper can make small rooms appear larger. Heavy embossed paper, which has raised surface areas as part of the design, is used to create a formal effect. Fabrics and natural fibers backed with paper can provide interesting textures. Some papers have cotton, silk, or rayon fibers added to the surface to provide added texture. Paintable wallpaper, which can be painted once it is in place, has a raised texture and is a good choice for covering uneven walls. Specially treated papers are used in commercial settings. They must meet government standards for flammability, wear, resistance to staining, and ease of cleaning.

Fig. 24-10 A chair rail adds an elegant touch to a room.

Buying and Installing Wallpaper

Before purchasing wallpaper, bring home a sample and hold it against the wall. Sometimes it's possible to have the retailer order a large sample piece. Before hanging, check that all rolls have the same batch number. Wallpaper that is printed at one time is given a number. Even though all the rolls of a given pattern have the same design, the colors may vary slightly from batch to batch.

The wallpapering process involves several steps. Walls need to be *sized* before hanging wallpaper. Sizing involves applying a very thin coating that makes the wall tacky, allowing the paper to stick better. Prepasted wallpaper is soaked briefly in water before hanging. Other papers require that paste be spread on the back. The strips of wallpaper are then cut, hung, and trimmed.

Some wallpaper is strippable, which means that it can be removed from the wall easily. Other types, especially older papers, must be removed by steaming and scraping.

Most wallpaper has a pattern repeat that must be matched from strip to strip. This must be taken into account when calculating how much to order. Some papers are designed to create murals. In this case two or more strips have different images that must be installed in the correct order to make a completed image.

Wallpaper Borders

Wallpaper borders are popular and relatively inexpensive. They can be pasted over coordinating wallpaper or a painted surface. Typically, borders are placed at the top of a wall, at a midway point, or above a countertop. Borders are easy to install, but it's helpful to have another person hold one end of the long strip. Most borders are sold in rolls containing 15 ft. (4.6 m).

Paneling

Paneling can provide a feeling of warmth. It can also camouflage imperfect walls. Available in many price ranges, paneling requires little maintenance. Most paneling is sold in 4 ft. x 8 ft. (1.2 m x 2.4 m) sheets.

- **Solid wood paneling.** Solid wood paneling is attractive but costly. It comes in many varieties, from white pine to dark walnut.

- **Manufactured paneling.** Manufactured paneling is a more economical option. It is created by bonding a thin layer of fine wood to a less expensive wood backing. This paneling, like solid wood paneling, requires a protective finish to seal it against stains and water.

- **Laminated plastic paneling.** This paneling is constructed much like the plastic laminate that is popular for countertops. It consists of layers of paper and resins baked at high temperatures and under extreme pressure. The top layer can be printed in any color or pattern, including wood grain.

Ceilings

Fig. 24-11 Ceilings with wood beams are a feature in some homes. How could you achieve the look of solid wood beams without incurring the cost?

Ceilings built long ago were sometimes painted with murals and designs or inlaid with tiles. In homes constructed since the beginning of the 20th century, however, less attention has been paid to the decorating potential of ceilings. Beams and other special treatments are sometimes used in modern homes, but they add to the cost of construction. See Fig. 24-11.

The average height of a ceiling is 8 ft. (2.4 m), although higher ceilings are common in older homes and in some rooms of many new ones. Higher ceilings lend a feeling of dignity, and sometimes freedom, to a room. Ceilings that are lower create a warm and less formal room. If they are too low, however, a cramped feeling can result. However, lower ceilings do lower the cost of heating and cooling.

Several tricks can be used to make ceilings seem higher or lower than they really are. Ceilings seem higher when wallpaper or paint is extended a short distance onto the ceiling. Wallpapers with vertical lines also create a feeling of added height. Ceilings appear lower when a border is applied at the top of the wall and when the ceiling color is extended a short distance down the wall. Painting a dark color or covering with patterned wallpaper also lowers the apparent ceiling height.

Acoustic ceiling tile has several benefits. The tiles can serve as insulation, absorb sound, and hide stained or cracked ceilings. Larger ceiling panels, 2 ft. x 2 ft. (0.6 m x 0.6 m) and 2 ft. x 4 ft. (0.6 m x 1.2 m), are commonly suspended from metal channels that form a grid in the ceiling. This system is often used to lower a high ceiling and to hide plumbing and wiring. Twelve-inch (30 cm) square tiles are typically stapled to strips of wood that have been nailed to the ceiling. They may be glued directly to an existing ceiling if it is level.

Window Coverings

Window coverings, also called window treatments, often play a starring role in a room's design. A dramatic window treatment can have a tremendous impact on the style of a room. Other designs create a more informal look. **See Fig. 24-12.** The style of the window itself and the view from the window both influence the choice of treatment. Window treatments can also help control the home environment by regulating the amount of light, cutting down on noise, and providing insulation and privacy.

Fig. 24-12 Tab-top curtains are often hung from decorative rods. **For which rooms or room styles would this style of curtain be a good choice?**

Types of Window Treatments

Consumers have many, many options for window treatments: dozens of types of curtains, draperies, shades, blinds, shutters, and valances. Often more than one type is used at the same window. Combining them with special window hardware multiplies the number of possible looks. **Figure 24-13** on pages 564-565 illustrates a sampling of popular window coverings.

Curtains

Constructed of unlined fabric or lace, curtains offer a variety of colors, patterns, and textures. They may be sheer to medium weight.

Sheer curtains may either stay closed or be drawn open on a rod. Sheers are often used behind draperies. They look best when they are very full.

Mainly used on doors, *sash curtains* are hung close to the glass and are gathered on rods at both the top and the bottom of the window. *Café curtains* are often used in kitchens and bathrooms. *Tiebacks* are another popular type of curtain. Tiebacks edged with ruffles are called *Priscillas*.

Fig. 24-13

Window Treatments

A Visual Guide

Draperies with Sheers.
Often found in formal rooms,
extending to the floor. The sheer
curtain lets light in.

Café Curtains with Valance.
Panels cover part of the window,
usually the bottom portion.
They are either shirred (gathered)
on a rod (shown) or attached
with rings, clips, or fabric
loops (tabs).

Tieback Curtains with Valance.
Two curtain panels may meet
at the center or cross over each
other and then be held back with
cord, fabric, or hardware.

Draped Scarves. Graceful
"scarves" are made of sheer or
semi-sheer fabric. Decorative
hardware is part of the look.

Swag and Jabots. Swags drape
across the top of a window.
Jabots (jab-OZE) or cascades
hang gracefully down the sides.
May be used over other window
coverings.

Valance. This very popular top
treatment may have pinch pleats
(shown), gathers, or hang from a
rod or mounting board. Typically,
valances cover no more than the
top third of the window.

Fig. 24-13

Window Treatments (continued)

A Visual Guide

Roman Shade. Accordion pleats are formed when Roman shades are raised; otherwise they are flat. They are made of various weights of fabric.

Roller Shade and Cornice. Roller shades may be plain or decorative and are often trimmed with fringe. A cornice is sturdier than a valance.

Balloon Shade. This shade balloons at the bottom when raised. An Austrian shade has rows of scallops from top to bottom.

Shutters with Valance. Shutters may cover an entire window or just the bottom half. They may be used with or without curtains.

Horizontal Blinds. May be wood (shown), metal, plastic, or fabric. Wood provides the best insulation.

Vertical Blinds. Often used at patio doors and large windows, the vanes or slats are wider than horizontal blinds. They may be rotated 180 degrees to control light.

Draperies

Draperies are typically made of heavier fabrics than curtains, giving a more formal look to a room. Most are lined. Traditional draperies have pinch pleats and are hung from a track called a *traverse rod*, which allows them to be opened and closed by pulling on a cord attached to the rod. Draperies may also be tied back at the sides of the windows. Stationary drapery panels hang at the sides of the window but can't be pulled across to cover it, making them most suitable when there isn't a need for privacy. **See Fig. 24-14.**

Draperies have decorating advantages, such as focusing attention on a window or changing the apparent proportions of a wall area. They can be used to hide uneven walls or unsightly pipes. Draperies can even suggest a window where there is none, or a wider window instead of a narrow one. Many are washable like most curtains, but some must be dry cleaned. Vacuuming helps keep them clean. Drawn draperies are energy efficient, especially when lined with a special insulating fabric. They also absorb sound.

Top Treatments

Top treatments are decorative and also serve to hide window hardware. The **valance**—a short length of fabric placed across the top of a window—may be used alone or with most other window treatments. It is often a gathered or pleated fabric that matches or blends with the rest of the window covering. There are many styles of valances. A *cornice* has the same purpose as a valance, but has more structure. It is often constructed of wood, which may be painted, stained, or padded and covered with fabric.

A **swag** is a piece of fabric that is draped gracefully across the top of a window. It is attached to both sides of the window frame at the top.

Shutters

Originally designed to keep out heat and cold, shutters give a simple, uncluttered look to a window. They work well with traditional decors. *Shutters* are vertical sections of wood or manufactured material hinged together, much like a folding door. The sections of traditional shutters have crosswise slats called *louvers*, which vary in width. Some use a fabric insert rather than louvers. Interior shutters are usually painted or stained.

Fig. 24-14 This combination of stationary drapes and sheer curtains let in light while providing privacy in this formal seating area.

Fig. 24-15 This roller shade is topped with an ornate cornice.

Shades

Shades range from very plain to very ornate. Most may be used alone or with another window covering. *Roller shades* come in a variety of colors. Usually mounted at the top of a window, they are made of cloth or vinyl and sometimes are trimmed with fringe. **See Fig. 24-15.** They can also be laminated with fabric or wallpaper. Roller shades may be made of room-darkening, light-filtering, or heat-reflective materials. Vinyl shades are washable.

A *Roman shade* is a shade that lies flat against the window when down and can be drawn up by a cord into a series of horizontal accordion folds. A *balloon shade* is similar to a Roman shade, but a puffed effect is created when the shade is raised. *Waterfall shades* fold in a softer, more graceful fashion than ordinary Roman shades. Other variations include Roman shades that are pleated into three vertical sections and those that have curved bottoms.

Pleated shades are usually made of a solid piece of fabric and are raised or lowered with cords. They have horizontal accordion folds that are evident even when the shade is down. *Cellular shades* are similar, but have a double layer of fabric with air space between, making them better insulators.

Some specialty shades are made to fit oval or arched windows or skylights. Others are designed to allow the user to lower the shade from the top instead of raising it from the bottom. This allows light into the room while still providing privacy.

Blinds

Blinds are made of a series of evenly spaced slats that may be opened or closed by cords. The entire blind may also be raised and lowered, or pulled across a window, by cords. One reason for their popularity is their ability to provide privacy or to let in almost full light. Blinds are more tedious to clean than other window coverings.

Horizontal blinds, traditionally called Venetian blinds, have horizontal slats. The narrowest slats are used in mini-blinds and micro-blinds. *Vertical blinds* are blinds with vertical vanes that are usually $3\frac{1}{2}$ in. (9 cm) wide. Most draw to one side of the window.

Window Hardware

Some curtain and drapery hardware is intended to be functional and not seen. For instance, combination rods have up to three rods in one, one curtain rod or traverse rod for each part of the window treatment. For example, a double rod can accommodate curtains and a valance.

Decorative hardware, on the other hand, is meant to be seen and enhance the window treatment. Most decorative wood or metal rods have a diameter of 1, 1½, or 2 in. (2.5, 3.8, or 5 cm). The ends of the decorative rods are called *finials* and endcaps.

Various types of hardware that hold fabric back to the sides of the window are called sideholders. They are used to tie back curtains or to hold back scarves. Brackets, sconces, and swagholders may be installed at the top of a window to hold rods or fabric.

Comparing Cost & Other Factors

Personal tastes, budget, and the necessary upkeep are all factors in choosing window coverings. Design details—the type of window and its placement, the scale and proportion of window coverings, and the color scheme of the room—also influence the choice. See Fig. 24-16. For some types of windows in certain settings, you may even decide not to have a window covering.

Custom and made-to-measure window treatments are the most expensive. Ready-made valances, curtains, and draperies are less costly because they're mass-produced. Many people hire a seamstress or make their own window coverings. Pattern companies have made the job easier than you might think. In most cases, valances and curtains can be sewn for a fraction of the cost of custom-made window treatments.

Fig. 24-16 The same window can look very different when the window covering is changed. Which of these two looks do you prefer? Why?

The Importance of Backgrounds

Backgrounds are easy to overlook. They are often designed in neutral colors and simple textures. Skilled designers pay much attention to them, however, because backgrounds help establish the style and identity of a room. Backgrounds that are out of proportion or that use colors that overpower the rest of the design upset the balance of the room.

Designers aim to coordinate their backgrounds to provide a consistent overall look. In doing so, they use the principles of design and keep in mind the color, texture, and weight of the materials they choose. **See Fig. 24-17.** A rough tile floor would probably not mesh with rich damask draperies in a dining room, but it could be used effectively in a kitchen or family room with more modern-looking shades. Of course, in choosing backgrounds designers need to think about a room's function, too. Intricately designed Oriental rugs are colorful and expensive, but they would look out of place and be impractical in a children's playroom.

When people enter a room, it is often the backgrounds that they notice first. Designing effective floorcoverings, wallcoverings, ceilings, and window treatments can make a strong and clear impression.

Fig. 24-17 The backgrounds in this room work together. They create a cohesive design that is very harmonious.

Careers in Focus

Profile of a Textile Specialist

Textile specialists use their knowledge of textiles to develop specifications for interior fabrics, including upholstery and window treatments. Their work involves studying flammability standards, energy conservation, and maintenance. They work with textile designers, researchers, and manufacturers to develop new products.

Education & Training

- A Bachelor of Science degree is required. Advanced degrees become more important as job opportunities decrease.

- Courses in chemistry, physics, textiles, CAD, principles of design, fire protection, and safety are helpful.

Skills & Aptitudes

- Knowledge of chemistry is important.

- Knowledge of research practices is helpful.

- Understanding of design principles and practices is critical.

Textile Specialist
Ann Loo-Shay

Textiles are both beautiful and technical. Being able to work smoothly with these two elements is what my profession is all about.

I became interested in this profession while I was working as an interior designer. I created almost all of the new fabric designs for our clients. Unfortunately, textile design was only one small division of the firm, and I wanted to work with fabrics all of the time. So I found a job with a company that designs and produces fabrics and wallcoverings. I work with our clients, fabric designers, and textile manufacturers.

My interior design background prepared me for this career. Taking advanced chemistry and textile courses helped too. The chemistry classes helped me understand the properties of different fabrics. Our firm sells a lot of fabric to designers specifying materials for commercial buildings. These fabrics must meet flammability standards by preventing ignition, flame spread, and smoke development. They also have to be durable.

My job is to blend these technical components with the beauty of a design. Each year our firm creates two new fabric collections. Each collection might have 20 new designs in a variety of colors. I work with the designers in developing these new collections. We get our inspiration from a variety of sources. Sometimes we refer to the textile museum here in New York, where we work. The museum has an enormous collection of fabrics from around the world. Some are extremely old. I can check out the fabrics that have inspired me and share them with our designers. If we develop new designs from these fabrics the library will reserve them for six months. That helps ensure that another textile manufacturer won't attempt to duplicate our designs.

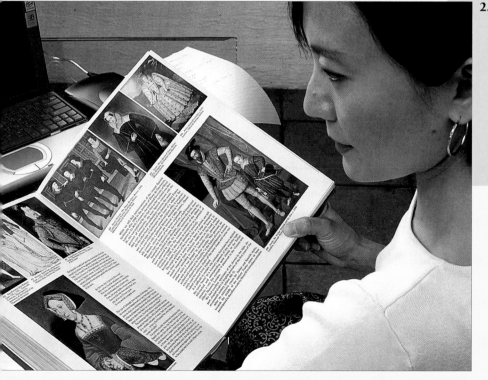

Design Portfolio

1. Obtain pictures of several upholstery and window treatment fabrics. Make a brochure that describes each in terms of weave, fiber content, and soil resistance.

2. Select upholstery fabrics and window treatments for a bedroom and create a sample board. Explain why you chose each fabric and window treatment.

Chapter Summary

- Backgrounds are an essential part of a room's design.
- Some backgrounds increase energy efficiency.
- A variety of **natural fibers** and **synthetic fibers** are used in home textiles.
- The type of floor covering should depend on the room's purpose, amount of traffic, and how much maintenance the floor covering needs.
- Paint, wallpaper, and paneling are common wall coverings.
- Decorative ceilings and **moldings** can add to a room's look.
- Homeowners can choose from many window coverings.

Checking Your Understanding

1. What are **backgrounds** and what roles do they play?
2. What is the difference between a **plain weave**, a **satin weave**, and a **twill weave**?
3. What type of weave is used to produce brocade and damask fabrics?
4. What are the advantages of **resilient flooring**? What is a disadvantage?
5. What does the grin test tell you?
6. How do **alkyd** and **latex** paints differ?
7. Why should all rolls of a wallpaper pattern have the same batch number?
8. What are the benefits of using acoustic ceiling tiles?
9. What is the difference between curtains and draperies?
10. What kind of **blinds** are preferable for a patio door?

Thinking Critically

1. **Suggesting Solutions.** What kind of fiber would you recommend for a family room carpet? Why?

2. **Identifying Alternatives.** Make a list of six different rooms in a home and analyze the typical traffic patterns and wear of each. Then recommend a floor covering for each room and explain each choice.

3. **Making Decisions.** What wall coverings would you pick for the following rooms: a master bathroom; children's bedroom; family room with brick fireplace?

Applying Your Knowledge

1. **Floor Coverings.** Assume you have been asked to recommend a new floor covering for your classroom. Create a chart that lists various materials and compares the durability and maintenance factors. Make a list of characteristics that you think have the most priority for this use. Recommend a floor covering based on those characteristics. Share your recommendation with the class.

2. **Wall Covering.** Assume you have been asked to recommend a new wall covering for your classroom. Create a chart that lists various materials and compares the durability and maintenance factors. Make a list of characteristics that you think have the most priority for this use. Recommend a wall covering based on those characteristics. Prepare a report summarizing your findings.

3. **Applying Wallpaper.** Obtain a sample piece of wallpaper and some wallboard. You might ask a home store for scraps. Find and follow instructions for installing the wallpaper on the wallboard. Would you enjoy installing wallpaper in a home? Why or why not?

4. **Planning Window Treatments.** Design a window treatment for your bedroom. Make a model of the window treatment. Research how much it would cost to have the window treatment custom-made.

Design Challenge

Your clients have asked you to design their kitchen and adjoining family room. The rooms are used by a family of five, including two parents, two young children, and an elderly grandparent.

1. Make a list of design requirements based on the family's needs.

2. Research different background materials and determine which would be most appropriate.

3. Use CAD software to show the floor coverings, wall coverings, and window treatments that you would use in these two rooms.

4. Write an explanation of why you chose the materials you did for each room.

5. Place a printed copy of each floor coverings, wall coverings, and window treatments in your design portfolio.

Recognizing Furniture Styles

Objectives

- Identify factors that influence changes in furniture design.

- Describe general points that can be helpful in understanding historical furniture styles.

- Compare formal and informal furniture styles.

- Identify and describe major styles of American furniture from 1600 to the present.

- Describe the types of furniture choices available to today's buyer.

Vocabulary

- reproduction
- antique
- turning
- chair table
- trestle table
- trundle bed
- veneer
- gateleg table
- highboy
- cabriole leg
- japanning
- wing chair
- reeding
- modular furniture
- distressing
- adaptations

Chairs, tables, beds, and other basic furniture pieces have been used for centuries, but their styles have changed significantly over time. Many things have influenced style changes. One example is changing expectations. At first people were concerned primarily about the function of furniture. In time, the way it looked became equally important.

Changing Styles

Some furniture styles are identified by the historic era in which they were first made. Such "period pieces" are often named for the king or queen who was in power when the furniture was built. Other styles are named for the person who originated the design or for the general design movement of the time. Some historical styles have become classics. Surviving examples are now found in museums or are owned by collectors. Other designs have been passing fads.

In this chapter you will learn how to recognize major furniture styles. Some will appeal to you more than others. Try to base your judgments on how well each piece meets its function and how well each style encompasses the elements and principles of design you learned about in Unit 5.

Why Designs Change

In addition to changing expectations, many other developments affect furniture design. Available materials, methods of manufacturing, and changes in lifestyles and tastes are a few examples.

Changes in Taste. The styles people prefer today are different from the styles people liked during other periods of time. Tastes change from era to era. These changes are influenced by several factors, including lifestyle, fashion, and needs. See Fig. 25-1.

Materials and Manufacturing. New manufacturing techniques and materials influence furniture design. Modern synthetic materials have different properties than traditional wood, thereby creating potential for new designs. Traditional wood chairs, for example, are carved. Some plastic chairs, however, are molded from liquid plastic. As a new material is developed, furniture makers experiment with different processes using that material. As processes are refined, new design possibilities may open up.

Lifestyle Changes. Furniture designs have often reflected the time during which the pieces were made and the lifestyles of the people who used the furniture. For instance, during the 18th century in France and England, much of the furniture was formal and elegant, reflecting the lifestyle of the royal courts. On the other hand, the furniture built by the early colonists in the New World was much plainer and more informal. What factors do you think influenced the designs of the colonists?

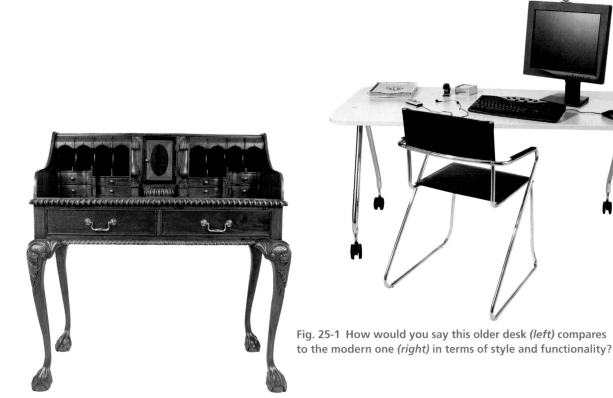

Fig. 25-1 How would you say this older desk *(left)* compares to the modern one *(right)* in terms of style and functionality?

Understanding Furniture Styles

Categorizing furniture styles by specific periods is convenient, but it can be difficult to place an unknown piece. You will have greater success in identifying furniture styles if you bear in mind with the following points.

Overlapping Style Periods. There is no definite beginning or end to any period. Typically, styles develop gradually. Often a certain country or region sets the fashion for others. In the 19th century, styles became popular in America later than they did in Europe.

Furniture that incorporates designs from two periods is referred to as *transitional*. When you study different periods, you will detect trends that indicate the general direction of change as one period blends into another.

The dates given in this chapter refer to the period when the styles were most popular in America. You'll get a better feeling for the period a style belongs to if you think of furniture in terms of the people who used it and the homes it occupied, not just the dates associated with it.

Going Through Stages. Most periods begin with simple, basic designs. As time goes by, designers tend to add more decorative features, and designs may become very elaborate. When people grow tired of these designs, a new cycle of designs begins.

Formal and Informal. Formal furniture styles originated mainly in Europe in the 18th century. Some formal styles were ornate. Others had classical lines. All formal styles were elegant, since they were created for the wealthy.

Furniture for the common people of the same era was usually made with simple hand tools. These pieces were plainer, smaller versions of formal styles.

Formal pieces of various periods can be grouped together successfully if they have similar lines. Simple informal furniture of various periods, sometimes called country-style furniture, also has a common bond. **See Fig. 25-2.**

Fig. 25-2 This room is furnished in a modern style. **Would you say it was formal or informal? Why?**

Designs That Last

Good design is not limited to a single period. Although only a small percentage of all furniture sold today is truly new, experimental, or contemporary in design, many people prefer a contemporary look. As time goes by, some of the contemporary styles will be successful. Those styles will be copied and in time become "traditional." Remember, at one time colonial style was contemporary.

Well designed furniture tends to survive over the years, partly because collectors recognize and value its excellence. Consumers help perpetuate good designs. There is a large demand for **reproductions**, or accurate copies of originals. Many people also buy antiques—furniture made in an earlier period. By law in the United States, a piece of furniture must be 100 years old to be classified as an **antique**. However, the term is often used informally to mean "old." Generally, if an antique has been refinished or changed significantly, it is less valuable.

 ## Consumer Considerations

Antique or Not?

Many people appreciate the beauty and character that antiques bring to a room. Yet most people aren't knowledgeable enough to distinguish an antique from a reproduction or a fake. The best advice is to buy only from reputable dealers. Knowing a few guidelines can also help you.

Techniques and Materials. The use of modern techniques or materials are sure signs that a piece is not an antique. Learn what carving tools were available to craftsmen of the time. What precision and detail were those tools capable of? Also be familiar with the materials typical of a certain time and place. For example, the bald cypress tree is rare in the Midwest today but was common two hundred years ago.

Signs of Age. Furniture that is newly made from old materials is not antique. An old-looking bench might be made with planks salvaged from an old barn that was recently taken down. Look for signs that the construction itself is old, like shrinkage that makes circles and squares lose their original shape.

Wear and Tear. In a true antique, signs of use should show around edges, handles, and other places where you would expect them. Marks in unusual areas may suggest the item was made, or at least repaired, using parts of other items.

Price. Price may be totally unrelated to authenticity. An unethical dealer may use a high price to convince buyers that a piece is rare and valuable. An inexperienced dealer may sell a valuable piece at far below its worth.

Colonial Period, 1600-1780

This chapter focuses on American furniture. You will see that most styles of American furniture, especially in the 17th and 18th centuries, were influenced by English styles. For this reason, this chapter concentrates on the English impact. Other influences came from France, Italy, Germany, and the Netherlands. Furniture reflecting all these styles can be purchased today.

The colonists adapted foreign styles to make furniture that was practical for everyday use. They used tools and materials that were available to them. Thus, furniture made in America during colonial times was often simpler than European furniture of the same style and period.

Seventeenth Century

English and other European styles were introduced in the colonies in several ways. Some were brought by trained furniture makers who emigrated from Europe. Others were copied from European designs. The distance and difficult communication between settlements in America and the differences in available materials caused regional differences in how particular styles evolved.

The furniture style of the 17th century is often referred to as *Jacobean* (jak-uh-BEE-uhn) style, after James I, England's reigning king. (*Jacob* is the Latin word for James.) Jacobean furniture was heavy and rectangular, with geometric or floral carvings. **See Fig. 25-3.** Rounded forms, such as legs and spindles, were made by a method called **turning**—adding shape by using a *lathe*. A lathe spins wood against a cutting tool, held by the furniture maker, which cuts away various parts of the wood to different depths. Modern versions of the lathe are used today.

Stools and benches were more common than chairs during this period. The few chairs that were used had straight backs and hard plank seats. Cushions were not introduced until the last half of the 17th century.

First, the colonists chose oak for their furniture, as they had in England. Then they turned to more plentiful hardwoods, such as maple, beech, ash, and hickory. Regardless of the wood used, the furniture was often painted black, red, or yellow.

Homes of this period were sparsely furnished and had little storage room. Since there were no closets, chests were especially important. Colonists used them mainly for storage, but also as seats, tables, and even beds. Chests were generally rectangular with hinged lids. The side panels could be either ornately carved or very plain.

Cupboards were also important for storage, but they were considered a luxury. Cupboards often contained shelves at the bottom for linens and clothing and an enclosed upper section for silver and glassware.

Fig. 25-3 This piece is from the Jacobean era. What characteristics identify it as Jacobean?

Tables were less common than chests. Some tables were designed to conserve space. For example, the draw-top table had leaves that could be pushed beneath the tabletop when the table wasn't in use. The **chair table** was also popular. It was a chair that had a large back that protected the occupant from drafts when upright and that could be tipped forward to form a table. Very large trestle tables were also used. A **trestle table** was a table with a long rectangular top and a wide vertical support at each end. To offset its size, the top could be removed, and thus the table was easier to move.

Because most houses were small, bed space was limited. Four-poster beds, wooden cradles and trundle beds were used. A **trundle bed** has a low bed that can be stored under a higher bed during the day.

William & Mary Style, 1700–1725

The next important furniture style—William and Mary—was named for the royal couple who began their rule of England in 1689. William, who was Dutch, brought Dutch traditions and craftspeople to England. The delicate furniture style that evolved was also influenced by the French court style of Louis XIV and by an earlier Italian design.

The chairs of the William and Mary period reflect a strong Asian influence. The curved back replaced the straight back of the Jacobean chair. Seats were often woven from *rushes*—the stems of marsh plants. These were more comfortable than the wooden plank seats of the previous periods. American furniture makers quickly adapted the William and Mary style.

In the American colonies, William and Mary furniture was marked by a lightness not found in Jacobean furniture. **See Fig. 25-4.** It featured fine carvings and trims, which reflected the growing prosperity of the colonists. Fine **veneer**—a thin layer of more expensive wood—was glued to less expensive wood furniture for a better appearance. Velvets and silks were used to upholster chairs made of deeply carved walnut, birch, and maple, creating an elegant look.

After the chair, the table was the most common type of furniture. The **gateleg table**—a table with legs on each side that swing out to support drop leaves that are pulled up from the sides—was popular during this period. **See Fig. 25-5.**

Fig. 25-4 This William and Mary highboy, with its delicate and intricate design, provided storage space for clothing.

As their wardrobes grew, colonists needed more storage space. For the first time, the chest of drawers became an important piece of furniture. The **highboy**, a chest of drawers mounted on legs, was developed in this period. The delicate William and Mary highboy is an example of a style being refined over time. For example, this furniture often had brass handles instead of wooden knobs. The highboy soon replaced the cupboard as the fanciest piece of furniture in the home.

Fig. 25-5 The gateleg table was introduced in the 17th century. The pull-out legs supported the expandable tabletop.

Queen Anne Style, 1720-1755

In the early 18th century, the colonists adopted a furniture style known for its graceful, curved lines. This style had become popular with the middle class in England during the reign of Queen Anne. The Queen Anne style was influenced by the furniture of the Netherlands and Asia. Queen Anne furniture was slender and flowing, featuring curved rather than straight lines. The **cabriole** (KAB-ree-ohl) **leg**, a leg that curves out at the middle and then tapers inward just above an ornamental foot, is a characteristic of the Queen Anne style. **See Fig. 25-6.**

Fig. 25-6 The cabriole legs of this Queen Anne table echo the curves of the tabletop.

Sometimes the wooden surfaces of this furniture were varnished with "japan," a glossy black lacquer. The process of applying glossy black lacquer to furniture is known as **japanning**. Furniture makers of the period felt that the technique gave the furniture an oriental look.

The Queen Anne style brought a number of innovations in sofa and chair design. For the first time, upholstered furniture became widely available. Queen Anne style furniture was more comfortable than that of any previous time. One popular style was the fully upholstered **wing chair**, an armchair with a high back and high sides (or "wings") designed to give protection from drafts. The wing chair remains popular today.

A simpler piece of furniture from this period, the *Windsor* chair, has also retained its popularity. The Windsor chair is a chair with turned legs and a spindle back inserted into a saddle-shaped plank seat. It was originally made in Windsor, England, but was soon produced throughout colonial America. See Fig. 25-7.

Fig. 25-7 Windsor chairs were often made from different woods and painted so all the parts would match.

Fig. 25-8 Note the decorative details on the inside, as well as the outside of this Chippendale desk.

Chippendale Style, 1755-1780

Around the middle of the 1700s, two developments changed the course of furniture design: the increasing popularity of mahogany wood and Thomas Chippendale's book of furniture designs.

Chippendale was a popular cabinetmaker and furniture designer in England. Chippendale's company produced furniture in a variety of designs, including his own. In 1754 he published a book of furniture designs—the first such book ever published. Although the book didn't introduce new styles, people found Chippendale's interpretations of existing styles very exciting. The book's influence on furniture making was widespread. Wealthy Americans wanted to furnish their homes with Chippendale designs.

Several distinctive details marked Chippendale's work. S-shaped chair and table legs ending in *claw-and-ball* feet were a common feature of his early work. His later oriental-inspired designs had straight legs. See Fig. 25-8. The *camelback sofa* was also his design. This well-known piece is distinctive for its curved back and sides. Decoration on Chippendale's furniture often included shells, leaves, and flowers carved into the wood. Some Chippendale features show Asian influence. Many cabinets in this style include Oriental fretwork on the tops and sides. *Fretwork* is fancy, open-cut patterns. Straight legs also reflected Asian styles.

Compared to the delicate designs of the Queen Anne style, Chippendale furniture appears heavier and more solid. Part of the illusion of weight comes from the use of mahogany. The properties of this wood, widely available for the first time, allowed craftspeople to produce elaborate designs more easily.

Postcolonial Period, 1780-1840

The colonists' declaration of independence in 1776 ushered in many changes in political thinking and lifestyle. After the Revolutionary War, there were changes in furniture styles. Designs in both Europe and America were influenced by the delicate, balanced lines of classical styles of ancient Greece and Rome. This overall style is often referred to as *Neoclassicism*. Two basic styles predominated during this time in America: the *Federal* and the *Empire* (ahm-PEER).

Federal Style, 1780-1820

The term *Federal* is often used to denote the furniture of the earlier of the two classical styles. As you read in Chapter 15, this was also the term used to describe the architecture of the time. The Federal style was most popular in New York, Washington, and Philadelphia, each of which served as the federal capital of the new country at different times after the Revolutionary War.

The architecture of the Federal period was straight-lined and uncluttered. Federal furniture was similar in style. Designs were small and rectangular, and the furniture was light, delicate, and symmetrical. **See Fig. 25-9.**

The first furniture to have features of the Federal style was actually designed in England in the 1760s by the Scottish architect Robert Adam. Adam designed furniture to harmonize with the delicate, airy rooms of his Georgian-style buildings. Adam's buildings emphasized function but were also decorative. He used plaster walls, ceilings decorated with classical designs, and raised moldings.

Two rival English designers—George Hepplewhite and Thomas Sheraton—simplified Adam's designs. This reduced manufacturing costs and made the furniture more accessible to the middle class. In no time, Adam's designs were famous.

Hepplewhite and Sheraton displayed both similarities and differences in their individual designs. One way to compare the two is to analyze their chairs. A typical Hepplewhite chair has tapered legs and a decorative back in the shape of a shield, an oval, or a heart. Sheraton's chairs had rectangular or square backs. The legs were slender and tapered, sometimes decorated with reeding. **Reeding** is decorative carving consisting of vertical lines that resemble thin reeds—stems of tall grass. Sheraton also favored painted surfaces and inlaid decoration.

Both Hepplewhite and Sheraton published important design books in the late 1780s and the early 1790s. These books had a tremendous influence on American furniture makers. By the beginning of the 19th century, the classical Federal style was the leading fashion.

Fig. 25-9 The Federal-style sofa shown here became popular after the Revolutionary War.

Empire Style, 1820-1840

The Empire style takes its name from the rule of the French emperor Napoleon I. The original Empire style was created by Napoleon's official court architects and interior designers. The style spread rapidly throughout Europe. In America, the Empire style flourished for about 20 years, during the last half of the Neoclassical period.

The Empire style is a continuation of the Neoclassical style, but with a much stronger emphasis on historical accuracy. Whereas the Federal style was mostly uncluttered and symmetrical, the Empire style was elaborate and much more dramatic. Designers began to copy ancient furniture directly. They also incorporated Egyptian decoration, because of Napoleon's campaigns in Egypt. **See Fig. 25-10.**

In America, the most famous of the Empire designers was Duncan Phyfe, a Scotsman who had emigrated to New York. Phyfe used such classical designs as leaves, swans, eagles, and dolphins, as well as urn-shaped pedestals and dog's-paw and lion's-paw feet. His shop was well known for pedestal tables with curved legs and brass feet. Phyfe was also known for his chairs with a back shaped like a lyre—a musical instrument resembling a small harp.

Fig. 25-10 This table is an Empire style.

As America's population grew, so did the demand for furniture. Phyfe is credited with incorporating the factory method into his workshop. Furniture makers began to standardize their designs and to keep some finished furniture on hand. Rather than ordering custom-made furniture, customers bought what was immediately available. With the industrial revolution, making furniture moved from being a craft to being an industry. In some cases, mass production caused the quality of furniture to decline.

Shaker Furniture

A plain and simple style of furniture existed along with Federal and Empire furniture. It was created by the Shakers, a religious group that had settled in New England. The Shakers emphasized utility, not ornamentation. Although the furniture was very plain, it had graceful lines and proportions. **See Fig. 25-11.** Shaker designs didn't achieve much popularity in the 1800s, but today they are popular.

Fig. 25-11 Shaker furniture is admired more today than it was in the 1800s.

Victorian Period, 1840-1900

Many different and often contradictory styles developed during the Victorian period, which coincided with the reign of England's Queen Victoria from 1837-1901.

Following a trend similar to that of Victorian architects, furniture makers of the day revived styles of earlier periods. Among the major revival styles of the period were Gothic, Elizabethan, Rococo (or "French Antique"), Louis XVI, and Italian Renaissance. Near the end of the period, some heavy, ornate pieces showed a Turkish influence. Actually, these so-called revival styles were not historically accurate. Inspired by earlier styles, Victorian furniture makers relied on their imaginations to create elaborate and fanciful designs. Many of these styles were little more than fads.

Advances in technology encouraged more elaborate details and fancy upholstery fabrics. Victorian sofas and easy chairs can be recognized by their curving lines, inlaid floral patterns, and rich upholstery. **See Fig. 25-12.**

Fig. 25-12 Victorian furniture is characterized by highly carved dark woods and curved lines.

Victorian tables, desks, and cabinets were also ornate and heavy-looking. There was a great demand for rosewood, a tropical wood with a dark, reddish brown grain. It was usually finished to a high luster. When it became possible to manufacture large pieces of veneer, furniture makers often applied a veneer of rosewood to a pine backing. Later in the period, many tables and cabinets were made of black walnut. Marble, iron, and brass were also used in Victorian furniture.

One of the most famous names of the Victorian period was a German cabinetmaker named John Henry Belter. In New York, Belter invented a technique for bending strips of wood around a wooden frame by using steam and pressure. The wood surface was then elaborately carved, giving an almost lace-like appearance. Belter's furniture was mass-produced, and his designs were popular and influential.

Design Reform

Toward the end of the Victorian period, some designers and furniture makers reacted against the excessive use of ornamentation. They called for a more natural use of materials and a return to hand-crafted furniture.

The most famous reformer was William Morris, an English artist and designer. Morris paid close attention to the basic line, structure, and proportion of furniture. Much of his furniture was hand-crafted and unaffordable for the average person. Nevertheless, his ideas of design reform had an important influence on other furniture makers and designers. Morris summarized the aim of design reform in a famous statement: "Have nothing in your house that you do not know to be useful or believe to be beautiful." Do you agree with this advice?

Modern Period, 1901-Present

In stressing the importance of function, Morris looked ahead to the Modern period. During the first two decades of the 20th century, furniture designers did not make a radical break from Victorian styles. However, many designers did become interested in simpler forms. Many of these forms were abstract; that is, they didn't resemble recognizable forms. Modern furniture used very little decoration. Furniture contained fewer parts and was built out of newly invented materials. Designers were also fascinated by the growing possibilities offered by modern machines.

International Style

Architect Walter Gropius founded the Bauhaus (BOW-hows) school of design in 1919 in Weimar, Germany. Gropius wanted to unify architecture, interior design, and furniture design. Followers believed that furniture should not include details that didn't contribute to its function.

The plain, functional style developed by Gropius spread to other countries, including the United States. Known as the International style, it is completely nontraditional.

Early designers in the International style abandoned the use of wood and other natural materials. Instead, they used chrome-plated steel tubing and manufactured materials. More recent furniture in the International style often makes use of molded plastic and glass.

Modern Scandinavian designers returned to the use of wood, this time with a natural, hand-rubbed finish. See Fig. 25-13. Many American furniture makers have also followed this trend. The combination of innovative designs and mostly manufactured materials gives most International-style furniture a distinctive machine-made look.

Fig. 25-13 This modern Swedish furniture has very clean lines. How does it compare to the earlier historical styles?

Fig. 25-14 This modular outdoor furniture can be regrouped in many configurations.

Contemporary Designs

Although the period in which we are now living can still be termed Modern, there is a general trend toward softening the harshness of early Modern designs. It is difficult to identify the leading contemporary style. We are too close to it to judge it yet. Nevertheless, most designs today do have certain characteristics. The following points apply to many pieces of contemporary furniture:

- Contemporary designs aren't confined to one nation or continent. Designs may originate in the United States, Italy, Germany, or other countries. This furniture rarely embodies traditional designs or national characteristics, so it's usually difficult for the average person to tell where a certain design originated.

- Contemporary furnishings usually utilize architectural materials such as marble, wood, glass, stone, and plastics. These contribute interesting textural contrasts. Furniture is arranged so that the shape stands out clearly against a simple background. Bold design, as well as color, may be used.

- Furniture shapes are designed for the human form. Before plastic came into use in furniture manufacturing, people had to adapt to the shape of the particular seat, whether it was a crude 17th century wooden bench or an overstuffed Victorian sofa. In each case, the material used for the seat limited its form. A plastic seat, however, can theoretically be shaped to fit any person who might use it. In practice, because of mass production methods, such individualized shapes haven't been made. Modern plastics, however, has provided designers a new freedom of expression.

- Freedom of design, along with an emphasis on convenience, has made modular furniture popular. **Modular furniture** consists of standardized pieces (modules) that can fit together in a variety of ways. **See Fig. 25-14.** Modular furniture can be arranged and rearranged to suit the changing needs of the people using them. Some pieces have been designed to serve more than one purpose. Sofas may convert into individual seats or beds. Storage units may be stacked to form room dividers. You'll learn more about modular furniture in Chapter 26.

- Furniture may now be influenced by the work of engineers and chemists. Finishes that are durable and almost indestructible are now available. Designers are experimenting with other new materials. They use clear, see-through plastic, for example, to make furniture that seems to take up little space in a room.

Although contemporary furniture is usually created of new materials such as plastic, glass, and metal, the use of such traditional materials as wood and fabric is not ruled out. These materials give a feeling of warmth that is lacking in furniture made solely of metal or plastic.

Most people strive to protect their furniture from wear, but others think that aged wood with wormholes, nicks, and cuts is aesthetically superior to new wood. Because the amount of antique wood is limited, techniques have been developed to make wood look as if it's from an earlier era. **Distressing** wood is one process in which new wood is made to look old. The color and the texture of the wood are changed by first scraping the surface of the wood and then rubbing it with a piece of smooth metal. This process is used when older furniture needs repair or a new part, or when a furniture designer wants to create the look of age.

Awareness of Different Styles

Designs from the past can be obtained in three ways. One is to furnish a home with antiques. This is difficult because scarcity and demand have made good antiques very expensive. Another method is to select reproductions—exact copies of originals. See Fig. 25-15. Reputable manufacturers identify their reproductions so they cannot be confused with antique originals. A third method is to use **adaptations**, that is, furniture made today in the style of old designs. For example, furniture in the Victorian style may have many features characteristic of the Victorian era without exactly copying any one piece.

Awareness of different furniture styles will help you choose styles that can be blended to create pleasing rooms. You will also be better able to judge new furniture styles as they become available.

Today, more furniture styles are available than ever before. For example, you can purchase a William and Mary gateleg table, a Windsor chair, a Chippendale cabinet, a Shaker chest, and a Modern-style dining set. **Figure 25-16 on pages 591-592** illustrates the array of chair styles from 1650 to date.

Fig. 25-15 This is a traditional piece of furniture. Can you tell if it is an antique or a reproduction?

Fig. 25-16

Chairs Through Time

A Visual Guide

What differences and similarities do you see in the various styles? What influences can you make from this timeline about changing lifestyles and tastes?

1650
Jacobean Style

- Straight, rectangular back
- Wooden plank seat
- Straight legs

1710
William and Mary Style

- Curved back
- Leather back and seat fastened with brass-head nails
- Elaborately turned front legs

1730
Queen Anne Style

- Decorative, rounded back
- Fabric seat
- Cabriole leg with ornamental foot

1745
Windsor Style

- Spindle-backed
- Saddle-shaped seat
- All wood parts

1770
Chippendale Style (Thomas Chippendale)

- Decorative, open back
- Fabric seat
- Carved leg with claw-and-ball foot

1785
Federal Style (George Hepplewhite)

- Decorative back in shape of shield
- Fabric seat
- Tapered legs

1825
Empire Chair (Duncan Phyfe)

- Decorative lyre-shaped back
- Fabric seat
- Curved, decorated legs

1889
Victorian Style

- Rounded, tufted upholstered back
- Rounded, upholstered seat
- Curved, carved legs

Fig. 25-16

Chairs Through Time (continued)

A Visual Guide

1898

Mackintosh Style (Charles Rennie Mackintosh)

- Tall backs
- Oval insets
- Pierced patterns

1909

Modern Style (Frank Lloyd Wright)

- Straight slat back
- Rectangular seat
- Straight, rectangular legs

1929

Barcelona Style (Mies van der Rohe)

- Chrome plated steel frame
- Leather strap suspension
- Leather-covered cushions

1946

Modern Style (Charles Eames)

- Molded to fit human form
- Plywood seat and back
- Molded, wooden legs

1957

Modern Style (Eero Saarinen)

- Molded plastic back
- Aluminum pedestal
- Cushioned seat

1984

Post-Modern Style (Robert Venturi)

- Bent plywood construction
- Wide, tilted seat
- Painted pattern

2003

Post-Modern Style (Herman Miller)

- Ergonomically designed
- PostureFit technology
- Novel appearance

Working with Furniture Styles

You can use your knowledge of different furniture styles in making design decisions. Suppose you're designing a room around a Chippendale chair. Knowing the characteristics of pieces from that period will help you identify other furniture items that would complement the room. Understanding the characteristics of each style can also help you combine pieces from different styles. A dark, heavy Jacobean style cabinet would not work well with a contemporary table made of lighter wood and with little ornamentation. That table would fit well with a plain looking colonial pine cabinet, though.

Mixing furniture of different styles—such as pieces of folk art, antiques, reproductions, adaptations, and handmade furniture—creates a uniquely American look. Natural wood, earthy colors, plants, and pottery are also typical of this look. Wicker furniture, twig furniture, refinished furniture, and American Victorian pieces can be combined in informal ways to provide comfort and beauty. Whatever look you want to create, there are plenty of furniture styles to choose from. **See Fig. 25-17.**

Fig. 25-17 This porch combines wicker furniture with a pine rocking chair and accessories for an American look.

Careers in Focus

Profile of a Furniture Restorer

A furniture restorer takes furniture that is old, broken, or damaged in some way and makes it look like new. This process includes sanding, stripping, cleaning, polishing, and repairing. Then the restorer uses stains, finishes, or paint to finish the piece. Restorers work with many different chemicals and power tools, so following safety precautions is important.

Education & Training

- No formal degree is required.
- Training takes place on the job.
- Courses in woodworking and cabinetmaking are very helpful.

Skills & Aptitudes

- A thorough knowledge of woods and other materials is needed.
- Patience, persistence, and a good eye for detail are important.
- Some strength might be necessary to move large pieces.

Furniture Restorer
Jaime Orduno

For several years I owned an antique shop. When I realized that repairing and refinishing the furniture was what I enjoyed the most, I sold the store so that I could specialize as a furniture restorer.

I do a range of work: from patching an old picture frame to replating a silver tray. I never get bored, for I rarely do the same thing two times in a row!

Furniture restoration is an art and a craft; yet it's a business, too. I have to listen carefully to what the client wants done. Some people have trouble describing what they want, so it helps if I can envision the finished product and convey that idea to the customer. Once the right method of restoration is determined, I write up a contract detailing the work to be done and the cost. I charge a deposit, usually 20 percent of the cost estimate.

An example will show what I do. Recently, a woman brought in a chest of drawers that had been hers as a child, and her mother's before that. The top and sides of the chest were made of maple, but the drawers were pine—not an unusual combination of woods 100 years ago. Wooden flowers were carved across each drawer front. The customer wanted me to strip the chest and repaint it to match her bedroom. I explained that antiques are worth more unstripped, but she said, "I don't want to sell it. I want to use it and enjoy it."

First I stripped off all the old layers of paint—eight of them. Next, I used a palm sander on the bare wood, though I had to sand the carved flowers and the vertical molding by hand. Then I painted everything except the top of the chest with two coats of cream-colored gloss paint. After it dried, I painted the carved flowers and vertical molding in pastels. Finally, I used a number of intricate techniques and some specialty paints and glazes to create the look of marble on the top.

When the customer came to pick up the chest, she was so happy. She said this heirloom combined her childhood memories with her adult taste. Moments like that may be the most satisfying part of this job—to think that I'm preserving not only furniture, but also heritage and history.

Design Portfolio

1. Suppose you are starting a furniture restoration business. Design a brochure that shows what you can do for customers. Be sure to include illustrations.

2. You have been asked to restore an Empire-style table. Assemble a file of information that you could use to guide your restoration of the table. Create a diagram showing the steps you would follow.

Review & Activities

Chapter Summary

- Furniture styles change over time due to several factors.
- Furniture style periods overlap and go through stages.
- Furniture styles can be formal or informal.
- Most traditional American furniture styles were influenced by styles popular in England or other European countries.
- Certain pieces of furniture, materials or methods, and ornamental details characterize different styles.
- People today can choose among and blend many different styles, including older and more modern ones.

Checking Your Understanding

1. What factors lead to changes in furniture styles?
2. What three principles help you understand styles?
3. Contrast formal and informal furniture styles.
4. What is the difference between an **antique**, a **reproduction**, and an **adaptation**?
5. What is **turning**, and for what style was it popular?
6. How does the William and Mary style differ from the Jacobean?
7. What style is characterized by each of the following kinds of legs: (a) **cabriole leg**; (b) S-shaped leg with claw-and-ball foot; (c) tapered leg; (d) tapered leg with reeding; (e) curved leg with brass feet?
8. How did mass production affect furniture design?
9. What are two characteristics of Victorian style?
10. What does **distressing** wood involve?

Thinking Critically

1. **Comparing and Contrasting.** How does the Shaker style compare to the Victorian style? What are the main differences?

2. **Defending Your Position.** Identify the furniture style that you prefer of all those covered in this chapter. Explain why—in terms of design and functionality— you prefer that style.

Applying Your Knowledge

1. **Analyzing Styles.** Make a chart with three columns. In the left column, list each of the furniture styles described in this chapter. In the right column, indicate whether you think the style emphasizes appearance or function. In the last column, give reasons why you think that style emphasizes appearance vs. function.

2. **Researching Designers.** Choose one of the designers mentioned in this chapter. Research more about that designer's furniture designs. Write a report that describes what the designer was trying to achieve and why. Include images of his or her designs. Describe any changes that occurred in that person's furniture designs over time.

3. **Dining in Style.** Use print resources or the Internet to find pictures of dining chairs currently sold by at least two different companies. Label each picture as to the historical style they most resemble.

4. **Designing a New Style.** Your design firm has asked you to design a new chair style. Create a design for a desk chair and a side chair that can be used in a living room or family room. Explain what materials you would use and why.

5. **Making a Style Brochure.** Create a brochure that highlights one historical style from the 1700s, one from the 1800s, and one from the 1900s. Include images and text descriptions for each piece of representative furniture. Discuss the impact of manufacturing methods and materials on each style.

Design Challenge

A client has asked you to design a formal dining room in an early American style. He hosts dinner parties on a regular basis. The room is only 8 ft. x 10 ft. and does not have any windows.

1. Determine what pieces of furniture you would place in the room.

2. Gather pictures of each furniture piece.

3. Research what background colors and accessories would be appropriate for a room of that period.

4. Prepare a design presentation of his dining room, showing the background treatments, furniture layout, and placement of accessories.

5. Place the completed design in your design portfolio.

Selecting Furniture

Objectives

- Describe the characteristics of different materials used to make furniture.

- Evaluate furniture by comparing methods of construction, materials, and cost.

- Identify common wood furniture joints and finishes.

- List factors to consider in evaluating and purchasing upholstery materials.

- Describe the options available when shopping for furniture.

- Summarize ways to care for furniture based on the type of finish.

Vocabulary

- case goods
- plywood
- particleboard
- wicker furniture
- bamboo
- wrought iron
- joint
- multipurpose furniture

Imagine life before furniture. You might have to lean your back against a rock and sleep directly on the hard ground. Today there's furniture for every purpose—sitting, eating, sleeping, studying, and storage. The challenge is choosing the most attractive, useful, and durable pieces for the available space—all within a budget.

Furniture Materials

The first step in evaluating any piece of furniture is to check the type and quality of the materials used. Of the variety of materials used in the construction of furniture, the most common are wood, metal, glass, and plastic. Each of these materials can be used alone or in combination with others.

Wood

Wood is the most common material, especially for case goods. **Case goods** are furniture pieces that are not upholstered. Chests, desks, and tables are examples of case goods. Wood is both beautiful and durable. It can withstand a great deal of weight and is fairly easy to repair. Both hardwoods and softwoods are used in furniture construction.

Hardwoods come from deciduous trees—the trees that lose their leaves each year. Common examples include cherry, maple, pecan, oak, walnut, mahogany, birch, and ash. Their strength, beautiful natural grain, and resistance to denting make them desirable for fine furniture.

Softwoods come from coniferous, or cone-bearing, trees. Examples are pine, fir, redwood, and cedar. Softwoods, generally speaking, dent more easily, have a coarser grain, and cost less than hardwoods. They are commonly used for interior parts of case goods. Pine is often used for constructing country-style furniture because the cracks and dents that may occur in pine give this furniture its characteristic rustic look. Redwood is coarse and splintery but is weather-resistant. For this reason, many outdoor furnishings are made of redwood.

Common hardwoods and softwoods are described in **Fig. 26-1**. Furniture makers select these woods for furniture construction based on the cost and the different properties of the wood. Possible furniture construction uses for various woods include veneer, solid wood, and particleboard.

Fig. 26-1

Hardwoods & Softwoods

A Visual Guide

TYPE	Cherry	Maple	Pecan	Oak	Walnut
Characteristics	Close-grained; durable; resembles unfinished mahogany; darkens with age.	Very strong; grain is usually straight and fine. Bird's-eye maple and curly maple have unusual grains.	Strong and tough; open-grained; machines well; glues moderately well.	Strong; durable; widely available; open-grained; glues well. White oak and red oak are used for furniture.	Medium hard; beautiful grain; strong; ideal for carving.
Use in the Home	Fine furniture; cabinets.	Early American and contemporary furniture; fine flooring.	Furniture.	Fine furniture; unfinished furniture; cabinets; and architectural details.	Fine furniture; cabinets.

TYPE	Mahogany	Birch	Pine	Cedar	Redwood
Characteristics	True mahogany is considered ideal for furniture and cabinets. Fine grain; uniform texture; strong; polishes well. Philippine mahogany (lauan) is coarser and inexpensive.	Fine texture; close grain; sands poorly; can be stained to resemble mahogany, walnut, or maple.	Lightweight; even-textured; soft; dents easily.	Durable; close-grained; easy to finish; pleasant scent.	Lightweight; moderately hard; resists decay; strong.
Use in the Home	Fine furniture; cabinets. Philippine mahogany is used for inexpensive furniture and trim.	Tabletops; furniture parts requiring strength; cabinets.	Early American, country, unpainted, and inexpensive furniture.	Chests; closets.	Outdoor furniture; fences.

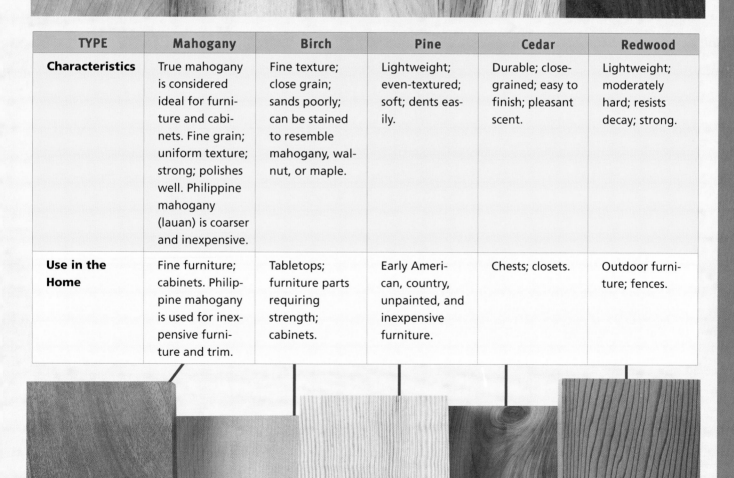

Fig. 26-2 Veneer can be used to create a beautiful piece of furniture.

Veneer. Most wood furniture produced today is made with veneer—an ornamental overlay placed over a base material. See Fig. 26-2. The veneer may be a thin layer of fine wood; several thin sheets of lesser quality wood that are dyed, glued, and pressed together; or plastic laminate. The base material is often plywood. **Plywood** consists of three, five, or seven layers of less expensive wood glued together. Some plywoods can be purchased with a fine veneer finish on one side.

Because of the high-quality glues used, veneered wood is strong. It also resists shrinking and warping. Veneers show off the unique characteristics of the wood used. Because it requires a smaller amount of expensive wood, veneered furniture is usually more economical than solid-wood furniture of the same type. A major disadvantage of veneered wood, however, is that it's difficult to repair if damaged. Sanding and refinishing are impractical because of the danger that the veneer might peel off.

Solid Wood. When furniture is made of solid wood, whole pieces of the same wood are used to make the exposed surfaces—for example, tops, sides, and door and drawer fronts. The interior construction of the furniture, however, may use a wood of lesser quality.

Unlike veneered wood, solid wood can be turned and carved. When it's damaged, solid wood can be sanded and refinished. One disadvantage is that changes in humidity may cause the wood to crack, swell, and warp. Its relatively high cost is another disadvantage.

Particleboard. Parts of inexpensive furniture and higher priced furniture are often made of **particleboard**—a combination of wood shavings, veneer scraps, chips, and sometimes sawdust that is mixed with glue and pressed together under heat. Particleboard, though less expensive and more durable than solid wood and veneer, is less desirable. Because of its appearance, it is widely used on parts of furniture that are concealed, such as the insides of doors and drawers and the backs of bookcases. Furniture makers use particleboard for the shelves of bookcases because it doesn't warp as easily as solid wood. Particleboard can be used as a base for wood or plastic laminate veneer.

Other Wood Products. Some styles of furniture use whole slender growths of wood. **Wicker furniture** is furniture that is woven of thin, flexible twigs, branches, and stems, often from willow trees. See Fig. 26-3. Wicker has been popular since the 1800s. Once the furniture has been woven, it is usually varnished or painted. The best quality wicker has smooth surfaces; neat, well-wrapped joints; and legs that stand evenly to provide stability. **Bamboo** is a fast-growing, woody, tropical plant. Its sturdy stems can be used in furniture making. Bamboo is particularly popular for casual furniture.

Fig. 26-3 Wicker furniture is lightweight, easy to carry, and can be used in almost any room.

Metal

Metals are also used in furniture construction. Some common furniture metals are iron, steel, aluminum, brass, and copper. All are strong and durable.

Iron is the most frequently used metal for furniture. **Wrought iron** is a tough, durable form of iron that can be hammered and bent into different shapes. It is suitable for decorative accessories, table and chair frames, and lawn furniture.

Steel can also be used for decorating purposes and, because of its strength, for exposed furniture legs and arms. When combined with chromium, steel becomes *stainless steel*. Stainless steel doesn't rust and maintains a shiny appearance. Brushed steel is currently popular.

Aluminum is one of the most adaptable metals. It is inexpensive, easy to care for, and lightweight. Because it doesn't rust, it is ideal for outdoor furniture. Aluminum can be formed into many shapes, making it especially suitable for such items as lamp bases. One drawback is that aluminum dents.

Copper is both durable and rust-resistant. Copper can be shaped by hammering or by heating and then casting the metal in a mold. You may find it in lamps and hardware, such as doorknobs and drawer pulls. Brass is made by mixing zinc with copper. Both brass and copper take a high polish but will tarnish if not protected by lacquer. Since they reflect nearby colors, brass and copper blend well with most interiors. They are chosen for their beauty, color, and texture and are commonly used in decorative accessories such as lamps and fireplace screens.

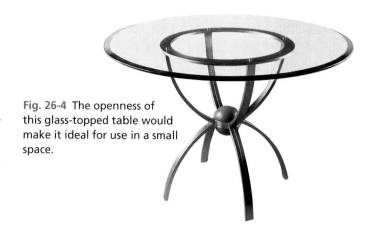

Fig. 26-4 The openness of this glass-topped table would make it ideal for use in a small space.

Plastic

The versatility of plastics has permitted many innovations in furniture design. Manufacturers and designers have experimented with plastic to form new shapes and surfaces. Plastic can be molded, for example, to form tables and chairs. See Fig. 26-5.

Plastic furniture is available in a variety of colors and can be made to look like other materials, such as wood or marble. It may also be transparent. Transparent objects give the illusion of space and help avoid an overcrowded look in a small room.

Thin sheets of plastic laminate can be glued to wood panels as veneer to form the tops or sides of tables, desks, chests, and other pieces of furniture. Because plastic resists spots, scratches, and other abuse, this process is especially popular for furnishings that are heavily used.

Glass

Glass is a popular material in the production of furniture. Glass used for furniture should be *tempered* (treated for safety and durability). It should be free of bubbles, scratches, and other defects. Glass is used for tabletops and for the doors of china cabinets and display cabinets. See Fig. 26-4. When using glass in furniture, designers usually combine it with a wood or metal frame to secure the glass.

Fig. 26-5 Plastic furniture comes in many colors and shapes.

Basic Furniture Construction

Once you understand the materials used to make furniture, it may be even more important to know how pieces are constructed. As you've learned, wood is the most common furniture material. It forms the structure of most case goods, as well as the frame for upholstered pieces. Knowing how to judge quality wood construction can help you make the best choices for the money you have available—your own or a client's. **See Fig. 26-6.**

Joints

A **joint** is the place where one piece of wood is connected to another. Some joints are concealed. Others are exposed and are part of the furniture design. Joint structure can be simple—placing one board against another—or it can be intricate and complicated. The structure of a joint and how it is held together determine its strength. **Figure 26-7** shows common wood joints, how they are used in furniture, and methods for strengthening them.

Fig. 26-6

Signs of Quality Case Goods

A Visual Guide

A. Sturdy; doesn't wobble.

B. Drawers and doors evenly meet the surface of the piece of furniture.

C. Drawers and doors open and close smoothly.

D. Center or side glides make drawers operate smoothly.

E. Drawer stops prevent pulling the drawer free.

F. Back panels are firmly screwed in place.

Fig. 26-7

Common Wood Furniture Joints

A Visual Guide

The most commonly used joints for furniture construction range in complexity from the rabbet to the dovetail. A rule of thumb is that the more complex the joint, the sturdier the construction.

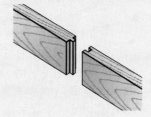

Tongue and Groove. The projection, or tongue, on one piece is inserted in a groove cut into the other. Used in flooring materials and paneling, as well as furniture, such as tabletops.

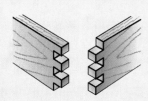

Finger or Box. Square notches are cut into the ends of each piece of wood and then fitted together. Because the notches are square, they can sometimes be pulled apart. Used on lower quality furniture.

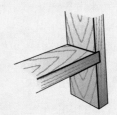

Dado. A groove is cut across one piece of wood so that the other piece fits snugly into it; generally used for holding shelves or drawer bottoms in fixed positions.

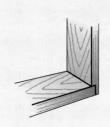

Rabbet. A groove is cut in one piece of wood to receive the other. Not a sturdy joint; should not be used on pieces that must withstand continual movement, such as a drawer. This joint is better if it's reinforced.

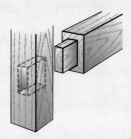

Mortise and Tenon. A projection on one piece of wood fits into a hollowed-out space on the other. When glued, this forms a strong joint that holds well under strain. Has many uses, such as attaching a bar between two chair legs.

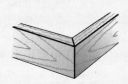

Mitered. Two edges are cut at 45-degree angles and joined to form a square corner. The joint is glued and sometimes reinforced.

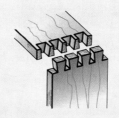

Dovetail. A series of flaring projections on one piece fit into a series of grooves in the other; can take strong pulls or strains. A good joint for drawers.

Joint Reinforcement

Rabbet and mitered joints are often reinforced to add strength to their weak structures. More stable joints are sometimes reinforced as well, especially in fine furniture. The illustrations below show some of the devices and methods available to strengthen wood furniture joints.

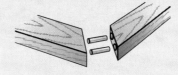

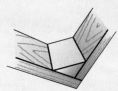

Spline. A thin strip of wood is inserted into grooves where two pieces come together.

Dowels. Small wooden dowels are glued into holes of the pieces being joined.

Glue Block. A small block of wood is attached with glue and/or screws where two sides come together.

Various methods are used to hold joints together. Wood joints are usually glued to add strength. Nails and screws may also be used. When evaluating wood furniture, check to see that appropriate joints have been used and that they are tight and strong. The drawers in a desk, for instance, must support the weight of the contents, as well as withstand frequent opening and closing. Check whether joints have been glued and nailed. Staples don't provide enough support. Also, check to see if joints are reinforced.

Some molded metal and plastic furniture may not have joints. Other pieces have joints that are bolted, welded, or riveted. Joints should be smooth and sturdy enough to hold up under normal use.

Finishes

Once constructed, the outer surfaces of wood furniture are prepared for receiving a finish. Finishes are applied to protect the wood from moisture, heat, warping, and abrasions that may occur during use. Finishes may also be used to enhance or change the color of the wood or to decorate it. **See Fig. 26-8.**

The minimum preparation for finishing requires sanding the wood smooth. In some cases, bleach is applied to wood for decorative purposes. Bleach removes some of the natural color of the wood and can give it a worn or weathered look. Other finishing substances include:

- Stain, which adds color without covering the natural grain.

- Clear varnish, which emphasizes the grain pattern and protects the wood.

- Clear lacquer and polyurethane, which provide a protective finish.

- Hand-rubbed oil, which penetrates the wood and brings out the natural grain. Oil used on fine wood furniture gives it a soft shine, or patina.

- Paint, which is generally used to cover the grain of less expensive woods.

Some pieces are finished to resemble a more expensive wood. For example, if you see a label on a piece of furniture that reads "oak finish," this means that another material or wood—usually an inexpensive wood—has been finished to resemble oak.

It is also important to check the finish of metal furniture. Brass and copper pieces may be lacquered. Those that aren't will require occasional polishing. Sometimes an entire piece may be made of the surface metal. At other times an underlayer of inexpensive metal is plated, or covered, with a more attractive metal, such as brass, chrome, or copper. Eventually, plated metals can wear thin and expose the underlayer. If the label doesn't mention the type of finish used on the furniture, ask the salesperson. Find out the best way to care for the finish.

Fig. 26-8 Various finishes can be used to change the appearance of a piece of furniture.

Upholstered Furniture Construction

Upholstered furniture—chairs and sofas with padding, springs, and cushions—provides a soft surface on which to sit and relax. See Fig. 26-9. Upholstered furniture was rare until the end of the 18th century. It became common after 1850, when more thought was given to comfort. Since then, many changes have occurred in upholstering.

The basic elements of all upholstery construction are the frame, springs, padding, cushions, and upholstery fabric. Check these features carefully. They indicate the quality of a piece of upholstered furniture. See Fig. 26-10.

Fig. 26-9 Upholstered furniture provides more comfortable seating than hard surfaces.

Fig. 26-10

Quality Upholstered Furniture

A Visual Guide

Look for these signs of quality construction when evaluating upholstered furniture:

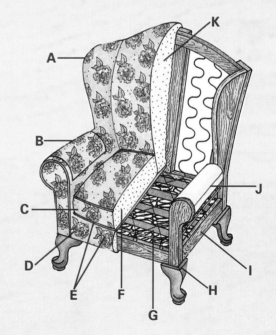

A. Durable, stain-resistant fabric.

B. Protective covers for arms.

C. Snugly fitting cushions.

D. Threads secure and trimmed.

E. Fabric patterns match.

F. Solid foam or down cushions.

G. Coil springs anchored to steel bands.

H. Reinforced joints.

I. Hardwood frame.

J. Padded edges.

K. Durable padding material.

Frames and Springs

The frame is the skeleton structure of a chair or sofa. It is a vital, but unseen, part of the furniture. The frame of an upholstered piece should be constructed of a strong hardwood, such as birch or maple. The wood should have been dried in a kiln to prevent warping. Look for joints heavily reinforced with dowels, corner blocks, and glue. Screws may also be used. (Nails or staples don't provide enough support.)

Springs are another important consideration. Coil springs are used to make high-quality furniture. Each spring is hand-tied and anchored to webbing or to steel bands at the back of the piece. Less expensive furniture uses the *convoluted spring*, which consists of zigzag strips of steel. Before purchasing, sit on the chair or sofa to test the "give" in the springs. They shouldn't strike the frame when bounced on lightly.

Padding and Cushions

Padding materials are used to cushion the frame, making upholstered furniture more comfortable. Similar materials are used to form or stuff cushions. Several types of fillings and padding are used today.

- Polyester and polyurethane foam are good materials that hold their shape well and resist moths and mildew. They are very durable and provide good support.
- Cotton and shredded foam compress over time.
- Down is the most expensive filling for cushions and gives a very soft feel.

Also look for features that can add extra durability. Loose back cushions and seat cushions give twice the wearing surface because they can be turned. Extra arm covers protect the arms of furniture, which tend to wear and show soil first.

Consumer Considerations

Alternatives to Buying New Furniture

Suppose you have an old sofa that you love but its covers have worn thin. Or suppose that a sofa has sentimental value but needs new padding. Do you have to buy a new piece of furniture? Not necessarily. Many people fix up the existing piece instead. This can be a wise choice if the piece has solid construction. You might get more years out of fixing up an older piece of furniture than from buying a newer piece.

Slipcovers. Slipcovers are shaped pieces of fabric that can be placed over furniture. They are made for everything from sofas to dining chairs. Some are ready-made pieces suitable for all furniture of a given size. Others are custom-made pieces tailored to a specific piece. Some people purchase or make two or three slipcovers, which they switch during the year for an easy design change.

Recovering. If you want a more permanent fix, you can go to an upholsterer to have the piece recovered.

Upholsterers offer a huge selection of fabric styles and patterns. This solution is more expensive than buying slipcovers, but a skilled worker can make the piece as good as new.

Reupholstering. Upholsterers use this approach to repair old furniture. They can fix frames, tighten springs, and replace padding. They usually recover the piece as well. This is the most expensive approach, but if the underlying frame is in good shape, you may find it worth the money.

Loose cushions may be stuffed with a block of polyurethane foam or a polyurethane core wrapped in polyester fibers, cotton, or down. Regardless of the padding used, you should not be able to feel the framework or springs through the upholstery. The fact that so much of the furniture construction is concealed by the outer covering makes selecting upholstered furniture difficult. Read labels carefully on the pieces you're considering.

Upholstery Fabrics and Materials

Upholstery fabrics are specially made for covering furniture. The major features that determine the suitability of an upholstery material are its appearance, feel, durability, color, pattern, and cost. Additional considerations may be the fabric's ability to resist fading and soil, along with its flammability. Upholstery fabrics are either woven or nonwoven. Tightly woven fabrics are the most durable choice for upholstered furniture.

When buying new upholstered furniture, it's often possible to choose the fabric. Generally, a store will offer many fabric choices. You can judge the quality of the fabric by looking at these factors.

- **Fabric Grade.** Upholstery fabrics are usually labeled by grades. Grade A is usually the most expensive fabric and Grade C the least. A higher grade doesn't necessarily indicate better quality, though. Expense depends on the cost of the fiber used, the construction method, and the difficulty of dyeing or printing the piece.

- **Color and Pattern.** How is color added to the fabric? Dyed threads that are woven to create a design will hold the color better than a design that's printed on the fabric.

- **Tightness of Weave.** Hold a sample of the fabric up to the light. Fabrics that allow less light to show through are woven more tightly and tend to give longer wear. Pull on opposite edges of the fabric. The threads of a good quality fabric will not be forced apart.

- **Texture.** Fabrics that have a texture, such as velvet or corduroy, may show more wear in spots. Flatter weaves wear more evenly. Check for pilling and other signs of wear by folding a fabric sample in half and rubbing the two sides together.

- **Fiber Content.** Check the label for the fiber content. Often upholstery fabrics are made from a blend of fibers, giving them some of the characteristics of both. Refer to Chapter 24 for the benefits and drawbacks of common fibers used in home textiles.

- **Stain Resistance.** Generally, fabrics made from natural fibers soil more easily but clean more easily. Synthetic fibers tend to resist soil more but may be harder to clean. Many upholstery fabrics are covered with a stain-resistant finish. This is often worth the extra cost.

- **Warranties.** Some manufacturers offer a warranty on their fabric. Learn what the warranty covers and how long it lasts.

Leather and vinyl are also used for upholstering. Although leather costs more, it gives a special look and feel. **See Fig. 26-11.** Well-made leather pieces are very durable, though stains, cuts, and scrapes can be a problem. Vinyl is durable, easy to clean, and much less expensive than leather. Some people don't care for it, however, because it can be very difficult to repair.

Fig. 26-11 Leather furniture is durable and, with proper care, will be attractive and comfortable for years.

Bed Construction

You spend about one-third of your life sleeping. A good bed supports your body as your muscles relax. If your body is not properly supported during sleep, your muscles may ache in the morning. A soft bed provides little support. For this reason, a firm bed is usually recommended, especially for people with back problems.

Generally speaking, an adult with a traditional bed should purchase a new mattress and springs every ten years. Evaluate bed frames as you would any other case goods. **See Fig. 26-12.** Use the following information to select a mattress and springs that will be comfortable and provide the support you need.

Mattresses and Springs

Choosing a mattress can be difficult because you can't see inside it. You must rely on labels and salespeople for much of your information. Stores often have cut-away models that show the interior construction of particular brands and models.

The most common mattress is the innerspring mattress. Its firmness and comfort are determined by a series of coil springs that vary in size, number, placement, wire thickness, and padding. A quality mattress should have at least 300 firmly anchored coils, good padding around each coil, and a tightly woven cover with a reinforced border to prevent sagging. The fabric must be fire-resistant.

Foam mattresses are popular choices for people with allergies. A foam mattress is about 6 in. (15 cm) thick. It's made of foam or plastic, with thousands of holes or cores cut in it. The more holes there are, the softer the mattress will be. Foam mattresses are light, distribute weight evenly, and rarely lose their shape.

The mattress of a bed rests on top of springs. The mattress should not be placed directly on the floor because air must circulate around it to keep it dry and free of mildew.

Fig. 26-12 A trundle bed is a great space saver in small bedrooms. The lower bed slides under the top one during the day to give more floor space. At night, that bed can be raised to the same height as the other.

Fig. 26-13 Futons look like a couch or chair during the day and transform into a bed at night. Modern futons have firm mattresses and quality frames to provide a comfortable night's sleep.

The size and number of springs determine their quality. *Box springs*—a series of coils attached to a base and then padded and covered—provide the most support, but they are also the most expensive. Less expensive coil springs are the same as box springs but are not padded and covered. Flat springs are attached to a frame and may have metal bands supporting them. Inexpensive flat springs provide the least support and often sag. Usually springs and mattresses are purchased as a set. Don't spend money on recovered and reprocessed mattress sets, however.

Water Beds

Some people find a water bed more comfortable and supportive than a standard mattress. When the heavy-duty plastic water bag is filled, it produces a mattress that conforms to the body's curves and gives good support. Water bed mattresses need to be heated.

A major disadvantage of water beds is their tremendous weight. A standard-size water bed weighs about 1,600 lbs. (726 kg). A strong foundation, as well as a special frame, is required to support it. Be sure that your home can support a water bed before you buy one. If you rent, check whether the landlord will allow water beds.

Futons

Another alternative to the traditional bed of mattress and springs is a futon. At night, a futon is a bed. During the day, it can be folded to serve as a sofa. **See Fig. 26-13.** For this reason, people can economize by buying a futon.

A futon has a wood or metal frame and one or more layers of mattresses. The highest quality futons come with a rope webbing, a 3-in. (7.6-cm) cotton mattress, and a 3-in. (7.6-cm) wool mattress. The webbing—firmly woven fabric strips that are interlaced—prevent the mattresses from falling between the slats of the frame.

Furniture in the Workplace

To a commercial furniture designer, a chair is not just a place to sit—it's a tool of someone's trade. It's as essential as any other equipment to a job well done. The same is true of a workstation. Concerns in commercial design are different from those you might use in judging home furnishings.

- **Ergonomics.** In some jobs, people spend most of their time in a chair behind a desk. Ergonomic designs can make the difference in their health and productivity. Office chairs with adjustable headrests and back supports ease stress on the neck and spine. Seats that tilt and swivel prevent possible injury from repeated twisting or stretching. In a meeting room, comfortable chairs and a table at the proper height contribute to productive discussions.

- **Efficiency.** Designers keep ease of care and repair in mind. Durable, stain-resistant fabrics and sturdy construction are more likely to stand up to daily use. Furnishings with long lifetimes are not only convenient, but also economical.

- **Accessibility.** Making public places accessible to people of different abilities is more than the law in the United States—it's also good business. Accessibility can be built into an existing design. For example, a computer workstation can have a desktop that can be raised or pulled out to accommodate a wheelchair.

- **Adaptability.** Designers try to meet as many needs as possible with the most useful, relevant features. Modular designs are favored for flexibility. Individual pieces can be used alone or combined in various ways for different situations. This quality grows more important as employers look for ways to save money.

Apply It!

Locate and photograph (with permission) a piece of office furniture at a business or public building in your community. Use the criteria described on this page to evaluate the furniture design. Recommend potential improvements and give reasons for each. Present your report to the class in a visual format.

Shopping & Caring for Furniture

Furniture, like other costly items, should be considered an investment. You don't want to waste your money on furnishings that won't last. Gather all the information you can before making a purchase. You can use your knowledge of materials and construction to help you choose durable, well-made pieces. Whatever your style preference, budget, or lifestyle, you have many options. Once you've made your purchase, take care of it. By maintaining your furniture, you protect your investment.

Shopping for Furniture

There are numerous ways to buy furniture for your home while sticking to a budget. You can choose among new or used pieces. You can also buy unfinished, unassembled, or modular furniture.

New Furniture. Try to shop for new furniture at reputable stores that carry brand names. Then you can be more assured of the quality of the furniture. Most manufacturers offer guarantees against flaws. At certain times of the year, most furniture stores reduce prices. You can cut the cost of new furniture by hundreds of dollars if you buy it on sale.

Used Furniture. Used furniture, especially case goods, can be a very good buy. The key is to check for signs of quality. Auctions, thrift shops, flea markets, estate sales, and garage sales are excellent sources of used furniture. Some stores specialize in used furniture. If you like the design of a piece, but not its finish or color, you can refinish or repaint it. Many products are available that give striking results.

Unfinished Furniture. Unfinished furniture has not been stained, varnished, or painted. **See Fig. 26-14.** Such pieces are usually less expensive than finished goods. They come in a wide variety of styles—and in different levels of quality. Use the same quality checks on unfinished pieces that you would on a finished product. If you do buy unfinished furniture, be sure to finish it right away to prevent the wood from becoming damaged or soiled.

Fig. 26-14 Unfinished furniture can be a good way to decorate a new home if the owner has the ability and time to finish the furniture.

Unassembled Furniture. Some stores offer ready-to-assemble furniture. These mass-produced pieces cost less than other furniture. Some pieces can be taken apart later for storage or moving. Many, however, require permanent gluing as part of the assembly process. Before buying this kind of furniture, look at an assembled model to make sure it will meet your needs. You may want to review the assembly instructions, too, to make sure that they are clear.

Modular Furniture. Modular furniture comes in sections that can be stacked or arranged in a variety of ways. Perhaps you've seen wall or storage units made up of interchangeable sections. Modular furniture is great for people who move often. Since the modules can be arranged in different ways, they can be made to fit in different rooms. Some modular furniture needs assembly. Follow the guidelines for buying unassembled furniture. The quality of modular furniture varies greatly. Check what you are getting. Are the pieces made of hardwood or less costly particleboard? What type of finish is used? Will pieces withstand the amount of use you'll give them?

Caring for Furniture

Both upholstered pieces and case goods require careful treatment and regular maintenance to keep them looking good and to make them last. Most manufacturers include instructions for the proper care of each piece of furniture. **See Fig. 26-15.**

Upholstered Furniture

All fabrics tend to fade if exposed to the sun for a long time. Position upholstered furniture away from sunny windows. If that isn't possible, close the window coverings.

Dirt and soil can damage fabric. Regular vacuuming of upholstery can prolong its life. Periodic dry cleaning by a specialist is recommended, or use a dry-cleaning foam.

No matter how careful you are, accidents occur sometimes. Remove spots immediately so the stain doesn't set.

Case Goods

Dust and soil are abrasive and can scratch a fine wood finish. Regular dusting will help. Waxes and polishes should be applied occasionally to provide a protective finish. Don't wax more than once every few months, however, to prevent wax build-up. Use only polishes recommended for furniture.

Occasionally, cuts and scratches occur on case goods. Some home remedies are helpful for blemishes on wood. Minor scratches can be treated with wax sticks. Choose a wax stick that matches the color of the furniture. Rub the wax into the scratch, then smooth the wax with a soft cloth. Finally, apply a polish.

If watermarks appear after a wet glass has been left on an unwaxed surface, use fine steel wool to gently rub in wax or polish. Another method is to place a thick blotter over the ring and press it with a warm iron until the ring disappears. The best solution, however, is prevention. Place glasses on coasters instead of putting them directly on wood furniture.

Fig. 26-15 Look at the beautiful finish on the furniture in this room. It clearly is well maintained.

Furnishing Your Home

Furniture is a major investment. It's easy to fall in love with the look or style of a piece and want to buy it. However, there are other considerations. Ask yourself if the piece is functional—will it serve your needs? Will it last? Will it fit in the space and the design plan that you have?

Since furniture is expensive, accumulating it is usually a gradual process. Start with an overall plan and set priorities for what is most important to buy first. For instance, is a new sofa a priority? Is furnishing a home office more important? If so, you might prefer putting a slipcover over an older loveseat and spend your money on a workstation and a good desk chair.

You can buy less expensive furniture, which allows you to furnish a home more quickly. Bear in mind, though, that less expensive items may need to be replaced sooner. If you buy more costly pieces, you will have to get by with less, but what you have should last longer. Which strategy is best for you?

Looking for versatile pieces is one way to compromise. You may be able to buy fewer items if they are **multipurpose furniture**—pieces that serve more than one need. A sofa bed can turn a living room into a guest bedroom. A table can be used for dining and for paperwork.

Improvising is another way to stretch your furniture dollars. You've probably seen shelves made from bricks and boards. A simple desk can be constructed by placing a flat door across a pair of filing cabinets. Outdoor furniture is yet another option. You can use it indoors now and outdoors later. See Fig. 26-16.

Fig. 26-16 Some outdoor furniture is so attractive and well made that it can be used as casual indoor furniture.

Profile of a Furniture Showroom Salesperson

A furniture showroom salesperson helps customers buy furniture. These workers explain furniture construction and design features and show various models and colors. Jobs exist in a variety of environments, ranging from large retail stores to smaller shops.

Education & Training

- A high school diploma is required. Advanced degrees are needed to advance to management positions.
- Courses in business, interior design, and furniture construction are very helpful.
- Retail sales experience is a plus.

Skills & Aptitudes

- Strong people skills are necessary.
- The ability to complete transactions and the related paperwork carefully and accurately is required.
- Thorough knowledge of the different product offerings is vital.
- The ability to assist customers with CAD-generated choices is increasingly important.

Furniture Showroom Salesperson
Zack Danz

Looking back, I'd say my interest in furniture began with my grandmother. When I visited her as a child, she told me fascinating stories about an old table that had been in the family for over a hundred years and about a chest that her grandfather hand-carved. Now my folks have those same pieces of furniture in their home, blended with new ones like the ones that I sell today as a furniture showroom salesperson.

I'm amazed by the huge number of furniture options people have today. Some people want pieces that reproduce older styles. Others prefer modern designs. I like helping customers find what they want.

While I was in high school, my interest in furniture led me to take a couple of classes in housing and interior design. What I learned comes in handy in the store when we create room arrangements.

My first job in this business was part-time in a large retail store's furniture department. Now I work full-time for a home furnishings store. To stay current, I take courses and workshops in furniture construction, preservation, and interior design. I have to know about furniture construction and safety, as well as appropriate care. You never know when you're going to have to talk about the hardness or softness of woods, or the security of a table's joints. People come in with budget limits in mind, so I also have to understand how different financing arrangements can work for them.

I've been learning to use CAD software that helps customers see what an upholstered piece looks like in the fabrics available. I put the sofa or chair on the screen, the customer chooses a favorite fabric, and with the click of a few keys, there it is. This really helps customers make decisions quickly.

If I come across as caring and helpful, the customer is happy and so is my supervisor. Receiving good sales commissions makes me feel good too.

Design Portfolio

1. Research how sofas are constructed. Create a brochure that highlights the features a person should look for to find a quality sofa.

2. Suppose a client asks you to recommend furniture selections for a family room that will include a home entertainment center and play space for a five-year-old child. Locate and price furniture that meets the client's needs. Use CAD software to create a design showing how you would arrange the pieces.

Review & Activities

Chapter Summary

- The most commonly used materials for furniture construction are wood, metal, glass, and plastic.
- Shoppers must look at **joints** and finishes to determine the quality of furniture construction.
- Details of the frames, springs, padding, cushions, and fabric reveal the quality of upholstered furniture.
- Checking the quality of a bed involves looking at the mattress and springs.
- Consumers have a number of options for buying furniture.
- Properly caring for pieces helps furniture retain its value.

Checking Your Understanding

1. Name an advantage and a disadvantage of each of the following wood uses: **veneer**, solid wood, **particleboard**.
2. What are the advantages and disadvantages of metal furniture?
3. Why should you buy glass furniture that's been *tempered*?
4. What are the benefits of plastic furniture?
5. What is a **joint**? Why are some joints reinforced?
6. What is the difference between a stain and a varnish?
7. What kinds of springs are best for upholstered furniture? Why?
8. What are three factors to use in judging textiles used in upholstered furniture?
9. How can a cutaway model help you when shopping for a mattress?
10. Is a futon a piece of **multipurpose furniture**? Why or why not?

Thinking Critically

1. **Making Decisions.** Suppose you were choosing furniture for a screened-in porch that is covered but sometimes receives wind and rain. What material would you choose for the furniture? Why?

2. **Identifying Alternatives.** Which characteristic would be most important in the choice of upholstery fabric for a family room sofa? Why?

3. **Establishing Priorities.** If you were furnishing an apartment on a limited budget, what furniture might you buy new? Used? Unfinished? Unassembled? Give reasons for your answers.

Applying Your Knowledge

1. **Furniture Display.** Using images you obtain from print sources or the Internet, create a report that compares and contrasts the advantages and disadvantages of at least three hardwoods and three softwoods.

2. **Analyzing Case Goods.** Using an example of case goods in your home, sketch the piece and identify the locations and type of each joint. Summarize the strong and the weak points of the construction.

3. **Comparing Finishes.** Research the application of and care for three different types of wood finishes. Give an oral presentation detailing your findings.

4. **Comparing Upholstery Fabrics.** Obtain samples of synthetic, natural, and blended upholstery fabrics. Find out about the care and cleaning instructions and the cost per yard of each fabric. Compare the various fabrics and identify which you would choose for different pieces of furniture and why.

5. **Designing Furniture.** Design a multipurpose piece of furniture that would be useful for a college student. Sketch the furniture being used for at least two uses.

Design Challenge

A couple with one young child has asked you to make furniture recommendations for their two-bedroom apartment with an eat-in kitchen. They don't want to spend too much on furniture because they are saving to buy a house.

1. Create a list of furniture needs for each room in the apartment.

2. Find two options for each piece of furniture, considering quality, construction, materials, and price.

3. Select the pieces of furniture you think the family should use.

4. Arrange the recommended furniture on a floor plan.

5. Place the completed furniture recommendations and floor plan in your design portfolio.

Choosing Lighting & Accessories

Objectives

- Explain the function of different kinds of lighting.

- Describe different types of light sources and fixtures.

- Summarize guidelines for choosing appropriate lighting.

- Plan lighting and select lighting fixtures.

- Suggest ways to use accessories to personalize an interior design.

- Describe how to display accessories.

Vocabulary

- direct lighting
- indirect lighting
- incandescent light
- halogen bulb
- fluorescent light
- fiber optic light
- light emitting diode (LED)
- downlighting
- uplighting
- valance lighting
- cove lighting
- soffit lighting
- wall washers
- cornice lighting

Have you ever noticed how lighting can affect your mood? Imagine a light bringing to life a brilliantly colored painting. Recall how a sunny room in December makes you forget about the winter wind. Lighting can turn an ordinary room into a work of art. Add your own special accessories, and you've created a welcoming space.

Lighting Rooms

Not only can you set a mood with light, you can create subtle drama with light. Properly used, lighting can emphasize the best features of a room and your furnishings. But if a room is too dark or too overlit, it will appear unattractive, no matter how beautifully decorated it is.

Lighting also affects the way a room can be used. For example, if the only light in a room is a dim bulb in an overhead fixture, chances are you won't be reading in that room at night. Inadequate lighting can cause eyestrain, affect your comfort level, and result in accidents. Proper lighting contributes much to everyone's comfort and safety.

In the daytime, lighting can come from sunlight. The sun's intensity depends on the time of day, the season, and the weather. This natural light is also affected by the number, size, and location of windows; the kind of window treatments; and the orientation of the room to sunlight.

As you read in Chapter 18, sunlight consists of a mixture of colors. The color of sunlight varies with the time of day and orientation of the room. Afternoon light from the south and west has a "warm" cast, toward the red end of the spectrum. Light from the north is "cool," which makes colors seem bluish.

Of course, at night, on cloudy days, or in rooms without windows, you must depend on artificial light. Some lighting fixtures provide **direct lighting**—light that shines on specific areas. **Indirect lighting** is reflected off ceilings and walls. It's also more diffused, or softer, than direct light.

Fig. 27-1 Attractive rooms combine lighting from different sources, such as this room's natural light from the windows and artificial light from a table lamp.

The Purposes of Lighting

Lighting professionals identify three main types of lighting in a home—general, task, and accent. Rooms need at least two of these types. **See Fig. 27-1.** Understanding the nature and purpose of each type of lighting, as well as the light fixture options available, will help you make effective lighting choices.

General Lighting. Also known as background or ambient lighting, general lighting provides just enough light so that you can see everything in a room. It also helps soften the shadows and harsh contrasts that can be caused by other lighting. General lighting is most effective when both direct and indirect sources of light are combined.

Task Lighting. Tasks such as reading require more intense light than general lighting provides. Task lighting focuses light on the area where it is most needed—for instance, a desk lamp illuminating a desk top. To provide the best task light, shades should be shaped so that more light is directed downward than upward.

Accent Lighting. A light aimed directly on a specific object to create a dramatic effect is called accent lighting. Accent lighting can be used, for example, to highlight a special painting. For the most dramatic effects, accent lighting should be three times brighter than general lighting. You can achieve that with increased bulb wattage or a light-focusing fixture.

What's in a Bulb?

The light you get from any fixture depends on the bulb used. Bulbs are categorized by their type and their wattage. The higher the wattage, the greater the intensity of light. Some fixtures can be used safely only at a certain level of wattage—check the labels on the fixture. Different bulbs produce different effects. Three-way bulbs allow a user to select from three levels of light. A dimmer switch allows the user to lower the light level and vary the mood of the room. The sources of artificial light are incandescent, halogen, fluorescent, fiber optics, and light emitting diodes.

Incandescent Light. Light produced by electricity passing through a tungsten filament in a glass bulb is called **incandescent light**. Light from an incandescent bulb tends to be warm and flattering. Bulbs are available in a variety of shapes and are either clear or frosted. A frosted coating reduces glare and produces a softer light. Small, clear bulbs—often used in chandeliers—produce a sparkling effect. Reflector bulbs have a silver or aluminum reflective coating inside that directs the light forward, giving better beam control. Reflector bulbs put approximately double the light on a subject as a regular bulb of the same wattage. Incandescent bulbs are available in 15 to 300 watts.

The Impact of Technology

LEDs Light the Future

Light emitting diodes, or LEDs, are already far more efficient and longer lasting than incandescent bulbs. In the future, they could also be brighter.

A diode is a semiconductor made of two materials bonded together. Each material has been altered by adding atoms of another substance. That addition gives the material either a negative or a positive charge. The negatively charged material is hooked to a battery's negative terminal and the positive material to the positive one. The pull between the opposite charges is strong enough that some electrons in the negatively charged atoms "jump" into the structure of the positive atoms.

The energy released by the transfer of electrons takes the form of visible light, which is trapped and concentrated inside small, sturdy plastic bulbs. Currently, LEDs don't give off much light—most of it is absorbed by the materials. In tests, a change in diode design allowed the bulbs to capture more light particles, boosting usable light by over 50 percent. Newer organic light emitting diodes (OLEDs) have greater surface area contact, making them more efficient and more adaptable. With improvements to the technology, efficient LEDs may light the way to the future.

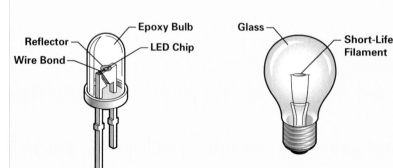

Tech Trends

Learn more about current and possible future uses of LEDs. What are their advantages compared to incandescent and fluorescent bulbs? What improvements are needed to make LEDs more practical?

Fig. 27-2 Track lighting gives flexibility to a lighting design.

Halogen Bulbs. A special type of incandescent light is produced by a **halogen bulb**—a bulb containing pressurized halogen gas, which makes it more efficient than a regular incandescent bulb. Halogen bulbs are usually smaller than regular bulbs, but they produce a whiter, more intense light. **See Fig. 27-2.** Although halogen bulbs are more expensive, they also last longer. Halogen bulbs have disadvantages. They become very hot when in use and can cause serious burns. A typical halogen bulb burns at 1000°F (450°C).

Fluorescent Light. A visible light produced when chemicals inside a sealed glass tube transform ultraviolet rays is called **fluorescent light**. Fluorescent bulbs produce various color casts, and some give off the true color created by natural sunlight. Fluorescent bulbs are usually long, straight tubes, but they may also be circular, U-shaped, or shaped like regular incandescent bulbs. Fluorescent tubes produce more light than the same wattage incandescent bulbs. Also look for the new, compact fluorescent bulbs (CFLs). They screw into regular incandescent lightbulb sockets. They cost more than incandescent bulbs but will last up to ten times as long. CFLs can create electronic interference and shouldn't be used with dimmers or electronic timers, however.

Fiber Optics. Fiber optic cable, consisting of hair-fine strands of glass, was developed for clear, high-speed communication. However, it's also being used for lighting. Currently, **fiber optic light** is used primarily in museums and for displays because it emits no heat and no ultraviolet rays. Light flows through the glass strands and is focused at the other end.

Light Emitting Diodes (LEDs). LEDs are considered by many to be the next major evolution in lighting. In each **light emitting diode** is a silicon "chip" about the size of a grain of salt and made of crystals. An LED bulb can last 100,000 hours or more. That's ten times longer than compact fluorescent bulbs and 133 times longer than incandescent bulbs. Residential use of LED technology is just getting started.

Types of Lighting Fixtures

The lighting fixtures in a home may be structural or nonstructural. Structural lighting fixtures are built into the home during construction or remodeling. Nonstructural lighting fixtures can be replaced or moved from one location to another fairly easily.

Structural Lighting

Structural, or built-in, lighting fixtures and their wiring are usually hidden from view. They are also permanent. **Figure 27-3 on the following page** shows examples of structural lighting that can be used in homes.

Fig. 27-3

Structural Lighting

A Visual Guide

Strip lights consist of a row of incandescent bulbs around the top or sides of a mirror. They are usually used in bathrooms or dressing areas.

Cove lighting is a concealed light source that directs light upward toward the ceiling. Cove lighting can give a room the appearance of added height.

Wall washers are recessed ceiling lights that spread light over a wall from ceiling to floor. For best effects, the fixtures should be placed the same distance apart and 2 ft. to 4 ft. (61 cm to 122 cm) from the wall (the higher the ceiling, the greater the distance).

Luminous ceiling panels consist of fluorescent tubes placed above plastic panels. They may cover all or part of a ceiling and provide good general lighting in kitchens, workrooms, and baths.

Downlights direct a beam of light from the ceiling downward. They may be used for accent lighting or general lighting. Downlights are set flush in the ceiling.

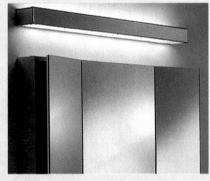

Valance lighting consists of a light source (usually a fluorescent tube) mounted over a window and hidden by the window valance. The valance is open at the top and bottom, allowing light to be directed both upward and downward.

Cornice lighting is mounted near the junction of the wall and ceiling and directs light downward. Cornice lighting is often used to highlight wall hangings or wall groupings.

Soffit lighting is enclosed in a box-like structure that directs light downward. Usually, a plastic panel at the bottom of the soffit diffuses the light. Soffit lighting is often used over kitchen and bathroom sinks.

Nonstructural Lighting

Nonstructural lighting consists of fixtures that can be moved or replaced. Nonstructural lighting includes various ceiling and wall fixtures, as well as portable lamps. Most nonstructural fixtures use incandescent, halogen, or compact fluorescent bulbs. Only buy light fixtures that have the Underwriters Laboratories (UL) seal, showing that the fixture meets safety guidelines. **See Fig. 27-4.**

When choosing nonstructural lighting, consider the following:

- Ceiling and wall fixtures are commonly used for general lighting. The fixtures come in a variety of styles ranging from an elegant chandelier to a modern hanging pendant to a wall sconce.

- Track lighting consists of a series of light fixtures called cans attached to a strip mounted on the ceiling. Usually these fixtures are spotlights that can be swiveled, rotated, and angled toward specific areas. They can be moved to different locations along the track. The light cans should be aimed at a 30-degree angle to prevent light from shining in anyone's eyes and to avoid disturbing reflections and glare.

- Portable canister spotlights can be placed on the floor to produce accent uplighting on specific objects. Some people use special bulbs in floor canisters to provide growing light for large plants.

- Lamps are very versatile forms of portable lighting—both direct and indirect—as well as task lighting. A well-equipped lighting store will carry table lamps, floor lamps, clip-on lights, mini-reflector spotlights, and desk lamps. An endless variety of lamp styles and shades are available.

Fig. 27-4

Decorating with Light

How much light is enough light? That depends on the purpose of the room. A kitchen or workshop needs brighter light than a family room. Generally five portable lamps can nicely light a 12 ft. x 20 ft. (3.7 m x 6 m) room.

Designing with light, though, is much more than just having enough light. Good lighting is usually made up of a number of effects that create a balance between areas of illumination and subtle pools of shadow. One of the biggest lighting mistakes is to overlight a room. On the other hand, too much contrast between bright and dark areas of the room tires the eyes. The decorating in a room will need to be considered when designing the lighting. Light is reflected by smooth surfaces and light colors and it is absorbed by textured fabrics and dark colors. Combinations of structural and nonstructural lighting that produce downlighting, uplighting, wallwashing, and accent lighting will help create the look you want.

Downlighting, the most common type of lighting, is usually accomplished with a ceiling fixture or one of the types of structural lighting. If there is only one downlight in the center of the room, you can end up with a gloomy appearance because the floor is well-lit but the ceiling and walls are dark. Combinations of track lighting and ceiling fixtures can help solve this problem. **Uplighting**, or reflecting light off the ceiling, can be achieved with many of the structural lighting fixtures, wall sconces, or tall floor lamps. Uplights enhance a sense of height, making a room appear spacious.

Wall-washing can make a room seem wider. To create dramatic shadows with wall washers, mount the lights closer to the wall, only 6 in. to 12 in. (15 cm to 30 cm) away, and space the lights evenly. Direct the lights downward to create pools of light.

When decorating with light, accent lighting shouldn't be confused with task lighting. Accent lighting highlights chosen features of a room, such as a painting or a stone fireplace. Accent lighting works best when the fixture and bulb remain hidden, so recessed ceiling fixtures or hidden upright can lights are ideal.

"Painting with light" is a talent you can master once you learn the basics. Each room of the house has its own lighting needs. There are even software lighting design programs that will help you plan how to light a room for the effect you want.

Entryways, Hallways, and Stairways

The entryway is the first introduction your guests will have to your home, so you want to make the lighting engaging and welcoming. A pendant light that hangs from the ceiling is a good choice. Hang it high enough to be out of everyone's way. You'll find dozens of attractive fixtures at a lighting store. If the entryway is large enough to accommodate a small table, a table lamp can be added to cast a warm glow.

Cove or bracket lighting achieves nice effects in hallways and helps provide a feeling of spaciousness. Accent lighting could illuminate artwork or family photos on the walls.

Lighting for safety is very important in the entryway, hallways, and stairway of a home. To prevent accidents, stairs should be lit at the top and bottom, with switches provided in both places. For safety in hallways, lighting fixtures need to be placed every 8 ft. to 10 ft. (2.4 m to 3 m). It's also an important safety precaution to keep light from causing a glare or shining directly into anyone's eyes. Recessed downlights are a good solution.

Living Room and Family Room

Consider all of the uses these rooms get and you'll understand the variety of lighting you'll need. A combination of structural and nonstructural lighting achieves the best effects. General lighting will work wonders when entertaining or watching TV. Dimmer controls allow you to pick the light level you want. Wall washers or valance lighting lend a dramatic flair to the room, or track lighting could be used as accent lighting to show off your favorite artwork. Upright can lights placed on the floor would spotlight plants and cast dramatic shadows on the wall.

Task lighting is needed for reading or working on projects. **See Fig. 27-5.** The ideal reading light in a living room or family room is a floor lamp placed to the right or left of your shoulder and slightly behind so it casts a beam on the seat of your favorite reading chair. Use a high-wattage bulb or choose a three-way bulb so that you can adjust the light level to the need. The bottom of the shade should be at eye level to reduce glare. Select a lamp style that works well with the room and add a dark shade to reduce overall light or a sheer lamp shade for maximum output.

Fig. 27-5 Task lighting is used in reading and study areas throughout the home.

Fig. 27-6 These four pendant lights add to the room's mood as well as serve their lighting purpose.

Dining Room

Dining room lights need to be attractive as well as functional. **See Fig. 27-6.** A chandelier or pendant light is used most often. Choose fixtures that work well together and complement the furniture. Track lighting can provide lighting accents. Cornice lighting can illuminate wall decorations. Wall sconces could set off a buffet or built-in cabinet. The most common lighting mistake in the dining room is to select a light fixture that looks out of scale. The rule of thumb for the appropriate size is to pick a chandelier that is no less than 6 in. to 12 in. (15 cm to 30 cm) smaller than the width of the table. The fixture should hang no more than 30 in. (76 cm) above the tabletop.

Kitchen

A large ceiling fixture or luminous ceiling panels will supply plenty of general downlighting. With only an overhead light, though, you may find that you're working in your own shadow at the sink or range. Soffit lighting can direct the light where needed. Small fluorescent lights under the cabinets put task light on the countertops.

Bedroom

An overhead light from a recessed fixture, a ceiling fixture, or a light that is part of a ceiling fan will take care of general room needs. In addition, a bedside light is a must for people who like to read in bed. To avoid having the light shine in the eyes, the bottom of the lamp shade should be at eye level when the person is reading.

Bathroom

A ceiling fixture or recessed downlights can provide overall room light. Add lights around the bathroom mirror to provide task lighting. To avoid shadows, use strip lights on either side or across the top of the mirror.

Lighting That Sells

Retail sales lighting is a kind of advertising. In order to get consumers to buy, commercial designers do more than shed light on merchandise. Through tailored strategies, they put the entire shopping experience "in its best light."

- **Supermarkets.** Fluorescent bulbs produce a bright, white light that shows off the natural colors of flowers and foods. However, food safety and quality can suffer from the added heat and ultraviolet radiation. Full spectrum bulbs use a wider range of rays to produce equal but less damaging light.

- **Department Stores.** Lighting invites shoppers even before they leave their car. Outdoor lights are located to provide a sense of security at night. By day, distinctive fixtures enhance the store's image. Inside, neon signs and brightly colored, blinking LEDs embedded in floor tiles bring a sense of high-tech fun to the shopping experience.

- **Billboards.** Billboard lighting has been criticized for contributing to light pollution, or "skyglow." Extremely bright lights increase glare and reduce contrast, making the advertisement harder to read. Instead, designers are setting bulbs in reflectors and louvers. Both of these features can be adjusted to focus lighting on specific areas and to adapt to changing advertisements.

- **Searchlights.** Few attention-getting techniques surpass a searchlight sweeping the sky. Powerful beams can cover up to 40 miles, with a narrow focus for clear nights or a wider one to compensate for fog or haze. Some lights rotate in a cloverleaf pattern. Others dazzle with the interplay of four beams simultaneously.

Apply It!

Imagine that you are designing the lighting for an indoor craft show. The show will include both demonstrations and works for sale. What facts do you need to know in order to choose the best lighting? How will this information affect your design decisions?

Fig. 27-7 Programmable lighting controls allow homeowners to present just the right balance of light in a room.

Lighting Controls

You may find as you arrange the lights in a room that the way to achieve the perfect balance is by dimming some lights and turning up others. In order to recall those level settings easily, you need lighting controls. A sophisticated dimming system allows you to create and save multiple preset lighting scenes. **See Fig. 27-7.** You could program the living room lights to dim to just the right level for watching a DVD on the home entertainment system or brighten the room for a family card game. In addition to automated systems, there are dimmers that allow you to manually adjust the level of light you want in a room.

Saving Energy with Lighting

On a typical energy bill, lighting accounts for 10 to 15 percent. Much of that is unnecessary consumption due to lights left on in unused rooms or the use of inefficient incandescent bulbs. Turning off the lights when you leave a room seems like an easy habit anyone could develop, but technology can help handle forgetfulness. Occupancy sensors can detect activity within a room and switch off the lights if no activity is detected. Occupancy sensors operate either by ultrasonic, which detects sound, or infrared, which detects heat and motion. Motion sensors are ideal for homes with children or others who may have trouble reaching a light. Motion sensors on outdoor lights are an energy-efficient way to have lights for security and safety without having to keep a light burning.

Incandescent lights are the most power hungry. If using incandescent lights, choose reflector bulbs for energy savings. A 50-watt reflector bulb can put as much light on an object as a 100-watt regular bulb. A better choice, however, is a compact fluorescent bulb using about 75 percent less energy while producing the same amount of illumination. These bulbs also last about ten times longer than incandescent bulbs. High-efficiency fixtures that use fluorescent light tubes are another alternative. They are often found in kitchens, laundry rooms, basements, and garages.

As the cost of LED bulbs drops, LEDs may become the most economical type of lighting to choose. An LED bulb currently has ten white light LEDs mounted in a standard light bulb base. It uses less than 1.5 watts of electricity.

Accessories

After you've finished selecting the furniture and lighting for a room, the next step is choosing accessories. These personal touches make it your home. They also tell your guests something about you. Accessories are the items that give a room personality. See Fig. 27-8.

There are endless possibilities for accessories. Maybe you have a collection of sports memorabilia you want to display. Perhaps you like plants and floral arrangements. It doesn't matter whether the objects are sophisticated or simple, elegant or rustic. What matters is that they mean a lot to you. What is important, though, is learning how to display your treasures in a way that shows them off while complementing the room. Although accessories are considered decorative, they can also be functional. A room divider, for example, separates living space, while its design makes a personal statement.

Wall Decorations

Paintings, posters, tapestries, prints, and even sculptures can be found adorning the walls of many homes. Pictures and other items hung on the walls give a room a warm, personal look. See Fig. 27-9. Wall mirrors make a space look larger while adding elegance. Wall clocks serve both design and functional purposes. A shelf display of brightly colored bottles sets a casual tone. A row of thick volumes of poetry might set a more formal mood.

When planning wall decorations, keep these basic principles in mind.

- Hang items approximately at eye level for most people. When hanging shelves and baskets, place them high enough to avoid being bumped by anyone.

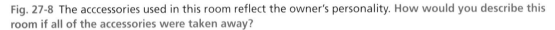

Fig. 27-8 The acccessories used in this room reflect the owner's personality. How would you describe this room if all of the accessories were taken away?

Fig. 27-9 This room's design is accented by well-chosen accessories that also serve to harmonize the space.

- Consider the proportion between the wall decoration, the wall, and nearby furniture. A single, small item will look lost on a large bare wall, but it might be just right over a small end table. The rule of thumb is that the art should not be wider than the piece of furniture under it and should be no smaller than half the piece's length.

- If the wall has a highly patterned background, use simple wall decorations, such as a mirror in a plain frame. If you want to hang a busy picture against patterned wallpaper, select a wide mat— a white or colored border between the picture and the frame.

- For art, pick a frame that complements both the room and the piece of art.

- Position a mirror where it will create an illusion of space and depth and where it will reflect something pleasing. For example, hang a mirror on the wall opposite a fireplace and everyone in the room can enjoy the glow of the fire.

- Use lighting to enhance the color and texture of wall decorations. The light shouldn't distort the colors or create glare on the item. Avoid fluorescent lights because they emit UV rays that can damage art. To avoid overheating artwork, use lighting of no more than 25 watts.

- Choose hanging hardware appropriate for the weight of each piece.

Wall Groupings

If you don't have a large item to hang on a large wall, create a grouping, such as several related prints or a collection of related objects. You can even group different subjects by using color to create a unified look. If you're working with pictures or photographs, frame them similarly and put the same color mat around them.

When creating a grouping, use an uneven number of items for a more pleasing arrangement. **See Fig. 27-10.** Arrange the items into a geometric shape, such as a rectangle, oval, or triangle. Position the pieces so there is one strong vertical or horizontal line in the grouping. If you want to add height to a room, use vertical arrangements. Use horizontal arrangements to add width to the room. The midpoint of the grouping should be at eye level. Balance light and dark colors throughout the grouping.

The space between the items is important, too. If the space is too narrow, the items lose their individuality. If the space is too wide, the group does not appear cohesive.

Before you start pounding nails in the wall, figure out the most pleasing way to arrange the items. Software drawing programs are a very convenient way to experiment until you achieve the look you want. There are also two simple methods you can use without a computer.

Method 1

1. Collect the items you want to group, trace their outlines on paper, and cut them out.
2. Tape the paper silhouettes on the wall, trying out different arrangements to see which is most appealing.
3. Insert the nails or hangers through the paper, remove the paper, and hang the wall decorations.

Fig. 27-10 Examine each wall grouping. **Explain why each of these different groupings works well.**

Decorating with Plants

Live plants are not only attractive, but can add to the health of your environment. They give off oxygen, making them natural air purifiers. However, because they are living things, the room where they are placed must meet each plant's particular need for heat, humidity, and sunlight. Also, plants need nurturing: food, water, and regular inspection. Some plants are poisonous. They should be kept away from children and pets. Here are some ways to make the most of plants:

Apply the elements and principles of design. Drape the long lines of creeping ivy over a tall bookshelf, for example. Add variety and unity to a Southwestern décor with a brightly blooming cactus against an adobe wall.

Be creative with containers. Pots are made in a range of materials, from porcelain to wicker. Consider nontraditional containers, like an old soup tureen or a plastic-lined cowboy boot. Use a plant stand to fill a bare corner.

Plant an indoor herb garden. Fresh herbs add color, texture, and aroma to a room design as well as a recipe. Dill is delicate and feathery. Sage is dusty green with hints of purple. Nasturtium's edible blossoms range from bright red to deep yellow. Choose herbs that suit your decorating and cooking style.

Method 2
1. Piece together newspaper to create the size of the wall space.
2. Lay the paper on the floor and arrange the wall decorations until you achieve a grouping that is balanced in size, shape, and weight.
3. Trace their outlines on the paper and tape the paper to the wall. Insert the nails or hangers through the paper, remove the paper, and hang the items.

Care of Wall Decorations

Hang paintings and other decorations away from sources of dirt or damage. Sunlight can damage photographs and artwork over time. Special UV-coated glass can help protect images, but even behind UV glass art and photographs will fade after years of sun exposure. Always hang treasured pieces or family heirlooms out of direct sunlight.

Mats on artwork can become dingy over time. You can learn how to cut mat board yourself or take the art to a framing shop to have the work done. Ask for acid-free mat board.

Fabric wall hangings, quilts, and other woven or cloth decorations may discolor if exposed to direct sunlight. They also require periodic cleaning to maintain their attractive appearance.

Additional Accessories

Many other types of accessories can be used to enhance a room's design. You don't have to search for expensive items to display. It's more important to choose items that reflect your personality and interests. Here are just a few ideas of accessories you might display:

- Family photographs, souvenirs, and other personal mementos.
- Simple, everyday objects such as candlesticks, bowls, baskets, and vases.
- Natural items, such as interesting rocks or branches.
- A small, dramatic piece of sculpture.
- A stack of your favorite books next to a sofa or on the fireplace mantel along with some candles and plants.

Try mixing different kinds of items and styles to achieve an eclectic look. For example, pair unlikely style partners such as antique with modern or rough with shiny. Accessories are also more interesting when placed in groupings. As with wall decorations, arrange the objects in uneven numbers for visual interest. Try organizing them by pattern, color, or theme. **See Fig. 27-11.** Careful thought will result in an interesting effect rather than an appearance of clutter. Think of tables or shelves in the home as an empty canvas just waiting to be filled with interesting colors, shapes, and textures. If you're unsure what goes together, color is a good guide. Then vary the heights. Place low objects toward the front and the taller ones in the back.

A decorative screen can serve as a backdrop to embellish a room's décor or to divide an area. Screens come in a variety of designs.

Spruce up a sofa with pillows to add softness to a room. Choose an accent color that picks up other accessories around the room to tie it all together. Rich fabrics that would be too overwhelming on large furniture can be introduced on decorative pillows. Use a variety of fabrics or choose pillows in your favorite color and vary the texture of the fabrics. A throw can add color and warmth.

Fig. 27-11 This painted armoire gives the illusion of additional accessories. **What would be the benefits and drawbacks of such a piece?**

Using Lighting & Accessories

Lighting and accessories are vital parts of design. You can use lighting to enhance your design by highlighting pieces of furniture or structural details that you want to emphasize. It can enliven colors and take away shadows. You can also use lighting to help display your accessories—the family pictures or collections or plants that you treasure and that help make your home reflect your personality. Those accessories are probably not the most important feature of a design. Still, they help give a home character. See Fig. 27-12.

Remember, too, that safety is a factor in choosing lighting and accessories. With many rooms, lighting should be accessible when a person first enters. Place a switch that controls ceiling lights or a lamp just inside each entrance to give people the chance to light the room immediately. Avoid placing accessories in locations that could cause accidents, such as in walking paths or at head level.

Fig. 27-12 This room exemplifies good use of lighting and accessories. Identify all the different types of lighting used and how each accessory complements the room's design.

Profile of a Lighting Specialist

Lighting specialists assist customers with their home or office lighting needs. They help the customer choose the lighting that will be most effective and comfortable in a particular area. A lighting specialist is familiar with the types of light needed for various activities, and can help in designing lighting for a new home or adding accent lighting to an existing home.

Education & Training

- A high school diploma is required.
- Courses in electrical or electronic engineering are required for management positions.

Skills & Aptitudes

- A knowledge of the properties of light and how light is best suited to different activities is useful.
- Sales experience is beneficial.
- Good questioning skills and problem-solving abilities are a must.

Lighting Specialist
Rod Walker

As a lighting specialist I visit the homes of clients to evaluate their lighting needs. The houses may be well built and the furniture of good quality but it may not have areas with sufficient light for specific tasks, like reading or working on a computer.

An important part of my job is to discuss my clients' lifestyles and then advise them on the amount and type of lighting they need for their various activities. As with furniture, lighting should contribute both to the overall effect of a room and to the comfort of its occupants.

My clients could easily go to a general merchandise store and pick out lights that fit their decorating scheme. However, when they come to my lamp and lighting fixture shop, they can get answers to their questions about correct lighting. I recommend minimum light levels for various tasks, following recommendations published by the U.S. Department of

Agriculture, the Illuminating Engineering Society, and the manufacturers of lighting equipment. For instance, a lamp with bulbs totaling 150 to 200 watts should normally supply ample light for studying. However, I know that if a room has dark walls, dark furniture, and little light from other sources, 200 watts may not be enough.

To determine just how much light each room has, I measure the amount of light in each area where activities take place. The amount of light is measured in units called footcandles. Each footcandle represents the quantity of light that would be produced by a candle as it shines on a surface one foot away. Reading requires 30 footcandles under normal circumstances. Ironing or shaving demands about 50. Writing a letter or working in the kitchen needs 70 or more. To find the exact amount of light in each area, I use a light meter. Then I can determine whether the client has enough of the correct type of lighting for her or his activities.

Design Portfolio

1. You've been hired to light a home library that has dark paneling, high ceilings, and a dark ceramic tile floor. Find pictures of lighting you would recommend and briefly explain why you made those choices.

2. You've been hired to light a country-style kitchen with a breakfast nook. The kitchen has light oak cabinets and a dark wood floor. Using CAD software, draw the kitchen and show your lighting design.

Review & Activities

Chapter Summary

- Lighting, whether from the sun or artificial lights, affects the mood and uses of a room.
- General, task, and accent lighting each have different purposes.
- Different types of bulbs have different characteristics.
- Lighting can be structural or nonstructural.
- Different rooms have different lighting needs depending on the activities that take place within them.
- Accessories add personality to rooms and should complement the design.
- Accessories can be organized by size, color, or theme.

Checking Your Understanding

1. What is the difference between **direct lighting** and **indirect lighting**?
2. What are the functions of general lighting, task lighting, and accent lighting?
3. How do **incandescent lights** and **fluorescent lights** differ?
4. What are the advantages and disadvantages of **halogen bulbs**?
5. Give an example of nonstructural lighting.
6. Name two structural lighting fixtures that provide **downlighting** and two that provide **uplighting**.
7. Why does a kitchen need task lighting?
8. What are the advantages of lighting controls?
9. What energy-efficient bulb choices do consumers have?
10. What do accessories reflect?
11. What rule of thumb can you use to place a wall decoration above a piece of furniture?
12. What are three examples of accessories?

Thinking Critically

1. **Suggesting a Solution.** Assume that you are converting a spare bedroom into a home office. At present the room has a single overhead light. What lighting would you recommend for the home office?

2. **Identifying Cause and Effect.** Why is safety a major factor when choosing lighting for stairways and hallways?

3. **Identifying Alternatives.** What lighting and accessories might you choose for a dining room with dark walls and flooring?

Applying Your Knowledge

1. **Evaluating Lighting.** Draw a floor plan of your home that shows the lighting as it is. Evaluate the use of general, task, and accent lighting and think about changes that would enhance the lighting. Prepare a list of suggestions and show your ideas on the floor plan in a different color.

2. **Researching Building Codes.** Do research or talk to an architect, builder, or interior designer to learn what local and state building codes require for residential lighting. Prepare a report of your findings.

3. **Planning Lighting.** Prepare a lighting plan for the living room, kitchen, and dining room of a family interested in conserving energy. Identify the type of fixtures and bulbs you would use and explain why you made each choice.

4. **Arranging Photographs.** Suppose you wanted to decorate a wall with 12 family photographs of different sizes. Choose frame sizes for the photos, and assume that half are horizontal and half are vertical. Make a drawing showing how you would arrange the photos.

5. **Making a Brochure.** Write a brochure that provides guidelines for selecting and arranging accessories.

Design Challenge

You have been asked to redesign the lighting and accessories for an L-shaped, 10 ft. x 18 ft. family room. It has a dining table at one end, and a seating arrangement at the other. They have a collection of Native American rugs and pottery, as well as several live plants that must stay in the room.

1. Create a floor plan showing the placement of the furniture.

2. Design a lighting plan that will highlight their collections.

3. Prepare illustrations to show the lighting placement and fixtures.

4. Present your design and explain how you would arrange accessories.

5. Place the completed design in your design portfolio.

Home Safety & Security

Objectives

- Identify common home health hazards.

- Describe ways to prevent home accidents.

- Describe ways to make a home safe for young children.

- Explain safe and effective use of smoke alarms and fire extinguishers.

- Identify ways to improve home security.

- Suggest strategies for improving home safety for people with special needs.

Vocabulary

- carbon monoxide
- asbestos
- asphyxiation
- flammable
- radon
- thermal burn

One of the basic human needs is to feel safe and secure. Most people feel safest in their home. Homes can, however, present risks of pollutants, accidents, and security problems. Fortunately, there are steps you can take to increase your home's safety and security. The information in this chapter will help you plan and implement strategies to make your home a safe and secure place.

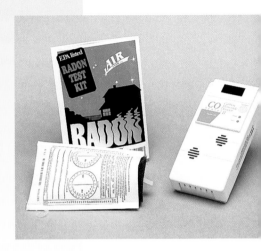

Reducing Health Hazards

People have become increasingly aware of the harm pollution causes to the natural environment. Pollution can also be a problem in the home. Some indoor pollutants may make people feel mildly ill. Others may have no noticeable effect at first, but, over time, they can cause serious health problems. By taking a few precautions, families can reduce the health hazards of pollution and enjoy greater peace of mind. See Fig. 28-1.

Pollutants in the Air

The majority of indoor pollution problems are airborne—carried by or through the air. There are several indoor air pollutants. Some are natural and some are the result of technology. How much indoor air pollution a home has is influenced by the building materials and equipment used, how the home is used, and where it is located.

Carbon Monoxide

Any furnace, heater, stove, fireplace, or water heater that burns gas, kerosene, or wood produces poisonous gases. One of the most dangerous of these gases is **carbon monoxide**—a colorless, odorless gas that is readily absorbed by red blood cells when breathed in. If the red blood cells absorb too much carbon monoxide instead of oxygen, the body doesn't get the oxygen it needs. The symptoms of carbon monoxide poisoning can range from headaches, nausea, and heart problems to **asphyxiation**—loss of consciousness or death from lack of oxygen.

All heating devices should be checked regularly to be sure they're working properly. Every home using gas appliances should have a carbon monoxide detector, which monitors the air and sounds an alarm if a dangerous level of carbon monoxide is detected.

Fig. 28-1 Families who take steps to prevent indoor air pollution can relax in the knowledge that they are protecting their health.

Radon

Radon is another dangerous gas to guard against. **Radon** is a radioactive gas that occurs naturally in some types of soil and rock. Usually radon escapes into the atmosphere and causes no harm. However, if it seeps into the home—through cracks in the foundation—it can build to harmful levels. Breathing high concentrations of radon increases the risk of lung cancer. Home test kits are available to measure radon levels. If tests show high levels of radon, simple steps such as sealing cracks can be taken to reduce the levels.

Asbestos

Many older homes contain **asbestos**, a flame-retardant mineral substance. Before 1978, asbestos was used in many building materials that were installed in hundreds of thousands of homes and buildings. Unfortunately, the discovery came later that tiny fibers of asbestos, when inhaled, could cause lung cancer. This danger arises when asbestos crumbles or is otherwise damaged. Homeowners should never try to remove or seal off suspected asbestos. That task must be performed by a professional.

Other Air Pollutants

Indoor air quality can be affected by chemical vapors from carpeting, insulation, and other materials. Other substances that pollute indoor air are molds and bacteria, tobacco smoke, and fumes from cleaning products and pesticides.

There are several steps you can take to preserve and improve air quality. First, keep your home clean and well ventilated. Try to keep moisture levels low to help prevent the growth of molds and bacteria. Discourage people from smoking indoors. Choose cleaning products and other materials that are free of known pollutants. An air purifier that removes dust, mold, bacteria, and odors from the air can also be used.

Lead

Lead is a toxic metal that can be found in old paint, water, soil, and air. Sometimes it penetrates a home's water supply. If lead enters the body, it can cause behavioral and developmental problems, particularly in young children.

In most cases of lead in water, the cause is traced to lead water pipes or lead-based solder (SAH-der) used to join the pipes. Lead solder has been prohibited since 1988, but many homes still have lead pipes. If you think your home has lead pipes, contact your local health department or water company to find out how to have your water tested. Meanwhile, before use, it is wise to let faucets run until the water runs cold to flush out any lead that might have accumulated in the pipes.

Homes built before the 1970s may have lead-based paint. Lead particles from the paint can get into household dust, which may be breathed or swallowed and can cause lead poisoning. Children may eat chips and flakes of peeling paint. To reduce the risk of lead poisoning, repair peeling paint and keep the house clean.

Consumer Considerations

Combating Mold & Mildew

Mold and mildew are more than unsightly. They're also a health hazard. Inhaling these single-celled organisms can adversely affect people who have asthma, allergies, and other breathing problems. Over time, mold and mildew can grow into colonies that can cause enough damage to make a home unlivable.

Molds and mildews thrive in warmth and humidity. They like to feed on "organic food" such as wood and cotton and wool fabrics. They frequently grow undetected inside walls near pipes, under carpets and behind wallpaper, and above ceiling tiles—anywhere moisture collects. An earthy, musty odor signals their presence.

You can remove small, isolated patches of mold yourself. Large-scale cases may require a certified mold abatement technician. Recurring problems may be a sign that structural changes are needed.

Fortunately, you can check mold and mildew through simple maintenance habits. Promote air circulation with open windows and closet doors, when possible. Keep bathrooms and kitchens well ventilated. Make sure all exhaust fans, like those in clothes dryers, vent outside the home, rather than into a crawlspace or attic. Repair leaking pipes and roofs promptly. Use adequate insulation around windows, pipes, and other areas that are prone to moisture condensation. Keep coils and drip pans of air conditioning units clean and replace the filters as needed.

Preventing Accidents

Every year more than 20,000 Americans die as a result of home accidents. Thousands more suffer long-lasting injuries, including lifelong disabilities. The most common types of accidents that occur in the home are falls, electric shock, and burns. Fortunately, most home accidents can be prevented by taking some simple precautions.

Falls

Falls account for most home injuries. Many falls occur because of defects in flooring, clutter, or lack of adequate lighting. Falls also result when people hurry or use poor judgment, such as standing on an unsteady chair to reach a high shelf.

To reduce the risk of falling, follow these home safety tips:

- Wipe up spills immediately.
- Repair loose tiles and tears in carpeting promptly.
- Anchor rugs firmly to the floor with double-sided adhesive tape or rubber backing.
- Use sturdy step stools to reach high places.
- Install grab bars on walls in tubs and showers and use nonskid bathtub mats. **See Fig. 28-2.**

Homes with steps and stairways present additional hazards. Make certain that any changes in floor level are obvious and that those areas are well lighted. Provide secure handrails. Avoid leaving items on stairs where they can be tripped over.

Outside the home, keep sidewalks swept and clear of trash and clutter. Cracks in the sidewalk should be repaired and uneven sections replaced. If you live where the winters are cold, keep sidewalks and steps free of ice and snow.

Fig. 28-2 Grab bars are especially important in homes where older people reside because they can suffer serious injuries from falls.

Electric Shock

Severe electric shock is powerful enough to knock a person down, cause unconsciousness, or interrupt breathing and heartbeat. Electric shocks in the home result mainly from the misuse of electrical appliances. Learning the safe way to handle appliances and making safe use an everyday practice will decrease your risk of electric shock. Each appliance comes with specific warnings, but some cautions apply to all. For example, never clean or service appliances while they are plugged in. When disconnecting an appliance, turn it off first. Don't pull on the cord to unplug it, as this tends to loosen or break the wires. Instead, grasp the plug with your thumb and forefinger and pull gently to remove it from the outlet.

Because water is a good conductor of electricity, never touch electrical appliances with wet or damp hands. Don't use electrical appliances near sinks or bathtubs. A hair dryer, for example, could accidentally fall into a bathtub or sink full of water. If someone tried to pick it up, an electric current might pass through the person's body even with the appliance turned off.

Plugging too many appliances into one outlet can overload the circuit and might damage the wiring. **See Fig. 28-3.** An electric circuit is the path electric energy follows from the source of electric power to one or more electrical fixtures or receptacles and back.

Faulty electrical systems can cause or contribute to electrical accidents. All electrical systems should be installed according to the National Electrical Code. Homeowners should arrange to have a professional check their electrical system about every five years and replace defective parts as necessary.

As you read in Chapter 11, fuses and circuit breakers are built-in safety devices in an electrical system. Both protect electrical circuits from damage caused by too much current. Whether the excess is caused by a fault in the wiring or by lightning, the fuse or circuit breaker protects the system by shutting off the flow of current. As you read in Chapter 11, ground fault circuit interrupters (GFCIs) work similarly. They are placed on some electrical outlets to cut off power when they sense a surge in current too low to trigger a circuit breaker or fuse but high enough to cause a shock. GFCIs are required in all kitchen, bathroom, and outdoor receptacles in new homes.

Burns

Becky Martello was cooking dinner for the family. As Becky removed a pan from the burner, her loose shirt sleeve swept across the flame and caught fire. Clothing is often very **flammable**, which means it is capable of burning quickly. Fortunately, Becky remembered what to do when clothes catch fire: STOP, DROP, and ROLL. She escaped with only minor thermal burns.

A **thermal burn** is an injury caused by hot liquids, hot surfaces, or flames. Other types of burns may be caused by chemicals and by electricity. Many thermal burns are caused by carelessness while cooking. Becky, for example, should have been wearing close-fitting clothing while working near an open flame. Long hair should be tied back. Keep flammable materials, such as towels, paper, and plastic, away from the range or cooktop. Turn pan handles toward the center of the range to prevent accidental spilling of hot food. Use potholders and oven mitts when handling hot containers of food. **See Fig. 28-4.**

28-3 Too many appliances plugged into an outlet (left) can overload a circuit and possibly damage the wiring. Instead, plug in only the appropriate number of appliances and use ground fault circuit interrupters in kitchen and bathroom receptacles.

Fig. 28-4 Following safety precautions in the kitchen can help prevent thermal burns. **What precautions has this person taken?**

Childproofing the Home

Very young children are naturally curious. Dozens of things attract their attention. They want to get close, to touch, and perhaps to taste each one before crawling, climbing, or running to the next attraction. Because they're unaware of the potential dangers in the home, their need to explore and experiment can lead to accidents. It's up to adults and older children to keep young children safe. Here are some ways to make a home safer for young children.

- Install a gate across stairway openings. See Fig. 28-5.

- Install safety catches on all windows.

- Insert safety plugs into all unused outlets.

- Arrange electrical appliance cords so young children cannot get tangled in them or pull down appliances by the cord.

- Keep small items out of reach. Children can easily choke on coins, marbles, and other small objects.

- Avoid using furniture with sharp corners or glass tops. If there are sharp corners, pad them by attaching strips of foam rubber. Special cushions can also be purchased.

- Fasten bedding so a baby cannot pull it over his or her head.

Fig. 28-5 Installing a gate across stairways is one safety precaution needed in homes with small children.

- Tie up cords from curtains, drapes, and blinds so that children cannot get tangled in or choked by them. Keep the crib away from windows with hanging cords.

- Keep pillows and stuffed animals out of the crib while the baby is sleeping.

- When carrying hot liquids or foods, make sure the baby isn't crawling nearby.

- Always test bath water to make sure it's not too hot.

- Use nonslip mats in the bottom of the tub. Never leave a baby alone in a tub, even for a second.

- Store medicines out of reach. Brightly colored pills and liquids may look like candy to a child.

- Keep houseplants out of reach. Some can be poisonous.

- Store poisonous substances such as cleaning products in high, locked cabinets.

- Put safety latches on the doors of low cabinets to keep children out.

Preventing Fires

Thousands of people die each year in residential fires and property losses are in the billions of dollars. Becoming familiar with the main causes of home fires can help you take actions to prevent them. Many fires are caused by:

- Careless smoking or children playing with matches or lighters.

- Faulty wiring or electrical equipment.

- Unattended or improperly extinguished wood stove and fireplace fires.

- Flammable liquids or oily rags stored near a heat source.

- A space heater too close to combustible materials, such as drapes or a bedspread. See Fig. 28-6.

- Combustible materials too close to hot surfaces of wood-burning stoves.

- Chimneys and flues clogged with soot and dirt.

- Use of flammable substances, such as aerosols, in cooking areas or near heating units.

- Grease in exhaust fans and vents.

- Ignition of a gas leak.

A fire goes through four stages. In the first stage, the fire smolders. Invisible, toxic (poisonous) gases may be produced even though there's no flame, smoke, or noticeable heat. A fire may smolder for hours. In the second stage, some smoke and more toxic gases are produced. In the third stage, flames erupt and begin to spread. During the fourth stage, there is high, uncontrolled heat. In this stage, toxic gases expand rapidly.

Fig. 28-6 Some people use space heaters to provide additional comfort. What safety precautions need to be taken with a space heater?

Most fires start in the kitchen. Three-quarters of the people who die in house fires are trapped upstairs by fires that start downstairs. The majority of these people don't die from burns; rather, they are asphyxiated in their sleep by the toxic gases produced by the fire.

No matter how careful people are about fire prevention, fires can happen in any home. To minimize the danger, you can purchase fire-safety devices.

Smoke Alarms. Fire experts believe that smoke alarms are the most important aid in saving lives and property. Smoke alarms detect poisonous gases in the first stage of a fire and sound a loud buzzer to alert residents to the danger. Small and relatively inexpensive smoke alarms can be wired into a home's electrical system, plugged into a receptacle, or operated by batteries.

Ideally, there should be a smoke alarm in every room except the kitchen and bathroom. (These rooms aren't good locations because smoke alarms can be set off by cooking fumes and steam.) At the very least, there should be one alarm on each level of the home, including one near the kitchen and each sleeping area, and one near the furnace and water heater. They should be installed near the ceiling, and away from windows, doors, or heating vents that might divert smoke from the unit. Once smoke alarms have been installed, they need to be tested regularly to be certain they are working. Replace batteries at least annually.

Fire Extinguishers. Several types of fire extinguishers are available for putting out small fires. Water extinguishers deliver water under pressure and are effective on ordinary combustible materials, such as wood, paper, or cloth. Foam extinguishers and dry-powder extinguishers will douse flammable liquids such as fat, oil, and alcohol. A third type of extinguisher contains a carbon dioxide to smother electrical fires. This last type must be used carefully, because the gas itself can asphyxiate people.

Fig. 28-7 The contents of many fire extinguishers lose their effectiveness after a period of time. Check your fire extinguishers to see if they have expired. If they have, follow the manufacturer's directions for renewal or recharging.

Because the kitchen range is the most likely place for a fire to begin, an extinguisher for smothering grease fires should be located in the kitchen. Place it where it can be grabbed without having to reach across the range. A grease fire can also be smothered by sprinkling it with baking soda or salt, or by covering the pan with a lid. Special "fire blankets" can also smother most fires that begin at the range. Some homeowners install indoor sprinkler systems that turn on in case of a fire emergency.

All adults and teens should know how to operate the fire extinguisher. See Fig. 28-7. Young children, however, should be taught to run for help if fire breaks out—not to fight it. Fire professionals advise everyone to use extreme caution when deciding to fight even a small fire. If the fire isn't immediately extinguished, their advice is to leave the building and call the fire department from a safe location.

Fig. 28-8 Plan a fire drill with your family to practice escaping from your home in a hurry. In case of a fire emergency, you'll be able to think more clearly if you have planned ahead.

A Home Fire Safety Plan

Schools and other public buildings are required by law to have a fire safety plan for evacuating the building. A fire safety plan is just as important for your home. When the smoke alarm goes off, you and your family must know how to get out of the home quickly and safely.

The first step is to plan possible escape routes. For each room or area of the home, plan at least two ways to get outside. Alternate routes are back doors, windows, balconies, and fire escapes. See Fig. 28-8.

If you live in a high-rise or other multifamily building, check the hallways for a diagram of possible escape routes from the building. Remember, never use an elevator during a fire. If the power goes out, you could become trapped in the elevator.

Make sure your escape routes are usable. Check all windows to make sure they open easily. If necessary, purchase escape ladders for upper-story windows. In a high-rise building, be sure that fire escapes are functioning and that fire exits are neither blocked nor locked.

Designate a place for all family members to meet after escaping from the building. People have lost their lives by going back into a burning building to look for someone who was already outside.

Once you have an escape plan, draw a diagram showing all escape routes and the location where you will meet. Post it where everyone in the household can see it. Make sure everyone is familiar with the escape plan. Explain these procedures for escaping from a fire:

- Don't stop to gather valuables or call the fire department. Leave immediately.

- Crawl on your hands and knees. Since heat and toxic gases rise, the cleanest air will be close to the floor. If you are in bed, roll to the floor instead of sitting up.

- Shout to alert others as you exit.

- Use the escape routes you planned ahead of time.

- When you come to a closed door, feel it first. If the doorknob is hot, DO NOT open it! Use an alternate route. If the door isn't hot, brace your body against it and open it slowly. If you feel a rush of hot air, close the door and use an alternate route.

- Close all doors behind you.

- Once outside, go to the designated meeting place.

- If you're unable to escape, close the door of the room first, then open a window a few inches and breathe through the opening. Wave your arms, a sheet, or a curtain out the window to attract attention.

To increase safety, ask family members to sleep with bedroom doors closed. A closed door will hold back a fire for a long time and slow down the passage of smoke.

Practice your escape plan by holding fire drills at least twice a year. Since many home fires occur at night, it's a good idea to hold at least some drills after dark. A fire safety plan and regular drills can greatly increase your family's chances of escaping a fire safely.

Promoting Security

How safe is your neighborhood? Some people believe that they live in a safe neighborhood where crime is unlikely. However, break-ins and robberies can and do happen anywhere. Fortunately, there are security devices you can install and several security measures you can take to help keep your home, family, and possessions safe. **See Fig. 28-9.**

Security Devices

Burglary is committed by people who take advantage of carelessness or neglect. Therefore, the more difficult you make it for burglars to break into your home, the less likely they are to keep trying. Of course, too many security devices can make it inconvenient to go in and out. In the end, you must compromise between what makes you feel secure and what level of inconvenience you're willing to put up with. Minimum protection begins with secure doors and windows.

Fig. 28-9 Every exterior door needs to have a security device. This horizontal lock prevents the door from sliding open.

Secure Doors. All entrances to a home or residential building should have a door with a solid wood or metal core. **See Fig. 28-10.** Hollow-core doors made of soft, thin wood are suitable for closets and interior rooms, but they are too weak to provide the security needed for an entrance door. The door frame should be solid as well. It should also be strong enough to prevent a burglar from easily prying it away from the door with a crowbar. If the garage is attached to the house, make sure the connecting door to the living area is secure.

Door Locks. Police recommend installing a deadbolt lock on each exterior door. The bolt should extend into the door jamb a minimum of 1 in. (2.5 cm). Unlike common spring locks, deadbolts can't be opened by a credit card or a screwdriver. **See Fig. 28-11.**

Fig. 28-11 Deadbolt locks provide extra security on exterior doors. Locks that can be opened from either side by a key are best.

Fig. 28-10 Even connecting doors in residential facilities, such as this nursing home, need to be secure. The alarm on this door is controlled by the main desk, which resets it each night when the visitor's entrance is closed.

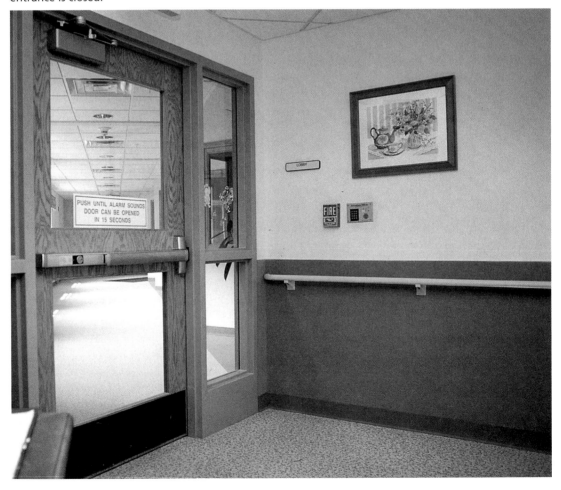

Fig. 28-12 Door viewers can be installed at a child's height as well as at an adult's height. *Why is it important not to open the outer door to your home if you don't know who is on the other side?*

Door Viewers. Some intruders ring the doorbell and try to get invited in. Others force their way inside once you've opened the door. Always identify a visitor before opening the door. If there's no window to look out, install a door viewer. A door viewer is a small hole in the door. The hole is fitted with a metal cylinder and a lens that allows a wide-angle view of the person at the door. See Fig. 28-12.

For safety reasons, it's best not to have windows beside exterior doors. If the doorknob is too close to a window, a burglar could break the window, then reach inside and unlock the door. Another solution is to use shatterproof glass in windows that are installed next to doors.

Window Locks. Most types of windows come equipped with locks, but these alone don't ensure security. For example, traditional double-hung windows with thumb-turn locks can be easily pried open. Keyed locks might be added for extra protection, especially for the first-floor windows. However,

keyed locks shouldn't be used on windows in sleeping areas, because they might slow down escape from fire.

Alarm Systems. Even the best of locks may not keep burglars from attempting to enter a home. The next line of defense is alerting residents, neighbors, or the police that a break-in is underway.

A number of electronic alarm systems are on the market. Some are as simple as an electronic barking dog that is triggered by attempts to force a door or window. Other systems are very complex and include electronic eyes and motion detectors. Control panels allow homeowners to set up the system. These systems often include an outdoor keypad where family members punch in a code that allows them to enter the house without triggering the alarm.

Once the alarm is triggered, responses vary widely. **See Fig. 28-13.** In some alarm systems the only response is a loud noise. The hope is that the noise will frighten the intruder away and alert someone else that there's trouble. Some alarm systems are connected to a central processing station that alerts the police when the alarm is triggered. Often, private companies send an armed response team to investigate triggered alarms.

To select an alarm system that will be right for your needs, consider several factors. First, think about your neighborhood. What is its history of burglary attempts? Consider the layout of your home. Is an alarm system appropriate? What about your budget? What can you afford? Your local police department is a good source of advice for making a decision about alarm systems.

Lights and Intercoms. Correctly placed light is another safety device. Place floodlights over exterior doors, including the garage door. Some floodlights have a motion detector that causes them to turn on whenever they sense movement. Parking areas and walkways should also be well lighted and clear of structures and foliage that could conceal someone. In multiunit buildings, every hallway and stairway should have adequate lighting. An intercom system can help keep unwelcome people out of multiunit buildings. The intercom allows residents to identify people who ring the main entrance doorbell. The residents then use a remote door-lock release to let authorized visitors enter.

Fig. 28-13 Electronic home security systems can detect when there is an attempted forced entry, sound an alarm in the home, and trigger an alarm that summons the police.

The Impact of Technology

Biometric Security Systems

Biometrics, which is now used for security in airports and ATMs, may be coming to a home near you. This technology promises almost foolproof security without another code to remember—or to be stolen.

Biometrics uses a person's unique physical features to verify his or her identity. Recognition software captures and records the trait in detailed digital form and translates it into an electronic template that is stored in a database. Every time a person wants to gain access, the software compares the user's features to the stored template. The system can modify the template over time to incorporate changes due to aging. This basic process takes different forms.

Fingerprints. Electronic fingerprinting is based on individual patterns of swirls, arches, and ridges in a person's fingertips. Some methods use sound waves rather than electronic impulses to identify and record the patterns. Fingerprint recognition is already being used on some safes and door locks.

Hand Geometry. A high-resolution camera equipped with a mirror photographs a hand to create a three-dimensional template. Up to 90 separate physical characteristics may be stored, including overall size, length of fingers, and skin folds.

Signature. A biometric pen measures pressure, pen angle, and other factors in the process of writing a signature, as well as the size and shape of the letters. Some biometric pens also recognize fingerprints.

Iris. The iris, the inner membrane of the eye, includes rings and other distinctive features. These are unique and are not changed by contact lenses or surgery. Recognition software can scan up to 200 of these points for comparison.

Tech Trends

Investigate the drawbacks and concerns associated with current uses of biometrics. Do you think these issues will affect the acceptance of biometrics in home security? Why or why not?

Fig. 28-14 Lights on the exterior of a home not only make it look attractive, they also add security.

Security Measures

There are several other security measures people can take to lower their risk of becoming a victim of burglary. For example, make the exterior of the home visible. Trim trees and shrubs so that they don't cover doors or windows. Planting thorny bushes underneath windows might also discourage burglars. See Fig. 28-14.

Try to disguise the fact that your home is vacant when you're away. Ask a trusted neighbor to pick up newspapers and mail and to open and close the shades or drapes. Use an automatic timer to turn lights on at dusk and off at the usual bedtime. The timer can also turn on a radio. Keep garage doors closed at all times.

There was a time when most people knew their neighbors and assumed that most of them would look out for one another's property. As lifestyles changed, home security increasingly became an individual endeavor. Some people have tried to regain the idea of shared responsibility by forming neighborhood crime watch groups. Neighbors attend regular meetings, get to know one another, and agree to watch out for one another's property. Thieves may be less likely to burglarize homes in such a neighborhood.

Meeting Special Needs

A home that is safe and secure for the "average" person may present problems for a person with a disability or someone with diminished abilities due to age. See Fig. 28-15. The following ideas for increasing safety and security are in keeping with the philosophy of universal design—designing homes for people of all ages and physical needs.

Impaired Mobility. For those who use a cane or a walker, or who simply have difficulty walking, falls are a constant household danger. A highly polished floor, a loose rug, or a chipped piece of tile can be especially treacherous. Safe floor coverings are essential. Throw rugs shouldn't be used. Here are some other home modifications to prevent falls:

- Trim doorway thresholds so that they are flush with the floor or extend no higher than ¼ in. (6 mm).
- Provide handrails on each side of a staircase and along hallways. Handrails should extend 18 in. (46 cm) beyond the last step.
- Install grab bars and rubber flooring in the bathroom.
- Provide a seat in the tub or shower.
- Provide sturdy chairs, preferably with arms, to make it easier to sit down and stand up.
- Provide a place to sit while preparing meals, in case the person becomes tired.

When designing to accommodate wheelchair users, safety and security are especially important. Devices such as sound- or motion-activated lights and wheelchair-height door viewers can help increase security.

People with limited mobility can benefit from a system that allows them to summon help easily. In case of an emergency, users simply press the but-

Fig. 28-15 A motorized lift can be installed to help a person with impaired mobility move from one level of the home to another.

ton on a device worn around the neck or wrist. The button signals the home telephone to dial a preset number automatically, which might be a hospital or a central dispatch office. The source of the incoming call is automatically identified, and assistance is sent.

Fig. 28-16 This telephone is especially equipped to assist a person with a hearing impairment.

Impaired Vision. People who have reduced vision and those who are blind have an increased risk of accidents. For those who have trouble distinguishing objects, it may be necessary to increase the amount of lighting in the home. Increasing the contrast between objects and their backgrounds increases their visibility. For example, placing a light object against a dark background makes it easier to see. The following measures can also make homes safer for the visually impaired.

- Mark the edges of steps with wide strips of contrasting adhesive tape.

- Clearly label and store any poisonous substances. Use very large type or braille, depending on the severity of the impairment.

- Remove furniture that has sharp corners, glass tops, or is easily tipped over.

- Install a telephone with oversize numerals or numerals printed in braille. Preprogram emergency and frequently used phone numbers.

Impaired Hearing. Certain measures can help people who have impaired hearing. An electrician can install wiring that substitutes a flashing light for the ring of the doorbell and telephone. See Fig. 28-16. Some smoke alarms have flashing lights as well as a warning sound. Another helpful device is a portable, vibrating timer, which can be used as a kitchen timer. By alerting a person with impaired hearing to check the progress of cooking food, the timer can help to prevent fires.

Dementia. People with dementia are easily confused. For this reason it is advisable to avoid rearranging furniture or making other changes that could disorient them. It may also be necessary to install some simple security devices. Dementia can cause people to lose track of time. They may get up in the middle of the night and try to leave the home. Sound monitors in their room and motion detectors outdoors can alert family members if they try to wander off.

A Safe & Secure Home

People want to feel safe and secure in their homes. Unfortunately, there are many dangers that can enter the home to cause illness, injury, personal loss, and even death. The risks posed by those dangers can be minimized with careful planning and thoughtful action. Certain tests and common-sense practices can be used to prevent and detect dangerous indoor pollution levels. Preventive home repairs and a few simple precautions can prevent the accidents that cause thousands of falls, shocks, or burns every year. Basic security measures—with or without the use of sophisticated alarm systems—can cut the risk of someone breaking into the home to take valuable possessions or threaten the occupants.

Creating a safe home environment also means making it safe for people of all abilities. Many families include people who have limitations due to illness, injury, or age. Some of those problems are physical; some reflect declining mental faculties. Various steps can be taken to make it easier for everyone to move around in and make use of all the rooms in the house. In such an environment, everyone feels safe, secure, and at home. See Fig. 28-17.

Fig. 28-17 Even from the outside, this home appears to be safe and secure. **How could you determine if the interior is safe and secure?**

Profile of a Space Planner

Space planners design the space and specify the furniture, equipment, and lighting for public buildings and commercial or institutional establishments, such as offices, restaurants, hotels, and stores. Space planners often work for architectural or interior design firms.

Education & Training

- Space planners usually hold a bachelor's degree.
- Courses in interior design, ergonomics, CAD, architectural drawing, and lighting are very helpful.

Skills & Aptitudes

- Excellent visual and spatial aptitudes are critical in this career.
- Both the ability to sketch freehand and CAD proficiency are required.
- Knowledge of the elements and principles of design is critical.
- The ability to handle detail work accurately is also required.

Space Planner
John Harding

The next time you are in a large office complex, look closely at the furnishings and how they are arranged. The design of such spaces is usually the work of an interior space planner, a specialized field within interior design. Space planners generally develop plans for commercial offices or other large institutions. We select and arrange the furniture, equipment, and lighting. In addition to applying the principles of good design, we aim to encourage productivity.

I became interested in space planning while an intern at an architectural firm. Our company was hired to redesign an office complex. What we found was a chaotic use of the space. The reception area was too far from the main entrance. People who needed privacy for conversations were sitting very close to other employees. Many workers had to stack files and paper on the floor.

It took us six months to transform the office complex. Some of the employees actually sent notes to thank us. I liked the idea of making a positive difference in peoples' attitudes, so I decided to become a space planner.

The firm I work for now specializes in office space planning. Corporations all over the world hire us to develop space plans and specifications. Specifications usually include choosing furniture, equipment, materials, and lighting.

International companies are especially exciting to work for. We have to gain an understanding of the culture of the country where the facility is placed. Cultures differ on such issues as how they view privacy and social interaction. I find it exciting to learn about these differences and plan accordingly.

My profession is always changing. We have to constantly keep up with new products, technology, and concepts. I read trade magazines and attend space-planning conferences. At those conferences I attend workshops and talk to manufacturers' representatives about new products. I'm sure that in the future the Internet and other technology will continue to transform how space planners work.

Design Portfolio

1. Study how space is arranged in your school library. Sketch a new design altering the use of the space and give your rationale for that design plan.

2. Design the lobby of a large hotel. Be sure to include comfortable sitting areas as well as a reception desk and any other needed facilities.

Chapter Summary

- Health hazards caused by indoor pollutants can be monitored and often prevented.
- Several steps can be taken to prevent the most common home accidents—falls, electric shocks, and fires.
- Childproofing makes a home safe for small children.
- Preventing fires and knowing how to respond to fire emergencies can save lives.
- Homeowners can use some devices and various basic behaviors to reduce the likelihood of a burglary.
- Homeowners can take steps to make a home safer for people with different abilities.

Checking Your Understanding

1. Identify at least three pollutants that can be found in the home.
2. What two steps can be taken to prevent falls in a kitchen?
3. What are two basic rules for preventing electric shock?
4. What causes a **thermal burn**?
5. What is childproofing a home?
6. What are two steps you can take to prevent children from swallowing something poisonous?
7. Where, at minimum, should smoke detectors and fire extinguishers be placed?
8. Why should families practice a home fire safety plan?
9. How do security alarms aim to prevent burglaries?
10. Why are motion detectors useful when someone in the home has dementia?

Thinking Critically

1. **Making Inferences.** Why might asbestos and lead pollution be less of a problem in the future?

2. **Synthesizing.** A young couple you know is raising their first child. Create a list of suggestions to help them childproof their kitchen.

3. **Comparing and Contrasting.** Why are door viewers more secure than door chains?

Applying Your Knowledge

1. **Indoor Pollution.** Research "sick building syndrome" and prepare a report on the causes, symptoms, and preventative steps that can be taken.

2. **Accident Prevention Checklist.** Create an accident prevention checklist aimed at preventing falls, electric shocks, and fires in the home.

3. **Fire Safety Plan.** Develop a fire safety plan for your home. Take into account routes each family member should take. Show the plan to a parent or guardian for approval. Once the plan is approved, encourage your family members to hold regular fire drills.

4. **Analyzing Your Home.** Analyze your home for security by checking all the doors and windows. Also think about how members of your family handle situations such as a stranger coming to the door. Recommend steps your family could take to make your home safer.

5. **Home Security Systems.** Research the various types of security alarm systems currently available and report on how different systems work.

6. **Neighborhood Watch.** Investigate starting a neighborhood watch program in your community. Report on the steps that must be taken to put this program in place.

Design Challenge

You have been asked to assess a two-bedroom ranch and recommend ways to make it safer and more secure. The occupants are an elderly couple who have been married for 55 years. The husband is visually impaired. They have not taken any special security measures beyond deadbolt locks on the exterior doors.

1. Obtain a floor plan for a two-bedroom ranch and make a list of features you would include to make the home more secure.

2. On the floor plan, label the safety and security devices that you recommend.

3. Present your recommendations and ask the class for feedback.

4. Make any needed changes and place the completed security plan in your design portfolio.

Measurement Conversions

Inches to Centimeters

inches	mm/cm	inches	cm	inches	cm
1/8	3 mm	13	33.0	32	81.5
1/4	6 mm	14	35.6	33	83.8
3/8	1 cm	15	38.1	34	86.4
1/2	1.3 cm	16	40.6	35	88.9
5/8	1.6 cm	17	43.2	36	91.4
3/4	1.9 cm	18	45.7	37	94.0
7/8	2.2 cm	19	48.3	38	96.5
1	2.5 cm	20	50.8	39	99.1
2	5.1 cm	21	53.3	40	101.6
3	7.6 cm	22	55.9	41	104.1
4	10.2 cm	23	58.4	42	106.7
5	12.7 cm	24	61.0	43	109.2
6	15.2 cm	25	63.5	44	111.8
7	17.8 cm	26	66.0	45	114.3
8	20.3 cm	27	68.6	46	116.8
9	22.9 cm	28	71.1	47	119.4
10	25.4 cm	29	73.7	48	121.9
11	28 cm	30	76.2	49	124.5
12	30.5 cm	31	78.7	50	127.0

Yards to Meters

yards	meters	yards	meters	yards	meters	yards	meters	yards	meters
1/8	0.11	2 1/8	1.94	4 1/8	3.77	6 1/8	5.60	8 1/8	7.43
1/4	0.23	2 1/4	2.06	4 1/4	3.89	6 1/4	5.72	8 1/4	7.54
3/8	0.34	2 3/8	2.17	4 3/8	4.00	6 3/8	5.83	8 3/8	7.66
1/2	0.46	2 1/2	2.29	4 1/2	4.11	6 1/2	5.94	8 1/2	7.77
5/8	0.57	2 5/8	2.40	4 5/8	4.23	6 5/8	6.06	8 5/8	7.89
3/4	0.69	2 3/4	2.51	4 3/4	4.34	6 3/4	6.17	8 3/4	8.00
7/8	0.80	2 7/8	2.63	4 7/8	4.46	6 7/8	6.29	8 7/8	8.12
1	0.91	3	2.74	5	4.57	7	6.40	9	8.23
1 1/8	1.03	3 1/8	2.86	5 1/8	4.69	7 1/8	6.52	9 1/8	8.34
1 1/4	1.14	3 1/4	2.97	5 1/4	4.80	7 1/4	6.63	9 1/4	8.46
1 3/8	1.26	3 3/8	3.09	5 3/8	4.91	7 3/8	6.74	9 3/8	8.57
1 1/2	1.37	3 1/2	3.20	5 1/2	5.03	7 1/2	6.86	9 1/2	8.69
1 5/8	1.49	3 5/8	3.31	5 5/8	5.14	7 5/8	6.97	9 5/8	8.80
1 3/4	1.60	3 3/4	3.43	5 3/4	5.26	7 3/4	7.09	9 3/4	8.92
1 7/8	1.71	3 7/8	3.54	5 7/8	5.37	7 7/8	7.20	9 7/8	9.03
2	1.83	4	3.66	6	5.49	8	7.32	10	9.14

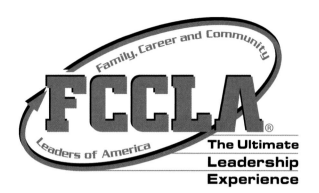

Family, Career and Community Leaders of America, Inc. (FCCLA) is a national student organization for students enrolled in family and consumer sciences courses. Involvement in FCCLA offers members the opportunity to develop life skills, expand their leadership potential, and explore careers.

FCCLA promotes personal growth and offers members opportunities to participate in a number of individual and chapter programs that strengthen life skills. Some examples of specific FCCLA programs follow.

Power of One

Power of One helps students find and use their personal power by setting and achieving goals. Members complete projects that focus on improving personal traits, getting along with family members, exploring career options, and developing leadership qualities.

Career Connection

This FCCLA program helps members target career goals. Students focus on six aspects of career development: Plug In to Careers; Sign On to the Career Connection; Program Career Steps; Link Up to Jobs; Access Skills for Career Success; Integrate Work and Life.

Community Service

FCCLA helps members strengthen their contributions to their community through this program. Students develop, plan, carry out, and evaluate projects that improve the quality of life in their communities.

Leadership Programs

FCCLA offers two leadership programs.

- *Dynamic Leadership* offers activities and project ideas that help students learn to model good character, solve problems, foster relationships, manage conflict, and build teams.

- *Leaders at Work* recognizes FCCLA members who create projects to strengthen leadership skills on the job in one of six career areas related to Family and Consumer Sciences.

STAR Events

Students Taking Action with Recognition (STAR) Events are competitive events in which FCCLA members are recognized for proficiency in individual and chapter projects, leadership skills, and career preparation. Here are a few of the *STAR Event* categories:

- Illustrated Talk
- Interpersonal Communications
- Career Investigation
- Job Interview
- Entrepreneurship
- Applied Technology

For more information, contact FCCLA at **www.fcclainc.org**

Glossary

A

ability. A skill a person has already developed. (Ch. 4)

accented neutral. A neutral color scheme that includes a small amount of bright color. (Ch. 18)

accessory. Complimentary decorative objects of art, lighting, plants, area rugs, and wall hangings added to an interior space to enhance the design.

achromatic color scheme. A colorless scheme using black, white and grey. A variation of this is possible, making a warm or cool achromatic by adding a hint of red yellow or blue.

acoustic tile. Square blocks made of soft material such as cork or plaster rather than hard reflective surfaces.

active solar heating system. A system that requires mechanical devices to collect and store the sun's heat and then distribute it throughout the house. (Ch. 12)

adaptable design. Design features that are temporary and can be easily changed. (Ch. 1)

adaptations. Furniture made in the style of old designs without being an exact copy of any one piece. (Ch. 25)

adaptive re-use. Utilize an existing space or structure for a new purpose.

Adirondack furniture. Rustic furniture made in North America in the mid 1800s from roughly hewn timber and bent branches and logs.

adjustable rate mortgage. A home loan in which the interest rate changes depending on current rates in effect. (Ch. 8)

adobe (uh-DOH-bee)**.** Clay formed into sun-dried bricks and used as building material. (Ch. 14)

aesthetic (es-THE-tik) **codes.** Codes that regulate the appearance of buildings in order to maintain the beauty and the desired look of an area. (Ch. 16)

airbrick. Perforated block built into walls to ventilate a room or the underside of a wooden floor.

alkyd (AL-ked)**.** A type of paint made from an oil or a synthetic resin that dries more quickly than pure oil paint. It produces a durable and washable surface. (Ch. 24)

amortization. Gradual elimination of the principal of a mortgage. (Ch. 8)

analogous. A color scheme using colors that are next to each other on the color wheel. (Ch. 18)

antique. A piece of furniture that is at least 100 years old. (Ch. 25)

antiquing. The process of artificially aging paint. It can be achieved by rubbing over the new paint with a darker glaze or color wash.

anti-slip paint. Paint that contains a grit such as sand, plastic chips, or cork dust that forms a grippable surface.

appraisal. An estimate of the value of a property. (Ch. 8)

apprenticeship. A program that combines on-the-job training from a skilled worker and classroom instruction. (Ch. 4)

apron. Horizontal panel or board underneath a window and projecting slightly into the room.

aptitude. A natural talent or a person's potential for learning a skill. (Ch. 4)

archaeologist (ahr-kee-AH-luh-jist)**.** Scientist who studies history through the relics and remains of old civilizations. (Ch. 1)

area. Typically refers to the length times the width of floor space. Cubic area refers to the length times the width times the height.

Arrowback chair. An American variation of the Windsor chair in which the spindles flare outwards. The chair was popular after 1830.

Art Deco. Popular decorative design style of the 1920s and 1930s. The style is characterized by stepped forms, rounded corners, triple-striped decorative elements, and the use of chromium and black trim.

asbestos. A flame-retardant mineral substance used in many building materials until it was discovered to be a health hazard. (Ch. 28)

asphyxiation. Loss of consciousness or death from lack of oxygen. (Ch. 28)

assign. To transfer a tenant's lease and all legal responsibility for a rental unit to someone else before the end of the lease period. (Ch. 7)

asymmetrical balance. A design effect in which elements on either side of an imaginary central line are unmatched but appear to be in balance. (Ch. 19)

attic fan. Large circulating fan mounted in the room or space just below the roof of a house.

Austrian shade. Fabric shade with vertical rows of swags from the head rail to hem.

automated management systems. Central computerized control units that oversee daily functions in a home, such as heating, cooling, lighting, and security. (Ch. 3)

awning. Lightweight roof structure typically constructed of fabric or metal installed over an exterior opening, such as a doorway, porch or balcony to provide shelter.

B

baby boomers. People born in the 20-year period immediately following World War II. (Ch. 2)

backgrounds. The floors, walls, ceilings, and windows in a room. (Ch. 24)

backsplash. Vertical area behind a counter, with or without a sink typically measuring 4 in. (10 cm) to approximately 18 in. (46 cm) for a full backsplash.

bagging. A textured finish, which is created by working a glaze over a base coat, using a cloth in a plastic bag and working over the glaze in a random pattern removing the glaze as you go.

balcony. Landing over 4 ft. (1.2 m) above the floor that projects from the wall of a building and is enclosed by a railing.

balloon shade. Fabric shade creating a gathered bottom edge when raised.

balustrade. The collection of rails and posts with a rail along the top that form the waist height wall to the sides of stairs or to a terrace or balcony.

bamboo. A fast-growing, woody, tropical plant. Its sturdy stems can be used to make furniture. (Ch. 26)

barrier-free design. Living spaces designed without structures that prevent access to people with special needs. (Ch. 1)

baseboard. Trim, often wood, used where the floors and walls meet.

bay window. A window in a formed wall that projects from the main wall line to form an alcove.

bid. An offer from a contractor to complete a building or remodeling project for a certain price. (Ch. 13)

biomaterial. Organically-based building material manufactured from recycled matter. (Ch. 3)

biometric. A security system that reads the physical characteristics of a person before allowing access. (Ch. 3)

bishop's sleeve. Drapery with side panels gathered with tie-backs to create multiple poufs.

blend. Fabric containing a mixture of two or more fibers or yarns.

blinds. Window coverings made of a series of evenly spaced slats that may be opened or closed by cords. (Ch. 24)

board and batten. A type of siding composed of wide boards and narrow battens. The boards are nailed to the sheathing so that there is a 1/2 inch space between them. The battens are nailed over the open spaces between the boards.

breach of contract. A legal phrase for failure to meet all terms of a contract or agreement. (Ch. 7)

building codes. Rules that regulate the quality of building materials and set standards of quality and safety for construction. (Ch. 16)

bungalow. A small, one-story house with an overhanging roof and a covered porch. (Ch. 15)

C

cabriole (KAB-ree-ohl) **leg.** A furniture leg that curves out at the middle and then tapers inward just above an ornamental foot; a characteristic of the Queen Anne style. (Ch. 25)

café curtains. A casual form of curtains which generally cover the lower portion of the window, and often have a scalloped heading and are hung from a rail.

candelabra. Multiple candle holders supported on a single decorative stand.

caning. Slim pieces of bamboo, cane, rattan or palm which are woven to form the seats and backs of furniture.

Cape Cod house. A house with a simple rectangular design, a central chimney, and a pitched roof. (Ch. 14)

capital. Decorative top member of a column, pillar, or pilaster.

carbon monoxide. A colorless, odorless gas that is readily absorbed by red blood cells when breathed in, thus interfering with the body's oxygen supply. (Ch. 28)

career ladder. Group of related jobs that can lead to more advanced positions. (Ch. 4)

case goods. Furniture pieces that are not upholstered, such as chests, desks, and tables. (Ch. 26)

casing. Trim around a window or door opening.

caulking. Applying a sealing compound to make a joint watertight and airtight. (Ch. 9)

ceiling rose. Generally made of plaster, a circular decorative molding fixed to the ceiling, often in the center. It often has a pendant light fitting suspended from it.

ceramic tile. A thin, flat piece of fired clay attached to walls, floors, or countertops with adhesive to create durable and decorative surfaces.

cesspool. A system that collects sewage and lets it gradually seep into the surrounding earth. (Ch. 11)

chair rail. Molding that runs horizontally across the wall about 3 ft. (0.9 m) from the floor. (Ch. 24)

chair table. A 17th century chair with a large back that protected the occupant from drafts and could be tipped forward to form a table. (Ch. 25)

chandelier. Ceiling mounted light fixture with arms branching out from a central support.

circuit breaker. A safety device that stops the flow of electric current in an overloaded circuit. (Ch. 11)

clapboards. Narrow, overlapping boards with one edge thicker than the other, used for siding. (Ch. 10)

clearance space. The additional space needed around furniture for ease of use. (Ch. 20)

closed plan. An interior layout in which rooms are separated and self-contained. (Ch. 16)

closed storage. A storage system in which doors or drawers conceal items. (Ch. 23)

closing costs. Fees due at the time a home purchase is finalized. (Ch. 6)

closing. The meeting at which legal papers are signed and money changes hands finalizing the sale of a home. (Ch. 8)

coffered ceiling. Recessed panels created in a ceiling.

colonnade. Series of evenly spaced columns supporting arches.

color scheme. A combination of colors selected for a room design in order to create a mood or set a tone. (Ch. 18)

color. The effect an object produces by absorbing and reflecting light rays; hue. (Ch. 17)

column. Round or square slender pillars, which are often used as structural supports, but can also be purely decorative.

combing. This paint effect is similar to wood graining. A notched card or comb is dragged over a painted or translucent glazed surface to achieve lines, squiggles, zig zags, or any pattern that is desired.

commode. Cabinet or chest, typically raised off the floor with legs, which can hold a wash basin or chamber pot.

complement. The color opposite another color on the color wheel. (Ch. 18)

complementary. A color scheme that uses two colors that are directly opposite each other on the color wheel. (Ch. 18)

computer-aided design (CAD). Software that enables designers, architects, and drafters to make construction drawings, interior designs, and other drawings using a computer. (Ch. 3)

condominium ownership. Individual ownership of a unit in a multifamily dwelling, such as an apartment or town house. (Ch. 6)

conduction. The transfer of heat from a body of higher temperature to one of lower temperature by direct contact. (Ch. 11)

contingency fee. An additional percentage of the total cost of a project to cover unexpected expenses. (Ch. 20)

contract. A legally binding agreement that states what work the contractor will do and the amount the homeowner will pay. (Ch. 13)

contractor. A person who oversees a construction project. (Ch. 11)

convection. The transfer of heat by means of air flow. (Ch. 11)

conventional construction. A building method in which materials are cut and assembled piece by piece at the home site. (Ch. 3)

conventional mortgage. A home loan in which the borrower pays a fixed interest rate for the life of the loan. (Ch. 8)

conversion. A type of major remodeling that involves buying a building for the purpose of converting it or changing its use. (Ch. 13)

cooperative ownership. A form of home ownership in which residents of a multifamily building purchase stock in a nonprofit corporation that owns the building and its grounds. (Ch. 6)

coquina (co-KEE-nuh). A soft porous limestone composed of shell and coral. (Ch. 14)

cornice (KOR-nuhs). A decorative strip at the area where the roof and the walls meet. (Ch. 15)

cornice lighting. A concealed light source that is mounted near the junction of wall and ceiling and directs light downward. (Ch. 27)

cove lighting. A concealed light source that directs light upward toward the ceiling. (Ch. 27)

crackle. Surface finish that creates a glaze of fine cracks on the top layer and exposes the base coat color underneath.

credit history. A person's record of paying loans and bills. (Ch. 8)

cresting. Ornamental ridge at the top of a wall or roof peak.

cross ventilation. Air flow created when air travels in one side of a home and out another. (Ch. 10)

crown molding. Molding installed where the wall and ceiling meet or applied at the top of case goods.

culture. A combination of all the customs, beliefs, and ideas of a group of people. (Ch. 2)

cupola. Roof with a dome shape.

cut length. Distance from top to bottom of drapery plus hems and top headings.

cutting in. Painting a clean edge, usually a straight line, at the edge of a painted area.

D

damage. As defined in a warranty, a problem that is the result of improper treatment by the buyer or the result of natural disasters. (Ch. 9)

deck. Coming out from a building it is a floor with no walls and roof; it is generally made of timber and supported by joists.

defect. As defined in a warranty, any flaw that exists in the product when it is sold, or that develops within a certain period of time. (Ch. 9)

demographics. Statistical characteristics of a population. (Ch. 2)

direct lighting. Light that shines on specific areas. (Ch. 27)

distressing. A process in which new wood is made to look old. (Ch. 25)

dormer. A structure that projects through a steeply sloping roof. The window set in this structure is called a dormer window. (Ch. 14)

double-complementary. A color scheme that uses four colors that are an equal distance apart from one another on the color wheel. (Ch. 18)

dovetail joint. Furniture construction technique using interlocking "V" shaped cut-outs.

down payment. A partial payment of cash made at the time of purchase. (Ch. 6)

downlighting. The most common type of lighting; usually accomplished with a ceiling fixture or a type of structural lighting. (Ch. 27)

downlights. A type of lighting that directs a beam of light from the ceiling downward. (Ch. 27)

dragging. A process which creates fine vertical irregular lines and a soft textured look to walls. It is achieved by applying a translucent color glaze over a base coat and then using a dry wide brush, dragging it over the glaze before it dries.

duplex. One building that contains two separate living units. (Ch. 5)

E

earnest money. A deposit a potential buyer pays to show that he or she is serious about buying a home. (Ch. 6)

eave. Lower edge of a roof extending beyond the exterior wall.

eclectic. A style of decorating that involves mixing furnishings of different styles and possibly from different periods. (Ch. 19)

efficiency apartment. A unit with one main room, a small kitchen area, and a bathroom. (Ch. 5)

egress. Vertical or horizontal means of escape from a building.

elevation. A diagram that shows vertical surfaces as if viewed from the ground; usually shows a house exterior or one wall of a room. (Ch. 10)

ell. An extension built at right angles to the length of the original house. (Ch. 14)

emphasis. In design, the center of interest or focal point that first catches the viewer's attention. (Ch. 19)

employability skills. Skills such as dependability, responsibility, and a positive attitude, that are required to acquire and retain a job. (Ch. 4)

energy audit. An inspection of a home to determine where heat loss may be occurring. (Ch. 12)

engineered wood product. Manufactured material formed from wood. (Ch. 3)

entrepreneur. A person who starts his or her own business. (Ch. 4)

entry-level job. A job that requires little training, although a high school diploma may be required. (Ch. 4)

equity. The difference between the market value of a piece of property and the principal owed on the mortgage. (Ch. 8)

ergonomics. An applied science concerned with designing and arranging things so they are safe, comfortable, and efficient for people to use. (Ch. 23)

escrow. Money held in trust by a third party until a specified time; often pertains to payments for property taxes and insurance. (Ch. 8)

étagère. Tall, open shelving unit for displaying accessories.

evict. To legally require tenants to move out before their lease has expired. (Ch. 7)

extended family. A family that includes other relatives in addition to parents and children. (Ch. 2)

F

fanlight. A semicircular, round, or oval window with fan-shaped panes of glass. (Ch. 15)

faux finishes. Finishes that give a false impression of a surface.

Feng Shui. The ancient Chinese practice of harmonizing the built-environment with spiritual forces.

festoon. A design often appearing on renaissance and neo-classical furniture that depicts a loop of drapery or a garland of fruit or flowers.

fiber optic light. A type of light that flows through glass strands and is focused at the other end of a tube; emits no heat and no ultraviolet rays. (Ch. 27)

fiberboard. Board of compressed wood shavings and glue.

filament. A single strand of any type of fiber.

finial. Decorative hardware used to cap drapery rods, newel posts, furnishings, woodwork, etc.

fire box. Open masonry area built in a wall at the base of a chimney to house a fire.

fixed expenses. Expenses, such as rent, that are fairly constant and that must be paid regularly. (Ch. 6)

flammable. Capable of burning quickly. (Ch. 28)

flashing. Strips of sheet metal placed around a chimney and other roof openings to prevent moisture leaks and insulate the roof from the chimney. (Ch. 10)

flax. Cellulose plant fiber used to create linen.

flexible expenses. Expenses that vary in amount and that do not occur regularly. (Ch. 6)

flock. This luxurious velvet feel is made by dusting powdered silk, wool or flock onto a tacky patterned surface paper, creating a piled effect.

floor plan. A diagram of a home or other structure that shows the arrangement of rooms, as if seen from above. (Ch. 7, 10)

flue. The vertical shaft of a chimney that carries smoke and hot gases to open air. (Ch. 11)

fluorescent light. A visible light produced when chemicals inside a sealed glass tube transform ultraviolet rays into visible light. (Ch. 27)

foam core board. Stiff sheet of Styrofoam sealed with laminated paper front and back.

footing. Continuous concrete base that supports the foundation walls of a house below ground level. (Ch. 10)

form. An element of design that describes the shape and structure of solid objects. (Ch. 17)

fossil fuels. Fuels such as oil, coal, and natural gas that were formed in the earth from the remains of prehistoric animals or plants. (Ch. 12)

foundation. The part of a building that sits below ground and supports the structure; the masonry substructure of a building.

fourplex. A housing unit that is attached at the side walls to three other units. (Ch. 5)

furniture. Any freestanding or custom-built article constructed to provide surfaces for sitting or storing objects.

fuse. A safety device that stops the flow of electric current in an overloaded circuit. (Ch. 11)

G

gable roof. A pitched roof that forms triangular end walls, or gables. (Ch. 14)

gables. Triangular end walls formed by a gable or pitched roof. (Ch. 14)

gambrel roof. A roof that has two slopes on each side, the upper slope being flatter than the lower slope. (Ch. 14)

garden apartment. A unit in a low-rise building that includes landscaped grounds. (Ch. 5)

garrison house. A house with a second story that overhangs or projects from the first story. (Ch. 14)

gateleg table. A table with legs on each side that swing out to support drop leaves that are pulled up from the sides. (Ch. 25)

gazebo. A free-standing, outdoor structure with a roof, typically octagonal and open on all sides.

geothermal energy. Heat from the earth's interior. (Ch. 12)

gilding. This is essentially the application of a gold finish. It can be achieved by applying gold leaf, or by using metallic powders.

gingerbread. Lacy-looking, cutout wood trim. (Ch. 15)

glaze. A translucent coating used to enrich or protect a surface.

gold leaf. Hand applied thin layers of gold leaf brushed onto a prepared adhesive surface, over a red primer to increase vibrancy and luster.

golden rectangle. A rectangle in which the ratio of the sides is based on the ratio of the golden section. (Ch. 19)

golden section. The division of a line at a point between one-half and one-third of its total length so that the ratio of the larger segment to the smaller segment equals the ratio of the whole line to the larger segment. (Ch. 19)

grab bar. A safety rail installed in showers, tubs or other areas to help prevent individuals from falling on slippery surfaces.

gradation. A type of rhythm in design achieved by a gradual increase or decrease of color, size, or pattern. (Ch. 19)

graduated mortgage payment. A home loan in which the payments start out low and increase in the later years of the loan when the owners are likely to have more income. (Ch. 8)

green building. Designing, building, and operating homes to use materials, energy, and water efficiently. (Ch. 3)

gross income. The amount a person earns before taxes and other deductions are taken out. (Ch. 6)

ground fault circuit interrupter (GFCI). A safety device used in receptacles near plumbing or water to guard people against electric shock. (Ch. 11)

ground wire. An electrical conductor that is connected to the earth, providing protection in case there is an abnormal flow of electric current. (Ch. 11)

grout. Thin mortar used to fill in spaces between tiles, bricks, or other surfaces.

H

half-timbered house. A style of house built by early English colonists in which the wood frame of the house forms part of the outside wall. (Ch. 14)

halogen bulb. A special type of incandescent light bulb containing pressurized halogen gas. (Ch. 27)

hand. The feel of a surface or fabric.

handrail. A waist-high rail installed as a support or guard on a balcony, stairway, or porch.

hardwoods. These trees are porous, and usually deciduous. They have broad leaves and covered seeds. Their wood is used to make fine furniture.

heading. The top of a curtain or drape.

highboy. A chest of drawers mounted on legs. (Ch. 25)

high-rise apartment. One of many separate living units in a multistory building generally equipped with elevators, most often found in cities. (Ch. 5)

hip roof. A roof with four sloped sides. (Ch. 15)

home equity loan. Money borrowed from a lending institution based on the current market value of a property, minus the amount owed on the mortgage. (Ch. 13)

homeowner's insurance. Insurance protection for a home and its contents. (Ch. 8)

household. All the people who live together in one housing unit. (Ch. 2)

housing. Any structure built for people to live in. (Ch. 1)

hue. The feature of color that makes one color different from others. (Ch. 18)

human resources. Personal qualities that people possess, including creativity, imagination, knowledge, skills, talent, time, energy, and experience. (Ch. 5)

I

incandescent light. Light produced by electricity passing through a tungsten filament in a glass bulb. (Ch. 27)

indirect lighting. Light that is cast off ceilings and walls. It is more diffused, or softer, than direct lighting. (Ch. 27)

inlay. To set one material into the surface of another creating a decorative pattern.

insulation. Materials, such as fiberglass, that protect a room from sound or heat.

intensity. The brightness or dullness of a color. (Ch. 18)

interest. The money a lending company charges a buyer for a loan. (Ch. 6)

interview. A formal meeting between an employer and a job applicant. (Ch. 4)

inventory. A survey a designer uses to identify characteristics that will affect a design plan. (Ch. 20)

island. A freestanding storage and countertop unit. (Ch. 22)

J

jabot. Side portion of a window treatment where fabric is draped in soft vertical folds.

jalousie window. Similar in movement to a Venetian blind, this window is comprised of horizontal strips of glass that move in unison to allow ventilation.

japanning. The process of applying glossy black lacquer to furniture. (Ch. 25)

job application. A form employers use to ask questions about an applicant's skills, work experience, education, and interests. (Ch. 4)

job shadowing. Spending time with a person at work and learning by watching as he or she performs the functions of the job. (Ch. 4)

joint. The place where one piece of wood is connected to another. (Ch. 26)

joist. A floor or ceiling beam support.

K

kick plate. Decorative plate installed at the bottom of a door to protect it from wear.

knee kicker. Tool used to stretch carpet.

knocked down. A description of components that are ready to be assembled.

L

laminate. To layer a number of items together and bond them with glues, heat, and pressure. Laminates may take the form of materials such as Formica or veneer.

landlord. A person who owns a property and rents it to someone else. (Ch. 6)

landscaping. The ways people use plants and objects to enhance or change the natural environment around their homes. (Ch. 12)

latex paint. A water-based, quick-drying paint. It is considered more environmentally safe than solvent-based paint. (Ch. 24)

lease. The legal document a tenant signs when agreeing to rent housing for a specific period of time. (Ch. 7)

lifestyle. A way of living. (Ch. 1)

light emitting diode. A type of light made of a silicon "chip" about the size of a grain of salt. A small electrical current passing through the chip generates the light. (Ch. 27)

line. An element of design that delineates space, outlines form, and conveys a sense of movement or direction. (Ch. 17)

loft. A room in the roof of a building.

louver. Horizontal slats framed-in on a 45 degree angle to shed rain and allow circulation; often operable.

low-rise apartment. An apartment in a building with few floors and no elevators. (Ch. 5)

lumen. This SI unit expresses the quantity of light output.

luminous ceiling panels. Consists of fluorescent tubes placed above plastic panels. (Ch. 27)

M

mansard roof. A roof that has two slopes on all sides, with the lower slope being steep and the upper slope almost flat. (Ch. 15)

manufactured home. A dwelling completely assembled at a factory and transported to the site. (Ch. 3)

marbling. The imitation of the natural product of marble, often called faux marble.

marquetry. Decorative wood veneer inlay.

master bath. A full bathroom that is part of the master bedroom area. (Ch. 22)

material resources. Tangible assets such as money, property, supplies, and tools. (Ch. 5)

medallion. Large ornamental panel featuring a crest or some other decorative element.

mentor. A successful worker who shares her or his expert knowledge and demonstrates correct work behaviors to new employees. (Ch. 4)

modular furniture. Furniture made from standardized pieces that can fit together in a variety of ways. (Ch. 25)

modular home. A systems-built home made up of separate boxlike sections, or modules, that are built at a factory and assembled at the site. (Ch. 3)

molding. Strip of shaped wood used for trim or ornamentation in a room. (Ch. 24)

monochromatic. A color scheme that uses tints and shades of one color on the color wheel. (Ch. 18)

mortgage. A home loan. (Ch. 6)

multipurpose furniture. Furniture pieces that serve more than one need, such as a futon that serves as a couch and a bed. (Ch. 26)

multipurpose room. Room used for many things. (Ch. 20)

N

natural fibers. Fibers made from plants or animals; cotton, wool, linen, and silk. (Ch. 24)

networking. Communicating with people you know or can get to know to share job and career information and advice. (Ch. 4)

newel. The central column around which the steps of a circular staircase wind.

newel-post. Decorative post used to support the beginning or intermediate intervals of a staircase railing.

niche. A recess in a wall.

nomads. People who wander from place to place in search of food for their grazing herds. (Ch. 1)

nuclear family. A family that includes a father, a mother, and one or more children. (Ch. 2)

O

open plan. An interior layout that has few dividing walls separating rooms. (Ch. 16)

open storage. A storage system in which stored items are visible. (Ch. 23)

opposition. A design effect in which lines come together to form right angles. (Ch. 19)

orientation. The position of a home on its site and the direction the home faces. (Ch. 10)

overlay. A sheet of transparent material that is placed over a basic drawing in order to add enhancements or special details without altering the drawing itself. (Ch. 21)

P – Q

Palladian window. Greek revival styled arched window flanked by two square windows, originally created by Roman architect Andrea Paladio.

panel box. A device that controls the distribution of electricity to the home wiring system; also called a service entrance or fuse box. (Ch. 11)

paneling. Wood panels applied continuously to an interior wall.

parquet. Wood floor laid in geometric patterns.

particleboard. A type of board made from a combination of wood shavings, veneer scraps, chips, and sometimes sawdust that are all mixed with glue and pressed together under heat. (Ch. 26)

passive solar heating system. A system that makes direct use of the sun's heat without mechanical systems. (Ch. 12)

patina. A green or brown film formed on copper and bronze by weathering or oxidization of the metal.

pedestal. A substructure used below the columns in classical architecture; a base supporting a column or a base supporting a basin or serving as a base for a statue.

pediment (PED-uh-munt). A triangular or arched decoration over a window or doorway. (Ch. 15)

pendant. A hanging electrical fixture mounted from the ceiling.

peninsula. A countertop that extends out into the room, with one end attached to a wall or a cabinet. (Ch. 22)

performance bond. A sum of money a contractor puts up to provide insurance that a job will be completed. (Ch. 13)

physical needs. All the things the human body needs to survive: air, sunlight, shelter, sleep, and food. (Ch. 1)

pictorial drawing. A drawing that shows the viewer several surfaces of objects in the room simultaneously. (Ch. 21)

pigment. A substance that absorbs some light rays and reflects others, affecting the color of an object. (Ch. 18)

pilaster. Decorative flattened column. (Ch. 15)

pile. The density of carpet or fabric; nap. (Ch. 24)

pillar. The column supporting an arch.

piping. A product that can be stitched into the seam of a curtain; a fabric covered cord in a pipe-like fold over cord with a narrow flange.

pitched roof. A two-sided roof with a steep angle. (Ch. 14)

plain weave. A simple weave pattern that is as strong in one direction as it is in the other. It wears evenly. (Ch. 24)

plywood. A building material consisting of three, five, or seven layers of less expensive wood glued together. (Ch. 26)

pocket door. An interior door that recesses into a wall cavity to disappear from view.

points. A one-time service fee charged by lending companies to increase their yield on a mortgage. Each point generally equals 1 percent of the mortgage amount. (Ch. 8)

polypropylene. A tough plastic used for furniture frames.

portfolio. A collection of examples of a person's best work; often used when applying for a job to show a person's abilities and accomplishments. (Ch. 4)

portico. (POR-tih-koh). A tall, open porch, supported by columns, over the front entrance. (Ch. 15)

primary colors. The basic colors—yellow, red, and blue—that cannot be created by mixing other colors. (Ch. 18)

primer. A sealant that makes a surface nonporous and keeps out humidity; a base paint. (Ch. 24)

principal. The original amount of a loan (not including interest); also the portion of a loan payment that goes toward reducing the original amount of a loan. (Ch. 6)

prioritize. To rate wants and needs in order of preference and importance. (Ch. 20)

private zone. The part of the home used for sleeping, relaxing, bathing, and dressing. (Ch. 16)

proportion. The size relationships that can be found within an object or design. (Ch. 19)

psychological (sy-kuh-LAH-jih-kuhl) **needs.** Needs related to thoughts and emotions. (Ch. 1)

pueblos. Adobe houses built on top of each other into cliffs and caves and on the level ground. (Ch. 14)

R

R value. A measure of insulation's capacity to resist winter heat loss and summer heat gain. (Ch. 10)

radiation. (a) The transmission of heat by means of rays traveling in straight lines from a source. (Ch. 11) (b) A type of rhythm that occurs when lines radiate, or move outward, from a central point. (Ch. 19)

radon. A radioactive gas that occurs naturally in some types of soil and rock and can seep into homes through cracks in basement floors and walls. (Ch. 28)

ragging. A finishing technique in which a translucent glaze is applied over a base coat and then removed by a rag that is bunched up and dabbed over the surface.

rail. Structural support used in various applications including stairs, balconies, doors, windows (top rail, bottom rail, side rail).

ramp. Sloped surface or walkway connecting two levels.

recovery rate. The average amount of water that will be heated in a water heater tank in one hour. (Ch. 11)

reeding. Decorative carving that consists of vertical lines that resemble thin reeds—stems of tall grass. (Ch. 25)

references. People who will recommend a person to an employer. (Ch. 4)

remodeling. Changing a home's structure or systems. (Ch. 13)

rendering. A drawing in which the designer adds realistic details, such as textures, shadows, shadings, and color. (Ch. 21)

renovation. The process of extensively repairing and modernizing a home. (Ch. 13)

renter's insurance. An insurance policy that covers personal property against loss by theft, fire, or other hazards. (Ch. 6)

repetition. A type of rhythm in design achieved when different elements are repeated. (Ch. 19)

reproduction. A furniture piece that is an accurate copy of an original design. (Ch. 25)

resilient flooring. Flooring with a semi-hard surface that returns to its original shape after stress. (Ch. 24)

resource management. The wise use of natural resources. (Ch. 12)

restoration. A type of renovation in which an older home is returned to its original state. (Ch. 13)

résumé. A brief summary of a person's education, skills, work experience, activities, and interests. (Ch. 4)

retrofitting. The process of making an existing home more energy-efficient. (Ch. 12)

rhythm. The design principle that suggests connected movement between different parts of a design by using colors, lines, forms, or textures. (Ch. 19)

rod pocket. A stitched pocket that holds draperies on drapery rods.

roller shade. A flat window treatment, typically made of fabric or vinyl, using spring rollers inside a window frame for raising and lowering.

Roman shade. Window treatment utilizing a series of tapes, or rings and cords stitched onto the backside for raising and lowering, which draws up the horizontal pleats when raised.

rosette. Round, elaborately detailed pattern resembling a rose.

S

saltbox house. A two-story, pitched-roof house in which the rear portion of the roof extends down to cover a first-floor addition. (Ch. 14)

sample board. A piece of illustration board with mounted samples of proposed wall coverings, floor coverings, fabrics, and window treatments. (Ch. 21)

satin weave. A fabric weave pattern distinguished by long "floats," which are formed when each warp (lengthwise) thread passes over a certain number of weft (crosswise) threads at one time before passing under one. (Ch. 24)

scale drawing. A drawing in which a given number of inches or centimeters represents a given number of feet or meters. (Ch. 20)

scale. The way the size of an object or a space relates to human beings and to other objects or spaces in a design. (Ch. 19)

sconce. A wall-mounted electrical or candle light fixture.

secondary colors. The colors orange, violet, and green, which are made by mixing equal parts of two primary colors. (Ch. 18)

security deposit. A fee paid by a renter to cover the cost of any future damage that may be caused to the unit. (Ch. 6)

septic tank. A large concrete box, usually buried underground, that is used for sewage disposal. (Ch. 11)

service contract. An agreement purchased from a dealer or manufacturer under which regular inspections and repairs of a product are made at no extra charge or for a small fee. (Ch. 9)

service zone. The part of the home where most of the household work is done. (Ch. 16)

setback. The distance a building must be from the property line. (Ch. 13)

settee. A medium-sized sofa or long bench.

shade. A hue that is darker than its normal value; created by adding black to a hue. (Ch. 18)

sheers. A window treatment constructed of translucent fabrics and materials.

shingles. Thin pieces of material that are laid in overlapping rows to cover the roof of a structure. (Ch. 10)

shutters. Window coverings made of vertical sections of wood or manufactured material hinged together, much like a folding door. (Ch. 24)

single-parent family. A family that has only one parent living with one or more children. (Ch. 2)

site. The land and surrounding environment on which a home is built. (Ch. 3)

skylight. A window installed in a roof to provide additional light to an interior space.

social zone. The part of the home used for activities and entertainment. (Ch. 16)

soffit. The underside of a structural member (i.e., a dropped ceiling or overhang).

soffit lighting. Built-in lighting that is enclosed in a box-like structure that directs light downward. The box-like structure often has a plastic panel at the bottom to diffuse the light. (Ch. 27)

softwoods. These trees are non-porous and are usually evergreen conifers. They have needle-like leaves and uncovered seeds.

solar panel. Panel installed to collect, store, and convert energy from the sun to electricity.

space. An element of design that is the three-dimensional expanse that a designer works with, as well as the area around or between objects within that expanse. (Ch. 17)

split-complementary. A color scheme that combines one color with the two colors on each side of its complement on the color wheel. (Ch. 18)

stairwell. The entire open area encompassing a staircase.

status. The way a person's importance in society is perceived by others. (Ch. 2)

stenciling. Patterns created by applying paint through cutout areas in a template. (Ch. 24)

stippling. Is achieved by dabbing a stippling brush over a wet glaze or layer of paint. It creates a soft dappled grainy texture and is ideal as a wall finish.

strip lights. Rows of incandescent bulbs or fluorescent tubes around the tops or sides of a mirror. (Ch. 27)

stucco. A plaster siding material made with cement, sand, and lime. (Ch. 10)

style. The overall characteristics of a design. (Ch. 21)

subcontractor. A worker hired by a contractor or homeowner to perform a specific function in the construction of a home. (Ch. 11)

sub-floor. Concrete base, or boarding laid over joists on top of which the flooring is laid.

sublet. To move out of a rental unit before the lease is up and rent the unit to someone else while retaining legal responsibility for the original lease. (Ch. 7)

subsidized housing. Private housing available at low cost to families with low incomes through programs in which the government pays part of the rent to the housing owners. (Ch. 7)

survey. A check to determine the exact boundaries of a property. (Ch. 8)

swag. A piece of fabric that is draped gracefully across the top of a window. (Ch. 24)

swag. Fabric or garland curving between two points that is used in drapery treatments or as an applied decoration.

symmetrical balance. A design effect in which the arrangement of forms on one side of an imaginary central line is the mirror image of the arrangement of forms on the opposite side. (Ch. 19)

synthetic fibers. Fibers made with chemicals and other materials; nylon, polyester, and rayon. (Ch. 24)

systems-built home. A dwelling whose parts are manufactured in a factory, with the building completed at the site. (Ch. 3)

T

tapestry. Fabric wall hanging usually depicting an image or a scene.

task lighting. A light source used to perform specific tasks, such as reading.

technology. The practical application of knowledge. (Ch. 3)

telecommute. To work from home while keeping in touch with an employer's office via electronic devices. (Ch. 2)

telecommuters. People authorized by their employers to work from home while keeping in touch with an employer's office via electronic devices. (Ch. 23)

templates. Cutout patterns of furniture and appliances drawn to scale and used to create floor plans. (Ch. 20)

tenant. Someone who pays rent to use or occupy property owned by someone else. (Ch. 6)

tenements. Apartment complex with minimum standards of sanitation, safety, and comfort. (Ch. 15)

terrazzo. This is a composite material made up of cement and marble aggregate that has a mosaic look.

tertiary colors. Colors such as yellow-orange and red-violet that are created by combining a primary color with a neighboring secondary color. (Ch. 18)

texture. The appearance or feel of an object's surface. (Ch. 17)

thatch. Bundles of reeds or straw used as roofing material. (Ch. 14)

thermal burn. An injury caused by hot liquids, hot surfaces, or flames. (Ch. 28)

thermostat. A temperature-activated switch that turns the heating or air conditioning system on and off to keep the temperature of a home at a set level. (Ch. 11)

tie-back. Any decorative element used to hold a drapery away from the center of a window.

tint. A hue that is lighter than its normal value; created by adding white to a hue. (Ch. 18)

tone. A color that is duller than its normal value; created by adding gray to a hue.

topography. The contour, or slope, of the land and its other physical features. (Ch. 10)

town house. One of several houses attached together at the side walls. (Ch. 5)

track lighting. Adjustable incandescent or halogen fixtures mounted along a track installed on the ceiling.

traffic patterns. The paths people take as they walk from room to room during everyday activities. (Ch. 16)

transition. A design effect in which lines change direction by flowing in a curve, or when curved lines lead the eye from one object to another. (Ch. 19)

traverse rod. A cord-controlled drapery rod used for opening and closing window treatment.

tread. Flat horizontal member of a step or staircase.

trellis. Horizontal joists supported by posts created to support vines or provide shade.

trestle table. A table with a long rectangular top and a wide vertical support at each end. (Ch. 25)

triadic. A color scheme that uses any three hues that are an equal distance apart on the color wheel. (Ch. 18)

triplex. A housing unit that is attached at the side walls to two other units. (Ch. 5)

trundle bed. A bed that contains a lower bed that is stored under the higher bed during the day. (Ch. 25)

turning. A method of adding shape to wood, such as legs and spindles, using a lathe. (Ch. 25)

twill weave. A fabric weave pattern with diagonal lines or wales. A wale is formed when a weft (crosswise) thread passes over two or more warp (lengthwise) threads before passing under a warp thread again. (Ch. 24)

U

U value. The measure of a window's capacity to resist winter heat loss. (Ch. 12)

unity. A principle of design that occurs when all the parts of a design are related by one idea. (Ch. 19)

universal design. A philosophy of designing interiors and products to accommodate all people with a variety of requirements, needs, and abilities. (Ch. 1)

upholstery. Materials used to make soft seating—including a wood or metal frame, springs, foam, batting, cording, and fabrics.

uplighting. A type of lighting that reflects light off the ceiling to give a sense of height and spaciousness. It can be achieved with many structural lighting fixtures, wall sconces, or tall floor lamps. (Ch. 27)

utilities. Services such as electric power, gas, water, and telephone. (Ch. 5)

V

valance lighting. A type of built-in lighting that consists of a light source (usually a fluorescent light) mounted over a window and hidden by the window valance that directs light both upward and downward. (Ch. 27)

valance. A short length of decorative material placed across the top of a window. (Ch. 24)

value. The lightness or darkness of a color. (Ch. 18)

values. The principles that you want to live by and the beliefs that are important to you. (Ch. 4)

vanity. A base cabinet in a bathroom. (Ch. 22)

vapor barrier. Materials added to walls and attic areas to help reduce drafts and prevent moisture from getting into a home. (Ch. 10)

variance. A license to waive a zoning law. (Ch. 13)

variety. A design effect that occurs when different styles and materials are combined. (Ch. 19)

vaulted ceiling. Ceiling forming an arched canopy.

veneer. (a) Any overlay material used to provide an ornamental finish. (Ch. 10); (b) A thin layer of more expensive wood glued to less expensive wood to create a better appearance. (Ch. 25)

volume. Space required by a three-dimensional object.

W

wainscoting. Decorative paneling or other materials applied to the bottom third of an interior wall as a lining.

wall washer. A recessed ceiling light that spreads light over a wall from ceiling to floor. (Ch. 27)

wallboard. Boards made for surfacing, rather than for insulating ceilings and walls, including plywood, plasterboard, and laminated plastics glued to a backing of hardboard or plywood.

wallcoverings. Flexible materials such as paper, vinyl, foil, fabric, felt, cork, carpet, or veneers applied to a wall.

wallpaper. Decorated printed paper sold in rolls to cover walls.

warp. Threads running lengthwise and parallel to the selvage in fabrics.

warranty. A written statement of the manufacturer's promise to replace defective parts of a product at no charge for a certain time. (Ch. 9)

weft. Threads running crosswise to the selvage in fabrics.

well. The space, or horizontal distance, between the flights of a stair.

welt. A seam in flexible-metal roofing.

wicker furniture. Furniture that is woven of thin, flexible twigs, branches, and stems, often from willow trees. (Ch. 26)

windbreak. A natural or manufactured item, such as a row of trees or a fence, that protects a housing site from strong winds. (Ch. 10)

windows. Glass enclosures designed to allow in natural light.

Windsor chair. A wood chair with stick legs and a spindle back inserted into a saddle-shaped plank seat. (Ch. 25)

wing chair. An upholstered armchair with a high back and high sides, or "wings," designed to give protection from drafts. (Ch. 25)

work center. An area of a kitchen especially equipped for a particular task. (Ch. 22)

work order. Document specifying work to be completed, including details and drawings.

work triangle. In a kitchen, the triangle formed by drawing imaginary lines to connect the sink, range or cooktop, and refrigerator. (Ch. 22)

workplace readiness. Ability to do the various tasks required for a particular job. (Ch. 4)

wrought iron. A tough, durable form of iron that can be hammered and bent into different shapes such as decorative accessories, table and chair frames, and lawn furniture. (Ch. 26)

X – Y – Z

xeriscaping (ZIHR-uh-skay-ping)**.** Landscaping to conserve water. (Ch. 12)

zoning laws. Laws that determine the type of building that may be constructed in a particular zone, or section, of a community. (Ch. 16)

Cover and Interior Design:
William Seabright & Associates

Cover Photo: Richard Bryant, Arcaid

Acme Brick, 62
Alamy, 306B, 376
    B.A.E., Inc., 399
    Richard Bryant/Arcaid Ed, 10, 574
    Creatas/Dynamic Graphics Group, 626BC, 658
    Frazier Cunningham/Mode, 520
    Florida Images, 646
    Ross Germaniuk/Design Pics, Inc., 626CR
    D. Hurst, 218
    V + A Images, 592
    Alan Weintraub, 361
Amana Appliances, 512
American Standard, 253T
Ann Sacks Tile & Stone, 578
    Todd Graf, 435B
Andersen Windows, Inc., 446T, 623
APA Engineered Wood, 459B
AP/Wide World Photos, 274B
Archive Photos, Popperfoto, 327
Aristokraft, 382
Armstrong Floors, 393, 431
Arnold & Brown, 87T, 205TR, 312B
Art MacDillos, Gary Skillestad, 132T, 222, 223, 224, 225, 226, 227, 238, 249T, 249B, 261B, 429B, 429T, 557, 605
Bassett Furniture Industries Inc., 395, 433, 550B
Beateworks, Inc., BrandX, 593, 614
Marshall Berman, 156, 198B, 231, 483
Bromonite Corporation, 266
Brookstone, Inc., 653
Bruno Independent Living Aids, Inc.®, 659
Butterick/Vogue, 421, 563, 564BL, 564TC, 564BR, 564TR, 565TL, 565BL, 565TR, 566, 567, 568,
California Redwood Assn./Saart & Forai, 228B
Dave Caves Construction, Inc., 282
Comstock Royalty Free, 147B
Container Store, 542
Corbis, 5, 18, 36, 201TR, 332B, 487B, 626C, 629, 660, 656
    Barton, Paul, 3, 45B, 49B, 283, 388-389
    Beck, Peter, 288
    Richard Bickel, 369
    Blank, James, 344
    Jon/Elizabeth Bouchier, Elizabeth Whiting & Assoc., 565BC
    CB Production, 332B

George Diebold, 84B
George Disario, 342B
Carlos Dominquez, 626TC
Najlah Feanny, 106T
Jon Feingersh, 119T
Gordon Gainer, 125B
Brownie Harris, 637
Ralf-Finn Hestoft, 120
Rodney Hyatt, 5, 58, 78
Harald A. Jahn, 630
Michael Keller, 140B
Rob Lewine, 178T
Lightscapes, 3, 212-213
Don Mason, 135B
Tom McCarthy, 112T
Jean Miele, 278
Kelly Mooney, 69B
Warren Morgan, 104T
Owaki-Kulla, 11, 642
Jose Luis Pelaez, 404
Javier Pierini, 5, 38, 56T
Jose Fuste Raga, 22B
John M. Roberts, 3, 108-109
Bob Rowan, Progressive Image, 52B
Pete Saloutos, 351
Chuck Savage, 172B, 354T
Ariel Skelley, 79B, 267, 657
Bruce Smith/Fratelli Studio, 534
Joe Sohn/ Chromosohm, 48B
Roman Soumar, 339
Tom Stewart, 97B
Wes Thompson, 43T
Larry Williams, 20T, 134B
Bo Zaunders, 23T
Don Couch, 34, 35, 336, 337, 488, 489, 496. 497, 638, 639
Davis Caves Construction, Inc., 282
Decks Appeal Custom Redwood Decks, Rick Paris, 291B
Luis Delgado, 126T, 127, 155T, 184B, 199T, 287, 362, 363, 438, 594, 595
Domehome, 360B
DuPont, Corian®, 504
DuPont Tyvek, 228T
Dyson Company, 192T
ECR International, 254
Elumens Corporation, 485B
Environmental Protection Agency's Energy Star® Program, 314, 540
Envision
    Andre Baranowski, 633
    George Mattei, 304 BL&R, 443, 569
    Melabee Miller, 415, 491B
    Sue Pashko, 6, 148, 164T, 328
    Madeline Polss, 547, 579
    Photononstop, 9, 11, 426, 442, 620, 635, 640
    RESO, 589

EPA, 509L
Esto, David Sundberg, 398
Ethan Allen Inc., 409T, 409B, 416T, 416B, 437, 478B, 530, 602B, 603T, 615
Curt Fischer, 95B, 96B, 142B, 151T, 312T, 524, 525, 535, 550T, 602T
Fisher & Paykel, 514
David R. Frazier Photolibrary/David Frazier, 44T, 47T, 67B, 68B, 121T, 123T, 216B, 243, 349T, 387, 474B, 484B
Tim Fuller, 9, 54T, 55B, 76T, 77B, 144T, 145B, 186T, 187B, 208T, 209B, 268, 269, 298, 299, 318T, 319B, 402, 403, 422, 423, 444, 464, 466, 490, 544, 545, 570, 571, 582L, 583, 584, 616, 617, 649T, 662, 663
The Futon Shop, 611
Ann Garvin, 150T, 204B, 221T, 413, 460, 480B, 508, 652
General Electric, 513
Getty Images
    Altrendo Images, 368
    Tony Anderson, Taxi, 373
    Gianni Cigolina, Image Bank, 308B
    Digital Vision Ltd., 8, 366, 386
    Flying Colours Ltd., 143B
    Pam Francis/Stone, 3, 492-493
    Peter Gridley, 6, 110, 128, 345
    Richard Leo Johnson/Beateworks, 6, 130
    Bill Losh, 6, 190, 210
    Ryan McVey/Stone, 631
    S. Meltzer/PhotoLink, 74B
    Doug Menuez/PhotoDisc, 263
    Neo Vision/Photonica, 628
    Brad Simmons, 591
    Stephen Simpson/Image Bank, 3, 322-323
    J. Scott Smith, 625, 626TR
    Stockdisc, 171
    Telegraph Colour, 8, 10, 27T, 122B, 340, 364, 494, 497
    Arthur Tilley, 305T
    Scott Van Dyke, 626BR
    VCG, 60B
    Phil Wegener, 626TL
    Andrian Wilson, 499
Michelle Gray, 378, 381
Habitat for Humanity/Kim MacDonald, 53B
Jon Haeme Construction, 63
James Hardie® Building Products, 49T, 177T, 292, 295
Hartco Quality Wood Flooring from Armstrong, 265
The Hartstone Inn, Camden, ME, 350B

Infilling, 372
Informal balance, 434
Inner city revival, 116
Inlay, 676
Inset sink, 521
Inspections
    fees, 139
    inside walls, 182
    home, 181-184
    for remodeling, 310
Installations, 487
Insulation, 201, 233-234, 676
    energy efficiency and, 283
    forms of, 233-234
    inspecting, 182
    siding systems, 233
    for water heaters, 254
    for windows, 236
Insurance
    homeowner's, 141, 181
    renter's, 139
Integrated circuit, 71
Intensity, of color, 412, 676
Intercom systems, 656
Interest, 47, 136, 170-172, 676
Interest survey, 82
Interior construction, 245-271
    cooling, 260
    designing functional, 377-382
    electric wiring, 248-250
    finishing, 262-266
    heating system, 256-260
    jobs in, 246-247
    plumbing, 252-255
    universal design in, 32
    ventilation, 261-262
    wall finishes, 263
Interior designers, 100, 402, 451
    contract, 440-441
    government, 488-489
    healthcare, 34-35
    hospitality, 462-463
    residential, 403-404
    working with, 449
Interior design projects
    budget for, 457-459, 479
    fees for, 457
    timeline for, 487
International style, 356, 588
Internet
    job hunting on, 90
    research on, 84

Interpersonal skills. *See*
    Communication skills; Client
    relationships
Interviews, 93-95, 449, 676
Inventories, 449
    family, 449-451
    home environment, 453-454
    nonresidential, 451
Inventory, 676
Iroquois, 328
Island, 676
Island, kitchen, 499, 501
Israel, housing in, 42
Italianate style, 350

J

Jabots, 564, 676
Jacobean furniture, 580-581, 591
Jacquard weave fibers, 554
Jalousie window, 676
Japan, housing in, 24
Japanning, 582, 676
Jefferson, Thomas, 347
Job readiness, 82-87, 91-98
Jobs. *See also* Careers
    advertisements, 90
    applications, 93, 676
    basic skills for, 87
    finding, 90-95
    leaving, 98
    offer, 95
    shadowing, 85
    work experience on, 95-98
Job shadowing, 85, 676
Joints, 676
    caulking, 198
    furniture, 604-605
    reinforcement of, 605, 606
Joists, 225, 676

K

Kacha, 43
Kibbutzim, 42
Kick plate, 676
Kitchen, fires in, 648, 651
Kitchen planner, 524-525
Kitchens, 24, 45, 496-507
    appliances in, 507-515
    cabinets in, 503

cleaning routine for, 193
commercial, 508
countertops in, 504
efficient layout in, 499-502
fire extinguishers in, 651
history of, 45-46
layouts, 500
lighting for, 629
remodeling goals, 311
sinks in, 505
storage in, 540
universal design in, 32, 46,
    506-507
ventilation for, 262
Knee kicker, 676
Knocked down, 676

L

Laminate, 676
Laminate floors, plastic, 555
Laminated plastic paneling, 562
Lamps, 627
Landlords, 132, 676
    relationship with, 158-159
Landscaping, 676
    designing, 292
    hiring, 296
    manufactured elements in, 295
    natural elements in, 292, 294
    planning, 293
    purpose of, 292
    security and, 658
    water conservation and, 296
Landscape architect, 298-299
Latex paint, 676
Lath, 263
Lathe, 580
Launching stage, 30
Laundry areas, 383
    planning, 517-518
    universal design and, 518
Laws
    discrimination, 51
    open space, 50
    textile, 554
    zoning, 217, 369, 531
Layout, designing efficient, for
    kitchen, 499-502
Lead, 646
Leadership, 96, 667
Lead testing, 184

Mood
    backgrounds in setting, 550
    color in setting, 408, 418
Moore, Charles, 358
Morris, William, 587
Mortgage loan officer, 186-187
Mortgages, 140, 170-172, 677
    prequalifying for, 172
    shopping for, 172
    types of, 126, 170-172
Mortise and tenon joint, 605
Motion-sensitive lights, 74
Motion sensors, 631
Moving, 49, 138
    costs of, 136, 138
    planning for, 157
Multifamily units, 122-124, 382
Multiple listing services, 179
Multiple roles, managing, 95, 97
Multipurpose furniture, 471, 615, 677
Multipurpose rooms, 24, 450, 677
Munsell color chart, 423

N

National Association of Builders, 174
National Electrical Code, 312, 648
Native American homes, 327-328
Natural elements in landscape, 292, 294
Natural fibers, 552, 677
Natural gas, 276
Natural materials, 61-62
    wise use of, 286-287
Needs
    housing as universal, 19-33, 36-37
    housing decision and, 113
    individual, 29-32
    physical, 23-25
    psychological, 25-27, 29
    special, 30-31, 659-660
Negotiation skills, 95
    in home buying, 180
Neighborhood associations, 372
Neighborhoods, 118-119
    condition of, 118
    convenience, 118
    drawbacks, 119
    planned, 373

Neighbors, relationships with, 159
Networking, 90, 677
Neutral colors, 408, 412, 416, 558
New homes, 174-175
    custom-built, 174
    development, 173
    homes built on spec, 174
    stock home plans, 174
New urbanism, 374
Newel-post, 677
Niche, 677
Nigeria, housing in, 41
Nineteenth century, housing in, 348-352, 375
Nomads, 21, 40, 678
Nonresidential interiors. *See* Commercial design
Nonstructural lighting, 625, 627
Novel designs, 99
Nuclear family, 41, 678
Nuclear power, 276
Nylon
    carpeting, 556
    fibers, 552, 553

O

Oak wood, 265, 601
Obscure glass, 236
Occupancy sensors on lights, 631
Occupational Outlook Handbook, 84
Occupational Outlook Quarterly, 84
Occupational Health and Safety Administration (OSHA), 314. *See also* Safety, workplace
Offer-to-purchase contract, 180
Offices. *See also* Home offices
    space planning for, 533-534
    design trends, 251
Older home, advantages of, 175
Olefin fibers, 553
On-demand water heaters, 254
One-level home, 380
One-point perspective, 480
One-wall kitchen, 499-500
Open floor plan, 379, 678
Open space laws, 50
Open storage, 540, 678
Opposition, 436, 678
Orientation, 219, 678
Oriented strand board (OSB), 228
Origination fee, 185

Outdoor furniture, 291
Outdoor lighting, 295
Outdoor living space
    constructing, 291
    designing, 290
Outdoor maintenance, 198-199
Outside walls, inspecting, 182
Ovens, 511-513
Overhang, 227
Overlay, on drawing, 483, 678
Owings Mills New Town, 374

P

Padding for furniture, 608-609
Painters, 247
Painting, decorative, 399, 560
Paint
    alkyd, 560, 668
    calculating amount, 458
    choosing color, 551
    for exterior walls, 230
    for interior walls, 560
    latex, 560
Palladian window, 678
Panel box, 248, 249, 678
Paneling, 562, 678
Parapets, 354
Parenting stage, 29-30
Parking, 139
Parking areas, lighting for, 656
Parquet, 265, 678
Particleboard, 600, 602, 678
Partnership for Advanced Technology in Housing (PATH), 67
Passive solar heating systems, 279, 280, 678
Patina, 678
Patio homes, 47
Pattern
    in fabric, 396, 609
    in rhythm, 434
Pavement (permeable), 289
Pecan wood, 601
Pedestal, 678
Pedestal sink, 521
Pediment, 344, 678
Pendant, 678
Peninsula, 499, 501, 678
Penn, William, 368
Perennials, 294

locks, 655
    parts and styles, 235
    storm, 236, 281
    types of glass, 236
Window treatments, 563-568
    calculating fabric for, 458-459
    factors in choosing, 568
    types of, 563-568
Wind power, 278
Windsor chair, 582, 684
Wing chair, 582, 684
Wireless technology, 537
Wiring, inspecting, 183. *See also*
        Electrical system
Wood, 61
    distressing, 590
    as energy source, 277
    engineered products, 63

for fireplace, 259-260
for furniture, 600-602
for outdoor space, 291
scarcity of, 63
types of, 600-602
Wood floors, 265
Wood siding, 229
Wool fibers, 552, 553
Work centers, 46, 497-498, 684
Work experience, 85. *See also*
        Apprenticeship
Work habits and attitudes, 87,
        95-98, 103, 106
Work order, 684
Workplace readiness, 87, 684
Work simplification, kitchen layout
        and, 496-502
Work-study programs, 85

Work triangle, 311, 498, 500-501,
        684
Wright, Frank Lloyd, 355, 356, 592
Written agreement, 155
Wrought iron, 603, 684

X Y Z

Xeriscaping, 296, 684
Zero-lot-line homes, 373
Zoning laws, 217, 286, 369, 370,
        684